"Judith Blau's Companion is an impressive collection by a sociologist/editor who clearly knows her field and has done her homework. The volume is comprehensive enough to serve as a lifetime sociological companion, and will be useful not only to researchers, teachers, and students, but to sociologically curious general readers."

Herbert J. Gans, Columbia University

"Judith Blau has assembled an impressive group of international scholars who have written essays on the cutting edge of sociology today. Not only are the chapters first rate, but the range of topics is creative and new. The book reflects some of the changes in sociology over the last decade, and it presents new agendas for sociology in the next decade, and beyond. This exciting book is a 'must read' for all sociologists."

Jonathan H. Turner, University of California-Riverside

BLACKWELL COMPANIONS TO SOCIOLOGY

The *Blackwell Companions to Sociology* provide introductions to emerging topics and theoretical orientations in sociology as well as presenting the scope and quality of the discipline as it is currently configured. Essays in the Companions tackle broad themes or central puzzles within the field and are authored by key scholars who have spent considerable time in research and reflection on the questions and controversies that have activated interest in their area. This authoritative series will interest those studying sociology at advanced undergraduate or graduate level as well as scholars in the social sciences and informed readers in applied disciplines.

The Blackwell Companion to Social Theory, Second Edition
Edited by Bryan S. Turner

The Blackwell Companion to Major Social Theorists
Edited by George Ritzer

The Blackwell Companion to Political Sociology
Edited by Kate Nash and Alan Scott

The Blackwell Companion to Medical Sociology
Edited by William C. Cockerham

The Blackwell Companion to Sociology
Edited by Judith R. Blau

The Blackwell Companion to Major Classical Social Theorists
Edited by George Ritzer

The Blackwell Companion to Major Contemporary Social Theorists
Edited by George Ritzer

The Blackwell Companion to Criminology
Edited by Colin Sumner

The Blackwell Companion to the Sociology of Families
Edited by Jacqueline Scott, Judith Treas, and Martin Richards

The Blackwell Companion to Social Movements
Edited by David A. Snow, Sarah A. Soule, and Hanspeter Kriesi

The Blackwell Companion to Law and Society
Edited by Austin Sarat

Forthcoming

The Blackwell Companion to Social Inequalities
Edited by Mary Romero and Eric Margolis

The Blackwell Companion to the Sociology of Culture
Edited by Mark Jacobs and Nancy Hanrahan

The Blackwell Companion to Sociology

Edited by

Judith R. Blau

Blackwell
Publishing

BLACKWELL PUBLISHING
350 Main Street, Malden, MA 02148-5020, USA
108 Cowley Road, Oxford OX4 1JF, UK
550 Swanston Street, Carlton, Victoria 3053, Australia

First published 2001
First published in paperback 2004 by Blackwell Publishing Ltd

Library of Congress Cataloging-in-Publication Data

The Blackwell companion to sociology / edited by Judith R. Blau.
    p. cm. – (Blackwell companions to sociology)
  Includes bibliographical references and index.
  ISBN 0–631–21318–X (hc : alk. paper) – ISBN 1–4051–2267–6 (pbk : alk. paper)
  1. Sociology. I. Series.

HM585 .B53 2000
301 – dc21   00-025860

A catalogue record for this title is available from the British Library.

Set in 10.5/12 pt Sabon
by Kolam Information Services Pvt. Ltd., Pondicherry, India
Printed and bound in the United Kingdom
by TJ International, Padstow, Cornwall

The publisher's policy is to use permanent paper from mills that operate a sustainable forestry
policy, and which has been manufactured from pulp processed using acid-free and elementary
chlorine-free practices. Furthermore, the publisher ensures that the text paper and cover board
used have met acceptable environmental accreditation standards.

For further information on
Blackwell Publishing, visit our website:
http://www.blackwellpublishing.com

For
Amartya Sen,
a companion in economics

SOLD TO:

BONNIE ERICKSON
SOCIOLOGY DEPT
TORONTO UNIVERSITY
725 SPADINA AVENUE
TORONTO
ON M5S 2J4
CANADA

Original
Quality is our bu

INVESTOR IN PEOPLE

MARSTON BOO

Marston Book Services Ltd.
PO Box 269, Abingdon, Ox
Tel: (01235) 465500 Fax: (0

VAT No. GB 787 4454 78

XXXXXXXX

Bank Accounts: Barclays, C
Account No. 00636835 Gi

85759000

85759000 AA;2701439 I78102847 OGI

Pick Batch					Batch/Doc.	Transac
GSS 48236		ERI/CAN		DSF 9000	66179/018	Gratis

Pub. Code	Edition Binding	Standard Book No.	Author/Title		
			GRATIS INVOICE		
			These title(s) are being sent with the compl		
BB	1P	1 40512267 6	BLAU\BLACKWELL COMP TO SOC		

E & OE

TOTAL
DUES

1.1

siness

K SERVICES

n OX14 4YN, U.K.
235) 465555

GB787 4454 78
xford. Code No. 20 65 18
Account No. 2366053

(006)

SHIP TO:

BONNIE ERICKSON
SOCIOLOGY DEPT
TORONTO UNIVERSITY
725 SPADINA AVENUE
TORONTO
ON M5S 2J4
CANADA

on Type	Account No.	Date/Tax Point	Payment Terms	Document No.	Page
nvoice	85759000	17-MAY-04	Terms: 30 Days	I78102847	1

Customer Reference	QTY	Retail Price	Net	Discount	Value	VAT	VAT Amount
iments of The Publisher							
ERI/CAN	1	19.99					

Total Quantity	1

VAT Codes	

SUB TOTAL	
CARRIAGE	
TOTAL VAT	
TOTAL TO PAY	

Contents

Preface

Sociology, like other fields, is undergoing rapid transformation owing to enhanced global interdependencies and changes in the underpinnings of social and economic life. The intensification of the global economy, the rapid development of new communications technology, and the declining robustness of modernity's structures and institutions pose new puzzles for inquiry. As Agnes Heller describes modern social arrangements, "nothing here fits perfectly with anything else. There are relatively separate spheres, many major discrepancies, several discourses, panels, fragments, and niches." Building on this premise, I want to suggest that modern social arrangements exhibit few solidities, as well as little specificity about accountability, organization, structure, and norms. Yet, paradoxically, there is more basis for solidarities as emergent global formations reveal important communalities.

Although sociology maintains a distinctive focus on groups, populations, and societies, the field is increasingly receptive to theories, concepts, and methodologies from other academic and applied fields. In addition to this growing acceptance of other approaches, sociology reveals several other trends. First, many of the classic analytical distinctions – such as macro versus micro and interpretive versus explanatory – no longer have the vigor they formerly did. An indication of this is that neither the macro–micro divide nor the interpretive–explanatory contrast applies to such current concepts as embeddedness, social construction, social capital, engagement, and contextualism. Second, although the quantitative–qualitative division does distinguish between current methodological approaches, it is often ignored because of an interest in advancing descriptive understanding and in achieving more synthetic accounts.

A third significant change is the more rapid pace of restructuring of subspecialties in sociology. An indication of this, at least in the USA, is that more than one-third (14 out of 39) of the sections in the American Sociological Association were founded in the 1990s, while the other two-thirds were formed at a relatively slow pace beginning in the early 1960s. Fourth, most significantly, sociology is increasingly international, which will have far-reaching consequences for knowledge and understanding in ways that cannot now be predicted. Currently, this internationalist focus is reflected in an interest in essentialist and universalistic categories, namely those of race, ethnicity, gender, and class. These are central in understanding how people construct their own and others' identities; they also underlie and shape persisting inequalities.

In selecting topics for this volume, I wanted to include areas that are well defined and highly robust, in which research and inquiry will long continue, as well as newly emerging specialties now taking shape, often around interdisciplinary concerns. In general, the chapters collectively achieve three major objectives. First, as globalization processes accelerate, as they no doubt will, knowledge about and understanding of aspects of globalization are especially important. A second objective was to provide readers with a perspective on established fields in which researchers are asking new and exciting questions. Areas in sociology that have such a rich and complex framework include political sociology, sociology of education and of health, and the study of inequality and poverty.

A third objective was to include various diagnostic approaches that provoke critique. What are the most pressing problems of human rights, and what are the conceptions and debates dealing with social and economic justice? There are clear indications that sociologists have veered from a value-free science – which was a myth at best – and are interested in questions of justice and rights. We should address these questions in an informed and thoughtful way, taking into account humanistic understandings of historical consciousness and contemporary narratives, and recent thinking about social variation and shared, or universal, needs and interests.

ORGANIZATION OF THE CHAPTERS

The chapters in part I deal directly with aspects of globalization and, in particular, how to achieve more freedom, and reduce people's constraints on space and time (Urry, chapter 1), as well as on institutions (Wagner, chapter 3). Peters (chapter 2) analyzes how media and communications foster shared symbolic worlds and discourses about what is universally shared and what is particularized, while Urry focuses on how places provide comparable constructions of centrality and dispersion through networks and diaspora. Wagner (chapter 3) discusses modernity in terms of its various "problématiques," including the tension between autonomy and mastery that emerged with the weakening of "organized modernity." One of the tragic aspects of modernization is the extent to which rich industrial nations have contributed to environmental destruction and the depletion of resources. The development of environmental sociology is outlined by Buttel and Gijswijt (chapter 4). They suggest that challenges raised in cultural studies to question the division between the natural sciences and the humanities may have led to the relativization of knowledge, but may also have created a broader base for inquiry about the environment. Blau seeks to clarify in chapter 5 how social interdependencies might help to overturn growing inequalities, such as those described in the chapters on immigration (chapters 10 and 27) and health (chapter 24), and in part III.

Part II deals with Relationships and Meaning in general ways – as embodied abstractly in civil society and as conceived in the abstract as human rights – and in concrete, lived forms. Misztal (chapter 6), after sorting through the various conceptualizations of civil society, expands its usefulness for sociology by indicating how it relates to institutions and the market, and how it is a sphere of autonomous individual actions. Another facet of civil society pertains to the rights of individuals and groups. An-Na'im, in chapter 7, shows how the human rights paradigm that pertains to the protection of individual civil and political rights is consistent with a broader conception about the rights of groups, communities, and other collectivities. He also invites sociologists to consider human rights from a social and political movements perspective.

The substance of civil society lies in political engagement (parts V and VIII), but also in other spheres of meaning, notably religion, and participation in voluntary associations. Smith and Woodberry (chapter 8) show the growing importance of religion throughout the world in providing identity and meaning. Religious convictions can leverage progressive social change, but they can also provide a defense for group protection. The expansion of autonomy and choice is nowhere more evident, perhaps, than in relationships. Dozier and Schwartz's chapter (9) on intimate relations brings this out especially clearly.

High rates of migration accompany globalization. In chapter 27, Rumbaut discusses overall patterns of immigration to the USA, with an emphasis on historical changes, and Suárez-Orozco (chapter 10) gives immigration a "face." A critical dimension of migration is how individuals cope, and in particular how children fare. Family relationships are especially important as buffers for immigrant children, and in examining the pressures that these immigrant children face, Suárez-Orozco indicates that it is important to understand developmental processes as well as parental and family relations, along with school experiences.

If the ideal of modernity is equal opportunities, there is nothing to suggest that we are moving steadily in a direction of promoting that ideal. Economic inequalities continue to grow both within and between nations, and, also, between particular groups. Chapters in part III deal with various aspects of economic inequalities. Osmani (chapter 11) considers two arguments. The first hinges on the goal of equal liberty versus that of equality in basic respects, such as freedom from hunger and the freedom to lead a healthy and active life. Osmani's second argument centers on the debate concerning growth versus equity. His chapter provides the philosophical perspective on justice for the empirical chapters in this section, and also provides a helpful background for the chapters on social action in part VIII.

Oliver and Grant (chapter 12) describe the "violence of poverty" in the USA and poor nations, but they also indicate how communities are involved in asset building, with examples from Indianapolis and Pilluseri, a small village in Tamil

Nadu. They show how remarkable change can be initiated and implemented at local levels. Their optimism is not, however, shared by other authors. The overall magnitude of racial economic inequalities in the USA is substantial and persistent, as described by Darity and Myers (chapter 13). Not all of the gap in earnings and income can be explained by educational differences, and the evidence suggests that discriminatory practices are not declining. During the 1980s, attention focused on poverty in inner cities of older industrial centers in the Northeast and Midwest of the USA, and little attention was paid to rural areas, particularly in the South. Dill provides an overview of rural poverty in the USA (chapter 14), and shows how women and their children are especially at risk of poverty in rural areas.

Together, the chapters in part IV indicate, despite their divergent approaches, the broad scope of creative inquiry in the areas of the sociology of science, ideas, and knowledge. Whereas earlier investigations in the sociology of science focused on the normative and organizational aspects of science, Duster (chapter 15) examines the knowledge base itself, specifically in the field of molecular biology. Its virtual autonomous development poses central dilemmas for society, and by treating the natural sciences as esoteric, sociologists have had little voice in their development and applications. Duster's main focus is the genetic mapping of race. Lee and Wallerstein (chapter 16) situate the importance of social scientists' probing the contents of science in a historical overview. They trace the trajectory from the division of knowledge between science and the humanities to a collapse of that division. The point of transition entails both the liberation of human action and a crisis in human relations. Camic and Gross (chapter 17) likewise underscore the demise of dichotomies in social thought and knowledge. They trace the development of the sociology of ideas, and highlight the importance of the local context in which ideas are produced, and how fragmentation and struggle develop among intellectual fields.

As the chapters in part V indicate, there is a new convergence between political sociology and the sociology of social movements. This is due to the deformalization of politics and other institutional spheres, the heightened importance of symbols and of identity in mobilization processes, and the ritualization of contention. Savage, in chapter 18, takes on a range of issues from the perspective of political sociology, including the role of social class, political realignments, and institutional theory. He describes how the repertoires of mobilization slip through groups, thereby destabilizing traditional divisions. Collective action is the focus of Klandermans's chapter (19). He indicates that cultural frames and identities provide the potential for mobilizing, but also stresses that actual participation involves other factors, such as incentives and networks. Social movement researchers alternatively favor cultural approaches and organizational approaches. Minkoff (chapter 20) argues that when one is considering global social movements, organizations and resources are especially important, although they cannot easily be disentangled from cultural dimensions.

The study of "structures," which has always been central to sociology, poses increasing challenges to researchers owing to variation in different contexts and the dynamic qualities of structures themselves. Three kinds of structures are exemplary in sociology: stratification, social networks, and organizations; these are the topics in part VI. Approaches to studying stratification were largely developed to account for occupational distributions and mobility in industrial societies, but Treiman (chapter 21) examines recent advances using cross-national and multilevel approaches. Networks are neutral structures from one perspective since any network can be described in purely formal terms: centrality, vacancies, sparseness, and so forth. In chapter 22, Erickson shows that a network framework provides distinctive ways of answering substantive questions about culture, power, and thinking, to mention just a few of her examples. Network theories and methodologies are especially suited to the study of contemporary organizations that are loosely assembled. Knoke (chapter 23) provides an overview of the conceptual and methodological power of network analysis in studying economic behavior of firms, ties among actors, and the consequences of organizational networks.

The chapters in part VII relate to research on individuals and their wellbeing. Schwartz (chapter 24) discusses how sociologists can make distinctive contributions to medical research, through, for example, studies of stress and health outcomes, and how the larger environment and, in particular, contextual inequalities, affect health. Like Duster (in chapter 15), Schwartz suggests that more collaborative research involving sociologists and scientists is greatly needed. DNA researchers, according to Duster, may prematurely draw naive conclusions about racial differences from genetic tracers without an understanding of the ideological construction of race and the overwhelming importance of people's circumstances. Schwartz draws attention to the contributions that sociologists can make in medical research, but also what social scientists can learn from medical researchers. He illustrates the latter with examples of laboratory research on the effects of maternal behavior on the brain physiology of young animals, suggesting possible parallels with the effects of nurturing parental behavior on health outcomes among humans.

Two areas that have long developed through interdisciplinary collaboration and been mindful of application and relevance are education and the study of aging. Hallinan organizes her discussion in chapter 25 in terms of two dominant foci in the sociology of education: organizational analysis of schools, and the transition from school to work. Madonna Harrington Myer and Pamela Herd provide the reader in chapter 26 with a general overview of the large field of aging. They discuss the current emphasis on the life course, and, among other aspects of aging, examine those that relate to inequalities of race, class, and gender.

Contemporary immigration patterns are examined from a historical and comparative perspective by Rubén Rumbaut (chapter 27). He shows how race, national origins, and immigration laws have played out in the USA in terms of public discourse and how immigration affects demographic and cultural pluralism. Social psychology is an enormous field, encompassing a great variety of perspectives and methodological approaches. Smith-Lovin (chapter 28) provides an overview of the field by centering attention on the tradition of group processes and on the research linking social structure and personality. She concludes her chapter with a discussion of recent work on the convergence between affective and structural processes.

The papers in part VIII raise questions about epistemology in sociology, social transformation, and social action. Not all sociologists would agree that social action and activism are appropriate extensions of scholarship, but most would agree that there is an epistemological hiatus involving the conception of social agency and that of social responsibility. One way this is bridged is through activist research in which a reciprocal relationship is established between the research-scholar and the "subject," which is especially important when the purpose is to gain an understanding of exclusion and domination. Hondagneu-Sotelo's (chapter 29) research examines immigrant women who work in domestic jobs. She shows how participant, activist research helps to transcend social spaces in ways that are impossible using conventional research methods, and how the process itself yields new understandings. The final two chapters, though strikingly different in their goals, raise critical questions about how emergent processes unfold through social action and transform consciousness. For Touraine (chapter 30), consciousness interacts within and opposed to society and involves a quest for identity and for social coherence. Collective social action is both interpretive and integrative. Fantasia (chapter 31) is more concrete, as he suggests that transforming "consciousness" must be broad-based, grounded in people's experiences. Social transformation involves the mobilization and construction of myths, namely a composite of shared knowledge, critique, and visionary thinking.

The chapters in this final section are provocative, as they raise questions about scholars in their roles as researchers, teachers, mentors, and colleagues. To mention one: how is our own vision of a better world – or our ease with, or our cynicism about, the present one – conveyed to students in the classroom? They also raise questions about the foundation of sociological inquiry and understanding. Through this century the academy is bound to become more diverse, with growing access to education by previously excluded groups. This diversity itself will no doubt provide the foundations for creative dialogues, contention, and new grounds for consensus.

Finally, the Appendix, "Data Resources on the World Wide Web," prepared by Kathryn Harker, is a listing of Internet sites for data sources for the purpose of research. It was designed, in part, to encourage international research. It includes listings of established research centers and government agencies that are likely to maintain and expand their databases. Therefore, we consider the listing as helpful for the purposes of research, and as a source for descriptive comparisons for teaching.

ACKNOWLEDGMENTS

Susan Rabinowitz, at Blackwell Publishers, suggested that I undertake this project, and after consulting with Karen Edwards, a friend at the American

Sociological Association, and Robert K. Merton, who questioned the wisdom of my doing it, I agreed. There is a great deal of exciting work in sociology these days, and, quite frankly, I thought of the venture as something like a sabbatical in which I would do an immense amount of reading. Because I did this for the fun of it, royalties will be donated to the Minority Fellowship Program of the American Sociological Association. Susan Rabinowitz was extremely helpful and, after launching the project, turned me over to Ken Provencher. He was my great ally and adviser. He is knowledgeable and wise, and was always gracious and helpful. He made all of the truly bad moments turn out perfectly fine, and I am truly thankful to him for his support. Rhonda Pearce and John Taylor brought the project into home base.

For their kind suggestions in the early stage of this project, I am especially grateful to Sylvia Walby and Gill Jones, and also Pierre Bourdieu, Hans Joas, Elihu Katz, Amartya Sen, and Angelika von Wahl. This book is dedicated to Professor Sen. His contributions to the social sciences are foundational.

The Department of Sociology at the University of North Carolina, Chapel Hill, provided support for the preparation of the Appendix, for which I thank the Chair, Arne Kalleberg. Several students, including John Hipp and Keri Iyall Smith, were helpful with the electronic retrieval of graphs and manuscripts. Most especially, I thank Anita Sharon "Shea" Farrell, who, with meticulous care and good cheer, logged the manuscripts, cross-checked many references, standardized the formatting, and kept up with the revisions as they arrived.

Judith R. Blau

Contributors

Abdullahi Ahmed An-Na'im is Charles Howard Candler Professor of Law, Emory University. He is the author of *Toward an Islamic Reformation: Civil Liberties, Human Rights and International Law;* editor of *Human Rights in Cross-cultural Perspectives: Quest for Consensus; Human Rights in Africa: Cross-cultural Perspectives* (with Francis Deng). He has also published numerous articles and book chapters on human rights, constitutionalism and Islamic law and politics.

Judith R. Blau is Professor of Sociology at the University of North Carolina at Chapel Hill and President of the US chapter of Sociologists without Borders, an international NGO. She is the author of *Architects and Firms* (1984), *The Shape of Culture* (1989), *Social Contracts and Economic Markets* (1993), and *Race in the Schools* (2003), and has published articles on organizations, networks, economic inequalities, crime, sociology of science, urban sociology, historical sociology, medical sociology, and sociology of education.

Frederick H. Buttel is Professor and Chair, Department of Rural Sociology, and Professor of Environmental Studies at the University of Wisconsin, Madison. He is currently the President of the Environment and Society Research Committee (RC 24) of the International Sociological Association, and was previously President of the Rural Sociological Society.

Charles Camic is Martindale-Bascom Professor of Sociology at the University of Wisconsin-Madison. Currently, he is also Co- editor of the American Sociological Review. He has written extensively on the interrelationship between the institutional and intellectual development of American sociology in the 1880–1940 period. He is completing a book on the early career of Talcott Parsons and has begun research on a new intellectual biography of Thorstein Veblen.

William A. Darity, Jr is Boshamer Professor of Economics at the University of North Carolina at Chapel Hill, Adjunct Professor in Sociology, and Research Professor at Duke University. His research includes cross-national investigations of racial and ethnic economic inequality, North–South models of trade and growth, the impact of financial crises on developing countries, economics of the Atlantic slave trade, and the social-psychological effects of exposure to unemployment. He has published more than 120 articles in professional journals and several books.

Bonnie Thornton Dill, professor of Women's Studies and Director of the Research Consortium and Gender, Race and Ethnicity at the University of Maryland, College Park, conducts research on African American women, work, and family. Her books include *Women of Color in US Society*, co-edited with Maxine Baca Zinn, and *Across the Boundaries of Race and Class*.

Raine Dozier is a graduate student in sociology at the University of Washington. She is working primarily in the fields of gender, sexuality, and culture.

Troy Duster is Chancellor's Professor of Sociology at the University of California, Berkeley, and Professor of Sociology, Institute for the History of the Production of Knowledge at New York University. He has been a member of the National Advisory Council for Human Genome Research, and the Assembly of Behavioral and Social Sciences of the National Academy of Sciences, and served as Chair of the Advisory Committee on Ethical, Legal and Social Issues of the Human Genome Project.

Bonnie Erickson is a member of the Department of Sociology at the University of Toronto. Her research interests include social networks, culture, work, gender, and health. She has recently studied the role of different forms of culture in the workplace and the roots of culture in social networks ("Culture, class, and connections," *American Journal of Sociology*, 1996), the widely varying gender outcomes in the security industry, and social networks in a large alternative economy.

Rick Fantasia is Professor of Sociology at Smith College in Northampton, Massachusetts. The author of *Cultures of Solidarity* and various other writings on labor and on culture, Fantasia is currently working on a study of the symbolic and material dimensions of American mass cultural goods in France and their relationship to traditional sources of cultural authority.

August Gijswijt has published in the areas of the sociology of housing, public administration, and environmental sociology. Between 1990 and 1998 he was board member and secretary of the Research Committee on Environment and Society of the International Sociological Association.

David M. Grant is an Assistant Professor of Sociology at Cleveland State University. His current research focuses on poverty and various aspects of urban inequality, particularly racial inequality in the labor market. He received his PhD from UCLA in 1998 and has published several articles on race and inequality in Los Angeles.

Neil Gross is Assistant Professor, University of Southern California. His work has appeared in *Sociological Theory*, the *Journal of the History of the Behavioral Sciences, Theory and Society*, and the *Annual Review of Sociology*. His dissertation is a case study in the sociology of ideas.

Maureen Hallinan is the William P. and Hazel B. White Professor of Sociology and Director of the Program on the Social Organization of Schools of the Institute for Educational Initiatives at the University of Notre Dame. She currently studies the determinants and consequences of the organization of instruction, and organizational effects on students' social relationships. Her previous research includes studies of cross- race friendships in middle and secondary schools.

Kathryn Harker is a graduate student in the Sociology Department at the University of North Carolina at Chapel Hill. Her research interests include race and ethnicity, immigration, and the psychological wellbeing of adolescent immigrants.

Pamela Herd is pursuing a PhD in Sociology at Syracuse University. Her main interest areas are aging, the welfare state, and care work.

Pierrette Hondagneu-Sotelo is Associate Professor in the Department of Sociology and in the Program in American Studies and Ethnicity at the University of Southern California. She is author of *Gendered Transitions: Mexican Experiences of Immigration*, co-editor of *Challenging Fronteras: Structuring Latina and Latino Lives in the US* and *Gender Through the Prism of Difference*.

Bert Klandermans is professor in Applied Social Psychology at Free University, Amsterdam. He has published extensively on the social psychological principles of participation in social movements and labor unions. He is the editor of the book series *Social Movements, Protest, and Contention*, and author of *The Social Psychology of Protest*.

David Knoke is Professor of Sociology at the University of Minnesota. His research interests are organizations and social networks. A current project is the changing network of strategic alliances in the global information sector.

Recently published books, with several co-authors, include *Comparing Policy Networks*, *Organizations in America*, and *Change at Work*.

Richard E. Lee is a Senior Research Associate at the Fernand Braudel Center and Assistant Professor of Sociology at the State University of New York at Binghamton.

Madonna Harrington Meyer is Associate Professor of Sociology, and Senior Research Associate at the Center for Policy Research, at Syracuse University. She is editor of *Care Work: Gender, Labor and Welfare States*. Her research emphasizes financial and health security for older Americans, particularly women and persons of color.

Debra C. Minkoff is Associate Professor at the University of Washington. She is the author of *Organizing for Equality: The Evolution of Women's and Racial-ethnic Organizations in America*, and articles on the organizational dynamics of contemporary American social movements, particularly the civil rights and feminist movements. Her current research is on the structure of the US national social movement sector.

Barbara A. Misztal is Senior Lecturer in the Faculty of Arts, School of Humanities at Griffith University, Brisbane. She is co-editor of *Action on Aids* (with D. Moss) and author of *Trust in Modern Society* (1996) and *Informality: Social Theory and Contemporary Practice* (2000).

Samuel L. Myers, Jr is the Roy Wilkins Professor of Human Relations and Social Justice at the Hubert H. Humphrey Institute of Public Affairs, University of Minnesota, where he conducts research on racial economic inequality. Recent co-authored publications include *Faculty of Color in Academe* and articles on family structure, race and earnings disparities, racial differences in child abuse reporting, and the effect of race on alimony and child support appeals.

Melvin L. Oliver is Dean at the University of California–Santa Barbara. He previously was Professor of Sociology at the University of California, Los Angeles and Officer at the Ford Foundation. He has published widely in the areas of race and ethnic relations, poverty and inequality, and urban studies.

Siddiqur Rahman Osmani is an economist whose research interests include poverty, inequality, nutrition, hunger, health, and generally the problems of economic development. He has worked at the Bangladesh Institute of Development Studies, Dhaka, and at the World Institute for Development Economics Research, Helsinki. He is currently Professor of Development Economics at the University of Ulster.

John Durham Peters is Associate Professor of Communication Studies at the University of Iowa. He is the author of *Speaking into the Air* (1999), and has received a Fulbright Fellowship to Greece, a Leverhulme Trust Fellowship to England, and a Research Fellowship from the National Endowment for the Humanities. He teaches courses on media, culture, and society, and social theory.

Rubén G. Rumbaut is Professor of Sociology at Michigan State University. He is the Founding Chair of the Section on International Migration of the American Sociological Association. He has two new books based on the Children of Immigrants Longitudinal Study, which he directed throughout the 1990s in collaboration with Alejandro Portes: *Legacies: The Story of the New Second Generation*, and *Ethnicities: Children of Immigrants in America*.

Mike Savage is Professor and Head of the Department of Sociology at the University of Manchester, UK. His recent works include *Social Change and the Middle Class* (edited with Tim Butler, 1995), and *Gender, Careers and Organizations* (with Susan Halford and Anne Witz, 1997).

Joseph E. Schwartz is Associate Professor of Psychiatry and Behavioral Science at the State University of New York at Stony Brook. While trained as a sociologist, his recent research is mostly in the area of behavioral medicine. He is the senior investigator of a longitudinal study of the relationship of work-related stress to blood pressure and cardiovascular disease.

Pepper Schwartz is Professor of Sociology at the University of Washington in Seattle. She is past president of the Society for the Scientific Study of Sexuality and author of books on intimacy and relationships, including *American Couples* (with Philip Blumstein), *Peer Marriage*, and *The Gender of Sexuality* (with Virginia Rutter).

Christian Smith is Professor of Sociology at the University of North Carolina, Chapel Hill. His studies of religion and social change include *The Emergence of Liberation Theology, Resisting Reagan: The US Central American Peace Movement, Disruptive Religion: The Force of Faith in Social Movement Activism*, and *American Evangelicalism: Embattled and Thriving*.

Lynn Smith-Lovin is Professor of Sociology at the University of Arizona. She is a former chair of the American Sociological Association section on the Sociology of Emotions and is currently co-editor of *Social Psychology Quarterly* and chair of the American Sociological Association section on Social Psychology. Her research focuses on identity, social interaction and emotion. She is currently completing a National Science Foundation funded study of identity and conversational interaction.

Carola Suárez-Orozco is co-director of Harvard Immigration Projects and a lecturer in education in the Human Development and Psychology area. She is co-author (with Marcelo Suárez-Orozco) of *Transformations* and *Children of Immigration*.

Alain Touraine was appointed Directeur d'études in 1960 at Ecole Pratique des Hautes Etudes, which later became Ecole des Hautes Etudes en Sciences Sociales. He has also taught at Paris-Nanterre University and in Chile, Brazil, the United States and Canada, and has served as President of the French Association of Sociology and Vice President of the International Sociological Association. The most recent of his many books that have been translated into English include: *Return of the Actor*, *Critique of Modernity*, *What Is Democracy?*, *Can We Live Together? Equal and Different*, and *How to Get out of Liberalism?*

Donald J. Treiman is Professor of Sociology at the University of California at Los Angeles. His research focuses on the comparative study of social stratification and social mobility. For many years he has carried out large-scale worldwide comparisons of systems of social stratification, and recently conducted sample surveys in South Africa, Eastern European nations, and the People's Republic of China, all designed to explore the effect of abrupt social change on stratification outcomes.

John Urry is Professor of Sociology at Lancaster University, and author or joint author of various books, including *The End of Organized Capitalism* (1987), *The Tourist Gaze* (1990), *Economies of Signs and Space* (1994), *Consuming Places* (1995), *Contested Natures* (1998), and *Sociology Beyond Societies* (2000). Research areas include service industries, the environment, leisure and tourism, urban sociology, and social theory. He is Chair of the UK's Research Assessment Exercise Sociology Panel in 1996 and 2001.

Peter Wagner is Professor of Social and Political Theory at the European University Institute in Florence and Professor of Sociology at the University of Warwick. Before 1996 he taught at the Free University of Berlin, and has held visiting positions at various European and American universities. His publications include *Le travail et la nation*, *A Sociology of Modernity*, and *Der Raum des Gelehrten* (with Heidrun Friese).

Immanuel Wallerstein is Director of the Fernand Braudel Center, Binghamton University; author, most recently, of *The End of the World as We Know It: Social Science for the Twenty- first Century*; and Chair of the Gulbenkian Commission for the Restructuring of the Social Sciences (1993–5), whose report is *Open the Social Sciences*.

Robert Woodberry is a sociology graduate student at the University of North Carolina, Chapel Hill. His research interests include global religious transformations, and he has also done research on the sampling and measurement of religious groups on surveys.

Part I
Referencing Globalization

1

The Sociology of Space and Place

John Urry

Introduction

In this chapter I shall show that space (and place) should be central to sociology. But the history of sociology in the twentieth century has in some ways been the history of the singular absence of space. This was an absence that could not be entirely sustained. Here and there space broke through, disrupting pre-existing notions which were formed around distinctions which had mainly served to construct an a-spatial sociology. Societies were typically viewed as endogenous, as having their own a-spatial structures. Furthermore, societies were viewed as separate from each other, and the processes of normative consensus or structural conflict or strategic conduct were conceptualized as internal to each society, whose boundaries were coterminous with the nation-state. There was little recognition of the processes of internal differentiation across space.

This was so although the beginning of the twentieth century saw a series of sweeping technological and cultural changes which totally transformed the spatial underpinnings of contemporary life (Kern, 1983; Soja, 1989). These changes included the telegraph, the telephone, X-rays, cinema, radio, the bicycle, the internal combustion engine, the airplane, the passport, the skyscraper, relativity theory, cubism, the stream-of-consciousness novel and psychoanalysis. However, these changes were not reflected within sociology at the time and they became the province of a separate and increasingly positivist science of geography that set up and maintained a strict demarcation and academic division of labor from its social scientific neighbors.

In the next section I summarize some of the early "classical" writings on space which developed within the context of geography's colonization of the spatial. In the section following I show what in the late 1970s changed this and brought space into sociology and social theory more generally. In the final section analysis is provided of the recent emergence of a research program of a sociology of place, which brings out the importance of diverse spatial mobilities across, into, and beyond such places.

THE "CLASSICS" AND SPACE

The sociological classics dealt with space in a rather cryptic and undeveloped way. Marx and Engels were obviously concerned with how capitalist industrialization brought about the exceedingly rapid growth of industrial towns and cities. In *The Manifesto of the Communist Party* Marx and Engels describe how fixed, fast-frozen relations are swept away, all newly formed relations become antiquated before they can ossify, and "all that is solid melts into air" (1888, p. 54; Berman, 1983). Marx and Engels argue *inter alia* that capitalism breaks the feudal ties of people to their "natural superiors"; it forces the bourgeois class to seek markets across the surface of the globe and this destroys local and regional markets; masses of laborers are crowded into factories, so concentrating the proletariat and producing a class-for-itself; and the development of trade unionism is assisted by the improved transportation and communication that capitalism brings in its wake. In his later works, especially *Capital*, Marx analyzes how capitalist accumulation is based upon the annihilation of space by time and how this consequently produces striking transformations of agriculture, industry, and population across time and space.

Some similar processes are analyzed by Durkheim, although the consequences are viewed very differently. In *The Division of Labor in Society* it is argued that there are two types of society with associated forms of solidarity, mechanical (based on likeness or similarity) and organic (based on difference and complementarity). It is the growth in the division of labor, of dramatically increased specialization, that brings about transition from the former to the latter. This heightened division of labor results from increases in material and moral density. The former involves increases in the density of population in a given area, particularly because of the development of new forms of communication and because of the growth in towns and cities. Moral density refers to the increased density of social interaction. Different parts of society lose their individuality as individuals come to have more and more contacts and interactions. This produces a new organic solidarity of mutual interdependence, although on occasions cities are centers of social pathology. Overall Durkheim presented a thesis of modernization in which local geographical loyalties will be gradually undermined by the growth of new occupationally based divisions of labor. In *Elementary Forms* Durkheim also presents a social theory of space. This has two elements: first, since everyone within a society represents space in the same way, this implies that the cause of such notions is essentially "social"; second, in some cases at least the spatial representations will literally mirror its dominant patterns of social organization.

Max Weber made very few references to space, although his brother, Alfred Weber, was a seminal contributor to the theory of industrial location. Max

Weber was relatively critical of attempts to use spatial notions in his analysis of the city. He rejected analysis in terms of size and density and mainly concentrated on how the emergence of the medieval city constituted a challenge to the surrounding feudal system. The city was characterized by autonomy and it was there for the first time that people came together as individual citizens (Weber, 1921).

The most important classical contributor to a sociology of space and place is Simmel (Frisby, 1992a, b; Frisby and Featherstone, 1997). He analyzed five basic qualities of spatial forms found in those social interactions that turn an empty space into something meaningful. These qualities are the exclusive or unique character of a space; the ways in which a space may be divided into pieces and activities spatially "framed"; the degree to which social interactions may be localized in space; the degree of proximity/distance, especially in the city, and the role of the sense of sight; and the possibility of changing locations, and the consequences especially of the arrival of the "stranger." Overall Simmel sees space as becoming less significant as social organization becomes detached from space.

In "Metropolis and the City" (in Frisby and Featherstone, 1997), Simmel develops more specific arguments about space and the city. First, because of the richness and diverse sets of stimuli in the metropolis, people have to develop an attitude of reserve and insensitivity to feeling. Without the development of such an attitude people would not be able to cope with such experiences caused by a high density of population. The urban personality is reserved, detached and blasé. Second, at the same time the city assures individuals of a distinctive type of personal freedom. Compared with the small-scale community, the modern city gives room to individuals and to the peculiarities of their inner and outer development. It is the spatial form of the large city that permits the unique development of individuals who are placed within an exceptionally wide range of contacts. Third, the city is based on the money economy, which is the source and expression of the rationality and intellectualism of the city. Both money and the intellect share a matter-of-fact attitude toward people and things. It is money that produces a leveling of feeling and attitude. Fourth, the money economy generates a concern for precision and punctuality, since it makes people more calculating about their activities and relationships. Simmel does not so much explain urban life in terms of the spatial form of the city as provide an early examination of the effects of "modern" patterns of mobility on social life wherever it is located. He shows that motion, the diversity of stimuli, and the visual appropriations of places are centrally important features of the modern experience.

These analyses were not much developed by the "urban sociology" established in the interwar period at the University of Chicago. This work involved the attempt to develop ecological approaches to the study of the city, such as the concentric ring theory. Theoretically important was Wirth's "Urbanism as a way of life" (1938; followed by Redfield's "The folk society," 1947). Wirth argued that there are three causes of the differences in social patterns between urban and rural areas. These are: *size*, which produces segregation, indifference and social distance; *density*, which causes people to relate to each other in terms of specific roles, urban segregation between occupants of such roles, and greater formal regulation; and *heterogeneity*, which means that people participate in different social circles, none of which commands their total involvement, and this results in discrepant and unstable statuses. Wirth and Redfield thus claim that the organization of space, mainly in terms of size and density, produces corresponding social patterns.

Much effort has been spent on testing the hypothesis that there are two distinct ways of life and that these result from the respective size, density and heterogeneity of urban and rural areas. However, the research has largely shown that there are no such simple urban and rural patterns. Indeed, urban areas often contain close-knit social groups, such as the urban villages of Bethnal Green in London or of the immigrant ghettos in North American cities. More generally, Gans (1986) questioned the thesis that most city dwellers are isolated, individualized and autonomous. Even inner-city areas can be centers of a complex sociality focused around, for example, gentrification. Other city areas are more suburban, where the focus of activity is the home and where the main forms of activity are car-based (see Sheller and Urry, 2000, on urban sociology's treatment of automobility). In such cases it is the forms of mobility that are important, and less the size and density of the urban area. Furthermore, rural life is not simply organized around farm-based communities, where people frequently meet each other, are connected in diverse ways, and tend to know each other's friends (Frankenberg, 1966). Studies of rural communities have shown that there may be considerable conflict and opposition in such places, especially around status, access to land and housing, and the nature of the "environment" (Newby, 1979).

To a significant extent, then, sociology took over such easy contrasts in its endeavor to construct a spatially determined analysis of the urban and rural way of life. Elsewhere it was shown that the concept of "community" can be used in various ways (Bell and Newby, 1976). First, there is its use in a topographical sense, to refer to the boundaries of a particular settlement; second, there is the sense of community as a local social system implying a degree of social interconnection of local people and institutions; third, there is "communion," a particular kind of human association implying personal ties, belongingness, and warmth; and, fourth, there is community as ideology, where efforts are made to attach conceptions of communion to buildings, or areas, or estates, or cities, and so on, in ways which conceal and perpetuate the non-communion relations that are actually found.

Finally here, sociology has tended to reproduce not just the distinction in popular discourse between the countryside and the city (Williams, 1973), but also Tönnies's opposition of *Gemeinschaft* and *Gesellschaft*. Such binary distinctions have been especially criticized by Schmalenbach (1977), who adds a third term, the *Bund*. The *Bund* involves community, but this is a community that is conscious and freely chosen on the basis of mutual sentiment and emotional feeling. And *contra* Weber, the affective basis of such a *Bund* is not irrational and unconscious but conscious, rational and non-traditional. Such *Bünde* are not permanent or necessarily stable (Hetherington, 1994).

BRINGING SPACE BACK IN: THE 1970S AND 1980S

In this section I outline the Marxist and post-Marxist critique of this treatment of space and place. Castells (1977, 1978) argued that any scientific discipline needed a properly constituted "theoretical object," and maintained that urban sociology (and by implication rural sociology) did not possess such a theoretical object. Such an object would be based on a distinctive "structuralist" analysis of the unfolding contradictions of capitalist relations. These relations are increasingly organized on an international basis and this gives a particular role to towns and cities which have become centers not of production, but of "collective consumption." This term refers to services generally provided by the state and necessary for the "reproduction" of the energies and skills of the labor force.

Castells, having identified a proper "theoretical object" for urban sociology, "collective consumption," uses this to explain particular kinds of spatially varied politics. He argues that collective consumption cannot be provided unproblematically since states are rarely able (and willing) to raise sufficient taxation revenues. All sorts of disputes arise over the forms and levels of provision, such as the quality of public housing, the location of health care, the nature of public transport, and so on. Each of these services becomes "politicized" because they are provided collectively. Thus a sphere of urban politics emerges focused around these forms of collective consumption. Castells devotes particular attention to analyzing "urban social movements." These normally comprise a number of different urban groups but come under the dominance of working-class organizations, to become in effect a new kind of class politics. Thus, he argues strongly against efforts to understand the urban in terms either of "culture" or "way of life" or of a spatial determinism.

A more geographical focus was developed by Massey (1984). She argued that spatiality is an integral and active feature of the processes of capitalist production; it has various aspects besides that of region, including distance, movement, proximity, specificity, perception, symbolism, and meaning; and space makes a clear difference to the degree to which, to use realist terminology, the causal powers of social entities (such as class, the state, capitalist relations, patriarchy) are realized (Sayer, 1992). In particular, there are a number of distinct spatial forms taken by the social division of labor; there is no particular historical ordering in the emergence of each of these forms of restructuring; that which develops depends upon the specific struggle between capital and wage labor; one important pattern of spatial restructuring involves the relocation of certain more routine elements of production away from headquarters and research and development functions; and these diverse patterns of spatial restructuring generate new patterns of inequality, which are not just social but also spatial. On this account a particular locality is the outcome of a unique set of "layers" of restructuring dependent upon different rounds of accumulation. How these layers combine together in particular places, and especially how international, national, and local capitals combine together to produce particular local social and political effects, became the subject of major research programs (for example, in the UK, Bagguley et al., 1990).

One implication of spatial differentiation is to challenge the notion that social class is a *national* phenomenon, that classes are essentially specified by the boundaries of the nation-state. The emphasis within the restructuring literature on local/regional variation has led analysts to rethink social classes through this prism of space (later, gender and ethnicity were subject to similar analyses). Thus, there are international determinants of the social class relations *within* a nation-state; there are large variations in local stratification structures within a society, so that the national pattern may not be found in any particular place at all; the combination of local, national, and international enterprises may produce locally unexpected and perverse commonalties and conflicts of class interest; there are marked variations in the degree of spatial concentration of class; some class conflicts are in fact caused by, or are displaced onto, spatial conflicts; and, in certain cases, localities emerge with distinct powers to produce significant social and political effects (see Urry, 1995; Fröbel et al., 1977, on the "new international division of labor").

Some of these points were developed into Harvey's (1989) concept of "time-space compression." He shows how capitalism entails different "spatial fixes" within different historical periods. In each capitalist epoch, space is organized in such a way as to facilitate the growth of production, the reproduction of labor power and the maximization of profit. And it is through the reorganization of such time-space that capitalism overcomes its periods of crisis and lays the foundations for a new period of capital accumulation and the further transformation of space and nature through time.

Harvey examines Marx's thesis of the annihilation of space by time and attempts to demonstrate how this explains the shift from "Fordism" to the flexible accumulation of "post-Fordism." The latter involves a new spatial fix and most significantly new ways in which time and space are represented. Central is the "time-space compression" of both human and physical experiences and processes. Harvey brings out how this "compression" can generate a sense of foreboding, such as when the railway first transformed the countryside. In the past couple of decades mobility has been carried to further extremes, so that time and space appear literally *compressed*: "we are forced to alter... how we represent the world to ourselves.... Space appears to shrink to a 'global village' of telecommunications and a 'spaceship earth' of economic and ecological interdependencies... we have to learn how to cope with an overwhelming sense of *compression* of our spatial and temporal worlds" (Harvey, 1989, p. 240). Interestingly, Heidegger in 1950 foresaw much of this "shrinking" of the distances of time and space, the importance of "instant information" on the radio, and the way that television is abolishing remoteness and thus "un-distancing" humans and things (Zimmerman, 1990, pp. 151, 209).

However, these dramatic ways in which time and space are compressed does not mean that places necessarily decrease in importance. People appear to have become more sensitized to what different places in the world contain or what they may signify. There is an insistent urge to seek for roots "in a world where image streams accelerate and become more and more placeless. Who are we and to what space/place to we belong? Am I a citizen of the world, the nation, the locality? Can I have a virtual existence in cyberspace?" (Harvey, 1996, p. 246). Thus, the less important the temporal and spatial barriers, the greater the sensitivity of mobile capital, migrants, tourists, and asylum-seekers to the variations of place, and the greater the incentive for places to be differentiated, albeit through processes which are highly capitalized.

Finally, Giddens, in his post-Marxist theory of time and space, argued that the movement of individuals through time and space is to be grasped through the interpenetration of presence and absence, which results from the location of the human body and the changing means of its interchange with the wider society (Giddens, 1979, 1981, 1984, 1991). Each new technology transforms the intermingling of presence and absence, the forms by which memories are stored and weigh upon the present, and the ways in which the long-term *durée* of major social institutions are drawn upon within contingent social acts. Presence-availability depends upon the degree to which, and the forms through which, people are co-present within an individual's social milieu. Communities of high presence-availability include almost all societies up to a few hundred years ago. Presence-availability has been transformed in the past century or two through the development of new transportation technologies and the separation of the media of communication from the media of transportation. Thus there is variation in "time–space distanciation," the processes by which societies are "stretched" over shorter or longer spans of time and space. Such stretching reflects the fact that social activity increasingly depends upon interactions with those who are absent in time-space. In contemporary societies there is the disembedding of time and space from social activities, the development of an "empty" dimension of time, the separation of space from place, and the emergence of disembedding mechanisms, of symbolic tokens and expert systems, which lift social relations out of local involvement. Expert systems bracket time and space through deploying modes of technical knowledge which are valued independent of the practitioners and clients who make use of them. Such systems depend on trust, on a qualitative leap or commitment related to absence in time and/or space. Trust in disembedding mechanisms is vested not in individuals but in abstract systems or capacities, and is specifically related to absence in time and space.

TOWARDS A SOCIOLOGY OF PLACE

In the contributions so far considered, space and time have been treated as Newtonian, as objective, linear, and absolute notions in which there are three dimensions of space and the separate dimension of time. It is presumed that objects are located within these objective dimensions of time and space, that objects are not intrinsically "spaced" and "timed." However, in recent years the challenges to these views from twentieth-century science have begun to trickle into the sociology of place and space.

Thus, for example, twentieth-century physics has shown that time is not a separate dimension along which objects may travel forwards or backwards. Time is now conceived of as irreversible and as constitutive of physical and social entities. This is clearly seen in the expansion of the universe through the cosmological arrow of time, following the singular historical event of the "big bang." There are many mundane examples of such irreversibility: coffee always cools, organisms always age, spring follows winter, and so on. There can be no going back, no reabsorbing of the heat, no return to youth, no spring before winter, and so on. Laws of nature are historical and imply pastness, presentness, and futureness. "The great thing about time is that it goes on" (Eddington, quoted in Coveney and Highfield, 1990, p. 83), while "irreversibility [of time] is the mechanism that brings order out of chaos" (Prigogine and Stengers, 1984, p. 292; see also Hayles, 1991; Adam, 1998).

More recently, chaos and complexity theories have begun to inflect sociological analysis (Byrne, 1998). Such theories involve repudiating simple dichotomies of order and disorder, of being and becoming. Physical systems do not, it seems, exhibit and sustain structural stability. The commonsense notion that small changes in causes produce small changes in effects is mistaken. Instead, there is deterministic chaos, dynamic becoming, and non-linear changes in the properties of systems as a whole rather than transformations within particular components. Time in such a perspective is highly discontinuous, and there are many non-equilibrium situations in which abrupt and unpredictable changes occur as the parameters are changed over time. Following a perfectly deterministic set of rules, unpredictable yet patterned results can be generated. The classic example is the famous butterfly effect, where minuscule changes at one location produce, in very particular circumstances, massive weather effects elsewhere. Such complex systems are characterized by counter-intuitive outcomes that occur temporally and spatially distant from where they appear to have originated.

Complexity theory emphasizes how complex feedback loops exacerbate initial stresses in the system and render it unable to absorb shocks in a simple way which re-establishes the original equilibrium. Very strong interactions are seen to occur between the parts of a system and there is a lack of a central hierarchical structure. Zohar and Marshall (1994) elaborate the implications of the concept of the *quantum society*. They describe the collapse of the old certainties of classical physics, characterized by rigid categories of absolute time and space; solid impenetrable matter made up of interacting "billiard balls" and strictly determinant laws of motion. In its place there is "the strange world of quantum physics, an indeterminate world whose almost eerie laws mock the boundaries of space, time and matter" (Zohar and Marshall, 1994, p. 33). They particularly develop analogies between the wave/particle effect and the emergent characteristics of social life: "Quantum reality" has the potential to be both particle-like and wave-like. Particles are individuals, located and measurable in space and time. They are either here or there, now or then. Waves are "non-local," they are spread out across all of space and time, and their instantaneous effects are everywhere. Waves extend themselves in every direction at once, they overlap and combine with other waves to form new realities (new emergent wholes), such as those changes occurring at the emergent global level (Zohar and Marshall, 1994, p. 326; Urry, 2000).

Many writers have directly or indirectly developed aspects of these arguments in relationship to the social world (Byrne, 1998; Cilliers, 1998). I shall now discuss three older writers whose ideas connect to such notions: Lefebvre, Bachelard and Benjamin. First, Lefebvre (1991) argues that space is not a neutral and passive geometry. Space is produced and reproduced and thus represents the site of struggle. Moreover, all sorts of different spatial phenomena – land, territory, site, and so on – should be understood as part of the same dialectical structure of space or spatialization. While conventionally these different phenomena are separated as a result of fragmented discipline-based analyses, they need to be brought together in a unified structure.

This comprises three elements. First, there are "spatial practices." These range from individual routines to the systematic creation of zones and regions. Such spatial practices are over time concretized in the built environment and in the landscape. The most significant spatial practices are those of property and other forms of capital. Second, there are representations of space, the forms of knowledge and practices that organize and represent space, particularly through the techniques of planning and the state. And, third, there are the spaces of representation, or the collective experiences of space. These include symbolic differentiations and collective fantasies around space, the resistances to the dominant practices, and resulting forms of individual and collective transgression. Lefebvre is particularly concerned with the production of space under capitalism. Different forms of space succeed each other through time. There is succession from natural to absolute to abstract space, the effect being progressively to expel nature from the social. Abstract space is the high point of capitalist relations, leading to extraordinary "created spaces." Shields's (1991) analysis of social spatialization develops Lefebvre's examination of the cultural construction of space. He examines the changing social spatialization of the beach, as it went from a medical zone to a pleasure zone; the social construction of the place-myths of Brighton and Niagara Falls; the construction of the "north" and "south" "spaces" of Britain; and the contested space myths of the north of Canada (see Urry, 1995, for other examples).

Bachelard (1969) likewise develops a conception of space that is qualitative and heterogeneous, rather than abstract, empty and static. He specifically considers the nature of the "house" and argues that it is not to be seen as a purely physical object. In particular, it is the site within which one's imagination and daydreaming can take place and be given free rein (Bachelard, 1969, p. 6). And the home is also a metaphor for intimacy. Houses are within us and we reside in houses. In particular, all sorts of spaces, such as the house in which one is born, are imbued with memory traces. And that belongingness derives from the materiality of the particular place in question. Moreover, Bachelard argues that the very duration of time is itself dependent upon such spatial specificity. Space is necessary to give quality to time. Or, as Game (1995, p. 201) expresses it, "Space transforms time in such a way that memory is made possible." Thus a space such as a house plays a particularly significant role in the forming and sustaining of memory. It shelters daydreaming. Further, our bodies do not forget the first house that we encounter. Bachelard (1969, p. 15) talks of a "passionate liaison" between the body and this initial house. Its characteristics are physically inscribed in us. Memories are materially localized and so the temporality of memory is spatially rooted. Bachelard spatializes the temporality of memory. Houses are lived through one's body and its memories (Game, 1995, pp. 202–3). Memories of places are embodied. The past is "passed" on to us not merely in what we think or what we do but in how we do it. And places are not just seen, as in the scopic regime of the "sightseer," but perceived through the diverse senses that may make us ache to be somewhere else or shiver at the prospect of having to stay put (see Urry, 2000, on the senses). Proust conveys this embodied character of memory: "our arms and legs are full of torpid memories" (Low-enthal, 1985, p. 203).

Benjamin (1979) draws on similar themes in his analysis of how people "read" the city (see also Buck-Morss, 1989). This is not a matter of intellectual or positivistic observation; instead, it involves fantasy, wish-processes, and dreams. The city is the repository of people's memories and of the past; and it also functions as a receptacle of cultural symbols. These memories are embodied in buildings that then take on a significance different from that intended by the architect. However, this is not simply a matter of individual interpretation, since buildings demonstrate collective myths. Understanding these myths entails a process of unlocking or undermining existing interpretations and traditions and of juxtaposing conflicting elements together. Even derelict build-ings may leave traces and reveal memories, dreams, and hopes of previous periods. Wright's *A Journey through Ruins* (1992) well demonstrates Benjamin's method, as he begins his journey with an old toilet in Dalston Lane in east London.

Benjamin was also concerned with the similarities between artistic perception and the reading of the urban text. Benjamin suggests that buildings are normally appreciated in passing, in a state of distraction, as people are moving on else-where. This is by contrast with people's "concentrated" absorption of paintings in a gallery. Most famously, Benjamin examined the role of the flâneur, the stroller, who wandered around the city sampling life in a distracted and unpre-meditated form (Buck-Morss, 1989). The voyeuristic and distracted nature of the encounter with the urban means that memories of the past can be ignited by some current event. It is only with distracted perception that this chance linking of past and present can occur and undermine the oppressive weight of past traditions. Benjamin also analyzes those places concerned only with entertain-ment, such as the expositions in Paris; they transform visitors to the level of the commodity as they enter a "phantasmagorical world."

Following on from these theories, a variety of crucial points about place have been developed by writers influenced in one way or another by these older contributions. However, the kinds of points now made are diverse and mean that the sociology of place has moved a long way from the simple and objective dimensionality of Newtonian space and time.

First, it is now more clearly seen that places are not necessarily static and unchanging (Massey, 1994, pp. 136–7). Places involve process and such processes involve more local and much wider sets of social relations. Massey states that what I have termed localness is a "distinct mixture together in one place [which] produce[s] effects which would not have happened otherwise" (1994, pp. 156, 138). Places can therefore be loosely understood as multiplex, as a set of spaces where ranges of relational networks and flows coalesce, interconnect, and fragment. Any such place can be viewed as the particular nexus between, on the one hand, propinquity characterized by intensely thick co-present interaction, and on the other hand, fast flowing webs and networks stretched corporeally, virtually and imaginatively across distances. These propinquities and extensive networks come together to enable performances in, and of, particular places.

In particular, places, we now know, are "gendered." Men and women can have different relations to the "city," which is often dominated by male interests and by the predominant forms of representation, such as monuments, commemorative buildings, and historic sites, that record male activities. We also know just how important urban design is for the safe dwelling and mobility of women, especially in those places dominated by automobility (Wilson, 1991; Ardener, 1993; Wolff, 1995; Sheller and Urry, 2000). There are, of course, complex interconnections between such analyses and those of ethnicity. Particularly in the USA, much focus has been placed on showing the changing spatial distribution of different ethnic groups and especially the development of a black underclass in the inner city (Wilson, 1987). Wilson argues that this has resulted from the spatial mobility of the black middle class that in large numbers left the black areas. This has helped to undermine the bases of community life, at the same time that such areas have been devastated by massive deindustrialization as jobs moved south and west and out to the suburbs. There is an "emptying out of the ghetto" (Wacquant, 1989; Davis, 1990).

Changing gender and ethnic character is associated with cities being reconstructed as centers for postmodern consumption (and employment); the city is becoming a spectacle, a "dreamscape of visual consumption," according to Zukin (1992, p. 221). She shows how property developers have constructed these new landscapes of power, stage sets within which consumption can take place, including especially wining and dining (see Bell and Valentine, 1997, on how "we are where we eat"). These dreamscapes pose significant problems for people's identity, which have historically been founded on place, on where people come from or have moved to. Yet postmodern landscapes are all about place, such as Main Street in EuroDisney, World Fairs or Covent Garden in London. But these are simulated places for consumption. They are barely places that people any longer come from, or live in, or which provide much of a sense of social identity. Somewhat similarly, Sennett (1991) argues that in the contemporary city different buildings no longer exercise a moral function – the most significant new spaces are those based around consumption and tourism. Such spaces are specifically designed to wall off the differences between diverse social groups and to separate the inner life of people from their public activities.

Objects are thus very significant in this construction of place. Various kinds of objects, activities, or media images may constitute the basis of such an "imagined presence." They carry that imagined presence across the members of a local community, although much of the time members of such a place may not be conscious of this imagined community. Various objects can function in this way – and not just the immense monuments of place and community. Oldenburg has described the significance of informal casual meeting places: bars, cafés, community centers, spaces under pear trees, and so on. He calls these "third places," places beyond work and households where communities come into being and neighborhood life can be sustained (Oldenburg, 1989; Diken, 1998).

Finally, even those places which are based upon geographical propinquity depend upon diverse mobilities. There are countless ways of reaffirming a sense of dwelling through movement within a community's boundaries, such as walking along well worn paths. But any such community is also interconnected to many other places through diverse kinds of travel. Raymond Williams in *Border Country* (1988) is "fascinated by the networks men and women set up, the trails and territorial structures they make as they move across a region, and the ways these interact or interfere with each other" (Pinkney, 1991, p. 49; Cresswell, 1997, p. 373). Massey similarly argues that the identity of a place is derived in large part from its interchanges with other places that may be stimulating and progressive. Sometimes, though, such notions depend upon gender-unequal relationships to the possibilities of travel. Massey discusses how "mum" can function as the symbolic center to whom "prodigal sons" return when the going elsewhere gets tough (1994, p. 180).

Finally, I shall consider two examples where research has shown how places are constituted through networks of movement. First, among British road protestors and travelers, dwellings are often impermanent and characterized, according to one participant, by "their shared air of impermanence, of being ready to move on...re-locate to other universities, mountain-tops, ghettos, factories, safe houses, abandoned farms" (Mckay, 1996, p. 8). There is a sense of movement, of continuous acts of transgression, as happens in the case of a peace convoy. Their dwelling spaces are constituted through various routeways and specific sacred nodes. Dwelling is intense, impermanent, and mobile. These cultures of resistance are constituted as "a *network . . .* of *independent collectives and communities*" (Albion Free State Manifesto, 1974; see Mckay, 1996, p. 11). Such groupings form a "loose network of loose networks," such as those involved in free festivals, rural fairs, alternative music, hunt sabotage, road protests, new age traveling, rave culture, poll tax protest, peace convoys, animal rights, and so on (Mckay, 1996, p. 11). These networks are reinforced by various patterns of travel, in which there is a kind of resistant mapping of key events, places, routeways, and so on (see Urry, 2000, on corporeal mobility).

Second, the literature on diasporas shows how cultures have been made and remade as a consequence of the flows of peoples, objects, and images backwards and forwards across borders (Bhabha, 1990). Gilroy specifically argues that: "In opposition to...ethnically absolute approaches, I want to develop the suggestion that cultural historians could take the Atlantic as one single, complex unit of analysis . . . and use it to produce an explicitly transnational and intercultural perspective" (Gilroy, 1993, p. 15). Diasporic societies cannot persist without much corporeal, imaginative, and increasingly virtual travel both to that home-land and to other sites of the diaspora (Kaplan, 1996, pp. 134–6). Clifford (1997, p. 247) summarizes:

> dispersed peoples, once separated from homelands by vast oceans and political barriers, increasingly find themselves in border relations with the old country thanks to a to-and-fro made possible by modern technologies of transport, com-munication, and labor migration. Airplanes, telephones, tape cassettes, camcor-ders, and mobile job markets reduce distances and facilitate two-way traffic, legal and illegal, between the world's places.

The sacred places and the family and community members to be visited are located in various "societies" linked through "structured travel circuits" (Clif-ford, 1997, p. 253). Such modes of travel and exchange – what Clifford terms the "lateral axes of diaspora" – reorganize the very sense of what is a social group's "heritage," which is never simply fixed, stable, natural, and "authentic" (Clifford, 1997, p. 269). In particular, the close-knit family, kin, clan, and ethnic connections within a diaspora enable the flows of migrants and income across national borders and the more general organization of diasporic trade.

The tendency for diasporas to live within major "global" cities means that they particularly contribute to, and profit from, the increasingly cosmopolitan character of such places (Hannerz, 1996). This can be seen with the overseas Chinese who have generated Chinatowns in many major cities across the globe. The largest is in New York and is a strikingly recent phenomenon. In the 1960s there were only 15,000 residents but over the next twenty years they had grown twenty-fold, with a staggering array of services, workshops, and increasingly professional trades. Chinatowns have of course become key nodes within the routeways of "global tourism," since they sell authentic "ethnic quaintness," a quaintness cleaned up and repackaged for the international tourist gaze (Cohen, 1997, p. 93).

Diasporas thus indicate the more general point about place, summarized by bell hooks (1991, p. 148) when she writes: "home is no longer one place. It is locations" – and, we might add, the mobilities between such locations. I have described sociology's journey to make sense of such places, a journey that involves traveling in and out of diverse intellectual homes, producing a hybrid analysis drawn from many locations.

2

Media and Communications

John Durham Peters

COMMUNICATION AND SOCIAL THEORY: LEGACY AND DEFINITIONS

Of all the social sciences, sociology has the most distinguished record of contributions to the study of media and communications. Throughout every decade of the twentieth century, important sociologists made them a central topic – Tarde, Park, Blumer, Ogburn, Lazarsfeld, Merton, Katz, Adorno, Habermas, Tuchman, Schudson, Gans, Luhmann, Bourdieu, among many others. Yet communication is not simply a specialty in sociology; it is in many ways the historical precondition of modern social theory. Its founding thinkers, such as Tocqueville, Marx, Durkheim, Weber, Simmel, and Tönnies, rarely called communication by name, yet their picture of modern society, with its individualism, participatory institutions, and new possibilities of large-scale social conflict, administration, and integration, centers on the symbolic coordination of individuals and populations. Concepts as diverse as Marx's class consciousness, Durkheim's collective representations, or Tönnies's *Gesellschaft* all point to social relationships that transcend the face-to-face. Neither ancient nor feudal society had any use for a notion of pluralistic, inclusive, and horizontal sociability. Modernity, with its political and transportation revolutions, foregrounds the symbolic aspect of social coordination. Communication becomes an axis of modern society. Association not anchored in place or in personal acquaintance is the central topic of both modern social theory and mass communication theory. Classic European social theory in this sense was always the study of communication without knowing it.

It was the Americans who made the explicit connection between sociology and communication. Drawing on German political economy and the evolutionary philosophy of Herbert Spencer, such first-generation American evolutionary sociologists as Lester Frank Ward and Franklin Giddings saw the movement of goods and ideas as the lifeblood of modern society. Even more emphatically, Charles Horton Cooley, Robert Ezra Park, and W. I. Thomas, along with their philosophical co-conspirators John Dewey and George Herbert Mead, saw society as a network of symbolic interactions. Communication was the secret of modern social organization. In Dewey's famous declaration, "Society not only continues to exist *by* transmission, *by* communication, but it may be fairly said to exist *in* transmission, *in* communication."

In its intellectual development, "communication" has meant many things (Peters, 1999), and this was no less true in sociology. Communication's sense could include the dissemination of symbols, cultural transmission, and also more intimate processes, such as dialogue, socialization, or community creation. For the Chicagoans, communication could mean the descriptive total of human relationships as well as an ideal of democratic participation. American democracy, they thought, depended on citizens becoming co-authors in the symbolic and material shaping of their worlds. Park and Burgess (1921, p. 341) offer a characteristic pair of sentences: "the limits of society are coterminous with the limits of interaction, that is, of the participation of persons in the life of society. One way of measuring the wholesome or the normal life of a person is by the sheer external fact of his membership in the social groups of the community in which his lot is cast." A straightforward descriptive statement (that communication defines social order) is followed by a normative one (that participation is the criterion of healthy social relations). This normative loading of communication persists in social theory to this day. For Jürgen Habermas, for instance, communication is not just linguistic exchange or social interaction, but a principle of rational intersubjectivity, even of social justice. For him, communication is much more than the sharing of information; it is the foundation of democratic deliberation. In seeing communication as the mesh of ego and alter, he is a clear heir to the early Chicago sociologists. "Communication" has always worn a halo, offering inklings of the good society.

Communication as a concept also splits along symbolic and material lines. In E. A. Ross's classic definition, "Communication embraces all symbols of experience together with the means by which they are swung across gulfs of space or time." *Communications*, in contrast to *communication*, often makes just this distinction, referring to the institutions and practices of recording and transmitting symbols rather than to an ideal of community. It typically includes telecommunications, such as the postal service, telegraph, telephone, satellite, and computer networks; sometimes railroads, highways, air and sea travel; sometimes also fundamental modes of human intercourse such as gesture, speech, writing, and printing.

We can also speak of these institutions and practices as *media*. The term has several senses. First, and least interesting, *media* in popular usage refers indiscriminately and often disparagingly to the personnel or institutions of the news media, taken as a lump. Second, *mass* media often refer to a complex of culture industries, especially the big five – radio, television, movies, newspapers, and magazines – which share the features of being for-profit institutions that use industrial-era technology to engage in largely monologic transmission to massive audiences. Media sociology arose in the heyday of these media, roughly the 1920s through the 1960s or 1970s, but it is now clear that these definitional criteria may be valid only for a passing historical moment. Hence a third definition of media is needed: any vessel of cultural storage, diffusion, or expression. In this sense, architecture, cities, sculpture, bumper stickers, sky-writing, or the human body could be media, in the same sense that one speaks of artistic media, such as oil, watercolor, or papier mâché. This expanded sense of *media* is used by thinkers outside of the mainstream of media sociology, such as Harold Adams Innis and Lewis Mumford, who link basic media forms with larger civilizational consequences. Though less precise, this more open definition is helpful for understanding current transformations in the social place of media and for broadening the historical and comparative vistas of media studies.

STANDARDIZING AND LOCALIZING TRENDS

In broad strokes, the fundamental task of twentieth-century media sociology has been to assuage the anxiety that modern communications homogenize culture and society. Sociological research has repeatedly minimized fears of media power. Although new communications media seemingly rupture social scale, local community life does not disappear, say most sociologists; instead, it takes different shapes.

In the early twentieth century, the main challenge came from the anxiety, deriving largely from crowd psychology and Tocqueville's notion of democratic leveling, that modern communication, thanks to its contagious sweep and increased radius of influence, would wash all personal, cultural, and geographic diversity into a standardized ocean of sameness. Cooley (1909, chapter nine) responded by arguing that improved communications enhance "choice" and weaken "isolation" as the basis of individuation. His point, familiar in turn-of-the-century social thought, was that communication had superseded geography as the chief constraint on human sociability. A community of isolation would differentiate, like Darwin's finches, in idiosyncratic directions, but a community of choice, one united by the interests rather than location of its participants, was a harbinger of a renewed democracy. In a sense Cooley theorized virtual communities by suggesting that new forms of communication allowed for remote associations based on interest rather than place. Thus Cooley, like his colleagues, identified countervailing tendencies against the supposed time- and space-destroying powers of new forms of communication. The first generation of American sociology answered the specter of assimilation with the hope of the great community.

Malcolm Willey and Stuart Rice, in a forgotten but highly suggestive early study of new transport and communication media, made a similar argument: "Contacts within the community are multiplied out of proportion to contacts at a distance" (Willey and Rice, 1933, p. 57). Rather than eviscerating local life, cars and telephones actually multiplied the intensity of contacts. Although new means offered an unprecedented opportunity to escape locality, they were more often used to link familiar people and places. "Individuals north, south, east, and west, may all wear the garments of Hollywood. At the same time each may hold with undiminished vigor to certain local attitudes, traditions, and beliefs. An increase in overt standardization may be accompanied by retention of inward differences" (Willey and Rice, 1933, pp. 213–14).

In a somewhat similar way, the tradition of work on media effects associated with Columbia University sought to check the fear that media were bulldozing collective bonds and individual judgment. The hallmark of the research done by Paul F. Lazarsfeld and his students at Columbia in the 1940s and 1950s was the proposition that media have strong influence only when mediated by such psychological variables as selectivity or such sociological variables as interpersonal relations. Work at the Columbia Bureau of Applied Social Research focused more on the short-term attitudinal effects of media campaigns than on the larger trends favored by the Chicagoans, although Lazarsfeld's blueprint, at least, of the mission of communications research did include the macro, long-term consequences of media for social organization.

The Columbia tradition's insight that the power of mediated messages is constrained by extant social-psychological conditions has proved remarkably influential and adaptable. Against the inflated fears (or hopes) of some propaganda analysts, Lazarsfeld and Merton (1948) argued that mass communication could be persuasive only under special conditions, such as the absence of counter-propaganda, the reinforcement of media messages by face-to-face discussion, and the strategic exploitation of well established behaviors. The power of unaided mass media to win wars, sway voters, or sell soap was, they argued, overrated. In their 1955 *Personal Influence*, Lazarsfeld and Elihu Katz argued the priority of personal over mediated influence. People, not radio or newspapers, turned out to be the key channels of communication. Opinion leaders first expose themselves to media, then talk to friends and family, thus serving as links in the larger network of communication, by dancing "the two-step flow" of communication. The "discovery of people" in the process of communication, as Lazarsfeld and Katz whimsically called it, was not only empirical; it was a gambit in the debate in 1950s sociology about whether postwar America had become a mass society of lonely crowds, disconnected from each other but connected by media. *Personal Influence* expounded people's immunity to media-induced atomization and assimilation, thus fitting the broader American legacy of understanding media as agents of social differentiation rather than homogenization. Localizing factors were again deemed as important as standardizing ones in the effects of mass communication.

The same argumentative logic appears in more recent work in the same tradition. In a study of the worldwide reception of the television program *Dallas*, Tamar Liebes and Katz (1990) argue against the widespread fear that a new imperialism of television, music, and film would lead to a global (American) monoculture. Instead, Liebes and Katz showed that different groups used their own cultural and ideological predispositions and resources to interpret *Dallas* in distinct ways. Russian Israelis, for instance, often read *Dallas* as a self-critical exposé of American capitalism, while Israeli Arabs often focused on its intricate kinship structures and clan loyalties. Against the classic fear of a powerful media stimulus, updated here to an international setting, Liebes and Katz affirmed the inevitability of diverse and local responses to a homogeneously disseminated text. (In this, they were in line with trends in the sociology of media audiences generally.) Although the context was different from the founding generation of American sociology – electronic media threatening national diversity worldwide versus national railroads and newspapers threatening island communities – the sociological response is similar: outward (media) standardization, inward (social) differentiation.

The equally venerable critical tradition of media sociology, whose chief archi-tects were scholars of the Frankfurt School and whose classic statement is "the culture industry" chapter in Horkheimer and Adorno's *Dialectic of Enlighten-ment* (1944), differs principally on this point. For critical theory, the standard-ization of culture cannot be separated from that of society. Whether cultural industries are totalities or differentiated formations is one of the great theoretical fault lines in media sociology, not only in the mid-twentieth-century face-offs between figures such as Lazarsfeld and Merton versus Adorno and Horkheimer, but also in more recent debates in feminist research and cultural studies about the interpretive autonomy of media audiences. For critical theory, the defense of popular autonomy serves as an apology for an invasive consciousness industry, by placing the responsibility for media effects on the individual rather than the system; for mainstream sociology, to ignore audience interpretation is to ignore facts. Lazarsfeld's tradition, like that of the Chicago School, ultimately sees the media as agents of social integration; Adorno's tradition agrees that media achieve integration – a forced reconciliation in the interest of a few. The Frank-furt School insisted that any adequate analysis of modern media had to link the social-psychological study of socialization, personality, and family with the historical-economic study of cultural-making institutions; the rationalization of culture went together with the duping of consciousness. A similar notion of media as linking personal dreams and social structures is found in the thought of Gramsci and Althusser and their disciples. Media sociology, whether critical or mainstream, has turned on the question of social homogenization and control.

CONTEMPORARY ISSUES

The National Frame

All complex societies, ancient and modern, organize communications in various ways and to diverse ends. For much of the past century, communications gen-erally and the mass media in particular have been designed to link the nation-state with the household. In Habermas's language, media have been a chief agent in coupling "system" (the market and the state) and "lifeworld" (civil society and the family). Modern media history, especially that of the press and broadcasting, is an open book of large-scale social integration. Modern media have had the task of tying micro-level parts of social life (taste, consumption, the household) to macro-level cultural, political, and economic structures (corporations, the nation). Raymond Williams (1974) coined the suggestive term "mobile privatization" for the contradictory historical processes shaping the emergence of broadcasting: increased mobility in goods, people, and ideas, together with the solidification of the household as a site of entertainment and consumption. (Note too the hint of political pathos: this was not public mobilization!) Newspapers, realist drama, brand names, opinion polling, mail-order catalogues, soap operas, call-in shows, or TV guides are diverse examples of practices that quite literally mediate feeling and structure, household and society. As media always involve negotiations along the border of public and private, their study raises explicit questions about the constitution of social order (Carey, 1989). What is significant about twentieth and twenty-first century media is not only the pervasiveness of their reach, but also the intimacy of the site in which they touch us.

In Anderson's (1991) thesis, the modern newspaper, even with local circulation, invited its readers to imagine themselves members in a vast national community. Network broadcasting, which did achieve national distribution, likewise operated in the frame of the nation state. The national focus is clear in such names as NBC, CBS, ABC, BBC, CBC, each of which indexes the polity: National, Columbia, American, British, Canadian. Radio first established the crucial arrangements in the two decades between the world wars: nationwide distribution of programs to a domestic audience trained to simultaneous reception. Despite differences between the market-sponsored system in the United States and the state-sponsored systems of Europe and elsewhere, something sociologically remarkable was achieved in broadcasting: the coordination of national populations over time and space. Perhaps what emerged earlier on Sunday mornings in Protestant countries, with the whole population effectively tuned to the same "program" (the vernacular Bible), was similar, but broadcasting was new in its conjuring of a simultaneously co-oriented national populace and in its address of a listenership at home. Cinema too, from the First World War through the 1960s or so, was organized nationally in production, content, distribution, and exhibition. In their heydays, both broadcasting and cinema were at once a mode of production, a set of stylistic conventions, and a set of social relations involving audiences and cultural forms (though these, as we will see, were importantly different for the two media).

Due to technical, regulatory, and economic developments, the national frame for cinema and television has been waning in the past quarter century. (Radio, in some regions such as sub-Saharan Africa, is still the medium of national integration, but in the 1950s United States, it became the medium of musically differentiated taste cultures or "formats.") The domestic box office is only one important source of revenue for Hollywood films today, along with foreign box office, video sales, and merchandising. Instead of a studio system churning out variations on well known genres for a national audience, one shift in the past quarter century has been to blockbusters (genres of one), such as *Jaws* or *Titanic*, for distribution (and merchandising) across the globe. Television audiences, while often still huge in relative terms, are increasingly fragmented into demographic segments thanks to channel proliferation. And in the transition to digital encoding of all content, media are increasingly inseparable from communications. The air once carried radio and television programming, but increasingly fiber-optic cables are the main medium for news and entertainment, just as the air is becoming the prime medium of voice and data transmission thanks to mobile telephony, in a rather stunning switch of the old order. In 1950, mails, telephones, phonographs, radios, televisions, and movie theaters were all separate channels with distinct content, such as print, interactive voice, sound, image, and money; now they are all carried on the Internet in digital form (Mueller, 1999). Broadcasting to a national audience, then, just like national cinema, may turn out to be a momentary historical deviation, as media now return to their origins in wires (the telegraph). When social scientists were minting concepts for media analysis at mid-twentieth century, mass communication had paradigmatic status. Today, different conditions, such as smaller audience size, differentiated niches, and altered social norms, raise new questions.

One such question is the fate of social integration amidst the proliferation of channels and fragmentation of audiences. As recently as the 1970s, the three American television networks, NBC, CBS, and ABC, shared up to 95 percent of the viewing audience. By the late 1990s, that figure has dropped to about 65 percent, shared among NBC, CBS, ABC, and Fox, owing to competition with cable services, but also satellites, video rentals, home computers, and the Internet. Since the 1970s, advertisers have sought purer demographic segments. This is clearly a radical shift in the national provision of news and entertainment – though not an utter meltdown. A common fear is that citizens will be isolated by their idiosyncratic tastes. Instead of national newspapers people will read the daily me; identity politics will vanquish the common good. Yet the potential to fragment into a Tower of Babel, each of us speaking a private cultural tongue, is a problem only for the very rich, as unlimited programming choices remain, for the time being, outside the reach of most. Clearly, channel-multiplication has created neither cultural nor cognitive chaos, as some postmodern writers on information blizzards fear. The statistical limits on human energy always centralize attention. Tastes in programming are not infinitely diverse, but cluster into taste cultures. In the case of Germany, Italy, and Greece, for instance, four television networks shared 65–75 percent of the television audience in the early 1990s, as in the United States. In Britain, just two channels draw a comparable percentage (Curran, 1998). Of the twenty-five or so radio formats in the USA, the top five have nearly half of the audience. Format concentration is found across media (Neuman, 1991), though we should not assume that popular demand alone is the controlling factor. The fear that media segmentation will cause citizens to retreat to a cocoon of private egoism (a fear in social theory that dates at least to Tocqueville) is checked by the habitual preferences of audiences for programming that engages a societal frame. Fragmentation has replaced homogenization as the chief fear aroused by media.

The Shifting Moral Economy of Media

The waning of a nationally organized schedule of programs as a cultural grid suggests a more significant, but more subtle, transformation of the place of broadcasting in the general moral economy. Because it entered the homes of the nation, broadcasting historically accepted constraints on topics and forms of expression. Radio, like television, was painted as a guest in the family circle, and was hence pressured to embody a culture of middle-brow mundaneness and normality, a tonality that continued from early radio through much of television, though never with full compliance. From Mae West's banishment from the airwaves in 1938 for inviting the puppet Charlie McCarthy to play in her "wood pile," through the 1978 Supreme Court case *Pacifica* concerning the broadcast of comedian George Carlin's satirical monologue about the "seven dirty words" that could never be said on the air – a case which found that broadcasting's "unique pervasiveness" justified tighter content controls than other media – radio and television have been bound by a thick set of normative, if obviously ideologically loaded, constraints (the nation as patriarchal family). Because they spoke to the nation at home, radio and television in their heydays were regarded, for better or worse, as forums whose tone should be suitable to all.

Film, in contrast, never quite assumed the same burden of public decency as broadcasting, despite an even more intense history of attack by the guardians of public morals. The theatrical exhibition of movies took place outside the home, in dark spaces set apart for collective fantasy on extraordinary topics such as romance, sex, crime, and adventure. The dangers of such fantasy were buffered by collective viewing; the assembled peer group of fellow citizens, as Cantril and Allport (1935) argued, immunized against anti-social consequences. Wandering eyes and hearts were cathartically reserved to the film palace. For both film and broadcasting around mid-twentieth century, the audience experience was intensely normed: one watched movies collectively and took part in broadcasting with the awareness that one's reference groups were also simultaneously doing so.

The division of media labor – broadcasting as normalizing the family circle, film as fantasizing the collective psyche – has crumbled. The multiplication of channels and shifting modes of exhibition and delivery suggest shifting constraints on the audience experience. The old standard of broadcast decency has weakened, as has the sense of a simultaneous collectivity of fellow watchers. Katz (1998) argues that proliferation of channels breaks the collective norm of obligatory viewing. Viewing becomes an asocial experience, not a simultaneous communion of reference groups that sets the agenda for water-cooler discussions the next day. The very notion of a "Home Box Office," the first dominant cable channel (1975) and a leader in getting content hitherto allowed only in theaters onto television screens, signals these changes.

The normative frame of much American television programming has shifted from common culture to private club, allowing forms and contents of expression adapted to homogeneous in-groups. No longer under the ideological and economic constraint of reaching general audiences, American television today includes R-rated prime time drama, explicitly indecent talk shows, and caught-on-tape programs such as animals (or police officers) attacking people. As programs proliferated into niches, television lost its halo as the collective hearth, even if still viewed by a plurality of citizens. Such programs as MTV's *Beavis and Butthead*, with its sophomoric humor and crudity, were even designed to scare away viewers over a certain age, thus purifying its demographics for advertisers in search of young buyers (Turow, 1997). Now programs can be designed to expel as much as to include.

The national-social logic of broadcasting taught viewers that there were other, unknown audiences out there. Hence, as a cultural field, broadcasting is a breeding ground for worries about effects on others (third-person effects). Broadcasting breeds offended viewers, if not for themselves, then for children or other vulnerable souls in the audience. In our age of increased fragmentation, this logic persists, as content once taboo for a national audience fills channels aimed at a few but available to many. Conservative backlash against cultural industries, and efforts to label, rate, or otherwise police the vast output of new film, television, and music commodities, will likely remain part of the political landscape. Such initiatives as the V-chip, a content-regulating device required by US law to be installed in all new TV sets, or the Communications Decency Act, which President Clinton appended to the 1996 Telecommunications Act in an effort to protect both children in cyberspace and his election prospects, and which was almost instantly found unconstitutional, are state-sponsored answers to the decline of moral inhibitions in the wake of splintering audiences and globalized programming flows. What some read as symptoms of large moral or civilizational decline reflect, in fact, changing industrial and technical conditions. As long as profit is the chief value that governs media production, new kinds of content will continue to appear that can make money from marginal audiences.

Channel-multiplication creates a huge demand for content. Prime-time television drama is still sometimes lavishly produced (or at least expensively, as in the case of *Seinfeld*), but talk, game, and caught-on-tape shows have the advantage of attracting salable audiences with low production budgets. The race for content also makes control over the rights to film, television, and music libraries industrially crucial (and worrisome to historians and purists, who fear such commercially motivated tampering as the colorization of old black-and-white movies). Amid the general frenzy of media mergers, a clear trend is union between producers of hardware (electronics or delivery systems) and software (programming): General Electric and NBC, Matsushita's short-lived purchase of Universal Pictures and MCA (later bought by Seagram), Sony and Columbia Pictures, Viacom and Paramount, AOL and Time-Warner. The scarcest commodity today is not channel capacity, as it was when broadcasting emerged; it is desirable programming.

The proliferation of channels, then, does not imply social fragmentation; it implies a changed social place of broadcasting and an attendant loss of moral inhibitions. Will stations and networks continue to exist? Will there be a need for a nationwide program schedule if video on demand becomes available?

Probably, given the social (and economic) value of centralized audiences and the utility of cultural packaging. Such changes have created an institutional identity crisis for European public service broadcasting, whose mission of providing quality programs to the nation is threatened by the transnational appeals of commercial television. Perhaps the unique mission of public service broadcasting should not be a national program schedule but a distinct kind of social contract with the audience: commercial-free quality programming available to all within a morally moderate national frame (Curran, 1998).

Globalization

Media flows have long been studied for their threats to national culture. In the 1970s, the common critique was that American film and television were agents of cultural imperialism, since national entertainment industries could not compete with their slick products. While such arguments could serve to fortify nationalist sentiments at home, they correctly saw Hollywood's comparative advantage in its production values and economies of scale. For the price of creating one hour of original TV, countries can lease from ten to one hundred times as much US prime-time drama. Audiences worldwide prefer local or national content, but the hitch is always production quality. Still, globalization and Americanization are not the same thing. Like everything else, media globalize unevenly. The media aren't as American as they used to be. Multiple centers of production trouble the old model of one center and one periphery: Brazilian telenovelas in Russia, Mexican programs in Latin America, Egyptian television in the Arab world, wordless Polish cartoons, Bollywood (Indian) movies in East Africa, Eastern Europe, and China, or Hong Kong action cinema in the USA. There is important regionalization of media flows, often based on common language and culture, but also mixtures and pockets (Chinese heavy metal, Franco-Maghrebi rap, karaoke in the Philippines, etc.). Even so, America still dominates, and without reciprocation. Compared to the vast majority of other nations, the USA is quite lacking in foreign media. Countries average about one-third foreign TV programming, but the USA has about 2 percent. The American market can absorb Power Rangers and Teletubbies, but in entertainment as in news, it remains isolated by its giantism. It is strange indeed that the world's chief exporter of cultural matter is blind to what every other nation sees constantly.

States often seek to protect national culture by building dams for media flows. France, Canada, and New Zealand, for instance, all have quotas for the radio play of nationally produced music. States also find other motives for blockage, usually sex and politics. Some Muslim nations ban dangerous performers (Madonna) or depictions (of kissing). Both China and Singapore police e-mail by way of firewalls. In all efforts to block media flows, the state walks a tight-rope between global political-economic pressures (since regulation erects a statist obstacle to global capitalism) and national-political ones (preservation of national distinctness).

Besides state intervention, there are other subtler impediments to media flows, such as cultural accessibility. Violence and sex travel readily across national and linguistic borders: the martial arts of a Jackie Chan or musclebound antics of an Arnold Schwarzeneggar, the beautiful people of *Baywatch* or *Beverly Hills 90210*, require little translation; culturally specific and dialogue-heavy programming such as comedy and drama do. Because of its topical references and involuted humor, *Seinfeld*, the number one rated program in late 1990s America, will probably prove a less profitable export than *Baywatch*, which never scored big at home.

The miniaturization and cheapening of media production also fuels transborder media flows. Much can be done at a desktop or in a basement, thanks to websites, CD pressing, color photocopying, video editing, etc. E-mail and the fax machine, which played a key role in the 1989 Tiananmen Square uprising and dissident movements since, are a bane of repressive governments. The ease of citizen production (and piracy) by-passes traditional gatekeepers. *Titanic* was banned in Iran, yet it was almost instantly available there in bootleg versions, recorded by hand-held video cameras in movie theaters abroad. Music tends to travel more readily than film or video, in part due to cheapness and the global compatibility of playback technology. "Small media" such as tape cassettes, samizdat carbon copies, or flyers can work more effectively for political agitation than traditional, capital-hungry media such as the press and television. The heavy artillery of media touted by modernization theory, which require not only capital investment but also a complex division of labor, vie with do-it-yourself media (Sreberny-Mohammadi and Mohammadi, 1994). As conceived by modernizers such as Rostow, Lerner, and Schramm, literacy, newspapers, and national broadcasting are the crown atop industrialization and infrastructural development (roads, schools, hydroelectric dams). Instead, relatively cheap, oral media such as mobile phones, radios, and VCRs have spread in such non-industrialized regions as South Asia or the Middle East. The relative autonomy of media from other modernization processes is a chief exhibit of the disjunctive character of globalization (Appadurai, 1996). Clearly, modernity is not a package deal.

Given shrinking cost and access to media production, how do we explain the unprecedented concentration in media corporations? The long muckraking tradition attacking media power that stretches from Upton Sinclair to Noam Chomsky, with its doctrine that concentration of control means uniformity in content, risks missing the curious ways that huge cultural industries have learned to allow, like the Catholic Church, all kinds of internal variety in cultural production. Likewise, Adorno's classic analysis of the integrated culture industry was quite apt for Hollywood in the 1940s, when vertical integration of film production, distribution, and exhibition was at its height, but finds only partial resonance today. Corporate power should be a foremost issue on the agenda of media studies, but *modi operandi* have changed. The recording industry majors, for instance, are not the monolithic trusts of yore. Oligopolistic organization is not incompatible with some creative independence, in order to insure flexibility and innovation. In recording, like other oligopolistic media industries such as film, television, and publishing, financial control is centralized but decision-making is decentralized (Rothenbuhler and Streck, 1998).

Digital Convergence?

Driving much of the transformation of media is the growing power and shrinking size and cost of computing. Some foresee a universal medium that digitizes all other media – indeed, the totality of recorded human culture – into a boundless ocean of zeroes and ones. The vaunted "convergence" of telephones, televisions, and computers is best seen not as a union of existing media but the assimilation of all media by the computer. The Internet is both a new medium and a zoo of diverse media species – raising again the paradox of simultaneous bigness and smallness in media today. Marshall McLuhan argued that the content of a new medium is an old medium. The Internet contains all previous media – telegraphy, telephony, phonography, radio, television, film, books, magazines, newspapers, and videogames – and, alas, advertising. It offers an interesting case of a still normatively unsettled medium of communication. On the one hand, the Internet seems to be as free from social obligations as home video viewing: anonymity and the lack of face-to-face acquaintance allow for uninhibited venom and narcissism in expression. Yet the leading Internet service provider, America On Line, with its significant name and policing of indecent material, may represent the revival of an older normative model. Indeed, in many ways the Internet is recapitulating radio's early transition from a culture of anarchic, technically minded renegades (amateurs/nerds) into a corporate engine of entertainment and commerce. The ongoing fight will concern access and intellectual property.

The Internet is a huge well of digitized code – sounds, texts, images – available for creative appropriation, raising fascinating questions for art and economics. One is the unprecedented manipulability of digital texts. Digital technology allows for editing *within* the frame, instead of between frames, blurring the formerly separate domains of production and post-production in film and video. The documentary or testimonial function of photography or sound recording is now more dubious, as they become less records of events than fabrications of art. The dephysicalization of entertainment, information, and other forms of programming also opens new problems in intellectual property, thanks to sampling technologies, intensifying questions such as "copyright of personality," which protects celebrities and their likeness, voice, or even gait from appropriation. Dead celebrities such as Elvis Presley, Marilyn Monroe, and John F. Kennedy have all been digitally resurrected in advertising and film. Monroe has even lent her voice to the London Underground's public address system (with a suitably anglicized accent). Digitization allows the uncanny practice of harvesting fresh images, words, and sounds from the dead.

Like channel multiplication in television, digitization raises questions of the public organization of cultural menus. What is to keep cultural consumption from being identical to cultural production, as people learn to treat digitized products as code to be manipulated? Again, the fear of private cocoons or the utopia of universal creativity should be limited by both the recognition of opportunity costs and the ongoing need for shared cultural experience.

Information is not scarce in a digital world, but intelligence is, one reason why search engine services are proliferating. The packaging (pre-processing) of information is always crucial, especially in situations of programming abundance. Information bottlenecks reinforce the principle that media are not just pipes, but have unanticipated consequences. As Innis insisted, new media create monopolies of knowledge and hence aid the formation of new power-holding classes, such as the operators of Internet portals like Yahoo!

Digitization intensifies an old principle of electronic media: economies of scale. In contrast to print media, which always had steep unit costs (paper and ink), audiovisual media generally often faced gigantic first-copy costs and cheap unit costs. Even a feature-film print, costing over ten thousand dollars, is inexpensive compared to the cost of the original; cutting a vinyl LP copy is cheap. Whereas analogue media require a physical connection to the original, digital media can be transported anywhere with enough bandwidth. Media industries are today principally in the software business. The recording industry is considering "digital kiosks" where customers may choose an album, download it, and have the CD burned on site, thus eliminating distribution and inventory, just as film distributors are developing digital projection to avoid the significant expense of transporting cans of 35 mm film. The etherealization of cultural commodities also provokes worries: the record industry wants to assess fees, similar to radio, for Internet airplay of music, instead of the Internet culture of unlicensed usage, an example illustrating some of the radical changes in distribution, ownership, and financing that digitization of content poses for large-scale media production.

The dream of universal accessibility of culture, of an Alexandrine library on the wires, is nowhere in sight. First, there are obvious impediments to access, in terms of access both to hardware and to competence or desire. (In the late 1990s, 70 percent of American homes did not have a modem.) Second, there are technological problems of incompatibility and turnover. Texts written in the 1980s and stored on $5\frac{1}{4}$ inch floppy disks are in some ways more irretrievable than those written 700 years ago on medieval parchment. Vinyl LPs are all but obsolete, and estimates vary on how long the current CD format will last. All recording media are subject to degradation, but people have lots of experience with writing and printing, whose (not inconsiderable) decoding apparatus is literacy, but little experience with digital storage in an economy of planned obsolescence. This age, eager to record everything, could ironically be a sealed book in the future if playback machines are not preserved. Digitization may mean traffic jams as much as information flows. Massive data-dumping is the flipside of gigantic downloading. As always, the sociology of digital media should recognize the centripetal as well centrifugal trends.

The Great Communications Switch

Perhaps one of the strangest and subtlest of the social consequences of twentieth-century media is a change in interpersonal interaction. A chief feature of modern interpersonal life is its mediation – by mail, phone, e-mail, and so on. At the same time, media discourse has grown increasingly conversational. In the 1940s, Adorno attacked "pseudo-individualization" in mass culture, the pretense of establishing one-on-one relationships with audiences in commercial forms of address like "especially for you." At the same time, Merton attacked the "pseudo-*Gemeinschaft*" of media-promoted communities. Both grasped, from distinct positions on the theoretical compass, the ways that media had assumed interpersonal features and vice versa. Just as broadcasting and telephony have switched media (from air to wires), perhaps the richer nations of the planet are in the middle of a great communications switch: in face-to-face talk intimates broadcast at each other, while media are full of strangers chatting with us.

A hallmark of twentieth-century cinema, drama and literature – and sociology – is the gaps between people; that is, the distortion and difficulty of dialogue. People are shown as sending messages to each other and never quite connecting. Broadcasting and the press, in contrast, have consistently imitated dialogical and intimate styles of talk, a development motivated by both domestic reception and commercial purpose (Scannell, 1991). Although some scholars have treated "parasocial interaction" (the sense that people can have personal relationships with media figures) as a pathology, it is clear that most relationships, face-to-face or otherwise, are mediated in some sense. There are elements of fictionalization in interpersonal relationships, not only in fan clubs or the more prototypical kinds of parasocial interaction. Knowing what is dialogue and what broadcast in daily interactions (i.e. what to take personally) is often difficult. E-mail's disembodiment of interaction represents a longer trend that theorists such as Luhmann and Giddens associate with modernity generally. Harvey Sacks's conversational analysis showed just how tortured and fraught – and intricately ordered – everyday dialogue could be. Interaction has become precisely something to be managed, not a natural reciprocity.

While everyday speech has grown more fraught, public discourse has grown more personal. In the nineteenth century, it was considered undignified for presidential candidates to make personal campaign appearances. Aloofness was honorable. Today it is a truism that leaders must photograph well and project their sincerity over television. From Teddy Roosevelt onward, the personalization of political leaders has grown massively, thanks to developments in the audiovisual capacities of the press and a more general process of social informalization, a process, once started, that did not stop with Reagan's smile and Clinton's tears, but made public the former's polyps and the latter's semen.

ACKNOWLEDGMENTS

For ideas, conversation, and advice I would like to thank Judith Blau, Kenneth Cmiel, Joy Hayes, Chul Heo, Elihu Katz, Franklin Miller, Stylianos Papathanassopoulos, Eric Rothenbuhler, Michael Sáenz, and Peter Simonson, without implicating them in any errors of fact or interpretation I have made.

3

Modernity: One or Many?

Peter Wagner

Half way through the fourth volume of his monumental tetralogy on the past two centuries of world history, historian Eric Hobsbawm unexpectedly uses an extraordinary phrase when he characterizes the period from 1945 to 1990 as "the greatest and most dramatic, rapid and universal social transformation in human history" (Hobsbawm, 1994, p. 288). Historians are usually quite reluctant to come out with such grand propositions. That is one reason why the assertion comes as a surprise.

The second reason for surprise is more strictly sociological. Even though no extended period of world history is without some important changes, the second half of the twentieth century could be considered one of unusual stability. In global terms, the most significant institutional transformation was certainly decolonization. But if the focus is on Western societies, all that seemed to happen was gradual change without major ruptures or unpredicted events. In striking contrast to the first half of the century, in which there were wars and revolutions of global dimensions and the establishment of novel socio-political configurations, notably socialism and fascism, the second half can be described in terms of the institutional consolidation of liberal-democratic market societies.

SOCIOLOGY AND MODERNITY

Assertions of Hobsbawm's kind are always contestable. How do we measure the magnitude of social change? Neither historians nor sociologists have a completely convincing answer to that question. But there is a conceptual question in the background of such assertion that needs an answer – or at least a reflective discussion. Sociologists have long tended to theorize contemporary Western societies as "modern societies." One can even take it to be the founding assumption of sociology that there was a rupture with earlier modes of social organization by which societies were put on an entirely different footing. The Reformation and the scientific, industrial, and democratic revolutions are the major points of reference, and even though the precise dating is debatable, at the very least the sum of all those transformations put modern society firmly into place. Importantly, this thinking went with the additional assumption – which often remained implicit, but was sometimes spelt out – that there could be no further major social transformation. When "modern society" was established, a superior form of social organization was reached that contained all it needed to adapt successfully to changing circumstances. If Hobsbawm was right about the second postwar period, then something was wrong with the sociological view of modern society.

What are the issues that are at stake? Assuming we accept his diagnosis of a recent major social transformation, there are several possibilities of interpretation. First, one can see this transformation as a rather comprehensive one that touches more or less all societies. This generates two further conceptual options. Either one can see this change as a major adaptation of modern society to new circumstances, or one can see it as the end of modern society and its transformation into something else. We shall see that both options have indeed been embraced. Second, there is the possibility that this transformation does not occur everywhere or not everywhere in the same way. Such an interpretation would cast doubt on the general applicability of the concept "modern society." Third, and radicalizing this idea, this transformation – which after all was unexpected by sociologists – may call for a reconsideration of the very way sociology approached the study of contemporary societies. Was the "modernity" of modern society ever understood?

Initially, our latter suspicions are confirmed by some peculiar developments in terminology. At some point some quarter century ago, the sociology of entire contemporary societal configurations – sometimes somewhat infelicitously called "macro-sociology" or also "political sociology" – lost its vocabulary. Around the end of the 1960s, it disposed of – as far as this can go in a pluralistic discipline like sociology – a coherent set of concepts, centered on terms like "industrial society" (Clark Kerr and others) or "modern society" (Talcott Parsons and others). In this framework, "modernization" and "development" were the terms for social change, which was thought to be as predictable as the structure of society was analyzable. From the 1970s onwards, however, in the light of observed changes that had not been foreseen, sociologists became inclined to add prefixes like "post-" or qualifying attributes like "late" to their key concepts, thus implicitly giving up on all theoretical coherence. For a certain time during the 1980s, the diffusion of the term "postmodernity," even more radically, signaled a momentous transformation by suggesting that the very core of Western self-understanding, namely being "modern" – which, etymologically speaking, means nothing but being up to the exigencies of one's time – was in question. And even worse (for sociology), the term carried with it the implication that the very intelligibility of the social world was cast into doubt.

Sociologists' response to this challenge was the introduction of the term "modernity" into their vocabulary. In this chapter, I try to show that what is at stake in this enigmatic terminological shift is the very possibility of analyzing entire societal configurations and their historical transformations. To provide a bit more of a background, I first sketch in some more detail the intellectual developments over the past three decades. Then I discuss the questions introduced above, namely: Was there a major social transformation? If so, to what new societal configuration(s) has it led? And what do these considerations entail for our understanding of "modernity" and "modern society"?

From "Modern Society" through "Postmodernity" to "Modernity": a Short Intellectual History

Sociology in general, and also the sociology of entire societal configurations at issue here, had its heyday during the 1950s and 1960s. Its knowledge was in broad demand, and the writings of its proponents exuded an enormous air of confidence and an exceptional degree of epistemic certainty about having firmly grasped that which held the social world together (Wagner, 2000, chapter one). The strength and coherence of this conceptual grip on the contemporary social world can easily be read from textbooks of the time. The greatest testimony to this period is probably the *International Encyclopedia of the Social Sciences* of 1968, edited by David Sills, but prepared under the guiding influence of Talcott Parsons.

In this view, the USA and some West European societies had reached the stage of "advanced industrial society" or "modern society." Other societies still had to undergo "modernization" and "development," leading up to where the more advanced societies already were. Major upheavals or ruptures were not envisaged, and all societies had basically embarked on the same historical path. The power of this interpretation, as exemplified in Parsons's work, stemmed not least from the fact that it managed to combine a broad empirical-historical observation on institutional stability in the West with two explanatory elements, which in their combination appeared unbeatable. As elaborated – somewhat too affirmatively – by Jeffrey Alexander (1978), Parsons started out from the voluntarism of human freedom, which historically led to the differentiation of social institutions. In a second step, he aimed at showing that those differentiated institutions would functionally interrelate to form an overall social system that was superior to others in all respects. He thus produced a sociologized version of the Enlightenment view that human affairs were self-regulating once freedom and reason were permitted to have their way.

Although not everyone agreed with this affirmative view, the major alternative approach or critical view painted a picture with similarly clear contours. From the 1940s to the 1960s, critical theory in the tradition of the Frankfurt School held that the reign of instrumental reason had succeeded in containing all social change in "administered society" (Theodor W. Adorno) or "one-dimensional society" (Herbert Marcuse). And Marxist social theory, which revived during the 1960s and 1970s, saw "capitalism" or "late capitalism" (Ernest Mandel,

Claus Offe, Nicos Poulantzas, and others) as neither harmonious nor stable, but contradiction-ridden. Mostly, however, these critical theorists argued that if capitalism could not control those contradictions, some form of socialism would evolve.

As stable as this double – *affirmative* and *critical* – image of contemporary Western societies still appeared by the mid-1960s, objections to it began to accumulate. I will just mention three important ones. First, historical sociologists were able to demonstrate that theorists of modern society had neglected historical information or downplayed its significance to an utterly unacceptable degree to arrive at their story of smooth and linear development. As Reinhart Bendix (1967, p. 312) put it, "Seldom has social change been interpreted in so managerial a fashion, while all contingencies of action are treated as mere historical variations which cannot alter the 'logic of industrialism'."

Second, events in Western societies themselves led to doubts about the inherent and unshakable solidity of those social orders. On the one hand, "1968" became and remained a symbol for the possibility of major unrest to emerge almost without any warning. The protest movements of the 1960s certainly did not achieve the major political revolution some of their protagonists were hoping for. But the significant cultural transformations of the ensuing decades – most prominently a new understanding of selfhood, sometimes called "new individualism" – are often traced to this period. On the other hand, the similarly unexpected economic crisis of the early 1970s led to a questioning of the sustainability of the postwar economic model. Standardized mass production was accompanied by growing mass consumption patterns and a mode of government regulation of the economy that mechanically protected capitalist expansion by fiscal and monetary policies. This model seemed to allow for projections of stable economic growth that stretched far into the future. As of 1975, those projections were no longer even worth the paper on which they were printed. It is not only that crises and recessions recurred; economists and economic sociologists also detected increasing signs of the transformation of the economy away from mass production toward "flexible specialization," and away from nationally controllable economic flows toward "globalization."

Third, the observation of those and other, more gradual developments, such as the changing composition of the workforce, started to demand revisions of the prevailing sociological image of society. The first major response came to be known as the idea of a transition from "industrial society" to "post-industrial society." This transition was characterized by a shift from industry to the service sector as the major employer and to scientific-technical knowledge as the major productive force. Although this new theory of post-industrial society initially tried to match its predecessor in terms of explanatory tools and precision, it never achieved the same coherence. Some of its proponents, such as Alain Touraine (1969), even made it a key point that post-industrial society is perpetually changed by the activity of social movements. Sociological analysis had to change in tandem with social change, in his view.

The power of these various objections to the predominant sociological way of representing contemporary society was brought together in a short report "on knowledge," commissioned by the University Council of Québec, that did not initially appear destined to become a classic (Lyotard, 1979). The philosopher Jean-François Lyotard started the report, which he chose to give the title "The postmodern condition," much like the kind of diagnosis of post-industrialism that was quite common by the late 1970s. As he went on, however, the radical nature of his analysis became clear. He criticized both affirmative and critical ways of conceptualizing the "social bond" as "no longer relevant" (p. 14). Alternatively, he proposed to restart the analysis of social relations as based on language games and without any presuppositions about societies as functionally coherent or inherently contradictory entities. Later, he added that this view indeed questioned the possibility of subsuming the multiple events of human history under one single meta-narrative. Similarly, he argued, the translatability from one language game to another in social life could no longer be presupposed; instead, it had to be made a topic of investigation itself (Lyotard, 1989).

Among sociologists and social theorists, this proposal has largely been considered as unacceptable. The critique of epistemology and of ontology that it presupposed was seen to make any analysis of entire social configurations impossible. If postmodernity meant the questioning of any possibility of providing a valid representation of the social world, then a postmodern sociology would be a contradiction in terms. Trying to domesticate the proposal somewhat, it has also been suggested that Lyotard is essentially diagnosing a major transformation of Western societies and is seeing this transformation as much more profound than it is analyzed to be in the theory of post-industrial society. That is why the term postmodernity is necessary, and a sociology of postmodernity – unlike postmodern sociology – then becomes a feasible project (see, for example, Bauman 1992, p. 111). The problem with this interpretation is that it far too easily divides the debate between one position, which holds that sociology can basically just carry on, and another one, which holds that everything is anyway in vain.

Sociological diagnosis suffered from such a divide during the 1980s and 1990s. As a field, sociology has lost much of its appeal to those who take the so-called postmodern challenge seriously; they have just moved to other genres of inquiry. And within sociology, partly as a consequence of this withdrawal, the consolidation and application of established methods and concepts has regained priority over the questioning of the mode of investigation and interpretation in the face of an often recalcitrant and unpredictably changing social world. Against this background, I intend to demonstrate that there are other ways out of this situation. In particular, I want to show that some strands of the sociological debate about "modernity" have tried to live up to the full impact of the so-called postmodern critique without abandoning the attempt to analyze contemporary societal configurations. My presentation proceeds along the lines of the issues at stake in this recent debate. By and large it moves from the more easily treatable issues toward the more difficult and risky ones. I start by coming back to Hobsbawm's question: has there been a major transformation in Western societies during the second half of the twentieth century, or can sociology work on the assumption of some basic continuity? And if there was a transformation, where have Western societies gone from there?

CONTINUITY OR RUPTURE?

Looking again at Hobsbawm's assertion, we find that he gives little attention to institutional restructuring but looks at phenomena that formerly were termed "socio-structural" and "attitudinal." That is why it is possible to diagnose a major transformation during the period in question despite the great stability of institutions. At the same time, this asymmetry helps us to understand why a more institutionally oriented sociology was rather reluctant to acknowledge major change – beyond its theoretical predilection to rule out the possibility of such change. This observation, however, still leaves open the question as to how one can diagnose a major social transformation – such diagnosis is always also a theoretical act – without any major institutional change. Surveying sociological literature that compares the closing decades of the twentieth century with the years following the end of the Second World War, one finds that recent emphasis is placed on the changing ways in which human beings relate to institutions. Those changes are considered to be more important than the constancy of institutional form.

In substance, such comparison shows that the "modern society" of the 1950s was characterized by a high standardization, even institutionalization, of the life course, not least due to state regulation in conjunction with economic rationalization. This order, however, has tended to break up in more recent years, when stages in the life course were destandardized and biographical perspectives emerged more strongly. During the 1970s and 1980s, those "highly standardized life trajectories have been 'shattered' by structural and cultural developments in all major social institutions." And such "transformation of the life course regime" can be connected to the emergence of "the formation of a highly individualistic, transient, and fluid identity," which is increasingly observed in Western societies (Buchmann, 1989, pp. 187–8).

Elsewhere (Wagner, 1994) I described this and related changes as the breaking up of a highly institutionalized social arrangement, namely "organized modernity." The institutions of organized modernity were formed as a response to the crises of capitalism at the end of the nineteenth century, with industrialization, urbanization, and "the social question." They were erected such that the increased demand for participation could be granted, in terms of both universalized political rights and broadened access to consumption. At the same time, such participation was channeled and, indeed, organized in such a way that the viability of the social order was not put into question. It was basically this social arrangement that Talcott Parsons and others described as "modern society" and mistook for a more general and universal model than it actually was. Their concern about (accomplished) functionality tended to overemphasize the consistency of the well ordered set of "modern" institutions and saw human beings as living their autonomy within that institutional framework. "Modernization" was then predominantly conceived as the building of functionally differentiated institutions and the securing of a consensus about compliance with rules.

The changes since the 1960s can then broadly be interpreted as a weakening of the grip of those institutions on human beings, or, vice versa, as a liberation of human beings from the institutionally suggested standards of behavior. More, however, needs to be said about the nature of the transformation and its impact on the overall societal arrangement. Much of current sociological observation converges on this weakening of the institutional grip on human beings, a process called "individualization," and a simultaneous weakening of the coherence of nation-and state-bound institutions, called "globalization." Both of these terms have created more confusion than clarification. Taken together, they tend to suggest that social phenomena "in between" human beings and the world are disappearing. This, however, is a claim that can hardly be empirically supported. The earlier overemphasis on a coherent social system within the boundaries of a state-bound society finds here its counterpart in a conceptual overreaction in the opposite direction. Significantly, such conceptualization of the transformation continues to carry implicit assumptions about the driving forces of social change. Whereas in Parsonsian structural-functionalism the maintenance of the social system was the key requirement, current revisions tend to see the requirements for the maintenance of the individual in the social order in a competitive environment as the driving force of social change in the "enterprise culture" of the "new individualists." Rather than organizing and planning, markets and flexibility are the means toward that end.

Like in the earlier period, different theoretical attitudes toward the new situation can be distinguished. The successorship to the affirmative theory of industrial society has been taken over by "neo-modernization" theories, which see individualization as a new expression of the emancipatory promise of modernity. The critical position now considers, in the overemphasis on the individual, the risk of a breakdown of social order. In older terminology, such a view would have been called conservative. Nowadays, however, it is often known as communitarianism, and it includes many authors who would not want to see themselves as conservatives. A third position – now also associated with the political slogan of the "third way" – recognizes the risks of the loss of "ontological security" (Anthony Giddens), but finds in the increase of reflexive monitoring of social arrangements also a possible remedy. Accordingly, the approach has become known as theorizing on "reflexive modernization" (Beck et al., 1994).

All three positions, which are necessarily presented somewhat schematically here, have one problematic feature in common. They all claim to understand what the ground-rules of the new societal configuration are. Each tries to re-establish intellectual hegemony and, as a consequence, epistemic certainty. In this sense, they mirror the intellectual constellation before the social transformation and they refuse the insight from the experience of the transformation that the ways to sociologically analyze contemporary society may also have to undergo a reflexive turn.

Such reflection on sociological knowledge itself (a question to which I return below) needs to address the question of what a sociological diagnosis of the present can achieve, in particular in terms of the possibilities for the future. In my own proposal, I suggested that the demise of organized modernity opens up the perspective of an "extended liberal modernity." This would be a societal configuration that, unlike nineteenth-century societies of "restricted liberal modernity," is fully inclusive, but at the same time needs no longer to rely on the channeling of human desires for the expression of interests and the realization of selfhood into pre-organized forms. Rather than providing a sketch of a likely – or desirable – future, however, I developed this image to demonstrate basic *problématiques* of human social life that do not disappear under conditions of alleged "late modernity." Major social transformations change the ways such *problématiques* are addressed; they do not solve them for good.

CONVERGENCE OR PERSISTENT DIVERSITY?

It is an understandable desire of human beings to be able to predict the future. However, sociology should not give in to the temptation to satisfy that desire. The former theory of industrial society claimed to know that "modernization" was the direction of history, and convergence of societies would be its outcome. This convergence theorem was based less on empirical observations than on the theoretical assumption that superior ways to meet the exigencies of industrial organization would eliminate inferior ones.

During the Cold War period, the convergence theorem took two forms. Some theorists held that socialism had made some achievements in terms of the conscious organization of society and that market societies were not unequivocally superior. Convergence would then take place somewhere between the two existing forms of social organization, though not necessarily in the middle. Others, including Parsons, insisted that socialist societies had not developed a sufficient degree of institutional differentiation and that their inferiority would become apparent once a higher state of development was reached. Convergence would take place towards the Western model, in this view. The collapse of socialism after 1989 is sometimes seen as a confirmation of the latter assessment.

Such an interpretation, however, is superficial, not least because it overlooks both the intellectual change and the social transformation since the 1960s. The convergence theorem resided on the requirement for social systems to functionally cohere. Now, both the social transformations in the West and the collapse of socialism can be interpreted as the breakdown of such coherence. And in its stead, as we have seen above, sociological theory came up with a new driving force and a new functional requirement – individualization and flexibility – that were now to explain the occurrences, but after the fact. Significantly, this adapted theory contains a version of the convergence theorem, although none would call it by that discredited name. On the one hand, exchange-oriented "individualization" is seen as the universal trend to which all collective arrangements have to adapt and which thus will make them all alike. And the outcome is described as "globalization," in the very name of which convergence is already presupposed.

If the idea of convergence outlives such major intellectual and societal transformations, should we then accept it as indubitably valid? One reservation is
based on the observation that the telos of the convergence trend has not
remained unchanged over the period in question. In addition, however, we
should also ask what it is about this theorem that allows it to outlast those
transformations. My answer to that question is that both versions of the theorem
are based on a problematic conception of modernity, and it is this conception
that tends to limit the possibility of conceptualizing societal diversity. In the first
version, "modern society" is the social entity that contains institutional forms of
autonomy. At the same time, the differentiation of those institutions allows the
effective mastery of the social and natural world in its various aspects. In the
second version, "modernity" is the societal condition under which human beings
realize their autonomy and, by doing so, increasingly master and control the
world. The main difference between the two versions is the reference point – a
collectivity or social system, on the one hand, and the individual human being,
on the other. Otherwise, the two views work with rather similar understandings
of modernity.

The reference to autonomy and mastery, which we find here, is indeed a
fruitful starting point to conceptualize modernity, but it has to be rethought.
Following Cornelius Castoriadis (1990, pp. 17–19, and elsewhere; see also
Arnason, 1989; Wagner, 1994, chapter one), I consider modernity as a situation
in which the reference to autonomy and mastery provides for a double imaginary
signification of social life. More precisely, the two components of this signification are the idea of the autonomy of the human being as the knowing and acting
subject, on the one hand, and the idea of the rationality of the world, i.e. its
principled intelligibility, on the other. Conceptually, to put it briefly, modernity
refers to a situation in which human beings do not accept any external guarantors, i.e. guarantors that they do not themselves posit, of the certainty of their
knowledge, of the viability of their political orders, or of the continuity of
their selves. Despite the enormous variety of specific conceptualizations of
modernity, the great majority of them agree in identifying the key characteristic
of modernity: human beings think of themselves as setting their own rules and
laws for their relation to nature, for their living together, and for understanding
themselves.

Starting out from some such assumptions, however, most sociological analyses
of modernity aim at deriving a particular institutional structure from this double
imaginary signification. And this is where they are led to profoundly miscon-
ceptualize modern social life. Terms such as "democracy" or "market" certainly
have one of their points of reference in the idea of the autonomy of human
action. But either they provide only such general indications as to be almost
devoid of content – when, for instance, the political forms of former Soviet
socialism are taken to be expressions of collective autonomy and therefore as
democratic – or, on the contrary, they are read in such a limiting way that the
current institutions of Western societies are considered to be the only adequate
interpretation of the idea of autonomy. Thus, it was the error of large parts of
the social sciences during the nineteenth and twentieth centuries to mistake a

historically specific interpretation of a *problématique* for a general *problématique* of modernity. Sociology tended to conflate the historical form of the European nation-state with the solution to the political *problématique*, or, as it was often called, the problem of social order, which was expressed in the concept "society."

To put the conceptual problem in other words, the basic ideas, autonomy and mastery, were taken to be of a universal character, and as such their socio-historical emergence marked the distinction between modernity and "tradition." The project of modernity, then, was the full permeation of the world by this double imaginary signification. Man was to be fully autonomous and in complete control over the world. Modern institutions, such as the democratic polity, the free market, and empirical-analytical science, in their ideal form would be completely emptied of any inherited, traditional features. The progress in the building of such institutions was a process of rationalization. There are many different and overlapping formulations for what ultimately is one single set of issues: modernity was seen as providing universal foundations that transcend all particularities of empirical situations. It can be considered as putting social institutions on a procedural basis and thus overcoming the need for any substantive grounding. And modern societies thus become accessible to a structural analysis, which underlines commonalities across societies, whereas cultural features are what make individual societies distinct.

Very broadly, such thinking has guided most of the sociology of modern societies, but it has repeatedly led it into dead ends. The basic flaw, to return to my formula above, is that it has been assumed that a modern set of institutions can be derived from the imaginary signification of modernity. The two elements of this signification, however, are ambivalent on their own, and there is tension between them. In contrast, one needs to see the relation between autonomy and mastery as instituting an interpretative space that is to be specifically filled in each socio-historic situation through struggles over the situation-grounded appropriate meaning. Theoretically, at least, there is always a plurality and diversity of interpretations of this space (see Skirbekk, 1993).

I attempted, as briefly mentioned, to provide historical illustrations for the diversity of modernity. Focusing on Western Europe, I contrasted the West European experience with the modernity of the USA, which at most times appeared comparatively more "liberal," and with the experience of Soviet socialism, which rather consistently appeared more "organized." Conceptually, the analysis limited itself to employing basically two registers. The oscillation between historically more "liberal" and more "organized" modernities, first, refers to the tension between individualist and collectivist interpretations of autonomy. The second focus was on the relation between procedural and substantive interpretations of collective arrangements, and in particular on the tension between the two main substantive resources for organizing European modernity, the culturally and linguistically defined nation and the socially defined welfare state (Wagner, 1994).

This conceptual limitation entailed that even this analysis could not fully unfold an understanding of what may be called the cultures of modernity, namely the variety of socio-historical interpretations of the double imaginary signification of modernity and the resources such interpretations draw on and mobilize. Within Western Europe already – for example, between France and Germany – or within the more broadly defined "West" – for example, between Europe and the USA – those resources are much richer and much more varied than this attempt of mine showed (see now Wagner, 1999; Zimmermann et al., 1999, for complementary analyses). Both richness and variety increase considerably as soon as one focuses on the so-called non-Western societies. Under names such as "varieties of modernity" or "multiple modernities," a research perspective has recently developed that aims at analyzing the plurality of interpretations of the modern signification (Arnason, 1998; Eisenstadt, 1998). Such sociologies of modernity break with any reasoning that associates modernization unequivocally with Westernization. Without disregarding the problem of the "specificity of the West" – that is, the Weberian *problématique* – interest is accordingly revived in the comparative-historical study of societal configurations.

MODERNITY AS A *PROBLÉMATIQUE*

In terms of the analysis of entire societal configurations, this seems to me to be the adequate response, all qualifications in detail notwithstanding, to both the classic-modern representation of society as differentiated into functional subsystems (which is by far not yet fully abandoned), and the spreading discourse on "globalization" and "individualization." The former sees modernity far too unequivocally as based on the pillars of an empirical-analytic approach to knowledge, a market organization of the economy, and plural democracy as its political form. It disregards or underestimates the variety of situations and experiences hidden behind those formulae and forecloses the possibility for sociology to grasp that variety. The latter far too often assumes that the increasing density of relations of communication and transport necessarily leads to the overall convergence of societies. In addition, its theoretical emptying of the space between the individual and the globe imposes on singular human beings the burden of continually creating and recreating their relevant connections to others. Thus, it disregards the capacity of "institutions" to provide relief from the need to act, or at least to guide action. Moreover, its skepticism toward collective concepts is matched by a reverse faith in the individual human being – in theoretical, in normative, and in empirical terms. It can hardly do other than lead into a view of the world shaped by individualist-rationalist social theorizing and then realized by neoliberal policy design. In the former – systemic theorizing – there is an *a priori* formula for the set of modern social institutions; in the latter – the rationalist-individualist one – there are no social institutions at all.

Both of these sociological representations of modern society are possible interpretations of the double grounding of modernity in the ideas of autonomy and mastery as guiding orientations for human social life. In different ways, however, they both overlook – or downplay – the inextricable relation of tension between the two parts of this self-understanding. In contrast, the approaches discussed above as "sociologies of modernity" underline a basic openness of modernity in terms of institutional forms, a constitutive openness that emerges precisely from the ambivalence of, and tension between, these two basic ideas. Over the past two centuries, sociology and social philosophy have mostly only provided variants of attempts at intellectually handling the advent of modernity by reducing or denying this openness (Wagner, 2000, chapter 2); the point, however, is to accept and think this very openness.

Now, one may object that openness as such is not a virtue. Accepting it as a principle would lead to sociology losing its analytic grip on the social world. It may be possible to convincingly demonstrate that contemporary societies are indeed not driven by technical-organizational requirements or that the rational individual is not the typical form of human being. But does it not remain the task of sociology to develop overarching concepts for all kinds of societies and for the beings that populate them? This is a question to which a full answer cannot be given here, but I sketch out a preliminary approach (for some more detail see Friese and Wagner, 1999).

Since the wave of critique, at the end of the 1960s, of a sociological representation of society that tended toward both objectivism and determinism, elements of two alternatives have emerged. Within the tradition of social theory, attempts have been made to bring human agency back in, as pursued in varieties of ways by Margaret Archer, Pierre Bourdieu, Anthony Giddens, and Alain Touraine, among others. Mostly from outside the social sciences proper, the linguistic constitution of the social world has been made a key topic. And importantly, the human sciences themselves have been analyzed in their form of text and writing by authors such as Michel de Certeau, Jacques Derrida, Michel Foucault, and Claude Lefort, among others. Taken seriously, both strands demand to put the question of the intelligibility of the social world explicitly on the agenda of the social sciences.

Unfortunately, and here I return to an earlier theme, these works have by and large not had that effect at all. The first strand has basically subsided. Except for replacing the term "modern society" with "modernity" and – vaguely and broadly – insisting on the shapability of the world, the call for agentiality has not considerably altered the ways of analyzing contemporary societies. Authors from the latter strand have often been accused of making social analysis impossible because of overloading it with concern for its epistemological and ontological conditions of possibility. With few exceptions, they have been too little interested in actual sociological analysis to actively refute that accusation. It is my contention that it is necessary to make and keep the concerns from both strands as central in sociology.

Joining together historical-empirical analysis and philosophical reflection, I advocate that such work on contemporary societal configurations cautiously withdraws from the explanatory overambitiousness of the theories of (post-) industrial society and of (late) capitalism. The historical-empirical observation of modernity's variety has its conceptual complement in some constitutive openness of modernity – or of the project of modernity, if some readers prefer this accentuation. It prefers a "weak" substantive social ontology to the strong ones of earlier sociological analysis.

In this context, the change of terminology from "modern society" to "modernity" becomes important. "Modern society" denotes a social order that gains its modernity from a particular structural and institutional arrangement. Modernity is here seen as a given and identifiable social form. "Modernity," in contrast, refers to a situation, a condition, which human beings give themselves and/or in which they find themselves. This situation is in need of interpretation; and such interpretation can always be contested. The term "autonomy," among other connotations, also stands for the human capacity for unpredictable beginnings. And the term "mastery" indicates that there is a relation of human beings to the world and to themselves that is always potentially problematic.

Under conditions of modernity, there is always a range of possibilities, even if some are unlikely. But if the history of modernity reveals both plurality and possibility, can there be a theorizing that captures all the present and past diversity as well as the possibilities that are open to the future without itself adopting some mode of plurality and possibility? This question has regularly been answered in the affirmative. Or, even more strongly, the necessity of a single and stable theoretical viewpoint has been asserted, for otherwise neither firm analysis nor critique would be possible. The view held here, in contrast, is that the historicity of modernity requires the development of modes of theorizing that are adequate to the variety of modernities and to the *problématiques* that the modern condition poses for social life.

In other words, socio-political modernity is constitutively characterized by *problématiques* that remain open, not by specific solutions to given problems. Among those *problématiques* we find, in particular, the search for certain knowledge and truth, the building of a viable and good political order, the issue of the continuity of the acting person, and ways of relating in the lived present to time past and time future. Without some assumption of human autonomy – i.e. the human ability to give ourselves our own laws – these questions would not arise. That is why they are fundamentally modern. But this assumption cannot be taken for granted, and it does not lead toward solutions. That is why the sociology of "modern society" unduly limits the variety of possibilities of conceiving these *problématiques*.

These *problématiques* co-emerge with modernity, and they can neither be rejected nor be handled once and for all by finding their "modern" solution. Societies that accept the double imaginary signification of modernity are destined to search for answers to these questions and to institute those answers. Temporarily stable solutions can thus indeed be found. But those solutions can always again be challenged, and then new ways of dealing with those *problématiques* have to be elaborated. Hobsbawm's "most dramatic" transformation was – and still is – such a transformative crisis of modernity. What the sociology of the contemporary world needs to take from this experience is that the constitutive *problématiques* of modernity will tend to re-emerge and they will always have to be interpreted in their concrete temporality, at their specific historical location.

4

Emerging Trends in Environmental Sociology

Frederick H. Buttel and August Gijswijt

The subdiscipline of environmental sociology has now has been in existence for a little over a quarter century. Beginning in the late 1960s and early 1970s, sociologists in a number of (mostly Western) countries began to recognize the importance of environmental issues, and initiated research relating to the natural environment. By the late 1980s, dozens of universities across the world were offering courses in environmental sociology, and many of these universities had designed undergraduate or graduate curricula in environmental sociology. In a number of countries environmental sociologists formed voluntary associations, typically within larger sociological associations. For example, in 1975 the Section on Environment (later renamed the Section on Environment and Technology) was formed within the American Sociological Association. In 1990 a group of 35 environmental sociologists formed a Working Group on Environmental Sociology at the International Sociological Association (ISA) World Congress in Madrid, and in 1994 it obtained official status as the Environment and Society Research Committee (RC 24). At each ISA World Congress since Madrid there has been continued expansion of RC 24 activities in terms of the number of participants, papers, and post-congress publications.

Despite this impressive expansion of environmental sociology, the subdiscipline has yet to achieve a prominent position in the larger sociological discipline. Nor does it have an influential position in national and international policy-making circles as do the physical and biological sciences at the Intergovernmental Panel on Climate Change (IPPC). This lack of centrality suggests the need to look historically at the emergence and institutionalization of environmental sociology and to do so critically.

In this chapter we survey some of the most important developments in environmental sociology since its establishment about a quarter century ago. In so doing we adopt a historical approach, and stress major trends in the subdiscipline since its founding in the early to mid-1970s. We place particular emphasis on the major debates in the field and how these controversies have shaped and contributed to its development.

THE ESTABLISHMENT OF THE MATERIALIST CORE OF ENVIRONMENTAL SOCIOLOGY

To a very considerable extent the course that environmental sociology took over its first quarter century was shaped by several interrelated convictions that were strongly held by the most influential founders. The first conviction was, of course, a tendency for environmental sociologists to have strong pro-environmental predilections, and to feel that sociology ought to be made relevant to achieving environmental goals. Second, it was held that conventional or mainstream sociology was seriously flawed because the discipline of sociology had ignored the role of the biophysical environment. The third strongly held conviction was that the inability of the discipline of sociology to address environmental issues was rooted in the classical tradition, which promulgated the "social facts" injunction, and which assumed that indefinite social, technical, and material progress was inevitable. (By "social facts" we refer to the general posture that sociological analysis must stress social explanations of social phenomena.) The fourth conviction was that environmental sociology ought to aspire for nothing less than to strive to reorient the larger discipline of sociology so that it could better understand the rooting of human actors and societies within their biophysical contexts.

Perhaps the most critical concomitant of these four convictions of the 1970s foundation generation of environmental sociologists was that the key problematic of environmental sociology was why there tended to be very strong, if not intrinsic, tendencies to serious environmental destruction within modern societies. Not only would persuasive theorization of environmental destruction help to launch the field as a distinctive area of inquiry, but such a theoretical emphasis was thought to be effective in pointing out that mainstream sociology was obsolete because of its failure to recognize the strong tendencies toward cataclysmic environmental changes. Thus, much of the formative literature consisted of explanations as to why contemporary societies tended to be locked into environmentally destructive tendencies. Riley Dunlap (1993) and William R. Catton Jr (1976), for example, posited that the four-plus centuries of abundance made possible by Western expansion resulted in cultural assumptions about the desirability of growth and the inevitability of progress. Catton posited in his influential book *Overshoot* (Catton, 1980) that the combination of the resources made available through the colonization by the West and the huge supplies of fossil fuels caused modern societies to engage in growth and expansion that is analogous to a species which no longer faces predation. In short, exuberant growth will continue until sustenance runs out, precipitating "crash" and "dieoff." Similarly, Allan Schnaiberg and colleagues (Schnaiberg, 1975, 1980; Schnaiberg and Gould, 1994) developed an influential notion of the "treadmill of production," which has been employed to explain why economic growth tends to be in the interest of state managers and agencies, as well as in the interest of private capital, and how and why state interests in growth reinforce the interests of capital in expansion. James O'Connor (1994) developed a related but distinct neo-Marxist perspective on the "second contradiction of capital." O'Connor has posited that in addition to there being a contradiction between capital and labor (the first contradiction, as elaborated by Marx), the expansionism of capitalism tends to cause environmental problems and create a second contradiction (which is manifested mainly as rising private costs of production). Raymond Murphy (1994) developed a neo-Weberian analysis that locates the causes of environmental problems in the increasing institutional sway of formal and instrumental rationality and the increased tendency for private accumulation to become the accepted end of private and public decision-making.

These early theoretical developments in environmental sociology tended to be couched in ambivalence toward or criticism of mainstream sociology. In addition, emphasis was typically placed on the claim that the inability of standard sociology to recognize the importance of the natural world had to do with the legacy of the classical tradition. The pioneering environmental sociologists felt that the nineteenth-century classical sociological theorists, in their quest to distinguish sociology from the rival disciplines of psychology, biology, economics, and geography, had shifted the pendulum of scholarship too far in the direction of handcuffing sociology with the "social facts" injunction. Catton and Dunlap (1978), Dickens (1992), Benton and Redclift (1994), Martell (1994), Murphy (1994), and many others insisted that nineteenth-century social thought has had the effect of steering the discipline of sociology in the direction of ignoring resources, nature, and the environment. Not only has there been sharp criticism of the classical sociologists (especially Marx, Durkheim, and Weber) within core environmental sociology, but Catton and Dunlap (1978) argued that the "human-exemptionalist" character of twentieth-century sociological thought presumes that social-organizational, cultural, and technological innovations exempt humans from the natural laws that govern other species. Conversely, Catton and Dunlap have argued that environmental sociology should strive for nothing less than to catalyze a fundamental reorientation of the discipline of sociology. They have suggested that the very nature of environmental sociology is that it represents a "new paradigm" (Catton and Dunlap, 1978), while the apparent divisions within sociology – for example, between Marxism and functionalism – are actually relatively minor variations on the larger tendency of sociology to ignore the natural environment (see Foster, 1999a).

These and other influential pieces of scholarship during environmental sociology's first two decades have very significant strengths and have been major contributions. Each of these scholarly traditions has been theoretically ambitious. Each has striven for a multi-institutional perspective that, for example, encompasses major literatures from such sociological specialty areas as political sociology, economic sociology, sociology of science, sociology of occupations and work, demography, and urban sociology.

At the same time, the core of environmental sociology exhibits some problems. First, the preoccupation with accounting for the causes of increasing environmental degradation has tended to foreclose consideration of ongoing social processes of responding to or providing solutions to environmental problems. As we will see below, the need for environmental sociology to be able to theorize the processes of environmental improvement has resulted in some major changes in the subdiscipline over the past five or so years.

A second issue is that these core or foundational works were written at a high level of abstraction and have tended to lead to a theoretical literature that is meta-theoretical in nature. Put somewhat differently, it has proven difficult for these core environmental-sociological scholars to deduce testable hypotheses from their work and apply them in a systematic, sustained research program. Many of the pioneers in environmental sociology have found themselves doing their empirical work at some distance from their theoretical views. For example, as is noted below, Dunlap's (1991) empirical work has tended to focus on public environmental attitudes (particularly the degree to which a "new environmental paradigm" can be found in public environmental orientations). Likewise, Schnaiberg's empirical work has focused on local environmental movements (particularly anti-toxics and recycling movements), albeit with attention to how the treadmill of production constrains movement strategies (Gould et al., 1996). But in the main the tendency has been for controversies in the field to be dealt with on the grounds of theoretical debate rather than empirical evaluation and comparison. Thus, there has remained a fairly wide gulf between theory and research, though the 1990s have arguably witnessed a number of major efforts to narrow this gulf.

Third, each of the core theories in environmental sociology has tended to have an overly general conception of what the environment is or how the environment should be defined. These theories tend to presume that the environment is a singular "thing" that is being degraded in essentially a cumulative fashion by extraction of materials from the earth and biosphere and by the creation of pollution. That is, "the environment" – even if it is acknowledged to be multi-dimensional and a highly complex system – is nonetheless seen in some ultimate sense as having some upper bound of long-term human-carrying capacity, and as having an underlying "unity" (Ophuls, 1977). Thus, mainstream environmental sociology has not tended to recognize the different levels or scales of environmental resources or environmental causality, nor has it been effective in recognizing the importance of what Benton (1989) has called "ecoregulatory practices" (by which he means renewable resource extraction systems based on ecosystems that have some degree of regenerative capacity). In addition, environmental sociologists have not done nearly as well as environmental geographers and other scholars in taking into account the fact that some habitats and ecosystems are more fragile, vulnerable, and ecologically significant than others (see, for example, Zimmerer, 1994).

In addition, the notion that the classical tradition has been problematic for environmental sociology and sociology at large has been de-emphasized. If anything, there has been a growing tendency in the 1990s for the appearance of contributions to environmental sociology that are explicitly labeled Marxist, Weberian, or Durkheimian (for example, Foster, 1999b; Murphy, 1994; Prades, 1999, respectively). Finally, a number of sociologists (for example, Buttel, 2000a) have suggested that a close reading of the texts of the classical theorists shows that they were much more aware of matters pertaining to resources and environment than many contemporary environmental sociologists give them credit for. Foster (1999a), for example, has written very forcefully to the effect that Marx's considerable work on soil fertility and land destruction led him to develop a concept of "metabolic rift" which remains useful in environmental sociology.

Environmental Attitudes and Orientations

While the first generation of environmental-sociological theoretical work was being fashioned in the mid-to late 1970s, a new phase of environmental policy-making had been in effect for nearly a decade, which was characterized by the establishment of separate administrative bodies for environmental protection, and by regulation and control of behavior by means of legislation. By the 1970s governments were actively exploring how to develop environmental protection based on affecting individual and collective behaviors through strategies such as education, attitude change, material incentives, and "internalization of externalities." Governments began to utilize public information campaigns to get people involved in environmental issues. Government-funded contract research stimulated the development of the research tradition on environmental attitudes and behavior (for a useful overview, see Tellegen and Wolsink, 1998, chapter six).

This tradition of research in environmental attitudes and behaviors has produced an impressive body of knowledge. Three important generalized results from studies in the tradition of the influential Fishbein–Ajzen (1975) model suggest the contributions as well as the limits of this research. First, while there is a direct causal relation between attitudes and behavioral *intentions*, there is little association between attitudes and *actual behaviors*. Second, attitudes explain intentions only if intentions are disaggregated according to particular "attitude-objects." There is very little connection between general environmental attitudes and environmentally related behaviors. Third, whatever environmental attitudes people have, at the individual level there are very strong links among affluence, consumer spending, and environmental impacts of consumption behaviors (Tellegen and Wolsink, 1998, pp. 127–38). Survey respondents tend to underestimate the environmental effects of their own behavior. They also tend to see themselves as having greater motivation to conserve and protect the environment than do other people, to feel powerless in changing the behaviors of others, and to find themselves in what might be described as a "prisoner's dilemma": if they change their behaviors, others will not, and overall environmental quality will fail to improve.

A second major focal point of research on environmental values and orientations has been the literature that tests the notion of postmaterialism. Developed initially by the political scientist Ronald Inglehart (1977), the notions of post-materialism and postmaterial values were based on Maslowian reasoning about the hierarchy of needs. Inglehart argued that as societies industrialized and became more affluent, the immediate economic and survival needs of most citizens would be adequately met, and that affluence would ultimately lead citizens to move up the hierarchy of "needs." Inglehart has suggested that "postmaterialism" characterizes the emergent value orientations of industrial-country citizens who have few, if any, remaining concerns about the basic material conditions of life. Respect for nature and interest in the quality of life rather than in the quantity of material goods are seen as the prototypical postmaterial values. Among the emerging lifestyle orientations stressed by Ingle-hart is environmentalism (see Inglehart, 1995). Inglehart has thus posited that growth in national income will be associated with growing support for environmental protection and environmental movements.

It was fortuitously the case that at the same time that postmaterialism was being advanced as a framework for understanding cross-national differences in environmental orientations, environmental attitude data were being collected from a number of developed and developing countries. Cross-national comparisons from these data were examined for consistency with the postmaterialism hypothesis. A number of authors noted that, contrary to the postmaterialism hypothesis, there is very little association between national income and environmentally related values (for example, support for pollution control, and concern about global warming and global environmental change; see Brechin and Kempton, 1994; Kidd and Lee, 1997). Thus, observers such as Dunlap (1997; Dunlap and Mertig, 1996) have argued that the urgency of global environmental problems of various sorts has essentially overridden whatever linkage there existed among income growth, postmaterialism, and environmental values.

Martinez-Alier (1995) has taken this line of argument a step further by noting that data of this sort suggest that there is no singular phenomenon of environmentalism. Thus, in the North, environmentalism's referents include matters of lifestyle and postmaterialism, while the level of environmental degradation or immediate threats from environmental destruction do not play major roles in shaping environmental orientations. In the South, on the other hand, environmentalism tends to be based more on immediate threats of environmental degradation to livelihood and personal well-being.

ENVIRONMENTAL SOCIOLOGY, ENVIRONMENTAL MOVEMENTS, AND ENVIRONMENTALISM

Environmentalism has become one of the most widely researched modern social movements. However, most research on the environment movement during the 1970s through the mid-1980s was done by environmental sociologists, rather than by social movement specialists. These early years of research on the "modern" (post-1968) environmental movement were dominated by survey research on public environmental attitudes, mostly conducted with little guidance from social theory. Also, this literature tended to have a partisan flavor, with much of the research being done by academics and non-academics who had strong commitments in favor of – and occasionally against – it.

As noted above, the major general theories of environment and society have tended to take the form of theorizing how it is that there are pervasive, if not inexorable, tendencies for capitalist-industrial development and modernization to lead to environmental degradation. Environmentalism and the environmental movement tend to be incorporated into these theories as the predominant social response to degradation, and as one of the principal mechanisms by which societies can escape the contradictions of growth and environmental destruction. Over the past ten to fifteen years, however, environmental movement researchers have been increasingly drawn from outside of environmental sociology, and their research has aimed at a higher level of generality. Recent analyses of environmentalism and ecological movements have been very strongly influenced by two interrelated trends in the sociological discipline. First, there has been a general tendency over the past decade or so for neo-Marxism and related materialist-structuralist perspectives to decline in persuasiveness, and for various cultural, subjectivist, or hermeneutic sociologies to be in ascendance. Second, as is discussed at more length below, there has been a broad "cultural turn" in sociology at large, and as a result many (for example, Beck, 1992; Giddens, 1994; see the reviews in Martell, 1994; Hannigan, 1995; Goldblatt, 1996) view environmentalism as one of the defining social forces in late twentieth- and early twenty-first-century societies. In particular, "ecology" is now commonly regarded as the prototypical "new social movement" (see the summary of this tradition in Scott, 1990).

Given the increasingly widespread view that environmentalism is an ascendant social force, the bulk of work in the field has been directly or indirectly aimed at understanding the factors in society and its environment that have contributed to this outcome. Three basic perspectives from the environmental sociology and related literatures have been advanced. One influential tradition is that pioneered by Riley Dunlap and colleagues (Dunlap and Van Liere, 1984). They argue that as industrial society developed over the past several centuries, this was historically propelled and accompanied by a set of beliefs and institutional patterns that can be referred to as a "dominant Western worldview" or "dominant social paradigm" (DSP). The DSP denotes the belief that human progress should be seen primarily in material (production and consumption) terms, which in turn legitimates human domination of nature. The DSP has accompanied the long-term development of industrial society across a variety of societal types (ranging from capitalism to twentieth-century state socialism) and across a wide range of institutions within societies (for example, the polity and popular culture, as well as the economy). But while the social institutions of growth have led to material abundance, they have also created environmental destruction. Environmental problems and the growth of environmental knowledge are seen to be engendering a growing questioning or rejection of the DSP among many social groups. The DSP is now seen by many citizens of the advanced societies, and increasingly in the developing nations as well, to be environmentally problematic, if not environmentally irresponsible. The result is that there is being nurtured a "new ecological paradigm" – an ethic that involves more and more social groups rejecting DSP assumptions and seeing themselves more as a part of nature. Thus, environmentalism is ultimately a social response to the biophysical realities of and scientific knowledge about environmental destruction.

A second view, that by Inglehart (1977, 1995), was discussed in the preceding section. Again, Inglehart's argument is that as industrial societies have developed, and as absolute scarcity has been conquered and most basic material needs have been met, public concerns tend to rise up a definite hierarchy of "needs" to a point where there is an articulation of "postmaterial," quality-of-life-oriented values such as environmentalism.

A third general orientation toward environmental mobilization locates the growing force of ecology within the transition from the institutions of mid-century Fordism and "industrial society" to the post-Fordist, postmodernist, or "risk-society" institutions of the late twentieth century (see the overviews in Scott, 1990; Martell, 1994). Beck's (1992) theory of the transition from industrial to "risk society," and the corresponding reflexive-modernizationist processes of subpolitics and new social movements, is another related form of this "political vacuum" approach to explaining the rise of ecology movements. The institutional disarray associated with the disintegration of Fordism has undermined traditional reservoirs of social meaning, and weakened associational and political-party vehicles of interest aggregation. These social vacuums have increasingly been filled by movements such as ecology. For many citizens these movements are more satisfactory vehicles than traditional political institutions (especially political parties) for enabling people to articulate post-industrial concerns (particularly concern about risks to health and about environmental integrity).

Each of these master theories of environmentalism has strengths and weaknesses. Their strengths derive from the fact that they have identified important overarching features of institutional and environmental change that are related to organized environmentalism. Their weaknesses are generally due to the fact that in the quest for overarching explanations they focus on certain particular forms or processes of environmentalism and downplay others. A comprehensive theory of environmentalism must be able to deal with a number of pivotal characteristics of ecology movements. First, the surges and declines of the movement since the late 1960s suggest that biophysical (or scientific-knowledge) factors do not play the predominant role in shaping movement mobilization (Hannigan, 1995). Second, as noted above, the relatively widespread expressions of Third World environmentalism in recent years cast doubt on the notion that environmentalism is primarily a phenomenon among rich countries and affluent social classes (Martinez-Alier, 1995). Third, a comprehensive theory of environmentalism must also be able to explain anti-environmentalism, and account for the fact that in this neoliberal era anti-environmentalism at times rivals environmentalism as a political force (McCarthy, 1998). Fourth, there is a need to theorize the enormous internal diversity of the movement; expressions

of organized environmentalism exhibit tremendous diversity in their class alignments, claims, goals, and political ideologies, and the coexistence of these groups
is often far more precarious than is recognized in academic treatments of them
(Gottlieb, 1994). By recognizing the internal diversity of the movement environmental sociologists will recognize that there is no underlying coherence to
the movement (or that it is a congeries of movements rather than a single
movement).

Fifth, there is a need to recognize that environmentalism is in large part a
social product. For example, many contemporary expressions of environmentalism (for example, indigenous resistance to rainforest destruction in the developing world) have existed for some time but were not defined as environmental
activism three decades ago. Sixth, there is a need to distinguish between public
support for the movement (which tends to be broad, but shallow and somewhat
transitory) and movement participation (which is much less prevalent but more
stable, and which tends to be drawn from well educated and/or politically
efficacious strata of civil society). In sum, environmentalism and environmental
movements are a heterogeneous set of phenomena which will likely need to be
explained through the use of multiple theoretical perspectives.

THE "CULTURAL TURN," SOCIAL CONSTRUCTIVISM, AND GLOBAL CHANGE

During the first fifteen or so years of North American environmental sociology,
until roughly 1990, there was an almost universal commitment of the environmental sociology community to a realist epistemology and materialist ontology.
In fact, prior to the late 1980s a sizable share of the North American environmental sociology community saw its mission as being to bring the ecological
sciences and their insights to the attention of the larger sociological community.
Some environmental sociologists had such strong commitments to the ecological
sciences that they felt it was appropriate to evaluate environmental-sociological
literature in terms of whether it supported or undermined the persuasiveness of
ecological-scientific positions on global environmental change and related issues
(Dunlap and Catton, 1994).

Since the mid-1980s there have been two social changes – one in sociology and
the other in world society – that have had contradictory implications for environmental sociology and that have led to some protracted controversies in the
field. The first change – the growing interest in environmental matters within
mainstream sociology – occurred primarily as a reflection of the cultural turn of
the discipline in the Anglo-American world, and because of growing discipline-
wide interest in ecology as an ideational phenomenon and as a focal point of
modern social movements. The second change was the growing national, and
especially international, attention to global environmental change in general and
atmospheric warming in particular.

The principal pivot of controversy over the cultural sociology of environment
and the environmental sociology of global change was the emergence of a

social-constructionist literature on global environmental change. Prior to the 1990s the social constructionism had been largely confined to the social problems and sociology of science literatures. Beginning around 1990, however, social constructionism was increasingly employed to understand "framing" processes within social movements. Also, sociologists of science were increasingly extending the tools of constructionism to the environmental and ecological sciences (for example, Yearley, 1991, 1996; Wynne, 1994). A number of environmental sociologists (for example, Taylor and Buttel, 1992; Hannigan, 1995) proceeded to apply constructionist insights to the processes according to which global environmental and climate change knowledge claims were being "framed."

The thrusts of the social-constructionist literature on global environmental change were several-fold. It was argued that global change served simultaneously as a scientific concept and social movement ideology, and that social movement claims and items of scientific knowledge were mutually constitutive. A number of analyses suggested that the way that environmental movement organizations appropriated knowledge from climate scientists was partial and selective (for example, placing great stress on Third World sources of global warming and biodiversity destruction, while saying very little about the likelihood that living standards in the affluent countries would need to be rolled back in order to reduce substantially greenhouse gas emissions). The selective appropriation of global change knowledge was suggested to be, at least partly, a strategy by environmental organizations to make the most attractive possible case to the public and to political elites about why there needed to be a strong policy response to global change issues. Social constructionists also argued that the movement claim – that the most significant environmental problems facing human societies are global ones – was as much a socio-cultural construct as a demonstrated scientific fact. A number of social constructionists also observed that there was a small but influential minority of climate scientists who were not in agreement with much or all of the stylized knowledge about the anthropogenic causes of global climate change. At a minimum, these scientific disagreements were predicted to provide the basis for many corporations, state officials, and interest groups whose interests were not well served by an agenda of reducing greenhouse gas emissions to make a persuasive case that there is "uncertainty" with regard to the validity of global circulation models of global warming that predict substantial atmospheric warming in the twenty-first century. "Uncertainty arguments" (see Hannigan, 1995) would indeed prove to be crucial to anti-climate change interest groups (such as the corporate-sponsored Climate Coalition in the USA) in making the case that the evidence about global climate change is not sturdy enough to justify major costly policy changes. In addition, the existence of differences of scientific perspective about global warming might imply that there was premature closure – by climate scientists, environmentalists, and environmental sociologists – on the consensus surrounding global environmental and climate change.

The social constructionist literature generated an immediate and very animated response from a number of environmental sociologists (Dunlap and Catton,

1994; Martell, 1994; Murphy, 1994, 1997; Redclift and Woodgate, 1997). The critics of constructionism, while conceding that there are social processes involved in translating climate science findings into a policy program, have nonetheless suggested that constructionism has served to distort the realities of how the climate science community perceives the global warming issues. It was suggested that portraying global warming predictions as a mere "knowledge claim" underestimates the degree to which there is scientific consensus around global warming. Relativizing knowledge about global warming can only serve to diminish its credibility within sociology and society at large. The critics of social-constructionist accounts of global warming were not only concerned with how these accounts might lead to distorted views about climate and environmental sciences; there was the broader concern that social-constructionism deflects attention from the material dimension of science and technology in general. Social constructionism's critics have also suggested that this approach serves to reinforce the "exemptionalism" of mainstream sociology, and to legitimate sociology's lack of attention to the biophysical environment. Finally, the critics have suggested that because social-constructionism is contradictory to the core postulate of environmental sociology – that the biophysical and social worlds are connected by webs of cause and effect – the growth of constructionism could serve to undermine the stature of environmental sociology.

As central as the debate over social constructionism was to the pulse of the field during the early and mid-1990s, our prediction is that a decade or so hence this debate will not be seen as particularly meaningful. The social constructionists and their critics have tended to talk past each other to a considerable degree. On one hand, the critics of social constructionism seem to have misperceived the degree to which constructionists are motivated by the goal of relativizing or challenging the facticity of global warming and related knowledges. While there are indeed some constructionists in the sociology of science and cultural studies who are so motivated, the constructionists in environmental sociology are primarily interested in how scientific knowledges are "represented," how environmental movements and environmental researchers interact in the representation of environmental knowledges, and how environmental issues are "framed" in the public sphere (see, for example, Capek, 1993; Hannigan, 1995). On the other hand, social constructionists have a tendency to exaggerate the degree to which this perspective is a coherent theory. In effect, social constructionism and related approaches (for example, discourse analysis; Hajer, 1995) are more a set of concepts and methodological conventions than they are a full-blown theory. As an example, the geographers Braun and Castree (1998) have published a highly influential anthology based on the notion that constructionism needs to be joined to more fully formed theories such as neo-Marxism in order to provide clear analytical leverage in understanding social processes that shape environmental issues.

While the high-visibility debate between the social constructionists and their critics was proceeding, a number of more empirically oriented environmental sociologists began to initiate a set of research activities on global change in association with official governmental and intergovernmental organizations, particularly within agencies such as the National Academy of Sciences in the USA, and through the Global Change Initiative of the UK's Economic and Social Research Council. The bulk of this research has focused on understanding the contributions of social or socially related "driving forces" that influence global environmental and climate change. Driving forces are the proximate causal factors that affect the global environment. Land use change and "industrial metabolism" (the flows of materials/goods into and out of production processes) are the most common type of driving forces that are analyzed. Sociologists have also contributed to research aiming to identify the socio-economic and socio-political factors (for example, the capital intensity of technological changes, social values, and globalization) that influence the driving forces underlying climate change. Sociologists have typically worked on interdisciplinary teams that include economists, geographers, and environmental scientists, as well as climate scientists (see Rosa and Dietz, 1998; Commission on Behavioral and Social Sciences Education and Policy Division, 1999).

Increasingly, the most influential type of interdisciplinary global change model of driving forces is that of the STIRPAT (STochastic Impacts by Regression on Population, Affluence and Technology) model developed by Dietz and Rosa (1997). Dietz and Rosa's application of this model to carbon dioxide emissions has resulted in some novel findings. For example, they have found that there are environmental diseconomies of scale at the largest of national population sizes. A few countries with very large populations have been found to contribute disproportionately to carbon dioxide emissions. Related research by Roberts and Grimes (1997) on world-systems processes, societal development, and the "environmental Kuznets curve" (the notion that there is an inverted U-shaped relation between national affluence and environmental impact) has found that over the past two decades the postulated inverted U-shaped relation between income growth and carbon dioxide emissions has pertained only in the case of the already industrialized countries. By contrast, the poorest world nations tend to be locked into a high and increasing level of environmental impact per unit of income or affluence.

STIRPAT and environmental Kuznets curve research has gotten off to a promising start. But as noted at the outset of this chapter, the vast bulk of the work of the IPCC continues to proceed with relatively little input from environmental sociologists. Rosa and Dietz (1998) have made the bold and constructive suggestion that the way forward for global change research is for the diverse community of environmental sociology scholars to recognize the complementarities between neo-realist research (typified by STIRPAT) and interpretive research (such as constructionist research on how climate science data are represented to the public and framed within environmental movement organizations).

ECOLOGICAL MODERNIZATION

The most significant trend in Anglo-American environmental sociology in the late 1990s has been the rise of ecological modernization. As noted above, the core of environmental sociology had long involved a predominance of perspectives that were aimed primarily at theorizing the inevitability of environmental destruction. To the degree that general environmental-sociological theorists saw a way out of the "iron cage" of environmental destruction, their solution was almost always that of radical environmental movement opposition. In general, then, there was little room for anticipating or explaining environmental improvement deriving endogenously from major societal institutions.

During the 1980s and early 1990s, however, various groups of environmental and social scientists began to dissent from these notions of "iron cage" and of radical environmentalism as being the only logical response. German and Dutch scholars became convinced that there were emerging tendencies toward environmental improvement being manifested in eco-efficiency improvements (for example, strategic environmental management and industrial ecology) in manufacturing industry. In addition, these scholars came to be increasingly skeptical that radical environmental groups (for example, the radical wing of the German Grünen) would be effective in spearheading environmental reforms.

Drawing on the pioneering German literature (Jänicke, 1986) and anchored in very general terms in Beck's and Giddens's (Beck et al., 1994; see also Giddens, 1998) perspective on "reflexive modernization," Mol and Spaargaren (Mol, 1995, 1997; Spaargaren, 1996; Mol and Spaargaren, 2000) have played key roles in articulating an ecological modernization perspective as an alternative to core theories in environmental sociology. Essentially, ecological modernization theory holds that capitalist liberal democracy has the institutional capacity to reform its impact on the natural environment, and that further development ("modernization" and "superindustrialization") of industrial economies and liberal democracy will tend to result in improvement in ecological outcomes. The growth of ecological modernization thought in the late 1990s was meteoric. Ecological modernization hypotheses and concepts have very rapidly become the most dynamic area of environmental sociological research. Interestingly, the influence of ecological modernization is not confined to environmental sociology (for example, Giddens, 1998).

While ecological modernization is widely thought of as a new and challenging theory, and the "ecological modernization hypothesis" – that one ought to expect ecological improvement over time in response to progressive modernization – is very commonly cited, ecological modernization is more variegated that many of its proponents and critics recognize. The ecological modernization notion, for example, is used in a variety of ways, ranging from the efforts of Mol and Spaargaren (2000) to construct a coherent ecological modernization perspective to Murphy's (1997) use of ecological modernization as a synonym for any state policies that make possible the "internalization of externalities." In addition, ecological modernization is not yet a well elaborated theory. With the growing number of practitioners of ecological moderization and the diversity of ways they employ this concept, there exists a large variety of explanations (for example, decentralization of environmental policy-making, enlightened self-interest on the part of industrial organizations, global diffusion of international environmental standards, strategic "framing" on the part of environmental bureaucracies and movement organizations) for why one would expect an ecological modernization trend (see Buttel, 2000b). For our own part, we feel that the logic of ecological modernization suggests that central to the explanation must be a political-sociological rationale. Elsewhere (Buttel, 2000b) we have suggested that theories of embedded autonomy and state–society synergy (Evans, 1995) are particularly promising in explaining why environmental-state bureaucracies would find it in their interest to shift toward a decentralized oversight role in environmental regulation and away from "command-and-control" regulation, which decreases corporate autonomy to experiment with alternative industrial ecology practices. The transformation of the role of the environmental state seems critical in explaining why private firms would find it advantageous to make environmental improvements in their production practices and why environmental groups would shift from a largely adversarial to a partnership role in private environmental decision-making (Buttel, 2000b).

The ascendant role of ecological modernization can be gauged not only by the explosion in the volume of its literature (see, for example, the special issues on the topic in *GeoForum* and *Environmental Politicism* in 2000), but also by the fact that it is increasingly obligatory for environmental sociologists of all stripes to refer to this perspective, even if only to criticize it (Benton, 1997; Schnaiberg et al., 1999; Redclift and Woodgate, 1997). These criticisms include the perspective's (Northern) Eurocentricity (the fact that its theoretical roots and empirical examples are largely taken from a set of Northern European countries that are distinctive by world standards), the excessive stress on transformative industry, the preoccupation with efficiency and pollution control over broader concerns about aggregate resource consumption and its environmental impacts, the potentially uncritical stance toward the transformative potentials of modern capitalism, and the fact that very fundamental questions raised about modernizationism within the development studies literature have not been addressed within ecological modernization theory. It should also be noted that while we can agree with the ecological modernizationists that radical environmentalism may not be *directly* responsible for many of the environmental gains achieved in Northern Europe and elsewhere, these non-mainstream ecology groups arguably play a significant role in pushing mainstream environmental groups and their allies in the state and private industry to advance a more forceful ecological viewpoint. Thus, radical environmental groups, by providing alternative vocabularies and "frames" of environmentalism, by stressing issues often ignored within mainstream environmentalism, and by providing new loci of personal identity for citizens, could well serve to strengthen the movement as a whole, and thus *indirectly* contribute to ecological modernization processes. It is worth noting, in fact, that in the USA the environmental groups that are most concerned about toxins and chemicals – the primary preoccupation of ecological modernizationists – are not the mainstream environmental groups, but rather local (particularly "environmental justice" oriented) groups which are most radical and often thought as being out of the movement mainstream (Capek, 1993; Gottlieb, 1994). In sum, as the social science community moves rapidly to explore the new ecological modernizationist viewpoint, it should do so with awareness of both its strengths and weaknesses.

CONCLUDING REMARKS

Environmental sociology can look back on its first quarter century with some satisfaction that the subdiscipline has been able to make slow, but perceptible, inroads into two types of influential circles: the discipline of sociology and the policy-making communities with responsibility for addressing issues within the purview of environmental sociology. To be sure, most sociologists today are no more interested in applying ecological concepts or more likely to see environmental sociology as one of the highest status specialties than they were in the 1970s. And sociological global-change research is still relatively marginal to the agendas of international organizations such as the IPCC. Nonetheless, there is now a stronger environmental-sociological foothold in both arenas than there was a decade ago.

A good share of this progress has been made during the past decade. Interestingly, though, the decade of the 1990s was not an entirely comfortable one for environmental sociologists. The 1990s witnessed invasion of environmental-sociological turf by new cadres of sociologists who did so with little regard for the subdiscipline's historical commitments and goals (see Macnaghten and Urry, 1998). The 1990s also witnessed a quickening pace of major controversies – over postmaterialism, the nature of environmentalism, social constructivism, and ecological modernization. The subdiscipline has grown in its ability to deal with external appropriations of its subject matter and in its capacity to be able to build on debate and controversy.

Almost from the beginnings of environmental sociology, the major axes of theoretical debate have revolved around its "double specification" – that environmental sociology draws from material-ecological postures about humans as a biological species in an ecosystem on one hand, and from the classical-theoretical emphasis on the distinctly social and symbolic capacities of humans and the social character of their institutions on the other. We have attempted to suggest, however, that instead of these rival views and perspectives being irreconcilably contradictory, there are some opportunities for cross-fertilization. The issues identified in this chapter – the environmental implications of political and economic institutions, whether further "modernization" is primarily an antecedent of or solution to environmental problems, and the origins and significance of environmentalism – are not only important in their own right, but are among the major areas in which environmental sociology is working toward syntheses of the biophysical and social dimensions of environmental change.

5

Bringing in Codependence

JUDITH R. BLAU

One way of assessing various schools in Western sociological theory is how in one way or another they have focused on how individuals incur risks and how they grapple with them. This is the case for functionalism, systems theory, symbolic interactionism, mass society theory, dramaturgical sociology, structural sociology, institutional theory, and rational choice theory. That is, for example, institutionalized rules and norms, social rewards for compliance and conformity, group memberships, and positions in various social structures reduce the risks individuals incur. Socialization, status incumbency, class membership, norms, and social control protect individuals from one another, and from society. Likewise, it is assumed that individuals deal with risks themselves through, for example, competition, domination, cooperation, and conformity.

In this way, too, Western capitalism provided a foundational linkage between self-interest and risk-taking. Its origins, according to Max Weber and Joseph A. Schumpeter, can be traced to the legitimization of economic risk-taking as the superior expression of rationality. Capitalism's ascent in the West and its global penetration were achieved because risk-taking entrepreneurs were protected by laws, administrative mechanisms, and technologies, which helped to keep their transactions costs – that is, their social costs – low (Coase, 1988). Western nation-states may have solved other problems, but their most critical role has been protecting economic risk-taking and risk-takers.

Alternatively, we might entertain a conception of risks as lying in spaces of codependence, as between or among individuals, groups, and communities, and within, more generally, civil society. To coin a phrase, *utility lies in the ties*. (To put this in the terms of economics, utility lies in the very transactions that are now considered to be the "costs.") That is, we can think of risks and responsibilities as being embedded in relational spaces rather than being precisely situated with individuals (or economic entities). I think this is heuristically useful because it reaffirms the axiomatic priority of social relations over economic abstractions, and might suggest that codependencies are more endangered the more markets and economic risk-takers are protected.

Market capitalism is based on the doctrine that there is a standard of utility common to all individuals. As initially advanced by Jeremy Bentham, and further elaborated by John Stuart Mills, Vilfredo Pareto, and Carl Menger, this doctrine can be summarized as follows: behavior is self-centered and rational; the desire for goods is dominant (that is, people value commodities above all else); and wants, needs, and utilities are equivalent. Sometimes this is refashioned in political rhetoric as "choice" and even "democracy." Most sociologists probably agree that social agents have more choice in contemporary life than previously, but "choice" in sociology has usually meant voluntarism rather than utility, or the singular pursuit of self-interest. I intend to advance a conception of choice as it is lodged in codependent relations, not individuals. Risks and responsibilities are, thereby, considered to be collectivized by groups, communities, social movements, and organizations.

I can point out two paradoxes that motivate my arguments. One is that social and cultural processes are promoting egalitarian social relations, through empathy and mutual regard, while simultaneously market forces give rise to increasing economic inequalities. Another is that heterogeneous publics and, also, post-national formations (composed of fundamentalist ethnic, racial and religious groups) are emerging despite an acceleration of homogenizing economic processes. To clarify these paradoxes, I suggest that economic processes, which have engulfed communities, societies, and regions, are driven by a logic that makes too-strong assumptions about individual utilities.

These globalizing economic processes encounter tenacious community solidarities, and local social diversities are stubborn roadblocks against homogenizing work and production routines. Some of these solidarities take the form of post-national formations (Appadurai, 1996), as nations and groups respond to protect their own identity in terms of ethnic or religious fundamentalism, but also in reaction to materialism and the threat that marketization poses to their social foundations. Others draw from liberation models and maintain fairly extensive ties throughout the world in their struggle for self-determination. Still others pose alternatives to marketization in ways that are not as dramatic, but are innovative and help to promote economic advance. These include collectivization of production, reappropriation of markets and suppliers, and the creation of demand for their own products, such as organic coffee, fish, hardwoods, crafts, or herbs and other natural products for medicine. Just as cultural entrepreneurs in Africa, Latin America, and elsewhere hybridize popular music and cast it back to the international community (Hannerz, 1991), economic entrepreneurs are beginning to hybridize products to reinsert them into international markets (Lutz, 1999; Oliver and Grant, chapter 12 in this volume). In other words, resistance against monopolies of global markets takes various forms, but the common theme is that capitalism poses threats to codependent relations around which groups and collectivities define themselves.

CRITICAL PERSPECTIVES ON THE THEORY OF UTILITY

According to Sen (1987; also see Osmani, chapter 11 in this volume), real difficulties with the assumption of utility are the following: (a) in diverse communities each person's utilitarian preference may not in fact maximize his or her own outcome and may impair the outcomes of others; (b) monist conceptions of economic models ignore the fact that people are responsible and that there are pluralities of goods; and (c) individuals have complex needs and wants, many of which, like responsibility, are interpersonal and intergroup in nature. For these reasons, outcomes ought to be evaluated in terms of their distributional consequences – in terms of the equalities and inequalities they produce – and also as they affect interpersonal and intergroup relations.

Sen's emphasis on the inherently relational aspects underlying individual and group well-being – which cannot be understood simply in the singular terms of utility, use-value, or rationality – challenges sociologists in important ways. Specifically, it suggests that we view individual rationality as a component of intention and wants, which are inseparable from individuals' group memberships. It also follows that owing to their inseparabilities, people admit ethical considerations into their actions and decisions. These assumptions verge on a rejection of an essentialist conception of the individual and instead suggest that social, economic, and civic institutions are built around relatively fluid, but irreducible, reciprocal relations.

These considerations help to unravel one paradox. Choice – through co-dependence – involves others, and to the extent that contemporary life offers more choices than ever before, choice promotes more reciprocal relations. Without strong institutional holds on choice, individuals are likely to err on the side of generosity or, at least, civility. In contrast, relations governed by utilitarian principles are not so constrained, and they, thereby, produce highly inflated and artificial inequalities. To further elaborate, I discuss aspects of economic globalization and its correlate, global communications, and then review evidence for increasingly decentralized political processes, and I argue that racism might be compared with post-national and ethno-national formations. Finally, I return to how emerging codependence and diversity go against the tide of economic homogenization.

ECONOMIC GLOBALIZATION

The penetration of market capitalism and commodified products into virtually every community in the world has transformed daily practices, social relationships, and people's consciousness in ways that we do not quite understand. While capitalism is not new, transforming Europe and regions that had been colonized over a period of several centuries, its global reach and societal depth was made possible by the collapse of the world order in the late 1980s. Foreign ownership, intense commodification, and staggering financial debts are part of the price incurred by developing nations. One cost to nations with competitive economies – notably the United States, but also Canada, the UK, and other European countries – has been a retrenchment in welfare and social services, increasing privatization of public goods, and the concentration of wealth. Another cost is the great and growing obligations that rich nations have to poor nations, incurred as the consequences of military incursions, social engineering, environmental degradation, and other forms of exploitation.

Global capitalism, or hyper-capitalism, has accelerating adverse effects on poor nations because both the rules and scope of capital circulation and investment have changed over the past decades. The flow of raw capital is virtually unregulated; unfixed currencies introduced high instabilities for nations that are import dependent; and trade liberalization after the 1980s eliminated many export subsidies. This has led to deepening poverty, soaring rates of unemployment, and widespread capital flight. It also has created increasing economic inequalities within and between nations. Galbraith (1999) examines the period of 1972–95, and finds that global economic inequalities increased steadily from 1972 to 1989, and then dramatically so between 1989 and 1995, particularly in Korea, China, Africa, the Middle East, Eastern and Central Europe, and Latin America. What is responsible for "economic havoc," he concludes, is "weak government, deregulation, privatization, and free global flows of capital" (p. 186). The dilemma for individual nations is that policies to protect the integrity of civil society by reducing poverty – fiscal discipline, tough regulations, and social benefits – frighten away foreign investors.

Neither have populations in industrialized nations especially benefited during the past decades of global expansion. In the USA, for example, over the past three decades, real earnings have declined and the distribution of income has become more unequal. In a close examination of possible reasons for increasing economic inequalities in the USA, Morris and Western (1999) report that the following play a role: the growth of low-paying service-sector jobs and stagnation in other sectors; a growing gap between the earnings of college graduates and those without a college degree; and the decline of union strength. They find little evidence that immigration and the changing demographic characteristics of the labor market play much of a role in contributing to economic inequalities. Similarly, in their analysis of developed nations, Gustafsson and Johansson (1999) find that inequalities have increased over recent decades, but this increase is less in countries with high union strength, and in those in which social welfare programs continue to be relatively strong.

It is useful to put this into a somewhat longer historical perspective, and although I refer particularly to the USA here, there are close parallels in other Western nations. Between 1945 and 1973 there was a growth in productivity and wages, and, in general terms, the well-being of adults and children improved quite dramatically, and the very poor were partially buffered by social welfare and health care plans. However, the growth of real family income had begun to fall by the early 1970s. The overall trend since then has been a decline in real earnings, a concentration of wealth, growing racial economic inequalities, and an increase in poverty rates of single-women with children (Bernstein and Adler,

1994; Wilson, 1996; Plotnick et al., 1998). To give one specific example, the percentage of children who live in poverty increased from 1960 to 1997, and now stands at over 20 percent (Hernandez, 1995, p. 289; Cornia and Danziger, 1997). To give a contrasting example, the richest person in America has a net worth of $100 billion, which is equal to the combined wealth of the bottom 40 percent of the American population (Thurow, 1999).

Another aspect of globalization has been the growth of already large firms and their growing prominence in global production (Harrison, 1994). A central feature of these firms is their ability to downsize, namely to eliminate workers and to replace bureaucratic hierarchies with networked coordination. While in the conventional view, market uncertainty is best dealt with by hierarchical bureaucratic structures, in which transaction costs associated with market exchanges are internalized (Williamson, 1975), global firms now operate in quite different ways. They are not hierarchical, entrepreneurial, or purely competitive in nature, but instead are knit together through networks (Powell, 1990; see Knoke, chapter 23 in this volume), increasingly possible owing to international communications, flexible production, and just-in-time technologies. Headquartered in a place with maximum tax shelters, firms use cherry picking strategies to decide where to locate their various production operations.

The picture that is emerging of the world's labor market is that it is organized in terms of four segments: (a) a transnational capitalist elite (Reich, 1991), or what Barnet and Cavanagh (1996) called the "casino masters"; (b) local markets that respond to competitive pressures and are increasingly based on services; (c) public sector employees; and, (d) a marginal labor market that includes informal economies, the self-employed, and low-wage workers.

GLOBALIZATION AND KNOWLEDGE

Thus, it appears that there is more than a grain of empirical truth in Marx's prediction that capitalists would fatten themselves off the resources of the globe, while governments would initially wink, then wither away. In this section and the next, I develop arguments that suggest that there are countervailing forces that stem the effects of capitalist expansion. I briefly indicate that an important one is the phenomenal growth of non-governmental organizations (NGOs) that work with communities on local projects. In this way, schools and clinics are built – village…by village… by village. NGOs tend to favor community empowerment over the classic "top down" development model, and when communities are empowered to come up with their own approaches, there are positive externalities and multiplier effects. That is, successful communities pass on leadership, know how, and strategies for other communities.

One of the most notable changes in the past decades is the increase in literacy, school enrollments, and access to information. UNESCO (1998) reports fairly dramatic gains in school enrollments since 1970. However, adult illiteracy rates in many nations are alarming high – over 60 percent in Benin, Burundi, Ethiopia, Gambia, Guinea, Liberia, Mali, Mauritania, Niger, Senegal, Sierra Leone,

Afghanistan, Bangladesh, Nepal, and Pakistan. Yet many of these countries with high adult illiteracy also have high school enrollment rates, so that the next generation will have higher levels of skills and resources. But an important caveat is that overall favorable rates of school enrollments often disguise huge gender gaps between boys and girls, sometimes close to double, in favor of boys.

Dramatically different motives drive educational expansion. Writing as the Chair of UNESCO's International Commission on Education for the Twenty-first Century, Jacques Delors (1996, p. i) states that education is "one of the principal means available to foster a deeper and more harmonious form of human development and thereby to reduce poverty, exclusion, ignorance, oppression and war." The World Bank has a different vision: "Knowledge... illuminates every economic transaction, revealing preferences, giving clarity to exchange, informing markets. And it is lack of knowledge that causes markets to collapse, or never come into being" (World Bank, 1999b, p. iii).

Thus, there are opposing assumptions about education that center on whether it relates to utilities and market demand, or to the expansion of choice leading to self-determination. Evaluations aside, there are several considerations that suggest that the UNESCO model may be superior to the one proposed by the World Bank. These considerations relate to the character of global interdependence, and also how awareness of this interdependence empowers communities. High rates of immigration and population movement accompany the transfer of remittances, but also the transfer of information technologies (cable, telephones, radios, televisions, VCRs, computers). They also facilitate the diffusion of cultural values about knowledge. Immigrants have a unique perspective on how knowledge and education in their host nation can bear on the educational needs in their home nation.

A new understanding of diffusion is that formal education, like technology, commodities, and foreign goods, adapts to local conditions (see Urry, chapter one in this volume). This mutability and recontextualization involves the localization or, as Howes (1996) terms it, the "creolization" of institutions, products, and practices. In a general way, alternative uses and meanings come to be conferred on institutions, products, and practices. Likewise, we can expect that Western models of schooling will not always, or even often, be cloned elsewhere.

The juxtaposition of universality and particularism is especially interesting in this regard. Consciousness of others' cultures – their understandings, myths, narrative possibilities – is expanding, and so is personal and group access to others' cultural products, social institutions and knowledge. As Augé (1994, p. x) notes, we all participate in creating "contemporaneous worlds" with discourses of consensus-seeking, community building, and interconnectedness. Finding common grounds, with lessening spatial constraints, greatly enhances our shared interests in identifying and acting on common objectives. In this sense we can speak and organize across national borders about justice and human rights (see An-Na'im, chapter seven in this volume). This addresses the issue of universalism.

This is not to suggest that cultural differences will become diluted. Existing differences among locales can be intensified for several reasons. First, emigration and immigration patterns vary from place to place, with distinctive consequences. Because each "module" of migration is associated with multiple networks, all of which embed interpretations, ideas, and practices, locales have many options. Contemporary global media help to exponentiate these options (see Peters, chapter two in this volume). In other words, locales appropriate very distinctive commodities, knowledge, and culture from elsewhere, and people construct their identities not only in terms of their locales, but also in terms of what they selectively choose from elsewhere. To be specific, every community becomes a cosmopolitan hodgepodge, with a unique mix of cuisine, music, labor, industry, ethnicity, religion, and so forth. Locales can keep the McDonalds and Burger Kings at bay with sushi bars, Chinese take-out stores, frankfurter and knish stands, and plantain and herring vendors. Each locale becomes a unique configuration; this speaks to the issue of particularism.

RETHINKING POLITICS

Accompanying globalization is the transformation of politics and political institutions. "Cosmopolitan democracy," according to Archibugi et al. (1998), helps to capture the idea that the international order is becoming increasingly democratic in the sense that there are many chains of negotiation, multilevel and multisited interconnections among population segments, and the expansion of many kinds of exchanges. The expression "everything is political" conveyed in the early 1990s that "everything is contentious." But I will attempt to put a different spin on what people might mean by that expression. Over recent decades, I propose, there was a shift in deep-seated understandings about social relations. This involves an emancipation of exchange relations from their traditional asymmetries of power and privilege. In daily practice, this notably means emancipation within intimate relations (Dozier and Schwartz, chapter nine in this volume), but it also involves reconfigurations in organizations, and the declining significance of status – but not class – in everyday social relations.

"Emancipation to what?" There is no direct answer to that, but I suggest that the processes underlying "to what" can be provisionally identified. Specifically, there is an increasing understanding that legitimacy is required of the process itself and that legitimacy must be bilaterally or symmetrically negotiated. This is different from legitimacy that is authorized to some by others, that is demanded by some through fiat, or that is claimed as a matter of tradition. Additionally, such exchanges and transactions are decentralized as loosely coupled and multi-layered networks and structures, so that we can think of multiple sites as each having different claims, stakes, and perspectives. The freedom accorded participants to exercise choice is not complete, since it is contingent on the process and, also, on others' choices. Unlike utility, which has a centered self and involves some certainty about means and ends, choice accompanies exchanges within matrices of groups and individuals, and involves considerable ambiguities and uncertainties.

How these processes work within the context of global market capitalism is complex in interesting and paradoxical ways. For example, small producers in poor nations that perform the work for large Western corporations are establishing alliances with consumers and organizations from Western nations to exert demands on corporate firms. This has been increasingly successful in cases involving firms with brand-dependent reputations, such as Nike, Starbucks, the Gap, Pepsi Cola, and many apparel manufacturers and petroleum companies (see Stallings, 1995; Conroy, 1999). This is because actions can be coordinated through far-flung networks that include not only the communities that are adversely affected by corporate practices, but also consumer groups from affluent countries that are opposed to abusive corporate practices. Communities (say, in Brazil) and consumers (in Europe and the USA) together can create chains of cooperation to bring public pressure to bear on companies around issues relating to sustainable communities, the environment, a living wage, child labor, health, and working conditions.

Traditional national politics are also undergoing transformation, with devolution and privatization of programs and the decline of "high politics," earlier configured around class divisions and distinctive ideologies accompanying those divisions (see chapters 18, by Savage, 19, by Klandermans, and 20, by Minkoff, in this volume). The difference between Conservative and Liberal/Labour, or between right and left, are confusing nowadays because they do not explain much about either voters or office holders. These distinctions within the USA are particularly confusing because they are confounded with an emergent political neoliberalism, the retrenchment and cutbacks in welfare and other programs, and the ascendance of a ideology that each individual bears entrepreneurial risks. The emerging inequalities are a consequence of the ways in which "risk-taking" has been "valorized" (that is, subsidized). As a consequence, those without the initial resources – and the subsidization – to take risks are put at risk.

In the early decades of the twentieth century in the USA, social diversity was decoupled from the economy and the workplace in a way that suppressed people's identities. Immigrant workers, by taking on American identities, solved problems for factory owners, corporate managers, and foremen. In a sense, that was what late nineteenth and early twentieth-century assimilation was all about. Assimilation is no longer a desirable solution, nor even a practical one. There are high rates of migration; new immigrants, at least in the USA, are primarily people of color who do not pass as white; people's communities involve long-chained connections around the world; and group identities have partially displaced identities bound up with the nation-state (see Kymlicka, 1995). Abstract allegiances to the nation-state have been displaced by more concrete ties to groups and locales, introducing into the social fabric a new social realism and heterogeneity.

The assimilationist paradigm has, to a great extent, been replaced by the paradigm of diversity, and this, in turn, is accompanied by a shift in social theory away from the individual, and toward the group and group relations, as publics, or as civil society. However, where these considerations run aground, at least in considering the American case, is around the issue of race. Black–white inequalities are usually considered as a home-grown problem, but I will explore the possibility that the social construction of race in the USA might be compared with other post-national, late twentieth-century formations.

RACE

Colonial experiences involved the construction of "alterity," or the construction of the Other as inferior, but also as exotic and erotic (Said, 1979). Yet globalizing experiences of the past decades involve dehierarchization of difference, the decline of categorical thinking about groups, and the affirmation of diversity. The US case is atypical because, though imperialistic at times, it was not a colonial power in the classic sense. Itself a colony, it became a nation of immigrants. However, initial settlers and early nineteenth-century immigrants defined the nation as "Anglo" and conferred on new immigrants from South, Central and Eastern Europe racial equality in exchange for their abandoning their cultural and linguistic practices. Through assimilation and the suppression of difference, immigrants became Americans. In contrast, whites reified differences between themselves and blacks, and also Native Americans.

About a century ago Frank Boas (1906) maintained that race does not exist – that it is a mere social construction of racists. However, Boas underestimated, as we now understand, the tenacity of social constructions. Glazer's (1997) recent argument that blacks are simply one grouping within many in a highly diverse society is not very helpful; it ignores how powerful and persisting are the forces of racial exclusion. Recognizing this, Omni and Winnant (1986), and critical race theory generally, describe the disparities between American whites and blacks as being ideologically constructed through racialization. This descriptive account implies that the plane of transformation will be on cultural grounds. Wellman (1993, p. 222) is more concrete: "White racism is what white people *do* to protect the special benefits they gain by virtue of their skin color."

Why do whites *do what they do?* One conjecture, based on my interpretation of W. E. B. Du Bois's *Souls of Black Folk* (1903), is that excluded racial minorities possess a deep-seated and complex culture, which is a consequence of adapting to exclusion while simultaneously being members of society. As a consequence, blacks understand mainstream culture from a perspective that whites do not, and can also navigate between black and the white-defined culture with a fine-tuned understanding of the differences. From this perspective, whites *do what they do* because they feel threatened by what they imagine those who are excluded might know, and, also, then, what they fear about those they have excluded.

A related interpretation of the persistence of racism can be derived from Appadurai's (1996) insightful argument, in which he compares being white in

America with other contemporary ethnic solidarities. With the transition out of modernity, ethno-nationalisms emerge as solidarity formations around "hot" first-order identities involving, for example, ethnicity, language, religion, and descent. As examples of such "hot" identities, he cites movements in Bosnia, Serbia, Sri Lanka, Namibia, Punjab, and Quebec. Such nationalisms serve to protect groups against corporate capitalism and to preserve societal integrity as it is defined by religious values, ethnic identity, and primary solidarities. The pursuit of community aptly describes groups and nations that seek such social-political alternatives to capitalism, such as Iran, but also ones that etch out strong identities in their adversarial relations with proximate groups. These include Bosnians, Croats, and Serbs, but also the Israelis and Palestinians, and the Protestants and Catholics in Northern Ireland. Such groups mobilize around "first-order" loyalties.

From this perspective, "whiteness" might be considered to be an earlier form of first-order tribal loyalty. Unlike contemporary post-national forms, it took root under the conditions of colonialism and in the context of nation-state formation. One implication of Appadurai's argument is that racism, which is fueled by "hot" whiteness, will subside only with the emergence of "cool" identities associated with dehyphenization, globalizing diasporic experiences, the discovery and affirmation of "roots," and the deepening of multiculturalism. More precisely, as white Americans come to discard their own socially constructed hyphens and accept distinctions as part of a broader, complex social fabric, black–white differences, as well those involving Native-Americans, Latinos, and Asians, will become mere components of a taken-for-granted cultural diversity.

Shifts in identities and culture do not, however, quickly solve the glaring gaps in educational attainment and economic resources between whites and blacks. Charles Tilly's (1998) analysis is clear about that. He contends that explicit categorical boundaries have been drawn and reified in America, especially in terms of race, but also in terms of other binary distinctions, such as gender and language. It is at these boundaries that deep inequalities develop by means of exploitation and the hoarding of opportunities. The boundaries that establish inequalities help dominant groups to solve organizational problems, such as loyalty, solidarity, control, and succession. In other words, whites *do what they do* because it is a winning game for them.

There are consequences of racism and racist practices. Namely, there are resulting differences in performance (educational achievements) and in outcomes (occupations and earnings), which thereby reinforce the categories, and come to justify what whites *do*. Tilly is not optimistic (see Darity and Myers, chapter 13 in this volume). On the other hand, along the lines of Appadurai's argument, contemporary identities are constructed not only in terms of first-order identities, such as race, gender, ethnicity, and religion, but also in terms of multi-stranded cosmopolitan and global connections that groups and individuals acquire. First-order identities become "cool," we might assume, as these connections, and codependencies, take hold.

DE-HIERARCHIZATION, DIVERSITY AND THE PUBLIC SPHERE

Contemporary theory about the public sphere (civil society) places great emphasis on the extent to which society is dynamically constructed around diversity, and through pluralistic and democratic participation (see Misztal, chapter six in this volume). It is assumed, moreover, that personal autonomy – that is, having choices – is compatible with a high degree of flexible interdependence. That is the case because autonomy is the consequence of membership in diverse multi-stranded networks patterned around socially meaningful identities and as "plural selves" (Coser, 1991; Blau, 1993). People also vest their identities in realms of meaning that accompany participation in community affairs, religion, and social and political movements.

This conception of how the self relates to society is different from earlier ones in which individuals were considered to be integrated into society through groups and status orders (Tocqueville), through larger differentiated social structures (Durkheim), functionally, through shared values and institutions (Weber, Parsons), for good or bad, in social classes (Marx), or in terms of their particular roles or statuses (Merton). Put simply, these groups, structures, institutions, societal values, and status configurations are not as stable as they once were, and individuals are liberated from the constraints that were understood to protect them from risks. To capture the dynamic character of social life, a general non-deterministic conceptual framework is needed that focuses on agency and choice, as well as interdependence and socially emergent and constructed meanings (see Wagner, chapter three in this volume).

It is consistent with our understanding of agency that individuals are no longer incorporated into modernity's hierarchies – namely, high church, high culture, high politics, bureaucratic organization, and status orders. Agency is as meaningful for groups as it is for individuals, which helps us to understand that locales uniquely micro-manage global influences and appropriate elements from global culture for their own particular uses. The contrasts between rural and urban places and between social classes are quickly eroding, as are those between the developed core and the dependent periphery, as earlier described by Wallerstein (1979). It is a flatter, but more variegated and complex, world than the modern one that was organized in terms of privilege, hierarchy, and status. Extraordinary differences in wealth and power, however, cut across this variegation and complexity.

Fortunately, there is new thinking within the social sciences and in philosophy about economic and social justice. It is initially useful to reconsider how fairness and justice have been colloquially understood. The term that immediately comes to mind is "tolerance." It conveys the meaning of charitable forgiveness and the entitled right to be tolerant. However, as taken-for-granted, traditional privileges are challenged, the term "tolerance" loses its moral bite (but see Walzer, 1997). Consider the alternative coinages. A factory owner must appeal to residents to be tolerant of the factory's depletion of community resources. As a homeowner, I inadvertently increase the local taxes that are passed on to poorer residents who live in rented apartments – for which I ask their tolerance. We might say that blacks are overly tolerant of whites who hoard superior schools. Evidently, the classic conception of tolerance, with its presumption of asymmetry and privilege, should be replaced with another conception that recognizes equality among people and pluralistically constituted selves.

In this context it is useful to reconsider diversity. There is a noticeable shift in public opinion in the USA to seeing that a monolithic Anglo culture is boring for Anglos and illegitimate from the standpoint of others. It is increasingly recognized that the treatment of indigenous populations was wrong; that it is better to encourage Latino youth to maintain ties with their language and culture than not; and that the social fabric is far richer with diversity than without. Democracy can only be maintained when groups are given the rights to insert their own distinctive perspectives into political processes (Torres, 1998). What lies behind these possibilities is a developing normative climate whereby groups are accorded freedom, autonomy, and responsibility for participating in democratic processes in terms of their own cultural and social identities. This is an ongoing project that rejects static individualism, but rests on common interests in finding universals across myriad of differences (Alexander, 1995).

Relevant to the social science understanding of changing conceptions involving the self, groups, and civil society is Sen's analysis, which I have already briefly discussed. To extend this a bit, his views suggest that cooperation can be institutionalized along new lines and with new understandings. First, people come to accept the idea of reflecting on their own agency and well-being as they are codependent on the agency and well-being of others. Second, people come to consider the consequences of their behaviors and decisions in intergenerational terms, which is to say, over the long run. Benchmarks for justice considerations include how outcomes and resources are distributed over groups and populations, and over time. Skewed outcomes that systematically favor one group over another are to be suspected from this perspective. Examples include: racial imbalances in prison populations; gender differences in wages; and educational, health, and other disparities between whites and non-whites. These examples highlight why codependence considerations are useful.

These conceptions originate in philosophy. Alasdair MacIntyre (1984) refutes the idea of a unitary self and contends that the individual is inseparable from his or her situation in relations with others, through engagement and empathy. Along similar lines, Emmanuel Levinas rejects ontological autonomy and independence in favor of irreducible social relations and discourse. What follows from this is an ethics, indeed, the *social necessity*, of responsibility. Simply put, we "are responsible beyond our intentions" (Levinas, 1998, p. 3). He contends that a contemporary ethical framework must be based on difference, not ontology; on responsibility, not tolerance; on interdependence, not independence. He writes: "it is impossible to free myself saying, 'It's not my concern.' There is no choice, for it is always and inescapably my concern " (Levinas, 1998, p. 237; see also Campbell, 1999). In my own words, social scientists, by investigating how people's utilities are vested in cooperation rather than in individual self-interest, will contribute to our understanding about how codependencies form and how they can be encouraged. As I have suggested, social and cultural diversities require these codependencies, and, no doubt, encourage them.

CONCLUSIONS

I raised two paradoxes initially. One deals with how social egalitarianism can emerge in opposition to economic inequalities. This is possible because globalization accompanies the decline in centralized structures and sturdy institutions that earlier had strong holds on behavior. Under these conditions, we can expect that people are more likely to err on the side of generosity and to be cooperative in their dealings with others. Social actors have great choice in contemporary societies, and choice possibilities are embedded in a tapestry of codependencies. Individual utility, in contrast, is defined from the perspective of each singular, competing self-maximizing actor. In globalizing markets, economic actors have few constraints except for their own initial assets, with the result that they amass great wealth. Economic inequalities among and within nations and groups, and among individuals, place undue strain on our proclivities to cooperate, just as the logic of utility has marketized the conditions under which we make choices.

Although the global economy introduces great uniformity in production, labor, consumption, media, and so forth, the trend toward uniformity is accompanied by increasing social and cultural diversities, as well as, importantly, an appreciation of their value. Such diversities provide weakly institutionalized structures around which people organize their codependencies and the responsibilities that accompany them.

ACKNOWLEDGMENTS

For their critical comments on an earlier draft, I would like to thank Vicki L. Lamb, Ted Mouw, Peter M. Blau, and Keri Iyall Smith.

Part II
Relationships and Meaning

6

Civil Society: a Signifier of Plurality and Sense of Wholeness

Barbara A. Misztal

Why Has the Concept of Civil Society Captured the Sociological Imagination?

During the past two decades the concept of civil society has been very popular in sociological writings and has become one of the most favored exports from sociological theory into the language of politics and journalism. Although the initial concern was with civil society as a purely abstract idea, the recent revival of interest in civil society has led to empirical studies of associational life as a realm of emancipation from state power, as a condition of the stability of democracy, and as a source of generalized reciprocity. In such sociological research the term "civil society" is interpreted in a variety of different ways and used to identify cases as diverse as the consequences of recent economic changes in China, the transformation of postcolonial states in Africa, and the vitality of democratic processes in Western democracies.

This wide dissemination of the idea of civil society has not, however, eliminated ambiguous definitions and conflicting interpretations of the concept. Consequently, the notion of civil society, presented as a panacea for all the problems of modern societies and used to identify a wide range of diverse cases, has been inflated to the point of losing much of its meaning. To continue to use this concept we need to recognize and confront more openly its ambiguous and seductive nature, as well as the different contexts to which this term is applied. By examining factors behind the popularity of (and resulting confusion about) the use of the concept of civil society, I shall show why the idea has captured the sociological imagination and evaluate the heuristic potential of different approaches to this issue.

While the origin of the concept of civil society is identified with eighteenth-century philosophy and the emergence of modern European societies, the rebirth of the idea of civil society in the twentieth century has been inspired by a wave of democratization in Eastern Europe and Latin America and the emergence of new social movements in the West (Keane, 1988). These developments have contributed to the attractiveness of a normative way of defining civil society and established its problematic understanding as "all that is desired in the making of democratic society" (Kumar, 1993, p. 388). Seeing civil society as "a noble hope rather than a possible reality" (Hall, 1998, p. 32) has, in turn, discouraged an empirically motivated search for the historical and sociological attributes of civil society, while the linkage of this idea to new social movements has limited this approach's usefulness as a general model (Kumar, 1993, p. 387). With the question about the nature of civil society unexamined, an inflation of the use of the idea has followed.

Second, the idea of civil society has captured the imagination of many social scientists because of a growing realization that formulae of citizenship have secured neither solidarity nor an expansion of the public sphere. With many symptoms of the decline of solidarity, the renewal of civic institutions has been perceived as a new way of constructing identities and enhancing responsibilities. As the task of protecting solidarity is seen to fall to non-state institutions, civil society becomes identified with the problem of constituting trust in society (Wolfe, 1989). Therefore, this perspective is confronted with many difficulties relating to how social trust is produced and to how social solidarity and cooperation are generated. These concepts, which date back to Durkheim's emphasis on group life and shared values as an antidote to anomie and self-destruction, have related the attractiveness of civil society solely with the positive aspects of social capital. Such a conception of civil society with strong assumptions about trust is, moreover, inconsistent with the notion of complex, highly specialized, and individualized societies where social cooperation does not presuppose shared norms (Gellner, 1994; Misztal, 1996). Consequently, by calling attention to the role of trust, this identification has contributed to a muddled understanding of the concept of civil society and has, therefore, jeopardized the term's heuristic value.

Third, the popularity of the notion of civil society is due to a conviction that civil society provides the synthesis of conflicting claims of abstract justice and shared norms. This belief accompanies the tendency for the language of civil society to avoid the problem of tensions between particular and universal interests, which, in turn, obscures strains between diversity and solidarity. Consequently, the concept of civil society is promoted by three opposing camps; those advancing a workable synthesis of conflicting claims of social diversity and solidarity, as well as "those who find exclusion inexcusable and those who find inclusion omnipresent" (Wolfe, 1992, p. 310). The accommodation of these three contrasting orientations, however, has not advanced the notion's analytical coherence.

Fourth, the revitalization of the notion of civil society is due to its fit with the current sociological interest in the shifting boundaries between private and public spheres. With the language of civil society reflecting a widespread desire to abandon the traditional public–private dichotomy and to close the gap between public and private domains, these new studies conceptualize civil society as "a realm of social life that contains elements of both the public and private without fully being equated with either one" (Wolfe, 1997, p. 196). Although the departure from the classical neutral view of civil society institutions and practices allows us to account for civil society as neither fully public nor fully private, the multiplicity of varied new ways of delimitating boundaries of civil society still presents an obstacle to a more clear use of the idea.

Fifth, the expansion of the notion of civil society is central to modern discourse because the idea of civil society as the "third way" between "the atomization of competitive market societies and a state dominated existence" (Gouldner, 1980, p. 370) seems to be the right response to the perceived weaknesses of the state and/or the excessive power of the market. In the context of the post-welfare state and the collapse of the Berlin Wall, all main political orientations search for a new solution to the failure of either the state or the market. Following the commonly accepted assumption that democratic systems are in jeopardy if too many citizens feel disconnected from organizational life, they all seem to agree that the quest for a new form of civil society is the adequate response to their discomfort with the deficiencies of the existing institutional systems. However, there is as yet no persuasive account of how to bring about the desired stocks of civicness, while recent attempts to that effect only increase the analytical redundancy of the concept of civil society.

Finally, the attractiveness of the notion of civil society can also be attributed to its presumed capacity to capture the widespread sense of change in the polity, the economy, the organization of work, and communication technologies. This capacity can be traced to the assumed quality of civil society as a sphere of complexity, dynamism, and choice that functions as the enemy of political despotism, while providing a foundation for post-industrial, information-based, global, and even expanding to cyberspace societies (Keane, 1998). The sociological emphasis on civil society can, however, be accused of relying on too many optimistic assumptions. It is not always realized that while the present changes have made civil society a more explicitly valuable asset, they have not made its attainment or maintenance any easier. It is impossible to believe that civil society can solve problems of limited resources and limited sympathies. It cannot be seen any more as an automatic by-product of macrostructures but needs to be perceived as an active political accomplishment. Furthermore, while civil society has traditionally referred to a national society, today we do not have a clear answer to the question of where "society" should be vested. Moreover, despite talk about a global civil society "there is yet no sign of any plausible alternative to the state as the primary institutional framework within which security and solidarity can be established" (Hann, 1996, p. 7). So the civil society approach is faced with many difficulties due to an increasingly undefined space for "society" and a lack of any answers to the question of how to create trust in "space" without clearly defined boundaries.

To sum up, the new studies of civil society tend to furnish this concept with many desirable qualities and to see it as the crucial antidote to all social problems. The lack of sociological realism and the diversity and ambiguity of many definitions, in turn, inflate the use of the idea of civil society itself. Yet the broadness of the concept of civil society is one of the reasons why this idea has captured the sociological imagination. This does not mean that the concept of civil society is popular for all the wrong reasons but that it risks taking on the role of a new grand narrative capable of explaining everything and, therefore, becoming "an empty shell" concept (Edwards and Foley, 1998; Hefner, 1998; Keane, 1998). To overcome the growing suspicion of the usefulness of this notion requires a more precise delimitation of historical and sociological attributes of the term "civil society."

VARIANTS OF CIVIL SOCIETY

Seeing civil society as the antithesis of the state is the common aspect of recent conceptualizations of this term. This widespread minimal definition of civil society identifies it as "a collective entity existing independent from the state" (Seligman, 1992, p. 5) or with "non-state institutions and practices which enjoy a high degree of autonomy" (Kumar, 1993, p. 283). Although this minimal definition of civil society is adequate for the purpose of decoding a despotic state, its usefulness is questionable when one is trying to reconstruct what role civil society plays in liberal democracies. While we cannot deny that civil society exists in this minimal sense in the West, this does not make it easier to answer questions about its independence and effect on public policy. Difficulties in addressing these issues are consequences of the continuous existence of arbitrary delimitations of the boundaries between civil and other spheres (for instance, whether civil society subsumes political society or economy or the public sphere) and of the absence of an agreement as to what civil society's independence from the state involves, i.e. whether it should be defined as the society's capacity to structure itself and coordinate its actions through free associations or whether it should be measured by its capacity to determine the course of state policy (Taylor, 1995, pp. 208–23).

Limitations of this predominant definition of civil society become visible when we examine two traditions that laid the ground for the emergence of the dichotomous vision of the state and civil society relations. These two traditions, the first labelled L-stream and influenced by John Locke and the second labelled the M-stream tradition and influenced by Montesquieu (and also Alexis de Tocqueville), consider civil society to be distinct from the state and examine conditions for constitutional forms of government. Both approaches suggest that political authority should respect the autonomy of society and stress the importance of the distinction between civil society and the state for the preservation of freedom (Taylor, 1995). In the L-stream's vision of society as a prepolitical community, civil society features individual rights and mutual sympathy that ensure the existence of freedom and civilized life. The M-stream perspective, which stresses the importance of self-rule as a vital condition of freedom, is concerned with civil society as the realm of associations, where "the feelings and ideas are renewed, the heart enlarged, and the understanding developed."

According to Tocqueville (1835, p. 514), although it is association that is a "seedbed of civic virtue," politics precedes civil society since it is politics that spreads a general habit and taste for association.

The L-stream proponents argue that societal cooperation might be achieved through both debates in the public sphere and organization of private interests in the economy. By stressing society's capacity to achieve unity outside the state, the model of civil society proposed by the writers of the Scottish Enlightenment bases the resolution of tensions between particularism and universalism in the achievement of a social connectedness grounded in natural sympathy and benevolence. However, the shift to a more individualistic and universalistic notion of citizenship has undermined the view that sociability promotes trust and civility. In contrast with philosophers of the Scottish Enlightenment, contemporary intellectuals are cynical about the capacity of persons to be benevolent in their relations and endowed with a capacity to have enriched social relations. This is reflected in the present minimal definition of civil society, with its impoverished understanding of social relationship. Now, however, we have significant evidence to suggest that such an understanding is not enough. While rethinking the old resolution to the tension between individual selfish goals and collective solidarity, I think, we should not overlook the importance of "informal sociability" or "insignificant communities" (Fleischacker, 1998) in fostering mutual respect, civility, and trust. On the other hand, the extrapolation of the L-variant suggests that we should avoid the anti-modernist nostalgia for a lost human unity, since the implementation of such a vision undermines freedom.

In contrast with the L-stream, which focuses on the idea of the non-political dimension of civil society, the M-stream demonstrates the role of intermediary associations for non-political purposes in teaching citizens how "to co-operate in their own affairs" (Tocqueville, 1856, p. 107) and thus in training responsible and trustworthy citizens suited for liberty. However, what really counts here is not that independent associations form a non-political social sphere, "but rather that they form the basis for the fragmentation and diversity of power within the political system" (Taylor, 1996, p. 222). So, if taken to its logical conclusion, this tradition results in the emergence of centralized, state-linked, and bureaucratic types of associations, which, as in the case of corporatist arrangements, do not encourage, and may even actually inhibit, the independence of civil society.

From this brief outline we can see that the recent minimal definition of civil society fails to do justice to the both traditions (Taylor, 1996, p. 219). The convergence of the L-and M-stream traditions into one approach, which Alexander (1998b) labelled *Civil Society I*, has resulted in an understanding of civil society as a complex web of institutions outside the state. In this vein, Putnam (1993) identifies civil society with dense networks of associations. However, such an arbitrary compression of the two approaches reduces their original, rich and distinctive legacies, while, at the same time, increasing – by using the notion as a general category abstracted from the particular tradition – a general confusion.

A different tradition, more concerned with the differentiated social forms functioning outside the ambit of the state, emerged with the development of the liberal state and was crucial through the first half of the nineteenth century. Its early versions comes from Hegel's attempt to synthesize two previous visions of civil society, while at the same time avoiding their potentially negative legacies of an undifferentiated homogeneity of common will and the unregulated and self-destructive play of blind economic forces. In Hegel's ambiguous version of the notion, civil society, seen as just a moment in the unfolding of the ethical idea, is "the achievement of the modern world," since it is modern's society way of reconciling universality and individual freedom (Hegel, quoted in Stillman, 1980, p. 623). On the other hand, civil society is a realm of particularity, difference and diversity where people recognize each other and grant each other respect. Civil society is seen as a separate but not self-sufficient sphere whose contradictions are resolved only with the appearance of the universal state that pursues the general interest. The purpose of civil society is the liberation of the individual, seen as "neither a passive nor an abstract universal but the union into distinctive individuality of the particular with the universal" (Stillman, 1980, p. 633), from domination of nature through socially interactive creative work within corporations of civil society, viewed as voluntary associations of those sharing vocation, purpose, or interests.

Hegel's ambivalence toward civil society totally disappears in the Marxist tradition, which rejects the importance of civil society as the condition of both the actualization of universal rights and the development of the particular and concrete individual, while accepting Hegel's vision of civil society as a sphere of conflicting egoistic interests competing or struggling with each other. Marx, by declaring that the presence of association-like corporations in Hegelian theory is a residue of the feudal past, renounces the difference between the civil society and the state, and reduces civil society to economic life as the main sphere of realization of private interest (Keane, 1988). The Marxist tradition's suspicion that civil society is a sphere of private egoistic interests of the capitalist class leads to the assumption that civil society is a temporary and historically specific sphere. This assertion is also present in Gramsci's idea of the accedence of hegemony in civil society that curtails the power of the state. While rejecting the economism of the old Marxist school and stressing mutual conditioning of the economy, polity, and culture, Gramsci, whose work has popularized the civil society tradition with thinkers on the Left, argues that the conflict between civil society and political society could gradually eliminate the domination of the capitalist state (Bobbio, 1988; Cohen and Arato, 1992).

This idea of resistance to the state finds its best expression in the Eastern European language of civil society, which, together with other Hegelian and neo-Gramascian ideas (such as the analytical separation of the non-state realm into economy and society), contributes to the revival of the idea of civil society among the Western Left. Such a conceptualization of the relationships between civil society and the state, where civil society is seen as a counterbalance to state power, is labeled by Foley and Edwards (1996) as *Civil Society II*, while Alexander (1998b) reserves this label for the Marxist tradition. This version, as expressed in Arato's (1981) phrase "civil society against the state," by reinforcing the idea of civil society as the antithesis of the state and linking it to new social movements, marginalizes political associations and underplays the conflictual potential of civil society. The weaknesses of this perspective became visible with the discovery that Latin American civil society is defined not as being opposed to a repressive state but as an alternative to political parties, while in the Western Europe civil society is a sphere of social autonomy or voluntary cultural and social organizations (Foley and Edwards, 1996).

Disillusionment with the vision of civil society as antithesis of the state, together with growing concern over the quality of interpersonal relationships and democracy in the West, has helped us to revise our understanding of civil society as the informal, non-state, non-economic realms of both public and personal life (Alexander, 1995, p. 34). However, when the project of civil society is reduced to the restoration of social bonds and self-organization outside of the official institutions, the importance of the state and its relations with civil society can easily be overlooked, while the role of the emotional dimension of participation can be overestimated. Without examination of all the main practices of civil society – that is, its autonomous institutions, the relationships between civil society and the state, and patterns of civil manners (Shils, 1991) – we are unable to determine whether civil society is committed to democratic practices and sentiments.

A lesson from historical traditions and theoretical debates is that we need to avoid being too ambitious in synthesizing these often contradictory meanings, being overly normative in describing civil society, or being excessively theoretical in delineating a history of ideas. It is necessary, therefore, to recognize more openly the overgeneralized and normative interpretations of civil society. We also need to confront the contradictory definitions, which can be explained by the political inclinations of writers, their particular social philosophies, the socio-political context in which they wrote, and the nature of political conflicts of the day (Alexander, 1998b; Edwards and Foley, 1998). The required operationalization of the term "civil society" has recently been made easier due to the development of both theoretical and empirical investigations of the phenomenon.

ATTEMPTS AT SOCIOLOGICAL REALISM

Sociological and anthropological examinations of the nature and task of various civil societies suggest that civil society should be particularized and made concrete (Hann, 1996; Berman, 1997; Bell, 1998). Critical discussions initiated by Habermas, Keane, and Putnam have also called for a greater sociological realism in approaching the notion of civil society and especially in studying how and under what circumstances a society's organized components contribute to political strength or political failure. Both empirically and theoretically oriented studies challenge the assumption about the significance of the decoupling of civil society from the state and question the assertion about the positive role of all types of associations. They claim that the vitality of civil society depends upon both the plurality of its structures and the preservation of shared norms.

Ignoring the importance of the state is now perceived as one of the main failures of the civil society perspective. Not all civil society theorists, to be fair, underestimate the role of the state. For example, Keane argues for "a secure and independent civil society of autonomous public sphere" which is protected and legally guaranteed by the state, and also argues that civil society and the state "must become the condition of each other's democratization" (1988, p. 15). Walzer (1992, pp. 103–4) notes that the state "frames civil society and occupies space within it," and that "civil society, left to itself, generates radically unequal power relationships, which only state power can challenge." Nonetheless, an easy dichotomy between "bad" state and "good" civil society has only recently been seriously put to question as a result of more critical debates about social capital (Portes, 1998) and empirical studies of the concrete mechanisms of ensuring the independence of civil society.

The discovery of what Walzer (1992) calls "the paradox of civil society argument" has helped researchers of postcommunist societies to realize the importance not only of the distinction between civil society and the state for the health of democracy but also of a strong democratic state for the stability of democracy and the preservation of freedom. Investigations of the postcommunist societies show that, on the one hand, the transition from communist rule involves state withdrawal from the public sphere, and, on the other hand, it demands that the state play an active role in the provision of legislation that allows social organizations to throw off party–state tutelage (Lowenhardt, 1995; Linz and Stepan, 1996). Considering civil society as "the arena of the polity where self organizing groups, movements and individuals, relatively autonomous from the state, attempt to articulate values, create associations and solidarities and advance their interest," Linz and Stepan (1996, p. 6) indicate that the development of postcommunist civil society requires political stability, unambiguous legislation, and a strong and efficient state which is able to contain conflicts, restrict particularism, and protect the rights for its own organization.

The importance of the state for the well-being of civil society is also the main element of the criticism of Putnam's thesis on the working of Italian democracy. Putnam (1993) argues that the organization of civil society precedes democratization, since strong democratic institutions only emerge once strong civic groups have been formed and have demanded to be represented. Unlike Tocqueville, who assumed that the establishment of a democratic polity and political activity were the primary conditions for a thriving civil society, Putnam argues that the prerequisite of a democratic society is the initial creation of voluntary associations because only their dense networks of interpersonal trust can overcome the free-rider dilemma. However, as his romanticized image of community precludes him from seeing that certain networks of civic engagement are a source of both trust and distrust, Putnam fails to supply a theory that identifies the mechanisms of production and maintenance of trust. Thus, while directly linking the quality of social life with civic engagement and norms of reciprocity, he argues that social connectedness is at its strongest when rooted in an old tradition. Consequently, Putnam's reformulation of the question of trust assumes that a society is indifferent to government action, and this leads him to overlook the role of the state (Woolcock, 1998, p. 157).

Many empirical studies question Putnam's deterministic view of democratization and suggest that the state can actually promote and strengthen civic organizations (Abers, 1998). Because the state influences the level of funding and subsidies to voluntary and non-profit groups and because of its involvement in economic infrastructures, it is also responsible for "the cross-class and organizational dynamics by which civic associations actually form and persist" (Skocpol, 1996, p. 22). Therefore, the state's role in securing conditions for the realization of citizens' rights and its intervention within the civic sphere cannot be ignored when one is examining the nature of civil society.

The significance of the state in shaping the nature of civil society can be fully understood by positioning civil society between the economy and polity. However, new approaches, especially ones examining civil society through the prism of social movements, have eliminated the market from their consideration. For example, post-Marxist researchers' focus their attention on civil societies as forms of "collective actions that are differentiated not only from the state but also from the market economy" (Cohen and Arato, 1992, p. 5). This departure from the classical view, where commerce and industry are central, although not exclusive, components of civil society, effectively eliminates economic power and economic inequalities as the basis for political change (Meadwell, 1995, p. 190). The consequences of such a removal of interest-representation from the ambit of civil society are best illustrated by recent studies of the diversity of postcommunist development which point out that the economy needs to be seen as a part of overall social relations essential for social mobilization and activism (Linz and Stepan, 1996).

The first usage of the idea of civil society connected it with the emergence of new commercial society and its associations, contracts, and property rights. Today, the liberal idea that a recognition of property rights is essential for sustaining individual freedom under a rule of law is increasingly perceived as a necessary but not sufficient condition for a healthy functioning of democracy. There is a growing understanding that this liberal view needs to be accompanied by the recognition that many divisions within civil society still "remain a source of inequality and instability" (Kumar, 1993, p. 389), and that this limits citizens' ability to exercise their rights and freedoms. The market economy, while specifying one necessary element, is not a sufficient condition for the existence of a strong civil society. In order for all individuals to actively participate in the public sphere, a democratic welfare state ought to take it upon itself "to equalize the worth of liberty to all its citizens" (Tamir, 1998, p. 223). Only civil society placed within the framework of a democratic welfare state can secure the conditions for its citizens' participation in public life.

However, the state and the economy not only shape conditions and opportunities for social mobilization activism, they are also essential for understanding the nature of associational life. If people do not have support from the state in their attempts to secure basic rights, goods, and services, they will join associations which can protect their particularistic rights (Reis, 1998). As the example of affluent and racially homogeneous residential community associations illustrates, this type of organization does not support civic virtues, distinguishes between insiders and outsiders, and may even have potentially destructive outcomes for democratic systems (Bell, 1998). Therefore, it can be said that not only can a decline in associational life jeopardize civic values, but the emergence of particular types of associations can determine generalized reciprocity and social trust. As not all kinds of associations are worthy of encouragement in a liberal democracy, so only an active state, ready to protect individual rights (including welfare rights) and ready to be attentive to the dangers embodied in civil society, although without interfering with the independence of the civil sphere, provides a real condition for the democratization of civil society.

The realization that civil society associations can not only mediate but also generate conflicts has brought the end of the dichotomy of "bad" state and "good" civil society and the realization that the proper functioning of democracy depends on a particular interaction between society and political institutions, and not simply on the maintenance of societal activity *per se*, and that the evaluation of the benefits of civil society in any given context depends, in turn, on a prior assessment of the political ends embraced by a particular community. So it is not enough to ask whether institutions are "macro" or "intermediate," one must also ask what ideas they "carry" and what interest they represent: civil–state institutions are good to the extent that they are animated by civic virtues (Berger, 1998, p. 362).

Consequently, we need to focus our attention on an examination of the conditions which ensure the translation of private particularistic identities and obligations into public universal civic solidarities. Solidarity and trust produce socially beneficial effects only among some groups, while among others they have exactly the opposite effect, such as a reduction of the privacy and autonomy of individuals, restrictions on access to opportunities, exclusion of outsiders, or downward leveling norms (Portes, 1998). Moreover, under certain circumstances a robust civil society may not produce positive political consequences but instead signal and accelerate a democratic regime's degeneration, as the disintegration of the Weimar Republic's democracy illustrates (Berman, 1997). So, to establish the sociological usefulness of the term "civil society," we should examine not only the formation of social capital but also the ends to which those assets are to be directed and the nature and strength of the political institutions. We need to go beyond the facile equation of solidarity and trust with the level of "civicness" in communities and to analyze particular societies by combining an analysis of societal and cultural factors with the study of political institutions (Hefner, 1998).

At present there are many perspectives on the age-old dilemma between diversity and solidarity. Some writers see civil society as "a signifier of plurality" (Keane, 1998, p. 53) and reject the need for a socially shared definition of the good, while others, such as communitarians, point to the need for some normative frameworks of shared purposes and consensus. A more pluralistic interpretation of democracy, which sees civil society as "based on a recognition of difference and diversity" (Hall, 1998, p. 34), criticizes calls for the moral reconstitution of civil society as realms of mutual trust for underestimating the importance of individualism and pluralism and for assuming that the perception of an attainment of solidarity and unity occurs "naturally," due to the existence of self-evident mutual obligations and common purposes. Understanding of civil society as a homogeneous unity or a harmonious community may result in considerable social and political losses, as illustrated by developments in post-1989 Poland, where the overunification of society has inhibited the emergence of a competitive pluralism and has made the differentiation of democratic institutions more difficult. However, seeing civil society as only a battlefield where interest meets interest can cause us to overlook the existence and sociological implications of shared identities that bind people as well the persistence of some boundaries. So, just as it "makes little sense to universalize a permanent particularity, it makes little sense to particularize a universal end result" (Wolfe, 1992, p. 315), and there is a need to understand that not all boundaries are the same and that not all types of solidarity produce the same effect. In the same vein, new debates stress the need for a plurality of structures of civil society and the preservation of some sense of wholeness.

Since there is a growing need to come to terms with the tensions inherent in democracy, sociological inquiry into the nature of civil society should be focused on how both the plurality of structures of civil society and the preservation of a sense of wholeness are realized. Such a reconciliation is always only incremental and never stable, since the balance of forces underlying a civil compromise shifts (Hefner, 1998). Seeing civil society as a space that opens the way for public participation, while preserving individual difference and diversity (Touraine, 1997), brings to center stage investigations into how both "inclusive democracy and exclusive group centeredness," as the necessary conditions "for a rich but just social life" (Wolfe, 1992, p. 311), are possible. It can be argued that the actualization of civil society means the reconciliation of tensions between democratic ideals and sociologically informed accounts of individual versus group obligations, or refers to a situation in which the acceptance of individual differences does not prevent the development of more universalistic identities of communicative rationality.

This can be realized when civil society becomes "a sphere of solidarity in which abstract universalism and particularistic versions of community are tensely intertwined" (Alexander, 1998b, p. 97). In order to identify conditions for the realization of civil society, we need to understand how inclusive citizenship rights actually are and how widespread is social acceptance of a normative framework of shared purposes and consensus within which diversity can be both cultivated and contained. This requires an examination of the relationship between universal individual rights and the particularistic restrictions on these rights, as well as general levels of civility and sociability. Civility, which underwrites pluralism, demands "that in all life outside the home we afford each other certain decencies and comforts as fellow citizens regardless of other differences between us" (Bryant, 1992, p. 111). Sociability creates a feeling of belonging and is necessary in democratic civil society, since informal bonds and communication, as the conditions of public opinion and identity formation, are essential for self-reliance, responsibility, and collective action. For civil society to be a realm of freedom, solidarity, and plurality it needs to be placed within the framework of a democratic welfare state and to be capable of nurturing civility and sociability, which assists the individual responsibility and participation demanded for democracy.

Stress on the crucial role of civility and sociability in democratic societies is based on the assumption that "Democracy depends upon the engagement of individuals, not only with the state, but with each other" (Hansen, 1997, p. 289). Due to the importance of these links between informal discursive sources of democracy and formal decision-making institutions, the revitalization of the complex world of civility and sociability requires overcoming the inadequacy of the public–private dichotomy as an analytical framework for the understanding of modern societies. Thus, to establish sociological usefulness of the term "civil society," we need to understand the overlapping nature of the private and public sphere. This means moving beyond Habermas's definition of the public sphere as based on the separation between the state, the private sphere, the market, and the public sphere (Calhoun, 1997; Wolfe, 1997).

Habermas's historical account of the rise of a "discursive public sphere" shows how "private people come together as public" (1989, p. 27), and describes the public sphere as the arena in which civil liberties and universal values could be expressed. Habermas's reliance on the distinction of private–public unnecessarily reintroduces a dichotomous vision of society and does not provide an adequate empirical description of the major contemporary institutions (Wolfe, 1997). In reality, the public is not separated from private, as it was assumed in the eighteenth-century model of the liberal public sphere, on which Habermas's ideal-typical construction is based (Calhoun, 1997, p. 82). Critical discussions of Habermas's treatment of identities and interests as settled within the private sphere and brought ready made into the public sphere show that such a theory does not take into account, for example, the gendered nature of the public sphere (Benhabib, 1992).

Habermas's claim that today's public sphere is under threat from the invasive logic of commodification leads him to insist on the importance of a "discursive ethic" in the process of democratization, as well as to identify the core of civil society as consisting of "a network of associations that institutionalizes problem-solving discourses of general interest inside the framework of organized public spheres" (Habermas, 1996, p. 367). Furthermore, the realization that the public sphere can no longer be contained within national boundaries informs his more pragmatic recent evaluation of the feasibility of a solidarity and cohesion in a modern, complex, functionally differentiated, and media-saturated global society. Although under such conditions civil society is highly fragile, the reshaping of relations between states and their more communicatively competent citizens and the structuring of a communicative sphere into a "sphere of publics" (Calhoun, 1996, p. 457) can, nonetheless, offer new hopes for further democratization – provided that the public sphere is underwritten by civility and protected by a stable state able to contain conflicts.

CONCLUSION

From its origin as "an invention from the conditions of European modernity" (Tester, 1992, p. 124), civil society has been a complex and contested concept. Now it is commonly recognized as a basis for democratic legitimacy and as an important ingredient in any effort to understand the conditions of modern democracy's cross-cultural possibility (Hefner, 1998).

However, while the discourse of civil society is "at the heart of a sea change in contemporary political culture" (Cohen and Arato, 1992, p. 3), its overly normative tone raises doubts about this notion's potential as an analytical concept. To secure a place in social theory and research, the term "civil society" needs to be converted into a more historically and sociologically informed concept. While undertaking efforts to maximize the level of "concreteness" of this idea, we should be aware of the impossibility of constructing a unifying category for all sociological analyses. So placing the idea of civil society in a particular tradition and developing the awareness of its actual usage and status in a particular presentation can be the first step to assist mutual understanding and exchange between different approaches to civil society. The second step in improving the usefulness of the notion should focus on enlarging its heuristic value. Civil society, to be the proper subject matter of sociology, should be operationalized in a way which allows us to examine it as a process securing democratic inclusiveness and social exclusiveness. To grasp the nature of a civil society means to understand its role in supporting and constraining the institutional spheres of the economy and the polity, and to reveal the extent to which it genuinely accommodates civility and sociability.

While it remains to be identified exactly how and by what mechanisms a program of revitalization of the public realm can be achieved, any project of reinvention of active citizenry as the basis of social solidarity needs to include the cultivation of a sphere of autonomous social actions valued for their ability to foster sociability and civility as well as nurture civil society's democratic dialogue with political institutions. The theory of civil society, understood as "the realm of fragmentation and struggle but also of concrete and authentic solidarities" (Walzer, 1992, p. 97), holds that a democratic civil society depends on finding a balance between social diversity and a sense of wholeness. Since people's opportunities for autonomy and participation depend on macrostructural factors, the promotion of such a compromise, which is neither easy to achieve nor stable, is one of the main functions of a democratic state.

7

Human Rights

ABDULLAHI A. AN-NA'IM

Human rights is not commonly accepted as a field in sociology, despite the clear overlap in subject matter and possibilities of mutual conceptual and methodological influence. In terms of the organization of this volume, for example, freedom from discrimination, as an overarching human rights principle, has obvious implications for fields in sociology ranging from citizenship and national identity to education, stratification and mobility, and health policy. Specific human rights, like freedom of speech and association, are clearly relevant to issues of political participation and labor. Gender, sexuality, children, and race are major themes among human rights scholars. The relationship between the state and civil society is central to the international articulation and national implementation of human rights in all societies around the world, and as such of interest to sociologists. Human rights considerations are also relevant to the mediation of competing claims to economic and social justice, identity, and communal autonomy, in global cross-cultural and comparative terms. These concerns join those of sociologists over such issues as globalization and postcolonial power relations, social movements, development, accountability of transnational corporations for labor relations, and environmental concerns.

To explore possibilities of collaboration and mutual influence between sociologists and human rights scholars, I begin with an overview of the human rights paradigm as the framework for the specification and implementation of rights through national politics and international relations. Since many of the main themes of human rights are commonly known in terms of constitutional or civil rights (subject to the crucial difference indicated later), sociologists might want to consider whether their familiarity with the working of domestic (national) civil rights could enable them to contribute to mediating what I call the paradox of international accountability for the domestic practice of sovereign states. Mediating that paradox also calls for some understanding of the debate over the universality and cultural/contextual relativity of human rights, discussed in the second section. In the third section of this chapter, I discuss the need for complementary legal and social science approaches to the implementation of human rights as a framework for justice; and provide a brief review of some of the ways in which sociologists have addressed human rights issues.

THE HUMAN RIGHTS PARADIGM

Human rights, in a generic sense, can be seen as a framework for an adequate response to the profound social concerns of persons and their communities. This primarily procedural sense of human rights is about creating and maintaining "the space" for individuals and groups to achieve justice, personal security and well-being, general political stability and economic development, and so forth. At the same time, however, human rights norms do have a specific normative content that reflects a certain understanding of what these individual and societal objectives mean, and how they should be realized in practice. In a substantive sense, therefore, human rights have a clear ideological orientation to what it means to be human, and how social and political institutions should work in order to achieve certain ends. However, there is a tension between these two dimensions of human rights. To inspire and motivate people to take them seriously, human rights need to have significant and relevant normative content in each specific context. Yet this is likely to be resisted by privileged and powerful persons and groups in any society precisely because of the potential to change existing power relations. Aspects of this tension and its implications will become clearer after a brief explanation of what human rights are commonly understood to mean, and how they are supposed to work.

By the human rights paradigm I mean the idea that the protection of certain individual and collective/group rights, as discussed below, is a matter of international concern, rather than the exclusive internal affair of states. Paradoxically, as explained below, the same states control the processes of determining these rights at the international level, and applying them within national jurisdictions. Moreover, what the so-called international community may do about a state that willfully and persistently disregards its international obligations to protect those rights is also subject to a complex interaction of legal principles and practical considerations. For instance, the notion of "humanitarian intervention" to stop serious human rights violations within a country (as claimed by the NATO governments who intervened militarily in Kosovo in 1999 against the government of Yugoslavia) involves balancing such factors as human concern about the suffering of the victims, the risks of action or inaction for international peace and security, and the political and economic interests of the intervening state(s), as well as the short- and long-term implications of violating the sovereignty of that country.

Much of the normative, as well as the procedural, dimension of human rights is traditionally supposed to be provided for in national constitutions and laws for domestic application by the judicial and executive organs of the state, as a matter of national sovereignty. Earlier attempts by some states acting collectively to extend such regimes into the boundaries of another state included international efforts to end slavery and to protect minorities during the nineteenth and early twentieth centuries. But the real launch of the human rights paradigm in the generally accepted sense came about around the middle of the twentieth century. The horrific events of the Second World War prompted strong agreement by the mid-1940s on the need to effectively check the serious failure of any state to protect the rights of all persons and groups within its territorial jurisdiction (Steiner and Alston, 1996, p. 59). That was the first time there has ever been such a broad consensus about the need to reconcile respect for the sovereignty of a state with the protection of certain human rights as rights due to every human being by virtue of his or her humanity, without distinction on such grounds as race, sex, belief, language, or national origin.

But since the process of determining the nature and scope of these rights, and approaches to their international protection, was confined to sovereign states which were members of the United Nations (UN) in 1945, only four African states and eight Asian states were included. The rest of Africa and Asia was colonized at that time by the same European powers that were proclaiming the universality of human rights at the UN. Moreover, some basic ambiguities in the original concept continue to frustrate the prospects of its practical application. For example, these rights are proclaimed in general terms as belonging to all human beings, while their realization is strongly associated with citizenship of a specific country. Although some general principles of international law still apply to how a state may treat non-citizens who happen to be within its territory, the distinction between citizen and non-citizen is sometimes difficult to justify from a human rights point of view (Turner, 1993b, p. 495; 1997). To avoid these complex issues in this brief overview, I refer to persons under the jurisdiction of a state, instead of identifying them as its citizens.

The consensus of the mid-1940s was strongly reflected in the Charter of the UN of 1945, which is the most authoritative document of the present international order. According to Article 1 of the Charter, "The Purposes of the United Nations are . . . (3) To achieve international cooperation in solving international problems of an economic, social, cultural, or humanitarian character, and in promoting and encouraging respect for human rights and for fundamental freedoms for all without distinction as to race, sex, language, or religion." While emphasizing this basic obligation in other Articles, the UN Charter left the task of definition and implementation of "human rights and fundamental freedoms" to subsequent developments.

That process began with the drafting and adoption of the Universal Declaration of Human Rights of 1948. But the Declaration is not binding as such because, according to the UN Charter, resolutions of the General Assembly are merely recommendations to member states of the organization. The drafting and adoption of detailed treaties, which are binding under international law, followed, to provide definitions of rights and their implementation. Moreover, some human rights norms can also be found in certain principles of what is known as customary international law, like the prohibition of genocide, war crimes, and crimes against humanity. These norms are binding on all states, regardless of their ratification of treaties on those matters. Some human rights scholars argue that certain aspects of the Universal Declaration have become binding as customary international law. For example, the prohibition of torture is generally accepted as binding on all states as a principle of customary international law, regardless of their ratification of the specific treaties on the subject.

The treaties setting the international "legal" standards of human rights range in scope from earlier Conventions on labor rights (1930), genocide (1948), and slavery (1956), to the broad 1966 International Covenants, one on economic, social and cultural rights, and the other on civil and political rights. There is also a growing number of specialized treaties, like the Conventions for the Elimination of All Forms of Discrimination, on grounds of race (1965) and gender (1979), and the Convention on the Rights of the Child of 1989. Similar standards appear in the regional documents of the European, Inter-American, and African systems (Steiner and Alston, 1996, p. 563). This legal regime also includes principles of humanitarian law regulating the conduct of armed forces in conflict situations, like the four Geneva Conventions of 1949, and the 1951 Refugees Convention. Human rights standards have also been elaborated through several major international conferences. During the 1990s, for instance, human rights principles and policies were elaborated in such documents as the Vienna Declaration and Programme of Action (1994) and the Beijing Platform for Action of the Fourth World Conference on Women (1995). Human rights are integral to the mandate of specialized intergovernmental agencies like the International Labor Organization (ILO), the World Health Organization (WHO), and the United Nation Development Programme (UNDP).

As the increasingly wide range of local, regional, and global actors and processes envisioned by this complex web of documents and institutions clearly shows, the development of an international legal framework cannot mean that the implementation of human rights be left to purely legal approaches. The basic idea of the human rights paradigm is now firmly established in international relations, as well as in the national politics of the vast majority of countries around the world, subject to differing assessment of its efficacy or consistency of its application. Nevertheless, the basic paradox remains: *how to achieve effective international supervision of domestic human rights protection without violating national sovereignty as the expression of the right to self-determination, which is itself a collective human right under the first Article of the 1966 Covenants.*

From this perspective, I suggest, social science approaches would be extremely important for understanding the processes of legal articulation and implementation of these rights as the proper and legitimate exercise of the right to self-determination, rather than its negation. Sociological analyses are needed, for example, for understanding the processes of social construction of rights, whose interests are served by those processes, and the role of civil society and social movements in generating the political will to adopt and implement international treaties protecting these rights. Such insights are essential for mediating the paradox of international protection of human rights through respect for sovereignty, instead of its violation, as explained below.

It is true that, by ratifying treaties and subscribing to international human rights policy statements, states are indicating voluntary acceptance of human rights obligations as limitations on their national sovereignty. But that notion itself can be seen as entrenching, rather than diminishing, the underlying paradox, because it is the state that decides when, how, and to what extent to limit its own sovereignty. First, the structure and content of any human rights treaty are negotiated and agreed among the delegates of states, before the treaty is opened for ratification. Second, and regardless of its publicly declared position, no state is legally bound until it formally ratifies the treaty according to its own internal constitutional and political process. Moreover, subject to the requirements of the international law of treaties, a state has the right not only to enter "reservations" limiting the scope of its obligations under a treaty, but also to repudiate a treaty that it has previously ratified. Third, the state is also intended to play a crucial role in the interpretation and implementation within its territory of the human rights treaties it has ratified. Where national legislation is required to incorporate international treaties into national law, as in the United States and United Kingdom, the domestic normative content of a treaty is effectively determined by the way it is expressed in legislative language, and interpreted through the judicial process, of the country (Steiner and Alston, 1996, p. 26). In other words, domestic compliance with a state's international obligations to protect human rights can only be achieved by the official organs of the same state.

Thus, while intended to ensure the protection of certain minimum rights, international protection is dependent on the active cooperation of states in limiting their freedom of action within their own domestic jurisdiction. The paradox of self-regulation by the state of its own behavior is, of course, also true of domestic constitutional and legal protection of rights. The crucial difference, noted above, is that constitutional rights are the product of internal dynamics, whereas the human rights paradigm seeks to influence domestic situations in favor of upholding certain internationally recognized standards. In other words, the paradox is sharper for the human rights paradigm because it has to overcome internal opposition within the country in question, without having the power to impose its will on states which refuse to comply. The need to mediate this enduring paradox calls for a clear understanding of the nature and functioning of social and political forces and institutions within each country, and in its relations with other countries.

It is not helpful to simply call for formal limitations on state sovereignty, because that is neither practically feasible nor necessarily good for the protection of human rights in the long term. Formal limitations on sovereignty are not feasible because sovereignty is integral to the foundations of the present international order, as entrenched in Article 2(7) of the UN Charter and other international documents, and fundamentally affirmed by national constitutions around the world. Since states are the principal actors at both the international and national levels, they are unlikely to relinquish their own autonomy by abandoning sovereignty or allowing other actors to achieve that result. Even if they were practically feasible, formal limitations might also be counterproductive because sovereignty is the essential expression of the fundamental collective right to self-determination, as the practical vehicle of domestic policy and the necessary medium of international relations.

A more realistic and desirable approach, I suggest, is to seek to diminish the negative consequence of the paradox of self-regulation by infusing the human rights ethos into the fabric of the state itself and the global context in which it operates. In that way, the protection of human rights becomes *the outcome of the free exercise of the right to self-determination, instead of being seen as an external imposition which violates that right.* This paradigm shift can best be achieved by upholding the universality of human rights as, in the words of the Preamble to the Universal Declaration, "the common standard of achievement for all peoples and all nations." Since external imposition will probably be resisted as a clear violation of sovereignty, while voluntary compliance with commonly agreed standards is likely to be seen as vindication of sovereign authority, the universality of human rights must reflect true consensus around the world. At a formal level, that is said to be achieved through agreement among states, as the representatives of their societies under international law. But according to the human rights paradigm itself, and as a matter of practical politics, international agreements are legitimate and sustainable only to the extent that they express the genuine consent of national societies and local communities.

THE QUANDARY OF UNIVERSALITY AND RELATIVITY

The issue of popular acceptance of the human rights paradigm is frequently discussed in terms of a binary of universality and relativity (Steiner and Alston, 1996, p. 166; Negengast and Turner, 1997), as if one has to either fully accept or completely reject the universality of certain rights for all human beings. At one end of this purported spectrum are said to be countries which claim cultural/ religious relativity or contextual specificity to justify rejecting or qualifying certain universal human rights norms, in contrast to those which are supposed to fully accept the universality of all human rights, at the other end. Whereas some Islamic and East Asian countries are commonly placed on the relativist side, Western countries are commonly assumed to be universalist. Upon reflection, however, one can see that such a binary view of this issue is both misleading and difficult to substantiate or maintain in practice.

A binary view is misleading in assuming either that human rights can be culturally and contextually neutral, or that a conception of human rights emerging within one culture or context can be accepted by other cultures for application in their context. To explain, I would first note that, as a normative system that seeks to influence people's behavior and direct the institutions which regulate their lives, human rights can only be the product of culture, to be interpreted for practical application in a specific context. In other words, human rights norms can be neither imagined nor understood in the abstract, without reference to the concrete daily experience of the people who are supposed to implement them. As indicated above, the human rights paradigm is founded on the belief in the possibility of universal rights, due to all human beings, everywhere, as the basis for international concern about how people are treated in any part of the world. Yet, since any conception of human rights as a normative system is the product of some culture(s), a given set of these rights can be perceived as alien or unacceptable to other cultures. That is exactly the quandary of universality and relativity: namely, how to determine universally valid and applicable human rights norms, which would naturally tend to reflect certain cultural values and institutions, without expecting one society to submit to the normative system of another.

It is difficult to substantiate a binary view of universality and relativity of human rights because that would ignore the realities of power relations in the world, and oversimplify the positions and behavior of countries on both sides of this alleged divide. For example, the criteria and process by which the present set of international human rights was established in the first place were not as inclusive as they ought to have been. As noted earlier, the vast majority of the peoples of Africa and Asia were not represented at the UN, except by the same colonial powers which had for decades violated the basic human rights of colonized peoples. Upon achieving independence, African and Asian states had no choice but to at least pretend to accept the pre-established concept, structure, and content of the human rights paradigm as a condition of membership in the international community. That is to say, the balance of global economic, military, and political power relations in the postcolonial world has enabled the developed countries to raise the human rights paradigm they have established themselves as the condition for membership in the international community. This does not mean that this paradigm can never become universally accepted and applied. Rather, the point is that efforts to promote universality should be founded on a clear understanding of the issues from different perspectives.

It is profoundly problematic, in my view, to assume that the universality of human rights is "self-evident" or has been "established," and all that remains is to "pressure" a few ruling elites in developing countries to abandon their "opportunistic" denial of the obvious. This view, on the hand, encourages hypocrisy among the governments of developing countries who have to pay lip-service to human rights in exchange for favorable treatment by developed countries in such matters as development assistance, support for credit from international financial institutions, and/or the grant of special trade status. The nature of existing power relations, on the other hand, enables the governments of developed countries to raise the human rights paradigm selectively, in the service of their own foreign policy objectives (compare the US positions regarding China and Cuba), without regard to the integrity and credibility of this paradigm as a whole. The application of double standards in judging similar situations is possible because of the lack of an independent check on the alleged commitment of developed countries to the universality of human rights. Since these states dominate international relations, they are the primary judge of their own behavior, as well as that of developing countries. In fact, developed countries have not shown consistent acceptance of the universality of human rights in their own national policies. This is reflected, for example, in the resistance of Western countries to accepting that economic, social, and cultural rights are actually human rights, as proclaimed by the Universal Declaration and numerous international treaties (Eide et al., 1994; Steiner and Alston, 1996, p. 256). For instance, Article 25 of the Declaration provides that everyone has a "right to a standard of living adequate for the health and well-being of himself and his family, including food, clothing, housing and medical care and necessary social services." Thus, these economic and social rights are as much human rights as the right to life, liberty, and security of person (Article 3), protection against torture, cruel, inhuman, or degrading treatment or punishment (Article 5), and freedom of opinion and expression (Article 19). No one would suggest that torture or suppression of freedom of expression be condoned or tolerated anywhere in the world today. Yet there is little objection to the denial of food, shelter, and medical care to the majority of human beings around the world, especially those living in developing countries. Western countries also find it difficult to accept the *possibility* of protecting any collective or group claim or entitlement as a *human right* within an existing state, although the first Article of both the 1966 Covenants provides for a collective human right to self-determination of "all peoples" (not nations, countries, or states). Since this Article clearly envisages political independence as a means to achieving such objectives as political participation, social development, and economic well-being, denying any group of people any of the essential elements of this right is a violation of the right itself.

It is true that some economic, social, cultural, and/or collective "interests" are substantially provided for within the national jurisdictions of developed Western countries through the normal political and legal processes of each country; sometimes with special constitutional or legal protection against easy violation. But the essence of the human rights paradigm is to ensure that such interests are safeguarded against the contingencies of national politics and legal processes. In fact, the idea emerged from the experience of Western countries which sought, through constitutional protection, to place certain fundamental civil liberties beyond daily politics. That is, recognition of a specific entitlement as a human right is supposed to enhance the prospects of its practical implementation more than can be expected from the normal political and legal processes of any country. To the extent that they do in fact respect and protect economic, social, and cultural rights, or collective rights, developed countries have nothing to fear from accepting those rights as human rights. Conversely, such acceptance is necessary whenever those rights are not sufficiently respected in the manner and to the extent required by international human rights standards.

It is true that economic, social, cultural, and collective rights are presently difficult to specify and enforce in the same way one can do with civil and political rights. For example, since the right to work cannot practically mean an obligation on the state to actually provide work for every person, the question is: what should be the content of this right and how can it be implemented?

Collective rights raise issues of human agency in determining membership and boundaries of groups, or more generally the dangers of elite appropriation of the collective voice of groups and communities. However, difficulties are only to be expected because formal recognition of these rights is much more recent, in comparison to civil and political rights. Moreover, these rights need not necessarily fit the model of civil and political rights to qualify as human rights. The processes of concrete definition and implementation of these rights, which require social scientific analysis as suggested here, are not likely to make significant progress unless they are taken seriously as *human rights*, rather than simply objectives of public policy.

The real reason for Western resistance to accepting these rights as human rights, in my view, is ideological or cultural. Subject to national and regional variations, the liberal ideology/culture of these countries tends to hold that economic, social, and cultural benefits or services should be provided for through the normal political process, instead of being given legal sanction as rights. Because of its emphasis on individual autonomy and privacy, against other social entitlements as well as the state, the liberal mind finds it difficult to conceive of collective entities or groups as bearers of rights. Liberals may see their views as obviously valid to every reasonable person, but that is exactly how ideological or cultural conditioning of human behavior works everywhere. In other words, liberal societies tend to resist accepting economic, social, and cultural rights or collective/group rights as human rights because that is the position of their own ideology or culture. If ideology or culture can exempt Western countries from accepting these rights as human rights, non-Western countries can claim the same regarding such human rights norms as equality for women or protection of freedom of expression.

Moreover, the persistence of some Western governments in asserting chauvinistic notions of national sovereignty can fairly be described as relativistic. For example, the United States is notorious for seeking to fashion international human rights treaties to fits its own ideological views and social institutions during the drafting process, only to fail to ratify and incorporate those treaties into its domestic law for application within the country itself. This is true from the 1948 Genocide Convention, which took the United States more than forty years to ratify, and only subject to reservations, to the 1989 Convention on the Rights of the Child, which is now ratified by every country in the world except the United States and Somalia. Since Somalia has had no government since 1992, the United States stands completely alone in refusing to ratify this Convention. It is difficult to see a significant difference between the position of the government of the United States and those of countries like China, Iran, and Saudi Arabia, as all of them are refusing to allow their own domestic practice to be judged by agreed international standards. Moreover, the position of the USA is especially damaging for the human rights paradigm, not only for its failure to live up to claims of global leadership in this field, but also because its economic and military power enables it to play a paramount role in shaping international relations, as well as influencing the domestic policies of other countries around the world.

Instead of insisting on a sharp dichotomy between universality and relativity, it is better to perceive the issues in terms of a constant mediation between the two poles. The realities of enduring cultural diversity around the world, on the one hand, and global multifaceted interaction and interdependence, on the other, challenge both the theoretical validity and practical viability of a framework of universality and relativity as polar extremes. An example of mediation between the excesses of both extremes can be seen in the doctrine of "the margin of appreciation" in the European human rights system – allowing states a degree of discretion in the interpretation and implementation of their human rights obligations (Steiner and Alston, 1996, p. 601). But as elaborated elsewhere, it is also important to strive to achieve wider and more sustainable global overlapping consensus on human rights norms through internal discourse within different cultures, and cross-cultural dialogue between them (An-Na'im and Deng, 1990; An-Na'im, 1992).

In conclusion for this section, I would emphasize the need to understand how the political will to uphold human rights is generated within civil society, or in response to its demands. State action is more likely to happen when human rights are accepted as culturally legitimate than when they are perceived as an alien imposition. It is also important to address the economic dimensions of the effective implementation of human rights, as underlying causes of violations as well as in the allocation of resources for practical implementation of rights. Even so-called "negative" civil and political rights, like freedom of speech or protection against torture, where the state is required to refrain from certain actions, still entail the deployment of material and human resources to implement the necessary policies. In any case, legal protection has to assume voluntary compliance as a general rule because no enforcement regime can cope with massive and persistent violations. Social scientists can make crucial contributions to addressing all these and other aspects of the human rights paradigm.

COMPLEMENTARY LEGAL AND SOCIAL SCIENCE APPROACHES

In view of the complexity of effective response to a wide variety of possible human rights claims in any society today, one should always consider as many approaches to the implementation of these rights as possible or advisable in one setting or another. Many factors affect the implementation of human rights, such as the level and quality of political commitment to the implementation of administrative, educational, and other policies, allocation of economic resources, and civil society activism. These and related factors cannot possibly be effectively addressed through purely legal approaches, though the latter will remain indispensable. In this final section, I offer an evaluation of legal approaches, followed by a brief review of how some sociologists have approached human rights issues.

The early emphasis on legal approaches to the protection of human rights will probably continue for the foreseeable future because of the universalization of European models of the state through colonialism, with its centralized powers over political processes, economic activities, social relations, provision of essential services, and so forth. As those models of the state persisted into the postcolonial world, thereby entrenching the central role of the state in national politics and international relations, the human rights paradigm adopted a legal approach for the protection of human rights. Indeed, the whole human rights system has generally emerged from the liberal approach to individual civil rights, as judicially enforceable limitations on the powers of the state in order to protect certain vital interests of the population. Accordingly, the judicial enforcement of these rights as a legal entitlement became the basis for the credibility of administrative, political, educational, and other policies and processes, as the source of operational definitions of each human right and as the mechanism for the mediation of competing claims of rights. But the limitations of purely legal approaches to constitutional rights at the national level are even more constraining for the international protection of human rights because, as noted above, the latter has to overcome domestic resistance without having the power to impose its will.

Generally speaking, the legal protection of rights assumes the prevalence of a certain conception of the rule of law, independence of the judiciary, and executive compliance with judicial determinations. The legal enforcement of rights also requires a certain degree of political stability for the proper development of an independent and credible judiciary, as well as a legal profession that is willing and able to represent all human rights litigants before the courts. These prerequisites are frequently lacking, especially when legal protection is most needed. For example, the legal systems of most African countries suffer from serious problems of poor legitimacy and accessibility, as well as lack of human and material resources (Ake, 1994). The complexity and procedural formality of postcolonial legal systems make it difficult for most Africans to have effective access to legal remedies. Structural and contextual difficulties include prolonged and complex political instability, economic underdevelopment, lack of independence and technical resources for the judiciary, and the inadequacy or poor quality of legal services. Under such conditions, it is not surprising that people will simply abstain from resorting to the courts for the legal enforcement of their rights.

This is not to say, however, that all prerequisites must be present at once before people begin to use the courts to vindicate their human rights. On the contrary, it seems to me, there is a synergy between the requirements of legal enforcement, on the one hand, and public confidence in the process, on the other. Since people will probably resort to the courts whenever there is the slightest chance of obtaining relief and justice, even a low level of public confidence may contribute to the development of an independent judiciary, and attract the necessary legal advice and representation, which may enhance public confidence further, and so forth.

But, as already indicated, even the best system for the legal protection of human rights will not be sufficient because the implementation of human rights requires different approaches. The mandate of the human rights paradigm in general is to simply provide effective redress, not only legal remedy, for every violation of human dignity and the rights of any person or group. Article 28 of the Universal Declaration provides that "everyone is entitled to a social and international order in which the rights and freedoms set forth in this Declaration can be fully realized." It is difficult to see how this original broad vision can materialize without substantial contributions of sociologists and other social scientists. The preceding analysis may have already suggested some ways in which social science approaches can make such contributions. As a human rights lawyer, I will now try to envisage how sociologists can improve our understanding of a set of interrelated issues of shared concern, by way of illustration, without presuming to speculate about specific ways in which they might do that.

Only a very few North American sociologists, like Rhoda Howard (1995), have consistently and systematically addressed human rights issues in their work in the past (Reynolds, 1998). But stronger interest seems to be emerging more recently, including efforts to examine the reasons for the earlier lack of sociological analysis of these issues in other parts of world as well. For example, Bryan Turner draws attention to the silence in sociology about human rights, and finds it puzzling, given the interest of sociologists in such subjects as social movements, social membership, and the general themes of globalization and mobilization (Turner, 1993b, p. 490). A discussion of Turner's outline of a theory of human rights, and the debate that followed (Waters, 1996b; Turner, 1997), is beyond the scope of this chapter. The point here is to note the sort of interrelated themes Turner is suggesting for analytical connections between sociology and human rights issues. For example, recalling that the human rights paradigm seeks to protect rights at the domestic level from an international perspective, without the power to impose its will over national sovereignty, one can appreciate the crucial role of social movements for and against this paradigm in different societies. However, while sociologists are familiar with the role of social movements in relation to domestic constitutional rights, as noted above, they now need to consider the impact of what is commonly known as "globalization" on the possibilities of international protection of human rights in the domestic context.

As the means for achieving and safeguarding the interests of their members, social movements have traditionally been engaged in the negotiation of competing claims among themselves, and in relation to the state as a hegemonic political institution. Some social movements succeed in substantially influencing the state, in pursuit of their own objectives. With the universalization of European models of the state through colonialism and its transformation of the postcolonial world system, as noted above, human rights non-governmental organizations (NGOs) have become the operational arm of social movements throughout the world, at both the national and international levels (Steiner and Alston, 1996, p. 456).

Social movements or groups, however, tend to perceive the human rights paradigm as either supportive of or antagonistic to their values and social objectives to varying degrees. All social actors need this paradigm for the "space" it ensures for them to organize and advocate their view, through freedoms of opinion, expression, and association, as well as the support it might give to their normative claims, such as freedom of religion or the rights of ethnic or cultural groups, and so forth. Yet social actors often try to claim the benefits of the human rights paradigm, while rejecting aspects of it that they deem to be contrary to their own values and objectives. This common inconsistency is at the heart of the universality/relativity debate discussed above, in that while all social actors would welcome the human rights paradigm to the extent that it affirms their own values and facilitates their own work, very few are willing to accept the totality of this paradigm and its implications, at least regarding matters they deem to be fundamental to their own position.

In their analysis of these social process at the domestic level, sociologists should also consider the international dimensions of the present age of multi-faceted globalization (Woodiwiss, 1996; Axtmann, 1997; Merry, 1997). The dynamics of social movements and NGO activism are increasingly influenced, if not shaped, by transnational forces and global processes. This is as true for the advocates of the rights of women and indigenous peoples as it is for those concerned with development and environmental issues. The human rights para-digm is contested by all these and similar social actors at the international as well as the national level. Indeed, since globalization itself is not a neutral phenom-enon, as it tends to enhance existing power relations, sociologists should seek to apply their conceptual and methodological insights to the working of global forces and processes at the local and national, as well as the international, levels (Cheah, 1997; Bauman, 1998).

CONCLUDING REMARKS

By the very nature of its subject matter, and the dynamic processes of the articulation and implementation of its normative content, the human rights paradigm offers sociologists and other social scientists a very rich and useful research agenda. As it seeks to negotiate the relationship between the local and the global, the human rights paradigm can benefit from sociological analysis at both the national and international levels. Moreover, the human rights paradigm raises questions about the conceptual possibility of the universality and validity of cross-cultural moral judgment. From a sociological perspective, these types of questions relate to such issues as the meaning and implications of personhood and human dignity in interpersonal or communal relations, gender and child–adult relations within the family and wider community, questions of race, ethnicity, and religion within and between communities, the nature and role of religion in public life, and the nature of the state and its institutions in relation to society at large. Sociological analysis is also necessary for mediating the tension between procedural and substantive aspects of the human rights paradigm; that is, their role in ensuring "the space" for struggles for justice, as opposed to being specific expressions of substantive justice in individual and communal relations, including questions of affirmative action or positive discrimination.

In conclusion, however, I wish to emphasize that even when judged on its own terms, the protection of human rights is only part of the answer to the major issues of social justice facing all societies. Other theoretical approaches and practical strategies for the realization of justice will of course always remain necessary. Accordingly, the invitation here is for sociologists to contribute to the further development and clarification of the human rights paradigm as a major component of the framework for justice within and between societies throughout the world. As sociological issues become increasingly transnational and globalized, it is clear that human rights are too important to leave to lawyers and a few political scientists.

8

Sociology of Religion

CHRISTIAN SMITH AND ROBERT D. WOODBERRY

Three decades ago, sociologists paid little attention to religion as an important force in social life, nor was religion considered to be of great significance. Anthropologist Anthony Wallace (1966, p. 265) summarized the then-prevailing view that "The evolutionary future of religion is extinction. Belief in super-natural beings and supernatural forces that affect nature without obeying nature's laws will erode and become only an interesting historical memory.... Belief in supernatural powers is doomed to die out, all over the world, as the result of the increasing adequacy and diffusion of scientific knowledge." But affairs have changed dramatically in the few decades since then. Peter Berger, one of an earlier era's most eloquent theorists of secularization, now proclaims a shift "from the crisis of religion to the crisis of secularity" and of "secularism in retreat" (Berger, 1983, 1996), concluding that "those who neglect religion in their analyses of contemporary affairs do so at great peril" (Berger, 1996, p. 12).

Sociologists' renewed interest in religion as a social factor is primarily the result of global events that spotlighted religion's vitality. Throughout the era of religion's academic neglect, there were sociologists who produced distinguished scholarship demonstrating religion's continued social significance. But instead it took a series of international political incidents to shock academia out of the old secularization paradigm. The crucial years were 1979 and 1980. In 1979, Muslim militants overthrew the Shah of Iran and installed an Islamic republic, which reverberated into a broad irruption of militant Islamic movements in many parts of the Middle East and beyond. At the same time, a Christian Right catapulted itself into American politics, as Christian fundamentalists – who for half a century had remained invisible on the political radar screen – publicly announced their intentions to mobilize a "moral majority" to counteract the forces of secular humanism and reclaim a Christian America. Then, in 1980, Salvadoran Roman Catholic Archbishop Oscar Romero was assassinated while saying mass, for his role in the Latin American liberation theology movement which committed the region's Church to progressive social activism and sometimes revolutionary insurrection on behalf of the poor; Romero's was only the most prominent of tens of thousands of political abductions, tortures, and murders of Latin American Christian social activists in the 1970s. Only months later, the Roman Catholic-based Solidarity movement initiated a wave of protest strikes against Poland's communist government, winning unheard-of concessions from the state, culminating in Lech Wałesa's signing of the Gdansk Accords with a Pope John Paul II souvenir pen while sporting a lapel pin of the Black Madonna of Częstochowa. Ensuing years would witness the emergence of a series of important religiously based movements around the globe: the anti-apartheid movement in South Africa, the anti-communist movement in East Germany, the Central America peace movement in the United States. With new eyes to see religion's social and political significance, sociologists have also increasingly noticed the high-intensity Pentecostalism sweeping Latin America, Christianity spreading in parts of East Asia, the panoply of religions multiplying in the USA through new immigration, the resurgence of religious identities in parts of post-communist Europe, and so on. By the 1990s, the University of Virginia's James D. Hunter (1991) was declaring a religiously infused "culture war" in America, and Harvard's Samuel Huntington (1996) predicted a global clash of civilizations with religious differences at the heart. Overstated, perhaps, but the point remains: religion is back.

Academic scholarship is now struggling to catch up with and make sense of the implications of these major events. For a long time, social scientists assuming secularization were lazy in thinking about religion. Now much empirical and theoretical work remains to bring our scholarship "up to speed" with our growing awareness of religion's social significance. This chapter is an attempt to map out some helpful recent work in that regard, and to suggest areas that need greater attention in future sociological scholarship on religion.

Much of the most interesting and important work in the sociology of religion in recent years has resulted from its scholars engaging theoretical influences from other fields, and from their shifting attention to varied levels of analysis. Stimulating debates have emerged, for example, as scholars have applied to religion theoretical insights from rational choice theory, cultural sociology, social psychology, institutional and organizational theory, studies of ethnicity, sociology of professions, and so on. The perceived failure of older categories of thought has given way to alternative conceptualizations of religion in social life. Here we observe some developments which we believe are among the most valuable and interesting.

RETHINKING MICRO-LEVEL SECULARIZATION

One area of ferment in the sociology of religion in recent years has been the reconsideration of secularization theory at the level of individual belief, consciousness, and practice. The apparent persistence of religious commitment and activity at the grassroots, particularly in the United States, has spawned attempts to better theorize religious growth and strength. This has revolved around two related theoretical approaches, both of which argue that religious and cultural pluralism does – or at least can – help religions to thrive.

One theoretical approach is the "religious economies" theory of Roger Finke, Rodney Stark, Laurence Iannaconne, and others (for example, Finke and Stark, 1992; Iannaconne, 1994; Young, 1997; Sherkat and Ellison, 1999; Stark and Finke, 2000; see also Warner, 1993), which employs a rational choice framework to try to explain: (a) the effects of religious competition and entrepreneurial mobilization on differential rates of church attendance; (b) the influence of religious capital formation on religious conversion and continuity; (c) the effect of religious strictness on church growth; and (d) the influence of the distribution of diverse religious products in a structured religious field on different religious organizations' ideologies, membership appeals, and growth and decline cycles. This theory's attempt to recast religion in economic terms, and especially its claim that religious pluralism and competition strengthen religion, has generated opposition from dissenting scholars, including Kenneth Land (Land et al., 1991), Judith Blau (Blau et al., 1993), Kevin Breault (1998), and Daniel Olson (1998). The jury is still out on the theory of religious economies, but the debate thus far has helped to push the sociology of religion into work using much stronger data, more sophisticated quantitative analyses, and more theoretical clarity.

The second theoretical approach emerging in the rethinking of micro-level secularization has been the "subcultural identity" theory of Christian Smith and colleagues (1998). Rather than taking an economistic rational choice approach, this theory synthesizes insights from literature on moral identity, reference group theory, the social psychology of group identity, the social functions of intergroup conflict, and structural approaches to deviant subcultures. It uses these insights to explain the positive effects of modern pluralism on the identity-work and symbolic boundary maintenance of thriving religious subcultures. It suggests that religion survives and can thrive in pluralistic, modern society by embedding itself in subcultures that offer satisfying morally oriented collective identities which provide adherents with meaning and belonging; and that those religious subcultures will grow strong which possess and use the subcultural tools to create both clear distinction from and significant engagement and tension with relevant outgroups. Like the religious economies theory, the subcultural identity theory advances an explanation for traditional religion's persistence in the modern world that turns on its head secularization theory's premise that cultural and religious pluralism is detrimental to religion. However, more empirical research and theoretical refinement are needed to assess the subcultural identity theory's enduring contribution and limitations.

RELIGIOUS TRANSFORMATION

Another avenue of investigation generated by the attempt to rethink individual-level secularization has been the effort to replace the old notion of religious secularization as decline, displacement, and extinction with the more open, less evaluative notion of religious "transformation." This can take many forms, but the key idea is that religion is neither declining, nor statically reproducing, but instead undergoing socially significant metamorphoses. Religions adapting to their environments is not a modern phenomena – it is evident throughout recorded history – and thus change should not automatically be interpreted as implying secularization or weakness. As with biological evolution, species that adapt to changing environments survive and those that do not often die out. In some cases, this transformation is expressed by what appears to be a growing popular interest in "spirituality," which is more individualistic, customized, and fluid than traditional, institutionalized religion (Wuthnow, 1998). Religious transformation is also evident in religious syncretism, in which believers unite adherence to different religious traditions or combine elements of multiple traditions into a personalized hybrid (for example, "I'm a Catholic-Buddhist-pagan"). A third form examines expanded religious transience; for example, the increase in church-shopping "religious seekers" and the entrepreneurial organizations that package themselves to appeal to that market – usually "seeker-sensitive" mega-churches, organizationally modeled on the shopping mall. Another focus of the religious transformation literature is the new wave of religious congregational studies that track the effects of neighborhood transitions and cultural movements on local congregational adaptation and restrategization (for example, Ammerman, 1997). Other cultural approaches to religious transformation analyze how traditional theological concepts – such as the "headship" of husbands and fathers, or the "stewardship" of possessions and wealth – are being modified by religious communities to make better sense of their changing structural and cultural circumstances (for example, Gallagher and Smith, 1999). It remains to be seen how profound an effect some of these religious transformations will have on the religious landscape. Meanwhile, work along these lines is helping to break down old categories of thinking, to retheorize religious change, and to track novel expressions of religious faith and practice.

RELIGIOUS PLURALIZATION

The USA is now undergoing a pluralization of religions, particularly in urban areas, which is made complex by issues of race and ethnicity, social class, subcultural identity, and generational change. The waves of "new immigrant groups" have arrived in North America since the USA and Canada lifted restriction on non-European immigration in the mid-1960s. These groups often carry with them the native (and sometimes missionary-planted) religions of their homelands. The substantially increased presence and visibility of Salvadoran Catholics, East Indian Hindus, Korean Presbyterians, Cambodian Buddhists, Pakistani Muslims, and so on is transforming and complexifying the US religious landscape. The simple days of Protestant, Catholic, or Jew are gone. And a new surge of sociological research is examining the implications of this new religious pluralization in the USA.

Recent scholarship by Warner and Wittner (1998), Stevens-Arroyo and colleagues (Stevens-Arroyo and Cadena, 1995) at the Program for the Analysis of Religion Among Latinas/os at the City University of New York, and an ongoing project by Helen Rose Ebaugh at the University of Houston (Ebaugh and Chafetz, 2000) suggests that religion plays a varied and vital role for new immigrants. The new immigration has brought greater religious pluralism to North America. Now mosques, temples, and ashrams sit alongside Protestant and Catholic churches in many parts of the country. However, it has not brought as much pluralism as many scholars suspect. This is partly because the vast majority of new immigrants to North America are at least nominally Christian. Much of this is because of the large waves of immigration from Latin America and the Philippines – both predominantly Catholic. But even immigrants from Korea, Vietnam, and the Middle East are disproportionately Christian. Persecuted religious minorities such as Jews, Ahmadia Muslims, and Bahais are also overrepresented. Thus, even with the new immigration, Kosmin and Lachman's (1993) *National Survey of Religious Identification* found 1.9 percent of Americans stating their religion as Jewish, and only 0.76 percent of Americans identifying with another specific non-Christian religious tradition (Muslim, Buddhist, Hindu, etc.). The Adolescent Health Survey of high school students gives similar results.

Religious affiliation helps immigrants to adapt to US life and preserve key elements of their cultures. However, religious traditions also often transform in the process. In most groups, religiosity increases after immigration. Groups also generally increase lay involvement and become more intentional – for example, children do not automatically pick up Hinduism from North American culture and so must be carefully instructed. Gender roles within religious groups also often change. In some groups (for example, Latin American Pentecostal converts), women gain more functional power; in others, the involvement of women is restricted. Among Indian Thomas Christians, men often counteract their decline in social status relative to their wives in the general society by maintaining stricter control of church leadership (Warner and Wittner, 1998). One of the most difficult problems for immigrant congregations is bridging the gap between the first and second generations. In churches, mosques, and temples that do not successfully bridge this gap, the young often leave their parents' faith. Tensions also develop between earlier and later waves of immigrants and between immigrants and their host religious denominations. Thus immigrant congregations provide a fascinating laboratory to study cultural and institutional change, and the selective process of cultural resistance and assimilation.

Yet immigration is not just a North American issue. Many Muslims, Hindus, and Buddhists have migrated to Europe, Latin America, and former British colonies around the world. Indian, Filipino, Korean, European, and North American workers also migrate to the oil rich Middle East. And wars, famines, and natural disasters force major cross-national migrations around the world. However, it is still unclear if religious groups play a similarly vital role for these immigrants and migrants. Future research should analyze such things as religion's possible influence on who migrates and to where, and how the religious context of host societies influences immigrant response. For example, does the religiosity of immigrants increase after migration everywhere, or is this particularly true in more religiously active societies like the USA?

There are also some weaknesses in the literature on new immigrant groups. In the past, research has been based almost exclusively on either small qualitative studies or quantitative data with awkward samples. Getting a national sample of small groups has been difficult; thus most scholars have used convenience samples, snowball samples, or samples of ethnic names in a telephone book. Fortunately, Guillermina Jasso and colleagues are now using administrative Immigration and Naturalization Service (INS) records to get a nationally representative sample of new immigrants to the USA for their New Immigrants Survey. This will help scholars to determine the actual religious composition of US immigrant groups and how this changes over time. Another weakness in this field is that the research has not generally been comparative. Researchers have not typically compared the same group of immigrants moving to two different countries, or gone back to the immigrants' place of origin to see how their religious traditions have changed.

RELIGION AND HEALTH

Although long neglected, research on the relationship between religion and health is growing rapidly. Much research suggests that religiosity has a consistent, moderate, positive influence on life expectancy, health, psychological well-being, and recovery from illnesses and surgery (for example, Ellison and Levin, 1998; Sherkat and Ellison, 1999). These salutary effects are consistent across several hundred studies and persist despite an impressive array of statistical controls for social ties, physical mobility, health behavior, and socio-demographics. They are consistent for a wide variety of illnesses and surgeries, for multiple age groups, social classes, races, ethnicities, and nationalities – although most of this research has been done in North America and Europe. The positive impact of religiosity seems greatest for the elderly and African Americans, but does not vary much by gender. There may also be some variation by religious tradition, as some studies suggest that certain conservative religious groups have greater positive health outcomes and greater life satisfaction (Ellison and Levin, 1998). Generally, church attendance has the greatest positive impact, although private prayer, subjective importance of religion, and religious coping strategies often have additional positive influence. Greater social support, more satisfying family relationships, and healthier behavior (for example, less smoking, alcohol abuse, and risky sexual behavior) account for some but not all of this positive impact. Scholars have begun to analyze a number of other possible mechanisms, such as the possible impact of religious meaning systems on stress.

Of course, not all forms of religiosity promote health and psychological well-being. A significant amount of research focuses on abusive churches, "toxic faith," and maladaptive religious coping strategies. And theorists like Sigmund Freud (1927), Albert Ellis (1992), and Nathaniel Branden (1994) have argued that religion is neurotic and damaging to self-esteem and self-efficacy. Most of this research, however, is based on anecdotal evidence and non-random samples. The overwhelming empirical evidence suggests that these cases are the exception rather than the rule (Gorsuch, 1988; Ellison and Levin, 1998).

However, there remain some important weaknesses in the field of health and religion. First, almost all the research has been done in North America and Europe, where Christian and Jewish traditions predominate. More data need to be collected to see if this impact is consistent across other religious traditions. Second, the generic religion questions on most surveys prevent scholars from modeling many possible causal mechanisms. Fortunately, researchers associated with the National Institute on Aging and Fetzer Institute (Idler et al., 1997) are currently developing better measures, and some appear on the 1998 General Social Survey. Third, most of the research only looks at the direct impact of religiosity, while controlling for social support, health behavior, and so on. However, much of religion's impact may be indirect (for example, through greater social support). With structural equations modeling, researchers could model both the direct and indirect impact of religiosity and use better latent measures of religious variables. Finally, because few longitudinal surveys include questions about religion on early waves, most of the conclusions are based on cross-sectional evidence. This makes it difficult to control for selection bias – perhaps the type of people who will be more healthy also choose to be more religious. It also means that researchers cannot measure the cumulative impact of religion, since they only have a snapshot of respondents' religiosity at one point of time. This is equivalent to knowing how many cigarettes someone smokes at the time of a survey, but not knowing how many he or she smoked previously. What researchers need is the religious equivalent to packs smoked per number of years. Duke sociologist Linda George (1999) and others are currently developing retrospective measures to gather this information. If religion's impact is so consistent with such weak measures of cumulative religiosity, it will likely be stronger with better measures.

CONSERVATIVE PROTESTANTISM IN THE UNITED STATES

Recently, scholars have carried out much interesting work about conservative Protestants (CPs) in the USA – that is, evangelicals, fundamentalists, pentecostals, and charismatics. To be clear about terms, "conservative" here refers to theological, not economic or political conservativism – CPs are typically more economically liberal with regard to government spending for the poor, for example, than are theologically liberal Protestants (Iannaccone, 1993; Clydesdale, 1999; Davis and Robinson, 1999). Long thought by scholars to be languishing in the backwaters of American religion, American CPs have become more socially mobile and culturally and politically visible since the 1970s. Inheritors of a religious tradition that consciously resisted the naturalism and liberalism of modernity, CPs represent an attempt to maintain a more intense religiosity and theological orthodoxy than much of American mainline religion.

As a group, CPs have higher levels of church attendance, attach greater importance to faith, and also are more successful in membership recruitment and
retention than most other American religious groups. And these characteristics
help to make CPs significantly different in a variety of other ways. For example,
when it comes to family, CPs are strict about premarital sex, generally marry
earlier than other Americans, have higher marital fertility rates, and report
higher levels of marital happiness and adjustment (see Woodberry and Smith,
1998). CPs tend to emphasize well defined, gendered, non-egalitarian parenting
roles, and are more likely than other Americans to endorse and use corporal
punishment of children. But they are also less likely to yell at, more likely to
express verbal and physical affection to, and more likely to spend greater time
with their children (Wilcox, 1998). CPs are more likely to say they support
patriarchal marital roles; but as a group they also comprise greater diversity on
gender attitudes than other Americans, and have more egalitarian marriages in
practice than their ideology would suggest (Woodberry and Smith, 1998; Gallagher and Smith, 1999; Sherkat and Ellison, 1999). Similarly, studies show that
CPs are also distinct when it comes to political attitudes and behaviors, workplace ethics, volunteering behavior, rates of giving to the poor, and other issues
of social and policy importance. Beyond merely demonstrating the sustained
social influence of a particular religious tradition, studies of American CPs
reveal interesting and important larger processes of collective identity construction, subculture formation, and the selective resistance to modernity (Smith et
al., 1998).

TOLERANCE AND PREJUDICE

As societies become increasingly globalized and pluralistic, religion's effects on
tolerance and prejudice grow ever more important to understand. In the USA,
research on tolerance is one area in which scholars have consistently analyzed
religious effects. The general relationship between religiosity and racial prejudice
in the USA seems to be curvilinear. Those who are only peripherally involved in
religion are the most racially prejudiced, and both the non-religious and those
who are heavily involved in religion are among the least prejudiced. People's
motivations for attending religious services are also important. Those who
report attending for religious reasons are less prejudiced, those who attend for
social reasons more prejudiced (Gorsuch, 1988).

Most past research on tolerance suggests that CPs are less tolerant than other
North Americans. However, a number of scholars suggest that most tolerance
scales (for example, on the General Social Survey) are biased against conservative religionists because they primarily test tolerance for left-wing and secular
groups (atheists, feminists, communists, homosexuals) and exclude most right-
wing and religious groups (fundamentalists, anti-abortion protesters, gender-
role traditionalists, "creationists"). Some evidence supports this claim. For
example, an analysis of the *1987 Freedom and Tolerance Survey*, which gave
respondents open-ended questions about their outgroups and intolerance, shows

that CPs are just as tolerant as other religious or non-religious groups (Busch, 1998). Certain groups within CPism are extremely intolerant, but they are not large enough to influence the overall CP mean significantly. Furthermore, CP intolerance seems to work against not only liberal and secular groups like atheists, feminists, and homosexuals, but also some right-wing groups such as militarists and racists. Generally, CPs are not less tolerant of Jews, blacks, Asians, Catholics, Hispanics, or immigrants than other Americans (Woodberry and Smith, 1998; Smith, 2000).

RELIGION AND SOCIAL JUSTICE

An important emerging dimension of recent work in the sociology of religion has focused on religion's role in movements of social justice. Moderns have inherited from the skeptical and revolutionary Enlightenment (May, 1976) the view that religion is naturally conservative, defensive, and allied with ruling elites – as, for example, the French Catholic Church was in the eighteenth century. Certainly in many cases religion has proved to be conservative, elitist, and allied with forces of oppression. But religion can cut both ways. It also readily inspires, mobilizes, and supports movements for social justice and democratization (Smith, 1996a). Historically, in the USA, religious actors and organizations were crucial in the fight for religious freedom in the eighteenth century and against slavery in the nineteenth century. In the mid-twentieth century, the black church in America was central in mobilizing and sustaining the black civil rights movement. People and organizations of faith in the USA in the decades since then have also played crucial roles in the anti-Vietnam War movement and in the Sanctuary movement that protected illegal Central American refugees, and were active in the nuclear freeze movement, the Central America peace movement against Ronald Reagan's sponsored wars in El Salvador and Nicaragua, the environmental movement, various progressive organizations such as Amnesty International, Habitat for Humanity, the American Friends Service Committee, and other peace, anti-poverty, and anti-discrimination movements and organizations.

Around the world, religion has played a significant role in the liberation theology movement in Latin America, Africa, and parts of Asia, the overthrow of the Somoza dictatorship in Nicaragua in 1979, the insurrection against El Salvador's military regime in the 1970s, Solidarity's resistance to the Polish communist state, the toppling of the Marcos dictatorship in the Philippines, resistance to the Pinochet dictatorship in Chile, the anti-Apartheid movement in South Africa, and the fall of the East German regime in 1989. In many movements for peace and justice, religion has often been crucial in providing activists with legitimation for protest rooted in the sacred, supplying insurgents with moral imperatives for love, justice, peace, freedom, and equality, and offering activists powerfully motivating icons, rituals, songs, testimonies, and oratory. Religion can secure in movements self-discipline, sacrifice, and altruism, furnish movements with trained and experienced leadership and financial resources, and supply congregated participants and solidarity incentives.

Movements often reduce start-up costs by using pre-existing religious communication channels, authority structures, and social control mechanisms. Religion can also provide potential common identification among gathered strangers, and shared transnational identities beyond nation and language. Finally, religion can offer movements transnational organizational linkages, provide the protection of "open spaces" in civil society, and provide activists with political legitimacy in public opinion (Smith, 1996a). Much exciting work remains to explore the role of religion not only in sustaining, but also often in challenging, social injustice around the world.

IMPROVING RELIGION MEASURES

Many of the standard religion measures used in survey research have become inadequate for the task. The significance of denominations, for example, in the American religious field has changed, such that many survey denomination questions have little analytical usefulness. Many standard theological indicators (for example, "literal Bible") yield invalid estimates of what researchers want to study. Improved measures of religious self-identity, practices, beliefs, and organizational location need to be developed and refined and used on surveys. Most surveys – especially longitudinal surveys – have no questions on religion or only a few poorly constructed ones. Fortunately, this is beginning to change. High quality data are becoming increasingly available and are starting to transform scholars' perceptions of religion.

In North America, surveys typically have asked if respondents are Catholic, Protestant, or Jewish. However, this distinction increasingly has little predictive power and researchers have developed more nuanced religion measures. The greatest progress has been in developing better ways to differentiate groups of Protestants. Little work focuses on differentiating types of Catholics – although David Leege and Michael Welch (1988, 1991) of Notre Dame have made progress in that direction. We still know almost nothing about how to identify different types of Muslims, Buddhists, Hindus, and other minority religious groups on surveys (see Leege and Kellstedt, 1993; Green et al., 1996; Woodberry and Smith, 1998).

In North America, religious denomination is probably the most common way scholars identify religious groups. With good denominational lists and categorization schemes, scholars can effectively differentiate mainline-liberal and conservative Protestant denominations, as well as pentecostals and black Protestants. Unfortunately, most denomination questions on surveys lack sufficient detail. Protestant denominations, especially small ones, can be tricky to code correctly. And many surveys do not distinguish subgroups within larger religious families. For example, Lutherans are very heterogeneous – the Evangelical Lutheran Church of America tends to be liberal, while Missouri Synod Lutherans are quite conservative. Good religion analysis requires getting these kinds of groups coded correctly. Fortunately, scholars (Green et al., 1996; Steensland et al., 2000) are developing useful schemes for recoding detailed denomination lists, which are being adapted by a number of major surveys, including the American National Election Survey, the Southern Focus Poll, and the Adolescent Health Survey.

Another way to identify different religious groups is with religious belief measures. In North America, "biblical literalism" or "biblical inerrancy" are the most common belief measures scholars use – in this case, to identify conservative Protestants. However, these Bible measures are crude. People vary widely in what they mean by "literal" and "without error." And since this measure excludes many better educated evangelicals who are not literalists or inerrantists, it makes "conservative Protestants" appear less educated and from a lower class than they actually are. Another problem is that scholars generally only use a single belief measure to categorize religious respondents, which can cause significant measurement error and biased coefficients. Or they use belief measures additively, such as identifying conservative Protestants as people who are biblical literalists, *and* 'born again," *and* have shared their faith with others. But this stringent procedure can confound the problem, excluding respondents who actually belong. Ideally, researchers should use multiple beliefs as indicators of a *latent* belief system (Woodberry and Smith, 1998).

Even so, denominational measures and most belief measures do not distinguish different subtypes of conservative Protestants or Catholics, between which there are actually striking differences. Recently scholars have begun asking respondents which religious tradition or movement they identify with – fundamentalist, evangelical, pentecostal, charismatic, traditionalist Catholic, liberal Catholic, etc. These generally predict attitudes and behaviors better than denomination or the religious belief measures. As to American religiosity, scholars typically use measures of church attendance, prayer, or subjective importance of religion. These religious measures work equally well for different groups of American Catholics and Protestants (Woodberry, 1998), though attendance typically has the strongest impact on people's beliefs and behavior. But it is not clear how well these measures work for non-Christian groups. As new surveys increasingly contact non-Christian respondents, scholars need to develop new measures that address other forms of religiosity.

Finally, several new methodological techniques promise to enhance our study of religion. For example, past research has tended to look at differences between religious traditions, but neglected the diversity within traditions. However, some scholars have developed ways to test whether the internal diversity is greater in some religious groups than others (DiMaggio et al., 1996; Gay et al., 1996). Scholars have also begun to mix qualitative and quantitative research more effectively. Past qualitative research on religion has suffered because it was hard to determine whether case studies, "insider documents," or interviews were representative or not. On the other hand, survey research often did not capture the important nuances, contradictions, and ambivalence in religious language and culture, and religion researchers often projected alien meanings onto their research subjects. Fortunately, several groups of scholars are beginning to bridge the gap between qualitative and quantitative research. For example, Christian Smith and colleagues (1998) conducted two-hour face-to-face interviews in 23 states with a random sample of churchgoing Protestants whom they had contacted in a national telephone survey of the United States. This directly linked national survey data with detailed information about how respondents understand concepts and the reasons they give for what they believe and do. Bradford Wilcox (1998) has combined broad reviews of religious family-advice books with careful quantitative analysis. These kinds of mixed-method strategies hold much promise for advances in religion research. Finally, religion research is just beginning to explore multilevel designs. For his *National Congregations Study*, for example, Mark Chaves and colleagues (1999) asked 1998 General Social Survey respondents where they attend church, then used this information to identify and investigate a representative sample of all US churches. This procedure could also be used to contact representative samples of religious-based schools, voluntary organizations, or political groups. Religion research will only improve by moving beyond simply cross-sectional surveys to creative mixed-method, longitudinal, and multilevel designs.

GLOBALIZING RELIGION

Religious transformation is taking place at a global scale. In the past two centuries, and especially since the Second World War, Christianity has spread rapidly in Asia, Islam and Christianity in Africa, Protestantism in Latin America, and Hinduism, Buddhism, and Islam have spread to North America, Europe, and former British colonies. Many new religious movements (NRMs) have also sprung up by combining elements of different traditions. Population migrations with religious implications are under way, and old religious cleavages are reasserting themselves anew in places like Serbia, Palestine, India, and Indonesia. Meanwhile, Pentecostalism – a native of the early-twentieth century US West coast – is spreading rapidly in many parts of the world. Large segments of many societies have changed their religions, and members of these "imported" religions have been disproportionately influential in their home societies, in both the West and the non-West.

We should remember that these religious transformations are not entirely new. Religious traditions have always been in flux, and sociologists have extensive historical data about religious and societal change. For example, Christianity originated and had much of its early strength in the Middle East and North Africa. Yet with the rise of Islam, much of Christianity in the Middle East and North Africa disappeared. Buddhism developed in India, but was then reabsorbed into Hinduism and disappeared from most of the subcontinent. Important strands of Tantric and Mahayana Buddhism developed in Central Asia, spreading from there to China and Tibet, and then on to Korea and Japan. But both traditions disappeared from Central Asia, replaced by Islam (see Robinson and Johnson 1997; Skilton, 1997). Nestorian Christianity entered China only slightly after Buddhism (circa CE 600). Both were initially banned and persecuted as foreign religions, but over time, Christianity faltered, and Mahayana Buddhism came to be viewed as an indigenous religion. Yet Christianity entered

India by the second century CE and China by CE 635, well before it entered much of Northern or Eastern Europe (Neill, 1986; Moffett, 1992; Hastings, 1999). Conversely, in the twentieth century Christianity spread rapidly in Mainland China and Buddhism gained influence in Europe. Everywhere, the great missionary traditions of Islam, Buddhism, and Christianity have spread at the expense of indigenous and tribal religions, although often these indigenous religions persist as folk traditions within global religions.

This raises many interesting theoretical questions. Why do some groups radically change their religious traditions, while others preserve their traditions for centuries despite missionizing, invasion, and persecution – like Jews, Armenians, Coptic Christians, Parsis, and Thomas Christians of India. Why do some missionary efforts succeed and others fail? How and why do people come to see some foreign traditions as indigenous, while continuing to see others as foreign? How do particular religious traditions or the competition between multiple religious traditions shape society?

Religious globalization has profoundly shaped existing religious traditions. Both "imported" and "indigenous" religions have transformed themselves in the process. As people adopt new religious traditions, they adapt them according to their culture and use them to meet their own interests. As dominant indigenous religions react to the importation of new value systems and competition for adherents, they are transformed as well. For example, in India and Sri Lanka, reaction to Protestant missions played a vital role in both the Hindu and Buddhist renaissances of the nineteenth century, and, in turn, these new forms of Hinduism and Buddhism have had important influences on the West. Reaction to neo-Hindu thought, for example, played an important role in the development of the theology of universal salvation within liberal Protestantism (Niell, 1986; Ariarajah, 1991; Robinson and Johnson, 1997; Hastings, 1999). These interactions of religious traditions provide another ideal laboratory for the study of cultural change – which parts of religious traditions are most malleable or resistant to change, which groups adopt or resist new religions, etc. This globalization of religious traditions also has important political and social implications. Imported religious traditions in various countries have influenced gender roles, the practice of slavery, drug and alcohol use, democratization, church–state relations, and concepts of political and religious rights. Whether religions spread along or across existing cleavages may also help to stabilize or destabilize societies.

Recently there has been a growing interest in global civil society and international non-governmental organizations (INGOs). Yet this literature seldom mentions religious INGOs – in fact they are often excluded from consideration – despite the fact that they continue to both dwarf and predate most of their non-religious counterparts. The literature that does analyze religion suggests that religious groups were central to the rise of INGOs (Boli and Thomas, 1999), as well as NGOs around the world; and that religious involvement is an important predictor for participating in both religious and non-religious voluntary associations. Moreover, comparative research suggests that religious context plays a substantial role in the number and type of voluntary associations around the world (James, 1987; Anheier and Salamon, 1998, pp. 11–17, 354–6).

One area inviting further research is on missionaries and missionary organizations, which are important for the massive number of personnel and amount of resources they have transferred to the developing nations. They invested massive resources in education and translation projects, creating the first written form of many languages, and often importing the first printing technology. They often established the first formal education for girls, and before the 1960s often provided the most widespread access to Western formal education. Well into the twentieth century, more Western missionaries went overseas than any other group other than tourists. They were also from among the most educated segments of North America and Europe. Moreover, missions dwarfed other NGOs in size. In 1900, for example, the American Federation of Labor (AFL) had a budget of $71,000, but the missions board of Northern Methodists (a single US denomination) had a budget of over one million dollars (Neill, 1986; Hutchison, 1987; Sanneh, 1989; Hastings, 1999). Protestant and Catholic missionaries wanted to transform societies, and they usually did – some for the good, some for the bad – and changed themselves in these encounters as well. Moreover, the number of Christian missionaries increased substantially over the twentieth century. And now Muslim, Hindu, Buddhist, Bahai, and NRM missionaries compete with Christian groups in spreading their messages, and religious mission work is increasingly being done by people from the developing world. Anthropologists have long conducted ethnographies of missions in tribal cultures, and in the past fifteen years historians have begun to do serious research on the impact of missions. But we still have little comparative sociological literature that broadly analyzes religious missions' impact on other societies, how they influenced colonial policy, postcolonial foreign policy, and so on.

CONCLUSION

Social scientists have increasingly come to realize that religion is not going to disappear with the advance of modernity. Nor is it going to be confined to a mere privatized existence without public influence. Traditional forms of religious belief and practice have remained resilient in the modern world, and new religions continue to emerge and spread with regularity. All of this has important consequences in many areas of social life. This realization opens up a host of research opportunities which recent scholarship is beginning to explore. The field remains wide open for development in ways that will enhance our understanding of the social significance of the sacred in human consciousness and practice.

9

Intimate Relationships

RAINE DOZIER AND PEPPER SCHWARTZ

The study of intimacy is, in some ways, the study of the history of human thought and a way of looking at the changing position of men and women in society. For intimacy to even be a concept, it first had to be seen as a capacity of human beings, a desirable state, and perhaps a right of human beings to exercise. It has been said that the emergence of the idea of the individual as an important actor with integrity of purpose and spirit occurred with the diffusion of capital and liberal democracy. Of course, in all times and in all places there have been one-on-one "intimate" relationships, but intimacy as a domain of importance, of personal meaning, and of societal consequence that merits the notice of the state and of seminal thinkers is placed as a product of the eighteenth-century European movement that historians have labeled the Enlightenment. During this period, the novel – that form of fiction that depends on the development of plot and character and personal striving – became a popular art form and philosophers like Rousseau gave voice to a vision of humanity that was translated during the American Revolution as the inalienable right of "man" to life, liberty, and, interestingly, the pursuit of happiness. The self became a preoccupation of that age and the nineteenth century as well when William James invented the discipline of psychology.

The nineteenth century in the United States and England was a period of rapid industrialization, intense migration, technological change, and urbanization. Viviana Zelizer (1985) has described how during this period intimacy was redefined between parent and child – as children, heretofore productive members of rural family, were sent out to apprentice at tender ages. This accompanied the shift from an agrarian to an industrial society, and children became less valuable workers at home as well. As children's economic contributions to the family declined and their need for education and training grew, they became a long-term emotional investment rather than an economic asset for the family.

These changes led to a significant decline in the birth rate. In 1800, a white married couple had an average of seven children; this rate was halved over the next hundred years (D'Emilio and Freedman, 1988). The useful child was transformed into the "precious" child and the turn of the nineteenth and twentieth centuries markedly romanticized the nobility of womanhood and the transformation of childhood.

With the mid-1800s came the proliferation of marriage books – on both sexual and emotional etiquette. In the early 1900s there were some of the first empirical investigations into female sexuality, and the Kinsey studies, published in the late 1940s and early 1950s, illustrated the extent to which intimacy was a part of personal relations. As personal life ascended in people's prioritization of needs, experts appeared to give them direction – and to sell them books and services. Childrearing books and maternal groups proliferated. Professionals of the 1920s advocated loving and nurturing children, while those in the 1940s advised strict regimentation with little physical affection (Grant, 1998). Styles of advice rotated, but the extension of the "helping professions" – first physicians, and later psychologists – into the intimate lives of families pointed to the centrality of intimate relationships and their transition from relationships of economic necessity to relationships requiring planning, nurturing, and remediation. Social scientists' role in family life had begun in earnest.

The rise of industrialization, the decline of agriculture, and the growth of cities during the twentieth century heralded another important transition – the flow of young people to cities and the creation of a dating culture. The twenties ushered in dancehalls, amusement parks, and growing numbers of automobiles that afforded young people privacy. Increasing numbers of young people left their families and had greater discretionary time and income. Dating became an end in itself instead of a step toward marriage, and multiple opportunities for a private, intimate life radically changed unmarried people's motivation from utilitarian relationships to ones based on love, sex, and pleasure.

The increasingly daring dating of the thirties and forties occurred within a traditional framework of male and female roles. Still, this was the soil from which great ideological and behavioral changes would be grown. This generation gave birth to the celebrated Baby Boom – a population that turned out to be determined to test the "double standard" and other gender guidelines of their parents' generation. The women's movement, the gay rights movement, and the rise of sexual liberation all changed conceptions about intimate life, especially for women. The rate of premarital sex increased rapidly for women; the rate of premarital sex for men increased slightly, but the real transition was in their choice of sex partner. Sexuality became an expression of sentiment and, then, play. By the 1960s, dating youth were likely to be sexual with a variety of willing partners. Women's premarital sexuality changed from fiancées to only "sex with meaning" to the sixties and seventies experience of recreational sex.

The sexual freedom espoused in the sixties created a greater focus on intimacy as well as sex for pleasure for both sexes. More women (and men) began to expect emotionally fulfilling relationships with some semblance of equality. This change was not just limited to college-educated liberals, but increasingly permeated the culture at large. Even working-class husbands of the seventies bewilderedly reported their wives' growing insistence on talking, sharing, and communication (Rubin, 1976). The search for intimacy became a cultural theme and altered expectations of sex and love. The quest for sexual and emotional fulfillment helped to create whole new professions of sexual and marital therapy that, in turn, created more and greater searches for sexual and emotional growth. Part of this search for individual authenticity and the exploration of the self led to a rejection of traditional modes of pairing – people left marriages, lived together before marriage, and questioned the hegemony of the heterosexual couple as the only normative model for intimacy. Many of the intimacy topics of interest to sociologists – premarital sex, gay and lesbian couples, cohabitation, egalitarian marriage, enhanced communication, divorce rates, single parenting, and non-marital parenting – can be linked to the movements of the 1960s and early 1970s.

Psychologists had, of course, fished in these waters before sociologists. But sociologists looked at differences in intimacy according to distinctions of gender, class, race, and ethnicity. We examine the social context of intimacy and the cultural contagion that has taken one model – the Western vision of romantic love and closeness based on personal disclosure – and distributed it via mass media and the social sciences to the rest of the world. There is a good deal of evidence to indicate that the Western vision of marriage, as a love match rather than as family maintenance of status and reproductive rights guaranteed to stay within class and religious and ethnic lines, has affected the most unlikely countries. Japan, for example, has a growing divorce rate, a significant majority of young people pick their own spouse, and marriage occurs later as young women join men in the work world. In China, 57 percent of women who married in 1987 reported choosing their husbands and the other 43 percent reported that they had had some choice in the matter. Even in India, researchers found that between one-third and one-half of their young adult sample believed they should have the freedom to choose their marital partner (Smith and Bond, 1998).

Other patterns of intimate association, such as cohabitation, seem to be increasing wherever personal liberty is allowed. Nearly all young people in Sweden live together before marriage (and most have children in these unions), the vast majority of the French cohabit at one time or another, and cohabitation experience in the United States has risen dramatically from less than a fifth in the 1970s to more than half of all people today. The most conservative countries – such as those that have established fundamentalist Muslim governments – have made a special effort to repress and extinguish these Western customs but other Muslim countries with non-theocratic governments, such as Turkey and Pakistan, have, for the most part, not followed suit. They too see changing family and relationship patterns as love and intimacy become central to a fulfilling life.

COMPETING PARADIGMS FOR A SOCIOLOGY OF INTIMACY

Psychoanalytic

Historically, the study of intimate relationships has been dominated by Freudian psychodynamic approaches. The Freudian assertion of anatomy as destiny implies an irreversible condition of gender. The corollary assertion that our earliest family experience of gender predicts our lifelong sexual and intimate lives establishes the centrality and immutability of gender to the human experience. This essentialist view pervades popular culture and supports inequality as the natural outgrowth of child development. Using "men are from Mars and women are from Venus" as a justification for the structural and relational position of men and women creates and maintains the vision of love and intimacy based on separate and unequal status of the sexes.

Social Exchange

Social exchange theory is derived from economic theory and behavioral psychology. Exchange concepts were initially used in studies of courtship and marriage before the term "social exchange" was coined. Willard Waller formulated the concept of the "marriage market" and examined the relative resources exchanged in love relationships; since then exchange in intimate relationships has been a major focus of social exchange theory. The theory has been popular because it doesn't rely on assessing individual motivations and psychological states; instead, it focuses on the exchange of resources, material and non-material, in the relationship. Richard Emerson expanded social exchange theory to include intimate relationships by exploring resource exchanges over time rather than restricted to a single interaction (Molm and Cook, 1995). Subsequent empirical work helped understanding of the complexity of exchanges involving multiple interactions. In couples, potential resources to be exchanged include both tangible and intangible assets, such as economic resources, housework, childcare, affection, and relative attractiveness. The *type* of intimate relationship (dating, marriage, cohabitation) often affects the relative worth of these resources.

If relationships are based on a mutual exchange of rewards, how do clearly unequal relationships endure? Many sociologists have documented the inequality of working wives' "second shift" (Hochschild, 1989; Brines, 1994); most women both participate in the labor market and are responsible for the majority of the domestic work and childcare. Michaels and Wiggins demonstrated that exchanges do not have to be equal; instead the value of the exchange must exceed any potential alternatives (see Molm and Cook, 1995). Still, the lack of analysis of the effects of power and coercion in dyadic exchange has been problematic for critics. By limiting social exchange theory to a reward-based system it has not adequately evaluated coercive power in discordant relationships. Recently, however, theorists have attempted to integrate reward-based and punishment-induced forms of power. This seems to be a more effective means of explaining coercive and abusive partnerships. Molm (Molm and Cook, 1995) found that in mutually dependent relations coercion is rarely used. She also found that coercion and punishment tactics are most often used by those lacking resource-based power – in other words, the power to reward.

Interactionist

Some sociological research examines how intimate relationships create and maintain gender stratification. This growing body of work claims that early socialization is less responsible for gender differences, styles, and goals than are current, ongoing interactions that both create and maintain difference and inequality. This view strays from psychoanalytic and sociobiological assertions of early, fixed gender identity and behaviors, and instead underscores people's shifting gender roles both situationally and over the life span. Risman focuses on a variety of family forms to explore how gender socialization takes place through interaction (Risman, 1998). She claims that gender structure so thoroughly organizes work, family, and community that rejecting gender directives is difficult because of the compelling "logic" of the gendered status quo. For instance, a couple may be committed to shared parenting which would require each working part-time, but if the man is paid significantly more then shared parenting economically penalizes the family. Since the structure supports the superiority of men economically, physically, and socially, the "logical" decision – that only he participates in the economic sphere – perpetuates gender stratification.

The structure of gender informs interaction in intimate relationships – how couples work, parent, love, and communicate. Necessarily, then, straying from prescribed gender roles changes intimate interaction. For instance, Risman's (1998) research on single fathers found that fathers become much like mothers when required to perform domestic tasks and nurture children, and even come to identify themselves as more feminine. This means that feminine characteristics are more strongly influenced by the performance of a social role than by early socialization, but since social position is usually determined by gender, the two become conflated.

These are a few of the primary ways intimate relationships have been examined: at a personal level through psychoanalysis and social exchange theory; and at a structural level examining how interaction creates and maintains the social structure of gender stratification. The sociological study of intimacy, then, can help to clarify the relationship between social structure and personal experience, both how structure creates the personal, intimate family experience and how the personal experience creates and maintains social structure.

Sociological methods for analyzing intimate relationships have been used in several domains. The rapidly changing roles of men and women in relationships, marriage, and the family have created numerous sites in which to study intimate relationships. In this article, we will focus on just a few: dual earner marriages, egalitarian marriages, cohabitation, and communication in intimate relationships.

SITES OF INTIMATE RELATIONS

Dual Earner Marriages

In the past fifty years, women's entry into the labor force has profoundly changed family structure, marital relationships, and attitudes about childrearing. Although some women have always worked outside the home, particularly African Americans, immigrants, and other poor women, now most women with children work outside the home. In fact, over 60 percent of women with children under one participate in paid labor (US Bureau of the Census, 1998b).

In order to accommodate women's entry into the labor force, families and couples have struggled to rearrange both their lives and their values. This rapid shift in values and identity has occurred within one generation, allowing few preceding role models for dual earner couples. Changing family roles and labor patterns leave both men and women struggling to redefine "good parenting" in the context of forty-or fifty-hour work weeks. Men grapple with their role in the domestic sphere and its relationship to masculinity; women wonder whether they can "do it all" – have a rewarding career, parent, maintain the household, and nurture a fulfilling relationship.

The concept of a "good marriage" has changed as well. No longer are husbands usually the sole breadwinner and wives happiest in managing the domestic sphere by themselves. In her interviews with working-class families in the early 1970s, Rubin often heard women report, "I have nothing to complain about. He's a steady worker; he doesn't drink; he doesn't hit me" (Rubin, 1976, p. 93). Her interviews twenty years later illustrate that the cultural shift in the definition of a good marriage had permeated the often traditional working class. Many of these wives worked full-time and came home to the "second shift," but they no longer felt it was fair. Many, in fact, deeply resented it (Rubin, 1994). Research has found a growing disenchantment among women regarding the household division of labor that has profound effects on both the health and future of a marriage.

Hochschild (1989) examined the lives of dual earner couples to discover under what circumstances men and women shared domestic responsibilities. She postulated that men's values would predict their behavior – that men who valued equity and espoused the equal division of domestic labor would be more likely to share in household tasks. She also believed that domestic work was directly exchangeable with money – men who were more dependent on their wives' wages would feel more obligated to help at home. Her empirical findings belied these logical assumptions: she found equitable relationships across the spectrum of both class and beliefs about gender equity. A working-class man with traditional beliefs was just as likely to participate in the domestic sphere as an upper-class man with a belief in equity. Instead of being a site for the expression of values regarding class or the division of labor, domestic work often became a site for the expression of power. Men who felt insecure economically were less likely to participate at home; those who felt their status most threatened because they earned less than their wives were the least likely to participate in domestic labor. Because of an inability to express traditional masculinity in the "provider role," masculinity was asserted by dominating at home and distancing from the domestic feminine sphere.

Wives also participated in "balancing" or the re-establishment of men's dominance and power (Hochschild, 1989). Since traditional models of intimate relationships between men and women rely on gender hierarchy, women who made more money than their husbands felt a need to restore his power by waiting on him or doing an even greater share of the domestic chores than non-working wives. This may sound counterintuitive, but additional research has strengthened Hochschild's findings. Brines's (1994) quantitative research supports the notion that men who are more dependent on their wives' income resist doing housework. She also describes this flight from domestic participation as a method of "displaying gender" when traditional masculine routes (economic success) are unavailable.

In addition to coping with conflicts regarding power and equity in the domestic sphere, the dual earner family might also lack the time and resources to accomplish all necessary tasks. With the rise in women's labor market participation, there has been a decline in their hours spent on domestic tasks without a commensurate increase by husbands. Assuming that all previous domestic tasks were necessary, certain tasks, then, must remain undone. Although some tasks like mopping the floor can be postponed, there is increasing concern that the nurturing and care of children will become a place to "cut corners," with unknown deleterious effects. In her later work, Hochschild (1997) found increasing numbers of parents working long hours at the office in order to avoid the stresses of home and family.

Hertz's (1986) work on dual career couples stressed the difference between the experiences of dual career couples and other dual earner couples. Her sample included high-earning, career-driven couples who, rather than struggling over domestic chores, delegated them to family outsiders – nannies, housekeepers, gardeners, and food service workers. In this manner, two demanding careers are supported through the low-wage work of people outside the family. However, for most dual earner families this type of extensive, external support is not available. For this reason, some couples have reported greater marital happiness in a more traditional marriage because of less stress and conflict in the family. Crouter and Manke's (1997) research supported the notion that couples reported greater love and less conflict in a traditional marriage than in a marriage where both had high-status careers. However, couples who reported the least conflict and the most love were partners who had lower levels of role overload – their careers were less ambitious, thus allowing for more time to fulfill family and relationship needs.

Dual earner couples have more harmonious marriages when the division of labor is fair (Hochschild, 1989; Schwartz, 1994), and those who reported lower marital quality were more likely to report that the division of domestic labor was unfair (Gager, 1998). In fact, the growing resentment of wives in inequitable marriages may be a factor in the rising divorce rate. The divorce rate doubled between 1970 and 1980 and women are usually the primary seekers of divorce. In a survey of 600 couples filing for divorce, Levinger (see Hochschild, 1989) found that the second most common reason why wives sought divorce (after mental cruelty) was neglect of household and children. For middle-class women, it was the most common complaint, cited by nearly half of women. Men also cited neglect of household and children as a significant factor in seeking divorce. Clearly, the battleground has been delineated; men and women are struggling with what it means to participate in a new form of marriage with few models to guide them. With women's growing economic self-sufficiency, abandoning unfulfilling and unfair relationships has become a plausible and increasingly common option.

Peer Marriage

Some couples have abandoned traditional roles and have attempted to create "fair" marriages. A few studies have examined the lives of couples involved in equitable marriages where each person is responsible for the family economically, emotionally, and domestically. Because equitable marriages are statistically rare, studies are few and rely on non-random samples. Increasingly couples are exploring more equitable relationships, particularly in the area of shared parenting. Perhaps more role models have become available or, as Risman (1998) believes, younger, postfeminist couples more often see themselves as being fulfilled only by a combination of career and parenting.

A common theme in egalitarian marriages is the significant cultural capital of the wife (Hertz, 1986; Hochschild, 1989; Schwartz, 1994; Risman, 1998). Regardless of career ambition, most women in "peer marriages" are the educational elite and many have rewarding jobs or careers. Perhaps the experience of having significant cultural capital allows women to bargain for equity. Additionally, wives in these relationships do not emotionally hoard the children (Hochschild, 1989; Schwartz, 1994; Risman, 1998) and are often the chief advocator of equality. For a fair marriage to succeed, men and women must both contribute significantly economically if men are to contribute emotionally and domestically. Although Schwartz (1994) found couples who regarded each other's contributions to relationship and family as equal despite their traditional division of labor, it was the exception rather than the rule.

In general, the literature indicates that achieving an equitable marriage relies on men's willingness to give up the power and position of head of the household. Risman points out that many women in "unfair" marriages are like the women in these equitable marriages – assertive, ambitious, not passive – and do not use the domestic sphere as a site to strengthen their identity as women. However, the key seems to lie in men's ability to redefine masculinity as including success and involvement in both the occupational and domestic spheres. If it were up to women, there would be many more equitable marriages, but it depends on men's willingness to give up male advantages in relationship and family structures.

Schwartz (1994) outlines both the advantages and challenges of egalitarian marriages. An outstanding feature of egalitarian or peer marriage is the opportunity for "deep friendship," an uncommon friendship shared by equals who hold each other in mutual high regard. Risman (1998) corroborates this tendency toward closeness; most couples voluntarily identified their partners as their closest friends. Egalitarianism, then, provides an opportunity for deeper intimacy and greater commitment. When partners define each other as irreplaceable and become so interdependent, marital dissolution becomes increasingly unlikely. If a decline in economic interdependency is responsible for the current high divorce rate, perhaps increasing emotional and domestic interdependency will help to sustain marital cohesion.

The costs of equality in marriage are mostly external – the response of the dominant culture to breaking with tradition and the subsequent internalized messages about what it means to be a successful man or woman. Friends, co-workers, and family may be unsupportive of "inappropriate" gender roles and may view the husband as faltering in his economic obligations or the wife as asserting control in areas where she should not legitimately have power, such as financial decision-making. On a personal level, it may be hard for career-oriented men and women to watch others gain career prestige while their ambition is tempered by shared family obligations. Indeed, the identity of men and women in egalitarian marriages may be challenged, since the usual gendered definitions of success may not be available to them.

A particular challenge for egalitarian marriages is a problem also commonly faced by lesbian couples who generally are committed to egalitarian relationships (Blumstein and Schwartz, 1983). Sexual intensity in egalitarian relationships often diminishes because of the priority of friendship in the relationship. Since much of the "charge" in sexual relations is based on power and dominance, an egalitarian relationship, particularly among heterosexuals, may have a difficult time retaining passion. The egalitarian couple is in a double bind: using power and domination may be problematic ideologically, but refraining from using it may lead to a feeling of having sex with your best friend. The level of intimacy between these close friends can lend itself to an "incest taboo," a feeling that sexual passion is inappropriate in the relationship. Egalitarian couples make a special effort to create a sexual life that is separate from their daily fusion of care taking and home making. Some couples accomplish this by banning talk of children and work, others preserve eroticism by introducing more fantasy into their love making and adopting sexual personas that are greatly different from their day-to-day selves.

The most remarkable aspect of egalitarian marriages is their rarity. Risman found that after she recruited seventy-five potential egalitarian couples, only fifteen actually qualified by equally sharing financial and domestic responsibilities. The paucity of couples available speaks to the difficulty of reaching the goal of egalitarian marriage, particularly when wives have not accumulated considerable cultural capital. Over time, though, there has been notable progress in both the quality and numbers of egalitarian relationships. Studies from the early seventies found the ideology of equality, but not the practice; research in the eighties found couples who were becoming increasingly equal, but in which men still relied on women for emotional tasks, scheduling, and organizing, and wardrobe management (Risman, 1998). Risman in her interviews in the nineties, however, found couples who never questioned women's equality or the appropriateness of egalitarian marriage and shared parenting. Perhaps couples are now finding a few role models and increased support for egalitarian relationships and shared parenting. Although these couples offer a vision of what marriage could look like, for the most part women are still largely responsible for household tasks and remain dissatisfied with an unequal division of labor.

Marital Communication

A further area of sociological exploration has been the study of communication patterns in couples, both how they are related to gender and power, and how they predict the success or failure of the relationship. Much research in couples' communication has been focused on delineating the differences between a masculine communication culture and a feminine communication culture (Wood, 1996). Men generally use communication to achieve instrumental goals, establish individual status and authority, and compete for attention and power. Women use communication to build connections with others, to include others, to cooperate, to show interest, and to support others (Wood, 1996). These differential conversational goals mean that men and women can choose both different topics and different interactional styles in conversation. For instance, women tend to discuss feelings and relationship issues in order to establish intimacy, whereas men prefer to discuss external topics and avoid personal topics. Women are more involved listeners, providing eye contact, facial expressions, and vocal feedback, whereas men engage much less actively in listening. Gendered differences in communication styles can lead to relationship conflicts between heterosexuals who use gendered strategies to create intimacy and closeness – women by talking, listening, and focusing and men through sharing activities or performing caring tasks. These differential gender patterns of communication are the basis of many popular relationship self-help books that attempt to give people, usually women, tools to "translate" the other sex's language and behavior.

Further research has added to a better understanding of communication dynamics in couples. Fitzpatrick and Mulac (1995) have found that although there are objective gendered language differences, these differences are subtle. They prefer to think of communication styles as gender preferential rather than gender distinct because differences within sexes and between sexes vary widely. Additionally, they find that where women's style remains fairly constant, men's communication style is both flexible and contextual. Men maintain the male interaction style, including more interruptions, directives, and sentence initial conjunctions/fillers ("Okay, the first thing we should do . . . ") when interacting with male or female strangers. However, when interacting with a spouse, men often conform to their wives' gender preferential language, using such strategies as questions, tag questions (" . . . , isn't it?"), justifiers, intensive adverbs ("very," "really"), and personal pronouns. While men do seem to maintain distance and autonomy in stranger interactions, they, too, seek connection and intimacy through communication with spouses. Incidentally, these findings are particular to casual, low-key conversation; conflict between spouses often generates the most substantial gender differences in communication, as men tend to distance while women pursue interaction and intimacy.

One of the advantages of research involving relationships other than marriage, such as cohabitation and same-sex relationships, is that it can provide a more lucid examination of the conflation of gender and power. For instance, same-sex relationships allow the issues of power to become more evident in the absence of gender difference (Blumstein and Schwartz, 1983). In their overview of research on same-sex partnerships, Rutter and Schwartz (1996) report that both gender and power have strong, separate influences on communication styles and that power rather than gender is a better predictor of "gendered" communication styles. The partner with more power uses the masculine style of communication, interrupting more, steering the conversation, and having more control over the decision-making process regardless of sex or sexual orientation.

Research has also been able to examine communication styles of lesbian, gay, and heterosexual couples and their different relationships to power. Heterosexual and gay men differ because gay men often attempt to equalize power using atypical gender/power responses. For instance, the more powerful man may use tag questions or attempt to involve the less powerful partner in decision-making processes. Lesbians, on the other hand, highly value egalitarian partnerships, and may often have conversations where neither partner enacts masculine gender responses in an effort to maintain a balance of power (Kollock et al., 1994).

Recently, research on communication has tried to predict the impact of communication style on marital satisfaction and durability. John Gottman has contributed substantially to the area of marital communication, specifically in analyzing conflict styles as a predictor of marital longevity. Interestingly, Carrere and Gottman (1999) found that quick escalation and high levels of conflict did not predict divorce. Instead, criticism, contempt, defensiveness, and sometimes stonewalling (withdrawal) were better predictors. Additionally, Gottman has found gendered differences in conflict resolution that predict success for marital couples. When husbands are able to accept wive's criticisms without defensiveness and work to de-escalate conflict, and when wives begin conflicts with less negative affect, they have a greater likelihood of remaining married. Gottman and his colleagues now claim to be able to predict divorces approximately 90 percent of the time by analyzing newly wed marital communication and its gendered characteristics (Carrere and Gottman, 1999).

Marriage and Cohabitation

Marriage in the United States is a declining institution across all races and classes. Fewer couples are marrying and at later ages and over half of marriages end in divorce. This decline in marriage, however, has been largely offset by the rising rate of cohabitation. In 1970, three-quarters of young adults under twenty-five had been in a marriage-like union and in 1985, 69 percent had

(Bumpass et al., 1991). The overall rate of union had not substantially declined, but the proportion that was cohabitation had increased dramatically.

Throughout the Western world there has been a dramatic increase in cohabitation in the past thirty years. In Sweden, cohabitation has become a common alternative to marriage. In the United States almost half of first-time married couples have cohabitation experience, and of those remarrying, 60 percent reported cohabitation experience (Bumpass et al., 1991). Cohabitation has often been portrayed in the media as a college student phenomenon, but it is most commonly found among the least educated. Additionally, 40 percent of cohabiting couples have children in the household, further evidence that this is not strictly a phenomenon of college students.

Sociologists have found that cohabiting unions are more likely to dissolve, and marriages subsequent to cohabitation are more likely to end in divorce – surprising facts that have spurred additional sociological research, especially in comparing cohabitors with married couples. Blumstein and Schwartz (1983) documented how couples, both married and cohabiting, negotiated money, sex, and power. Brines and Joyner (1999) have further explored the differing implications of equality and the division of labor on the likelihood of marital and cohabiting relationship dissolution.

There have been many attempts to explain the high rate of dissolution in cohabiting couples. Some believe that those who self-select into cohabitation are generally non-traditional people who are already prone to unstable marriages, have higher expectations for marriage, and have a generally weaker commitment to the institution of marriage (DeMaris and Rao, 1992). Others have documented that cohabitors are more tentative about their relationship than those who choose to marry. Rindfuss and Vandenheuvel (1990) argue that dissolution rates are high because cohabitation in the United States is unlike marriage and more similar to being single. Cohabitors have rates more similar to singles in home ownership, financial dependence on parents, and plans for children in the near future (Rindfuss and Vandenheuvel, 1990). However, the data used for this study excluded high school dropouts, the group most likely to cohabit, and may have given a non-representative view of cohabitors. It seems that if 40 percent of cohabitors have children in the household, cohabitation, rather than a version of being single, may be becoming a new family type and perhaps, in the future, will even become a predominant one. Rindfuss and Vandenheuvel posit that the rise in cohabitation, just like that in non-marital childbearing, reflects the centrality of individualism in the United States and is an attempt to adopt the appealing components of family life without impinging on individual freedom.

Brines and Joyner (1999) cite some evidence that cohabitation is not just a trial marriage, but that cohabitors and married people seek very different rewards from their relationships. By looking at each type of relationship as a valid form rather than marriage as the "conceptual ideal type," they are able to explore the different factors in relationship cohesion and dissolution. Primarily, they find that the division of labor, with husband as primary wage earner, encourages marital cohesion, whereas for cohabitors equality in income and hours worked is most important. Because of a lack of contractual obligation,

cohabitors find specialization in economic or domestic labor and joint investment in the relationship too risky. The principle of stability for cohabitors, then,
is not joint investment, but equality in resources and power allowing for individualism and strengthening commitment in the cohabiting relationship.

CONCLUSION

Sociological research regarding intimacy has grown to include a variety of
households, such as egalitarian and traditional marriages, cohabitors, single
parent families, gay and lesbian couples and families, and step families. The
growing literature reflects the increasing segmentation of household styles and
diverse patterns of intimacy. Instead of focusing only on heterosexual, married,
nuclear families with a traditional division of labor as an "ideal type," and
exploring other family and relationship forms as deviant, sociologists increasingly examine varied forms of intimate relationships in order to understand and
explain more generalized topics such as power and gender.

In this chapter, we have discussed some of the major topics of inquiry in the
field of adult intimacy; but we have not given substantial attention to intimacy
between children and parents. There is, however, a substantial amount of interest in the changing nature of parent–child relations and the relationship of these
new patterns of intimacy to broader societal changes, such as changing family
forms.

While we do not have the space in this chapter to address all these important
topics, clearly large-scale social change, such as the rise in single parent families,
alters the nature of the dynamics of intimacy in the family. The change in family
structure also brings about societal challenges we have become all too familiar
with, such as the need for daycare and child support enforcement, and the
increasing number of unsupervised children. The relative poverty of single
parents, in both time and money, deeply affects relationships between parents
and children. However, these challenges are largely contextual; countries such as
Sweden have a large number of single parents, yet do not face the same social
problems experienced by single parents in the United States. As social policy in
the USA lags behind social behavior, family relationships are adversely affected.
Governmental policies have direct implications for the level and quality of
intimacy experienced in individual homes.

Increasingly, couples are no longer staying together out of economic or moral
necessity. They are marrying later and have a high divorce rate, and cohabitation
has become an increasingly viable long-term option, especially for the previously
married. These alterations in relationship patterns have also generated a change
in family patterns, with children being raised in a variety of family forms by a
variety of primary caretakers. Also increasingly, we see families of choice,
particularly among gays and lesbians, where kinship ties are created without
blood or formal legal ties (Weston, 1991). Voluntary kinship ties have grown
increasingly popular as they reflect the Western ideal of individualism by allowing people to acquire the advantages of family ties based entirely on choice.

With the decline of joint economic dependence, relationship forms may take precedence that foster emotional interdependence, such as egalitarian marriage and voluntary kinship. This new interdependence – based on intimacy, volunteerism, and love – will, we maintain, facilitate family and kin cohesion, and enhance the quality of all intimate relationships.

10

Immigrant Families and Their Children: Adaptation and Identity Formation

Carola Suárez-Orozco

Introduction

Immigration involves over 130 million adults and children worldwide. In the United States, one out of every five children is the child of an immigrant. In New York City schools today, 48 percent of all students come from immigrant-headed households. This is not just an urban phenomenon – schools across the country are experiencing a large influx of children from immigrant families. It is increasingly clear that how these children adapt will be an important factor in remaking American society.

For many, migration results in substantial gains. This is particularly so for those escaping political, religious, or ethnic persecution and for those seeking reunification with their families. Whatever their motives, immigration is considered worthwhile for many. Still, the gains of immigration come at considerable costs, which could not have been anticipated at the moment of departure.

The social and psychological costs of migration are profoundly felt by the children of immigrants. These children experience a particular constellation of changes and experiences that are likely to have an impact upon their development and personalities. Yet, surprisingly, little research has focused on the psychological experiences of immigrant children (Garcia-Coll and Magnuson, 1997). In this chapter, I summarize the current state of knowledge and my views about immigrant youngsters' adaptation and identity formation.

Stresses of Immigration

Transitions of any kind are regarded by social scientists and mental health professionals to be stressful (Schlossberg, 1984). Events such as moves, job changes, and ruptures in relationships are known to be highly disruptive, often triggering a variety of reactions, including anxiety, anger, depression, somatic complaints, and illness (Dohrenwend, 1986). By any measure, immigration is one of the most stressful events a person can undergo. Immigration strips individuals of many of their sustaining social relationships, as well as of the roles which provide them with culturally scripted notions of how they fit into the world. Without a sense of competence, control, and belonging, they may feel marginalized. These changes are highly disorienting and nearly inevitably lead to a keen sense of loss (Grinberg and Grinberg, 1989; Ainslie, 1998).

On the most dramatic end of the stress spectrum are the stresses that result from experiencing or witnessing killing, rape, or torture. Recent arrivals originating from the former Yugoslavia, Somalia, Indochina, Central America, and Haiti often have experienced such trauma (Somach, 1995). Symptom clusters resulting from such trauma (post traumatic stress disorder) include reoccurring nightmares, numbness, intense anxiety, irritability, outbursts of anger, difficulty concentrating, and insomnia (Smajkic and Weane, 1995). In addition to the violence experienced prior to migration (in the cases where families are fleeing war or civil unrest), all too many immigrant children witness a disconcertingly high level of violence in their new neighborhood and school settings. Furthermore, the actual border crossing is often a traumatic event for adults and children alike. Immigrants who experience trauma will often suffer recurring waves of these symptoms over a period of time; the severity of the symptoms will depend on the extent of the trauma and the psychological, social, and material resources available to the victims. These symptoms add significantly to the stresses of immigration.

A form of stress specific to immigration has been termed "acculturation stress" (Berry, 1998). This is the process whereby individuals learn and come to terms with the new cultural "rules of engagement." The individual's place of origin provides her with familiar and predictable contexts; these predictable contexts change in dramatic ways following immigration. As Polish immigrant Eva Hoffmann notes in her exquisitely written memoirs, immigration results in falling "out of the net of meaning into the weightlessness of chaos" (Hoffman, 1989, p. 151). Without a sense of competence, control, and belonging, migrants often have a keen sense of loss and marginality. A 23–year-old Mexican informant insightfully summed up the experience: "I became an infant again. I had to learn all over again to eat, to speak, to dress, and what was expected of me."

Responses to the Stresses of Immigration

While anticipating migration and during the initial period following arrival, many immigrants experience a sense of euphoria (Sluzki, 1979). Expectations are often high as the anticipated possibilities may seem boundless. Energies are focused on attending to the immediate needs in becoming oriented to the new environment, including finding work and a place to live. As the realities of the new situation are confronted, individuals normatively begin to experience a variety of psychological problems (Sluzki, 1979; Arrendondo-Dowd, 1981; Grinberg and Grinberg, 1989). Most frequently, the cumulative losses of loved ones and familiar contexts lead to feelings along a spectrum from sadness to depression to "perpetual mourning" (Volkan, 1993). The dissonances in cultural expectations and lack of predictable contexts lead many to experience an anxious disorientation (Grinberg and Grinberg, 1989). Disappointed aspirations and dreams, when coupled with a hostile reception in the new environment, may lead to feelings of distrust, suspicion, anger, and even well founded paranoia (Grinberg and Grinberg, 1989).

Migration has destabilizing effects on the family (Sluzki, 1979). It is not unusual for there to be an increase in conflict between family members following migration (particularly if there was pre-existing marital tension). Migration often creates changes within the family structure: former family leaders may be "demoted" (Shuval, 1980) and the nature of the gender relationships may shift. Espin (1987, p. 493) argues that "immigrant families may become entrenched in traditional social and sex role norms as a defense against the strong pressures to acculturate." In other cases, as immigrant women move into the workplace, their new role as family providers may at once provide them with new found independence but create tensions within the family.

Many immigrant families incorporate extended family members and are more interdependent and hierarchical than traditional Anglo-American families (Smart and Smart, 1995). To some extent, this can be traced to their distinctive cultures, but it also can be secondary to migration. Extended families will often live together to share both the financial and the childcare burdens. In the absence of other social support networks, they may rely on each other considerably more than most non-immigrant families.

Immigrant parents often have to make dramatic sacrifices for what they hope will be a better future for their children. They are frequently fiercely protective of their children, with deep-seeded concerns about the perceived dangers of the new environment (including the potential of becoming too Americanized). Within the new context, they may set limits that are significantly more stringent than they would have been had they stayed in their country of origin. At the same time, immigrant parents are often quite dependent upon their children, who may develop language skills more quickly than they do. As a result they often serve as interpreters and errand-runners for the family. Alternating between "parentifying" the children and, at the same time, severely constricting their activities and contacts might create significant tension within the family.

Many immigrant parents (particularly those coming from poorer families) have several jobs. These multiple obligations lead them to be relatively unavailable to their children. For example, because their work schedules do not permit much flexibility, immigrant parents are often unable to attend school functions: as a result, educators lament the perceived lack of interest in their children's education. It is a mistake, however, to automatically interpret this as lack of interest or concern. Immigrant parents often tell us that they feel that working hard is the best way they can help their children; yet these long work hours leave the children unattended. This physical absence compounds the psychological unavailability that often accompanies parental anxiety and depression (Athey and Ahearn, 1991), and such absence and unavailability frequently leave immigrant children to their own devices long before it is developmentally appropriate. While in some cases this leads to hyper-responsible internalized children, in other cases it leads to depressed kids who are drawn to the lure of alternative family structures, such as gangs (Vigil, 1988).

The time frame for adaptation to the new culture is usually quite different for children than for adults. Schools represent an important first host-culture site encountered by the children. There, they meet teachers (who are usually members of the dominant culture), as well as children from both the majority and other minority backgrounds. Hence, they are forced to contend more quickly and more intensely with the new culture than are their parents, who are likely to work in jobs that do not require much in the way of language skills, or work in places where there are many others from the same immigrant background (M. Suárez-Orozco, 1998). The relative rapidness of the children's adaptation may create particular tensions in the household. Parents may try to slow the process by warning children not to act like other children in the new setting. Children may also have feelings ranging from vague to intense embarrassment with regard to aspects of their parents' "old country" and "old fashioned" ways.

It is important to understand the potential for miscommunication in immigrant families. Children often learn the new language more quickly than do their parents. Most children long to be like others: many will quickly show a preference for the language of the dominant culture. Furthermore, even if the child continues to speak the home language, the level of fluency is likely to be influenced by the fact that after a number of years in the new culture, without a concerted effort, the vocabulary and literacy level of the language of origin usually lags far behind that of the host culture. Hence, while the child may easily communicate about basic needs in her language of origin, she is likely to have more difficulty communicating subtleties of thought and emotion in that language (Wong-Fillmore, 1991). By the same token, often the opposite is true with the parents. Hence, one of the parties in the conversation is likely to be at a disadvantage in complicated communication sequences. Furthermore, in complex discussions, subtleties of meanings are likely to be missed and miscommunication may result. It is not uncommon to overhear discussions in which parents and children switch back and forth between languages and completely miss one another's intent.

My current research suggests that tensions between parents and children are particularly heightened in cases when the children have been separated from their parents for long periods of time. The majority of immigrant children are separated from one or both parents for several months to several years. During this time, the child can become attached to the caretaker, which complicates the child's later departure. If the child succeeds in attaching to the new caretaker, the separation from this caretaker in order to be reunited with the parent can be quite painful (compounding the mourning and loss that follows the immigration). If the separation was painful and the child was neglected or abused, this too will complicate the adjustment following migration. In any case, there is likely to be some fall-out following these years of separation prior to migration (particularly within the Caribbean immigrant community, as well as, increasingly, within the recent Central American community and those from some areas in China).

Separations resulting from immigration are also responsible for children being raised in single parent homes. In staggered migrations, where one partner goes ahead of the other, new families are often found, dissolving families that were intact in the country of origin. Although, overall, immigrant children are more likely to be raised in two parent homes than their non-immigrant counterparts (National Research Council, 1998), increasingly women who have been widowed, abused by their partners, or abandoned, or who simply never married, are coming to the new country to seek employment in order to offer their children a better life. This, of course, places children at great risk of being raised in poverty, by mothers who are overwhelmed and depressed and thus psychologically less than optimally available to their children (Weissbourd, 1996).

THE SENDING AND RECEIVING CONTEXTS

A number of factors may significantly attenuate the severity of response to the transitions and stress of immigration (Laosa, 1989; Garcia-Coll and Magnuson, 1997). These mediating variables can roughly be broken down into two categories: sending factors and receiving factors.

Each individual brings with him characteristics, traits, and experiences that are referred to as sending (or antecedent) factors. The circumstances surrounding the migration can play a key role. Was the individual "pushed or pulled" out of the country of origin? If the immigrant is pulled out of his homeland by the promise of opportunity and adventure, he is likely to be more positively disposed to the experience than if he is "pushed" out by ethnic, religious, or political conflict, chronic hardship, or famine in the homeland. By the same token, at least initially, the individual initiating the migration is likely to be more enthusiastic about the experience than a reluctant spouse, elderly parent, or child (Shuval, 1980). We have found that children in particular often have little understanding of the reasons for migration. As a result they may not pass through a stage of anticipating migration and may experience the move as a sacrifice.

Pre-immigration stress and trauma may be critical to the subsequent adaptation of immigrants. Individuals and families who flee conflict-torn areas may have witnessed traumatic events and been subjected to torture and other forms of physical and psychological violence (M. Suárez-Orozco, 1989). This is almost always true of refugees, a special kind of migrant. In addition, as noted above, these traumas may be compounded with further violence during the actual process of migration

Socio-economic background has been found to be a consistent mediator of the stresses of the migration process (Flaskerud and Uman, 1996). Higher levels of education as well as economic resources play a decisive role in minimizing structural impediments (C. Suárez-Orozco, 1998). On the whole, upper middle-class immigrants sustain the least loss. They may be able to retain much of their prestige and be able to travel back and forth to maintain their social relationships.

Immigrants of middle-class backgrounds often experience significant losses in prestige: they frequently find employment in positions far below their training and qualifications because of language difficulties, lack of connections, or lack of certification in certain professions. In addition, middle-class immigrants may suffer for the first time the painful experience of prejudice and discrimination in the new country. The poorest immigrants, who are largely members of the lower classes in their country of origin, often suffer tremendous adversity as a result of immigration. Despite these difficulties – which may include xenophobia, racism, and fierce competition for the least desirable jobs – they often achieve relative improvements in their economic and social circumstances. In addition, while they certainly suffer from discrimination in the new country, social disparagement may not necessarily be a new experience. As members of the lower socio-economic class, they are likely to have suffered such treatment in their country of origin.

A variety of other sending factors can also help to mediate the migration process. Possessing the language skills of the new country is clearly an asset. Religiosity and connection with a church may also play a positive role. The rural to urban shift, which is not an uncommon pattern for many immigrants, may complicate the transition. Many immigrant children in our study report to us that they find it very difficult to adjust being closed into their apartments. While they may have had considerable freedom to play and roam their neighborhoods in their earlier experiences, they often lose such freedoms in an urban environment.

Just as a number of factors related to the sending situation will ease or impede the adjustment to the new context, conditions in the new host milieu will also play a significant role. At the top of the list is the availability of effective social support networks. The presence of a healthy social support network has long been regarded as a key mediator to stress (Cobb, 1988). Social relationships provide tangible aid, such as running an errand or making a loan, as well as guidance and advice (including information, and job and housing leads) so much needed by disoriented newcomers. Social relations also serve to maintain and enhance self-esteem and provide much needed acceptance and approval. A well functioning social support network, quite predictably, is closely linked to better adjustment to the new environment. Of course, in part, the availability of an effective social support structure will be influenced by the individual's pre-existing social competence. Individuals with highly developed social skills are likely to be better able to establish and draw upon interpersonal relationships (Heller and Swindle, 1983).

A number of other factors within the host environment play a role in the adaptation of the immigrants. Whether or not the immigrant is "documented" or "undocumented" will obviously impact the opportunity structure in which she is able to participate (Chavez, 1992; Smart and Smart, 1995), as well as the general quality of life. Feeling "hunted" by the Immigration and Naturalization Services is highly stressful (Padilla et al., 1988) and leads to anxiety and (well founded) paranoia. For adults the availability of jobs will be key. Here, social networks will play a key role as employers often rely on migrant networks to provide them with a constant referral source of potential new employees (Waldinger, 1997; Cornelius, 1998). Ability to find work, questions of pay, seasonal availability, safety, and unpleasantness of the job will also play a role in adjustment.

For children, the quality of their schools will play a key role in the ease of transition. Unfortunately, many immigrant children find themselves in segregated, poverty-stricken, and conflict-ridden schools (Orfield, 1998). Fear of violence is a central concern in the lives of many new immigrants. Obviously, neighborhood safety will do much to influence the quality of life for children and adults alike. Many immigrants move to inner-city areas in search of housing they can afford. Unfortunately, "affordable" urban housing is often located in areas which may be characterized as "war zones." Parents, too, fear for their children's safety. They often require them to stay within the confines of their (often cramped) living spaces, out of harm's way in the streets. Many of our informants lamented the resulting loss of freedom following immigration.

The general social climate of reception to the new immigrants plays a critical role in their adaptation. At the present time in the USA there is considerable prejudice against immigrants, and particularly against immigrants of color (Garcia-Coll and Magnuson, 1997, p. 119). In recent years, widespread concern about the influx of new immigrants has led to several dramatic initiatives designed to prevent immigrants (largely undocumented but also documented) in the United States from receiving benefits or public services (M. Suárez-Orozco, 1998). Tightened restrictions initially involved border controls, but later were extended to services, including education, health, and welfare (Eschbach et al., 1997; Brown et al., 1998). These policies and practices are generating patterns of intense exclusion and segregation involving the workforce (Portes and Zhou, 1993; Waldinger, 1996), schools, and residential patterns (M. Suárez-Orozco, 1998). Furthermore, for many minority youth, while they have made gains in terms of level of completed education, those gains are not being rewarded proportionally in terms of wages in the market place (Myers, 1998).

EXCLUSION AND SOCIAL MIRRORING

While the structural exclusion suffered by immigrants and their children is detrimental to their work and social roles, racism and prejudice also play a toxic role. How does a child incorporate the notion that she is "an alien," "an illegal," unwanted and not warranting the most basic rights of education and health care? Even for legal residents, the hostility prevalent in the current climate in the USA adversely affects all children with accents and darker complexions.

The fear of the cultural dilution of the USA's Anglo-Saxon institutions and values is a enduring preoccupation, feeding the anti-immigrant ethos (Espanshade and Balinger, 1998). Citizens today feel more positive about immigrants from Europe than they do about immigrants from Latin America and the Caribbean. Immigrants who do not speak English and who "look" different from the dominant Anglo-European majority make many non-immigrants uncomfortable. The fact that 80 percent of the "new immigrants" (post-1965) are of color (coming from Asia, Latin America, and the Caribbean) is clearly a further complicating factor in the USA's race-polarized society. When it comes to immigration, race and color do matter. Immigration is an enduring concern that lurks just below the surface of public consciousness in the United States. Opportunistic politicians have long found immigrants to be convenient scapegoats onto which to direct righteous anger about all sorts of chagrins (Jones-Correa, 1998). At best they are viewed as competitors and at worst they are seen as sinister.

As a result, a range of negative attributes are projected onto them. De Vos and Suárez-Orozco (1990) developed an interdisciplinary, psychocultural framework to explore the experience of self in cultures where patterned inequalities shape social interaction. They argue that, in addition to the obvious structural inequalities they face, some minorities are also targeted for "psychological disparagement." They become the object of symbolic violence which stereotypes them as innately inferior (lazier, prone to crime, and so forth). These attributes make these "disparaged minorities," in the eyes of the dominant society, less deserving of sharing in the society's dream and justifies their lot in life.

When immigrant and minority children look into the societal "mirror" they see predominantly negative and hostile images. This distorted mirror communicates prejudiced expectations of sloth, irresponsibility, low intelligence, and violence. Such reflections as these can be further intensified by the media. Even when the parents provide positive "mirroring," it is often insufficient to compensate for the distorted images that children encounter in their daily lives. Even strong parental support may not be enough to compensate for the intensity of the distortions of the House of Mirrors immigrant children encounter in their everyday lives.

My recent research suggests that immigrant children are keenly aware of the prevailing ethos of hostility of the dominant culture (C. Suárez-Orozco, 2000). Psychologically, what do children do with this reception? Are the attitudes of the host culture internalized, denied, or resisted? The most positive possible outcome is to be goaded into "I'll show you. I'll make it in spite of what you think of me." This response, while theoretically possible, is relatively infrequent. More likely, the child responds with self-doubt and shame, setting low aspirations in a kind of self-fulfilling prophecy: "They are probably right. I'll never be able to do it." Yet another potential response is one of "You think I'm bad. Let me show you how bad I can be."

NEW PATTERNS OF ASSIMILATION

A number of theoretical constructs have been developed over the years to explore the immigration experience in American society. Historically, models developed to examine immigration were largely based on the European experience. These studies described patterns of assimilation and upward mobility (Gordon, 1964). The argument was quite simple: the longer immigrants were in the United States the better they did in terms of schooling, health, and income.

Most recently, a number of distinguished sociologists, such as Waters (1990, 1996a), Gans (1992), Portes and Zhou (1993), and Rumbaut (1996), argue that a new "segmentation" in American society and economy has been shaping new patterns of immigrant adaptation into American culture. This research suggests what might be broadly termed a "trimodal" pattern of adaptation. Some immigrants today are achieving extraordinary patterns of upward mobility – quickly moving into the well remunerated knowledge-intensive sectors of the economy in ways never seen before in the history of US immigration. At the other end of the hourglass economy, large numbers of low-skilled immigrants find themselves in increasingly segregated sectors of the economy and society – locked into low-skilled service sector jobs without much promise of mobility (Portes and Zhou, 1993). In between these two patterns are yet other immigrant groups which seem to approximate the norms of the majority population – "disappearing" into American institutions and culture without much notice.

This trimodal socio-economic pattern seems to be related to how the children of today's immigrants tend to do in school. In the past few years, there have been several studies on the performance of immigrant children in schools. The research suggests a complex picture. In broad strokes, we can say that the immigrant children of today also fit a trimodal pattern of school adaptation (a critical predictor of success in this society). Some immigrant children do extraordinarily well in school, surpassing native-born children in terms of a number of indicators, including grades, performance on standardized tests, and attitudes toward education (De Vos, 1973; Kao and Tienda, 1995). Other immigrants tend to overlap with native-born children (Rumbaut, 1995; Waters, 1996a). Yet other immigrants tend to achieve well below their native-born peers (Kao and Tienda, 1995; Rumbaut, 1995; Suárez-Orozco and Suárez-Orozco, 1995).

In addition to this pattern of variability in overall performance between groups, another disconcerting pattern had consistently emerged from the data. For many immigrant groups, length of residency in the United States is associated with declining health, school achievement, and aspirations (Kao and Tienda, 1995; Rumbaut, 1995; Suárez-Orozco and Suárez-Orozco, 1995; Steinberg, 1996; Vernez et al., 1996; Hernandez and Charney, 1998).

A recent large-scale study considered a variety of measures of physical health and risk behaviors among children and adolescents from immigrant families – including general health, learning disabilities, obesity, emotional difficulties, and various risk-taking behaviors (Hernandez and Charney, 1998). Interestingly, the researchers found that immigrant youth were healthier than their counterparts from non-immigrant families. The researchers pointed out that these findings are "counterintuitive" in light of the racial or ethnic minority status, overall lower socio-economic status, and higher poverty rates that characterize many of the immigrant children and families that they studied. They also found that the longer youth were in the United States, the poorer their overall physical and psychological health became. Furthermore, the more "Americanized" they became, the more likely they were to engage in risky behaviors, such as substance abuse, violence, and delinquency (Hernandez and Charney, 1998).

Those results are also supported in studies of education. Rubén Rumbaut, working with Alejandro Portes (Rumbaut, 1997), surveyed more than 15,000 high school students in San Diego, California, and Dade County, Florida. They found a *negative* association between length of residence in the United States and both academic achievement and educational aspirations. A similar pattern was found in another large-scale study of adolescents across the country (Steinberg, 1996). In a different voice, Reverend Virgil Elizondo, rector of the San Fernando Cathedral in San Antonio, Texas, articulates this same issue: "I can tell by looking in their eyes how long they've been here. They come sparkling with hope, and the first generation finds hope rewarded. Their children's eyes no longer sparkle" (quoted in Suro, 1998, p. 13).

NEGOTIATING IDENTITIES

At no time in the lifespan is the urge to define oneself *vis-à-vis* society as great as during adolescence. According to Erickson (1964), the single greatest developmental task of adolescence is to forge a coherent sense of identity. He argued that for optimal development, there needs to be a certain amount of complementarity between the individual's sense of self and the varied social milieux he or she must transverse. This model made a great deal of analytical sense to explain the experiences of individuals living in more homogeneous worlds across their lifespan.

However, in an increasingly fractured, heterogeneous, transnational world, there is much less complimentarity between social spaces. Hence, today we are concerned less with theorizing identity as a coherent, monolithic, and enduring construct than with understanding how identities are implicated in the ability to transverse increasingly discontinuous social, symbolic, and political spheres. The children of immigrants must construct identities that will, if successful, enable them to thrive in incommensurable social settings such as home, schools, the world of peers, and the world of work.

In this complex world, most children are required to move across discontinuous social spaces. For the children of immigrants, however, these discontinuities can be dramatic. Immigrant children today may have their breakfast conversation in Farsi, listen to African American rap with their peers on the way to school, and learn in mainstream English about the New Deal from their social studies teacher. Therefore, the experience of the children of immigrants offers us a particularly powerful lens through which to view the workings of identity.

Given the multiple worlds in which immigrant children live, they face particular challenges in their identity formation (Aronowitz, 1984; Vigil, 1988; Grinberg and Grinberg, 1989; Phinney, 1998). When there is too much cultural dissonance, negative social mirroring, and role confusion, and when the cultural guides are inadequate, an adolescent will find it difficult to develop a flexible and adaptive sense of self. Many are torn between the attachment to the parental culture of origin, the lure of the often more intriguing adolescent peer culture, and aspirations to join the American mainstream culture (which may or may not welcome them).

Optimistic hopes for the future are often tempered by pessimism borne of deprivation and disparagement. While immigrant and second-generation youth may believe that the "American Dream" should be attainable with sufficient effort, the many limits to this dream become increasingly evident with experience. High school graduation no longer guarantees earnings sufficient to lead a good life; college tuition is prohibitively expensive; and networks and connections – which their parents may not have – do indeed make a difference in youth's opportunities.

To further encumber the process of identity formation, the children of immigrants are a dissonant combination of precocious worldliness and sheltered naiveté. They are often vested with responsibilities beyond their years. They may be called upon to act as interpreters, to care for siblings, and to attend to chores at home while their parents work. They may be able to manipulate two languages and have insight into two different worlds. At the same time, particularly for girls, forays into the New World are often overrestricted by their anxious parents, which contributes to a relative naiveté. With a limited network of informed individuals to provide adequate information and advice, many immigrant children have difficulty navigating the turbulent waters of adolescence.

Given this multiplicity of factors, it is clear that immigrant adolescents face special struggles in the formation of identity. Each individual forges an identity, finding ways to adapt to the vicissitudes of being a stranger in a new land. In 1937, Stonequist astutely described the experiences of social dislocation. He aptly described cultural transitions, which leave the migrant "on the margin of each but a member of neither" (Stonequist, 1937, p. 4). He emphasized that the common traits of what he termed the "marginal man" (he wrote in pre-feminist consciousness-raising 1937 after all) evolved from the conflict of two cultures rather than from the "specific content" (Stonequist, 1937, p. 9) of any particular culture. Stonequist contended that cultural differences create the most difficulty in circumstances where there are sharp ethnic contrasts and hostile social attitudes. His observations on the psychological costs of marginal status are as useful today as when he first wrote them.

The majority of immigrant children, coming from a variety of countries and social classes, arrive with extremely positive attitudes towards schooling and education (Suárez-Orozco and Suárez-Orozco, 2000). Yet a number of new studies have shown that the longer the children are in the new environment, the less positive they are about school and the more at risk they are to disengage from academic pursuits. Kohut (1971) theorized that loss, mourning, and the narcissistic injuries of humiliation are linked to destructive tendencies such as aggression and violence. I would argue that the losses and mourning resulting from immigration coupled with the narcissistic injuries of the host culture's reception are a dangerous combination which may in large part account for this disconcerting pattern of decline.

Given that one in five children in the USA is a child of immigrants, how these children adapt to their new country should be a crucial societal concern. The pathways they take and the identities they form are multiply determined. The resources, experiences, stresses, and trauma, as well as coping strategies, they bring with them play a key role. The structural environment – including neighborhood, employment opportunities, and schools – within which they find themselves must not be overlooked. The social mirroring that children encounter is also critical. Immigrant children suffer a variety of forms of stress and loss, which are only compounded by corrosive social disparagement. We should not underestimate the toll that these erosive experiences and shattered dreams take upon the souls of developing children. The positive attitudes of recent immigrant children are a remarkable resource; as a society the USA would be best served by harnessing rather than crushing those energies.

Part III
Economic Inequalities

11

On Inequality

Siddiqur Rahman Osmani

Introduction

Few would deny that any morally defensible social arrangement must be based on some notions of impartiality and fair play. In popular perception at least, equality seems to be a very similar type of notion. It is true that the old adage "all men are born equal" fails utterly to reflect the human condition in the real world, where the accident of birth routinely drives a wedge between fellow human beings by bestowing unearned privilege on some and undeserved misery on others, but at least it echoes a deeply felt human aspiration for how things ought to be. Yet neither in intellectual discourse nor in practical politics does equality appear to command the same universal appeal as do the notions of impartiality and fair play. There are in fact many champions of inequality, and they are not in the most part evil people reveling at the misfortune of others. This chapter is in part an attempt to explain this apparent paradox and in part an attempt to reiterate the demand for egalitarianism. I take a critical look at some of the major theoretical and empirical issues that have figured prominently in the debate on equality, especially on economic equality.

The arguments for inequality fall generally into two groups. The first group of arguments is concerned with the object of equality. The demand for equality must refer to the equality of something – the object of equality – and the debate is about whether that object is really of fundamental value to the society.

Take, for instance, the idea of equality of income. Traditionally, income has been seen as a means of achieving utility or satisfaction; so when equality of income is sought, the true object of equality, at least in the traditional view, is human satisfaction. Now, it can be argued, as it has been argued by many, that utility or satisfaction cannot be the ultimate object of value for a good or just human society, so equality of utility *per se* cannot be a fundamental goal worth pursuing. For many of these critics, liberty or freedom is a more genuine object of value; so, if one wants equality in something, then, they would argue, one should want equal liberty rather than equal income. If the pursuit of equal liberty were to result in equal income, that would be fine, but the critics point out that in general that would not be the case, i.e. the goal of equal liberty may conflict with the goal of equal income or utility. In that case, equality of income will have to be jettisoned, for the sake of equal liberty.

In this example, inequality of income has been justified by invoking the supposedly superior claim of equality of liberty. This is a specific illustration of a general point that demanding or at least tolerating inequality in one dimension may be perfectly consistent with demanding equality in another dimension. In fact, Amartya Sen (1992) has made the stronger claim that most of those who advance a reasoned case for inequality do actually favour, either explicitly or by implication, equality in something else. So the debate, in the first set of arguments, is not really for or against equality but on the question of "equality of what." This debate is reviewed in the next section.

The second set of arguments can be more properly characterized as a debate for or against equality. Here the focus remains fixed on the same dimension or the object of value, and the question is asked whether equality in that dimension is really what is demanded by the conception of a good society as judged by that object of value. Consider again the example of equality of income, where the object of value, in the traditional view, is utility or satisfaction that one derives from income. While accepting utility as the ultimate object of value, and income as its proxy, one can argue, however, that equality of income is not necessarily the best way of promoting that value. A utilitarian would argue, for instance, that a society's goal should be maximizing the sum total of utilities enjoyed by its people, and if a more equal distribution of income leads to a lower aggregate income (and hence lower aggregate utility), then equality is not consistent with that goal. The debate here is not about the plausibility of utility as the ultimate object of value, but about an alleged conflict between a more equitable distribution and the aggregate sum of that object of value.

This is the context of the classic debate on "growth versus equity." There is a point of view, of considerable pedigree, which argues that unequal distribution of income is a necessary condition for faster growth of the aggregate income of a nation. Any attempt to make the distribution more equal will, in this view, only serve to reduce the total amount of economic resources that will be available for distribution. In the extreme case, the quest for equality can even be self-defeating, in the sense that people might end up with less income than they otherwise would. In particular, even the poor, who are intended to be the beneficiaries of a more egalitarian distribution, may end up with less income in absolute terms than they would have, had economic growth not been slowed down for the sake of equality. Thus, equality, in this extreme case, can be an enemy of the poor, and inequality a friend.

This view, of course, has been hotly contested. The argument that a more equal distribution of income will hold back the rate of economic growth has been criticized on both theoretical and empirical grounds. According to an emerging, and what might be called a revisionist, view, greater equity in income distribution may even be conducive to a faster rate of growth. If so, a move toward greater equality will be doubly beneficial to the poor: first, by helping to increase the aggregate amount of resources available for distribution; second, by tilting the distribution in favor of the poor. Below, I review these debates on the relationship between equality and growth.

EQUALITY OF WHAT?

Any argument for equality must specify an object, the distribution of which is desired to be equal. But that object itself must be of some fundamental value to the society, as otherwise a claim for equality in its distribution would not constitute a fundamental moral claim. What, then, is the object that is of fundamental value to the society? There is no single answer to this question, because the answer depends on one's conception of what constitutes a good or just society, and there are many such conceptions corresponding to many alternative ethical theories.

The resulting plurality in what is taken to be an object of fundamental value leads inevitably to a corresponding plurality in the dimension or "space" in which different people demand equality. And, as we shall see below, equality in one space may coexist with inequality in another space. What is more, equality in one space may demand inequality in another. One can, therefore, consistently be a champion of inequality in any particular space, while claiming to be an egalitarian in a general sense. Much of the debate on inequality stems from this plurality of spaces, which in turn stems from a plurality of ethical theories about what constitutes a good society.

One of the best known ethical theories, one that has had a powerful influence on economic as well as social and political discourse in the past two centuries, is the utilitarian philosophy. According to this philosophy, a society should strive to achieve the greatest possible satisfaction, or utility, for the largest number of people, which in practice means maximizing the sum total of all individual utilities. As stated, this principle does not show any egalitarian concern, indeed it does not say anything about distribution at all, concerned as it is solely with the aggregate or sum total of utilities. Implicit in the doctrine, however, there lies a special kind of egalitarianism, which some modern utilitarians have tried to highlight.

This can be seen by noting that maximizing the sum total of utilities requires that every individual has the same marginal utility – defined as the additional utility derived by a person from the last unit of income received. If at a given distribution of income, the marginal utility of person A exceeds that of person B, then clearly the society's aggregate utility can be increased by transferring some income from B to A, because the utility gain of A would more than offset the utility loss of B. Therefore, as long as marginal utilities are unequal, there will remain scope for increasing aggregate utility by redistributing income. Or, to put it differently, aggregate utility will be maximized only when all the marginal utilities are equal.

According to one interpretation, marginal utility reflects the "urgency of human needs" – the higher the urgency of needs, the higher the value of marginal utility (Harsanyi, 1975). On this interpretation, utilitarianism ensures equality of different individuals' urgency of needs, by demanding equality of marginal utilities (as a necessary condition for maximizing the aggregate sum of utilities). But equality of urgency of needs must imply that in some sense everyone is enjoying the same degree of need-fulfillment, so that no one is left with a greater urgency of needs compared to others. In this sense, the utilitarian principle of maximizing aggregate utility has been claimed to satisfy the fundamental egalitarian principle of "giving equal weight to the equal interests of all the parties" (Hare, 1976).

One consequence of accepting the utilitarian principle is that one cannot make a fundamental moral claim for equality of income. This is because equality of marginal utility – which is the only kind of equality demanded by this principle – does not necessarily entail equality of income. Only in the special case, when all individuals have the same capacity to derive satisfaction from any given level of income (in economic jargon, when they all have the same utility function), will equality of marginal utility entail equality of income. However, since it is entirely plausible to assume that different people have different capacities to enjoy and to derive pleasure from the same consumption of goods and services, the utilitarian principle will seldom demand equality of income in practice. Instead, it will actually demand inequality of income in this general case. Yet, as has been noted above, utilitarianism has been claimed to be egalitarian in its own right – in the space of urgency of needs.

There are, however, many problems with the utilitarian's claim to egalitarianism. In the first place, serious questions have been raised about the plausibility of interpreting marginal utility as reflecting an individual's urgency of needs (Scanlon, 1975). Furthermore, critics have demonstrated how the application of the utilitarian principle can lead to obviously inegalitarian outcomes. Sen (1973) makes the point vividly by giving the example of a disabled man who needs more resources than others to maintain any given level of mobility, and also has a lower capacity to enjoy any given income, owing to his disability. The utilitarian principle will discriminate against this person in distributing income (because, from the point of view of maximizing total utility, it is better to give the marginal income to someone else who is better able to enjoy it), yet it is obvious that such discrimination will accentuate his disadvantage by denying him the resources required for gaining mobility – hardly an egalitarian outcome, by anyone's moral criteria.

This example illustrates a particularly onerous implication of accepting the utilitarian concern with aggregate utility. But there are other ethical systems, which, in common with utilitarianism, accept utility as the fundamental object of value but do not judge the goodness of a society in terms of the sum total of utilities. The whole class of ethical systems that take utility as the fundamental object of value is known as welfarism, of which utilitarianism is a special case

(Sen, 1979). The example of the disabled man, which is such an embarrassment for utilitarianism, need not be so for other systems of this class.

Consider, for example, a welfarist system that judges the goodness of a society in terms of equality of utility distribution across the population rather than by the sum total of utilities. Since the disabled man finds it difficult to convert income into utility, a system that demands equal utility will have to encourage positive discrimination in favor of him so as to give him higher income than others. Higher income will then enable him to better overcome his problem of mobility. The disabled man will not, therefore, embarrass a welfarist system that demands equal utility.

Can we then say that welfarism in the broader sense provides an egalitarian principle – equality of utility – that is morally defensible? Not so, according to many a moral philosopher. One problem arises from a kind of consideration that is in a sense opposite to that of the example of the disabled man discussed above. Some people may be able to derive large satisfaction even from wretched conditions of life. This is especially true of those who have come to accept their entrenched deprivations as the normal way of life and have therefore learnt to come to terms with their lives by trying to be happy with the smallest of mercies. Equality of utility in this situation will serve to perpetuate and legitimize the entrenched deprivations that one segment of society may have imposed on another and then made them accept with equanimity through a process of cultural conditioning.

There is another line of criticism which takes a rather different approach. The issue at stake here is a feature of welfarism known in moral philosophy as consequentialism. Welfarism judges the moral force of any action simply by its consequence – in terms of the amount of pleasure or satisfaction. The process whereby the satisfaction is derived – whether by giving food to the hungry or by torturing an innocent man – plays no role in moral evaluation. For obvious reasons, this particular feature of focusing exclusively on consequence, with no regard for the rightness or wrongness of procedures, has long been a standard criticism of utilitarianism. Clearly, the criticism applies equally to all variants of welfarism, not just utilitarianism.

At the other extreme, new ethical theories have been developed which focus exclusively on procedures, with no regard for the consequences. It is instructive to explore the implication of these theories for the debate on inequality. One of the most elegant theories of this nature – one that is of particular relevance in the economic sphere – is due to Robert Nozick (1973, 1974). In this theory, the justness or goodness of an economic arrangement depends on the justness of the procedures whereby property rights are acquired.

Nozick has laid down some principles of justice in acquisition and transfer, and argued that people are entitled to, i.e. they have a right to own, the holdings that are acquired through repeated applications of these principles. According to these principles, people are entitled, in the first instance, to what they produce with their own labor. Next, they are entitled to what is produced by resources owned by them and what they can acquire by free exchange of what they legitimately own. Finally, they are entitled to what is legitimately passed on to them through inheritance or gift, provided the person making the transfer was entitled to the holdings that have been transferred.

Two features of this theory of entitlement are worth noting. The first feature relates to the justification of the procedures that give rise to entitlements. According to Nozick, the justification comes from the moral intuition that these procedures are in some sense intrinsically right – it seems intuitively obvious to him that a just society must be based on these procedures. No reference is made to the consequence of following these procedures in order to justify them. This deontological or non-consequentialist nature of justification is an essential feature of Nozickian rights.

The second feature relates to the duties and obligations that the Nozickian rights entail for others. Every right entails some obligation for others. In this case, the obligation takes the form of a constraint. My right to property entails that no one may prevent me from acquiring property as long as I follow the just procedures, nor may anyone take away from me any property I have so acquired. My right thus imposes a constraint on other people's behaviour. In this, Nozickian property rights fall neatly in the general category of libertarian rights, all of which emphasize the importance of freedom from coercion.

In this conception of a just society, the object of fundamental value is people's liberty to acquire goods and services through the just procedure. No fundamental moral value attaches to the consequence of following those procedures, i.e. what people can or cannot do with the goods and services they acquire, what utility or satisfaction they derive from them, etc. To put it simply, once we have accepted the procedures as morally right, then we have to take the consequences, no matter what they are. Therefore, we cannot attach a moral claim to the demand for equality of those consequences. In particular, we cannot demand equality of income, because the distribution of income is nothing other than a consequence of following the procedures for acquisition of property. As long as the procedures that were followed are deemed to be just, the resulting distribution of income is also just, no matter how unequal it might be.

A certain kind of equality can still be demanded, however, even within this framework. It is the equality of liberty to acquire property through the just procedure, because that is the fundamental object of value in this system. Equality of liberty will not, however, lead necessarily, or even typically, to equal distribution of income. Given equal liberty, differences in people's physical and intellectual abilities will result in unequal acquisition of resources in the first round; and these inequalities will be perpetuated, in the second round, partly through inheritance and partly through the greater bargaining power that attaches to concentrated wealth when it comes to the transfer of resources through free exchange. Thus, once again, equality in one space may be perfectly consistent with, and may even necessitate, inequality in another. A libertarian can thus oppose or at least fail to attach any value to the demand for equal distribution of income (or of utility, for that matter), while claiming to be egalitarian in a fundamental sense.

As in the case of welfarism, however, in this case too one must ask whether the object of value taken as fundamental in this system can indeed be accorded an overriding moral importance in preference to everything else. The critics have raised moral doubt on this issue by invoking Isaiah Berlin's (1969) famous distinction between negative and positive freedoms. To make the distinction concrete for the present context, consider the case of a person engaged in the task of acquiring food for her family by following the just procedures of acquisition as laid down by Nozick. The justness of the procedures being followed entails that she is entitled to the food she acquires and that no one must obstruct her pursuit of food. If she is indeed allowed by others to acquire food in a legitimate manner without let or hindrance, then she can be said to enjoy the negative freedom of acquiring food. If the food she so acquires is enough to allow her family to stave off hunger, then she can also be said to enjoy the positive freedom from hunger.

In reality, however, the negative freedom to acquire food in a legitimate manner need not go hand in hand with the positive freedom from hunger. As Amartya Sen (1981) has pointed out in his famous study of contemporary famines, millions have died in famines not because they were denied the negative freedom to acquire food in a legitimate manner, but because the food acquired through legitimate means was simply not enough to ensure survival. Because of this lack of a necessary correspondence between negative and positive freedoms, any moral system that might want to attach value to positive freedoms cannot be satisfied with negative freedoms alone. This is precisely the problem with the Nozickian system. Note that negative freedom is a matter of respecting procedures, whereas positive freedoms lie in the domain of consequences. So, by attaching fundamental moral importance to procedures and denying any independent moral value to consequences, the Nozickian system ascribes exclusive value to negative freedom with no regard whatsoever for positive freedoms.

It is arguable that an ethical system that disregards the moral status of consequences must be fundamentally inadequate. Yet, as was noted earlier, the most celebrated consequentialist system, utilitarianism, and its generalization, welfarism, whose essential characteristic is to focus on utility consequences, have severe problems of their own. What one needs, therefore, is a system that pays due regard to consequences, but defines consequences broadly enough to go beyond the narrow confines of utility and to encompass more fundamental objects of value such as freedom, including positive freedom.

The ethical framework proposed by John Rawls (1971) for devising just sociopolitical institutions meets these criteria neatly. Rawls starts from the premise that the justness of institutions cannot be determined by the value system of any one group of people in a society; all groups must agree upon rational reflection that the institutions devised are in conformity with their self-interest. However, an ethically defensible system cannot accept the outcome of reflections that people might make from the vantage points of their respective stations in life, because being self-interested they will try to advance their own stations even if it causes grievous harm to others. For instance, the rich and the powerful might propose institutions that would perpetuate their hold over the rest of the society. The point is, the existing distribution of powers and privileges is seldom fair, and a system that is not devised from a fair vantage point cannot be just.

Rawls suggests that the only "fair" vantage point is an "original position" that is covered by a "veil of ignorance." This is a hypothetical situation, obtaining prior to the formation of society, where we imagine individuals coming together to devise institutions for a future society without knowing who is going to occupy which station in life once that society comes into existence. According to Rawls, only the rules and institutions that would be agreed upon in this situation would be just, and therefore these are the only ones that would be able to claim a fundamental moral force. He then goes on to argue that rational reflection from the original position would lead individuals to agree upon the following general conception of justice: "All social primary goods – liberty and opportunity, income and wealth, and the bases of self-respect – are to be distributed equally unless an unequal distribution of any or all of these goods is to the advantage of the least favoured."

The reasoning through which Rawls reaches this conclusion is a complex one, involving comparison of this principle with other plausible ones in terms of their implications for rational self-interested individuals, who are about to make an inviolable commitment to a principle that would determine their entire life prospects without having any knowledge of the exact social station they will eventually find themselves in. Rawls proposes this particular principle because, by testing against moral intuition, he finds that self-interested people are likely to consider its implications more appealing than those of other principles.

Two features of Rawls's general principle are worth noting in the present context. First, equality in the distribution of what he calls "social primary goods," of which income and wealth are a part, is the benchmark of a just social order. Second, deviation from this benchmark, in the form of inequality, may be tolerated only if everyone in the society benefits from it, and when there are more than one unequal orders that would allow everyone to benefit, then that particular order must be chosen which will give the maximum possible benefit to the least advantaged person. The second feature thus qualifies the demand for absolute equality as expressed in the first, by allowing inequality when everyone benefits, but in so doing it again raises the flag of egalitarianism by insisting that the benefit to the least advantageous person must be the criterion for choosing among alternative social orders.

Thus, from the Rawlsian perspective, egalitarianism – in the space of social primary goods – emerges as a necessary consequence of self-interested people reflecting rationally from a "fair" vantage point. These primary goods are defined as "things that every rational man is presumed to want." However, they are not wanted for their own sake – "these goods normally have a use whatever a person's rational plan of life." These uses obviously include the negative and positive freedoms that people will enjoy by having access to the various components of primary goods, such as liberty, opportunity, income, and wealth.

Here is an ethical theory that attaches fundamental value to the consequences of actions and institutions, not in terms of the narrow conception of utility, but in much broader terms encompassing both negative and positive freedoms that people can achieve via the possession of social primary goods. Furthermore, this theory demands, as an essential part of the ethical framework, an egalitarian distribution of those primary goods.

In an important extension of Rawls's work, Sen (1980, 1992) has argued that if freedoms are indeed the ultimate object of value, then Rawls's demand for egalitarianism in the space of primary goods may be unduly limiting – one should focus on the space of freedom itself. His argument can be best understood in terms of two related concepts of "functioning" and "capability." Functioning refers to a person's ability to be and to do the things she has reason to value, such as the ability to be free from hunger, or to lead a healthy active life; and capability refers to all possible functionings she can choose to achieve given her resources and any other constraints she might face. Higher capability implies greater scope to choose a valuable functioning. The concept of capability thus corresponds to the notion of freedom in a broad sense – the freedom to choose the valuable functionings of life.

Sen argues that human well-being consists in their capabilities, not in their utility or happiness as assumed in much traditional thinking. Happiness is not irrelevant, of course; "to be happy" is, after all, one of the functionings people obviously value. To that extent, happiness is subsumed within the concept of capability, but the point is that there are other valuable functionings, which a utility-focused approach ignores but a capability-focused approach would not. An ill-fed, ill-nourished person who has resigned herself to her fate and learnt to take pleasure in small mercies may not seem to have a particularly low level of well-being if happiness is taken as the sole content of well-being. But if well-being is conceived as capability, then her deprivations in terms of the capability to be free from hunger and to lead a healthy active life will have to be considered along with her high level of happiness. This broader evaluation will not yield the same reassuring picture of well-being as before. Intuition suggests that the latter is a more revealing approach to understanding human well-being.

If capability is accepted as the content of well-being, then any ethical system that judges the goodness of a society in terms of human well-being must accept capability as the fundamental object of value. In that case, the demand for equality must mean the demand for equality in the space of capabilities. Sen (1992) does make a strong case for equality in the space of at least the "basic capabilities," such as the capabilities to be free from hunger, to be able to lead a healthy active life, to be able to participate actively in the society, and the like.

Insofar as income, or resources, or more generally, Rawls's primary goods, are a means of achieving capability, one might think that equality in the space of these resources would be equivalent to equality in the space of capability. But that is not so. The reason lies in the fact that for physical, biological, and social reasons, different people may have different capacities to convert primary goods into capabilities. Because of these differences, equality in the space of primary goods will not ensure equality in the space of capabilities. For example, if people with different metabolisms or people living in different environments of health and hygiene consume the same amount of food, they will end up with different nutritional capabilities to lead a healthy active life. Therefore, if freedoms are valued, then equality should be demanded in the space of capability, at least of basic capabilities, and not in the space of resources that yield capability.

The demand for equality of basic capabilities has a very important policy implication. Experience from different parts of the world shows that with appropriate policies it is possible to achieve remarkable equality in the distribution of basic capabilities even when the distribution of income is not very equal nor the level of income particularly high. Some of the celebrated examples are Sri Lanka, Costa Rica, and the Indian state of Kerala. What all of them have in common is a very high level of basic nutritional and educational capabilities that are enjoyed almost equally by the majority of the population, at levels of income that are quite low and with inequality in income distribution that is average by international standards. This extraordinary achievement has been made possible by conscious intervention by the state – in the form of public provisioning of food, health care and education. (For more on these case studies, see Dreze and Sen (1989) and the references cited therein.) Comprehensive coverage of public provisioning has ensured that many have achieved respectable levels of basic capabilities, who would not have been able to do so relying on their personal incomes alone. The result has been a remarkable equality of basic capabilities across a rather unequal income scale.

The demand for equality in basic capabilities thus calls for an active role of the state in providing access to food, health care and education. This does not mean, however, that the perspective of capabilities can afford to be indifferent to the distribution of personal income. To the extent that people must try to develop their own capabilities, and not rely on the state to do everything for them, they will need resources or income. So, if income happens to be distributed extremely unequally, especially at very low levels of per capita income, it may not be possible for the entire population to develop their basic capabilities equally. The demand for equal capabilities would thus set limits to permissible inequalities in income distribution.

THE GROWTH VERSUS EQUITY DEBATE

The preceding discussion suggests that the concern with income inequality remains valid even when one takes a broader view of equality, like the equality of capability. So even with the broader view, an egalitarian must grapple with the argument that the demand for greater equality in income distribution may come into conflict with the demand for economic growth – the so-called growth–equity trade-off. If such a trade-off really exists, then there is a danger that the quest for equality may turn out to be self-defeating by impoverishing everyone. This danger need not compel one to abandon the goal of equality altogether, but it will certainly call for tempering the demand for equality when the trade-off seems particularly onerous. It is, therefore, of great importance to unravel the true relationship between equality and growth.

Since the 1950s, the conventional wisdom regarding the relationship between equality and growth had been embodied in an empirical phenomenon known as the Kuznets curve, named after the Nobel laureate economist Simon Kuznets, who was the first to observe and document this phenomenon (Kuznets, 1955). While studying the historical data of the Western developed countries, he noted that the pattern of income distribution within a country changes in a specific way as the country becomes richer: as it begins to grow from a low level of income, inequality first rises; and only after it has reached a certain level of affluence does inequality begin to fall. Inequality thus appeared to be a necessary concomitant of growth in the early stage of development. The message then got across that a "premature drive for equality would only mean sharing of poverty," or more colorfully that "you must let the cake grow first before sharing it equally." Politicians in the rich and poor countries alike began to justify inegalitarian policies by using such metaphors.

As it happens, the empirical basis of the metaphor was never very firm. Kuznets himself was keenly aware that much of the information on income distribution that he had at his disposal was of uncertain quality, to say the least. Many subsequent studies that have tried to rediscover the Kuznets curve from more recent and somewhat more reliable data have come up with mixed results: some of them support his original insight, others don't; mostly, they don't (Fields, 1989).

Nevertheless, the belief in the trade-off between equality and growth has proved remarkably resilient. Actually, this belief predates the Kuznets curve by a long way, not so much on the basis of actual data, however, as on economic theory. Almost all the great classical economists – from Adam Smith to Karl Marx – propounded the theory that capital accumulation was the key to growth, and that accumulation was driven by the savings of the people, which in turn depended on the level and distribution of income. They also assumed that the rich capitalists tended to save a bigger proportion of their income than the poor workers. This was a crucial assumption, for it meant that a more unequal distribution, giving more income to the rich, would result in bigger savings, and hence to a faster rate of accumulation and growth. It is this chain of reasoning – linking distribution with savings, accumulation, and growth – that has served more than anything else to underpin the view that there exists an inevitable conflict between equality and growth.

This theory was never subjected to any rigorous empirical test by the classical economists; presumably, its truth seemed self-evident to them. In any case, they did not possess at that time the necessary data to test their theory. But the same cannot be said today. An impressive body of evidence has accumulated over time, and it has not been kind to the classical view. This evidence may be best summarized by dividing up the classical chain of reasoning into two parts: the first part says that a more unequal distribution of income results in higher savings and accumulation because the rich tend to save proportionately more, and the second part says that the more you save the faster you grow.

A couple of considerations weigh heavily against the first part (Lindert and Williamson, 1985). To begin with, numerous studies have shown that the rich and the poor do not differ markedly in their saving propensities. Second, even to the extent that saving propensities do differ, greater inequality will merely enable the economy to save more; it will not ensure that more will actually be saved in the form of productive capital. After all, savings can be utilized in many different ways, some of which – like building a factory – lead to the creation of productive capital, while others – like buying real estate for speculative gains – do not. The actual pattern of utilization depends on the structure of incentives that exists for encouraging investment into different forms of assets. These two considerations together suggest that greater inequality does not necessarily lead to a higher rate of capital accumulation, thus casting doubt on the first part of the classical proposition.

The second part, linking capital accumulation to growth, is also subject to considerable doubt. The initial ground for scepticism emerged quite a long time ago, in the 1950s and 1960s, as a consequence of a series of studies that have come to be known as "growth accounting." The objective of these studies was to quantify the contribution of different sources of growth, in particular to see how much of the observed growth in per capita income was attributable to capital accumulation and how much to the growth of the labor force. To their utter surprise, economists then discovered that historically capital accumulation had made a relatively minor contribution to the growth of developed countries, and by far the major contribution had come from technological change and an assortment of other factors whose nature was not well understood. Moses Abramovitz, the pioneer of growth accounting, called this part the "measure of our ignorance," so as to underline the message that we knew very little of the forces that actually promote growth. More sophisticated techniques of growth accounting employed by subsequent writers have reduced the "measure of ignorance" to some extent, but they have not overturned the finding that capital accumulation, at least as conventionally measured, may not be the key to growth (Abramovitz, 1993).

An even more serious reason for skepticism has emerged in the past few years. While the "growth accounting" literature had cast doubt on the supposedly overwhelming importance of capital accumulation, it did not dispute the claim that accumulation did after all contribute to growth. By contrast, some recent studies seem to strike at the very root of the classical proposition by demonstrating that accumulation appears to have no causal effect on growth at all! By analyzing the experience of a large number of countries, these studies have shown that faster growth precedes, rather than follows, higher rates of savings and accumulation (Blomstrom et al., 1993; Carrol and Weil, 1994). The causality thus seems to run in the opposite direction; it is growth which raises savings and accumulation, and not the other way round.

It should be noted that these studies are by no means conclusive. The methodology, the database and the interpretation of findings are still being debated. But the important point is that taken together they cast enough doubt on the old argument that inequality promotes growth by encouraging savings and accumulation.

The opponents of equality do, of course, point to other mechanisms through which inequality is supposed to promote growth and equality to stifle it. The most prominent of these is the incentive argument. The essence of this argument

is that economic growth occurs as a result of people working hard and entrepreneurs taking risks, which everyone is not capable of doing equally. Those who
can will naturally be rewarded more than those who cannot. If you do not allow
these unequal rewards, so the argument goes, then those who can will not have
the incentive to work hard or to take risks; as a result, the fountain of growth
will run dry.

This argument obviously has some merit. Indeed, some people find its merit so
overwhelming that they are prepared to ditch the cause of equality altogether in
the name of incentives. But extremism of this kind is totally unwarranted
because the incentive of differential reward is only one of a variety of ways in
which income distribution may affect growth. Against this incentive effect, one
must weigh the effect of a number of other channels through which, according to
some recent research, greater equality may actually promote rather than retard
growth.

To a large extent, this new research has been inspired by the experience of the
East Asian miracle economies. The two main stars of this miracle, South Korea
and Taiwan, started from a base of exceptionally equal distribution of income by
developing country standards, brought about half a century ago by some radical
land reforms that took away vast amounts of farming land from rich landlords
and redistributed it equally to poor peasants. Evidently, equality did not harm
the cause of growth in these countries! Indeed, many have argued that equality
may well have helped them achieve the exceptionally high rates of growth that
earned them the reputation of miracle economies in the subsequent decades. (See
the discussion and the references cited in Birdsall and Sabot, 1995.)

Much work has recently been done to understand the pathways through
which greater equality may actually promote growth. Four main channels have
been identified so far. These may be described as the theories of: (a) endogenous
fiscal policy; (b) capital formation under credit constraint; (c) endogenous
schooling and fertility decisions; and (d) socio-political instability. (For extensive
reviews of these theories, see in particular Alesina and Perotti, 1994; Perotti,
1996; Benabou, 1997.)

According to the endogenous fiscal policy theories, distribution of income
determines a government's choice of fiscal policy, which in turn affects the rate of
growth. The particular fiscal policy in question may be either taxation or
expenditure, but in either case, the point of these theories is to demonstrate
that a more equal income distribution will lead to a kind of fiscal policy that
would be more conducive to growth. Consider the case where a government
wants to pursue a redistributive fiscal policy by imposing a tax on capital income
and by redistributing the proceeds uniformly across the population. Since the
poor have less capital than the rich, they will pay less tax than the rich for any
given rate of tax. By contrast, everyone will receive the same amount of money
when the proceeds are distributed uniformly across the population. So a fiscal
scheme of this kind will entail a redistribution of income from the rich to the
poor. The government wants to choose as high a tax rate as possible in order to
maximize the scope for redistribution, but at the same time it wants to be careful
about public opinion because it knows that people don't like to pay tax. In

particular, it wants to ensure that the chosen rate is not considered too high by the majority of the people. So the question is: what does the majority want?

The answer is found by applying a trick known in economic theory as the "median voter theorem." Note that since redistribution will take place at the expense of the rich, they will want to keep the tax rate low. In general, the richer a person is the lower a rate he or she will prefer, and the poorer a person is the higher a rate he or she will prefer. Given this pattern of preferences, the tax rate preferred by the person located in the middle of the income distribution – the so-called median voter – will play a crucial role. It is clear that a tax rate that is marginally lower than the one preferred by the median voter is the highest possible rate that will not be considered too high by the majority. (The majority in this case will consist of the poorer half of the population plus the person whose income is marginally higher than that of the median voter.) This, then, is the rate that will be chosen by a government that wants to maximize the scope of redistribution while keeping the majority happy.

The chosen tax rate will depend, among other things, on the existing distribution of income. For any given level of per capita income, a more equal distribution will imply higher income for the poorer half of the population. The tax rates preferred by the poorer half, including, say, the median voter, will then be lower. So, if the government wants to keep the majority happy, it will have to choose a lower tax rate under a more equal distribution than under a less equal one. The chosen tax rate in turn will impinge on the rate of growth of the economy by affecting the incentives to invest – a lower tax rate will damage incentives less, encourage investment more, and stimulate faster growth. Thus, greater equality of income distribution will result in faster growth by raising the income of the poor, which will lead to a lower tax on capital, which in turn will foster more rapid investment and growth.

The second group of theories also link equality with growth through capital accumulation, but unlike the endogenous fiscal policy theories they focus on capital accumulation by the poorer segment of the population. The basic point is that with a more equal distribution of income the poor will be able to accumulate more capital, without impairing the ability of the rich to do the same, so that the society as a whole will be able to accumulate capital faster and grow faster.

The key to understanding the argument lies in the widely observed feature of the real world that credit and capital markets generally discriminate against the poor. There are a number of reasons why a profit-maximizing lender would want to discriminate against poor borrowers, even if many of them are potentially creditworthy. Whatever the reason, the fact is that the poor find themselves credit-constrained in a way that the rich do not. It is this feature of the credit market that establishes a link between distribution and growth.

The argument goes something like this. Since the poor have lower levels of capital than the rich, they would have a higher marginal return to capital, given the standard assumption of diminishing returns. Normally, therefore, the poor would want to invest more than the rich. But the problem is that the size of optimal investment typically exceeds what people can afford to spare from their own earnings. This is not a problem for the rich because they have access to the credit market, but it is a problem for the poor who are credit-constrained. The poor will therefore be forced to invest less than the optimal level. The actual size of their investment will depend on their command over self-finance, which in turn will depend on their income and wealth. This is where distribution comes in. The poor's command over self-finance will be higher in a society with greater initial equality of income distribution than in one with less equality, for any given level of per capita income. It is of course true that, while enhancing the poor's command over self-finance, a more equal distribution will also reduce that of the rich, but this will not have any adverse effect on capital accumulation, as the rich have ready access to the credit market. On the whole, then, a more equal society will be able to accumulate more capital and grow faster, other things remaining the same.

The third group of theories draw the link between distribution and growth via people's decisions to have children and to educate them. An equal distribution of income is supposed to affect the schooling and fertility decisions in a manner that would help to promote economic growth. To see how this link works, first note that schooling and fertility decisions are usually intertwined. The decision to give more education to children usually goes with the decision to have fewer of them. This is known in the literature as the "quantity versus quality" trade-off – when people want to improve the "quality" of children, they tend to reduce their quantity.

The extent of this trade-off depends on the cost of raising children on the one hand and the cost of educating them on the other. And these costs are often related to the level of household income. For a poor family, the cost of educating children can be quite high, especially in terms of opportunity cost, i.e. income forgone. Young children of poor families are known to contribute significantly to household income, especially in the rural areas of the developing world. If these children are to be sent to the school, household income will go down substantially at least in the immediate future. For richer families, however, this opportunity cost is negligible relative to their total income. On the other hand, the cost of raising an extra child is pretty low for a poor family, given the bare minimum of food, clothing, and shelter with which they are accustomed to get by. For richer families, this cost is not so small. Besides, their opportunity costs of raising children will also be high if working mothers have to give up well paid jobs, or if they have to employ paid workers, to look after the children.

These relationships suggest that as a family climbs up the income scale, the cost of raising children will go up while the cost of educating them will go down. Parents will then be more inclined to limit fertility and to educate their children, i.e. to trade off quantity for quality. It follows, then, that, for a given level of per capita income, a society with a more equal income distribution will have lower fertility and higher education than one with a less equal distribution, because a more equal society will have fewer poor families. Both these consequences – lower fertility and higher education – will in turn help a poor economy to grow faster.

The final category of theories – the socio-political instability theories – basically formalises the age-old idea that gross inequalities are likely to incite violence, rebellion, or attempts to sabotage the established social order by those who feel severely deprived. The resulting breakdown in the rule of law will create uncertainty in the enforcement of property rights, and in the absence of certainty about property rights investors will have little incentive to invest. As a result, the economy will grow more slowly. By contrast, a more equal society will enjoy greater certainty of property rights and hence more robust growth.

The proponents of all these theories have tried to test them statistically by using data drawn from a large number of countries. The test essentially involves an attempt to discern from cross-country data whether countries with lower initial inequality enjoyed a higher rate of growth, other things remaining the same. The initial tests almost invariably lent support to the hypothesis that equality promotes growth, but they were subject to a couple of problems. First, the inequality variable was measured from poor-quality distributional data, in the sense that the data were hardly comparable across countries and sometimes even in the same country at different points in time because of wide differences in the nature of surveys used to collect income distribution data. Second, the tests were done in a manner that made it impossible to discriminate between the alternative theories.

Both these problems have recently been addressed in an important work by Perotti (1996). He has used carefully screened distributional data, and tried to discriminate among alternative theories by deriving testable implications that are different for different theories. Using a sample comprising both developed and developing countries, he has confirmed the earlier finding that equality does appear to have a positive effect on growth. He also finds that among the four mechanisms discussed above, there is strong empirical support for the instability mechanism and somewhat weaker support for the endogenous schooling and fertility mechanism, but not much support for the other two.

An interesting result emerged when Perotti tried to test the hypothesis separately for rich and poor countries. He found that equality had a strong positive effect on growth in the rich countries, but no significant effect, either positive or negative, in the poor countries. This finding would seem to strike a severe blow to the cause of egalitarianism in poor countries. It used to be said in the olden days, when most people believed in a trade-off between equity and growth, that equity is a luxury only the rich countries can afford, because only they can afford to make the necessary sacrifice in terms of growth. Perotti's findings would now seem to suggest that the rich countries are even luckier than that – they don't need to make the sacrifice after all. They can eat the cake and still see it grow, while the poor countries are still left out of the party.

Further reflection shows, however, that such a negative conclusion may not really be warranted. In the first place, as Perotti himself notes, the negative effect of inequality on growth could be true as much for the poor countries as for the rich, and it is only some statistical problems that hide the fact for the poor countries. Even if this is dismissed as a triumph of hope over facts and the finding is taken at its face value, one can still argue that there is no support for the traditional view that the quest for equality will actually retard growth. This argument provides at least a weak case for adopting egalitarian policies, even in poor countries. It is arguable, however, that the case for egalitarian policies is in fact much stronger, Perotti's finding notwithstanding. There are two fundamental reasons why his finding cannot be taken as decisive evidence for the inability of equality to promote growth in poor countries, even if all the statistical problems are left aside.

The first reason lies in the very nature of the statistical exercise – regression analysis – that forms the basis of this finding. All one can infer from this kind of exercise is that *incremental* changes in inequality have no effect on growth. That leaves open the question of what happens when radical reforms are undertaken to bring about large changes in the distribution of income. There are in fact some plausible models in which small reductions in inequality will not promote growth, but large reductions will. These models are characterized by the so-called threshold effect. For example, in the models of capital formation with credit constraint discussed above, it is possible that in order to make any worthwhile investment it will be necessary to spend a large sum of money to pay for large fixed costs. In that case, a small-scale redistribution resulting in a small increase in the income of a credit-constrained poor household may not be enough for it to overcome the minimum threshold of fixed costs. Greater equality will then do nothing to promote growth, but a large-scale redistribution will solve this particular problem.

In fact, when one recalls that the recent theoretical interest in the growth-promoting effect of equality has its origin in the experience of East Asia, one should realize that it is large-scale redistributions that are really relevant. What happened in East Asia was not marginal changes in tax-expenditure policies that can do no more than tinker with the distribution, but radical land reforms that fundamentally altered the distribution of income. It is arguable that if greater equality did have a growth-promoting role in East Asia, it was only because distribution was altered so radically.

The second reason why Perotti's finding cannot be regarded as decisive is that it deals exclusively with the distribution of private income. This focus may be too narrow, especially in the context of human capital formation. For improving the education and health of poor children, public provision of good quality services may be more important than small increments in the private incomes of their parents – the celebrated examples of Sri Lanka, Costa Rica, China, and the Indian state of Kerala prove this point. In poor areas, where private schools and health facilities have not developed because the potential clientele are too poor to make the necessary investment worthwhile, a slight increase in private incomes of the poor will fail to buy any extra education or health services. Public provision will be much more effective in this situation. This line of argument suggests that egalitarian policies that take the form of greater public provisioning for the poor may well be growth-promoting, even though redistribution of private incomes may not be.

It follows from the preceding argument that if one wants to test the effect of inequality on growth, then it may not be enough to look only at private income distribution. One would need to test whether growth is related to a measure of inequality that reflects the distribution of both private income and public provisioining – for example, inequality in educational achievement. Such a test has recently been carried out by Birdsall and Londono (1997). Their results show that while income inequality has no significant effect on growth, educational inequality has a significantly negative effect. This finding indicates that a broader concept of equality may well be growth-enhancing.

This broader concept is of course nothing other than the equality of basic capabilities discussed above. It was noted there that on the grounds of ethical plausibility equality in the space of capabilities can arguably claim superiority over equality in any other space, such as utility, income, or resources. The arguments of the present section suggest that equality of capability has much to commend itself also on the grounds of economic interaction between distribution and growth. Policies aimed at achieving equality of basic capabilities can not only allay the traditional concern about the growth–equity trade-off, but may even lead to a virtuous circle in which economic growth and equitable distribution reinforce each other.

12

The Persistence of Poverty in a Changing World

Melvin L. Oliver and David M. Grant

> Poverty is pain; it feels like a disease. It attacks a person not only materially but also morally. It eats away one's dignity and drives one into total despair.
> **A poor woman, Moldova (World Bank Group, 1999, p. 25)**

Globalization is rapidly changing the world we live in and the social context within which poverty exists. On the one hand, technological innovations are bringing people closer together in both the real and virtual worlds. Expansion of the global economy has brought an increasing number of people into formal economies and created a growing interdependence among people, nations, and international institutions. Democratic institutions are proliferating along with ideologies that endorse citizen participation. The Internet has dramatically improved access to information and is eliminating boundaries and borders to revolutionize the distribution of goods and services. Yet one of the world's oldest social problems – poverty – remains stubbornly present despite rapidly shifting global institutional and organizational structures. The prophesy of the New Testament, that "ye have the poor with you always" (Mark 14:7), seems as true today as ever.

From a sociological perspective, confronting the issue of poverty raises a number of challenging questions concerning the social forces responsible for the persistence and intractability of poverty. What is poverty? Who is poor? How can poverty be measured? Why are people poor and why do people remain in poverty? And what strategies are most effective in reducing poverty? Providing complete answers to these questions is far beyond the scope of this chapter.

Rather, we highlight recent trends and dimensions in the incidence of poverty in the United States, one of the most advanced technological societies, and in a number of the world's least developed regions and societies. This strategy, we believe, reveals much about the multidimensional, complex web of factors responsible for poverty, as well as some of the common poverty-reducing strategies that seek to provide and build resources among those in need.

To understand the extent of poverty, we first address definitions and measures of poverty, focusing on the difference between absolute and relative measures of poverty. We then move to a discussion of poverty in the USA and in less-developed societies. Each of these sections addresses broad trends in the incidence of poverty to identify who are poor and the complexity of factors related to why they are poor. The final section of the chapter considers novel strategies to reduce poverty that go beyond traditional income transfers policies. To reduce the violence of poverty, we argue, requires a focus on developing and building assets among those in need. We use illustrative examples from the USA and India to demonstrate the relationship between assets and shifting people from economic marginality to economic security.

Defining and Measuring Poverty

The concept of poverty appears to be quite straightforward: poverty simply means to be poor, to be lacking in the basic material resources for an adequate human existence. At base, poverty is a function of the impact of macroeconomic forces as they are mediated by the mechanisms of governmental and institutional structures. Poverty is associated with expansive forces far beyond the reach of the poor themselves, such as economic trends, technology, financial institutions, the division of labor, political structures, infrastructure, health care, courts and criminal justice systems, the military, and much more. Yet the experience of poverty is personal, amorphous, and multidimensional. As a normative social concept, poverty can be applied to a vast array of conditions and circumstances, varying tremendously across time and place.

Definitions of poverty are themselves revealing of a given society's material standards, as well as providing an indication of why poverty exists. That is, how a society conceptualizes poverty tells us something about why that society thinks people are poor. Since poverty is a normative concept, levels of poverty and the causes of poverty cover a broad range of human conditions from developed to less-developed societies. A family of four in the USA may live on $15,000 per year, while a similar family in India exists on a mere $100 a year; on what basis do we consider these very different circumstances poverty? Poverty can be conceived and defined in either relative or absolute terms (see also Ruggles, 1990; Fürster, 1994). An absolute measure sets a fixed poverty threshold in which those below the threshold are considered poor and those above are not. An example of an absolute poverty measure is the United Nations "extreme poverty" construct, which considers any individual living on less than one dollar per day as extremely poor. A relative concept of poverty is based on the distribution of resources among all members of a society. Defining poverty in relative terms, for example, might consider the poor as the poorest 10 percent of a society.

Both absolute and relative poverty measures have advantages and disadvantages. From a social policy perspective, absolute poverty has the advantage of being fixed and thus providing a yardstick with which one can measure changes in poverty cross-nationally, over time, and due to various interventions, such as social policy initiatives or economic change. An absolute measure may become problematic, however, if the standard upon which it was originally based no longer corresponds to the material reality of a society. And, of course, the establishment of a poverty threshold is itself a political process that reflects the values and judgments of those with the power to define a social problem. Relative measures of poverty place a greater emphasis on the distribution of resources in a society and thus provide a better sense of social inequality. Social inequality, rather than absolute poverty, is often more closely related to violence and social, economic, and political instability than absolute poverty. However, relative poverty measures are often resistant to change over time by definition and make the impact of policy, or other, interventions, difficult to evaluate.

POVERTY IN THE UNITED STATES

The official poverty line in the USA was established in the 1960s, based on an estimated annual minimum dollar amount for a family to procure adequate food and housing. Thus, poverty in the USA is defined quite simply as a lack of money. Conceptually, this definition is based on the cost of food and housing, not simply for survival, but for an "adequate" standard of living. The calculus of this absolute poverty measure in the USA has remained virtually the same since its creation, adjusted for inflation, with families considered above or below the poverty threshold based on family income and family size. In 1998, the poverty line was $16,660 for a family of four (Dalaker, 1999). More than 34 million Americans (12.7 percent) were estimated to be below the poverty line in 1998.

Trends in poverty in the USA are reported in figure 12.1. The proportion of persons in the USA who were below the poverty line declined steadily following 1959, until stagnating during the economic recession of the mid-1970s. The incidence of poverty increased through 1983 and then averaged about 14 percent through the 1990s. The strong economic performance of the USA in the 1990s pushed poverty in 1998 (12.7 percent) to its lowest rate since 1979.

Poverty does not, however, affect groups equally. Fifty-seven percent of the poor today, for example, are women. Since poverty statistics have been tracked in the USA, certain groups of Americans, in addition to women, have experienced poverty at a higher incidence than others; racial and ethnic minorities and children, have been, and continue to be, overrepresented among poor Americans. Poverty among black and Hispanic Americans have persisted at a far higher rate than the national average, as shown in figure 12.1. The poverty rates of racial and ethnic minorities generally follow national trends over time,

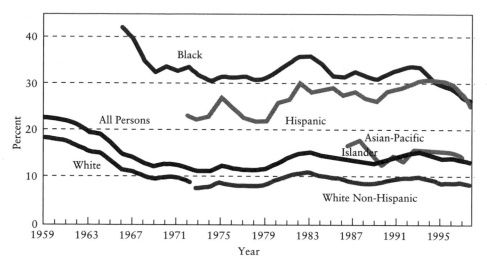

Figure 12.1   Percentage of persons below the poverty line in the USA by race,
1959–1998.

Source: US Bureau of the Census, Current Population Reports, Series P60–207.
Washington DC, US Government Printing Office, 1999.

except that the trends tend to be much sharper for minorities than for whites. These trends suggest that African and Hispanic Americans are at greater risk of becoming impoverished during periods of economic dislocation. On a more positive note, the most recent data report the lowest level of black poverty on record (26 percent), yet it remains more than three times greater than the incidence of poverty among non-Hispanic whites (8 percent).

In contrast to the persistent higher incidence of poverty among African and Hispanic Americans, a dramatic shift has taken place in the age composition of the poor. As shown in figure 12.2, the elderly, those aged 65 and over, were much more likely to be poor than other Americans until the mid-1970s. Poverty among the elderly, however, has dropped consistently, falling, and remaining, below the national poverty rate since 1982. Since official poverty records have been kept, the rate of children (those under age 18) in poverty has always been higher than that of the total population. As poverty fell throughout the 1960s and early 1970s, the rate of children in poverty closely followed the decline. While the poverty rate held steady for other groups during the 1970s, the rate of child poverty increased. More than one in five American children has been below the poverty line for the past two decades and roughly two in five black and Hispanic children are below this line.

What accounts for these trends? Certainly the expansion of social security coverage for elderly Americans and the increase in private and corporate retirement programs play a major role in the declining incidence of poverty among the American elderly (Treas and Torrecilha, 1995). Poverty reductions among the elderly are particularly impressive and important to overall poverty rates in the USA, since they are the fastest growing age group in the population. That is,

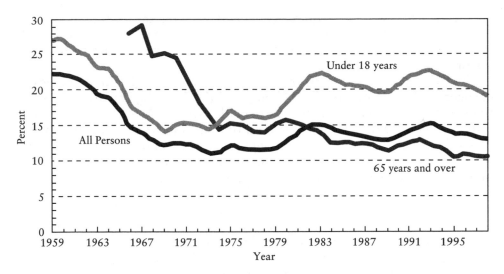

Figure 12.2 Percentage of persons below the poverty line in the USA by age, 1959–1998.

Source: US Bureau of the Census, Current Population Reports, Series P60–207. Washington DC, US Government Printing Office, 1999.

without policies and programs to reduce poverty among the aged, the USA would be facing a tremendous surge in poverty levels due to the aging of the population.

Explaining the persistence of poverty among racial and ethnic groups, as well as the high incidence of poverty among children, is a complicated affair. Since poverty in the USA is defined on the basis of income and family size, explanations of poverty focus largely on labor market participation and household structure. The persistently higher poverty rates among African and Hispanic Americans are undoubtedly linked in part to the long legacy of discrimination and exclusion in the USA; the contemporary role of racial discrimination in such outcomes, however, is subject to considerable debate.

For many years, following anthropologist Oscar Lewis's study of poverty in Mexico (1959), the culture of poverty was the dominant explanation of poverty in the USA and elsewhere. In short, this perspective argues that living conditions among the poor lead to a set of adaptive behaviors that function to help the poor survive the experience of their impoverishment. These non-normative behaviors, such as an inability to defer gratification and drug abuse, however, ensure their poverty will continue and that of their children as well, since these cultural attributes are transmitted in the family from one generation to the next. More recent variations on the culture of poverty theme suggest that the well intentioned, but misguided, policies which expanded the welfare state during the 1960s created an incentive for people to be poor and actively discouraged marriage and family formation (Murray, 1984). The decline in marriage and increase in child poverty are, from this perspective, the result of generous welfare payments and eligibility requirements. Furthermore, the culture of poverty paradigm contends that welfare has destroyed both the work ethic and the self-esteem of the poor, rendering them incapable of responding to economic opportunity (Mead, 1992).

The principal alternative to the culture of poverty explanation emphasizes changes in the structure of the economy and the declining employment opportunities for low-skilled workers, particularly African American men concentrated in central cities. The combination of residential segregation and the loss of good-paying jobs for persons without a college education has led to high rates of unemployment and joblessness. As jobs, economic development, and the middle class have left the cities for the suburbs, those left behind became increasingly isolated from mainstream lifestyles, values, and aspirations (Wilson, 1987, 1996). Declining marriage rates, particularly of African American women, are thus due to the lack of attractive marriage partners (i.e. men with stable employment) because of economic dislocation and expansion of the criminal justice system (Wilson and Neckerman, 1986). Nonetheless, liberal proponents of this economic restructuring perspective argue that the poor prefer work to welfare and are willing and able to respond to employment opportunities. The principal obstacles to employment in this scenario are the availability of jobs paying decent wages, transportation, medical insurance, and childcare.

The tight labor market of the booming American economy in recent years has pulled many young black men into the world of work. Gains in employment and earnings were most pronounced among young black men in cities with unemployment rates below 4 percent. And crime rates fell most dramatically in those metropolitan areas with the lowest unemployment rates between 1992 and 1997 (Freeman and Rodgers, 1999). Such findings are consistent with the liberal view that poverty and social dislocation results from limited opportunities, and solutions to poverty should focus on the expansion of employment opportunities. A recent study conducted in Milwaukee, Wisconsin, however, shows that even guaranteed employment with comprehensive support structures cannot fully overcome the complex obstacles that often keep the poor from stable employment. "The problems that kept people from maintaining steady employment comprise a catalog of inner-city ills: drug and alcohol abuse; jealous and or violent boyfriends and husbands; conflicts with employers; unreliable baby sitters and cars, and generally flagging spirits" (DeParle, 1999).

We briefly raise these examples of recent studies on poverty and employment to document the importance of opportunity and economic growth to employment and reducing poverty, but also to suggest that there are real limits to current and past poverty reduction policies in the USA that stress work and family formation (Katz, 1986, 1989). Neither welfare payments nor forcing the poor to work in low-wage jobs significantly improves the material conditions of the poor (Bane and Ellwood, 1994). Indeed, the fastest growing segment of children in poverty are the children of working parents (Annie E. Casey Foundation, 1996). And despite sustained economic growth and the widely celebrated trimming of thousands of persons off the welfare rolls, there is persistent hunger in the USA. A recent study by the US Department of Agriculture found that during the years 1996 and 1998, 10 million households (9.7 percent) experienced food insecurity each year, with more than one in three of these households experiencing hunger at some point during the year (Nord et al., 1999).

Policies that fail to address the broader social context in which the poor are situated condemn another generation to the risks and violence of poverty, such as hunger. In addition to a strong economy and opportunity, we contend that policy to reduce poverty in the USA and elsewhere must seek to build resources in those persons at greatest risk from the devastating consequences of poverty. Policies to build assets and resources to fight poverty in the USA need to address the complex obstacles related to poverty among adults and their children. Following a discussion of poverty in less-developed regions, we will return to this theme of asset building to reduce human suffering.

POVERTY IN DEVELOPING REGIONS AND COUNTRIES

As complex and multidimensional as poverty is in the USA, shifting our focus from poverty in the USA to poverty in less-developed societies exponentially ratchets up the complexity factor. Not only is the magnitude of poverty incomparably greater, but the contours and causes of poverty throughout developing regions are far more varied. Measurement issues are more complicated too, because of the lack of comparable data across nation-states and over time. In this section, we discuss poverty measures and broadly sketch poverty trends in developing regions and countries, revealing some of the stern challenges to poverty reduction in the twenty-first century.

In contrast to absolute poverty thresholds developed for single societies (national poverty lines), several measures have been devised for comparisons across regions and nations. The World Bank's one dollar a day "extreme poverty" measure and the United Nations Development Programme's (UNDP) "human development" indices are both useful constructs that inform the magnitude and contours of poverty in comparative settings. We use the first measure of extreme poverty as a crude, though effective, yardstick of economic deprivation.

Table 12.1 contains the most recent data on the incidence of extreme poverty, reporting the staggering number of persons and percentage of the population living on less than one dollar per day in developing and transitional economies over the decade 1987–98 (World Bank, 1999a). In 1998, an estimated 1.2 billion people subsisted on less than one dollar per day. The incidence of extreme poverty increased since 1987, fluctuating considerably over the decade. The regions of South Asia, particularly India, and sub-Saharan Africa accounted for two of every three persons living in extreme poverty in 1998. The most rapid increase in the incidence of extreme poverty has been in Eastern Europe and Central Asia, although it appears to have stabilized. Rapid social, political, and economic change in the former Soviet bloc countries has clearly led to a dramatic rise in material deprivation.

The major exception to worsening regional poverty trends took place in the East Asia and Pacific region until 1996. The reduced incidence of extreme

Table 12.1 Distribution of extreme poverty by region in developing and transitional economies, 1987–1998

Region	Number (millions)					Percent				
	1987	1990	1993	1996	1998 (est.)	1987	1990	1993	1996	1998 (est.)
East Asian and the Pacific	415.1	452.4	431.9	265.0	278.3	26.6	27.6	25.5	14.9	15.3
(excluding China)	(109.2)	(76.0)	(66.0)	(45.2)	(55.6)	(22.9)	(15.0)	(12.4)	(8.1)	(9.6)
Eastern Europe and Central Asia	1.1	7.1	18.3	23.8	24.0	0.2	1.6	4.0	5.1	5.1
Latin America and the Caribbean	63.7	73.8	70.8	76.0	78.2	15.3	16.8	15.3	15.6	15.6
Middle East and North Africa	25.0	22.0	21.5	21.3	20.9	11.5	9.3	8.4	7.8	7.3
South Asia	474.4	495.1	505.1	504.7	522.0	44.9	44.0	42.4	40.1	40.0
Sub-Saharan Africa	217.2	242.3	273.3	289.0	290.9	46.6	47.7	49.6	48.5	46.3
Total	1,196.5	1,292.7	1,320.9	1,179.9	1,214.2	28.7	29.3	28.5	24.3	24.3
(excluding China)	(890.6)	(916.3)	(955.0)	(960.1)	(991.5)	(29.6)	(29.3)	(28.5)	(27.3)	(27.3)

poverty in this region was impressive between 1987 and 1996, although China lagged behind the rest of the region until 1993. The recent economic recession in Asia reversed the post-1993 decline in extreme poverty, yet the number and proportion of persons living on less than one dollar per day in this region today are one-third to half their level in 1987. In sum, the one dollar per day extreme poverty measure indicates that there is wide regional variation in the extent of extreme poverty in developing and transitional economies. The numerical incidence of extreme poverty has increased, while the proportion of persons in such regions living in extreme poverty declined, from nearly one in three in 1987 to one in four in 1998. Most regions have experienced either stagnant or rising numbers of persons subsisting on one dollar per day, with the exception of the East Asia and Pacific region.

The growing number of persons in the world living on less than a dollar a day is a worrisome trend given the expansion of global linkages, economic growth, and a full decade of post-Cold War international relations. The dust of political, economic, and social upheaval has yet to settle, and hundreds of millions of people continue to suffer the consequences of impoverishment. In addition to global macroeconomic forces, ethnic conflict has wreaked havoc in numerous countries in Africa and Central Europe, while climatic dynamics in Southern Asia, Africa, and South America have undermined food security. In many countries, particularly in sub-Saharan Africa, the HIV/AIDS crisis is causing widespread devastation with generational repercussions. Clearly, poverty indicators based on income alone, such as the one dollar per day extreme poverty measure, are wholly inadequate to reflect the multidimensional features of poverty.

In terms of the quality and adequacy of material conditions, income among the poor in developing nations is often less important than access to resources. Recognizing the limits of income measures and that economic development by itself did not necessarily improve people's material living conditions, the UNDP has recently created several new indices based on the concept of "human development." These indices, which include the human development index, the gender empowerment measure, and the human poverty index, are not simply summary consumption measures, such as gross national product per capita. Instead, these measures attempt to more broadly capture dimensions of the human experience and are based on three concepts: longevity, knowledge, and a standard of living measure (UNDP, 1999). While certainly limited, this more comprehensive conceptualization of poverty by the UNDP is a shift toward a deeper and better understanding of poverty and its underlying causes. Unfortunately, the UNDP human development indices are not directly interpretable and, therefore, we do not report them here. Instead, we briefly consider some of the non-monetary resources used to create the UNDP indices that are associated with poverty and their differential impact on men, women, and children.

Among the basic central resources affecting the lives of the poor are access to safe drinking water, access to health care, and adequate sanitation systems that reduce the threat of disease. Nearly one-third of the population in developing countries is without access to safe water and nearly six in ten are without adequate sanitation (UNDP, 1999). Access to health care is critical, particularly for infants and children, to ensure long, productive, and fulfilling lives; in many poor nations, only small proportions of the population have such access, including Cameroon (15 percent), Nepal (10 percent), Yemen (15 percent), and the Central African Republic (12 percent). While poverty is intimately connected with access to health care resources, there is wide variation among poor nations, with important consequences. Currently, some two million children die each year, for example, from diseases that could be prevented with low-cost vaccinations (World Health Organization, 1999).

The incidence of HIV/AIDS in many poor countries has completely overwhelmed already inadequate health care facilities, particularly in sub-Saharan Africa. The impact of HIV/AIDS in sub-Saharan Africa is horrific and projected to worsen. Eighty percent of AIDS deaths worldwide took place in sub-Saharan African (1.8 million deaths in 1998), possessing one-tenth of the world's population, and resulted in the orphaning of one-fifth to one-third of the children in nine sub-Saharan African countries by the end of 1999 (UNAIDS, 1998). The impact of AIDS and related infectious diseases reduced life expectancy at birth in sub-Saharan African to less than fifty years in 1997. While the past century has witnessed a "health revolution" due to the eradication of communicable diseases and a near doubling in life expectancy worldwide since 1900, a number of countries in sub-Saharan Africa experienced substantial declines in life expectancy over the past decade (World Health Organization, 1999).

While the HIV/AIDS crisis will worsen in the future, it is, unfortunately, not the only, or even the worst, of health threats to the poor. Sexual behavior (2.2 percent) ranked a distant fourth among risks that contributed to global mortality, behind tobacco use (6 percent), hypertension (5.8 percent), and inadequate water and sanitation (5.3 percent) according to a recent World Health Organization study. The biggest health threat, tobacco use, has been rapidly increasing in developing nations, while decreasing in industrialized nations. "[B]y the third decade of the next century, smoking is expected to kill 10 million people annually worldwide – more than the total of deaths from malaria, maternal and major childhood conditions, and tuberculosis combined. Over 70% of these deaths will be in the developing world" (World Health Organization, 1999, p. 67).

Education is a key resource in the fight against tobacco, HIV/AIDS, and other health-related risks, as well as poverty more generally. Unfortunately, women in the developing world are less likely to receive access to adequate health care and education and are disproportionately poor. Like their sisters in the industrialized world, women in poor regions are more and more frequently finding themselves heading households in the absence of men; these women and their children are more likely to be poor (Buvinic, 1997). Adult literacy rates and child mortality rates demonstrate the additional burden associated with being a female in many poor countries. Child mortality rates over the past decade show a disturbing trend toward gender imbalance at birth. In a handful of the world's largest developing countries, the ratio of girls' to boys' mortality rates were particularly high: Nigeria (1.7), India (1.4), and Bangladesh (1.3). Adult literacy rates in

1997 universally favored men (80 percent) over women (63 percent) throughout the developing world (UNDP, 1991).

AN ASSET BUILDING STRATEGY FOR POVERTY REDUCTION

Poverty trends in the USA and in developing regions do not generate much optimism. Many people believe that poverty is intractable and that the poor will always be with us. They cite the multidimensional character of poverty, the impersonal nature of global economic forces, and the belief, sanctioned by religion, tradition, or personal worldviews, that the poor are the cause of their social conditions. These beliefs, among both the powerful and the powerless, are among the major impediments to the development and application of comprehensive strategies for poverty reduction around the world. While macroeconomic trends, which lead to cyclical changes in local, regional, and world economies surely play a significant role in material development, institutional arrangements and social policies also mediate income redistribution, other resources, and opportunities to affect the level and extent of poverty in a given society.

An "asset building" strategy for poverty reduction starts with the assumption that poor people need to be empowered to become a part of their own solution to poverty. As we have stated, most discussions of poverty are concerned with income poverty – the lack of sufficient cash income to meet basic household needs. Policy responses that involve temporary subsidies to income (or consumption) generate little change in the fundamental ability of families to escape poverty and may, in fact, lessen the likelihood of reducing poverty in the long run. For example, many welfare systems around the world are premised on providing poor people with the income to consume and spend at poverty levels. The present focus on putting "welfare" mothers to work in the USA does not address the fact that they work in poverty wage jobs. Thus, the resources that will enable people to invest in their capacities, to seize opportunities, and to move from economic insecurity and poverty to economic security and self-sufficiency are unavailable when the goal is to always keep people consuming at poverty and below poverty income levels.

Asset building as a poverty alleviation strategy refers to a mixture of activities by which the poor are assisted to acquire individual or collective control or ownership of assets, to effectively manage the assets in hand, and to sustain or improve the quality of their assets. Public and private groups often aid in the asset building process and pressure the state to pursue policies that facilitate the acquisition, control, and protection of these assets among the poor.

Poor people everywhere must manage a set of limited assets, among them financial capital, human capital, natural capital, social capital, and cultural capital. They are involved in a strategic use of these "bundles" of assets in which they substitute, trade off, and draw on these assets, accumulated individually or collectively, toward three strategic goals: making a living, making living meaningful, and challenging the structures under which one makes a living

(Bebbington, 1999. p. 5). While each of these five types of assets is important, many contemporary commentators give special attention to *social capital*. Social capital refers to "the norms and networks facilitating collective action for mutual benefit" (Woolcock, 1998, p. 155). Social capital is of unusual import-ance because the collective actions that it underpins often are the means by which people:

- gain access to or defend natural assets like trees or water;
- transform assets into income;
- connect with the market, state and civil society organizations that struc-ture the ways in which assets are acquired, protected, and transformed (Bebbington, 1999, p. 39).

Assets are distinguished from income by being a valuable stock that can be conserved, expanded, or improved and drawn upon as needed. Many assets have the important characteristic of being transferable from one generation to the next. Poor people are characterized by their lack of these assets and thus are unable to take advantage of opportunities or to guard themselves from risks and uncertainties that threaten their economic and social well-being. Moreover, without these assets they also cannot create a sound legacy for future genera-tions.

The asset building framework's message is that poverty is about more than material well-being and that alleviating poverty requires gaining access to a bundle of assets – financial, natural, human, social, and cultural. Below we provide two example of asset building strategies in the USA and India.

BUILDING ASSETS: THE AFRICAN AMERICAN CASE

African Americans have not shared equally in the prosperity of the USA. They earn less than whites, but most importantly they possess far less wealth. The data are both striking and consistent (see Oliver and Shapiro, 1995):

- whites possess nearly twelve times as much median net worth (all assets minus liabilities) as blacks, or $43,800 versus $3,700;
- half of all white households have at least $6,999 in a net financial asset nest egg (these are liquid assets that exclude homes and vehicles), whereas nearly two-thirds of all black households have zero or negative net finan-cial assets.

From an asset building perspective the general conclusion to be drawn from these straightforward yet very revealing facts is that the long-term life prospects of black households are substantially poorer than those of whites, even when we compare blacks and whites in similar income brackets. Sixty-one percent of all African American households have zero or negative net financial assets. If they were to lose an income stream, they would not be able to support their families without access to public support. Nearly eight out of ten African American families would not be able to survive on poverty level consumption with their level of net financial assets for three months. Comparable figures for whites are one-half those of African Americans. Thinking about the social welfare of children, these figures take on more significance. Nine out of ten black children live in households that have less than three months of poverty level net financial assets (NFA); nearly two-thirds live in households with zero or negative NFA.

What are the sources of this enormous racial wealth disparity? A sociology of wealth situates the social context in which wealth generation occurs. Racial differences in wealth holding are a function of the unique and diverse social circumstances that blacks and whites face. One result is that blacks and whites also face different structures of investment opportunity, which have been affected historically and contemporaneously by both class and race. These different social situations have been structured by racialized state policy that has impaired the ability of many African Americans to accumulate wealth – and discouraged them from doing so – from the beginning of slavery throughout American history. This has included restrictions and laws that barred African Americans from business participation, as well as violence that curtailed community economic development. The consequence is that in central ways the cumulative effects of the past have seemingly cemented blacks to the bottom of society's economic hierarchy. A history of low wages, poor schooling, and segregation affected not one generation of blacks but practically all African Americans well into the twentieth century. Wealth is the best indicator of the material disparity that captures the historical legacy of low wages, personal and organizational discrimination, and institutionalized racism. The low level of wealth accumulation evidenced by current generations of African Americans best represents the economic status of blacks in the American social structure.

How do we link the opportunity structure to policies that promote financial asset formation and begin to close the wealth gap? One idea revolves around the concept of individual development accounts (IDAs). First promoted by Michael Sherraden in the late 1980s, IDAs have captured the imagination of many federal policy-makers, state legislators, foundations, and most importantly local communities. In the words of Sherraden (1997), "An IDA is like an individual retirement account (IRA) except that it can begin as early as birth; it can be targeted to a specific population; savings can come from any source (i.e., not limited to income); savings should be matched progressively (i.e., higher matches to those with less income and wealth); the matching partners can be public, non-profit, or private; and the purpose of the account can include education, home ownership, and business capitalization."

The adaptability of IDAs to different contexts make them appealing to a broad range of purposes and circumstances. Experiments have taken root in places as different as Tupelo, Mississippi, and Chicago, Illinois, with small and large matches. Legislative initiatives are under way on the state and federal levels that encourage the use of IDAs in conjunction with welfare reform, and national funding of IDAs is a topic of community-based agitation, public policy discussions, and scholarly debate (Sherraden, 1997; Shapiro and Wolff, 2000).

In Indianapolis, Eastside Community Development Corporation's IDA program has enabled people to leave welfare, to start a small business, or to complete their education. It has created among many participants a different, more long-term and strategic view of their lives. As one participant noted, "IDAs give people who don't think they have a chance for anything to do something.... Before I got in [to the IDA program], I didn't figure on getting my high school diploma, but now I have my diploma and eventually plan on going to college" (Serafini, 1996, p. 935).

While IDAs will not solve the problem of low wealth and poverty in the African American community, they are a potentially important instrument in the policy toolbox to close the racial asset gap. It needs to be combined with other asset based interventions, among them renewed attention to the systematic discrimination of African Americans by the banking industry, workforce development to link people with jobs, and community economic development.

BUILDING ASSETS: THE WOMEN OF PILLUSERI

From this portrait of a marginalized minority in the USA, we now turn to India, where we focus on women belonging to a scheduled caste in the small village of Pilluseri, located in the state of Tamil Nadu. In 1997, the first author's visit to Pilluseri provided a firsthand account of the transformative potential of an asset building program. These women reflect some of the poorest of the poor in India. Their village, which houses 92 households with a population of 327, is wracked by caste distinctions. The families of the women in the scheduled caste own no land, are only allowed to live on the edges of the village, and can only interact with other castes in functional roles. Clearly, the long shadow of subordination casts a dark pall on the lives of these villagers.

The scheduled caste women of Pilluseri are wage laborers, selling their labor power to local villagers and those immediately outside Pilluseri. In this context, assets reflect a very narrow range of resources. Land to be sure is the most important asset, but homes, farm animals, and farm and cooking utensils are also assets. Important common resources that have important asset-like qualities are the natural resources that are central to the social and economic reproduction of the community. The resource focused on here is water.

In a region in which rainfall is no more than 850 millimeters (34 inches) a year, water harvesting has been an essential part of Southern India. For generations, farmers in Tamil Nadu have depended on literally thousands of small and medium-sized water tanks for their irrigation needs. Tanks are little more than a natural, low lying area, which is dammed on one side by an earthen bund, catching and storing run-off during the monsoon season. The tank is a crucial source of irrigation for watering fields and feeding farm animals. It has traditionally been a sustainable water source for innumerable village communities for centuries (Ford Foundation, New Delhi Office, 1994).

A key issue for local social welfare and for the economic security of villagers has been the ability of the tanks to meet the villager's needs. While tanks that can serve areas of over 40 hectares (99 acres) are traditionally under the control of the Public Works Department, smaller tanks are left to the local villages for their upkeep. Since this system of irrigation can produce optimally only one crop a year, to have a failed tank is to invite famine (Coleman, 1997).

We begin with the efforts of a developmental non-governmental organization (NGO), Professional Assistance for Professional Action (PRADAN), to organize more participation around the upkeep and maintenance of the tank in Pilluseri by the villagers. PRADAN is a group of professionals trained in agriculture, engineering, management, rural management, and social work who work with the poor to "enhance people's capabilities to take care of their development and lead a life of dignity" (Martin, 1996). They are the hallmark of the new interest in "civil society" and prime examples of the difference that NGOs and people-centered activism and development can make. They are both community builders and asset builders. (See Martin, 1996, for a case study of PRADAN.)

In India, a system of centralized banking, initially set up to aid the poor, has recently collapsed under its own administrative and bureaucratic weight and given rise to a reprivatization of banking services. PRADAN's grassroots engagement with the women of Pilluseri uncovered credit as one of the central needs of marginalized caste women. Paying exorbitant interest to local money lenders, women found that they were in perpetual debt, working not for the consumptive needs of their families, but for the money lender. Working with these village women, PRADAN enabled the self-organization of borrowing groups, similar to the Grameen model, where groups take responsibility for paying loans, thus creating a strong incentive for individual repayment (Yunus, 1998). These groups, with technical assistance from PRADAN, "administer the loan themselves, serving in effect, as account managers and loan officers for the group." Once the group perfects these technical skills it achieves financial and managerial independence from PRADAN.

By depositing only small amounts, women in Pilluseri managed to save considerable sums. While many continued to be unable to completely pay back the local moneylender (usually interest rates are over 100 percent), the idea of savings became a powerful motivator for the women. These women were able to build and manage their assets by using them both as collateral for more loans and as a cushion during the off-season, when many families go into debt with local merchants for food. The capability to be and to act was clearly present for these women. With the security of savings, women were able to take on activities beyond their previous imagination.

One of the remarkable accomplishments of the scheduled caste women in Pilluseri was their active involvement in terms of a conflict over access to the tanks. Traditionally, tank maintenance and access to the fish in them was controlled by the dominant castes in the village. This usually meant exclusion and further marginalization for the lower castes. When the government devolved more authority for the tanks to the local level, they deemed the tanks "common property" for the use and benefit of the whole population. When the lower castes of Pilluseri demanded these rights, the upper castes responded in an outraged manner at their assertiveness and refused to hire them. They were forced to leave the village for employment and to work in villages within close walking distance. But the lower caste women of Pilluseri continued to save.

With their collective savings, the women became long-term, strategic thinkers about their livelihoods and options. The tank became not just a source of water, but an opportunity to increase the livelihoods, incomes, and assets of the women. The idea that the women could buy fish and stock the tank was no less than revolutionary. To do so, they would have to apply to the state government for authority to stock the tank with fish. As common property, the water was available to all; but the fish would be the property of the women were they to gain the franchise. They could use the fish as food during the off-season and, more importantly, they could sell fishing rights to the upper castes and earn income.

With the power of collective assets behind them, newly developed social capital, and the technical expertise of PRADAN, the women set out to accomplish this task. Men from their caste laughed at them, the upper caste ridiculed them: "who do these women think they are," they would say, "they have never before even been to the regional city, let alone, talked and negotiated with government officials." Through a long and winding process the women did gain the franchise for stocking the tank. They used their collective savings to buy more goods. With assets they were able to develop a long-term plan; to strategize and take advantage of opportunity. More importantly, they also changed the terms of power, gender, and caste in their community.

CONCLUSION

As we have seen, poverty is a resilient feature of the human experience. Tremendous global changes in recent decades promise greater freedom and access to resources, yet the incidence of poverty has increased. The poor remain most susceptible to the worst aspects of poverty, particularly women and children. And as free market-based societies become the norm, those who are left in global capitalism's wake become increasingly marginal and superfluous. Old-fashioned human suffering, including hunger, disease, and death, remains far too common throughout the world today.

As contemporary understandings of poverty recognize its complexity and multidimensionality, poverty measures and interventions increasingly focus on access to non-monetary resources, such as water and education. Typical income-transfer policies, we contend, do little to improve the material conditions of the poor. Instead, strategies that build assets among the poor have the potential to alter the pattern of social relations in which poverty is generated and reproduced. The absence of wealth among African Americans and women in Southern India is central to not only their impoverishment, but also their inability to transform their circumstances. We present the asset building programs above as concrete examples of how such policies can have a lasting and broad-based impact on the lives of the poor.

The history of poverty's persistence and the legacy of programmatic failure to effectively reduce poverty appropriately give one pause when considering interventions such as asset building. The greatest failure of all, however, would be to fail to use our resources to combat the ravages of impoverishment. Poverty, wealth, and knowledge are all created by human interaction – and it is only there that the solution to poverty can be found.

13

Racial Economic Inequality in the USA

William A. Darity, Jr and Samuel L. Myers, Jr

Racial economic disparity in the United States of America centers on the gap in outcomes in labor markets and financial outcomes between blacks and whites. Blacks constitute about 12 percent of the American population and primarily are descendants of Africans who were enslaved in the USA until Emancipation in 1863. Indeed, we estimate, based upon data from the 1990 decennial census, that at least 90 percent of the extant black population in the USA has traceable ancestry among the nation's historic slave population.

The vast majority of the American population, approximately 80 percent of the total, identifies itself racially as white. But the racial category "white" obscures substantial variation in economic outcomes among them. For example, in 1990 the mean per capita income for the US population as a whole was $14,196, 13 percent of Americans lived below the poverty line, 26 percent of men aged 25–54 held professional-managerial jobs, and 29 percent of women aged 25–54 held professional-managerial jobs.

However, the group that identifies itself racially as white and ancestrally as Russian had a per capita income nearly twice as high as the national mean, a poverty rate half of the national average, and more than 45 percent of both men and women in professional-managerial occupations. Other whites with per capita incomes significantly above the national mean were those of Austrian, Rumanian, Lithuanian, Hungarian, and Scottish ancestry. Indeed, virtually all the 35 racially self-declared white ethnic groups had an economic profile at or above the national mean in the 1990 census (Darity et al., 1996, pp. 413–15).

The rapidly growing Latino population in the USA, regardless of ancestry or phenotype, tends to disidentify with blackness and to more strongly identify with whiteness. For example, among persons reporting Cuban ancestry in the 1990 census, less than 3 percent indicated their race as black. The Cuban respondents in that census year included the Mariel boatlift refugees who disproportionately ascriptively resemble persons who customarily would be socially identified as black in the USA.

Furthermore, fewer than 1 percent of Mexican ancestry respondents reported their race as black, as did fewer than 4 percent of Puerto Rican ancestry respondents (Darity et al., 1999). Angelo Falcón's (1995) study utilizing data from the Latino National Political Survey reveals that over 30 percent of Puerto Ricans in the sample that interviewers classified as "dark" or "very dark" and over 50 percent of those that interviewers classified as "medium" or brown-skinned classified themselves as white. Indeed, the Latino preference for a white racial identity over a black racial identity is so strong that anthropologists Warren and Twine (1997) doubt that there ever will be a self-identified non-white majority in the USA, despite popular demographic forecasts that "minorities will be a majority" in, say, the year 2030.

Racial inequality is understood as a problem of "minorities" in the USA. This is by no means universally the case. In Malaysia, the native Malays (the Bumiputera) still lag behind both the ethnic Chinese and East Indians and still suffer significant discriminatory losses in earnings after more than 20 years of affirmative action on their own behalf (Gallup, 1997). The "Bumi" are the numerical and political majority in Malaysia. Of course, South Africa represents another important case where a majority racial group holds markedly inferior economic status. In the last census taken under apartheid, blacks, who constituted 60 percent of South Africa's population, had a mean income only 16 percent of that of whites there and only 40 percent of all South Africans, as well as substantial discriminatory losses in earnings (Treiman et al., 1996).

In the US context the minority that is black holds center stage as the central group for whom the condition of racial disadvantage is rooted historically. This is hardly to dismiss the destruction of native American civilizations with westward expansion of the USA, but the exterminative thrust of the expansion sharply reduced the native presence in the US population. An interesting phenomenon evident between the 1980 and 1990 decennial censuses is growth in the numbers of whites who report themselves as of American Indian ancestry, growth inconsistent with natural increase. Hence, more whites are finding it desirable to identify with or declare native American ancestry. Other ethnic/racial groups of Asian origin, particularly those of Japanese, Chinese, Korean, and East Indian descent, actually have a superior economic profile to most Americans, whether black or white.

ECONOMIC DISPARITIES: CAUSES AND TRENDS

The largest economic gap between blacks and whites in the USA involves the wealth differential. Economists have tended to focus on labor market outcomes, particularly on income generated from employment and on occupational status, but the deepest gulf is in holdings of property, such as real estate, including home ownership, and of financial assets, such as stocks and bonds. One sample, the Survey of Income and Program Participation (SIPP), demonstrated that in 1988 the *mean* black family had $31,678 in wealth, whereas the *mean* white family had $127,237 in wealth. The black–white ratio was a mere 0.25. Furthermore, the *median* level of wealth for black families in the sample was zero. Moreover, the SIPP mean ratio actually was the *highest* among four major surveys reporting on wealth (Chiteji and Stafford, 1999).

These huge racial differences in wealth are *not* attributable to racial differences in propensities to save. The best available evidence indicates that, after controlling for income, there is no significant difference in black and white saving rates. In fact, the black rate might be slightly higher than the white rate at each income level. The key to the racial wealth gap is the gulf in capital resources acquired via inheritance, which is now the major source of wealth (Blau and Graham, 1990). White households are much more likely to receive inheritances than black households (Menchik and Jianakopolos, 1997).

What are the effects of the racial wealth gap? Wealth provides access to greater security of well-being when income fluctuates, access to superior schooling and academic enrichment opportunities, and access to resources that facilitate the pursuit of the self-employment option. A lack of wealth can produce cumulative disadvantages across generations. A large wealth gap can be a pernicious factor in sustaining racial inequality. Indeed, the racial wealth differential is a paramount factor in explaining racial differences in patterns of self-employment rather than black "cultural" aversion to self-employment (Bates, 1997). When we turn from wealth to income, we find very different pictures if we consider per capita income versus considerations about labor market earnings or hourly wages. The persistence of the black–white gap is dramatically evidenced by the fact that Vedder et al. (1990, p. 130) estimated that the *black–white per capita income ratio was 0.59 in 1880, identical with the estimate produced from the 1990 US census!*

There also has been a pattern of worsening of the relative income position of black *families* in the USA. The black–white disparity in family incomes has widened over recent decades. As figure 13.1 graphically demonstrates, the family income ratio, hovering at 0.61 and 0.62 in 1989 and 1990, was at or below the ratio attained in *every single year from 1967 to 1980*. The ratio rose from 0.625 in 1967 to almost 0.65 in 1970. It declined during the early 1970s, falling to a little more than 0.62 in 1973. It rebounded in the mid-1970s, reaching about 0.645 in 1976. However, by the early 1980s that changed. The sharp nose-dive in the ratio of black–white family incomes reached a decades-low point during the 1982 recession, when black families received less than 60.5 cents in income for every dollar that white families received. Even though the ratio rose after the recession, black families have never fully recovered their relative position. They still had incomes in 1990 that were below the relative position in 1970. There is no marked evidence of a change in relative family incomes throughout the 1990s.

The most obvious explanation for the relative decline in black family incomes in the 1980s is the increase in the share of black families headed by females. However, the evidence is far from clear that the major causal factor contributing to the widening earnings gap between black and white family heads is the increased presence of female family heads among blacks. Even among

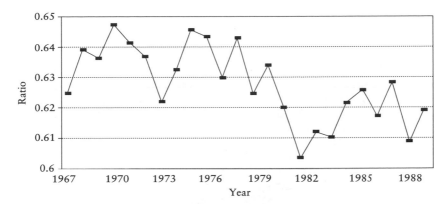

Figure 13.1   Black–white family income ratio, 1967–1990.

Source: US Bureau of the Census, *Money Income of Households, Families and Persons in the United States, 1996.* Current Population Reports, Series P60–184. Washington DC, US Government Printing Office, 1997.

male-headed families, there are substantial differences in earnings that are linked to age and education. The kernel of truth rests in the observation from figure 13.2, displaying the earnings gaps between young black and white family heads between 1970 and 1988. This figure maps the ratio of annual wage and salary incomes of high school drop-outs to the annual wage and salary incomes of college graduates among 16- to 24-year olds. The figure shows the ratios among blacks, among whites and between blacks and whites. For all pairings, of course, the earnings of young uneducated heads of families are lower than the earnings of young college graduates, revealing, on the face of it, a conventional skills gap effect.

But for white heads of families these differentials largely remained stable from 1970 to 1988. While young white uneducated heads of families only earned about 25 cents for every dollar that young white educated family heads earned, the wage premium for having a college degree remained largely stable throughout the nearly two decades among whites. Among blacks, however, the wage premium grew. Whereas young uneducated black male heads of families earned 25 cents for every dollar that young educated black male heads of families earned in 1970, by 1988 they only earned 5 cents for every dollar that young educated black male heads of families earned.

Thus, when a comparison is made between the earnings of young uneducated black male heads of families and those of young educated white male heads of families, a sizable increase in disparity is evident from 1970 to 1988. This suggests that the widening of the income gaps between black and white families may not be just a simple result of the growth of female-headed families among blacks – families whose heads earn less – but a more complex effect of changing returns to skills that differs between blacks and whites.

If the only effect were an overall decline in the returns to skills among young, uneducated family heads, the technological factors contributing to the rise in

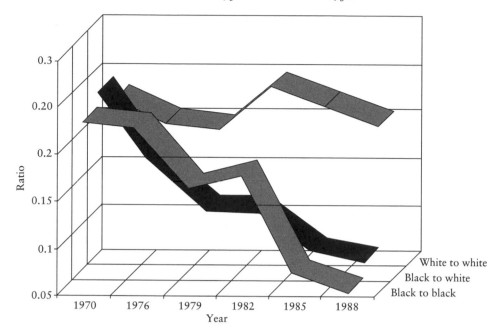

Figure 13.2   Earnings disparities among young men, high school dropouts versus college graduates, 1970–1988.

Source: Authors' computations from 1976, 1985 and 1993 IRP Family Extract Files (CPS March supplement tapes).

wage premia for highly educated workers would explain the rise in the racial earnings gaps because of the high concentration of black family heads among the young and uneducated. But more factors must be at play when there is a divergence between the earnings of family heads who are black male college graduates and those who are black male high school drop-outs, but no change in the gap between college graduates and high school drop-outs among white male family heads.

If anything, the differences between the races in the impact of changing returns to skills or education must be attributable to continuing labor market discrimination – a market that consistently values a black male high school drop-out differently from a similarly uneducated white – or to aspects of pre-labor market discrimination that lower the value of the black high school drop-out's education below that of a similarly situated white. In short, either equally uneducated blacks and whites with identical skills have unequal returns to those skills or equally uneducated blacks and whites have unequal skills because of disparities that originate outside the labor market.

The most recent debate about the pattern of divergence away from racial economic parity in the USA comes after two decades of research on the causes of an alleged movement toward parity. To appreciate the complexity of the current debate, one must understand the earlier body of research. Below, we summarize the main contours of the "black–white convergence" dispute, a dispute that emerged when economists and other social scientists debated the existence and causes of the narrowing of the earnings gap between blacks and whites. Note that the case for convergence centered on labor market outcomes, earnings and wages, *not* wealth, per capita income, or family income.

The main explanations offered for the alleged narrowing of the earnings gap were twofold: the improvement in black human capital, especially as a result of migration from the South and desegregation of Southern schools (Smith and Welch, 1977), and the passage and enforcement of civil rights laws (Freeman, 1981). A more agnostic perspective held that there was no real narrowing of the gap, only an illusion of racial progress (Butler and Heckman, 1977; Lazear, 1979; Darity and Myers, 1980). Reasons given for the "illusion" of progress differed among authors, but one major explanation indicated that the lowest earners were drawn out of the labor force, causing the mean earnings of the positive earners to rise.

Subsequent research has indicated that while the labor force drop-out effect partially accounts for the change, it does not fully account for it (Brown, 1984; Vroman, 1986); the first two arguments remained as contender explanations for the residual closure in the gap. Presumably, then, the more recent renewed widening of the earnings gap must be the result of: (a) the reversal of the positive effects of human capital gains during the 1960s and 1970s; (b) a decline in enforcement of affirmative action; or (c) altogether new factors not operating during the earlier era.

The evidence used to support the case for convergence in black–white earnings was drawn from aggregate data on relative labor market earnings. The mean income ratio for black males and white males rose from about 55 percent for all workers in 1950 to 66 percent by 1975 (Smith and Welch, 1977, 1978). The mean income ratio for black females and white females rose from 61 percent in 1950 to 95 percent by 1975, close to parity (Smith, 1978).

Figures 13.3 and 13.4 show these upward trends. Figure 13.3 plots the ratio of black–white mean incomes for all male workers and for full-time, year-round male workers. The steady increase in the earnings ratio is sharpest for year-round, full-time employees after 1964, the year of the passage of the most comprehensive US civil rights law since the Reconstruction period. Thereafter, and into the 1980s, the ratio levels off for all workers but maintains a slight positive slope for year-round, full-time workers.

Figure 13.4 reveals a sharper upward trend in the ratio of black–white mean incomes among females, a trend that began its upward climb well before the enactment of the 1964 Civil Rights Bill and that levels off and even turns downward by the late 1970s. The data from these two figures are the source of the claim during the late 1970s and early 1980s that black–white earnings were converging. The upward trends were extrapolated forward in time to envision the prospect of complete elimination of the gap. The debate then turned to how to explain the change in the economic status of blacks. What accounted for the improvement?

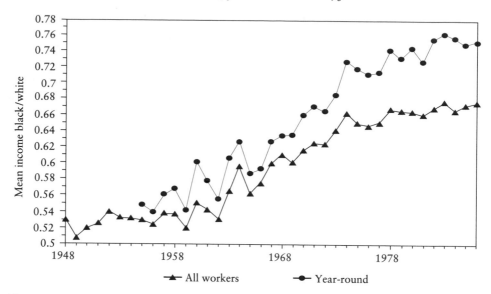

Figure 13.3   Ratio of black to white mean income, males, all workers and year-round
full-time workers, 1948–1986.

Source: Authors' computations from US Bureau of the Census, *Money Income of Households,
Families and Persons in the United States, 1987.* Current Population Reports, Series P60–162.
Washington DC, US Government Printing Office, 1988.

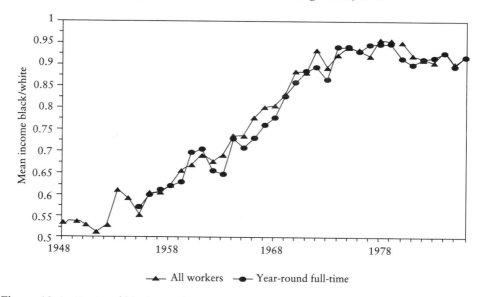

Figure 13.4   Ratio of black to white mean income, females, all workers and year-round
full-time workers, 1948–1986.

Source: Authors' computations from US Bureau of the Census, *Money Income of Households,
Families and Persons in the United States, 1987.* Current Population Reports, Series P60–162.
Washington DC, US Government Printing Office, 1988.

Two major competing hypotheses were advanced. The first was the position taken by James Smith and Finis Welch (1977, 1978) at RAND and UCLA respectively. They argued that the improved quantity and quality of black education, combined with South–North and rural–urban migration of blacks during the 1940s, 1950s, and 1960s, led to a decline in the average productivity differential between blacks and whites. This in turn led to a decline in the earnings gap. At the core of the Smith and Welch view was the decisive role they gave to "human capital" differences (which they associated largely with years of formal schooling in explaining average racial wage differences). The human capital gap was being closed as black schooling improved, ostensibly due to the rising quality of Southern schools attended by blacks as well as the beneficial effects of black migration to other regions where schools were superior.

Smith and Welch also argued that there was a "vintage effect," claiming that younger cohorts of blacks had educational experiences more similar to comparably aged whites, and therefore had more similar human capital endowments and more similar labor market experiences. The earnings gap for younger blacks, then, would be expected to be narrower than the earnings gap for older blacks. In general, Smith (1978) concluded, "Blacks are becoming less distinguishable from whites in at least one relevant index of performance – market earnings." The underlying reason, for Smith and Welch, was the closing of the gap between blacks and whites in terms of human capital acquisition.

Smith and Welch's Panglossian vision of black economic progress is rooted in a perspective that downplays any significant role for discrimination in labor markets as the source of racial economic inequality. Discrimination was, in their estimation, solely a *pre-* or *extra*-market phenomenon and an important factor in the historical disparity in schooling opportunities for black and white youths. In their view, the labor market generally processes all individuals with reasonable fairness (or *market* fairness) based on the individual's productivity-linked characteristics. Thus, as the historical differential in schooling opportunities apparently declined, so did the fundamental basis for earnings inequality decline as well.

The Smith and Welch perspective leads to the conclusion that the labor market generally affords equal opportunity. As the pre-market environment comes to provide equal opportunity as well, Smith and Welch's analysis suggests that equal results will be the outcome. For Smith and Welch there is no necessary inconsistency between equal opportunity and equal results. Furthermore, there is no need for any special programmatic intervention for blacks, aside from continuing to ensure that educational opportunities for blacks move toward matching those available for whites. The labor market works and needs no corrective measures such as affirmative action or anti-discrimination measures.

An alternative explanation was provided by Harvard economist Richard Freeman (1981), who argued that the trend toward economic convergence was attributable to a decline in labor market discrimination engineered by government anti-discrimination enforcement measures. In short, Freeman also took the position that equal opportunity would lead to equal results, but for equal opportunity to prevail government intervention would be required in employment markets.

Although disagreeing on the causes, Freeman, and Smith and Welch agreed on the "fact" of a positive trajectory for black economic progress in the 1960s and 1970s. But there were dissenters, especially the authors of this chapter, who argued that the evidence used to make the case for convergence was misleading at best. An initial basis for the dissent was the discovery that the data on which Smith and Welch, and Freeman based their findings did not account for zero earners – persons continuously unemployed or out of the labor force during the year. Black experience of long-duration joblessness is much higher than that for whites. Consequently, earnings and income ratios calculated exclusively from data on working persons will be biased by the selection effect. The bias tends to work by raising black–white earnings ratios artificially.

For males, black labor force drop-outs are disproportionately from the lower end of the income spectrum, while white labor force drop-outs are disproportionately from the higher end of the wage spectrum. When the earnings time series is corrected to account for males with no earnings in a given year, the change in the black to white mean ratio vanishes during the decade 1967 through 1977. Indeed, the black–white earnings ratio for males was slightly lower in 1977 (55 percent) than in 1967 (57 percent) after the correction (Darity, 1980, p. 164). By 1990 the black–white male earnings ratio for full-time, year-round workers was 70 percent, but for all males, with or without earnings, it was only 60 percent (US Bureau of the Census, 1992, p. 57, table 11).

For females, the Freeman and the Smith and Welch black–white earnings and income ratios were biased by the dramatic growth in the entry of white women into the labor force after the 1950s. Black women had long had high labor force participation rates (Darity, 1980, pp. 159–67). The time-series data from 1953 through 1977, unadjusted for zero income recipients among females, give the impression that the earnings ratio of black–white females soared remarkably from 55 percent in 1955 to 94 percent by 1975. When the series is adjusted to account for women with no incomes in a given year it flattens significantly; the ratio already was 84 percent as early as 1953, never dips below 70 percent during the interval, and was at 94 percent by 1977. Again, by 1990 the black–white female earnings ratio for full-time year-round workers was 90 percent, and for all women it was a slightly lower 87 percent (US Bureau of the Census, 1992, p. 57, table 11). If anything, both types of time series indicated evidence of a decline in the ratio in the 1990s. To extrapolate on the basis of current trends would lead one to conclude that divergence, not convergence, is the trend for the future.

We reiterate that an additional basis for skepticism about the convergence hypothesis is the fact that data on black family incomes have never displayed the same pattern of gap closure as have the data on individual earnings or on income for persons with earnings or income. Between the mid-1960s and 1980 the black–white family income ratio stayed in a rather narrow range between 61 and 64 percent. During the 1982 recession the ratio dipped below 60 percent. By

1990 the mean black–white family income ratio was 62 percent and the median black–white family income ratio was only 58 percent (US Bureau of the Census, 1992, p. 56, table 10). In 1980 one of the authors of this chapter made the following observation, suggesting the superiority of relative family income as a gauge of relative racial well-being:

> Although neither income nor earnings inequality between black and white women measured in per capita terms have been great in the postwar era, inequality in living conditions is probably quite substantial. This is a consequence of one of the short-comings of per capita income as an index of relative well being. It ignores how people come together socially and hence economically. White women combine their incomes with white men far more frequently than black women combine their incomes with white men. In fact, the large proportion of single parent, female-headed black families indicates that black women combine their incomes with those of black men less often than white women combine theirs with white men. (Darity, 1980, p. 176)

The incidence of females heading black families underwent a sharp upturn in the 1970s, accelerating throughout the 1980s, with no evidence of a peak in sight. We computed comparative estimates of the percentage of black families headed by women from the Census Bureau's *Current Population Survey* for 1976 and 1985. Nationally, the incidence of female-headed families rose from 36 to 45 percent of all black families. Particularly dramatic increases took place in the West and North Central regions. In the West the incidence rose from 25 to 47 percent and in the North Central region the incidence rose from 39 to 52 percent. For white families, the direction of movement was the same but the magnitude was not the same. White families headed by females rose from 11 percent in 1976 to 13 percent in 1985.

Data from the *Current Population Survey* (see US Bureau of the Census, 1992, Table 10, p. 56) indicate that the racial income disparity is much narrower among married couple families. In 1991, the black–white ratio of mean income for married couple families was 80 percent; the ratio of medians was 83 percent. However, less than half of all black families, 47 percent (3.57 million out of 7.47 million), were married couple families. Since a near majority of black families are now female-headed, evidence about approaching parity in relative incomes between black and white two parent families is misleading. The growing incidence of female-headed black families signals the effects of a process we refer to as the marginalization of black males. This process bears an intimate relationship to the fragile status of the entire black population in the United States, whether male or female. Economic manifestations of the marginalization process are plentiful.

Consider the absolute decline in labor force participation rates (LFPRS) for males of both races that began in the early 1960s and the relative decline that occurred after the mid-1960s. Between 1954 and 1966 the ratio of black–white male LFPRs held fairly constant at 98 percent. But over the course of the next decade LFPRs fell much faster for black males than for white males. As a result, despite the fact that after 1976 LFPRs for black males seem to have bottomed out, while white male rates continued to fall, a wide gap persists because of the sharp difference in rates of decline between 1966 and 1976, the very period that Freeman and Smith and Welch have touted as the period of dramatic progress for blacks.

By 1985 the employment–population ratio for adult black males was only 55 percent, while it was 70 percent for adult white males. Almost one out of every six black men between the ages of 25 and 54 reported zero earnings for 1984. By 1990 one out of every three black men 15 years old and over reported no earnings (US Bureau of the Census, 1992, p. 57, table 11). There also appears to be a bifurcation among black males based on credentials, between those with a college education or better and those with a high school education or less. The former group has far more earnings experience in the labor market than the latter. Pecuniary prospects are dim for young black males with a high school education or less.

In a very interesting and revealing study, Bluestone et al. (1991) have provided a typology of Metropolitan Statistical Areas (MSAs) based on growth rates of total non-agricultural employment and total manufacturing employment in the 1980s. They classified (1,1) cities as those with the slowest growth rates in overall and manufacturing employment, (2,2) cities as those with mid-range growth rates in both categories, and (3,3) cities as the fastest-growing in both categories. They then compared unemployment rates by race for males 20 years old with less than a college education in each type of city.

The results that they report are provisional because the sample cell sizes become relatively small for black males. But in the (1,1) cities they find that among 20-year-olds the black male unemployment rate was 42 percent while the white male unemployment rate was 4.1 percent. In (2,2) cities the black male unemployment rate was 26.5 percent while the white male unemployment rate was 3.5 percent for the same age group. Finally, in (3,3) cities the black male unemployment rate was 17.9 percent while the white male unemployment rate was only 1.5 percent, twelve times lower than the black rate! (Bluestone et al., 1991).

Conditions became so patently bleak that even Richard Freeman performed a complete flip-flop on his research agenda. In the 1970s Freeman sought to explain what he labeled the "dramatic economic progress"of black Americans. Now he was asking, in collaboration with John Bound, "What went wrong? Why have relative earnings and employment fallen for young black males?" (Bound and Freeman, 1992).

Exposure to college education does not alter comparative conditions substantially for black males. Black males 25 years of age or older with one to three years of college education and with positive earnings received, on average, $22,979 in 1990. White males 25 years of age or older with earnings, *who had dropped out of high school*, had mean earnings of $19,270, about $3,700 less. White males who completed high school earned more than $3,000 more than black males with some college education. Nor does completing college close the gap. A black male with four years of college and positive earnings in 1990 would have received mean earnings of $32,259, more than $10,000 below the mean of $43,919 earned by white male college graduates with positive earnings (US Bureau of the Census, 1992, table 12, pp. 47, 52).

Convergence in educational characteristics need not translate into convergence in earnings. Bound and Freeman (1992, p. 16) acknowledge that the increasingly depressed labor market experience for young black males is not due to a corresponding deterioration in their relative quality as potential employees: "We find little support for the hypothesis that deteriorated labor market skills of young blacks due, say, to poor schooling, worsened family background resources, or increased drug use explains their declining economic position."

Two key points need to be made. First, the Bound–Freeman (1992) discussion implies that the current trajectory will only worsen as more and more black males come into the labor market from younger cohorts that are now experiencing even greater resource deprivation. Second, and more fundamental, independent of the relative quality black males present to the labor market, processes persist that exclude them from comparable participation with non-black males with similar productivity-linked characteristics. To put it bluntly, discrimination in a comprehensive sense lies at the core of matters, not just at the point of employment but throughout an entire range of stages that affect labor market outcomes. American society is quite distant from attaining a pure equal opportunity environment, never mind correcting for historically inherited inequalities.

Current discrimination, while creating a disadvantage for the group against which it is directed, necessarily creates a corresponding advantage for another group. In 1991 the Urban Institute conducted an audit study of entry-level job access in the cities of Chicago and Washington, DC. The researchers paired young black and white males (19–24 years of age) with fake, identical credentials and had them apply for the same jobs. The subjects applied for a total of 1,052 jobs. Treatment of the applicants appeared to be neutral 73 percent of the time, but black males faced discriminatory treatment 20 percent of the time, while white males faced discriminatory treatment only 7 percent of the time. Therefore, black males were three times as likely to face job bias. There were also higher rates of discrimination against black males in white-collar jobs or jobs involving direct client contact (Lawlor and Pitts, 1991, p. 1A).

Gerald Jaynes has written, "The heralded recovery of the mid-1980s apparently improved the position of white low skilled men but not black. Why? We do not know" (Jaynes, 1990, p. 24). But we can make a highly educated guess. The changing structure of the US economy was narrowing the availability of well paid blue-collar jobs, jobs that pay well without requiring advanced educational credentials. White labor's discriminatory behavior would naturally intensify under such conditions, particularly if the heralded recovery of the mid-1980s did not mean a sharp reversal of the deindustrialization of the US economy. It was simply a classic case of protecting one's occupational turf from darker rivals, and it reveals the endogeneity of discriminatory practices. While much economic research proceeds as if discrimination operates at a constant level of intensity or does not exist at all, a more plausible analysis would indicate that the degree of discrimination fluctuates, in part, with the nature of aggregate conditions of employment, without disappearing.

The only period where measured levels of in-market discrimination against blacks declined significantly since Emancipation was during the decade immediately following passage of the Civil Rights Act of 1964. Thereafter, the level of labor market discrimination has shown no further tendency to decline significantly. From about 1975 to the present black men typically have lost 12–15 percent in earnings due to labor market discrimination (Darity, 1998).

THE WIDENING OF THE RACIAL EARNINGS GAP

More recent studies on black–white economic inequality have focused on the reversal in the pattern of alleged convergence in earnings between black and white males in the 1980s. The puzzle is: why is there now evidence of a renewed widening of the gap in black and white male earnings? The thrust of a substantial portion of recent work on black–white economic inequality is to explain divergence in the 1980s by restoring the pure human capital explanation of racial economic disparity. Correspondingly, the operation of the labor market is immunized from playing a role in directly producing racial economic inequality. The upshot is the claim that the persistent black male lag in earnings is due to deficiencies in productivity characteristics of black males, rather than a failure of the market to offer them rewards parallel to those of white males with equivalent productivity characteristics.

The skills mismatch hypothesis is used in this context in several studies. According to this line of argument, black males possess significantly fewer skills on average than white males. In the 1980s relative rewards for highly skilled workers rose vis-à-vis less-skilled workers. Since black males are disproportionately represented among less-skilled workers, their earnings have fallen relative to white males as relative rewards for skills have moved in favor of those with higher levels of skill acquisition.

Skills are measured in many of these studies by Armed Forces Qualification Test (AFQT) scores available in the 1980 National Longitudinal Survey of Youth (NLSY). Inclusion of these scores in regression analyses that seek to examine racial earnings differences virtually eliminates unexplained residual differences in earnings between blacks and whites. Studies by O'Neill (1990), Maxwell (1994), Ferguson (1995), and Neal and Johnson (1995) all reproduce this same result: skill differentials (or, for O'Neill and for Maxwell, "schooling quality" differentials) obviate any important role for discrimination in labor markets as an explanation for earnings gaps.

The "returns to skills" explanation for widening earnings gaps has received prominent attention. According to this line of argument, black males possess significantly fewer skills on average than white males. Part of the reason for the focus on black and white males is that these groups show the largest earnings disparities. Black–white disparities among females are not as pronounced (Darity, 1980).

Support for the argument is not unequivocal. Using the Panel Study of Income Dynamics (PSID) data, Card and Lemieux (1996) estimate the returns to unobserved and observed skills for males with earnings from 1979 to 1985. Their hypothesis is that if the cause of the widening racial wage gap between blacks and whites in recent years is due to the increase in returns to skills, then one would expect to find that the black–white wage gap is proportional to the returns to skills across various years for a common cohort of workers. Therefore, they conclude that the racial wage gap cannot be due to productivity differences because in their sample they estimate little change in the wage gap even in an era when returns to skills were increasing from 5 to 10 percent.

The fact that Card and Lemieux do not find an increase in the wage gap for a common cohort of workers suggests that the observed increase in the wage gap among different cohorts of workers must be attributable to the differing experiences of younger black workers. This issue is addressed explicitly by Holzer (1994), who examines a variety of explanations for the deterioration of earnings among young blacks. He concludes that productivity-related or skills explanations are insufficient to account for the rising racial wage gaps and points at least in part to discriminatory processes (via networks) that must be at play.

The reversal in the narrowing trends in racial earnings gaps has brought forth new efforts to explain the phenomenon. Explanations include shifting industry and regional employment, a decline in the real minimum wage, deunionization, a growing supply of black educated workers relative to white workers, and increased criminal activities among school drop-outs (Bound and Freeman, 1992). Another explanation, the *spatial* mismatch hypothesis, flows from the ghetto dispersal versus ghetto development debate of the 1960s (Kain, 1968; Harrison, 1972, 1974).

The question for the 1960s was whether residential segregation or employment discrimination caused the low incomes of blacks. The question for the 1990s is whether concentration in inner cities and/or industries where there are job losses or supply-side factors, such as high reservation wages and/or the inducements of crime, is the cause. The spatial mismatch debate has many of the features of the black underclass debate, where the issues of contention are structural/demand-side factors versus behavioral/supply-side factors (Fainstein, 1987; Darity et al., 1994).

The key piece of evidence underlying the spatial mismatch hypothesis is the apparent loss of inner-city, low-wage jobs as employment expands in the suburbs (Kasarda, 1985; Wilson, 1987). David Ellwood (1986, p. 181) tested the hypothesis and concluded: "The problem is not space. It's race" (Ellwood, 1986, p. 181). Ihlanfeldt and Sjoquist (1990) do find a positive effect of proximity to a job on black and white youth employment rates. They find that 33–54 percent of the racial gap in youth employment rates can be explained by spatial separation from jobs. They conclude: "poor job access is a significant contributor to the joblessness of black youth" (Ihlanfeldt and Sjoquist, 1990, p. 268).

Still, a comprehensive review of the recent evidence provides mixed support for the spatial mismatch hypothesis (Moss and Tilly, 1991). In contrast, the evidence against the *skills* mismatch hypothesis is more compelling. This hypothesis states that technological change has been biased against low-skilled workers, suggesting a decline in the demand for young blacks, who are disproportionately low-skilled. However, the greatest shifts in demand away from low-skilled workers occurred during the period when racial earnings gaps were narrowing. In more recent years, while racial earnings gaps continue to widen, the pace of skill restructuring has slowed markedly (Howell, 1994).

An incidental finding of many of the human capital-based studies of racial earnings inequality is that factors such as neighborhood or census tract characteristics, percentage black, or degree of segregation enter as statistically significant variables in earnings regressions. The justification for inclusion of measures of segregation or concentration of minorities appeals to the social isolation conjecture of William J. Wilson (1993) and/or the residential segregation thesis of Douglas Massey (1990). Because the effects of concentration of blacks on employment or earnings tend to be negative, the *ex-post* theory about the signs obtained relates to the various alleged disutilities associated with living in segregated or predominantly black neighborhoods.

Directions for Future Research

Clearly, there are numerous unresolved issues in the labor econometrics literature concerning the reasons for the increase in racial inequality in recent years. Five stand out prominently, on which we comment below.

Skills Mismatch and General Inequality

Is the skills mismatch hypothesis valid as an explanation for changes in general inequality? If not, then it cannot motivate the analysis of black–white male earnings disparity in the 1980s. In particular, if a shift toward the demand for skills did take place, given the claim of these researchers that there was convergence before the 1980s, the shift must be timed precisely with the 1980s.

Times Series and Test Scores

There is an anomaly in time-series results in contrast with cross-section results. Time-series data indicate that black standardized test scores rose relative to white scores in the 1980s, but earnings did not do so. The regression results that appear to vanquish the effects of discrimination all are based on cross-sectional data.

Test Scores as Proxies for Race

Take any standardized test on which blacks do worse on average than whites. One suspicion is that any of these scores included in a regression analysis would have the effect of eliminating evidence of discriminatory residuals. But if, for example, AFQT scores are endogenous outcomes generated by processes similar to those generating earnings, these models are misspecified (Oust-like models that use IQ as a proxy for "ability"). Rodgers and Spriggs (1996) demonstrate how powerfully results are altered by recognizing the endogeneity of AFQT scores. Moreover, when *psychological capital* is also taken into account in the process of wage determination (by psychological capital we mean motivation and self-esteem), discriminantory residuals re-emerge even when AFQT scores are included in wage equations (see Goldsmith et al., 1997).

Unmeasured Effort

Patrick Mason (1994) argues that a previously unobserved variable that had been excluded from wage equations is effort. He attempts to demonstrate that black effort is greater for attainment of given characteristics because blacks face greater obstacles. The obstacles are embodied in disadvantageous "social capital," not in the narrow sense of neoclassical economists, but in the richer sociological sense. For Mason (1994), "social capital" should be understood as: "The importance of having access to individuals embedded...in positions of power and authority. Consequently, equivalent scores between black and white males may actually correspond to *greater* black male personal productivity-linked skills."

Rodgers and Spriggs (1996) show that there is a systematic racial difference in the capacity of AFQT scores to predict earnings when they estimate separate structural equations for AFQT for blacks and whites with education, age, school quality, and family background measures as the independent variables. AFQT is a much weaker predictor of earnings outcomes for blacks than for whites. This is consistent with the general observation that most standardized tests are weaker predictors of black than white performance in a variety of areas. Previous research has been predicated on the assumption that there is no racial difference in the predictive power of AFQT scores.

Coupled with the fact that employers would not observe the AFQT scores in the NLSY, Rodgers and Spriggs (1996) argue that AFQT is a biased predictor of black skills, since the coefficients in the black AFQT equation tend to generate lower scores for given education, age, school quality, and family background characteristics. They propose that a non-discriminatory weighting of African American characteristics would involve generating hypothetical black scores on AFQT by using the coefficients from the white equation. When the hypothetical scores are inserted in the wage or earnings equation, racial wage gaps re-emerge that point toward indirect statistical evidence of discrimination against blacks (see also Maume et al., 1996, for a similar finding). Rodgers and Spriggs (1996) also point out that the military itself "does not use the AFQT score as the only indicator in placing military personnel in different occupations" because it is a far from comprehensive predictor of performance.

Wealth as an Omitted Variable

We remain curious about what results would be generated in earnings equations that decompose racial earnings differentials if another omitted variable entered into the analysis: wealth. However, oddly enough, in a case where reported wealth from the 1978 NLSY is included in a simultaneous equation model of wages and psychological well-being, the wealth variable is grossly insignificant (Goldsmith et al., 1997). It remains to be seen if that result holds with an older cohort with self-reports on wealth. The most powerful adverse effects of the racial wealth disadvantage fall on patterns of self-employment, access to higher education, and access to quality health care.

CONCLUSIONS

In summary, the recent explanations for the widening gap between black and white earnings have focused on the alleged human capital roots of low black wages and salaries. Alternative explanations that focus on institutional and structural deficits of labor markets and employers have largely been ignored. While many analysts claim by deduction that the widening earnings gaps between whites and blacks must not be caused by discrimination, racism, or other institutionalized factors, we remain unconvinced. There is persuasive evidence that the US anti-discrimination effort was nearly dismantled precisely during the period when racial gaps earnings reopened in the 1980s. We are also dissuaded because the process of eliminating explanations by focusing on individual deficiencies of minorities themselves leaves much to be desired.

More reasonable as an explanation of how and why racial earnings gaps widened is that white males lost jobs. Put simply, the widening of the racial earnings gap is inextricably linked to the widening of overall inequality and the loss of white middle-class employment opportunities. White males were squeezed out of the vanishing middle-class jobs, which had been their purview, especially well paid blue-collar jobs. They, in turn, were then crowded into a lower tier of occupations that they would not otherwise have held. They squeezed black males out of those jobs.

In fact, white males have begun to appropriate a set of jobs that were previously held by blacks and are making them "white male" jobs. Black males and females in the most tenuous labor market positions have been pushed out, both by whites and by immigrants from South America and Southeast Asia. Furthermore, those black males who had held blue-collar jobs and made the transition into white-collar employment actually went from operative positions to sales positions that paid less. In contrast, white males who made a similar transition went from blue-collar operative positions to sales positions that paid them more (Cotton, 1988).

In a sense, the argument here is that exclusion (discrimination) is endogenously linked to the employment needs of non-black males. As the occupational distribution eliminates jobs traditionally held by white males, they secure less attractive jobs at the expense of black males. The force of discrimination is then seen as instrumental. Its application intensifies when the dominant group's status is threatened, either because of improved productivity-linked characteristics of members of a potential rival group or because of a diminution in the job opportunities of members of the dominant group.

The endogenous model of discrimination also finds support in other contexts. For example, a study by Dhesi and Singh (1989) of economic inequality between religious caste groups in Delhi, India, in 1970 revealed negligible evidence of discriminatory earnings differentials for the lowest Hindu caste members despite a wide gap in earnings between them and higher caste members. Their educational levels were so low that they would rarely be direct rivals of members of the higher castes for preferred occupations. In a sense, there was no "need" for upper-caste Hindus to exercise direct discriminatory actions in the labor market toward the lowest-caste members because the latter could not even get in the game. In contrast, Dhesi and Singh found substantial evidence of discriminatory differentials in earnings between Sikhs and upper-caste Hindus. Sikhs, unlike lower-caste Hindus, on average possessed the education levels that would make them stronger and immediate rivals for the occupations typically held by upper-caste Hindus.

The endogenous model of discrimination suggests a rich and as yet largely unexplored research agenda with US data. One way to approach this is to estimate discriminatory earnings residuals over time and then see if the variation through time can be explained by changing labor market conditions for white males. Do the discriminatory residuals for blacks become larger when economic times are harder for whites (and white males in particular)? If so, there would be strong evidence to support the linkage we hypothesize between widening interracial inequality and widening general inequality.

14

Rediscovering Rural America

Bonnie Thornton Dill

Although concern about poverty in the United States has focused attention primarily on urban neighborhoods where the largest number of poor people live and where poverty is most visible, poverty in rural communities is severe and connected in many ways to the urban issues that capture attention. For decades, central cities have been the destination of choice for displaced rural workers seeking better wages, opportunities, and living conditions. Appalachian coal miners, black sharecroppers, Native Americans who left the reservations, and Latino farmworkers flocked to urban America in search of jobs and economic opportunity. Economic transformations of the past two decades, however, have created a much more complex flow of human resources.

Sizable numbers of Northern blacks are returning to Southern rural home-places (Stack, 1996). Latinos are moving from cities to rural communities: in California they are seeking agricultural work (Allensworth and Rochin, 1996); in the Midwest they are finding jobs in manufacturing (Green, 1994; Gouveia and Stull, 1995; Stull et al., 1995; Amato, 1996); in New York they are leaving cities in search of more affordable rural housing (Fitchen, 1995). At the same time, educated rural youth continue to leave their home communities and migrate to cities in search of improved employment opportunities (Pollard and O'Hare, 1990; Lichter et al., 1995). Some rural communities are experiencing a growth in newly arrived professionals, vacation home buyers, retirees, and commuters. The impact on poor women, children, and families who live there, however, is often mixed (Bradshaw, 1993).

Prolonged economic growth in the USA since 1945 has resulted in a pattern of bifurcated development in rural areas, with some areas growing and flourishing and others remaining economically stagnant or declining. This chapter focuses on the people and communities that have been hardest hit by industrial changes and contemporary economic restructuring. The stresses in these communities are characterized by a decline in resource-based industries, the loss of manufacturing jobs, increases in low-wage service sector work, limited economic development, precipitous declines in family farms, a steady decrease of small-scale rural entrepreneurs, a shrinking rural middle class, and a widening gap between rural and urban income.

Finally, rural areas are also characterized by patterns of long-term, persistent poverty concentrated in particular rural places: the southern black belt, the Lower Rio Grande Valley, in Appalachia and Native American Indian reservations in the West and throughout the country. The poverty that has engulfed these and other communities like them affects the live of hundreds of thousands of men, women, and especially children.

In this chapter, the term rural is used interchangeably with the term non-metropolitan. The metropolitan–non-metropolitan distinction refers to terminology developed by the US Office of Management and Budget in 1983. Metropolitan statistical areas usually include an urbanized area with a population nucleus of 50,000 or more, as well as nearby communities or counties that are economically and socially integrated with that nucleus. Non-metropolitan counties are not linked with large cities or with communities closely tied to large cities (Duncan, 1992).

Rural poverty is concentrated in the South, where over one-half (53.6 percent) of the rural poor live (US Department of Agriculture (USDA), 1997). Its rates also tend to be highest in areas with high proportions of minorities, children, elderly, the less educated, and workers employed in extractive industries and government (Lichter and McLaughlin, 1995). Native Americans, blacks, and Latinos living in rural communities are among the poorest people in the United States. Their poverty rates are almost three times greater than those of rural non-Hispanic whites (USDA, 1997).

Rural children have a higher risk of poverty than urban children. In 1995, 3.2 million rural children under the age of 18 (22.4 percent) lived in families with incomes below the poverty level (USDA, 1997). Although rural children are more likely than urban children to live in two parent families with at least one employed adult, 59.9 percent of rural poor children live in single parent families. And rural family incomes remain at or near the poverty line.

Many of the places where these children and their families live are places that have had high concentrations of poor people over long periods of time. In 1990, these long-term, persistently poor counties had an average poverty rate of 28.5 per cent – a rate more than double that of all other rural counties and many central cities – and were home to 30 percent of the rural poor (Summers, 1995). The poverty of these communities is the result of years of disinvestment. In some places, it represents the continuation of patterns of subsistence that resulted from the mechanization of agriculture and natural resource production generations earlier. In other cases it reflects a legacy of racial segregation and disenfranchisement (Swanson et al., 1995). In still other cases, it is the result of more recent structural transformations in the manufacturing and service sectors accompanied by slow economic growth and high unemployment. In most places today, it is the result of the intersection of several of these factors.

Links between children, families, and communities are vital to understanding and addressing poverty in rural America. This chapter seeks to provide a framework for beginning to understand rural poverty – specifically the poverty of rural children, women and families, and communities.

RURAL ECONOMIES IN THE 1980s AND 1990s: THE EFFECTS OF RESTRUCTURING

Despite popular imagery, rural communities today are not organized primarily around family farms and agricultural production. In fact, fewer than one-third of the jobs in rural communities are in any way related to agriculture. The other two-thirds of rural workers are employed in the manufacturing or service-producing sectors of the economy (Pulver, 1995). The result is that rural economies were as deeply affected by global economic restructuring of the past two decades as were urban economies. Beginning in the late 1970s, rural communities experienced an accelerated loss of farms and farm jobs, a loss of factory work and jobs in natural resource extraction (such as mining, forestry, and fishing), and a growth in low-paid service jobs (Gorham, 1992). Thus, while rural workers were more likely to be employed than urban workers, low wages combined with low levels of transfer benefits kept many rural workers below or near the poverty level (Adams and Duncan, 1992; Tickamyer, 1992).

The income gap between urban and rural workers increased in the 1980s as a result of economic restructuring. Rural areas particularly hard hit by restructuring were those whose economies were not diverse but were structured around one or two industries. Additionally, restructuring had a significant impact in rural communities because service sector growth generated mostly low-tech, low-wage jobs. The 1980s ushered in another pattern in rural communities. The flight of industries and people from the snowbelt to the sunbelt meant that some rural communities experienced considerable economic growth, while others declined (Bradshaw, 1993). According to a report by the Economic Research Service of the USDA (1997), rural economies have benefited from the economic expansion of the 1990s, in that they have experienced slightly greater employment growth and wage gain than urban areas as a whole.

Despite these encouraging signs, however, rural communities still lag far behind urban ones. For example, rural median household income is only about 77 percent of that of urban areas, and for black households and female-headed households rural income is only half the rural median. The poverty rate for rural children has remained virtually unchanged, in part because rural workers are still more likely to receive wages that either maintain their family in poverty or lift them only slightly above the poverty line (USDA, 1997, p. 5). In fact, rural communities may still be distinguished from urban ones by several basic features:

- higher poverty rates;
- more long-term, persistent poverty;
- less spatial concentration of poor people;
- fewer of the behavioral patterns associated with concentrated urban poverty;
- people of color are poorer than both their urban counterparts and their non-Hispanic white rural neighbors.

EXPLANATIONS OF RURAL POVERTY

In explaining rural poverty there are two approaches in the recent literature. One approach is examining the opportunity structures of rural places, through the study of the historical and contemporary patterns of economic and social organization. The second approach is assessing the human capital resources of rural people, through analyzing education, work experience, family structure, and cultural patterns.

In providing an overview of rural poverty in the 1980s, Deavers and Hoppe (1992) state unequivocally that its causes involve an underinvestment in both the human capital of rural people and the economic structure of rural places, which relied heavily on low-skilled, low-paid manufacturing jobs. Tickamyer (1992) focuses her research on the structure of labor markets, arguing that "people are often poor because there are limited opportunities to work and receive wages in their own labor market" (p. 55). Based on her analysis, race and gender differences were more likely a result of differences in the opportunities for work within various labor markets than of the characteristics of the people themselves.

Lichter et al. (1993) find that although individual rural workers have human capital deficits in education, cognitive skills, and work experience, they receive fewer economic rewards than their urban counterparts for the work experience and education that they do have. Lichter and Costanzo (1987; see also Shapiro, 1989) show that non-metropolitan poverty levels are higher than metropolitan poverty levels, regardless of education, and that at each educational level non-metropolitan rates of underemployment and unemployment exceed metro rates. Rural communities offer low returns to human capital because rural labor markets are characterized by a proportionately higher share of jobs in periphery or competitive industries, low rates of worker unionization, a lack of diversity of employment opportunities, and high levels of occupational and industrial segregation by race and gender in geographically and socially isolated locations (Summers et al., 1993).

Living in rural communities increases the likelihood of experiencing long-term poverty. Using the Panel Study of Income Dynamics data from 1967 to 1985, Adams and Duncan (1992) examined long-term poverty in metropolitan and non-metropolitan areas and found that, in contrast to the long-term urban poor, rural people who experienced long-term poverty had higher labor force participation rates. Low earnings, low transfer benefits, a large gender gap in wage rates, and a growth in the number of female-headed families are some of the factors which suggest that labor market strategies alone will not raise wages sufficiently to end rural poverty.

Lichter and McLaughlin (1995) sought to examine the impact of deindustrialization and the shift to a low-wage service economy on rural communities through the 1980s. Using 1980 and 1990 census data, they found that deindustrialization had both direct and indirect effects. Its direct effects were most visible in the declines in rural income and the shift from manufacturing to low-wage service jobs. However, employment data alone do not explain the differences in rural and urban poverty rates. Instead, they found that the growth of female-headed families in rural communities had a larger single effect on poverty rates than the demographic profile of community residents (which included race, age, mobility, education, and region), the industrial structure, or the percentage employed. In their view, "the effects of industrial restructuring are partly indirect." Restructuring has affected female employment opportunities. For example, it has caused a decline in factory work and increased the number of low-wage service jobs. When combined with a growth in female-headed families, the result is an increased likelihood of single mothers working for below poverty wages or choosing to rely on welfare.

Lichter and McLaughlin (1995) conclude that addressing the problems of poor rural people and places will require more than traditional labor market or human capital development strategies. It will require developing strategies that meet the needs of women and children. Citing the work of Janet Fitchen, in which she showed that rural single mothers were not being reached by anti-poverty strategies that stressed job growth, Lichter and McLaughlin (1995) suggest that special attention should be paid to developing policies that will facilitate the entry of women into the labor market, especially policies that would address such needs as childcare and health benefits.

Brown and Hirschl (1995) offer an analysis similar to many others, but they conclude that while both the concentration of people with limited education, skills, and other human capital and the organization of local economies around low-paid work are commonly associated with poverty in both rural and urban areas, a full explanation must also include other aspects of rural community life. In their view, such an explanation would require an examination of the effects of social isolation on access to and use of social welfare benefits and the effects of historical patterns of class and race.

The intersection of race and class is also central to the thesis of Hyland and Timberlake (1993). In their essay on the rural Mississippi Delta, they concluded that understanding the social conditions in that region requires paying considerable attention to the social groupings whose identities, actions, and relations have been formed within a rigid system of race, ethnic, class, and gender stratification. For example, they argue that the role of race and class relations in determining access to educational and political resources in the region has been fundamental (p. 77).

THE CONTINUING LEGACY OF RACE

Questions of labor market structure and human capital have been central to examining the socio-economic well-being of people of color living in non-metropolitan areas. Although urban–rural differences have moderated some-what in the past thirty years (Jensen and Tienda, 1989), the poverty rates of rural minorities exceed or equal those of both their urban counterparts and non-metropolitan whites.

According to Jensen and Tienda (1989, p. 529), rural minorities are particu-larly vulnerable to shifts in the economy. They "sit toward the bottom of the hiring queue" (see also Sayer et al., 1998). They are the last hired during periods of economic expansion and the first fired during economic retrenchment. For the most part, however, researchers agree that while improved human resources and enhanced labor market opportunities are necessary to enhance the position of rural minorities, they are not sufficient.

Consistent with the idea that "development is the result of more than a market-based economic process and involves a set of economic relations operat-ing within a historical, sociopolitical and spatial setting," Swanson et al. (1995, p. 82) seek to account for historical patterns of social relations which have relegated blacks to marginal positions in the Southern rural economy. They use the concept "legacy" to capture the history of slavery, sharecropping, segrega-tion, marginal employment opportunities, limited educational options, forced migration and labor, social ostracism, and systematic discrimination that has characterized the black experience in the South. And, in contrast to most researchers who treat racial concentration as an independent variable, they treat it as a dependent variable, examining the relationship of legacy to the concentration of African Americans in a county. They find, as a result of their analysis, that legacy persists as an explanation for high poverty rates of both metropolitan and non-metropolitan areas in the South that have high concentra-tions of African Americans. They argue that their findings provide support for social policies that focus on region as a basis for public entitlements in order to correct injustices of the past (Swanson et al., 1995, pp. 107–8; see also Allen-Smith, 1995).

Most critical of the limitations of traditional explanations of rural poverty to understanding or offering solutions to the needs of rural minorities is the essay on racial and ethnic minorities written by Snipp et al. in *Persistent Poverty in Rural America* (1993). The authors argue that given the rates and intractability of poverty among rural minorities, the subject has been given far less attention than it deserves among rural poverty scholars, particularly regarding the status of Native Americans and Mexican Americans. Their essay points up the limita-tions of economic analyses focused on supply and demand as a way of accounting for the unique status and history of rural minorities. While they do not discount the importance of either human capital or economic resources, they argue convin-cingly that those explanations are too often focused only on individuals, families, and households without placing them in the context of communities.

They argue that a history of discrimination, colonial domination, and economic exploitation cannot be reduced to a residual category in an economic
model. It is, in their view, a historical legacy that shapes both human capital and
labor markets in these locations. The fact that rural Mexican Americans, Native
Americans, and African Americans "share the experience of living nearby the
historical remnants of institutions designed to conquer and oppress them" (Snipp
et al., 1993, p. 193) has resulted in long-term patterns which have systematically
denied opportunities and rights to people of color remaining in those locations.
This, in part, explains the overrepresentation of minorities among poor rural
people in poor rural places.

The legacy of racial exclusion and exploitation that people of color experienced from their entry into the United States has shaped their current status in
rural communities. The fact that rural poverty rates tend to be highest in areas
with high proportions of minorities (Lichter and McLaughlin, 1995) and that
blacks, Native Americans, and Latinos living in rural communities are among
the poorest people in the United States is not coincidental. Nor can these
inequities be eliminated through policies that address only labor markets or
individual characteristics. Rectifying them requires a deeper look at the structure
of rural communities and at the place of rural people within them.

WOMEN, CHILDREN AND FAMILIES

Among studies of the relationship between declining rural economies and the
well-being of children and families is the work of Lichter and Eggebeen (1992),
whose oft-cited essay studies this issue from a social demographic perspective.
Examining demographic changes since 1960, they find that changes in family
structure in the rural USA – specifically the increase in female-headed households – accounts for almost two-thirds of the increase in child poverty. In 1989,
Porter concluded that the poverty risk of female-headed families is as high in
rural areas as it is in central cities (cited in Fitchen, 1992, p. 176). And as Ross
and Morrissey point out, rural single parent families are apt to be poorer and to
remain poor for a longer duration than do urban single parent families (cited in
Fitchen, 1992, p. 176).

Although in a demographic analysis family structure stands out as a primary
explanation for child poverty, other analyses suggest that the reasons for recent
increases in rural child poverty are quite complex. Sherman (1992, pp. 38–9), in
his report on children in rural America, suggests that the nationwide trend of
declining wages, combined with inadequate government transfer programs, is at
least as important as the growth of female-headed families in explaining the
impoverishment of rural children.

Anthropologist Fitchen (1995) argues that the focus on households as a
measure of family structure ignores community and regional factors, as well as
the role of extended families and kin, in explaining family poverty. Finally, in
addition to Fitchen, a number of other scholars, including Lichter and Eggebeen
(1992) and Tickamyer et al. (1993), argue that women in rural areas are

especially vulnerable to poverty and that their low wages and limited employment opportunities are key elements in the production and maintenance of child poverty.

Rural Women: Implications for Single Parent Households

Scholars studying women's poverty (Abramovitz, 1996; Albelda and Tilly, 1997) have demonstrated convincingly that women and children make up the majority of this country's poverty population. In fact, the two poorest groups in the USA are women raising children alone and women over 65 living alone. Women living in rural communities are especially vulnerable to poverty. Employment opportunities for women in non-metropolitan areas are limited by discrimination, traditional attitudes, and a lack of flexibility in home–work schedules (Dill and Williams, 1992; Tickamyer et al., 1993). In addition, women perform a substantial amount of unpaid labor in the family that is not acknowledged. Often this unpaid labor, which includes cooking, sewing, gardening, self-employment, and piecework, stretches a meager paycheck to make survival possible.

Women in non-metropolitan areas experience higher poverty rates than women in metropolitan areas, and African American, Native American, and Latino women experience greater levels of poverty than White women. While metropolitan areas still have higher proportions of poor female-headed households, growth of these families has continued in non-metropolitan areas, while slowing down in metropolitan areas. Wages for rural workers are low and it appears that women's wages, which are often earned in the service sector, are among the lowest of these low wages. Unfortunately, the lack of information on women workers in a number of labor studies makes computing accurate estimates difficult. It is known, however, that economic restructuring has provided little relief to these women because the sectors of the economy that have grown, such as service industries and retail trade, are ones where women earn considerably less than men (Tickamyer, 1992, p. 206).

Thus, work is not likely to bring rural women with children out of poverty. If they are single parents, their low wages and limited options in the workplace will be a source of their children's poverty. If they are members of a two parent household, they still have a high likelihood of remaining among the working poor. The poverty of rural children is inextricably linked to the economic circumstances of parents, especially their mothers, who increasingly find themselves raising their children on their own.

Well-being of Rural Children and Families

In his 1992 report on rural children for the Children's Defense Fund, Sherman (1992) provides data and an assessment of the lives of rural children using five broad indicators of well-being: accessible health care, affordable childcare, quality public education, safe and adequate housing, and public assistance. His discussion helps to convey a fuller picture of living conditions for rural children, women, and families, and reminds us that rural children indeed face additional hardships when compared with their urban counterparts. I draw on Sherman's discussion to provide a preliminary overview of some of the needs of rural children and families.

Health Care

Geographic isolation and dispersion, a small supply of health care providers, a declining number of less well equipped hospitals, and a greater likelihood of being without health insurance coverage make rural residents especially vulnerable to poor health. These deficiencies jeopardize child development and achievement and have a particularly negative affect on the health status of minority children (Sherman, 1992, pp. 69–92). According to Garrett et al. (1993, pp. 246, 256), poor health care and poverty reduce people's capacity to work, place children at risk for developmental delay, and increase the likelihood of preterm or low birth weight babies.

On most indicators of child health (low birthweight, infant mortality, prenatal care, perceived health status, and acute and chronic health problems), the rates for rural children are comparable to or worse than the rates for poor urban children. This is the result of a number of factors: "rural children are more likely than metro children to have no health insurance coverage" (Sherman, 1992, p. 79); Medicare and Medicaid reimbursements to physicians and hospitals are half those in urban areas (DeLeon et al., cited in Garrett et al., 1993); and rural areas have a smaller supply of health professionals, including specialists, hospitals, and clinics, than metropolitan areas. Research in the 1980s suggests that "within the US, areas with poor prenatal care, limited health care, and lower socio-economic levels have a greater incidence of mental retardation and learning disabilities" (Schrag et al., 1983, cited in Garrett et al., 1993, p. 247). Taylor (1999, p. 3) suggests that there is still very little research on rural mental health and family functioning and that this lack is largely a result of "geographic isolation, variability across different types of rural settings, the insular nature of many small communities and the stigma associated with formal service use."

Childcare and Education

Rural families experience greater childcare shortages than urban and suburban ones. In the rural USA, a smaller supply of regulated group and family-based childcare is accompanied by a slightly higher need for services because a greater proportion of rural mothers work. Additionally, inadequate transportation makes accessing these services especially difficult. Finally, on a number of measures, including staff training and credentials, child-to-staff ratio, and salaries, the quality of childcare is lower in rural areas (Sherman, 1992, pp. 93–106).

In my own research in rural Mississippi in the late 1980s and early 1990s, I discovered that Headstart, an extremely popular program among the mothers whom I interviewed, was designed to overcome some of the problems of isolation, transportation, and staff quality that Sherman (1992) identifies. However, as a result of limited funding the program was not serving all the children who were eligible to participate. In addition, in Mississippi, the founding and introduction of Headstart was tied to civil rights activity and the program was initially introduced into the state through the Child Development Group of Mississippi (Payne, 1995). One outcome was that Headstart was seen as a black program and eligible white families chose not to take advantage of it.

"Rural children are poorer and attend poorer schools where teachers have less training and experience . . . and schools offer fewer alternative programs and advanced classes" (Sherman, 1992, p. 107). As discussed above, the education levels and perceived educational competence of the population affects economic growth and development. Many rural communities find themselves in a "Catch-22" situation. They attract only low-wage industries because of a poorly educated workforce, yet they lack the economic resources necessary to improve school quality. The need for resources is compounded by the fact that in rural areas the costs of education are often higher than in urban areas as a result of lower economies of scale which result from serving a small, but geographically dispersed, population. The educational outcomes for rural children, when compared with their urban and suburban counterparts, are lower levels of achievement, higher drop-out rates, an increased likelihood of the outmigration of high school graduates, and lower rates of college enrollment (Sherman, 1992, pp. 107–26).

Again, data from my own research in Mississippi provide an example of the educational liabilities that characterize persistently poor rural counties. Overall funding for public schools is substantially less in Mississippi than in all but two other states. In 1994–5 Mississippi's per pupil public education expenditures were only $3,798, compared with $5,528 for the USA. Low levels of local financing for public education explain much of this difference. Local communities in Mississippi rely more heavily on state and federal funds than the US average (US Department of Education, 1997).

This lack of local support for public education is the result of a number of factors; a weak tax base is a contemporary one, but, as Duncan (1999a) points out, the denial of equal access to education has a long history in some rural communities. In the Lower Mississippi Delta and in Appalachia in the late nineteenth and early twentieth centuries, controlling elites deliberately restricted access to education as a means of controlling their workforce. That legacy has influenced the willingness of many of these communities to invest equally in the education for all of their children (Dill, 1998; Duncan, 1999a).

Housing

Low-income families in rural communities face serious housing shortages. As poverty has increased, the number of low-rent housing units has dropped sharply (Lazere et al., cited in Fitchen, 1992). And although housing in rural communities is less expensive than in urban communities, approximately 42 percent of the rural poor pay more than half their income for housing (see Fitchen, 1992).

The result is that an increasing number of rural families face the threat of homelessness.

Although less prevalent than in urban areas, homelessness does exist in rural communities, and it is estimated that the rural homeless are younger and more likely to be female and in families (Hirschl and Momeni, cited in Nord and Luloff, 1995, p. 462). The housing problems that many poor rural families face are the result of a number of factors, including a growing demand for low-income housing accompanied by a diminishing supply, declines in home owner-ship, a proliferation of land use regulations and housing codes, rising rents, and a volatile housing market in which low-income tenants become extremely vulner-able to changes in the local rental market. In these circumstances, the housing patterns of rural families which Fitchen (1992) identifies are characterized by doubling up in short-term arrangements, accepting housing that is seriously inadequate or unsafe, and moving frequently. Nord and Luloff (1995), in a study of homeless children and families in rural New Hampshire, found that homelessness and near homelessness caused children to suffer serious academic and social setbacks. Among these were exhaustion, lack of designated time and place to do homework, instability, absences, frequent school changes, and stig-matization. These and other patterns related to housing cause children to suffer serious setbacks and create hardships for families and children, especially single parent families.

Public Assistance

The literature on public assistance and rural communities, for the most part, was written before implementation of TANF (Temporary Assistance to Needy Families, a provision of the Personal Responsibility and Work Opportunity Reconciliation Act of 1996). Nevertheless, the findings are useful to convey the context surrounding public assistance in many rural communities and to provide a contrast with urban settings.

In 1990, fewer than 47 percent of rural poor families with children received Aid to Families with Dependent Children (AFDC) or related benefits (Sherman, 1992). The usage of food stamps was slightly higher and almost on a par with urban communities. According to Jensen and Eggebeen (1994), rural children's parent(s) are more likely to work. However, working was also likely to make families ineligible for welfare. In their 1994 study of the ameliorative effects of public assistance on the economic well-being of rural children between 1970 and 1990, Jensen and Eggebeen conclude that, "compared with metro poor children, non-metro poor children are less likely to receive public assistance and receive less in total benefits when they do. Both factors conspire to produce a sizable non-metro disadvantage in the poverty alleviating impact of public assistance."

However, because rural wages are low, the greater engagement of rural par-ents in the workforce did not reduce poverty for rural children. Thus, even before TANF was initiated, Jensen and Eggebeen (1992) cautioned that "the ameliorative effects of work should not be overestimated." This conclusion was based on a study by Lichter and Eggebeen (1993), which found that a 50 percent increase in employment among poor, female-headed families led to only a 26 percent reduction in their poverty rate.

My own work (Dill, 1998) and that of Taylor (1999) provide some insights into the resources and barriers to implementing work opportunity programs in rural communities. Rural women we studied have both work experience and a desire for employment. Many also have a support network that facilitates working and, according to Taylor, strengthens mental health by reducing depressive symptoms. But at the same time, the women face significant barriers to work, including geographic isolation and lack of transportation, limited access to childcare, and, most significantly, the lack of availability of work that pays a living wage and makes it possible for them to support their families over an extended period of time.

RURAL COMMUNITIES: UNRAVELING THE LEGACY

In an effort to draw attention to the plight of rural America and to the growing similarities between persistently poor non-metropolitan areas and urban central cities that garner most of the nation's attention regarding poverty, rural scholars and writers have adopted the language of urban poverty. Terms like ghetto and underclass have been used to highlight the depths of rural poverty. Certainly, an examination of the data on rural poverty suggests that these problems are profound and that they are not isolated from the poverty of urban communities. In the long run, however, the borrowed terminology may obscure more than it clarifies. Poverty in rural communities derives from many of the same sources as urban poverty and has many similar aspects, but rural poverty also has a distinctive character. To a large extent, this character is the result of a historical legacy shaped by the organization of work, the role of race and gender, and the structure of class relations. The industries that were central to the formation of these communities and the ways in which social, political, and economic life were organized around them have had a tremendous impact on the prospects and possibilities of rural communities today. This heritage which has shaped the present must be understood and accounted for if interventions for change are to be successful.

The peculiar character of rural communities is well demonstrated in Cynthia Duncan's recent book, *Worlds Apart* (1999a). The book is a study of three poor rural communities: Blackwell, in Appalachia; Dahlia, in the Lower Mississippi Delta; and Gray Mountain, in Northern New England. In it, she argues that studying rural communities provides a unique opportunity to view, in microcosm, the relations between macroeconomic processes – such as restructuring, local political and social arrangements, and the daily lives of individuals. This face-to-face, personalized view of the interactions of race relations, class structures, and daily life helps to penetrate surface similarities between urban and rural communities and reveals a detailed patterning of relationships that must be understood before social change can take place.

In her study, Duncan (1999a) finds that the poor communities in the Delta and Appalachia are made up, essentially, of two classes: the haves and the have-nots. The haves are upper-class families who control the resources and participate in mainstream economic and political life. The have-nots are lower-class families who are powerless, dependent, and do not participate. These patterns of social life are rooted in the historical economic organization of the communities. In Blackwell Appalachia, the power of the haves derives from that of the coal barons; in Dahlia, Mississippi, it derives from the plantation bossmen (Duncan, 1999a, pp. 191–2).

Civic relations in these communities are permeated by distrust and greed. In Appalachia the primary schism is along class lines, with the small group of middle-class professionals and entrepreneurs aligning themselves with the upper class. In Dahlia, the community divides along both racial and class lines. The upper class is white, and the small white middle class identifies strongly with them. The lower class is predominantly (and in some counties, almost exclusively) black. Middle-class blacks find themselves divided between an old guard with long-standing ties to the white community and the maintenance of the status quo and a new group of professionals, former civil rights activists and return migrants who are working to bring about change and improve conditions for themselves and the lower class. Life in Dahlia and Blackwell contrasts sharply with that in Gray Mountain, "a blue-collar mill town where mill workers, civic leaders and business owners have worked together and invested in community-wide institutions for many decades" (Duncan, 1999a, p. 152).

The strong sense of civic life that exists in Gray Mountain has existed in the face of both class and ethnic differences. The differences are not minor, but they did not become the dividing lines along which resources and political and economic participation were distributed. Duncan (1999a) explains this as a result of the community's tradition of public investment, limited economic inequality, and a large, stable middle class. She attributes the differences between Blackwell, Dahlia, and Gray Mountain to differences in the "political economy and the social relations that economy generated" (p. 200).

Duncan's argument suggests the need to examine closely the social relations of rural communities and the nature of political, economic, and civic participation in an effort to understand why and how change occurs or is blocked. The legacy of inequality and racial exclusion provides the basis for social relations that are still in place today. In some areas, particularly in the rural South, these relations have remained in place despite government interventions (Hyland and Timberlake, 1993, p. 87). In some instances, as she points out in the cases of Dahlia and Blackwell, new industries did not invest in these areas, not because of the skills of workers but because the coal and plantation owners actively discouraged them in order to limit competition for their workforce. In my own research in the Mississippi Delta, I found that economic development was often centered on maintaining the traditional paternalistic relationships between traditional white elites and poor blacks. In these counties, economic developers specifically sought low-wage industries. These minimum wage industries, such as the catfish processing plants in Mississippi, tended to employ a disproportionately large number of women until unionization became more widespread and/or wages increased. In the case of catfish processing, the percentage of female workers in unionized plants dropped from approximately 90 to 50 percent after 1987 when some plants were unionized and wages rose.

CONCLUSION: RURAL BUILDING BLOCKS

The literature on rural poverty clearly indicates that place matters. Living in rural communities subjects children, women, and families to greater risks of poverty. In the case of children of color, these risks are compounded because many of them and their families live in places where institutions historically designed to oppress and exclude their people still shape economic, political, and social relations.

Improving outcomes for children will require improved economic opportunities for families, especially for mothers on whom so many solely depend. And improving economic opportunities will require a reinvestment in communities and in the people who live there. While the challenges to this kind of rebuilding are great, there are people, programs, and institutions which can provide a basis for beginning this work. The aspirations of many local people and their willingness to work hard is the first building block for improving the lives of poor rural children.

Most low-income rural families, like families throughout the United States, aspire to have their children, if not themselves, participate in the mainstream of the economy. Although they might not know all of the means to that end and may lack the social capital to facilitate those outcomes, education is generally recognized as an essential first step. In my research in Mississippi and Tennessee, the overwhelming majority of the women identified education as an important goal for themselves and especially for their children. The women we interviewed saw education in this way despite the fact that the route to educational uplift is a difficult one, and its rewards, in the counties we studied, were limited (Dill, 1998).

Duncan (1999a) argues that the one policy that would immediately help the poor in both rural and urban America is creating good public schools. According to Duncan, however, education is important not only for individual mobility but also as a catalyst for political change (p. 206). When one reads this argument, in light of Stack's (1996) work on return migration, it is apparent that education includes schooling but goes beyond that to include exposure to new ideas, new ways of working together, and a willingness to challenge the status quo. What Stack (1996) finds in her research is that the millions of migrants and return migrants who have moved from the Midwest and East to the rural Sunbelt have brought with them new ways of thinking and acting that have changed the South.

In addition to the return migrants, some members of the elite and of the middle class recognize that change and enhancing opportunities for poor residents are in the long-term interest of the community. The presence of small groups of people who are willing to work collectively toward change is a second building block for improving the lives of poor rural children.

Rural communities have been actively engaged in economic development strategies for some time now, and there is considerable knowledge and expertise about community capacities, needs, and employment-generating opportunities. In combination with improving schooling, these communities also need to generate jobs that will provide a better return on education and experience for the residents. The effort and interest of a number of local people in economic development is a third building block for improving the incomes of poor families and the lives of poor rural children.

Initiatives designed to improve outcomes for children by addressing the needs of families and communities are required to facilitate change in persistently poor rural communities with high concentrations of people of color. Yet, in many of these places, creating change will require overcoming the historical barriers and entrenched control that local elites have over community economic and social resources. Convincing elites that they should support and promote broad-scale community investment will be even more difficult than convincing poor people that change in their communities is possible. Yet the active engagement of segments of each of these groups is essential to improving the lives of poor children in the rural USA today.

Part IV
Science, Knowledge, and Ideas

15

The Sociology of Science and the Revolution in Molecular Biology

Troy Duster

While there are many avenues, the "natural trajectory" of the sociology of science would seem to follow most closely those developments and disciplines in science and technology that alter, or are most likely to alter, social relations. From mid-twentieth century and into the 1970s, physics and attendant developments with atom-splitting nuclear power, and later the microelectronic revolution, commanded the greatest attention. In the past decades these fields have been rivaled and in some instances eclipsed, at least in media attention and the popular imagination, by developments in molecular biology.

Yet the two major scientific revolutions that have taken off in the past three decades have produced strikingly different responses from social analysts of science. The first – the microelectronic revolution, with its ever-increasing presence in everyday life, from the worksites to the educational and leisure activities of more and more people – has been fairly well chronicled and analyzed. The second major revolution – the revolution in molecular biology and molecular genetics – has not received even a fraction of the attention from social studies of science that the microelectronic revolution has. This is something of an oddity, given both the current and the potential impact of the genetic revolution on how individuals, members of families, and social groups think about each other. Indeed, it has already had demonstrable impact upon how we avoid, insure, stigmatize, and "explain" each other.

There are a number of important markers to highlight both the speed and the drama. These include the more sensational developments and breakthroughs, such as the technique of somatic nuclear cell transfer (with the realization of mammalian cloning and the specter of human cloning), and germ-line gene therapy (with its specter of altering the genetic make-up of future generations). But there is the more current and even more likely prospect of growing organs from animals genetically engineered to produce greater compatibility with the new human host's immunological system.

In the last half of 1996, the boundary of legitimate gene therapy intervention was drawn at the genetic engineering affecting somatic cells. The latter is a potential therapy for a person with a genetic disorder – but a therapy that affects *only the body of the person being treated*. But in only 18 months, molecular biologists began to claim in a widely publicized public forum that work with stem cells is the easiest and best way to intervene in genetic disorders. In March 1998, at a conference at the Los Angeles campus of the University of California, a group of leading molecular geneticists convened to support this position with near unanimity. A few months later, in September 1998, the National Institutes of Health Recombinant DNA Advisory Committee received a proposal to fund *in utero* gene therapy for the treatment for a specific genetic condition:

> treatment of adenosine deaminase (ADA) deficiency. We propose a direct injection into the 13–15 week fetus of a retroviral vector carrying a normal copy of the human ADA gene controlled by human genomic ADA regulatory sequences. Because it is a direct in vivo injection, an occasional vector particle may enter an egg or sperm, thereby resulting in germline gene transfer. The magnitude of this risk will be determined by animal studies over the next 2–3 years. (Anderson, 1999)

The implications of this would, if fully understood, catch the attention of the laity, because with "germ-line" interventions (as noted above) there can be deliberate and conscious impact upon future generations, with the manipulation of the genetic make-up. The American Association for the Advancement of Science immediately convened two national panels to reflect upon these developments and requested that they produce position papers with recommendations in the year 2000.

While there will be some general public interest in the content and outcome of these deliberations and recommendations, for sociologists of science, an even more remarkable saga has suddenly surfaced for the nation of Iceland. Foreseeing an important window to the future, a number of social analysts of science are shifting their focus and their intellectual and research interests to that site. Here is why.

ICELAND AS A POTENTIAL GENETIC GOLDMINE

On December 17, 1998, the Icelandic Parliament passed a Bill that provides legal access for a private company to obtain a comprehensive genetic database for the entire population of the country. (The entire nation of Iceland has a population of only about 270,000). Only one among the 41 members of the coalition government voted against the Bill (Berger, 1999). The expressed purpose of the legislation is to encourage research on the molecular basis of twelve genetic disorders, where exclusive access to the database has been provided to a USA-based biotechnology firm. This company is based in Delaware, and has major financial backing from both American investors and the Swiss pharmaceutical company Hoffman-La Roche.

Just one month before the vote in the Parliament, a Gallup poll reported that only 13 percent of the nation's adults felt that they were sufficiently knowledgeable about the Bill to have an "informed" opinion. Nonetheless, 82 percent of the respondents said they were in favor of the database being generated (Enserink, 1998, p. 891). One of the big issues is personal privacy. Health data and medical detail will be taken from hospital records, and new data will be added from time to time. While the identity will be encrypted, this is quite a departure from making the data entries completely anonymous. (This permits one to conjure up the Tuskegee syphilis experiments. For example, what if an Icelandic patient is diagnosed with a condition for which there is possible treatment? The Icelandic Medical Association opposed the Bill.) But that is only the surface of some of the intractable ethical and social concerns that reverberate around this development. Scientists not working with the private companies will have no access to these data. Another transparently controversial aspect of the deal is the fact that the biotechnology company, named *deCODE*, need not obtain informed consent from those in the database.

Iceland has kept medical data on its population for more than a century, and the database would also contain the records of the deceased. When combined with both stored and newly collected blood and tissue samples, and further supplanted by detailed genealogical charts and records, the biotechnology company that will mine these databases believes that it has a head start in searching for genes that are implicated in human disease. But there is another element to this story that captures the attention of social analysts of science, and that is the putative "ethnic purity" of the database. The *Science* magazine reporter who covered the story had this to say about why Iceland would be a potential genetic gold mine: "Thanks to its isolated position and several bottlenecks that wiped out large parts of this population, the island has a remarkably homogenic gene pool, making it relatively easy to track down disease-causing mutations that might form the basis for new tests and therapies" (Enserink, 1998, p. 891).

The degree to which this is true, of course, is an empirical question that awaits an answer with potentially volatile economic and political consequences. The major point to be made here is that this development has generated a considerable amount of interest from a number of sociologists and anthropologists of science. They have been joined by bio-ethicists and political scientists in a Great Trek northward to monitor and study these developments. While the molecular geneticists are concerned primarily with tracking down what they regard as "disease genes," the social analysts of science are focusing on the wider set of issues that can have a large impact on a full panoply of social relations – not only in Iceland, but as a harbinger of things to come, globally. So it is the case that work in the laboratory of the biological scientists has "taken off" and refocused the attention of the sociology of science.

Katz Rothman (1998) has pointed out how communication (or lack of it) of the technical intricacies of the molecular genetics revolution is often silencing and disempowering – intimidating to those not able to follow closely developments at the vanguard laboratories of the field. Yet these technologies are driven by profoundly social, political, and economic questions and concerns. It is therefore both useful and necessary to demystify the complexity, and to be able to cut to the core of basic elements of the scientific work. Then we will be better able to understand what the Iceland adventure is all about, and why it has such a powerful grip on the imagination. We will then see why issues of race and ethnicity, health and medicine, and crime and violence will all be impacted in new ways.

A Short but Necessary Primer on SNiPs

Although the work is named The Human Genome Project (the mapping and sequencing of all human genes), no one particular DNA sequence constitutes *the* human genome. Rather, each person (with the exception of monozygotic, or identical, twins) has her or his own unique human genome, or set of complete genes.

DNA is made up of four chemical components, called nucleotides. These are strung together in a chain, much like beads on a necklace. The four different nucleotides are represented as "G" (guanine), "A" (adenine), "T" (thymine), and "C" (cytosine), and a DNA sequence could look like GCGCATTAGCTACGG. Each molecule is in the form of a disc, and is called a "base." Rungs of the now famous DNA ladder are constructed when two of these nucleotides are connected in a spiral and form what is called a "base pair." The DNA of humans is made up of approximately three billion nucleotides that are packaged into 23 nuclear chromosomes and one mitochondrial chromosome. Approximately 10 percent of these base pairs are called genes. Each of these codes for the production of a particular protein.

If someone is missing a "correct" sequence of DNA in one of those segments, that particular protein will not be made. That could prove vital, fatal, or painful. For example, hemophilia is a condition where blood does not clot properly. Those with hemophilia have stretches of the DNA with "errors" that inhibit the protein that would instruct blood to clot properly. Quotation marks have been placed around "correct" and "errors" for an important reason. While there may be a relatively high consensus about what constitutes a debilitating or fatal disease condition (e.g. Tay-Sachs is a neurological disease that is fatal by age four), that consensus falls away for many other conditions. Setting a single standard of "normality" is always about the power and position to do so. In the United States and Europe, many communities of deaf persons resist the idea of being "corrected." This raises the question of who will set the standard of the "normal" human genome.

Maps of the genome allow researchers to locate a piece of DNA somewhere in the genome, but that map will not indicate the precise arrangement of the nucleotides in that piece of DNA. The precise arrangement, or linear order, of nucleotides is called the *DNA sequence*. The DNA sequence is important because different sequences encode different information. One of the main reasons for studying DNA is because it encodes information that specifies how cells should make biologically useful molecules, such as proteins.

If we compare the complete DNA sequence of any two people we will find a difference approximately one time in every thousand nucleotides. The simplest kind of difference is when one nucleotide differs between the two people; for instance, when one person has a G at a certain position in the sequence and another person has a T there. In some cases, such differences will cause a slightly different protein to be made. In other cases, these differences have no known impact on which protein is made or on any other biological functions.

Places where people's genomes differ by one nucleotide are called "single nucleotide polymorphisms," commonly shortened to SNiPs. The search for SNiPs is now in full bloom because these SNiPs can be used as "markers" on chromosomes. These markers can be used to make genetic maps which may allow us to locate genes of interest, such as genes involved in diseases. But they can also be used to identify and mark both individuals and groups of individuals, a technological capacity that will prove to be of extraordinary significance and consequence to social studies of science.

SNiPS on Chips

Many things that molecular geneticists want to study, including many (if not most) human diseases, are caused by a complex interaction between things in the person's environment and the person's biology, including many different genes. In the past decade, media accounts of "the gene for" this or that disease, condition, attribute, or behavior have become common, sometimes weekly, reports. This has led many lay persons to believe that a single gene is the cause of a host of diseases, attributes, and conditions. Yet it is only in rare cases that a single gene has a very strong, identifiable effect on whether or not a person contracts or develops a disease. Such cases are generally called "single gene disorders."

In most cases, when genes play a role in the development of a disease, such as a particular kind of heart disease, the role of any single gene will be very small. To study the genetics of complex conditions such as heart disease, methods must be devised for finding a constellation of genetic differences between people that correlate with that disease. One method for examining many different pieces of DNA all at once, and for detecting more than one genetic difference in a single experiment, is to put many different genes or parts of genes on a computer chip.

DNA chips are useful for doing the equivalent of 100 or even 1,000 experiments all at one time, in one simple procedure. The chip with dimensions less than one square centimeter may have 1,000 or 10,000 different sectors. The technology is now available to attach DNA of a slightly different sequence to each sector. For instance, suppose that a group of researchers had found 2,000 different SNiPs; that is, 2,000 identifiable places in the genome where people's DNA sequences could differ by one nucleotide. Then, someone could make a DNA chip that would have all the possible SNiPs (at least 4,000, but it could be more because each SNP will have between two and four possibilities), each in its own separate and identifiable place on the chip. Then, if my DNA were exposed to the chip (actually, DNA or RNA are hybridized to the chips), one experiment could determine which SNiP I had at all 2,000 different places in the genome. We could make a "SNiP profile" for me. If we did this for 5,000 people, 2,500 of whom had a certain kind of heart disease and 2,500 of whom did not, then we might be able to find five to ten SNiPs that were correlated with a high likelihood of developing heart disease. That is the core of the methodological strategy of SNiPs on chips.

SNiPs, Human Diversity, and Social Groupings

Approximately 85 percent of human genetic diversity can be found in any population, even a very small, village-sized population (Cavalli-Sforza, in Smith and Sapp, 1997, p. 55). For instance, if we were looking at SNiPs, we would find that most are in all populations throughout the world. However, there will be some SNiPs that are found in some people from Finland but probably not in people of Native American descent. This does not mean that a certain sequence is found in all people from Finland, or that it is never found in people who are not from Finland.

There are social implications of creating SNiP profiles if these can be used to suggest increasing likelihood of a person's ancestry and appearance, for example. As we shall see, forensic studies that attempt to provide the criminal justice system with strong leads to probable suspects are now being developed. Because phenotypical stereotypes of "race" have played a large role in such identification, we must first turn to the literature that sets the stage for the re-emergence of "race" in molecular biological clothing.

CONTEXT AND CONTENT FOR FEEDBACK LOOPS: SETTING THE EMPIRICAL PROBLEM

By the mid-1970s, it had become abundantly clear that there is more genetic variation *within* the most current common socially used categories of race than *between* these categories (Polednak, 1989; Bittles and Roberts, 1992; Chapman, 1993; Shipman, 1994). The consensus is a recent development. For example, in the early part of the twentieth century, scientists in several countries tried to link up a study of the major blood groups in the ABO system to racial and ethnic groups (see Schneider, 1996). They had learned that blood type B was more common in certain ethnic and racial groups – which some believed to be more inclined to criminality and mental illness (Gundel, 1926; Schusterov, 1927). They kept running up against a brick wall, because there was nothing in the ABO system that could predict behavior. While *that* strategy ended a full half-century ago, there is a contemporary arena in which hematology, the study of blood, has had to resuscitate a concern with "race."

In the United States, there has been an increasing awareness developed over the past two decades of the problem that blood from Americans of European ancestry (read mainly white) tends to contain a greater number of antigens than blood from Americans of African or Asian ancestry (Vichinsky et al., 1990). This means that *there is a greater chance* for hemolytic reactions for blacks and Asians receiving blood from whites, but *a lower risk for whites* receiving blood from Asians or blacks. Here we come to a fascinating intersection between the biological and social sciences. In the United States, not only do whites comprise approximately 80 percent of the population, but proportionally fewer blacks and Asian Americans donate blood than do whites. This social fact has some biological consequences, which in turn have some social consequences.

Approximately 400 red blood cell group antigens have been identified. The antigens have been classed into a number of fairly well defined systems: the most well known are the ABO and Rh systems, but there are other systems, such as P, Lewis, MN, and Kell (standard hematology texts note ten systems, including ABO and Rh). The clinical significance of blood groups is that in the case of a blood transfusion, individuals who lack a particular blood group antigen may produce antibodies reacting with that antigen in the transfused blood. This immune response to alloantigens (non-self antigens) may produce hemolytic reactions, the most serious being complete hemolysis (destruction of all red blood cells), which can be life threatening. Once generated, the capacity to respond to a particular antigen is more or less permanent, because the immune system generates "memory cells" which can be activated by future exposures to the antigen. For those who have chronic conditions, which require routine blood transfusion, this aspect of the immune response is critical, because it increases the likelihood of future transfusion incompatibility. The clinical goal is to minimize immune responses to antigens in transfused blood, in part because a crisis (such as trauma surgery) may require transfusion of whatever blood is available, regardless of its antigen composition.

Most blood banks only test for ABO and Rh – the most common systems. Testing for the other systems is considered inefficient and will increase the cost of blood. It is essential to minimize the antibodies against blood group antigens for everyone. However, the way in which blood typing is done puts members of racial and ethnic minorities at greater risk for the negative consequences of frequent transfusions. The term *phenotypically matched blood* basically means that it is possible to use the social appearances of race as a rough approximation (of likely antigens) to screen to minimize antibodies (along with ABO and Rh).

Transfusion therapy for sickle cell anemia is limited by the development of antibodies to foreign red cells (Vichinsky et al., 1990). In one important study, the researchers evaluated the frequency and risk factors associated with alloimmunization, and obtained the transfusion history, red cell phenotype, and development of alloantibodies in 107 black patients with sickle cell anemia who received transfusions. They then compared the results with those from similar studies in 51 black patients with sickle cell disease who had not received transfusions and in 19 non-black patients who received transfusions for other forms of chronic anemia.

We assessed the effect that racial differences might have in the frequency of
alloimmunization by comparing the red-cell phenotypes of patients and blood-
bank donors (n = 200, 90 percent white). Although they received transfusions less
frequently, 30 percent of the patients with sickle cell anemia became alloimmunized, in contrast to 5 percent of the comparison-group patients with other forms of
anemia (P less than 0.001). Of the 32 alloimmunized patients with sickle cell
anemia, 17 had multiple antibodies and 14 had delayed transfusion reactions.
Antibodies against the K, E, C, and Jkb antigens accounted for 82 percent of the
alloantibodies.

They then go on to conclude: "These differences are most likely racial. We
conclude that alloimmunization is a common, clinically serious problem in sickle
cell anemia and that it is partly due to racial differences between the blood-
donor and recipient populations" (Vichinsky et al., 1990).

Note that Vichinsky and his colleagues conclude "that it is partly due to racial
differences between the blood-donor and recipient populations." True enough,
this may not be "race" in any essentialist conception, but that is precisely the
point. Over eighty years ago, Hirschfeld and Hirschfeld (1919, p. 675) posited
that when introducing the blood of one species into that of the same species
"those antigen properties which are common to the giver and receiver of blood
can not give rise to antibodies, since they are not felt as foreign by the immunized
animal." While the Hirschfelds were talking about dogs, they were drawing a
straight line toward humans, human classification, and racial taxonomy: "If we
inject into dogs the blood of other dogs it is in many cases possible to produce
antibodies. By means of these antibodies we have been able to show that there
are in dogs two antigen types. These antigen types, which we recognize by means
of the iso-antibodies, may designate two biochemical races" (Hirschfeld and
Hirschfeld, 1919, p. 675–6).

Using this hypothesis, they went on to perform the first systematic and
comprehensive serological study of a variety of ethnic and racial groups. As I
indicated above, their classification system did not survive the test of time, but "a
way of thinking" persists (Marks, 1995). Moreover, with the data reported in the
Vichinsky study (given that the increased blood donations from "blacks" is a key
policy goal for those suffering from a relatively common genetic disease, sickle
cell anemia), the resuscitation of "race" through blood antigen theorizing and
empirical research cannot be far behind. That persons who are phenotypically
"white" can and do have sickle cell anemia complicates any essentialized racial
theorizing, to be sure – but for the purposes of further action (blood donation
requests and transfusion direction), racial phenotyping as a "short-hand" is back
with us at the beginning of the twenty-first century.

This provides a remarkably interesting intersection. While the full range of
analysts, commentators, and scientists – from postmodern essayists to molecular
geneticists to social anthropologists – have been busily pronouncing "the death
of race," for practical clinical purposes the concept is resurrected in the conflation of blood donation frequencies, by "race." I now want to make it clear that I
am not merely trying to resurrect "race" as a social construct (with no biological

meaning) – no more than I am trying to resurrect "race" as a biological construct with social meaning. Instead, I am arguing that when "race" is used as a stratifying practice (which can be apprehended empirically and systematically) there is often a reciprocal interplay of biological outcomes that makes it impossible to completely disentangle the biological from the social. While that may be obvious to some, it is completely alien to others, and some of those "others" are key players in current debates about the biology of race.

In late September 1996, Tuskegee University hosted a conference on the Human Genome Project, with specific reference to the Project's relevance to the subject of race (Smith and Sapp, 1997). In attendance was Luca Cavalli-Sforza, a pre-eminent population geneticist from Stanford University and perhaps the leading figure behind the Human Genetic Diversity Project. (This project has been concerned with tracing human populations through evolutionary history of many centuries, and is not be to be confused with the Human Genome Project, the goal of which is to map and sequence the entire human genome.) Cavalli-Sforza had appeared on the cover of *Time* magazine a few years earlier, as something of a hero to the forces that were attacking the genetic determinism in *The Bell Curve*, a popular book by Richard Herrnstein and Charles Murray (1994). At this conference, he repeated what he had said in the *Time* article: "One important conclusion of population genetics is that races do not exist" (Smith and Sapp, 1997, p. 53).

> If you take differences between two random individuals of the same population, they are about 85% of the differences you would find if you take two individuals at random from the whole world. This means two things: (1) The differences between individuals are the bulk of the variation; (2) the differences among populations, races, continents are very small – the latter are only the rest, 15%, about six times less than that between two random individuals of one perhaps very small population (85%). Between you and your town grocer there is on average a variation which is almost as large as that between you and a random individual of the whole world. This person could be from Africa, China, or an Australian aborigine. (Smith and Sapp, 1997, p. 55)

Cavalli-Sforza is speaking here as a population geneticist, and in that limited frame of what is important and different about us as humans he may be empirically correct. But humans give meaning to differences. At a particular historical moment, to tell this to an Albanian in Kosovo, a Hutu among the Tutsi, a Zulu among the Boers, or a German Jew among the Nazis may be as convincing, *for the purposes of further action*, as telling it to an audience of mainly African Americans at Tuskegee University, as Tuskegee was the site of the infamous syphilis experiments on black males, where the Public Health Service of the US Government studied the racial effects of how disease ravages the body of blacks in contrast to whites (Jones, 1981). Indeed, David Botstein, speaking later in a keynote address, had this to say about *The Bell Curve*:

> So from a scientific point of view, this whole business of *The Bell Curve*, atrocious though the claims may be, is nonsense and is not to be taken seriously. People keep

asking me why I do not rebut *The Bell Curve*. The answer is because it is so stupid that it is not rebuttable. You have to remember that the Nazis who exterminated most of my immediate family did that on a genetic basis, but it was false. Geneticists in Germany knew that it was false. The danger is not from the truth, the danger is from the falsehood. (Smith and Sapp, 1997, p. 212)

David Botstein is also a pre-eminent molecular geneticist at the vanguard of his field. In this statement, he takes the position that if people just understood the genetic truth, that would be sufficient and even corrective of racist thinking and action. But he acknowledges that the German geneticists knew that Nazi claims about Aryan racial purity were false. Even though people may someday come to understand that they are basically similar at the level of the DNA, RNA, immunology, or kinds of blood systems, it is the language group, kinship, religion, region, or race that is still far more likely to generate their pledge of allegiance.

THE AMERICAN ANTHROPOLOGICAL ASSOCIATION STATEMENT ON "RACE"

In May 1998 the American Anthropological Association issued its own statement on "Race." It attempts to address myths and misconceptions, and in so doing takes a "corrective" stance toward folk beliefs about race. The statement strongly states the position that "physical variations in the human species have no meaning except the social ones that humans put on them." But in casting "the problem" in this fashion, it gives the impression that the biological meanings that scientists attribute to race are biological facts, while the social meanings that lay persons give to race are: (a) either errors or mere artificial social constructions; and (b) not themselves capable of feedback loops into the biochemical, neurophysiological, and cellular aspects of our bodies, which in turn can be studied scientifically. The statement of the Anthropological Association is consistent with that of the UNESCO statement on race. However, formulating the matter so that "it is *only* the social meanings that humans provide" implies that mere lay notions of race provide a rationale for domination, but have no other utility.

There is profound misunderstanding of the implications of a "social contructivist" notion of social phenomena. How humans identify themselves, whether in religious or ethnic or racial or aesthetic terms, matters for their subsequent behavior. Places of worship are socially constructed with human variations of meaning, interpretation, and use very much in mind. Whether a cathedral or mosque, a synagogue or Shinto temple, those "constructions" are no less "real" because one has accounted for and documented the social forces at play that resulted in such a wide variety of "socially constructed" places of worship (Fujimura, 1998). "Race" as social construction can and does have a substantial effect on how people behave. One important arena for further scientific exploration and investigation is the feedback between that behavior and the biological functioning of the body. It is now appropriate to restate the well known social analytic aphorism of W. I. Thomas, but to refocus it on human taxonomies of other humans: *if humans define situations as real, they can and often do have real biological and social consequences.*

MOLECULAR GENETICS AND THE NEW CONFLATION OF RACE AND FORENSICS

If "race" is a concept with no scientific utility, what are we to make of a series of articles that have appeared in the scientific literature over the past seven years, looking for genetic markers of population groups that coincide with common sense, lay renditions of ethnic and racial phenotypes? It is the forensic applications that have generated much of this interest. Devlin and Risch (1992a) published an article on "Ethnic differentiation at VNTR loci, with specific reference to forensic applications" – a research report that appeared prominently in the *American Journal of Human Genetics.*

> The presence of null alleles leads to a large excess of single-band phenotypes for blacks at D17S79 (Devlin and Risch, 1992b).... This phenomenon is less important for the Caucasian and Hispanic populations, which have fewer alleles with a small number of repeats... it appears that the FBI's data base is representative of the Caucasian population. Results for the Hispanic ethnic groups, for the D17S79 locus, again suggest that the data bases are derived from nearly identical populations, when both similarities and expected biases are considered.... For the allele frequency distributions derived from the black population, there may be small differences in the populations from which the data bases are derived, as the expected bias is .05. (Devlin and Risch, 1992a, pp. 540, 546)

Some explanations are in order. Alleles are different versions of one gene. For example, while the "generic gene" will instruct the proteins and cells to make an eye, a particular allele may produce a blue, brown, or grayish-green eye. The same can be said for the allelic variation that produces the epicantic fold (or lack of it) over the eye, and a wide range of other human physiognomic characteristics, including hair texture and skin color. While some aspects of skin color are of course environmental, these account for only about 20 percent of the variation. Moreover, this is not to suggest that single genes determine skin color, but that allelic variations even from full siblings can produce considerable variation.

When researchers try to make probabilistic statements about which group a person belongs to, they look at variation at several different locations in the DNA – usually from three to seven loci. For any particular locus, there is an examination of the frequency of that allele *at that locus, and for that population.* In other words, what is being assessed is the frequency of genetic variation at a particular spot in the DNA in each population.

Occasionally, these researchers find a locus where one of the populations being observed and measured has, for example (let's call them), alleles H, I, and J, and another population has alleles H, I, and K. For example, we know that there are alleles that are found primarily among sub-populations of Native American Indians. When comparing a group of North American Indians with a group of Finnish people, one might find a single allele that was present in some Indians but in no Finns (or at such a low frequency in the Finns that it is rarely, if ever, seen). However, it is important to note and reiterate again and again that this does not mean that all Native American Indians, even in this sub-population, will have that allele. (This is a major and important point that is made in sets of statements about race from UNESCO and the American Anthropological Association.) Indeed, it is inevitable that some will have a different set of alleles, and that *many of them will be the same alleles as some of the Finns*. Also, if comparing North American Indians from Arizona with North American Caucasians from Arizona, we would probably find a low level of the "Indian allele" in the so-called Caucasians, because there has been "interbreeding." This leads to the next point.

It is possible to make arbitrary groupings of populations (geographic, linguistic, self-identified by faith, identified by others by physiognomy, etc.) and still find statistically significant allelic variations between those groupings. For example, we could simply pick all the people in Chicago, and all in Los Angeles, and find statistically significant differences in allele frequency at *some* loci. Of course, at many loci, even most loci, we would not find statistically significant differences. When researchers claim to be able to assign people to groups based on allele frequency at a certain number of loci, they have chosen loci that show differences between the groups they are trying to distinguish. The work of Devlin and Risch (1992a, b), Evett et al, (1993, 1996), and others suggests that there are only about 10 percent of sites in the DNA that are "useful" for making distinctions. This means that at the other 90 percent of the sites, the allele frequencies do not vary between groups such as "Afro-Caribbean people in England" and "Scottish people in England." But it does not follow that because we cannot find a single site where allele frequency matches some phenotype that we are trying to identify (for forensic purposes, we should be reminded), there are not several (four, six, seven) that will be effective, for the purposes of aiding the FBI, Scotland Yard, or the criminal justice systems around the globe in highly probabilistic statements about suspects, and the likely ethnic, racial, or cultural populations from which they can be identified – statistically.

In the July 8, 1995 issue of the *New Scientist*, entitled "Genes in black and white," some extraordinary claims are made about what it is possible to learn about socially defined categories of race from reviewing information gathered using new molecular genetic technology. In 1993, a British forensic scientist published what is perhaps the first DNA test explicitly acknowledged to provide "intelligence information" along "ethnic" lines for "investigators of unsolved crimes." Ian Evett, of the Home Office's forensic science laboratory in Birmingham, and his colleagues in the Metropolitan Police, claimed that their DNA test can distinguish between "Caucasians" and "Afro-Caribbeans" in nearly 85 percent of the cases.

Evett's work, published in the *Journal of Forensic Science Society*, draws on apparent genetic differences in three sections of human DNA. Like most stretches of human DNA used for forensic typing, each of these three regions differs widely from person to person, irrespective of race. But by looking at all three, say the researchers, it is possible to estimate the probability that someone belongs to a particular racial group. The implications of this for determining, for legal purposes, who is and who is not "officially" a member of some racial or ethnic category are profound.

Two years after the publication of the UNESCO statement purportedly burying the concept of "race" for the purposes of scientific inquiry and analysis, and during the same time period that the American Anthropological Association was deliberating and generating a parallel statement, an article appeared in the *American Journal of Human Genetics*, authored by Ian Evett and his associates, summarized thus:

> Before the introduction of a four-locus multiplex short-tandem-repeat (STR) system into casework, an extensive series of tests were carried out to determine robust procedures for assessing the evidential value of a match between crime and suspect samples. Twelve databases were analyzed from the three main ethnic groups encountered in casework in the United Kingdom; Caucasians, Afro-Caribbeans, and Asians from the Indian subcontinent. Independence tests resulted in a number of significant results, and the impact that these might have on forensic casework was investigated. It is demonstrated that previously published methods provide a similar procedure for correcting allele frequencies – and that this leads to conservative casework estimates of evidential value. (Evett et al., 1996, p. 398)

These new technologies have some not-so-hidden potential to be used for a variety of forensic purposes in the development and "authentication" of typologies of human ethnicity and race. A contemporary update of an old idea of the idea of deciding upon "degree of whiteness" or "degree of Indianness" is possibly upon us, anew, with the aid of molecular genetics. The Congress of the United States passed the Allotment Act of 1887, denying land rights to those Native Americans who were "less than half-blood." The US government still requires American Indians to produce "Certificates with Degree of Indian Blood" in order to qualify for a number of entitlements, including being able to have one's art so labeled. The Indian Arts and Crafts Act of 1990 made it a crime to identify oneself as a Native American when selling artwork without federal certification authorizing one to make the legitimate claim that one was, indeed, an authentic ("one-quarter blood" even in the 1990s) American Indian.

As noted above, it is not art, but law and forensics, that ultimately will impel the genetic technologies to be employed on behalf of attempts to identify who is "authentically" in one category or another. Geneticists in Ottawa, Canada, have been trying to set up a system "to distinguish between 'Caucasian Americans' and 'Native Americans' on the basis of a variable DNA region used in DNA fingerprinting" (*New Scientist*, 1995, p. 37).

In 1989, Virginia was the first state to pass legislation requiring all convicted felons (not just sex offenders) to provide blood samples for use in a state DNA database. In the next three years, several states followed the lead of Virginia, and in 1993, the FBI initiated a national DNA databank to link the DNA profiles of convicts across state jurisdictions. The Omnibus Crime Control Act of 1994 included a provision for coordinating DNA databank systems nationwide. Soon thereafter, the Department of Justice awarded nearly nine million dollars to state and city agencies to improve their DNA testing capacities and to encourage uniform standards (Butterfield, 1996). As a direct result, all fifty states have adopted laws requiring "specified offenders to provide blood samples for forensic DNA testing" (Nelkin and Andrews, 1999).

For practical purposes, the issue of the authentication of persons' membership in a group (racial/ethnic/cultural) can be brought to the level of DNA analysis. The efficaciousness of testing and screening for genetic disorders in risk populations that are ethnically and racially designated poses a related set of vexing concerns for the "separation" of the biological and cultural taxonomies of race. In New York City, Mayor Giuliani has been an advocate of the use of DNA testing of those arrested by the police. He has been joined by others, who have convinced Attorney General Janet Reno that she should appoint a commission to bring back recommendations on this matter. A report is due in 2000, but a preliminary draft has already concluded that such data collection would pass constitutional muster. Critics have pointed to the fact that who the police stop and arrest is not a neutral matter, but heavily politically biased, and, in particular, "racially" biased. Indeed, the American Civil Liberties Union has filed a lawsuit to stop the police from targeting primarily African Americans.

The technology to use "SNiPs on chips" to group, identify, categorize, and marginalize is with us, but it is still at a relatively early stage. The Department of Energy awarded a contract to IBM in early 1998 to produce a chip that can hold more than eight times the amount of information available and permit analysis at more than ten times the speed now possible with current chip technology. That technology is due to become operative in the year 2000.

ACKNOWLEDGMENT

I thank William H. Schneider for references to the German literature.

16

Structures of Knowledge

Richard E. Lee and Immanuel Wallerstein

The "Two Cultures": the Long-term Trend

The trend to secularize authoritative knowledge began in the Western world at the end of the Middle Ages. The resulting intellectual and institutional structures of knowledge production have been constitutive of, and constituted by, the modern world-system. These structures have been fundamental to the operations of this world-system, alongside the transformed relations of production and distribution (which form together a core–periphery axial division of labor) and the reorganized structures of sovereign states within an interstate system (which seek to monopolize collective decision-making and legitimate coercion).

Previously, knowledge in the Western world had been thought to reside in two realms, the earthbound and the heavenly, each constituted in different ways. About each, however, one could have knowledge of both the true and the good. To secularize knowledge meant to exclude theological judgments and authority from the search for knowledge about nature, but nature was now considered to behave by the same set of rules on earth and in the universe beyond. In effect, this separated knowledge about a heavenly world that was extra-natural and was the domain of theology, from knowledge about the natural/human world which was to be the domain of secular specialists. Had the secularization stopped there, it would merely have underpinned increased autonomy for natural philosophers. This did not, however, satisfy those oriented to systematic observation and empirical verification of knowledge about the physical world. They insisted on separating knowledge of what was true from knowledge of what was good, because they claimed that the latter was not realizable with scientific methods. This radical separation of two kinds of natural knowledge represented a departure from conceptions of knowledge hitherto espoused in any part of the world. There has consequently been a continuing intellectual debate in the modern world as to whether there could be any links whatsoever between what were now considered two quite different forms of knowledge.

The study of natural things was said to be only the study of the true, and it was progressively privileged over the arts or humanities, wherein one pursued the study of the good and of the beautiful. Proceeding from the knowing subject of René Descartes, the two domains came to be grounded in the asserted dualism of (non-human) nature and humans, of matter and mind. Descartes was motivated by the search for truth as an activity of the rational mind during a time marked by religious conflict, not by a consideration for values and accumulated learning. This set his project against rhetoric and the priority of willing the good over knowing the truth. Francis Bacon was also looking for a way of producing valid knowledge without either depending on received authority or falling prey to personal bias. Half a century later, Newton synthesized Bacon's empirical and experimental approach and method of induction capable of producing natural laws with Descartes's project based on rationalism and a deductive method.

This program reached its logical conclusion and social triumph over the course of the nineteenth century, which saw the proclamation of a doctrine of total determinism by Pierre Simon de Laplace, who considered himself a faithful disciple of Newton. The defining characteristic of modern science, as it came to be conceived and practiced, was that the world was one in which the discovery of universal laws explained change and permitted accurate prediction (and postdiction). Natural processes were linear and theoretical explanations were time-reversible. Laplace's demon, as an outsider theoretically perceiving the universe, could know everything.

From the beginning of the nineteenth century, one could say that "science" – as a world view, as a set of claims on truth-value, as a series of institutions – had effectively displaced natural philosophy and was becoming acknowledged as the pinnacle of the hierarchy of knowledge, and the principal mode of validation of intellectual activity. The "scientization" of authoritative knowledge was no doubt deplored by scholars who feared the social implications of this model. In the wake of the French Revolution, their reaction became organized in the form of anti-Enlightenment thought and romanticism, and was institutionalized in universities as the "humanities"; that is, eventually as multiple and autonomous departments of philosophy, of languages and literature, of art history and musicology. History was usually also classified as one of the humanities. While the sciences were concerned with the regularities and certainties they attributed to the natural world, the humanities took as their purview the uniqueness and unpredictability they argued was characteristic of the human world. This division of perspective and tasks is what has come to be known as the "two cultures."

Despite a continuing strong opposition by the humanities throughout the nineteenth century, the sciences maintained their lead and marched to dominance in the structures of knowledge. This represented the triumph of universalism, with its corollary, the irrelevance of time and space. The superiority of science, furthermore, received massive social confirmation in the twentieth century at the level of popular belief as a result of its very real accomplishments in terms of inventions and techniques, and, consequently, at the level of state support as well, because of its promise of economic development and military security through "big science."

Never did the sciences seem to be held in higher esteem than in the period 1945–70, and thereby the hierarchical organization of the disciplines of knowledge production they anchored. Nevertheless, beginning in the 1960s, the validity of the structures of knowledge came under renewed serious challenge from many quarters. Many of these recent challengers, however, did not merely reassert humanistic concerns. Some now began to express a skepticism concerning the very logic of the long-term division of knowledge into two cultures (see Wallerstein, 1991; Gulbenkian Commission, 1996). Given the fact that the structures of knowledge are both constituted by and constitutive of the modern world, the pertinent question this raises for social analysts is whether the contemporary sharp debate about the structures of knowledge may not itself be considered to be one of the signals of a structural crisis of historical capitalism.

THE SOCIAL SCIENCES: CONTRADICTION AND RESTRUCTURING

The contradictions driving the historical development of the two cultures took form in the early nineteenth century in political projects, the three modern "ideologies" of conservatism, liberalism, and radicalism/socialism. They claimed legitimacy in part on the basis of their interpretations of work in the humanities tradition, but also in part on the claimed scientific quality of their arguments. They did this, of course, while asserting antagonistic, mutually exclusive, value orientations. The social sciences – that is, the study of social reality as it was remolded, invented, and most of all institutionalized in the late nineteenth century and early twentieth century – represent a reorganization of the structures of knowledge in large part in response to this political debate.

During the nineteenth century, the intellectual as social critic began to play a central role in policy-oriented interpretations of a world in which change had come to be seen as normal and requiring management. The extension of the Enlightenment ideal of rationality to all individuals had the corollary that such social subjects consequently could, and for some should, exercise their rationality not only to confirm, but also to question, or even transform, time-honored social relationships or systems of rule. Values justifying change were the rallying cry of the radicals in particular – the eternally valid values of the Rights of Man and of Democracy, values which, however, were yet to be achieved or at least to be fully implemented.

This strand of social criticism was explicitly political in nature and was, of course, anathema to conservatives. Although romanticism embraced the Enlightenment ideal of individuality through creativity and difference, the romantics preferred to stress not only the artist's but even the common people's access to "truth" through imagination, personal experience, and the values of the community, as opposed to the scientific rationality of the *philosophes*. Responding in kind to the thrust of the radical critique, conservatives put forth notions of authenticity, tradition, and the organic community, in this case the defense of a vision of values coded as "culture" and extolled as "order" in opposition not only to revolution but also to democracy and *laissez-faire* liberalism, disparaged as "anarchy."

The scientization of social knowledge represented the medium-term resolution to the contradiction involved in the separation of knowledge into general statements that were value-neutral but confined to the world of nature, and multiple, particular assertions that were value-laden and limited exclusively to segments of human reality, and thus not amenable to external resolution and thereby general consensus. This was the dilemma posed to knowledge producers in their efforts, allied with those of policy-makers, to come to terms with the evolving material and political structures of the nineteenth century.

It was in this context that positivism as a methodology began to encroach steadily on the domain of social inquiry. John Stuart Mill argued for the application of the methods of the physical sciences to the moral sciences, and Auguste Comte attempted to establish positivism as the methodological basis for the analysis of human relations. As a result, the divorce of systematic knowledge from human values deepened. Both Mill and Comte were politically aware and understood the implications of a positivist methodology. Of course, not all students of the social world agreed. Against those who, following Mill and Comte, wished to apply so-called scientific methods to the study of the social world, there were those who continued to insist on a hermeneutic approach, emphasizing qualitative differences and particularistic patterns. This came to be known as the difference between a nomothetic and an idiographic epistemology. In organizational terms, these approaches found their strong bases in different disciplines. Looking at the social sciences as a super-domain in the structures of knowledge, in between the natural sciences and the humanities, one could say they were torn apart by the two strongly contending currents and failed to develop an autonomous "third" epistemology.

In the context of the English debates which posed order and anarchy as an irresolvable antinomy articulated in the ideologies of conservatism and radicalism, T. H. Huxley invoked the objective, value-neutral, problem-solving spirit of science to realize (a liberal centrist version of) progress without moralism: "men will gradually bring themselves to deal with political, as they now deal with scientific, questions" (Huxley, 1881, pp. 158–9). Nonetheless, humanist critics like Matthew Arnold and socialists like William Morris would continue to oppose the scientization of social inquiry, the individualism and reductionism of which they rejected in favor of holism and organicism.

In the middle of the nineteenth century, the Germanies had institutionalized a form of social science called *Staatswissenschaften* that rejected the transnational universalizing propositions put forth by the English and French positivists, and insisted on a holistic understanding of differently instituted social complexes, the *Staat* of *Staatswissenschaft*. The so-called *Methodenstreit* of the late nineteenth century began as an attempt to convert this major citadel of social science work, the *Staatswissenschaften*, to a positivist approach to social knowledge. Those who resisted this attempt made a philosophical defense of a connection between meaning or values, *Wert*, and systematic knowledge, *Wissen*, which they said positivism subverted. That this debate was especially strong in the Germanies was probably no accident, beset as Germany was by an internal controversy about whether the way to catch up with and contest Great Britain was by imitation or by difference. By analogy, in the structures of knowledge, the question was whether they should imitate a positivistic social science on the model of Mill and Comte such as that advocated by Huxley or pursue an original approach like that of *Staatswissenschaften*.

Wilhelm Dilthey (1883, p. 142) stated that "we must meet the challenge to establish human sciences through epistemology, to justify and support their independent formation, and to do away definitively with subordinating their principles and their methods to those of natural sciences." He considered it philosophy's task to demonstrate that the *Geisteswissenschaften* were not less fundamental, or comprehensive, or objective than the *Naturwissenschaften*, but were nonetheless not positivist either. In 1883, the very year of the appearance of his *Einleitung in die Geisteswissenschaften*, the *Methodenstreit* erupted in economics. The neoclassical marginalists challenged the rejection by the "historical school" of the universality of deductive theory in favor of inductive history.

The advocates of the marginalist revolution succeeded in overcoming the historicists' stronghold in the Germanies, and Germany would fall in line with the Franco-British structures in the twentieth century. Economics would be clearly demarcated as a "value-free" discipline. The historicists' project was also eventually frustrated by Max Weber, in part unintentionally, in his attempt to institutionalize sociology. Weber, like Descartes, labored in a milieu of ideologically driven conflict, this time concerning issues of nationalism rather than of religion, and therefore was similarly seeking a way of producing knowledge freed from the imperatives of (patriotic) value imperatives. Although Weber argued against both the positivists and their opponents and tried to hold on to the axiological dimension, operationally he lifted his "ideal type" out of time and context, thus *de facto* separating historians from the world of human relations they sought to explain.

Overall, the outcomes of the order and anarchy debates and of the *Methodenstreit* determined the intellectual and institutional arrangements for the subsequent construction of knowledge in the social sphere. Although it did not go unchallenged, the resulting organization of the disciplines was firmly in place and largely taken for granted during the 1945–70 period. (Lee (1996) explores the disciplinary organization of knowledge over the post-1945 period and the differing types of challenges that were advanced on either side of the 1967/1973 turning point.) It had set universal science, empirical, positivistic, and the source of truth, in opposition to the humanities, particularistic, impressionistic, anarchic, and expressing human values. Occupying a tenuous space in between, the social sciences remained very much torn between nomothetic and idiographic forms of universalism. The appeals to universalism and the sectorializing effect separating market, state, and civil society into independent domains tended to have the political effect of obscuring underlying organizational arrangements and historical feedback mechanisms, and thereby made organization to effect social change much more difficult. In fact, already by the end of the nineteenth century, the social sciences had become the indispensable instrument of the linear, predictable reformism that replaced the real, but defeated, political altern-atives of the left and the right, as they were swallowed up in the new liberal consensus and its promise of gradual progress.

SECULAR CRISIS AND SYSTEMIC TRANSITION

The term "two cultures" has been much discussed and repeatedly debunked, but the phrase lives on in contemporary epistemological debates as a commonsense classification. During the past three decades, however, there have been chal-lenges to the very concept, and they have occurred simultaneously across the entire gamut of the disciplines.

From its inception in the 1950s, cultural studies – a politically motivated intellectual movement that originated in the humanities and moved into the intellectual and institutional space of the social sciences – consciously challenged the validity of the separation of the disciplines of knowledge formation. It dismissed the high–low culture divide, applied literary methods to the analysis of social reality and insisted on the social bases of canons of taste, and re-evaluated the intellectual history of the ideologies. Cultural studies reasserted the values of the culture of everyday life. This was a conception of a culture that both offered the nourishment of tradition and served as the springboard for action. It represented an attempt to steer a course between the value-neutrality of the liberal model of quantitative social science and the reduction-ism of the Marxist base–superstructure mode of social analysis. Privileging a concept of culture that was ordinary and historically constructed, it under-mined the high culture canon on which traditional literary criticism rested. If culture could no longer be counted on as a stable resource, then the organization of the institutions (and implicitly of society) reproducing it, and reproduced by it, was also thereby severely challenged. The widening acceptance of the various structuralisms and the turn to "reading" the social text only aggravated the rejection of the traditional norms of the humanities and the social sciences.

From the late 1960s, developments at the level of theory were mirrored on the ground of practice. Those groups which had theretofore lacked a "voice" gained admittance to the academy and began to transform it from the inside. Multiple, not always harmonious, varieties of feminism have contested received premises of knowledge formation through a conception of values expressed in hierarchies of difference and power. They challenged the division of the two cultures by directly undermining what they saw as the male universalism and objectivity by which science laid claim to a distinctive arena of knowledge production. Their work disputed the "essentialist" categories of man and woman, and situated the female body as a pivotal site positioning women in society through scientific discourse. In a fashion similar to the way feminists have questioned the struc-tures of knowledge formation, scholars and activists working in the areas of race and ethnicity and non-Western civilizations have, in the course of producing their own empirical studies, elaborated theories of difference that likewise challenged Western universalism and objectivity. Their work also unveiled how the essentialism of received categories of difference functioned to inscribe whole groups into subordinate positions.

For the past three decades, social studies of knowledge ("science studies") have offered exogenous analyses of the historical development of science. They argued that (social) scientific methods could be applied to scientific work and that science was not a privileged domain exempt from historical/social explanation and interpretation. Initially, in the tradition of the classical sociology of knowledge, the emphasis was on the ways the social field, or "interests," shaped or influenced science, thus reproducing the Cartesian duality of nature and the human. Very soon, however, the accent shifted to the degree to which the construction of scientific knowledge was contingent and situated in local contexts. Cultural studies of science have emphasized the possibilities of participating in the construction of authoritative knowledge by engaging critically with scientific practices of making meaning.

These developments led to a strong backlash on the part of those committed to traditional epistemologies. The result was the so-called "culture wars" and "science wars." In the culture wars in the humanities, the defenders of traditional norms argued that the proponents of culture studies – especially various strands of race and gender studies, deconstruction, and poststructuralism – intended the politicization of all thought via the breakdown of objectivity located in canons of taste. The tone of the exchanges attests to the far-reaching consequences of the critiques from within the humanities and the social sciences and the position of authority and power occupied by the intellectual and the university in public debates.

In similar ways, some scientists have been denouncing what they see as a serious shift toward relativism put forward by what defines an "academic left" located in the humanities and the social sciences. This relativism is said to constitute a challenge to rationality itself. This high-pitched defensive attack has gone under the label of the science wars. In response to these attacks, others have alleged that what is really at stake in this scientific side of what is actually a single epistemological controversy is the fear of the undermining of the legitimacy of scientific authority (carefully defining scientists in very specific terms) and the allocation of societal funds that has gone with it.

It is thus particularly significant that the premises of classical science, the anchor of the true associated with universal legitimacy and authority in the structures of knowledge, has been put into question endogenously, via developments within the natural sciences and mathematics themselves. The sciences of complexity have attacked the universal validity of Newtonian dynamics, insisting that it represents a special case of the processes of the natural world. This new standpoint sees the world quite differently from the Newtonian worldview, which emphasized equilibrium and stability. Rejecting the presumed generality of determinism and linearity, which had allowed the discovery of universal laws, dynamical-systems research has reconceptualized the world as unstable and complex, explicable but unpredictable, one in which irreversibility (the "arrow of time") is as fundamental to nature as it is to humans.

Investigations in complexity studies fall into three interrelated categories: order-in-chaos, associated with strange attractors; order-out-of-chaos, associated with self-organization and dissipative structures; and fractal geometry, associated with visual representations exhibiting non-integer dimensions. Studies in these areas constitute implicit calls for a reappraisal of the assumptions of classical science. Scientists are now providing us with alternative models of physical reality in the form of relationally constituted self-organizing systems and fractal geometry, and alternative models of change and transition expressed in complexity theory and chaos theory. These defy the law of the excluded middle so fundamental to classical science, classical logic, and (as a result of long socialization) current common sense. This synthetic, non-reductionist approach questions the sacrosanct concept of natural laws that permit predictions, and emphasizes in their place the permanent reality of contingency and creativity.

Re-evaluations of the conceptual centrality of contingency, context-dependency, and multiple, overlapping, temporal and spatial frameworks are moving the humanities in the direction of the analyses of the historical social sciences. Studies of embedded order in both stable and chaotic systems and bifurcations leading to unpredictable new structures in far-from-equilibrium systems are moving the natural sciences in the same direction. Amidst the turmoil, the social sciences are becoming more concerned with the "stuff" of the sciences rather than their methods. Scholars across the disciplines are recognizing the centrality of broad "cultural" issues common to them all. As a result, the previous intellectual justification for those disciplines based on assumptions of radically different and independent domains or proprietary methods is collapsing.

Certainly there is some evidence of organizational rethinking. Of particular note is how studies embodying fresh intellectual approaches have transgressed not only particular disciplinary boundaries but those of the super-categories as well. The establishment of centers of advanced study and the deliberate restructuring of disciplinary/departmental relationships in new institutions or in rehabilitated ones are important developments. New disciplinary/departmental groupings have also emerged, directly challenging the fact–values divide. For instance, ecology takes a relational approach to the natural world and reaches down through the sciences to the social sciences and the humanities to reintegrate our understanding of the relation of human reality to the non-human world. A new form of stratification studies has built on work focusing on race and gender inequality, seeking to show how the historical construction of particular identities was associated with specific sets of values, and then legitimated by scientific, and social scientific, justifications of existing hierarchies.

Overall, we observe processes today in the structures of knowledge which seem to confirm evidence from developments in the "politics" and "economics" of the world-system that what we are living through in the contemporary world is the vastly increased possibility for human action to effect change offered in a period of systemic transition (see Lee, 1999). As complexity studies has made apparent, moments of transition, "where the system can 'choose' between or among more than one possible future," are historically rare and arise only when dynamical systems, including social systems, become unstable because they have been driven far from equilibrium by their own internal development (Prigogine and Stengers, 1984, pp. 169–70). It appears that we may be experiencing the beginning of such a secular crisis – that is, a crisis of the material structures and social relations of the Europe-centered world as it has developed since the sixteenth century (see Hopkins and Wallerstein, 1996) – and therefore are living in one of those unstable moments of transition, comparable to the transition from feudalism, when the future becomes an open future, rather than a law-bound Newtonian one, a future determined only by creative choices and contingent circumstances. The study of the structures of knowledge, with its emphasis on the secular trends and cyclical shifts in the cognitive limits on human action, offers a means of modeling interpretative studies directed at imagining possible futures for a world in transition.

17

The New Sociology of Ideas

Charles Camic and Neil Gross

Over the course of the past twenty years, an important field of study, which we call "the new sociology of ideas," has been quietly taking shape. The field focuses on women and men who specialize in the production of cognitive, evaluative, and expressive ideas and examines the social processes by which their ideas – i.e. their statements, claims, arguments, concepts, beliefs, assumptions, etc. – emerge, develop, and change. For much of the twentieth century, interest in these processes fell, along with many other concerns, to the often marginalized specialty area of the sociology of knowledge, where they suffered relative neglect. Recently, however, a major turnabout has occurred, as a result of the work of scholars in a number of specialty areas, including – in addition to the sociology of knowledge itself – the sociology of science, the sociology of culture, and general sociological theory, as well as intellectual history.

Rich in new theoretical formulations, methodological proposals, and empirical findings, however, this work has generally lacked consciousness of itself as a unified social-scientific undertaking, as specialists in each area have tended to operate in isolation from developments in related areas – thus retarding the growth of the sociology of ideas as a recognized area of theory and research.

The goal of the present chapter is to help to rectify this situation. We aim to do so not simply by pointing out that scholars in a variety of fields have, in relative isolation from one another, employed the tools of sociological analysis to explain why thinkers make the intellectual choices they do. In addition, we seek to characterize the contours of the intellectual transformation that the sociology of ideas has, despite conditions of fragmentation, undergone in recent years. On the whole, the sociology of ideas as it has been developing since the 1970s is substantially different from its approximate counterpart in earlier eras, and we can think of no better way to encourage contemporary scholars to recognize that they are at work on a common project – and that they would benefit enormously from a dialogue with one another – than by identifying some of the main theoretical and methodological principles that they seem increasingly to share. Taken together, these principles distinguish the new sociology of ideas from earlier sociological approaches to the development of ideas, or what we will schematically term the old sociology of ideas.

But a clarification is in order before we proceed. Ideas are the monopoly of no one social group: claims, beliefs, arguments, etc. are symbolic configurations formed and expressed by all members of human societies in all domains of human activity. Because a field of study so unbounded would exceed the scope of any social-scientific inquiry, the sociology of ideas focuses primarily on those who are relatively *specialized* in the production of scientific, interpretive, moral, political, or aesthetic ideas. In contemporary societies, such specialists often have academic locations; they are natural scientists, social scientists, or humanists working in university settings. But at the present time they are also found in many other social locations, in both the public and private sectors, and historically they have occupied an even wider range of social roles. As a shorthand for this broad array of specialist knowledge producers, we will sometimes speak of *intellectuals*, though we caution against reading into this term any of the many additional connotations that it has frequently been given (see assumption 5 below).

THE OLD SOCIOLOGY OF IDEAS

Since its inception, sociology has shown an interest in understanding the social basis of intellectual life. This interest can be found in the work of thinkers as disparate as Comte, Marx and Engels, Durkheim, and Weber. It was not, however, until the 1940s that the sociological study of ideas began to crystallize as a coherent project under the banner of the sociology of knowledge. Responding to the work of Mannheim, a number of scholars turned explicit attention to developments in the intellectual arena. Although there were major differences among the approaches to the sociology of ideas taken by thinkers like DeGré (1939), Znaniecki (1940), Mills (1942), Merton (1949), Stark (1958), Parsons (1959), Coser (1965), Gouldner (1965, 1970), and such first-wave sociologists of science as Hagstrom (1965), Ben-David (1971), Crane (1972), and Mullins (1973), there were also important commonalties. In this section, we identify five assumptions shared by many of these scholars.

Assumption 1:   The Sociology of Ideas is a Means, Not an End

With the notable exception of early works in the sociology of science, the old sociology of ideas typically viewed the study of ideas not as an end in itself, i.e. not as a legitimate arena of social inquiry that formulates and tests claims about the social bases of ideational production, but as a means to other ends, especially social-critical ends. This was somewhat ironic, since the area was indebted to Mannheim, who insisted on the need to depoliticize the Marxian approach to ideology (see Frisby, 1983, pp. 107–73; Thompson, 1990, pp. 44–52; Eagleton 1991, pp. 107–10). As Mannheim often complained, Marx's engagement with the sociology of knowledge did not extend beyond a desire to discredit bourgeois thought; it thus saw economic "interest [as] the only form of social conditioning of ideas" (Mannheim, 1925, p. 183). Mannheim's alternative agenda proposed that sociologists of knowledge attempt to understand the "existential basis" of *all* forms of thought, whether "ideological" in Marx's sense of the word or not, by means of an analysis of the socio-historical experiences of groups of intellectuals (see especially Mannheim, 1962). (But, as discussed below, Mannheim subsequently denied that some forms of thought have any social basis.)

Yet this depoliticization was by no means as thorough as it could have been. For Mannheim, the ultimate aim of the sociology of knowledge was not to understand knowledge production processes, but to inject a new kind of rationality into political and moral life, forcing individuals to interrogate the social bases of their beliefs and helping them avoid "talk[ing] past one another... overlook[ing] the fact that their antagonist differs from them in his whole outlook, and not merely in his opinion about the point under discussion" (Mannheim, 1929, p. 280). This view of the political aim of the sociology of knowledge was consequential for Mannheim, for it inclined him to analyze those worldviews, such as utopianism or conservatism, that seemed to underlie the most pressing political disputes of his day.

In the years following the publication of Mannheim's *Ideology and Utopia* (1929), sociologists followed the book's lead, conceiving the sociology of ideas to have critical aims and selecting research topics accordingly. In Gouldner's view, for example, the sociology of ideas was a form of critical hermeneutics. The sociologist of ideas may "contribute to an empirically testable social theory about social theorists," but his or her ultimate aim is to "assist us in taking possession of our own intellectual heritage, past or present, by appraising it actively – which is to say, critically – in terms of our viable interests" (Gouldner, 1965, pp. 171, 170; 1970). Similarly, Stark argued that "it is not the least valuable service which the sociology of knowledge has to render that it can teach all men humility and charity" by showing that "the truth is the truth only in its proper sphere" (Stark, 1958, p. 159). On these grounds, he suggested that researchers focus their attention upon major societal disagreements (Stark, 1958, pp. 208–9). Even Parsons (1959) touted the sociology of knowledge not as an end in itself, but as subsidiary to the task of understanding the relationship between the social and the cultural system.

Assumption 2:   The Internal/External Distinction

The old sociology of ideas assumed an unproblematic distinction between the content of ideas, their "internal" substance, and the social and therefore "external" factors that condition this content. Having made this distinction, it was assumed further that the content of thought, represented in terms of logical propositions, or what DeGré (1939, p. 3) called "thought signs" – "manifestations of thinking as embodied in scientific, philosophical, theological, logical,

mathematical and magical systems, propositions, and concepts" – was (in varying degrees) the realm of an asocial, scientific rationality about which sociology
could have little to say. From this it followed that the sociology of ideas should
restrict itself to those non-scientific arenas of thought in which rational considerations have little sway, or, insofar as it wished to treat science, forswear the
content of science and analyze the socio-historical conditions under which the
institutions of science were able to grow and develop.

The notion that sociology can only explain the content of ideas in some fields
was suggested by Mannheim, who argued that there exist "a few propositions in
which the content is so formal and abstract (for example, in mathematics,
geometry, and pure economics) that in fact they seem to be completely detached
from the thinking social individual." In his view, social life conditions only those
forms of thought "in which every concept is...from the first" ripe with social
meaning. For Mannheim, political, moral, religious, and social thought fell in
this category, but the "exact" sciences did not (Mannheim, 1929, p. 43).

Merton took a similar position: "A central point of agreement in all
approaches to the sociology of knowledge is the thesis that thought has an
existential basis in so far as it is not immanently determined and in so far as
one or another of its aspects can be derived from extra-cognitive factors." This
thesis, according to Merton, has its roots in Marxism, which tends "to consider
natural science as standing in a relation to the economic base different from that
of other spheres of knowledge and belief. In science, the focus of attention may
be socially determined but not, presumably, its conceptual apparatus." While
Merton was open to the possibility that "the cultural and social context [does]
enter...into the conceptual phrasing of scientific problems," he made no
attempt to explain the content of scientific thought. Instead, his influential
version of the sociology of science problematized the external normative climate
that governs the process of scientific inquiry (Merton, 1949, pp. 516, 523–4,
539–40).

Nor did those who accepted the notion of an asocial realm of immanent
determination limit it to the natural sciences. Even when dealing with ideas in
the humanities and social sciences, the point remained that many intellectual
choices rest on free and rational grounds – that "the process of [intellectual]
creation itself has always been a process of free choice and adaptation" (Shils,
1958, p. 10). From this perspective, the sociologist of ideas could do little more
than show how social factors incline thinkers to certain topics, general worldviews, or stylistic conventions. For example, Coser's analysis of eighteenth-
century French social thought focused on how the salon "helped shape the
literary style of the eighteenth century." Because success in salon circles
depended on "wit and grace,...the literature that emerged was eminently a
literature of sociability, a literature of playfulness, liveliness, and sparkle
...eschew[ing] the deeply personal and the philosophically profound" (Coser,
1965, p. 15). As to the social origins of the substance of any of the French
thinkers' actual arguments, however, Coser had nothing sociological to say.

Not surprisingly, sociologists whose primary interests lay with the natural
sciences were even less willing to treat the content of ideas sociologically.

Ben-David's view was representative: "the possibilities for either an interactional or institutional sociology of the conceptual and theoretical contents of science are extremely limited." Consequently, the sociology of science should restrict itself to "the conditions that determine...the level of scientific activity and shape...the roles and careers of scientists and the organization of science" (Ben-David, 1971, p. 14). That sociologists were still of this opinion a decade after Kuhn's (1962) influential, and quasi-sociological, historical study of the content of scientific revolutions is significant. For, though open to Kuhn's work in some respects (see Hagstrom, 1965; Crane, 1972), first-wave sociologists of science devoted little energy to explaining how social factors affect "the actual substance of the scientific ideas that are developed in the laboratory and then evaluated by the scientific community" (Cole, 1992, p. 33).

Assumption 3:   The Transparency of Ideas

When it did deal with intellectual fields whose substance was *not* immanently shaped, the old sociology of ideas treated the content of the ideas that it subjected to sociological analysis in a characteristic way. It assumed that the basic meanings of these ideas were more or less transparent to the sociological investigator, i.e. that a correct interpretation of the substance of the ideas could be achieved simply by reading this off from the writings of the intellectuals who produced them. Two brief examples will illustrate the practice.

In one of the most famous studies in the area, Gouldner examined the social theory of the young Talcott Parsons, seeking to reveal Parsons's ideas as "a response to the social conflicts...of the Great Depression." To establish the content of Parsons's ideas, Gouldner's procedure was simply to draw on scattered statements in Parsons's early writings and classify these according to Gouldner's own theoretical and political categories. This mode of analysis neglected to take account of Parsons's other work at the time and the writings of the contemporaries who made up his intellectual context, thereby overlooking the contemporary meaning of Parsons's statements and imputing to him ideas he never held. To be sure, since Gouldner was concerned to expose Parsons's deeper ideological message – his "tacit ideological apologetics" for capitalism – he had ample reason not to restrict himself to Parsons's self-understanding. The assumption of this approach, however, was that the sociologist of ideas could so immediately grasp Parsons's basic arguments that no interpretive effort was even necessary before one moved on to their ideological reinterpretation (Gouldner, 1970, pp. 141, 348; see also Marcuse, 1964).

Likewise, a study in the sociology of science by Mullins (1973) sought to account for changing theoretical orientations in American sociology. Seeking to identify the various "theory groups" making up American sociology, Mullins's method was to read the existing theory literature, categorizing some theorists as symbolic interactionists, others as functionalists, etc., based primarily on whether their statements and assumptions appeared on the surface to fit Mullins's own views about the ideas that defined each group (a procedure Mullins complemented with citation and co-authorship analysis). This method gave no attention to the contextual meanings of these intellectual orientations and failed to consider whether the intellectual positions whose developments Mullins sought to explain were those actually occupied by the theorists in question.

Assumption 4:   The Focus on Macrosocial Factors

When Znaniecki (1940) called attention to the effects of a thinker's "social circle" on his or her ideas, he gave voice to a micro-level focus that would remain recessive in the sociology of ideas until the 1970s. Proponents of the old sociology of ideas like Stark might concede the "great service the micro-sociology of knowledge can render the historian of ideas," but they tended nevertheless to assign explanatory weight to "the total historical movement of the social system" (Stark, 1958, pp. 26, 30). Insofar as ideas admitted of sociological explanation, such explanations involved appeals to macro-level economic, political, and cultural factors, cited separately or in combination.

Examples of this mode of explanation were plentiful. According to Mannheim's analysis of Greek philosophy, for example, it was the "process of social ascent... in the Athenian democracy [that] called forth the first great surge of scepticism in the history of Occidental thought," while sophism "was the expression of an attitude of doubt" arising from the collision of "a dominant nobility already doomed to decline" and "an urban artisan lower stratum, which was in the process of moving upwards" (Mannheim, 1929, p. 9). In a similar vein, Merton attributed the substance of the sociology of knowledge itself to its development in an era of "increasing social conflict" and growing "distrust between [social] groups" (Merton, 1949, p. 511). Likewise for Gouldner, "Plato's social theory [was] a response to the [economic and political] problems and tensions current in his historical period" (1965, p. 171), and Parsons's work an alarmed reaction to the "mass meetings, marches, [and] demonstrations" of the Depression era (1959, p. 146). For practitioners of the old sociology of ideas, any and all macro-level factors might easily be cited to explain intellectuals' concepts, beliefs, and arguments.

Assumption 5:   Intellectuals as an Objective Social Category

The old sociology of ideas was much occupied with conceptualizing "intellectuals." Efforts in this direction ranged from Shils's definition of intellectuals as those "with an unusual sensitivity to the sacred, an uncommon reflectiveness about the nature of their universe and the rules which govern their society" (Shils, 1958, p. 3); through Coser's reference to "special custodians of abstract ideas like reason and justice and truth, jealous guardians of moral standards that are too often ignored in the market place and the houses of power" (Coser, 1965, p. xvi); to Gouldner's description of intellectuals as part of an authoritative "New Class," "a new cultural bourgeoisie whose capital is not its money but its control over valuable cultures" (Gouldner, 1979, p. 21; see also Aron, 1955). What these formulations have in common is the assumption that in most societies, and certainly all modern societies, groups of persons can be found exhibiting the defining properties of intellectuals. The sociologist interested in knowledge producers proceeds, therefore, by locating these groups and examining how their macro-historical circumstances affect their various intellectual activities.

But by approaching intellectuals in this way – i.e. as an objective social category – the old sociology of ideas tended to efface important forms of variation among specialized knowledge producers. To be sure, those in the area were sometimes well aware that different fields of knowledge production exhibit different forms of social organization, which might condition ideas in different ways (see especially Merton, 1949, p. 521). Nevertheless, insofar as they considered intellectuals an objective social category, those working in the old sociology of ideas tended to occlude the extent to which the attributes identified in different definitions of intellectuals may systematically vary across groups of knowledge producers. This is so because attributes such as intellectual standing and authority, rather than inhering in all intellectuals as a category, are valuable and scarce resources, resources for which knowledge producers vie, individually and collectively, with profound effects on the ideas that they espouse.

THE NEW SOCIOLOGY OF IDEAS

This brief review of the old sociology of ideas is not intended to question the importance of some of the individual works discussed, nor to deny their combined success in establishing the sociology of knowledge as an active specialty area until the late 1960s. As early as 1968, however, Coser observed fewer explicit references to the sociology of knowledge and a tendency for the field to "merge...with other areas of research" (p. 432). This trend toward dissolution continued in the 1970s and 1980s, with the sociological study of ideas increasingly concentrated in five other more or less disconnected domains of inquiry: (a) the sociology of science, as reconstituted originally in Britain as the "sociology of scientific knowledge" (for review see Lynch, 1993; Hess, 1997); (b) the study of ideology, pursued now under the cross-cutting rubrics of Marxism, poststructuralism, and feminism (for review see Thompson, 1990; Eagleton, 1991; McCarthy, 1996); (c) the sociology of culture, a vibrant new American specialty area focused on "how kinds of social organization make whole orderings of knowledge possible" (Swidler and Arditi, 1994, p. 306); (d) the field of intellectual history, reshaped by a growing emphasis on intellectual discourses (for example, Foucault, 1969; White, 1973) and on contextualist methods (for brief reviews see Tuck, 1991; Miller, 1997); and (e) general sociological theory, where prominent figures such as Bourdieu (1984a) and Collins (1975, 1998) turned attention toward the intellectual sphere. By no means are these diverse lines of work concerned exclusively with the social processes by which ideas grow, emerge, and change – the central problem of the sociology of ideas. Nonetheless, not only have scholars in all these areas addressed this problem, they have done so on the basis of a common set of principles which differ markedly from the assumptions of the old sociology of ideas. In the section that follows, we identify the five major tenets of the new sociology of ideas. Although not every thinker who works in the area embraces every tenet, we believe that, taken together, these tenets characterize the current state of the field.

Tenet 1:   The Sociology of Ideas Is an End in Itself

New sociologists of ideas tend to view their research as an end in itself, taking the question "How do intellectuals come to hold the ideas they do?" as a legitimate concern in its own right and choosing their objects of investigation accordingly. This is not to characterize the new sociologists of ideas as naive positivists committed to "value-free" social science and blind to the connections between scholarship and power. To the contrary, most reject this outlook, even as they oppose selecting their research questions because of their immediate relevance to social-critical aims. (Of course, not every work in the area takes this view. Feminist sociologists of science and knowledge, for example, explicitly adopt a standpoint aimed at "countering eurocentric and androcentric science and technology policies and their effects" (Harding, 1998, p. 18), and choose empirical foci that help advance this aim.)

Bourdieu's work on intellectuals illustrates the general trend. His *Homo Academicus*, for example, is a hard-nosed analysis of the modern French university field, a multidimensional space where agents are distributed on the basis of prestige and capital and where academics jockey with one another for position, thus gravitating toward topics and arguments that are in their professional interest. Despite this conception of academic life, however, Bourdieu has nothing but derision for thinkers like Gouldner who would use the concept of "ideology" to commit "symbolic aggressions" on behalf of their own political positions (Bourdieu, 1979, p. 12). Bourdieu's own forays into the sociology of ideas aim, accordingly, to examine sociologically neglected aspects of the knowledge production process – e.g. the historical conditions under which the French intellectual field attained relative autonomy (Bourdieu, 1966), or cross-national knowledge transfer in the age of globalization (Bourdieu and Wacquant, 1999) – *not* to advance some critical interest in the particular ideas under investigation.

Contemporary sociologists of scientific knowledge have likewise insisted that cases be selected on the basis of their value for sociological understanding. This is one of the main themes of the "strong program" for the sociology of scientific knowledge (discussed below), with its injunction that sociologists attend impartially to all scientific claims, regardless of their own attitude toward these claims and their truth or falsity (see Bloor, 1976; Collins and Pinch, 1993).

The same point is evident in Gieryn's (1999) recent analysis of scientific "credibility" contests. Examining episodes such as the nineteenth-century debate over the relationship between science, religion, and "mechanics," or the modern controversy over cold fusion, Gieryn portrays science as an ever-changing, locally variable cultural construction whose boundaries "will be drawn to pursue immediate goals and interests of cultural cartographers, and to appeal to the goals and interests of audiences and stakeholders" (Gieryn, 1999, p. 23). Here, too, sociological interest in understanding the process by which ideas develop drives object choice.

Tenet 2: Rejection of the Internal/External Distinction

In a recent account of the science studies field, Shapin (1992) observes a transformation: until the 1970s, a majority of scholars viewed the distinction between internal and external explanatory factors as legitimate and doubted that external factors could affect the content of scientific knowledge; contemporary researchers, in contrast, decisively reject the internal/external distinction. While warning against overdrawing this contrast, Shapin reports that by the 1980s the internal/external distinction, eclectically mobilized through the 1960s, had "passed from the commonplace to the gauche" (Shapin, 1992, p. 333). We believe that this shift has taken place not only among sociologists of science, but among other sociologists of ideas as well. (For a parallel line of thought, see the discourse-centered intellectual historiography of Foucault, 1969; White, 1973.)

There can be no question, however, that developments in the sociology of scientific knowledge precipitated important aspects of this broader turnaround. Particularly relevant in this regard has been the work of Bloor. Laying out the so-called "strong program" for science studies, Bloor urges sociologists not only to develop causal explanations for why some scientific claims (rather than others) come to be made, disseminated, accepted, and rejected, but to develop explanations that are symmetrical in that they treat "true" and "false" scientific claims in the same way. Bloor grants that the objective nature of the world is not irrelevant to explaining why a particular scientific claim comes to be made or accepted. But he refuses to set true scientific ideas apart in an asocial realm of "immanent determination." In Bloor's view, the scientific process itself – the rational process of hypothesis formation and testing, of communicating experimental results to colleagues, and of having those results accepted by the scientific community – is shot through with sociality, in particular with rhetorical tactics and vocabularies that acquire their efficacy and meaning within historically specific frameworks of scientific convention and understanding (Bloor, 1976). From this point of view, the social is as much internal to science as it is external, and the distinction loses its cogency.

This view is not peculiar to Bloor. Since the articulation of the strong program, the sociology of scientific knowledge has grown tremendously and taken many different directions. On the whole, however, its practitioners have agreed that both institutional *and* rational factors are thoroughly social and that, for this reason, there is no justification for the construction of a firewall around the content of scientific claims (Lynch, 1993; Hess, 1997; for important foundational statements, see Barnes, 1977; Lynch, 1977; Latour and Woolgar, 1979; Knorr-Cetina, 1981).

The internal/external distinction has retreated as well in the work of sociologists who study ideas outside the natural sciences. Kusch (1995), for example, places the content of philosophical ideas squarely on the sociologist's plate. He does so through an analysis of an intense controversy that arose (c.1880–1920) among German philosophers over psychologism – the belief that logic and mathematics rest on psychology. To account for the substance of this debate, Kusch links it to the academic emergence of German empirical psychology, relating the claims of both psychologistic and anti-psychologistic thinkers to their institutional position in the German university system. "Pure" philosophers, threatened by empirical psychology, which was then housed in departments of philosophy, reacted to its growth with abstract arguments denying that psychology could advance the study of philosophical issues; in contrast, psychologists, still attempting to legitimate their work as a contribution to philosophy, towed the psychologistic line (Kusch, 1995).

An even more ambitious effort to subject philosophical ideas to sociological explanation is the work of Collins (1998b). This work builds on Collins's earlier skepticism about the internal/external divide: "The distinction between explaining background conditions and explaining content is not so easy to maintain... [for to] state when and where science will exist in an historical analysis is to give conditions under which particular kinds of ideas are formulated and believed in" (Collins, 1975, p. 474). Collins's recent work elaborates this position into a full-fledged theory of intellectual production, which (among a large number of other claims) maintains that "conflict [for] attention space is a fundamental fact about intellectuals" – a fact entailed by the very structure of the intellectual world, which "allows only a limited number of positions to receive much attention at any one time" (Collins, 1998b, pp. 876, 75). Faced with this situation, intellectuals necessarily "thrive on disagreement, dividing the attention space into three to six factions, seeking lines of creativity by negating the chief tenets of their rivals, rearranging into alliances or fanning out into disagreement" (Collins, 1998b, p. 876) – a sociological proposition that Collins uses to cut to the substantive core of intellectual life and to explain the range of philosophical positions that has taken shape the world over, from antiquity to modern times.

To be sure, rejection of the internal/external distinction remains far from a matter of universal agreement. Critiques of various aspects of the "strong program" have been numerous and have brought forth alternative research agendas in which the internal/external distinction remains more or less intact (see Cole, 1992; Schmaus et al., 1992). With little doubt, however, such critics are currently swimming against the tide.

Tenet 3: Contextualism

New sociologists of ideas insist that the meaning of ideas is not transparent: that meanings are always embedded in socio-intellectual contexts which must be opened up to in-depth investigation before the ideas themselves can be understood. The formation of this viewpoint has been stimulated principally by trends in the field of intellectual history, which has become more sociological in recent decades. This is not to say that contextualist intellectual historians now regard themselves as sociologists of ideas; few have taken the social processes by which ideas develop as their central topic, and many hold to the traditional particularist/generalist division of labor between history and sociology. Nevertheless, contextualist intellectual historians have played an important role in shaping the new sociology of ideas.

They have done so by developing a contextualist methodology. Rejecting the view that "the *text* itself should form the self-sufficient object of inquiry and understanding" for the intellectual historian, proponents of contextualism – such as Skinner, Pocock, and Dunn – insist that "the proper way to read an historical text is as an historical product, in which the actual intentions of the author (in so far as they can reasonably be reconstructed) should be our principal guide as to why the text took the particular form it did" (Skinner, 1969, p. 4; see also Tuck, 1991, p. 194). To understand these intentions, contextualists argue further that texts must be situated in the immediate socio-linguistic contexts where they were produced – contexts that can be reconstructed by careful examination of the writings of a thinker's contemporaries. The aim of such a reconstruction is not merely to pin down "the sense and reference allegedly attaching to words and sentences." The goal instead is to "identify what their authors were *doing* in writing them," i.e. to recover the illocutionary dimension of textual statements, understood as stemming from authorial intentions to make "moves in an argument" – a procedure Skinner applies in his research on Hobbes to "indicate what traditions [Hobbes] reacts against, what lines of argument he takes up, what changes he introduces into existing debates" (Skinner, 1996, pp. 7–8). (Also pushing intellectual historiography in the direction of contextualism is the "New History": see Chartier, 1982; LaCapra, 1983; Burke, 1991.)

To date, contextualism has entered sociology mainly through revisionist work on the history of sociology by Jones (1986), Camic (1995), Strenski (1997), and Abbott (1999). Of these contributions, Camic's work (discussed in the next section) on the social processes by which American social-scientific thought developed is the most explicitly concerned with the problematic of the sociology of ideas. But works by other contemporary sociologists of ideas, such as Bryant's (1996) study of moral codes in Ancient Greece and McLaughlin's (1998) research on the development of neo-Freudianism, also make fruitful use of contextualist methods, demonstrating the inadequacy of the assumption that the meanings of texts are transparent and understandable without reference to the contexts where they were produced.

Tenet 4:   Localism

Closely linked to contextualism is an increased emphasis on localism. In insisting on the need to reconstruct the context where ideas were produced, new sociologists of ideas generally hold as well that this reconstruction must have a strong local focus. Without discounting the relevance of the macrosocial, the context ordinarily considered most fundamental for analyzing the development of ideas is no longer taken to be the general economic, political, and cultural milieu but the particular local institutional settings in which intellectuals find themselves when formulating their ideas.

Present throughout the new sociology of ideas, this emphasis on the local derives in part from work in anthropology. Most important here has been Geertz's dictum that "to an ethnographer, sorting through the machinery of distant ideas, the shapes of knowledge are always ineluctably local," and his extension of the same idea to the analysis of modern intellectual communities. In Geertz's view, "thinking (any thinking: Lord Russell's or Baron Corvo's; Einstein's or some stalking Eskimo's) is to be understood 'ethnographically,' that is, by describing the world in which it makes whatever sense it makes" – bearing in mind that "most effective academic communities are not that much larger than most peasant villages and just about as ingrown.... Laboratories and research institutes, scholarly societies, axial university departments, literary and artistic cliques, intellectual factions, all fit the same pattern: communities of multiply connected individuals" (Geertz, 1983, pp. 4, 152, 157). From this perspective, understanding the social contours of these local institutional settings is a prerequisite for understanding the ideas generated within them.

This perspective informs Shapin's work on seventeenth-century science. Holding that "epistemic judgment depends upon local contexts of use," Shapin focuses upon the face-to-face interactions of British philosopher-scientists – a local context in which judgments of the validity of scientific claims were made in relation to assessments of the gentlemanly character and veracity of the claimant. In this context, the scientific statements of a man like Robert Boyle easily acquired truth-status, according to Shapin, because Boyle's gentlemanly identity led others to trust his claims to such an extent that "his factual testimony was *never* negated by the Royal Society or by those whom it recognized as competent practitioners" (Shapin, 1994, pp. xix, 291).

This stress on localism also appears in the work of Camic, which proposes that "the factor of *localism*...be incorporated into the study of the history of the American social sciences – understanding by 'localism' the pattern of relations obtaining among different [academic] disciplines at this or that particular university" (Camic, 1995, p. 1011). Examining the development of the discipline of sociology in the 1890–1940 period, Camic notes that the field faced, in all American universities, the "newcomer's dilemma": the problem of establishing its legitimacy according to prevailing conceptions of science, while simultaneously differentiating itself from more established sciences. On Camic's account, however, this common dilemma was resolved very differently at different institutions, as distinctive local interdisciplinary conditions structured the different conceptions of the sociological enterprise that took shape. This emphasis on local institutional factors also appears in Camic's (1991, 1992) work on Parsons, which traces the process by which Parsons's theoretical and methodological ideas emerged in response to the credibility demands made on him by local academic conditions at Harvard University. Further examples of this growing micro-level focus would be easy to multiply (for example, Collins, 1998b; Harding, 1998; Abbott, 1999).

Tenet 5:   Struggles for Intellectual Position and the Importance of Fields

In much of the work considered so far, we have already glimpsed the importance that new sociologists of ideas assign to contests for intellectual position and scientific credibility. Whereas contributors to the old sociology of ideas tended to view intellectuals as "special custodians of abstract ideas," new sociologists of ideas see the women and men who produce ideas as engaged in historically specific struggles with one another, and with various audiences, to establish their legitimacy and respectability as intellectuals of particular types (scientists, humanists, etc.) – struggles that can have significant effects on the ideas that these actors produce and on the fate of the ideas that they generate.

Two brief examples will illustrate this point. Consider first Collins's explanation for the rise of idealism in Germany. According to Collins, German academics in the late eighteenth century faced a serious crisis. Universities, long intellectual backwaters in the hands of the Church, were suddenly confronted with the educational demands of the expanding Prussian state bureaucracy. This situation gave academics the opportunity to elevate their standing by transforming the universities into real centers of intellectual activity. To this end, philosophers like Hegel and Fichte, who were active participants in this struggle, fashioned philosophy along idealist lines: conceiving it as a lofty domain of inquiry distinct from theology; yet making it the source of the dialectical methods that they defined as indispensable to "all the fields of knowledge opened up by the academic revolution" (Collins, 1998b, p. 660). A second example is furnished by Lamont's (1987) analysis of the spread of Derridean ideas in contemporary France. Lamont suggests that the decisive factor in this development was the legitimation of Derrida's ideas through the packaging of his work "as a sophisticated cultural good" (Lamont, 1987, p. 595) attractive both to the upper middle-class public and to academics embroiled in the structuralist controversy, a controversy in which Derrida skillfully positioned himself.

These examples should not be interpreted to suggest that new sociologists of ideas view struggles for legitimacy and credibility as occurring willy-nilly, as intellectuals of different stripes fight out some no holds barred contest. To the contrary, contemporary research insists that status struggles occur within distinct "fields" of intellectual production; that the credibility of intellectuals is typically assessed in relation to other thinkers in the same field; and that the field itself establishes the range of tactics that are deemed acceptable to achieve legitimacy within it. The production of ideas may be primarily a local affair, but it is the thinker's intellectual field that links local sites together in what most sociologists of ideas regard as a hierarchical structure.

The concept of structured intellectual "fields" has been developed by Bourdieu (1975) and Whitley (1984). For Bourdieu, as summarized by Ringer, "The intellectual field at a given time and place is made up of agents taking various intellectual positions. Yet the field is not an aggregate of isolated elements; it is a configuration or a network of relationships. The elements in the field are not only related to each other in determinate ways; each also has a specific 'weight' or authority, so that the field is a distribution of power as well. The agents in the field are in conflict with each other. They compete for the right to define or codefine what shall count as intellectually established and culturally legitimate" (Ringer, 1990, p. 270). In Bourdieu's view, each intellectual field is relatively autonomous from the other fields of social life; although it is "influenced by the concerns and conflicts of the larger society, its logic is its own" (Ringer, 1990, p. 271). (Contemporary sociologists of culture and analysts of ideology also stress the relative autonomy of cultural fields: see Wuthnow, 1989; Thompson, 1990; Eagleton, 1991.) In addition, Bourdieu argues that the workings of each field give rise to particular intellectual contents, for to each field attaches what he calls a "habitus," a distinctive "scheme...of perception, thought, and action" (Bourdieu, 1980, p. 54). Using other terms, Whitley's position is similar. Intellectual fields, on Whitley's account, "are the social contexts in which scientists develop distinctive competences and research skills so that they make sense of their own actions in terms of...collective identities, goals, and practices as mediated by leaders of employment organizations and other major social influences" (Whitley, 1984, p. 8). So understood, intellectual fields vary from one another along a number of basic socio-organizational dimensions, which Whitley identifies and then relates to the content of the intellectual work produced in any particular field. For Whitley, as for other new sociologists of ideas, struggles for credibility and reputation – and their effects on the substance of ideas – are thus always structured by the social properties of the specific intellectual fields where these struggles occur.

CONCLUSION

Despite broad consensus around these tenets, the new sociology of ideas is plainly not an internally cohesive area of scholarship at the present time. Pursued, in little mutual awareness, by researchers in a variety of existing academic specialties, both in and out of sociology, work in the area has thus far focused on different intellectuals, different intellectual fields, different times and places, and the development of different ideas – inevitably bringing forth different conceptions of the social processes by which ideas emerge and change. Insofar as scholars in the area overcome their current fragmentation, more clearly articulated theories of these social processes and more rigorous assessments of such theories will, in all likelihood, take shape. The new sociology of ideas can already be credited, however, with having cleared the ground for this exciting possibility.

Part V
Politics and Political Movements

18

Political Sociology

MIKE SAVAGE

Until the 1980s political sociology was one of the leading subdisciplines within sociology. Between the 1950s and 1970s the vitality of political sociology could be seen in its contribution to studies of the social bases of political alignments and party systems (for instance, by Seymour Martin Lipset and Stein Rokkan), research on community power systems (by Lloyd Warner, Bachrach, and Steven Lukes) and elites (by C. Wright Mills, Anthony Giddens, and Tom Bottomore), and historical studies of revolution and social change (by Barrington Moore and Theda Skocpol).

Despite such intellectual dynamism, the past two decades have seen political sociology in retreat. Today political sociology is a subdiscipline in crisis. New kinds of sociology have developed – such as sociology of social movements and of the state – which cover similar territory to political sociology, but there is relatively little connection with older traditions of political sociology. This chapter is a critical study of the reasons for this change of fortunes and a consideration of possible ways of reviving interest in political sociology.

My argument will be that the contemporary problems of political sociology need to be seen in terms of the unraveling of limitations of what I will term the "classic political sociology paradigm." I begin by exploring the main features of the paradigm, which I claim is organized around a "social base" perspective. This paradigm can be seen as the dominant approach to political sociology during its golden age between 1945 and 1975. It explored the relationship between social interests and political mobilization, mainly through the ways in which established political parties and organizations structured class interests. As early as the late 1960s, Sartori (1969, p. 68) could write, "There is a widespread feeling that while political sociology has emerged as a core social science discipline, political science is in a serious plight."

The second part of my chapter examines the challenge to this paradigm. My main argument here is that the crisis of the classic paradigm is inextricably associated with the problems of class analysis as a viable intellectual project. The third part of the chapter explores how we might reinvigorate political sociology by exploring the sociology of the political field. Rather than looking at the social determinants of political alignments, as in the classic paradigm, this involves examining how the political field itself is socially constructed and "boundaried."

In the last part of this chapter I develop this argument by showing how social movement theory might be drawn upon to revive the terrain of political sociology. I argue that we might develop a viable political sociology that is concerned with the contested and socially specific boundaries between the "social" and "political."

THE CLASSIC "SOCIAL BASE" PARADIGM OF POLITICAL SOCIOLOGY

As numerous writers have observed (for example, Nisbet, 1966; Greer, 1969; Therborn, 1980), the development of sociology as a discipline involved distinguishing specifically social relationships from political institutions and processes on the one hand, and from various kinds of "economic" process on the other. A recognition of the political had been central to the emergence of disciplines of "statecraft" from the sixteenth century onwards. From the later eighteenth century, the maturing of political economy led to a recognition that the political was articulated with the economic. It was not until later in the nineteenth century that claims for the distinctiveness of the "social" emerged. Common claims in this nascent sociology were the significance of "community" (as in the arguments of de Tocqueville and Tönnies), the role of a distinctive "collective conscience" (as in the writings of Durkheim, later adapted by Parsons and American structural-functionalists to mean norms and values), and the irreducibility of microsocial interaction to broader economic and political structures (as in the writings of Weber and their development by phenomenologists and ethnomethodologists). What united all these different approaches was a concern to establish that the "social" was different from and irreducible to the political or the economic. It was around this recognition that the claims of sociology as a discipline were founded.

Establishing the "social" as a distinct and irreducible realm led logically to reflections on the relationship between the "social" and the "political." Political sociology emerged as the subdiscipline that depended on the idea that politics could be distinguished from social relationships and that social processes were related to politics. Political sociology thus emerged as a way of reflecting on the linkages between "society" and "politics." The main mechanism which linked society and politics was generally that of "interests," and in particular class interests (see Sartori, 1969). In both European and American research, social class interests were the crucial conduit between social relations and political mobilization. Social position gave rise to interests which led to distinctive types of political mobilization. Class became the linchpin of the classical political sociology paradigm.

Admittedly, class was used in different ways, and indeed it was this mutability of class analysis that was part of its appeal. For some writers, such as Mosca and Pareto, as well as later writers in the Weberian tradition, the association between political elites and social classes was distinct, and the autonomy of the "political" from the "social" recognized. But insofar as political sociology was seen as having a clear purpose, it was in exploring how class linked the social and political. Of fundamental significance in this work was the recognition of the fundamental division between middle and working class as the key axis of class politics. This recognition could be found in the USA, where studies such as that of *Middletown* documented how community politics was riddled by class. In Britain the emphasis on the central role of working-class culture in defining politics was evidenced by numerous community studies (see Frankenberg, 1966), and writers such as T. H. Marshall (1950) emphasized the role of working-class movements in establishing citizenship rights.

While British research in the 1950s and 1960s emphasized the sheer importance of class as the mediating force between politics and society, American political sociologists led the way in developing more sophisticated analyses for thinking through the relationship between class and politics. The arguments of Lipset (1959) concerning the "democratic class struggle" were especially important. For Lipset (1959, p. 220), "in every democracy conflict is expressed through political parties which basically represent a democratic translation of the class struggle." He showed persistent tendencies across a number of nations in the political alignments of working-class and middle-class voters. By staging an alliance between the Marxist emphasis on the centrality of class and pluralist political science's emphasis on the role of democratic processes, Lipset helped to develop a fertile research agenda that energized not just political sociology but political science in general during the 1960s and early 1970s.

The social base paradigm depended on defining a spatial frame within which social bases operated. Whereas earlier community power research focused on the local level, the political sociology of the 1960s championed the nation as the arena in which social forces mobilized. Thus, Lipset was concerned with explaining the differences (and similarities) between nations, rather than explaining why nations emerged as the "natural" political unit. The intersection between class, politics, and the nation-state defines the intellectual frame of classical political sociology. This emphasis on the nation-state was adopted even by more radical political sociologists. Barrington Moore's (1966) classic book, *The Social Origins of Dictatorship and Democracy*, for instance, offered a historically sensitive account of how democratic polities emerged in some countries and not in others. Moore argued that the three distinctive paths to modernity (democratic revolution, fascism, and communism) were each related to different kinds of class coalition. In this historically sensitive way, Moore was able to show how political change was anchored in social process. His work took a similar line to that of E. P. Thompson (1963) and a number of neo-Marxist writers in championing a form of socially based accounts of political change. Thompson's path-breaking account of the *Making of the English Working Class* was primarily couched as a critique of functionalist sociologist Neil Smelser's (1959) arguments about how the working class developed passively as a response to modernizing pressures.

Present in all these different works was an interest in the politics of the working class. Lockwood (1995) refers to the power of the "problematic of the proletariat" in orienting early sociological studies of class and politics. Drawing upon Marxist influences, political sociologists were especially interested in the potential of the working class to effect political change. Orthodox political sociologists, such as Lipset (1959), tended to be critical of arguments suggesting the inherent progressiveness of working-class politics, and emphasized the significance of working class authoritarianism. Nonetheless, it was the politics of the working class which was of central importance to the classic paradigm. Since the 1970s there has been a steady decline in the appeal of the social base paradigm. There is increasing difficulty in defining a distinct territory of the "social" which is irreducible to politics or the economy. The crisis of political sociology is a crisis of the social itself.

Three currents of recent work indicate this trend clearly enough. First, and most important, is the hegemony of institutionalist approaches to politics. Such approaches emphasize the autonomy of organized politics and state formation, and dispute the idea that there are social determinants of political change. The roots of this new institutionalism run back into the 1960s. Lipset's own work, and especially that with Rokkan (1967b), ushered in this new institutionalist approach. Lipset and Rokkan developed a sensitive historical model of the development of political alignments which recognized that political alignments could not be simply reduced to class processes, but were related to this historical sequencing of cleavages between center and periphery, state and church, land and industry, and (only latterly) owners and workers. Thus, while party cleavages were found in every democratic nation, the specific constituencies which were represented in party cleavages depended on the historical development of the nation-states, and in particular the period in which modern party systems were formed. This argument concerning the autonomy of party alignments from their social underpinnings has been developed by a number of political scientists, perhaps most interestingly by Mair (1997). Mair notes that Lipset and Rokkan's observations that the party alignments formed in the 1920s persisted until the 1960s can be extended up to the 1990s. He discusses "the freezing of party alignments," the capacity of party alignments to absorb new kinds of political issues within them, and notes that during the 1980s and 1990s there was relatively little change in the appeal of the main parties in most Western democratic countries. The implication of Mair's argument is that politics operates largely autonomously from the social.

During the 1970s and 1980s this argument was developed not just to apply to part alignments but also to shed light on other political phenomena. Theda Skocpol became a leading exponent of "state-centered" accounts of politics, and she was explicit in her repudiation of "society-centered" accounts of politics. Skocpol's work developed since her account of revolutions in 1979 as a critical engagement with the arguments of Barrington Moore (1966) concerning the social determinants of revolutionary change. Skocpol argues that revolutions were related to the internal breakdown of the state apparatus, especially the way that foreign tensions led to intense demands on state organization. Such situations could lead to revolutions not as a result of social pressure based around the mobilization of economic interests, but more as a result of internal institutional pressures.

Skocpol's research during the 1980s became a fully fledged attempt to champion a "state-centered" account of political change. In the course of this work she has pioneered accounts of the New Deal (Skocpol et al., 1985) and American welfare policy (Skocpol, 1992). Her work has a further angle, undermining attempts to root political change in the concept of class, and is especially influential in developing a gender-focused approach to politics. Skocpol is perhaps the best known publicist of a much deeper movement within political sociology which doubts the value of rooting political mobilization in economic and social interests, and which has been termed a "new institutionalism."

By the later 1990s it was clear that political sociologists had largely abandoned the idea of rooting politics in social bases. For Boli and Thomas (1997) and Ramirez et al. (1997), the globalization of politics entails the declining significance of nation states and by implication the classic arena in which social forces mobilized. For other writers, such as Korpi and Palme (1998) and Gornick and Jacobs (1998), it is the structure of the nation-state that determines social processes and not the other way around. Korpi and Palme's paper is a particularly interesting example of how the institutionalist approach undermines the classic paradigm. They argue that political movements determined to reduce inequality are actually counterproductive and end up by increasing inequality. Thus, there is no social logic by which progressive social forces can effectively implement change through social action.

A second trend toward the dissolution of the "social" can be found in the work of social historians. During the 1960s and 1970s, social historians, following the lead of Edward Thompson, Herbert Gutman, and Barrington Moore, championed a mode of class analysis which examined how class mediated between social structure and political mobilization. Intellectual currents in the 1980s indicated a growing unease with this approach. In a well known study of Chartism, Gareth Stedman Jones (1983) emphasized the need to examine carefully "languages of class," that is to say the precise way that class was operationalized in language. Jones's arguments had an explosive effect in generating what has been termed the "linguistic turn." This current, associated particularly with the historians Patrick Joyce (1990, 1993, 1994), James Vernon (1994, 1993), and Bill Reddy (1987), situated political movements in terms of the linguistic categories available to people in different cultures and at various times and also suggested that the causes of class inequality were political rather than economic.

A third important development during the 1980s was the rise of a new kind of systems-based state theory. This was indebted to the structuralist currents of the

1970s, notably those associated with Louis Althusser and Nicos Poulantzas (see Jessop, 1983), and during the 1980s this matured as a distinct Regulation School (notably Aglietta, 1979; Boyer, 1990; Jessop, 1995). Writers within this school developed powerful sociological interpretations of political change, with Jessop et al.'s (1988) analysis of Thatcherism being especially well known. The key features of this approach lay in a different understanding of the relationship between society and politics to that found in the "social bases" approach. Rather than relating political movements or forces to specific social groups, the emphasis was on showing the interrelationship between changing modes of political regulation and the dynamics of the capital accumulation process. For Jessop et al. (1988), the decline of social democratic politics and the rise of Thatcherism could be seen as related to the transformation from Fordist to post-Fordist politics, and an attempt to establish a new kind of political hegemony.

The foregoing discussion suggests that the crisis of political sociology is closely related to the erosion of the idea of the "social" itself. In different disciplines and for varying theoretical reasons, the "social" is elided, and the autonomy of politics is reasserted. Even attempts such as those of cultural historians or political economists have tended to follow the same road (sometimes unwitting) to institutionalism. All these approaches have provided valuable, though contradictory, ways of reflecting on social and political change, but all of them have moved away from the classic paradigm of political sociology. In the next section I discuss how the defense of the classic paradigm has become attached to debates about the relevance of social class, and evaluate the lessons of recent research for considering whether the classic paradigm can be salvaged.

The Working Class and Politics: the Linchpin of the "Classic" Paradigm

In the classic paradigm class became central to political sociology because of its ability to offer a way of linking society and politics. Classes were rooted in social relationships but had political expression. Thus, when Sartori reflected on the nature of political sociology in the late 1960s, it was not accidental that his remarks were almost exclusively concerned with the relevance of class. Needless to say, there were very different ways of examining class, with some writers anchoring political processes more firmly in class structures than others did. What is important for our discussion is the recognition that the crisis of political sociology is also the crisis of class analysis.

It is within British research that the defense of class-based approaches to political alignments has been most trenchant, and I therefore focus on it here. In the mid-1960s, class-centered analyses of politics clearly held sway, expressed most memorably by Pulzer (1967) in his phrase that "class is the basis of British politics: all else is embellishment and detail." This argument was backed up by Butler and Stokes's (1969) study – the first using the British Election Surveys, which were first commissioned in 1964 – which underscored the centrality of class. From the 1970s, the consensus that class was fundamental to political alignments has faded, and during the 1980s a bitter dispute broke out concerning the idea of class dealignment. This debate has been instructive, since it clearly pitted sociologists against political scientists, and thereby revealed key differences in the methodology of political sociologists and mainstream political scientists. The rallying cry was that of class, especially the politics of the working class, but the debate on class dealignment also involved complex methodological issues about how to understand the relationship between class and politics, as well as substantive arguments about how social change was eroding the relationship between class and politics. In the early 1980s in the UK, attention focused on the shifting politics of the working class rather than that of the middle class. For political scientists such as Crewe and Sarlvik (1983), Kavanagh (1990a), and Crewe et al. (1991), the declining propensity of manual workers to vote Labour, and the general hegemony of Conservative politics during the 1980s, appeared to sunder the traditional association between class and politics.

Political sociologists defended class analysis in a number of sophisticated ways. One of them was by invoking a more rigorous definition of class structure. In place of the crude division between manual and non-manual workers that had dominated in older literature (Alford, 1967), Heath et al. (1985, 1991, 1994) and Marshall et al. (1988) emphasized that if the manual working class and non-manual middle class are "decomposed," it is possible to demonstrate that class and voting continue to be associated. Thus, in 1983, the middle class could be divided into small employers, who voted 71 percent Conservative, and routine non-manual workers, who voted 53 percent Conservative.

One innovation was to examine class politics in terms of relative class votes rather than absolute numbers. To illustrate, although Labour voting by manual workers declined between 1966 and 1983, support among middle-class voters fell far more, indicating, according to Heath and his colleagues (1985, 1991, 1994), that there was no general trend toward dealignment. However, on the basis of recent studies there are general questions raised about this thesis of "trendless fluctuation" (see Weakliem, 1995; Evans et al., 1999), and the 1997 election marked a further striking drop in class voting.

Furthermore, to the extent that relative class voting does persist, this cannot be taken as evidence for the importance of class cultures in political alignments (Heath et al., 1985). Crewe and Sarlvik (1983) and Franklin (1985, 1992) emphasize that the decline of class-based solidarities is linked to the tendency for voters take on a "consumerist" and "reflexive" approach to politics (see also Dunleavy and Husbands, 1985). Crewe and Thompson (1999) show that there has been a remorseless decline in strong party identification over time (in 1966, 44 percent of the electorate were strong supporters of a political party, a figure which dropped to 16 percent by 1997). Bartle (1998) has also shown that social class is not an especially important determinant of people's party identification or political outlook.

The debate on class dealignment has had relatively little international impact. In the USA, studies of voting and political alignments have over a number of years shown relatively little interest in class (for example, Campbell, 1960). However, some intriguing studies of American voting and politics which draw on British approaches have appeared in recent years (Brooks and Manza, 1997a, b). Brooks and Manza argue that relative odds of members of one class rather than another voting for one president rather than another did not change significantly between 1960 and 1992. They argue that the relative importance of gender and race increases, and class is at the very least stable. However, although they show that there are significant class effects, these turn out to be rather unusual ones. Professionals support Democrats, while managers support the Republicans, indicating that it is political division within the middle classes, rather than between working and middle class, which is significant to political alignment. There is some British research pointing in the same direction (Savage et al., 1992). Some professional groups (especially teachers, social workers, and academics) lean more to the left than do private sector managers, members of security services, and large employers (see Heath et al., 1991; Heath and Savage, 1995). Furthermore, Heath and Savage (1995) show that there is some evidence that professionals have been shifting their allegiance away from the Conservatives since the 1970s.

In concluding this section I finish with a general point and a rider. The general point is that even the most stubborn defenders of class analysis have had to modify their arguments so much in the face of recent political change that it is now implausible to claim that a clear class-based approach to politics remains intact. But my rider is this. As Brooks and Manza (1997b) show, and as is also clear in the British case, there is evidence that in place of the traditional divide between working and middle class, fractures within the middle classes may be becoming more politically important (see also Savage, 2000). In the 1997 British general election, Labour won back the level of support from the working class which it enjoyed in the 1960s, but also won unprecedented support from the middle classes. Indeed, the shift of middle-class support to Labour in 1997 was far larger than the shift of the working classes to the Tories in the 1980s. This point is interesting because it suggests that if we accept that the traditional social base approach to political sociology is dead, there is at least the possibility that one way of salvaging elements from it is to consider not how political alignments between working class and middle class energize the political field, but how relationships within the middle classes now play a central role. This is the idea I wish to develop in the remainder of this chapter, though I want to emphasize that taking this idea seriously means rethinking a new form of class analysis (see Savage, 2000).

NEW DIRECTIONS IN POLITICAL SOCIOLOGY

An interesting way of re-energizing the agenda of political sociology is to focus not on the social bases of political alignments, but on the sociology of the "political field" itself. The crucial difference between these two perspectives is that whereas the prime interest of the former is the sociological determinants of political alignments, the latter focuses on the relationship between the legitimate sphere of organized politics as a whole and other kinds of social relationships.

Instead of examining the determinants of voting for specific parties, people or causes, it examines how the social relations and networks involved with legitimate political activities (voting, organizing, campaigning, etc.) intersect with those of other social practices. This offers the prospect of a new kind of political sociology which examines the social construction of the boundaries between the "political" and the "social," and is attuned to divisions not within the political, but between the social and political.

This is a complex argument which I can hardly do justice to here. A starting point is to emphasize the extent to which formal political activity has been removed from everyday life. A good example is in voting. Undoubtedly, in liberal democracies, voting is the most important way in which the majority of people interface with the world of formal political activity. Nonetheless, voting is a rather unusual, even odd, kind of political activity. Whereas many forms of political activity, especially those which appear to transform or modify social structures – revolutions, protest movements, reform campaigns, etc. – involve mobilization and organization, voting in most contemporary liberal democracies has been constructed as an inherently individualized act. People vote in private booths, secretly. It need not be so. In early nineteenth-century Britain voting took place in a communal, public realm, where people's votes were openly recorded, and where elaborate rituals and ceremonies accompanied the process of polling (Vernon, 1993). However, as part of the general processes by which liberal capitalist states individualize citizenship rights and obligations (Turner, 1993a; Hay, 1996; Runciman, 1997), the act of voting, as the formal embodiment of the link between citizen and the polity, has been stripped of these communal underpinnings.

This process of the "individualization" of politics has also come to define politics as increasingly an activity for the middle classes. One of the best instances of this argument comes from studies of political activism. There has been dramatic convergence between the two main parties in the social background of party activists. Seyd and Whitley's research indicates that in both Labour and Conservative parties a clear majority of party activists – 58–60 percent – come from the "salariat." The only difference between the two parties in their social class composition is that Labour has a larger tail of manual working-class activists (18 percent of the total), while the Conservatives have rather more self-employed petit bourgeois aboard (14 percent of their total). This point can be broadened if all kinds of activism are included. Parry et al. (1992) show that the middle classes are consistently most likely to be activists of one kind or another. Parry et al. (1992) attribute this not to the role of class as such but to the way in which active individuals are able to draw on resources such as those linked to education, money, and social contacts. This argument has overlaps with the idea of "social capital," which the American political scientist Putnam (1993) claims to be a key determinant of the efficacy of democratic institutions. Putnam defines social capital primarily in formal institutional terms. Social capital is related to the existence of voluntary associations, where people meet others, so allowing them to have resources that enable people to act politically. In his well known study of political culture in Italy, Putnam argues that the long history of civic associations in the north of the country allows the emergence of a democratic polity that it not possible in the south, which lacks the requisite social capital. Putnam stages a reconciliation between an American Tocquevillian approach to political mobilization, which places emphasis on the role of voluntary associations as a guarantor of democracy, and network approaches to social mobilization, whereby attention can be directed toward the sorts of connections people can forge to allow them to act collectively in various ways.

What is lacking from Putnam's perspective, as well as Parry et al.'s (1992) account of the resources necessary for political activism, is a sense of the relational character of social capital, and a recognition that the social capital of some groups may be at the expense of others. This is an issue that Bourdieu (1979) squares up to, in his recognition that social capital is related to cultural and economic capital. Bourdieu emphasizes that the political field is one that only those with social capital feel comfortable operating within. Rather than search for class differences within the world of formal party politics, he defines formal party politics itself as an exclusive terrain.

> [There are] social agents, occupying different positions in the field of class relations and defined by a greater or lesser specific political competence – a greater or lesser capacity to recognize a political question as political and to treat it as such by responding to it politically... this capacity is inseparable from more or less strong feelings of being *competent* in the full sense of the word, that is socially recognized as entitled to deal with political affairs, to express an opinion about them or even modify their course. (Bourdieu, 1979, p. 399)

Bourdieu's argument is that social capital is not a neutral resource. The creation of social capital involves social closure that excludes some as it empowers others. If we take this line of argument it becomes possible to argue that contemporary organized politics has increasingly been structured as a field in which only those with economic or cultural capital are able to participate. Older forms of political activism which allowed popular entry to the political field have been increasingly eviscerated and diminished, with the result that organized politics has become largely a province of "middle-class" activism.

This is consistent with much research on political activism. Parry et al. (1992) show that that maximum political involvement for the vast majority (77 percent) of the British population is voting. Rather than being seen simply as lacking the resources to become politically active, they might be seen as excluded from the political field, since those with social and cultural capital define politics as an activity for those with particular kinds of attributes and resources. There is ample historical evidence pointing to significantly higher levels of political participation in earlier periods (Savage, 1987; Vernon, 1993; Lawrence, 1998).

The general conclusion would appear to be that the world of formal party politics is largely inhabited by members of the middle classes and that little popular energy is expended through this kind of political form. The limited but significant presence of the working class in the polity which can be demonstrated in the middle years of the twentieth century has largely been eclipsed. Very large numbers of people thereby have only very slight connections with politics of any kind, while the political field itself is differentiated between different fractions within the middle classes. It is possible to argue that the difference between party activists can best be seen as embodying tensions between those drawing upon economic capital (predominantly Conservative or Republican), and those drawing upon cultural capital (predominantly Labour and Liberal Democrat or Democrat). Party politics can thereby best be seen as embodying rival claims concerning the respective values of these two capitals. This is consistent with the observed differences in voting between state professionals and private sector managers. Historically, the Conservative Party represented the established professional middle class, and presented itself as the party of cultural distinction. The shift of the professional middle class away from the Conservative Party (Savage et al., 1992; Heath and Savage, 1995) appears to be due to the way that Thatcherism challenges the close association between the welfare state and the reproduction of cultural privilege, and has led to a reconciliation between the Labour and Liberal Democratic parties and the professional middle classes. Such a process has helped to marginalize the position of working-class activists in those parties.

Bourdieu's argument suggests that we might be better off searching for meaningful class divisions in the political realm not so much between political parties but between orthodox formal politics, on the one hand, and other, informal political modes, on the other.

SOCIAL MOVEMENTS AND POLITICAL SOCIOLOGY

In this section I briefly touch on how social movement theory (which has developed largely autonomously from political sociology in the past two decades) may contribute towards a re-energization of political sociology. There are two contrasting ways of viewing social movements from the perspective I have used in this chapter. One way is to see social movements as offering an alternative to established politics. If organized modern politics is premised on specific kinds of "middle-class" cultural competencies, there may be alternative forms of political mobilization that allow the otherwise excluded groups access to the polity. Piven and Cloward (1979), for instance, argue that working-class Americans, largely excluded from the American polity, have organized in "poor people's movements" that allow them to press their political agendas in different ways. There are parallel discussions about the role of new social movements as conduits for new kinds of political claims. Giddens (1991) sees new social movements as creating a new agenda based on "life politics," in place of the "emancipatory" politics associated with class. On the other hand, another view of "new social movements" would be to see them as a form of "middle-class" politics (Parkin, 1963; Eckersley, 1989; Bagguley, 1995). If this argument is true, it dovetails with my observations in the previous section concerning the dominance of the middle classes within the political field as a whole.

In reality, it would seem that a more nuanced view of social movements is required, which emphasizes their role in generating particular repertoires of mobilization. Repertoires are modes of activity which become recognized as effective ways of politically mobilizing. They are "a limited set of routines that are learned, shared, and acted out through a relatively deliberate process of choice. Repertoires are cultural constructions but they do not descend from abstract philosophy or take shape as a result of political propaganda: they emerge from struggle" (Tilly, 1994, p. 42). Tilly argues that Britain invented the first modern social movements. In the period between 1790 and 1830 new modes of political activism developed, which included the public meeting, the petition, the demonstration, the single establishment strike, and the national social movement, and which marked the onset of modern modes of mobilizing. These movements escaped from parochial, local politics, and built up support between places: "such a form as the public meeting transferred with relative ease from group to group, place to place, issue to issue. In comparison with the relatively parochial, particular and bifurcated eighteenth century forms of action they were cosmopolitan, modular and autonomous" (Tilly, 1994, pp. 61–2).

These repertoires emerged at the same time that the industrial working class developed as a major political force in British society. Tilly's argument is, in fact, rather similar to that of E. P. Thompson, who showed how the formation of the British working class depended on the development of new forms of organization – such as the formal association with "members unlimited" – which came to be the main mobilizing vehicle for radical politics. It is striking that today many of the repertoires which are still routinely used by protesters in diverse forms of social movement are those which were first developed two hundred years ago, around recognizably "working-class" politics. The meeting, the petition, and the demonstration all remain in common use, and indicate the power of the political movements of the late eighteenth and early nineteenth centuries in setting the mold for subsequent political action. This suggests that social movements and more organized political forms develop in interaction, not as alternatives to each other. In viewing the importance of current trends, we should see the emergence of new kinds of social movements as indicating the transformation of the political field itself, rather than the simple eclipse of working-class by middle-class politics.

One way of developing this point is to show how repertoires of political mobilization can "slip" between social groups. A fundamental point about the Labour movement is that its strategy depended on mobilizing large numbers of people, whether this be to organize effective strikes, to force collective bargaining arrangements, or to elect Labour candidates to elected offices. It therefore was not simply a class-based movement. It also sought to make alliances to maximize its command over numbers (Przeworski, 1977).

As Offe and Wisenthal (1980) show, this explains why trade unions placed such emphasis on maximizing their membership, since this was the crucial way in which they could try to outsmart their opposition. In the period from around

1900 to the 1960s there was a congruence between working-class political repertoires and the mobilization of large numbers of workers into coherent and organized interest groups. However, there are now indications that this congruence has come to the end of its useful life, and with it, the classic working-class repertoire for political action.

There are a number of reasons why this repertoire is fading, but this also relates to my earlier point that working-class politics as organized through the Labour movement has been incorporated into formal party politics. Historically, the Labour movement is best seen as embodying multiple political repertoires, including local campaigns around the provision of services, neighborhood mobilization, trade union struggles, and mobilization through national electoral politics. However, the difficulties in sustaining trade union politics, with the defeat of the coalminers in 1984–5 being an especially important point, and the centralization of local politics through government reform have led to national politics becoming the prime field on which Labour has organized.

Fundamentally, one of the main resources available to the Labour movement was its ability to mobilize numbers. However, this process depends less on face-to-face mechanisms of workplace and neighborhood communication, and more on the use of technologically advanced procedures which individualize while they also mobilize individuals. Targeted mailings, opinion polling, market research, and so forth create mechanisms for the mobilization of large numbers of individuals without recourse to face-to-face, informal discussion. Rather than mobilization through numbers being important, the use of visual signifiers takes on a much greater role. As the electronic media, especially those based around television, become of prime importance in disseminating information and imagery, so repertoires of action which are directly "visualizable" may take on a more significant mobilizing role. In many cases these modes of organizing do not benefit by having particularly large numbers of people involved, since these can be difficult to construct in a dramatically visual way. What matters more is the organization of action in a locale bounded by time and space so that it can be readily visually recorded and transmitted, organized, for instance, around specific occasions (Hetherington, 1998). Notable examples include movements against road building in Britain, ecological protests (especially those organized by Greenpeace, which have been highly original in devising effective visualizable protests), debates around new age travelers, as well as various kinds of riots, whether these be semi-organized (as in the Carnival against Capitalism) or more responsive to police interference.

The important point to emphasize here is that new repertories of action draw very little on traditional modes of formal political organizing, based upon the maximization of numbers. In this respect, and regardless of the actual class composition of the members of these new kinds of political movements, they are culturally and symbolically distinct from the old modes of working-class politics. A further implication of this point is that fractures open up within political campaigns themselves. Visually dramatic or extraordinary actions may not appeal to potential activists without cultural capital, who may therefore react against the movement itself (see Skeggs, 1997, on the issue of feminism and class). Class divisions develop within social movements, between those with the confidence and skills to develop novel campaigns and those who feel threatened by the challenge to respectability and ordinariness that such politics invokes. New kinds of social movement do indicate the rise of a new kind of political field, in which symbolic and visual presence, which can be associated with modes of cultural capital, hold increased sway. This testifies to a very different kind of political field to that which was studied by political sociology during its golden age in the 1960s.

CONCLUSION

In this chapter I have explored the limits of the classic political sociology paradigm, with its emphasis on the representation of class interests. In the latter parts of the chapter I have sketched out some ideas which might point toward a new, though hesitant, agenda for the re-energization of political sociology. The starting point for this revised approach is the recognition of the demise of traditional class politics, with the working class seen as occupying a privileged position as social actor. We might instead define a new kind of politics, in which the political field indeed operates largely autonomously from other social and cultural fields. However, it is then possible to redefine this field as one which is occupied by actors with significant amounts and kinds of cultural and social capital. To be sure, by seeing politics as a field, we should note that the definition of legitimate politics cannot be taken as given but is contested and fluid over time. We can then see the relative autonomy of the political from the social not as a "natural" phenomenon testifying to the inherent irreducibility of the political to the social, but as a historically constructed and policed process that involves the association between the world of legitimate politics and claims to cultural and symbolic dominance.

We can argue, somewhat schematically, that the politics of early industrial societies tended to be on a communal, "dramatic" basis, with all social groups having particular roles in the spectacles and rituals of political life. The process whereby more democratic political forms were developed also marked the stripping down of this communal element of politics, but it allowed the working class to emerge as a powerful force in organized political alignments. It would be wrong to exaggerate this, but there can be no gainsaying the significance of the organized labor movement and working-class activity in defining twentieth-century politics. We see instead the emergence of a new kind of politics that marks the numerical dominance of various groups of the middle classes, and new kinds of tension between different forms of economic, cultural, and social capital. As Bourdieu rightly points out, the political differences between these groups rarely lead to outright challenges to the status quo.

Where, then, might we find the sources of more radical politics? To some extent we can see them in various social movements that eschew or have a critical relationship to organized politics, though even here I have suggested that the salience of cultural capital for these kinds of activities cannot be doubted. Perhaps we might look again at the politics of the private realm. For as the world of organized politics becomes remote from the networks and routines of everyday life, so new kinds of informal, everyday politics develop in the interstices left open to them. We might even argue that the retreat into the private, into the domestic world, and into the burgeoning area of enthusiasms, leisure, and lifestyle (Bellah et al., 1985) is a form of political statement. Bourdieu's argument that refusing to have an opinion, refusing to become involved in the "legitimate" world of politics, might be more genuinely subversive than to become involved in formalized and sanitized political modes, which might include involvement in both established political parties and new social movements. Ordinary people stay aloof from the strange world of politics. But how long can they continue to do so?

19

Why Social Movements Come into Being and Why People Join Them

Bert Klandermans

In 1965, Mancur Olson published his *The Logic of Collective Action*. The core of the book was the argument that rational actors will *not* contribute to the production of a collective good unless selective incentives persuade them to do so. Olson's reasoning was soon applied to social movement participation. It helped to explain why so often people do not participate in social movements despite the interest they have in the achievement of the movement's goals. It was argued that movement goals typically are collective. If the goal is achieved people will enjoy the benefits irrespective of whether they have participated in the effort. In view of a goal whose achievement is uncertain, but whose benefits – if materialized – can be reaped anyway, rational actors will take a free ride, Olson reasons.

The problem with Olson's logic of collective action is that it provides an explanation for why people do not participate, but fares much worse in explaining why people *do* participate. A recurring criticism is that Olson's model assumes that individuals make their decisions in isolation, as if there are no other people with whom they consult, with whom they feel solidarity, by whom they are kept to their promises, by whom they are put under pressure; in short, as if all those factors that make people fight together do not exist.

Olson's dilemma of collective action is a good starting point for a discussion of two questions that have always occupied students of social movements: why do social movements come into being, and why do individuals participate in social movements? Despite its limited significance for the explanation of movement emergence and participation, it can serve well to argue that neither the development of social movements nor movement participation can be taken for granted. Indeed, movement participants are most of the time a minority. Even mass social movements most of the time do not mobilize more than a few percent of the population.

Our two questions hover between the sociology and the social psychology of social movements. The first question, about the emergence of social movements, typically concerns the sociology of social movements; social psychologists have little to say about it. The second question, on movement participation, brings us to the heartland of social psychology. Social psychology is best in proposing answers to the question of why individuals choose to make the sometimes considerable effort to participate in a social movement. Students of social movements have sought the answers to both questions in different directions. This chapter clarifies these different directions and thus explores the interface of the sociology and social psychology of social movements. But there is an obvious question waiting for an answer first.

WHAT ARE SOCIAL MOVEMENTS?

"Social movements are collective challenges by people with common purposes and solidarity in sustained interaction with elites and authorities" (Tarrow, 1994, p. 4; see also Klandermans, 1997, p. 2). This definition includes three key elements that deserve some elaboration. First, social movements are *collective challenges*. They concern disruptive direct action against elites, authorities, other groups, or cultural codes. There is an obvious reason why this is the case. Social movements typically encompass people who lack access to politics. Had they had access there would have been no need for a social movement. Disruptive collective action forces authorities to pay attention to the claims brought forward. Second, it concerns people with a *common purpose* and *solidarity*. Social movement participants rally behind common claims, they want authorities to *do* something, to change a state of affair or to undo changes. Such common claims are rooted in feelings of collective identity and solidarity. Third, isolated incidents of collective action are *not* social movements. Only by *sustaining* collective action does an actor turn a contentious episode into a social movement.

Meyer and Tarrow (1998) observe that the movement type of action has become much more frequent over the past thirty years. These authors wonder whether this is because movement action has become part of the conventional repertoire of participation, in other words whether this is a matter of institutionalization of movement type of activity. Neidhardt and Rucht (1993) and Jenkins and Klandermans (1995) have made a similar observation. Increasingly, these authors argued, social movement organizations are replacing political parties as intermediaries in interest representation between citizens and the state. These authors are interpreting this not so much as institutionalization of social movement action but as the "movementization" of politics. Some facts: Russell Dalton (1996, p. 76), for example, observes that, in 1975, 22 percent of the British people signed a petition. In 1990 the figure was 75 percent. In 1974, 9 percent of the British participated in a demonstration, against 25 percent in 1990. Between 1979 and 1993 the number of protest events in the French city of Marseille more than doubled, from 183 to 395 events per annum (Fillieule, 1998). Rucht (1998) reports considerable increases in protest events in Germany in that same period, a result that is confirmed by Kriesi et al.'s (1995) study on new social movements in Europe. These authors report a similar pattern for the Netherlands and Switzerland. In their study France is the exception, as it reveals a decline in the number of protest events, a finding the authors relate to the specifics of French politics during that period. On the whole, then, Meyer and Tarrow's observation is supported by other empirical studies. Meyer and Tarrow continue to argue that this diffusion of protest is a matter not only of growing numbers – that is, of more protest events within a set amount of time – but of diffusion to broader sectors of the population as well. Across age groups, and gender lines, from the left to the right, among workers and students, and in Western and non-Western societies alike, movement type actions have become a common phenomenon. Whether this is a matter of institutionalization of movements or movementization of politics remains a matter of interpretation, but this does not change the factual observation that movement type activity expanded considerably over the past decades. This raises all the more the questions as to why social movements come into being and why people join them.

WHY DO SOCIAL MOVEMENTS COME INTO BEING?

The social movement literature has offered three types of answers to the question of why social movements come into being: because people are aggrieved, because people have the resources to mobilize, and because people seize the political opportunity. These three answers parallel theoretical approaches that have successively occupied the field. It started with grievance theories such as relative deprivation theory, which basically hypothesized that discontent generates protest. But it was too obvious that many people who are aggrieved never engage in protest. Indeed, protagonists of resource mobilization theory began to argue that grievances are ubiquitous and that the real question to answer is not so much what makes people aggrieved but what makes aggrieved people participate in social movements. Their answer to that question has been the availability of resources. But soon social movement scholars, some of whom had a background in political sciences, questioned whether the availability of resources was sufficient. They proposed that political opportunities that present themselves to aggrieved groups make the difference.

Because People are Aggrieved

In a society there are all kinds of social and cultural cleavages. Some of those cleavages may become manifest and generate a social movement, others remain latent. Several attempts have been made to distinguish cleavages. The first that come to mind are the four classic cleavages distinguished by Lipset and Rokkan (1967a): *center versus periphery*, which concerns the conflict between the central nation-building culture and the increasing resistance of the ethnically, linguistically, or religiously distinct subject populations in the provinces and the peripheries; *church versus government*, which concerns conflicts between the centralizing and mobilizing nation-state and the historically established privileges of the church; *urban versus rural*, which concerns the conflict between the landed interest and the rising class of industrial entrepreneurs; and *class conflict*, which concerns the conflict between owners and employers on the one side and tenants, laborers, and workers on the other (Lipset and Rokkan, 1967a, p. 14). Kriesi et al. (1995) distinguish these "traditional" cleavages, as they depict them, from so-called "new" cleavages, such as gender, generation, peace and war, and ecology. Finally, Sisk (1995), in his discussion of politics in divided societies, distinguished between three types of cleavages: ascriptive cleavages, such as race, caste, and ethnicity; attitudinal cleavages, such as ideological orientation; and behavioral cleavages, such as membership of an organization or voting behavior. (Obviously, ascriptive cleavages, as defined by Sisk, are akin to Lipset and Rokkan's cleavages, but also to Kriesi et al.'s gender and generational cleavages. Kriesi et al.'s peace, war, and ecology cleavages, on the other hand, are akin to Sisk's attitudinal cleavages.)

The key question is, of course, how do cleavages turn into grievances? Relative deprivation was the answer given by grievance theory (Gurr, 1970). The theory pointed to the discrepancy between expectations and outcomes to explain why cleavages generate grievances. Rising expectations and outcomes that are lagging behind was the basic principle these authors proposed. Social psychologists would undoubtedly wonder if and how individuals are actually aware of the discrepancy. All too often such discrepancies are not observed simply because people do not make the relevant comparisons. Moreover, even if they are aware of the discrepancy they need not necessarily define it as illegitimate. The social psychology of relative deprivation or injustice has pointed to these two processes of comparison and legitimization as crucial for the generation of grievances (Tyler and Smith, 1998).

Grievance theory in the social movement domain initially had very little to say about the process of grievance interpretation. It took until the 1980s for social movement literature to show awareness of the problem. Klandermans (1984) coined the term consensus mobilization, Snow and his colleagues introduced the process of framing in the social movement domain (Snow et al., 1986), and with the appearance of the concept of collective action frame (see Gamson, 1992b; Klandermans, 1997, for synthetic treatments), grievance theory had become much more sophisticated, not only because the collective action frame was a far more elaborated conceptualization of grievances as determinants of social movement activity than relative deprivation, but also because processes such as consensus mobilization and framing added a dynamic component to the theory. Today's general consensus in the social movement literature is that grievances are socially constructed.

Collective action frames are "sets of beliefs that serve to create a state of mind in which participation in collective action appears meaningful" (Klandermans, 1997, p. 17). Collective action frames are conceived of as consisting of three components: *injustice*, *identity*, and *agency* (Gamson, 1992b). Injustice specifies a sense of injustice, moral indignation, and outrage about the way authorities are treating a social problem. Identity specifies a "we" – that is to say a group or social category that feels deprived and angry – *and* a "they" – that is to say authorities that are held responsible for the adverse situation. Agency concerns perceived opportunities, the belief that collective action may succeed in changing the situation. Thus a collective action frame specifies some authority that is doing injustice to a group or category people identify with, plus the belief that it is possible to take action as a group.

The transformation of social and cultural cleavages into collective action frames does not occur by itself. It is a process in which social and political actors, media, and citizens jointly interpret, define, and redefine states of affairs. A variety of conceptualizations have been proposed to account for the process. In an attempt to systematize (Klandermans, 1992, 1997), I proposed to distinguishes three different processes: (a) public discourse, i.e. the interface of media discourse and interpersonal interaction; (b) persuasive communication during mobilization campaigns by movement organizations, their opponents, and countermovement organizations; and (c) consciousness-raising during episodes of collective action. Public discourse in principle involves everyone in a society or a particular sector within a society. Persuasive communication affects only those individuals who are targets of persuasion attempts; and consciousness-raising during episodes of collective action concerns primarily participants in the collective action, although bystanders can be affected as well. In each setting the processes of forming and transforming collective beliefs take place in different ways: in the first setting, through the diffuse networks of meaning construction; in the second setting, through deliberate attempts by social actors to persuade; and in the third setting, through discussions among participants in and bystanders at collective actions who are trying to make sense of the events of the struggle.

Although grievance theory over the past few decades has become far more sophisticated, it has never provided a satisfactory answer to the question of why at a specific point in time and space a specific grievance becomes the focal point of a social movement. Grievance theory explains the "demand side" of social movement activity but has very little to say about the "supply side." It helps to understand why people are aggrieved, but not how aggrieved people mobilize into social movements. Resource mobilization theory took this assessment as its point of departure and argued that it is the availability of resources that makes the difference.

Because People Have the Resources to Mobilize

Resource mobilization theory distanced itself from grievance-based conceptions of social movements. Grievances are seen as ubiquitous and thus the key question is whether aggrieved groups have the resources to mobilize. Such resources include money, time, technical infrastructure, expertise, and so on, including the structures and organizations to mobilize and deploy those resources. Indeed, organizations and mobilizing structures are crucial according to resource mobilization theory. McCarthy and Zald (1976), who are generally seen as the founding fathers of the approach, deliberately used organizational theory and introduced concepts such as social movement sector and industry, and movement entrepreneurs in their attempt to theorize about resource mobilization by social movements. In a way, resource mobilization by movement organizations creates a vicious circle. You need resources to maintain the structures needed to mobilize those resources. Obviously, movement organizations do not only mobilize resources, they also make use of the acquired resources. In fact, an important aspect of organizational management and therefore internal conflicts relates to the deployment of resources. Decisions must be made about which part of the resources will be used for organizational maintenance, which part for interactions with opponents and countermovements, and which part for the mobilization of resources.

Movement organizations play a central role in the "supply" of social movement activities to aggrieved people. They organize activities, they stage protest events, they collect fees, they ask for time and effort from their members to maintain the organization, and so on. Most movement scholars see organization as a structural necessity to step up from loosely related protest events to sustained collective action, one of the distinguishing features of social movements. Movement organizations may be crucial in mobilizing resources but they are not the only mobilizing structures. Any kind of societal organization or structure can become involved in mobilization campaigns: friendship and neighborhood networks, but also formal organizations such as churches, unions, and professional associations. Perhaps one of the most significant contributions of resource mobilization scholars has been overwhelming evidence that social movement participant are *not* marginalized. On the contrary, precisely because any societal structure can be employed to mobilize, people who are involved in such structures run a better chance of being targeted by mobilization attempts (Marwell and Oliver, 1993).

If, then, the availability of resources is making the difference, a question of strategic importance becomes: is the emergence of a movement dependent on the availability of internal, indigenous resources; that is, resources that are available to the aggrieved population? Or are external resources needed from conscience constituencies who feel solidarity with the aggrieved population? Originally, McCarthy and Zald (1976) believed that external resources are needed, as aggrieved populations by definition tend to lack resources. Morris (1984), however, demonstrated that in the case of the civil rights movement indigenous resources were more important than external resources. Jenkins and Eckert (1986) concluded that a movement first needs indigenous resources to gain some visibility and success. It is only then that external resources are made available. Crucially or not for their emergence, social movements do receive external support as movement organizations are embedded in multiorganizational fields.

Multiorganizational fields consist of the organizations with which a movement organization might establish specific links (Klandermans, 1997). From the point of view of a movement organization, a multiorganizational field is composed of supportive, antagonistic, and indifferent sectors. Supportive sectors can be described as the movement organization's *alliance system*, consisting of groups and organizations that support the organization; antagonistic sectors can be described as the organization's *conflict system*, consisting of representatives and allies of the challenged social or political system and including countermovements; indifferent sectors consist of organizations that are not (yet) involved in the controversy. The boundaries between these sectors remain fluid and may change in the course of events. Specific organizations that try to keep aloof from the controversy may be forced to take sides. Coalitions can fall apart, and former allies can become part of the conflict system. Mobilization takes place within the boundaries of a multiorganizational field. Accordingly, the impact of mobilization attempts is influenced by the dynamics of that field. Finally, the composition of a movement organization's multiorganizational field is also determined by the original social or cultural cleavage the movement emerges from. If we take a specific social or cultural cleavage in mind, let us say ethnicity, we can for some organizations, though not all of course, predict on what side they will end if that cleavage generates a conflict.

Resource mobilization's emphasis on resources, be they indigenous or external, meant a concentration on the movement's internal life. To be sure, movement organizations were defined as open systems in interaction with their environment to either acquire or employ resources, but little was said about the environment itself. Questions such as what impact characteristics the political environment has on social movements or to what extent movements impact on the political environment remained largely untouched. It was no accident that scholars who have their roots in the political sciences, such as Kitschelt, Tarrow, and Kriesi, did formulate these questions and proposed a third answer to the question of why movements come into being: because people seize the political opportunities they perceive.

Because People Seize the Political Opportunity

Sidney Tarrow defines political opportunities as "those consistent – but not necessarily formal or permanent – dimensions of the political environment that provide incentives for collective action by affecting people's expectations for success and failure" (Tarrow, 1998, p. 76). The important difference from grievances and resources is that political opportunities focus on the *political* environment of a social movement. What makes people move is not the presence of aggrieved populations, or the availability of sufficient resources, but a political environment that promises success. Such a focus is so obvious for a phenomenon that is as political as social movements that it is amazing that it took so long for politics to become an integrated part of the social movement literature. Interestingly, Tarrow's definition is about expectations and *not* about structures. Hence, by definition only those dimensions of the political environment that are *perceived* are part of the political opportunity structure of a social movement. Indeed, opportunities can only be seized if they are perceived.

Which dimensions of the political environment are relevant? Opportunities can be *structural*, i.e. refer to relatively stable characteristics of political systems,

and *conjunctural*, i.e. refer to political changes. The first type of stable characteristics is especially useful for comparisons between systems, or states, in other
words for making comparisons of *space*. The second type of transitory characteristic is especially useful for investigating the impact of political change, i.e. for
making comparisons of *time*.

Comparisons of Space

Four structural aspects have been applied in comparisons of space: state
strength, repression and facilitation, party systems, and neocorporatism.
Kitschelt (1986) referred to the strength of the German, Swedish, French, and
American states in his attempt to explain the diverging fate of the anti-nuclear
movement in these countries. Strong, centralized states such as France, he
argued, draw protest to the political center and create weak opposition. But
because of their policy-making strength, they may actually be very effective in
implementing change. Hence, if a movement happens to prevail it may win
major victories, as was the case with the anti-nuclear movement in Sweden.
Weak, decentralized states such as the United States, on the other hand, are much
more accessible and therefore encourage mobilization, but because of their
policy-making weakness may be unable to implement concessions made to
movements. Repression, according to Tilly (1978, p. 100), is "any action by
another group which raises the contender's costs of collective action. An action
which lowers the group's costs of collective action is a form of facilitation."
Although states sometimes try to repress any kind of opposition, it is more
common to find some movements or movement organizations repressed, and
others tolerated or even facilitated. The structure of the political representation
system (Jenkins and Klandermans, 1995) is an important aspect of the institutional arrangements movements encounter. A movement facing a one-party
system with a strong, monolithic political party must accommodate itself to a
completely different structure than a movement facing a multiparty system.
Electoral systems differ as well. Whether a movement faces a few larger parties
that alternately take office (as, for example, in Great Britain or the United States)
or a larger number of smaller parties that must form coalitions (as in many other
European countries) makes a real difference in terms of movement strategy; and
so do such differences as proportional representation versus districts, winner
takes all systems, high or low thresholds. A final important aspect is the presence
of neocorporatist forms of interest representation; that is systems of institutionalized bargaining between the state and interest organizations (Nollert, 1995).
Neocorporatism reduces the level of political protest because there is less room
but also less need for protest, according to Nollert, because neocorporatist
countries performed economically better and reduced economic inequality.

Comparisons of time are about political changes that open windows of
opportunities for social movements that were closed before: increased access to
polity, destabilizing political alignments, changes in a movement's alliance structures, elites that become divided. Because these opportunities are not the same
for every movement, and not every movement is equally successful in seizing

opportunities, various movements within a country and similar movements in different countries may take different trajectories. Examples abound of the paradoxical finding that protest increases when access to polity increases and political systems become more open and responsive. Recent examples are Eastern Europe and South Africa, where protest only increased when repression relaxed. It is not difficult to understand why this is the case. Obviously, expectations of success become greater if access to policy increases. Changes in the political alignments that control the state create opportunities for challengers as well. In this regard, Kriesi (1995) refers especially to the distribution of power in the party system and in other parts of the system of interest intermediation. The make-up of these systems may change, some parties or interest associations may grow, others may decline or break down altogether. Such changes may open opportunities for some movements and close opportunities for others. For example, the odds of the pro-life and pro-choice movements changed dramatically when Reagan entered office. Political changes may make influential allies available. Kriesi et al. (1995) provide evidence of the facilitation of new social movements by established political actors, especially by organizations of the left. However, depending on whether the left is in or out of government, its magnitude varies considerably. The European movements against cruise missiles certainly exploited the fact that the elite were divided on the issue of deployment. For example, in the Netherlands and Belgium for a long time it was unclear whether there was a majority for deployment at all in the parliament.

In Conclusion

Grievances, resources, and opportunities have all been mentioned as factors that generate social movements. They have sometimes been proposed as competing explanations, but I don't belief that one would fare very well without the others. *Social movements come into being because people who are aggrieved and have the resources to mobilize seize the political opportunities they perceive.* Before I elaborate this any further, let me shift perspective and provide an answer to the second question that occupies us here: the question of why individuals join social movements. In a way, this question concerns the same process as the question of why social movements come into being, namely mobilization, but at the individual level of analysis. Obviously, social movements come into being because individuals join them.

WHY DO PEOPLE JOIN SOCIAL MOVEMENTS?

The question of why individuals participate in social movements brings us to the individual level of analysis, more specifically to the individual characteristics, and the social psychological dynamics, that make an individual decide to take part in social movement activities. The social psychology of protest suggests three fundamental motives for participation: a desire to change circumstances, a desire to belong to some group, and a desire to give meaning to one's life.

Succinctly formulated, these are instrumentality, identity, and meaning. Each individual motive has been proposed as the core of a theory of movement participation. Instrumentality is the key motive for theories that define movement participation as an attempt to influence the political environment. Social movements are seen as politics by other means and movement participation as a form of instrumental behavior. Others have argued that a search for identity is the key motive of movement participation. Groups that are marginalized or disadvantaged seek through their movement activity to find a new identity. Again others have argued that a search for meaning is the most important motive; a collective attempt to understand the world and to make sense of it. Different theories are associated with these three angles. Instrumentality is related to rational choice theory and the theory of planned behavior; identity is related to sociological approaches that emphasize the collective identity component of social movements and to the social psychological social identity theory; meaning comes with the framing and narrative approaches in social movement literature and more psychologically oriented theories of meaning construction.

I defend the view that we need all three motives to understand participation. Why would someone take the costs and risks of participation if not motivated by the desire to change social or political circumstances? At the same time, it is obvious that the more someone identifies with a group, the more likely it is that he or she will act as a member of that group. After all, social movement type activities are forms of *collective behavior*, that is to say, activities by individuals who act as members of their group. Finally, as far as meaning is concerned, a basic assumption of modern social psychology is that individuals live in a *perceived reality* and have no choice but to select, interpret, and give meaning. Elsewhere, I have tried to bring the three basic principles of movement participation together into three models: the generation of collective action frames, the motivation to participate in collective action, and the transformation of potentiality into action (Klandermans, 1997). The first model is an attempt to theorize about identity and meaning and about the way identity formation and meaning construction influence political protest. The second model focuses on instrumentality. Indeed, movement participation is defined as instrumental behavior, *but* instrumental in the situation as *perceived* by the participant. Hence, processes of identification and meaning construction determine which forms of behavior are instrumental and which are not in the eyes the participants. The third model is a *mobilization model*. Whereas the first model is about processes that generate the potentiality to participate, and the second about the decision to actually participate in social movement activities, the third model is about the process that turns potentiality into actual participation. This can be thought of as *demand* and *supply*: potentiality can be seen as demand for protest, but for such demand to turn into actual behavior a supply of attractive protest opportunities is needed. Such supply presupposes organizers and/or movement organizations that offer such opportunities and make the individual the target of a mobilization attempt. Protest participation is, then, defined as the positive response of an individual to such mobilization attempts.

The Generation of Collective Action Frames

We can conceive of collective action frames at different levels of analysis: the collective action frame of a social movement, the collective action frame of a movement organization, and the collective action frame of an individual. At the level of a movement or a movement organization this concerns *collective beliefs*; that is, beliefs that are *shared* by a set of individuals. At the individual level this concerns *individual beliefs*. Such individual beliefs are idiosyncratic remakes of the collective beliefs. Each individual adheres to his or her own version of the collective action frame. Yet, it *is* the same set of shared beliefs they are drawing from. Compare it to a language: a language community – let's say the Dutch – shares a language. Each individual member of the community speaks his or her own version of the language, yet we have no difficulties recognizing that it is the same language they are speaking.

The generation of collective action frames can be studied at two levels as well. At the level of movements and organizations it concerns the process of the *social construction* of collective action frames, involving the processes of public discourse, persuasive communication, and consciousness-raising discussed above. At the individual level it concerns the process of the *appropriation* of collective action frames. It is this process that I concentrate on here.

In the course of their life and due to processes of socialization in the family, at school or work, and by peers individuals develop sympathy for some movements and antipathy for others. This is obviously related to their position *vis-à-vis* the social and cultural cleavages in their society. Interpersonal interaction plays an important role in these processes. Such interaction may involve friends or colleagues, or it may occur during encounters between people in buses, on the train, in bars, at parties, and in today's world over the telephone, by fax, and by e-mail. Much of what goes on in such interactions concerns the formation of consensus. People tend to validate information by comparing and discussing their interpretations with significant others, especially when the information involved is complex – as is always the case with social and political issues. Social psychological research has shown repeatedly that people prefer to compare their opinions with those of like-minded individuals. As a rule, the set of individuals interacting in one's social networks – especially friendship networks – is relatively homogeneous and composed of people not too different from oneself.

However important interpersonal interaction is for the appropriation of collective beliefs, it is not the only context in which this appropriation occurs. Collective beliefs can be incorporated and conveyed in persuasive communication or media discourse, and can be assimilated independently of interpersonal interaction. Of course, these sources of information are also used in interpersonal interaction. In *Talking Politics*, Gamson (1992b) reports the results of a study of conversations conducted within groups of friends and acquaintances whom he asked to discuss such issues as the Israeli–Arab conflict and affirmative action. One of his findings was that in these exchanges people use any kind of information source available: newspapers, movies, advertisements, novels, rumors, their own and others' experience, and so on. Gamson distinguishes three types of sources of information: media discourse, experiential knowledge (direct, from one's own experience, or indirect, derived from other people's experience), and popular wisdom (shared knowledge of what everyone knows). It is through any of the resources that an individual can learn about the collective action frame of a social movement or a social movement organization and appropriate his or her own version of the injustice, identity, and agency frame. Gamson suggests that the integrated use of all three sources facilitates the development of such frames. Media discourse provides information especially about who is to be blamed for the situation; the two other sources, it turns out, are crucial for the interpretation and emotional loading of that information.

The Motivation to Participate in Collective Action

Adherence to a collective action frame at best produces the potential to participate. Actual participation requires a supply of activities individuals can take part in. There is a virtually endless variety of activities individuals can take part in: signing petitions, walking on demonstrations, wearing buttons or other symbols, taking part in meetings or site occupations, taking part in strikes or boycotts, paying money, writing letters to political elites, being an officer of a movement organization, and so on. In order to create some system in this variety several taxonomies have been proposed: moderate, militant, violent; high versus low costs or risks; limited versus unlimited in time, etc. I hold that each form of participation has its own motivational dynamics depending on its specific characteristics. Moreover, individual sympathizers differ in terms of the activities they find attractive. In general, I maintain that social movement participation must involve not only attractive goals, but attractive activities as well. Therefore, it is in the movement's interest to develop a broad supply of activities that attracts a variety of sympathizers.

The attractiveness of an activity is dependent on the *selective* and *collective* incentives an individual believes to be associated with that activity. Selective incentives relate to costs and benefits that differentiate between participants and non-participants. You are only spending time or money if you participate, you only run the risk of being beaten up by the police if you participate, your friends will only blame you for not participating if you stay at home, and so on. Sometimes movement organizations try to make participation more attractive by providing selective benefits: a popular music group, a train ticket to the city where the demonstration is held, a T-shirt, etc. Authorities or opponents on their part can try to make participation less attractive by imposing costs upon participants. Collective incentives are related to achievement of the movement's goals and the extent to which participation in a specific activity contributes to goal achievement. Obviously, it is not enough for a goal to be important to a person, what is also needed is some likelihood of success. The problem with collective action is that it is difficult to know to what extent an activity will have any influence on authorities. In any event, the chances are low that an activity will have any impact if only a few people participate. Therefore, the likelihood of success is dependent upon the expected behavior of others. If too few people participate it is unlikely that the activity will make any difference. As a consequence, it has been hypothesized that expectations about the behavior of others play an important role in the decision to participate. If someone expects that only a few people will participate his or her motivation to participate will be low. In a way, the expectation about other people's behavior functions as a self-fulfilling prophecy: if people believe that only a few will participate they will not be motivated to participate, and will thus make their own expectation true.

The Transformation of Potentiality into Action

Demand – that is, people who adhere to a collective action frame – is not automatically turned into actual participation. Demand and supply must be brought together. This is in fact what most action mobilization campaigns are about: targeting potential participants and turning them into actual participants. Obviously, a campaign will never be 100 percent successful in that regard. In the course of a campaign people may lose their sympathy for the movement. I have labeled this *conversion*; a phenomenon that is more likely if countermovements and/or authorities are mounting countercampaigns. On the other hand, organizers may fail to convert sympathizers into participants because they fail to target or to motivate them. This I have called *non-conversion*. As the previous section concentrated on motivating, I now focus on targeting.

Targeting sympathizers implies finding an answer to two strategic questions: who are the sympathizers, and how can they be reached? These are, by the way, two questions every attempt to persuade must find an answer to. Indeed, sophisticated movement organizations such as Greenpeace have learned to employ many of the strategies that have been developed in advertising. Social networks are of crucial importance in this regard. Movement organizations have two options here: they can try to co-opt existing networks or they can build new networks. Both strategies are mobilization efforts in themselves. Co-option is the easier strategy of the two, because it builds on existing commitments to organizations and networks that are part of the movement organization's alliance system. There are risks, however. The co-opted organization may use the campaign for its own ends or the leadership may for whatever reason decide not to collaborate. The latter makes it more difficult for the rank and file to cooperate. Yet co-option of existing networks, such as churches, unions, political parties, youth organizations, and the like, is frequently used, if only because it implies an answer to both strategic questions at the same time. On the one hand, it works from the assumption that most members of the organization sympathize with the movement; on the other hand, it is assumed that these sympathizers can be reached through the organization's networks.

Building new networks implies the recruitment of people who are willing to spend sometimes considerable amounts of time for a prolonged period as movement activists. It will, therefore, require more effort on the part of the organization than co-option of existing networks, but once established the networks are more reliable. The recruitment of movement activists is a process which is determined, on the one hand, by factors that influence who is being asked, and, on the other hand, by factors that influence who agrees to serve as an activist when asked. As for the first type of factors, a crucial determinant is someone's position in networks linked to the movement organization, or more specifically to the movement organizer who is undertaking the recruitment effort. Movement organizers tend to recruit first among the people they know, and often that suffices (Marwell and Oliver, 1993; Klandermans, 1997). After all, they don't need many. According to Marwell and Oliver (1993), long-term activism is a typical example of an activity with a decelerating production function. You need a few to maintain the network, but once you have those few the return from having additional activists diminishes rapidly. Indeed, Marwell and Oliver argue that long-term activism is one of the forms of activism that must cope with free rider behavior. The latter point is of importance for the decision to serve as an activist or not. I maintain that the people who are asked to serve as activists understand perfectly well that they are giving most of the sympathizers of the movement a free ride, but they are prepared to do so because they care. Only people who really care a lot are prepared to sacrifice for the others. In the words of Oliver (1984), they make the effort because they feel that "If [they] don't do it, nobody else will." I hold that only people who strongly support the movement's ideology and who feel responsible for maintaining and proselytizing the movement and its ideology are prepared to make the effort of serving as movement activists.

CONCLUSION

Social movements come into being because people who are aggrieved and have the resources to mobilize seize the political opportunities they perceive. People join social movements because it gives meaning to their lives to fight together with people they identify with for some social or political change. All these different aspects are important in order to understand why social movements come into being and why people join them. Grievances, resources, and opportunities on the one side, instrumentality, identity, and meaning on the other, are pieces of a puzzle we are only beginning to solve. Each of these concepts can be conceived of as the focal variable of a theoretical framework designed to investigate that variable. Grievance theory attempts to understand the demand side of political protest; resource mobilization theory the supply side; and opportunity theory the interaction between the resulting social movement activity and its political environment. Similarly, theories of identity formation and meaning construction try to understand the generation and appropriation of collective action frames by individuals; motivation theories the instrumentality of social movement participation; and mobilization theories how potentiality is turned into actuality. In this chapter, however, I have taken a synthetic approach and discussed the ways in which these theories combine in the explanation of social movements and social movement participation.

20

Social Movement Politics and Organization

Debra C. Minkoff

In the popular imagination, social movements are conceptualized as dynamic and dramatic mobilizations oriented toward such objectives as challenging the state to recognize group rights, seeking public goods to improve the (middle-class) quality of life, or stemming the tides of progressive social change. Periodic outbursts of activism – from black civil rights protests in the United States to student democracy movements in China and anti-immigrant campaigns in Western Europe – lend credence to this view of social movements as spontaneous and emotional surges of collective action. In contrast, close to three decades of sociological research on social movements demonstrates the many ways that movement politics are structured organizationally at the local, national, and increasingly transnational or global levels.

The juxtaposition of spontaneity and organization has been at the heart of academic debates about social movements at least since the initiation (and temporary ascendance) of the resource mobilization paradigm in the 1970s. In the intervening years, organizational perspectives on social movements have moved in and out of favor, as the field has embraced a broader turn in the discipline toward concerns with identity, discourse, and culture. The limitations to such cultural perspectives are evidenced by the fact that, after cumulating fairly detailed empirical knowledge of both contemporary and historical social movements, scholars are beginning seriously to revisit the central insight of early resource mobilization theory: that organization matters. This "return to organization" makes sense in the context of a central practical reality facing contemporary movement-building and activism: the institutionalization of social movements in the politics of advanced capitalist societies.

In seeking to understand this tension between social movement spontaneity and institutionalization, the challenge is to re-establish the importance of organizations in social movement analysis without losing what we have learned about identity, culture, and spontaneity. This chapter seeks to intervene in this project by reviewing the growing body of research that is explicitly organizational in its focus and conceptualizes movement politics and organization as interlinked. Such work promises to move social movement theory beyond such simple dichotomies as spontaneity versus organization and culture versus structure. At the same time, organizational approaches need to consider the concerns currently associated with more culturally oriented frameworks.

The first part of the chapter briefly reviews the original resource mobilization paradigm and describes some of its elaborations and criticisms. The remainder of the chapter focuses on recent work that emphasizes the more organized dimensions of social movement politics, examining the organizational processes that promote institutionalization and the implications of what has recently been called "the social movement society" (Meyer and Tarrow, 1998) for the relationship between spontaneity and organization. The chapter concludes with a provisional treatment of what I think is a central problem for future social movement theory: how to integrate organizational and cultural processes in the study of social movement dynamics. This issue is particularly important in light of the transnational context of many contemporary efforts at social change.

THE RESOURCE MOBILIZATION PARADIGM

The original resource mobilization (RM) paradigm staked out its terrain boldly by proclaiming that in contemporary (that is, advanced capitalist) societies discontent is relatively constant and therefore cannot explain the emergence and development of social movements. Instead, the availability of resources external to the movement accounts for the ups and downs of mobilization. According to McCarthy and Zald (1977), social movements (which they define as preferences for change) are increasingly reliant on formalized social movement organizations (SMOs) established by "issue entrepreneurs" (who might go so far as to manufacture grievances), directed by a professional staff, and more concerned with securing external support (both financial and moral) than creating a mass-based membership of the disenfranchised and aggrieved. McCarthy and Zald also introduced such concepts as social movement industry and social movement sector to make the point that social movements can be fruitfully analyzed using concepts drawn from organizational sociology.

This new focus on organizations as a critical dimension of social movements created something of a growth industry for sociologists concerned with extending (and legitimating) the study of those protest movements of the 1960s and early 1970s in which many of them had actively participated. Resource mobilization theory offered a compelling alternative to the then dominant view that social movements were manifestations of system breakdown, alienation, and participant irrationality, only slightly more organized than panics, crazes, and fads. An emphasis on resources and rationality provided a seemingly more accurate, and less derogatory, portrayal of what the civil rights, feminist, antiwar, and new left movements were all about.

Mayer Zald, in an essay titled "Looking Backward to Look Forward: Reflections on the Past and Future of the Resource Mobilization Research Program," summarizes the core assumptions of the RM perspective: (a) since all behavior entails costs, discontent is not automatically translated into social movement activity but entails some (at least "primitive") weighing of costs and benefits; (b) resources are mobilized from a range of sources, including but not limited to the aggrieved group; (c) organizing activity is critical since resources need to be aggregated and deployed; (d) state and societal facilitation or repression influences the costs of participation; and (e) movement outcomes are problematic since there is no simple relationship between the mobilization of social movements and their success (Zald, 1992). This summary combines the premises of the early McCarthy–Zald formulation of resource mobilization theory and what some would consider a distinct theoretical development – the political process model.

Early political process theorists, while also emphasizing the importance of organization and rationality, noted that even if resources are widely available, political conditions also influence the costs and benefits of collective action. To understand the emergence of social movements, it is therefore critical to consider changes in the political context, especially the vulnerability of authorities to outside challenges and what their incentives are to repress or facilitate collective action. The focus of these political approaches is on varieties of collective action and outcomes and not on organizational dynamics *per se*. Organizations matter, but mainly insofar as they provide local networks that can be used for mass recruitment and support the development of an insurgent consciousness or "cognitive liberation" (McAdam, 1982).

In the political process model, internal group resources (organizations, institutions, constituents) are more central to movement emergence (although not necessarily development) than external support, which is thought to channel insurgency in more moderate directions. In addition, the actions of state officials and other political contingencies are determinant. Recent work in the political process tradition has tended to de-emphasize organizational processes, focusing instead on macropolitical issues such as the patterning and dynamics of protest cycles and cross-national comparisons of state structures and protest action.

The Critics

Whether resource mobilization theory and political process models are considered to be of one piece or separate approaches, both have come under fire for being too structural and inattentive to psychological and cultural processes. As Steven Barkan succinctly puts it, "In the world of resource mobilization theory, ideology, culture, interpretation, emotions, the minutiae of daily interaction, and other nonstructural aspects barely existed" (Barkan, n.d., pp. 7–8). A second criticism has faulted resource mobilization theory for privileging organization over spontaneity and shifting attention from the disruptive potential of mass protest to the more institutionalized, and less transformative, world of conventional politics.

These criticisms have been taken up in a variety of ways. Some researchers have sought to modify the rational actor assumptions of resource mobilization and political process theories by developing a more nuanced and contextualized social psychology of mobilization. Here the focus has shifted from interests to identity, and, more recently, to the role of emotions in social movement dynamics. Others have responded to the dominance of resource mobilization theory by arguing for the importance of cultural processes, both at the macro-level of political discourse and the framing of movement demands, and at the micro-level of meaning construction. Finally, a number of researchers have attempted to integrate the new social movements perspective that, although it developed roughly in tandem with resource mobilization approaches in the United States, was shaped by a Western European political context and theoretical sensibility. This work posits the centrality of collective identities in contemporary social movements, drawing a contrast to the redistributive concerns of earlier class-based movements.

Taken together, these various approaches portray recent social movements as predominately cultural phenomena that emphasize processes of identity construction and are embedded in locally based social networks and less organized forms of social interaction. Activists are defined less by what they do in the political or legislative arena and more in terms of cultural or symbolic transgressions in the form of individualized lifestyle commitments and collective actions that attempt to challenge and change cultural discourse and consciousness. "The media" and "the public" are the main targets of these cultural challenges and strategic action has been replaced by symbolic action – which can sometimes appear as the antithesis of strategy.

Although this summary portrayal is certainly overstated it is meant to convey the extent to which recent advances in social movement theory have eschewed the field's earlier emphasis on social movement politics and organization. Barkan (n.d.) offers a cogent critique of the emerging cultural paradigm, especially that it has deflected attention from more strategic questions about movement outcomes and success. Still, as he notes, it is worthwhile to consider these theoretical developments sociologically: "The elements of the emerging paradigm perhaps hold particular appeal for scholars who have taken part in the women's, gay and lesbian, and other "new" movements, just as the elements of resource mobilization held special appeal for scholars who took part in the 1960s movements. If today's movements are indeed more about identity than about strategy, more about culture than about politics, then it's no accident that the emerging paradigm appeals to many of today's movement scholars" (Barkan, n.d., p. 12).

By the same token, it is important to situate future movement scholarship in the substantive realities facing social movements today. In the remainder of this chapter I suggest that among the many concerns that activists face one stands out: the need to negotiate a heavily institutionalized political environment that has "normalized" contention so much that it is considered fairly routine. In this new political context, where even many "spontaneous" demonstrations are highly scripted, organizational analysis provides analytic leverage on the processes by which movements become incorporated into national political structures and the implications of movement institutionalization for mounting sustained challenges against the state.

Social Movement Institutionalization

In some ways, McCarthy and Zald's early portrayal of social movements is even more accurate today. Social movement issues and actors have been incorporated into the polity to a striking extent. Movement organizations look and act very much like interest groups in the US system; green parties have gained considerable visibility and, in some cases, influence in Western Europe; and many of the opposition social movements that propelled East European and Latin American democratic transitions are now established political actors (if not political parties). In contrasting takes on the same phenomenon, David Meyer and Sidney Tarrow introduce the concept of the "social movement society" to capture the idea that "classical social movement modes of action may be becoming part of the conventional repertoire of participation" (Meyer and Tarrow, 1998, p. 4), whereas Paul Burstein (1998) argues that social movements and interest groups are essentially the same, and that even differences between these "interest organizations" and parties have diminished.

The institutionalization of social movements is part of a longer historical trend in the nationalization of social movements. As both Tilly (1984) and Tarrow (1994) have argued, the centralization of power in national states in the eighteenth century brought a concomitant shift in the repertoire of collective action from sporadic, spontaneous and, local forms of protest (bread riots, strikes) to more organized modes of action (mass demonstrations, petitions) better suited to putting pressure on national authorities. As a result, social movements, especially national ones, are more organized – in the sense of being both less characterized by spontaneous events and, well, more comprised of organizations.

A related feature of movement institutionalization is a convergence in forms of action and organization: "one of the characteristics of the movement society is that social movements can combine disruptive and conventional activities and forms of organization, while institutional actors like interest groups and parties increasingly engage in contentious behavior" (Meyer and Tarrow, 1998, p. 25). At the same time, so-called contentious behavior has been subject to redefinition as the legitimate repertoire of collective action has changed. Demonstrations and mass protests are more likely to take place by advance arrangement with authorities and, although such events garner desired media attention and provide an opportunity for increasing solidarity, this "policing of protest" certainly undercuts spontaneity and the disruptive potential of collective challenges (della Porta and Reiter, 1997).

One major implication of these trends is that formal organizations are now more central than ever to movement politics in most democratic polities. And movement organizations, unlike occasional outbursts of dissent, are burdened with the requirements of organizational survival. They need resources

– members, leaders, money – to establish and sustain themselves. They also need a minimal level of institutional legitimacy to convince powerful actors and potential contributors that they should support – or at least not repress – their efforts. Such resource and institutional dependencies fundamentally shape movement developments, as do competitive pressures that determine processes of organizational founding, survival, and change.

Early work on the "radical flank effect" of foundation funding was predicated on this insight. As this argument goes, in order to offset civil rights protest, foundation patronage was successfully directed in support of more moderate efforts, ultimately promoting the creation and maintenance of professional movement organizations. Jenkins (1999) develops this channeling argument by mapping trends in foundation funding for different movements and organizational forms, arguing that social movement philanthropy encourages professionalization by supporting groups with more formalized structures. Whereas some critics might consider this a form of co-optation, Jenkins suggests that the result cuts both ways. On the one hand, foundation funding provides "technical resources for consolidating movement victories and ensuring that these gains remain in place" (Jenkins, 1999, p. 15). On the other hand, more democratic, participatory organizations are underfunded and organizers may have more incentive to professionalize than engage in grassroots mobilization, potentially blunting movement effectiveness. Again, the trade-off between spontaneity and organization looms in the background.

McCarthy et al. (1991) extend the channeling metaphor to the "institutional channeling" of social movements by the state, noting the "strong tendency toward structural uniformity... among social movement organizations in the recent American context" (p. 47). They build on neo-institutional theories of organization, pointing to the sometimes subtle and indirect institutional pressures that channel organizational action into a limited set of choices. In addition to statutes that circumscribe the legality of various modes of associational activity, there are federal and state tax laws, postal regulations, and monitoring agencies that provide incentives to organize according to official standards and to limit innovation. Although compliance with such norms is voluntary, a "tangle of incentives" provides advantages to certain organizational forms over others. These are the groups that get the funding and the credibility; they also have better chances for survival.

I have analyzed processes of institutionalization from an ecological perspective on organizational evolution. My work focuses attention on how competitive and institutional pressures shape the contours and viability of organizational populations by influencing patterns of organizational founding, failure, and change. Environmental selection and changes in the political environment establish the legitimacy of organizational constituencies and forms, thus setting parameters around how social movements develop. To the extent that new constituencies or methods become legitimate, they establish an institutional niche; that is, an arena of activity that provides them with necessary resources for mobilization and organizational maintenance and protects them from the vagaries of political transitions or shifts in the public agenda.

Applying this framework to the contemporary civil rights and feminist move-ments in the USA, I demonstrate that social movement development is contin-gent on levels of inter-organizational competition for resources and the way this competition shapes the legitimacy of different models of organization (Minkoff, 1994). I argue that organizational density-dependence is a key mechanism driv-ing the development of these movements. My findings indicate that increases in the number of both service and protest organizations promoted the founding and survival rates of groups pursuing advocacy, an intermediate strategy that com-bines conventional lobbying and educational efforts with more confrontational activities. As this organizational form gained legitimacy, competitive pressures became dominant after 1970. One result was that the continued growth of protest and service organizations diminished as advocacy organizations began to dominate this sector of movement activity.

The key insight from these studies is that, without some baseline of legitimacy, the organizational models adopted by movement actors are not likely to be viable for long. Organizational ecology models suggest that early investments in organization-building pay off, not only because resource flows become rou-tinized and available for use by other constituencies, but also because the successful maintenance and growth of organizations increases their acceptance by powerful third parties. Such legitimacy affects the willingness of funders to support new constituencies, of authorities to tolerate their dissent, and of the media to broadcast their claims in a favorable light. As critically, organizational models must also be accepted by the movement constituency. As we know from the more visible and better documented contemporary social movements, there is often conflict among activists and constituents about what are the most appropriate methods and forms of activism (for example, see McAdam, 1982, and Polletta, 1997, on the civil rights and black power movements).

Elisabeth Clemens (1997) is one of the few researchers who has given such internal and external legitimation processes serious attention. Drawing on cul-tural-institutional arguments, she looks at two sides of the problem: how social movement actors adopt and adapt organizational models in ways that gain them political leverage and how this promotes innovation in the prevailing "repertoire of organization" and the political system more generally. One important insight of Clemens's work is that organizational forms can be thought of as social movement frames that must resonate with movement participants and potential activists in order to be accepted. This is likely to entail something of a cultural or cognitive stretch – for both activists and authorities – since not all organizational models are considered fitting for all social actors. As she notes, there are *"logics of appropriateness* that specify who should use what form for what purpose" (Clemens, 1997, p. 49; emphasis in original). To the extent that unfamiliar movement actors can deploy familiar organizational forms they increase not only their chances of success but, also, "through such oblique approaches, the roster of recognized political claimants and claims expands, transforming the relation of state and society" (Clemens, 1997, p. 12).

Using late nineteenth-and early twentieth-century activism by women, farm-ers, and workers as her cases, Clemens demonstrates that their ability to adapt existing non-political organizations – clubs, unions, corporations – for political purposes provided them with legitimacy and access to authorities. In the case of women, this was especially significant, since at the time they were not politically enfranchised. Clemens takes the argument one step further by demonstrating that, as these social groups gained a credible voice in the political arena because of their successful organizational innovations, they fundamentally transformed the institutional structure and promoted the rise of interest group politics in the USA – a critical step toward the development of a "social movement society" a half century later.

SOCIAL MOVEMENT ORGANIZATIONS AND POLITICS

If social movements are now as organized and institutionalized as these arguments suggest, the obvious question is: what are the implications for "contentious politics" (McAdam et al., 1996b)? This brings us back to the orienting theme of this chapter: the juxtaposition between spontaneity and organization. Piven and Cloward (1992) have been the most vocal opponents of resource mobilization's emphasis on the organized dimensions of social movements, arguing (on both normative and descriptive grounds) that it not only provides a recipe for the cooptation of dissent since formal organizations are essentially conservative, but also marginalizes the efforts of those groups unable (or unwilling) to establish formal organizations to press their claims. Nonetheless, the fact remains that contemporary protest movements are, in a number of ways, dependent on a formal and professionalized organizational infrastructure. In this section I argue for a renewed emphasis on movement organization by highlighting some of the direct and indirect ways in which formal movement organizations remain central to protest politics.

As a first point, social movement organizations are essential for the initiation and diffusion of protest. Tarrow (1994) has argued that competition among social movement organizations accelerates the spread of protest cycles. In the beginning of a protest cycle, successful collective action by "early risers" broadcasts to other movement groups that certain forms of collective action are viable and that the risks of repression are not prohibitive. At the peak of the protest wave, competition for members and supporters leads social movement organizations to escalate protest. New organizations emerge and conventional interest groups become active. The creation of new SMOs increases interorganizational competition as groups try to outdo each other by adopting radical forms of action to gain public support and attention. This "competitive spiral" is the dynamic behind the protest wave, encouraging tactical innovation.

Although Tarrow theorizes the importance of movement organizations as vehicles for protest, his emphasis is on the information provided by successful collective action and how this drives the development of protest cycles. In analyzing the relationship between the civil rights movement and the feminist movement, I show that increases in the number of civil rights *organizations*, not civil rights protest events, promote feminist collective action (Minkoff, 1997a). In fact, it appears that protest by initiator movements is likely to increase activism by other groups only when political allies are in positions of power. These findings suggest that organizational expansion is critical in creating protest opportunities for other challengers. Organizational effects operate both directly and indirectly: activists cross movement boundaries, taking organizing templates with them; resource-sharing and information-sharing transmit advantages to new movements and their organizations; and processes of legitimacy-building by initiator movements establish a resource base that becomes available to a wider set of challenging groups.

European social movements researchers are also beginning to analyze the relationship between protest and organization, although this research remains fairly descriptive and is limited to detailing the kinds of organizations that sponsor protest events and how this changes over time (Kriesi et al., 1995; Rucht, 1998). Rucht (1998), for example, documents a notable shift in organizational sponsorship of protest events in Germany since 1950 (including East German protests since 1989): whereas most demonstrations were organized by large formal pressure groups in the 1950s and 1960s, after 1970 informal groups and networks, along with political parties, also became key sponsors. Formal pressure groups are still the dominant sponsors (they organized 46 percent of protests in 1990–2), but not exclusively so. Importantly, the volume of mass protest also increased over this period, despite occasional declines. This is particularly the case with "demonstrative" events (demonstrations, marches, rallies, and strikes), but there is also some indication of a recent rise in violent protests (consisting of property damage, physical aggression, and personal injuries). One conclusion Rucht draws is that although many protest groups have become more professionalized and institutionalized, the result has not been a "deradicalization of protest" (Rucht, 1998, p. 52).

Organizations, particularly formal ones, also promote the stability and continuity of social movements. Staggenborg's (1988) analysis of the consequences of professional leadership and formal structure in the pro-choice movement demonstrates that formally structured and professional movement organizations help to maintain the movement under restrictive political conditions when mobilization is difficult. They are also more effective than informal groups at organizational maintenance because they can rely on paid staff to manage routine organizational activities and because the existence of a formal structure ensures continuity despite changes in leadership and external conditions. Staggenborg also makes the point that, although formalization is correlated with the institutionalization of movement tactics (lobbying over protest, for example), there is no evidence that goals necessarily become less radical or that organizations necessarily become more conservative in their use of tactics. At the same time, her comparative analysis suggests that "nonprofessional leaders and informal SMOs remain important in initiating movements and tactics that are critical to the growth of insurgency" (Staggenborg, 1988, p. 603). A diversity of organizational forms – both formal and informal – is thus critical for movement stability and innovation.

Continuity in movement organizations can also function as an "abeyance structure" (Taylor, 1989) that maintains movement ideology when political conditions become restrictive. For example, the contemporary US women's movement benefited from the feminist commitment and activist identities maintained by a small group of women involved in the National Women's Party in the 1940s and 1950s (Taylor, 1989). Available social networks, provided by traditional women's associations, and relationships among younger feminists forged in the civil rights and new left student movements, were also critical in promoting ideological continuity and movement emergence. Although informal networks can also function as abeyance structures, formal movement organizations, to the extent that they establish a resource niche, may be less vulnerable to political downturns, so that even as protest declines they can survive as a locus for future activism (Minkoff, 1997b).

I want to draw attention to two additional functions of formal SMOs that have not received much attention, largely because they shade over into discussions of culture and collective identity. And, as I noted earlier, collective identity approaches tend to overlook the importance of formal organization. As I have argued elsewhere with respect to the USA (Minkoff, 1997b), the intentional visibility of national social movement organizations and their efforts at publicizing movement goals and activities are conducive to the formation of a mediated form of collective identity among otherwise isolated individuals. Contemporary social movements are more likely to represent groups with "weak infrastructures," such as women, the elderly, lesbians and gay men, the disabled, and peace or environmental activists. These groups are not necessarily constituted by, for example, shared patterns of daily life or even the opportunity for face-to-face interactions through which to build solidarity or shared cultures. In their absence, individuals are tied together by common symbols and shared ideologies. That is, their relationship to each other is mediated by the organizations and movements with which they affiliate (and in which they may or may not participate). Importantly, national SMOs act as carriers of these collective definitions and play a role in disseminating them more widely.

A final function is the role formal SMOs play in shaping and expanding the public sphere by promoting debate on issues of concern to their constituencies. In the process, these movement organizations raise questions about what constitutes the public good and promote the diffusion of new ideas. So, for example, the activities of national civil rights organizations, public conflict between pro-choice and pro-life organizations, and efforts by environmental organizations have put a diversity of issues onto the public stage, challenging the assumptions guiding social and material relations and, in some cases, even influencing legislative and policy change. The visibility of national organizations may also contribute to the formation of "counterpublic spheres" in which subordinate groups are able to debate and construct alternative analyses, collective identities, and agendas for action (Fraser, 1992). Even less directly active members have access to these debates through a variety of media forms, such as movement-affiliated newspapers and, increasingly, Internet resources such as web sites and "chatrooms," that can ground the kind of symbolic affiliation discussed briefly above.

Social Movement Organization, Politics, and Culture

The last two points about collective identity and the public sphere can be read as a step by a neo-resource mobilization analyst onto the terrain of culture and identity. I want to suggest some additional ways in which analyses of movement organization and institutionalization can benefit from increased attention to questions raised by cultural approaches (broadly defined) and vice versa. To date, synthetic efforts have emphasized the framing function of social movement organizations (McAdam et al., 1996a), but we need more research on how organizational structures and processes reproduce or enable conceptions of legitimate action, the formation and maintenance of collective identities, and innovations in broader cultural understandings about social movement politics.

Clemens's work on the cultural meanings embedded in, and conveyed by, organizational forms represents one important direction for future research. If the professional SMO form has, in fact, become so widespread and legitimate – i.e. acceptable for use by almost everyone – what are the sources of further innovation in both organizational and collective action repertoires? Do social groups without the necessary resources to adopt this dominant model organize nonetheless – combining less familiar practices under the rubric of "organization" and, in the process, changing conceptions of what it means to participate in politics and civil society? These questions raise the need for more attention to how movement organizational forms become more conventional and widespread. Following Clemens, answers to these questions have potentially important consequences for the practices of social movements and institutional life more generally.

A second line of inquiry builds on the question of how ideological commitments delimit the choice of available organizational models and define how groups understand the very purposes of strategy and organization. The accepted view is that a radical social change orientation lines up with the use of informal, participatory organizational structures and that reform movements are more likely to adopt the standard SMO model because they are motivated instrumentally rather than ideologically. However, as Francesca Polletta (1997) argues, styles of decision-making have "powerful symbolic connotations" and what is seen as the best way to organize is open to continual redefinition. It is not sufficient, then, to simply posit a one-to-one relationship between organizational choices and ideological commitments without further research.

We also know much less than we should about how internal debates over goals, strategies, and identities – as well as their representations to a wider public – are shaped by the structure of movement organizations in terms of governance, administration, and the exigencies of resource procurement. We need to look at internal organizational processes with the understanding that cultural practices and collective identities are not free-floating, but develop within structural parameters that prescribe patterns of interaction and modes of power. However, there has been only limited attention by social movement researchers to the organization–identity nexus and how this shapes activist identities and organizational projects (but see Gamson, 1996).

Finally, there is the question of the broader cultural significance of movement organization and institutionalization. In arguing for the relevance of the growth and differentiation of movement-related organizations (a category that includes formal SMOs and affiliated service or cultural organizations, self-help groups, and other voluntary associations that serve the movement base), Meyer and Tarrow (1998, p. 20) point out that organizational diffusion "suggests ways in which movement-originated identities, goals, and personnel may be blending into the structures of civil society without necessarily producing a higher visible level of protest, violence or contention." That social movements and movement organizations are more institutionalized does not *ipso facto* mean that political dissent is contained or that activism is not taking place outside of conventional political structures. We just need to know where to look for it, whether on the more cultural terrain of civil society or in the organizational structures of the "social movement society."

MOVEMENT ORGANIZATION IN A "GLOBAL" WORLD

In the account of movement organization and politics that I have presented here, organizations are discretely bounded and identifiable social units that mobilize (more or less) discretely bounded and identifiable social groups and target their activities toward (somewhat less) discretely bounded or identifiable targets. Yet, as recent scholarship suggests, social movements have become increasingly transnational in scope, presenting unique conditions for resource mobilization and the mobilization of protest (McAdam et al., 1996b). Thus, at the same time that movements have become more institutionalized within national polities, they have also begun to transcend national boundaries in ways that challenge the very concepts that have animated social movement research in the past three decades – organization, opportunities, and collective identity.

In considering the transnational dimensions of social movements, there is a particular need to be clear about the object of study, which doesn't necessarily conform to our understanding of "social movements." Constituencies are harder to specify, as are targets and tactics that distinguish them as "social movements," as opposed to, for example, advocacy campaigns or networks. If we are interested in something called a "transnational SMO," do we look for an international SMO with national affiliates, an interorganizational network of international non-governmental organizations (NGOs), or local movement groups supported by international NGOs of some sort? A companion issue is how we conceptualize the targets of transnational challenges – are they national states, transnational authorities, or global conventions? What kinds of organizational forms and strategies make sense given the nature and mix of targets?

We also need to rethink the meaning and role of collective identity and cultural-institutional constraints. My earlier discussion of the way that formal movement organizations influence collective identity processes implies the hypothesis that there are correspondingly new forms of mediated collective identities that bridge interested individuals across political and social space. But if what gives social movements their distinctive character is the presence of interpersonal bonds of some sort (McAdam et al., 1996b), we need to understand the ability of movements to build such connections in a sustainable way. And if "logics of appropriateness" determine which groups can legitimately deploy specific organizational forms, what are the sources of such conventions and how do they influence transnational movement activists as they try to establish organizations both locally and across national domains?

Social movement scholars have recently begun to address the theoretical and practical complexities of organizing in a transnational context, as well as the difficulties inherent in challenging political systems where modes of dissent have become less spontaneous and more institutionalized. It is clear that we need additional research – that which takes movement organization seriously and that which takes up the meaning of "organization" as both a structural and cultural phenomenon. Perhaps less obvious is the need for such research to be more explicitly interdisciplinary, both within sociology and across the social sciences and humanities. Such a suggestion is certainly not novel, but it has been recently muted by debates within the social movement field over the relative importance of culture (identity, emotions) versus structure (political opportunities, organizations) (see the exchange following Goodwin and Jasper, 1999). But just as tactical and organizational innovation come from mixing familiar forms with unfamiliar actors, future social movement research is likely to benefit from work that mixes the accepted wisdom about resources, opportunities, and identities with concepts and theories located in less familiar disciplines and subdisciplines. Despite the professional constraints posed by disciplinary organization, intellectual spontaneity is nonetheless possible.

Part VI

Structures: Stratification, Networks, and Firms

21

Occupations, Stratification, and Mobility

Donald J. Treiman

INTRODUCTION

Social stratification refers to the unequal distribution of the rewards society has to offer and the resources individuals and families use to obtain such rewards. Conceptually we can summarize both the rewards and resources under the rubrics of power, privilege, and prestige; but, in practice, most research on social stratification is concerned with the distribution of, and relations among, education, occupational status, and income, both between generations and over the life course of individuals. There are two reasons for this. First, it is difficult to directly study power, privilege, and prestige. Power is difficult to measure and its measurement is seldom attempted. The prestige of individuals depends on a combination of personal characteristics and "deference entitlements" (objective status characteristics), but personal characteristics are salient only in the context of interpersonal relations; there is, however, a well developed tradition of research on the prestige of occupations, which is reviewed below. Some aspects of privilege, such as wealth and perquisites, also are difficult to study – wealth because individuals often are reluctant to reveal their wealth, and perquisites because they are difficult to compare across individuals, much less across societies or over time. Thus, students of stratification often settle for information on education, occupational status, and income, which can be readily gathered in sample surveys and censuses and which can be used both to compare different groups within a society and to make both cross-temporal and cross-national comparisons. Second, in the modern world these three attributes are very powerful indicators of the life chances of individuals and families; singly and together, they substantially define the position of individuals and families in hierarchies of advantage, or "socioeconomic status."

The field of social stratification is concerned with three central questions:

1   What is the shape of distributions of education, occupation, income, and
   other aspects of socioeconomic status in a population. For example, how
   much income inequality is there, are most people relatively poor and a few
   relatively rich, are most people in the middle of the income distribution, or
   does it have some other shape?

2   What factors affect who gets ahead; that is, who acquires high education,
   occupational status, and income? This question, in turn, can be divided
   into two: (a) what determines to what extent and in what ways socioeconomic advantage is transmitted from generation to generation; (b)
   what determines how some attributes are converted into others over the
   life course – for example, what is the relationship between education and
   subsequent occupational status, what is the relationship between occupational status and income, how orderly are careers, and so on? Together,
   these two questions constitute the study of "status attainment" or "social
   mobility."

3   What are the correlates and consequences of position in the stratification
   system? That is, to what extent and in what ways does socioeconomic
   status affect the way people think and act: whether and how they vote,
   how many children they have, how often they visit their relatives, how
   tolerant they are of other kinds of people and different points of view,
   what kinds of life styles they adopt, and so on?

All societies organized above the level of small independent bands are stratified because, as Treiman (1977) has argued, all societies of any degree of
complexity have a division of labor – that is, the tasks and duties that have to
be carried out are done by different people, who specialize in one occupation or
another, and differences in tasks, duties, and responsibilities inherently create
differences in power, which in turn give rise to differences in privilege, and hence
to differences in prestige. Connections between the power, privilege, and prestige
of occupations can be found throughout history: in Egyptian and Chinese
dynastic records, in the ordering of castes in India and Nepal, in the marching
order of guilds in medieval Europe, and in modern societies at all levels of
economic development.

Although wealth and power traditionally have been important dimensions of
social stratification, in the modern world two other attributes have come to
assume a central role: how much education people attain, and the kind of work
they do, their occupations. Indeed, wealth and power have come to be dependent
on education and occupational position. In industrialized societies, the primary
source of income for most people is wages and salaries. Moreover, in the absence
of hereditary distinctions of rank, occupations are the primary basis of both
power differentials and prestige distinctions. Finally, in the modern world, where
relatively little wealth is inherited, and income is substantially variable over the
life course, intergenerational status reproduction is mostly determined by the
similarity in the educational level and occupational status of successive generations. Thus, educational achievement and occupational status are central to
social status in the modern world, and their determinants, correlates, and

consequences, including their relation to each other, within and across generations, are the primary foci of social stratification research.

Although there are some important precursors (for example, Sorokin, 1927), the serious study of social stratification and social mobility is barely a half century old, dating to the work of the first Research Committee of the then newly organized International Sociological Association, which promoted a series of national intergenerational occupational mobility studies (recounted by Ganzeboom et al., who in 1991 identified three generations of stratification research). Over the past half century research in this field has become increasingly sophisticated, as a result of advances in statistical methods, solutions to the problems of measurement comparability, an explosion of new data sources, and the development of new, multilevel, research designs that have made it possible to rigorously investigate variations in stratification systems across societies and over time. The result has been a vast expansion of our understanding of how stratification systems function in the modern world. This chapter reviews developments with respect to the first two of the three core questions identified above: the shape of status hierarchies (focusing on the measurement of occupational status) and the process of social mobility and status attainment (with a separate section devoted specifically to educational attainment). Research on the correlates and consequences of socioeconomic status is as yet too fragmented to permit a systematic review. The chapter concludes with a brief review of the methodological developments that have lead to these advances.

THE MEASUREMENT OF OCCUPATIONAL STATUS

In the United States there are about 100 million employed persons and hence about 100 million jobs – specific positions in specific enterprises. For these to become tractable for analytic purposes, they must be aggregated into a small number (no more than a few hundred) of categories. Of the many ways in which it is possible to aggregate the specific jobs that people do, occupational categories – groupings of jobs with respect to the similarity of their content, i.e. the skill and knowledge it takes to do them, their duties, and their responsibilities – have the greatest currency in sociology. While economists have tended to aggregate jobs into industries – on the basis of the goods and services produced by the enterprises in which people work – sociologists have recognized that the relative status of jobs is best summarized by attending to their requirements and their responsibilities, i.e by forming occupational classifications.

There are three fundamental ways of classifying occupations with respect to their status, and each has culminated in a widely accepted internationally standardized scale or category system: occupations may be aggregated on the basis of their prestige, their socioeconomic status, or their class position.

Prestige scales assign scores to occupations on the basis of evaluations by the public of their relative "prestige" or "social standing" or "respect" – terms that for practical purposes are synonymous. While prestige ratings studies have been carried out in many nations since early in the twentieth century, the bulk of the research has been done since the Second World War. In the USA an important early study was conducted by researchers at the National Opinion Research Center in 1947, which was replicated and expanded in the early 1960s in a series of surveys, and still another replication was carried out in 1989 (Nakao and Treas, 1994); at the same time, similar studies were conducted in a large number of other countries. It turns out that people in all walks of life – that is, regardless of education, ethnic identity, gender, age, or their own occupational position – on average rank occupations in the same way with respect to their prestige, with high government officials and learned professionals at the top and unskilled laborers at the bottom. Moreover, members of different societies throughout the world perceive the relative prestige of occupations in essentially similar ways (the average intersocietal correlation, across 60 societies, is about 0.8), and the prestige ordering of occupations hardly changes over time (Treiman, 1977). In an important article, Kraus et al. (1978) demonstrate that prestige is not simply an invention of sociologists, since when individuals are asked to group occupations on the basis of their "similarity" (not further specified), the principal basis of similarity is how close occupations are with respect to their prestige rankings. As noted above, Treiman provided a theoretical explanation for these findings, suggesting that the enormous cross-national similarity in prestige evaluations reflects cross-national similarities in the relative power and privilege associated with different occupations, which in turn reflects inherent features of the organization of work in all complex societies.

The great cross-national similarity in occupational prestige ratings led Treiman to devise an international prestige scale, which has become the internationally accepted standard for occupational status measurement when a prestige scale is desired.

Socioeconomic Status

Seeking a way to generalize prestige scores from the relatively small number of occupation categories for which prestige ratings were available to the several hundred detailed occupations included in census classifications, Duncan (1961) showed that prestige scores could be quite accurately predicted from the average education and income of occupations. He then used the predicted scores to construct a Socioeconomic Index (SEI) of occupations. It was subsequently recognized (Featherman et al., 1975) that rather than serving as simple proxies for prestige, socioeconomic status scales were valid indicators of occupational status in their own right. Indeed, for studying social mobility and status attainment they are superior to prestige scales. There are two reasons for this. First, as was noted above, prestige appears to be substantially but not perfectly dependent upon differentials of power and privilege, and it is these resources that promote status attainment; thus, prestige is an imperfect indicator of the features of occupations that create a transmittable advantage – their socioeconomic characteristics. Second, prestige scales display one distinctive anomaly with respect to intergenerational occupational mobility: the typical mobility path for those from agricultural origins is into unskilled or semi-skilled non-agricultural work. In most societies, agricultural work typically enjoys average prestige, whereas laboring work has low prestige; but both types of occupations have low socioeconomic status. Thus, movement off the farm, which was pervasive throughout the twentieth century, is downward mobility with respect to prestige but not with respect to socioeconomic status, and is typically upward mobility with respect to income, material well-being, and life chances – since otherwise there would be little incentive to move out of agriculture. The result is that when intergenerational occupational status reproduction is measured with prestige scales it is understated relative to the degree of consistency in occupational socioeconomic status across generations.

The need for an occupational status scale that could be used for international comparisons of occupational socioeconomic status attainment led Ganzeboom et al. (1992; see also Ganzeboom and Treiman, 1996) to devise an International Socioeconomic Index of occupations (ISEI); the scale maximizes the association between the average education of occupational categories and their status, and between their status and their average income. It is thus conceptually distinct from prestige scales (although in practice corresponding socioeconomic and prestige scales of occupations tend to be highly correlated, on the order of 0.8 to 0.9). This scale has become the standard way of measuring occupational status for international comparisons. Recently, however, Hauser and Warren (1997) have challenged the practice of combining information on occupational education and income, arguing (and demonstrating for the USA) that status attainment depends far more heavily upon the average education of occupational categories than on their average income. This finding is quite consistent with the growing consensus that the driving force in intergenerational status attainment is family cultural capital, which is strongly reflected in the educational requirements of the father's occupation. This point is discussed further in the next section, on status attainment.

Occupational Classes

There is a long tradition of measuring occupational status by dividing occupations into a set of discrete categories, distinguished on the basis of the type of work performed. Although such classification schemes varied widely, most incorporated, in one way or another, a tripartite distinction between non-manual work, manual non-agricultural work, and agricultural work, and many schemes further distinguished upper non-manual occupations (professional, technical, and managerial positions) from lower non-manual occupations (clerical and sales positions), skilled from semi-skilled and unskilled manual jobs, and farm owners from farm laborers. Still, differences in the placement of specific occupations, particularly sales and service occupations, rendered the comparability of such schemes quite suspect even when the categories were nominally similar.

However, in recent years a set of class categories devised by Erikson, Goldthorpe, and Portocarero – and hence known as the EGP scheme – has emerged as the most widely accepted international standard. The EGP scheme organizes jobs on the basis of the employment relations they entail, using information on the occupation performed together with employment status and supervisory responsibility (Evans, 1992). An important feature of the scheme is that it is conceptually multidimensional. This point is discussed further below.

The result of these developments is that there are now three internationally standardized scales of occupational status available to the research community, all of which can be created from the categories of the 1968 and 1988 versions of the International Standard Classification of Occupations (International Labour Office, 1969, 1990), a classification of several hundred occupational categories that forms the basis of many national census classification schemes. This is a major accomplishment of the past quarter century, which makes possible valid comparisons of occupational status attainment and mobility across nations and over time.

SOCIAL MOBILITY AND STATUS ATTAINMENT

The publication of *The American Occupational Structure* (Blau and Duncan, 1967) revolutionized the study of social mobility and created the field of status attainment. Although research on the extent to which socioeconomic differences are reproduced from generation to generation had long been of central concern to students of social stratification, the typical approach was to construct a two-variable cross-tabulation showing, for a representative sample of the male population, the relationship between the occupations of men and those of their fathers. In the same way, cross-tabulations of educational attainment by father's occupation and of occupation by educational attainment were constructed, but three-way tabulations were seldom made, mostly because samples typically were too small to permit reliable estimates.

Blau and Duncan radically altered the way intergenerational social mobility was studied, both conceptually and methodologically. They reconceptualized the problem of the intergenerational transmission of status from generation to generation (the classic mobility formulation) as the problem of the determinants of the status attainment of individuals, where social origins (father's occupational status, parental education, etc.) were only some among several factors that accounted for the status outcomes of individuals. For example, in figure 21.1, which expresses the core of Blau and Duncan's approach, social origins, measured by father's occupational status (SEI) and father's years of schooling, influence the years of schooling of the respondent; father's occupational status plus years of schooling influence the status of the respondent's first job; and all three factors influence the status of the respondent's current job (at the time of data collection). Note that father's education has no indirect influence on the status of the first and current job, but operates entirely through education. Of course, the explicitly identified factors do not completely explain any status outcome; the unexplained portion is represented in the diagram by the "residual" paths – the arrows with no determinants. Methodologically, Blau and Duncan applied structural equation modeling and the algebra of "path analysis" to

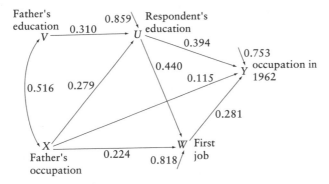

Figure 21.1 Path coefficients in basic model of the process of stratification.

quantify the relative importance of various paths to status attainment. For example, in Blau and Duncan's data the correlation between the status of the respondent's occupation and that of his father when he was age 16 (a standard measure of the extent of status reproduction) is 0.4. This correlation can be decomposed into a portion that reflects the fact that the sons of higher status fathers go further in school and hence obtain higher status jobs and a portion that reflects the transmission of occupational status independently of education. Such decompositions can reveal how the stratification system works. In Blau and Duncan's data (for the USA in 1962) the correlation between the occupational status of fathers and sons depended more on the fact that those whose fathers had high status occupations tended to go further in school and those who went further in school acquired higher status jobs than on the direct inheritance of occupational status; 56 percent of the correlation was due to the paths that involved education.

The combination of conceptual and statistical advances embodied in Blau and Duncan's analysis unleashed an enormous body of subsequent work that refined and expanded the status attainment model, on the one hand, and challenged it on the other. Central findings include the following.

First, there is only a loose connection between the socioeconomic status of parents and their children. With a handful of exceptions (for example, South Africa, with its history of racial oppression), the correlation between the socio-economic status of successive generations is quite modest in most nations: about 0.3–0.4 between the occupational status of men and that of their fathers when they were growing up; about 0.4–0.5 between the years of schooling of parents and children; and, for the limited number of places for which there are adequate data, about 0.2–0.3 between the incomes of men and their parents. Thus, from fewer than 10 percent to no more than 25 percent of the variance in socio-economic status characteristics is shared by successive generations. Moreover, even when multiple determinants of each status outcome are considered, it is seldom possible to account for as much as half the variance. Similar evidence is to be found in social mobility studies (discussed in more detail below). In industrial societies fewer than 10 percent of the male population work in the same specific occupation (for example, truck driver or school teacher) as their fathers did when they were growing up. Moreover, even when jobs are grouped into a small number of occupational classes (for example, the six-category version of the EGP classification), the majority of men are in different categories from their fathers.

The implication of these facts is profound: modern society is quite open. The achievement of socioeconomic status – going far in school, obtaining a high status job, earning a lot of money – is determined as much by a combination of individual traits (cleverness, charm, drive, etc. – or their lack) and chance events (being in the right place at the right time, having an especially supportive teacher, stumbling upon crucial information about a job or financial opportunity – or their opposite) as by systematic social factors, despite the best efforts of parents to ensure the success of their children. A little reflection suggests that this is a happy state of affairs, when one considers the alternative; imagine what it would be like to live in a society in which (as noted by Blau and Duncan, 1967, p. 174) some people are destined to poverty and others to affluence, some to work as laborers and others to enjoy professional careers, and so on, simply because of the circumstances of their birth.

Second, education has become the primary vehicle for occupational allocation. Given that industrialized societies are bureaucratically organized, that offspring generally do not take up the same jobs as their parents, and that schooling has become extensive, education has turned from a "consumption good" that inculcates the style and manner appropriate to maintaining one's station into a means of preparing people for work. To a considerable degree, people learn occupationally specific skills in school. But even when they don't, their level of schooling is the most important determinant of the kind of occupation they will be able to obtain.

Third, educational attainment promotes social mobility. The relatively modest association between the education of parents and their offspring has already been noted. Even when other attributes of parental status, such as father's occupational status, are considered, less than half of the variation in educational attainment can be attributed to social origins. On the other hand, as also noted, the connection between education and subsequent occupational status attainment is quite strong. The implication is that education serves to weaken the connection between social origins and destinations – that is, to increase the likelihood of social mobility.

Fourth, the more industrialized a society, the greater the importance of education for status attainment and the smaller the importance of social origins. Over the course of the twentieth century virtually every nation in the world industrialized as rapidly as possible. The consequence has been a very substantial decline in the proportion of the labor force in agriculture and, within the nonagricultural sector, an increase in the proportion of the labor force in nonmanual jobs relative to the proportion in manual jobs. In most countries there has been a concomitant increase in the level of education of the population and the proportion of school age children enrolled in school as educational credentials have become more important requirements for jobs. There is suggestive, but not yet definitive, evidence that as a result of these shifts, education has a stronger influence on occupational status attainment in industrialized than in non-industrialized societies, while the direct transmission of occupational status is weaker in industrialized societies.

Apart from these generalizations, which derive from application of the core status attainment model to data from many countries and at different points in time, the basic model has been elaborated in two additional directions. One elaboration has been the inclusion of additional variables, which has documented: the importance of intelligence, motivations, and other individual level factors; the influence of teachers and peers; and the increasing stability of careers over the life course; and also has been used to assess the extent and consequences of measurement error – a topic that deserves more attention since, contrary to the way most analysts behave, virtually all data used in social research are measured with some degree of error. A second elaboration has been the comparison of status attainment processes across subgroups within a society. This work has demonstrated convergence in the average education of men and women over time, a strong similarity between men and women in the link between social origins, education, and occupational status, but also a substantial gender gap in incomes, which is an unhappy but real cross-cultural universal. It has also been used to disaggregate racial and ethnic differences in status attainment in order to identify the locus of such differences. In South Africa, for example, there are very large racial differences in education, small racial differences in occupational status returns to education, but strong racial differences in income returns to education and occupational status. Thus, it is evident that, contrary to previous assumptions, the main effect of apartheid was not to block the access of non-whites to jobs for which they were qualified but to block access to training and also to discriminate in pay rates on the basis of race.

Despite these successes, the status attainment approach, which relies heavily on unidimensional measurements of status attributes, has not gone unchallenged. The most important challenge has been mounted by Erikson and Goldthorpe, in the CASMIN (Comparative Analysis of Social Mobility in Industrial Nations) project, which culminated in a 1992 monograph, *The Constant Flux*. Erikson and Goldthorpe analyzed intergenerational occupational mobility tables derived from 12 large-scale national surveys conducted mainly in the 1970s which they had carefully recoded into the categories of the EGP classification. By taking seriously the discrete nature of social stratification and social mobility, and using log-linear modeling techniques, Erikson and Goldthorpe, and others working in the same tradition, were able to demonstrate, first, that occupational inheritance – the propensity for men to work in the same occupational class as their fathers – was very strong for those categories that involved the transmission of property (farming, small business, and professional practice); and, second, that there is a sharp distinction between agricultural and non-agricultural occupations, with substantial mobility out of agriculture but virtually no mobility into agriculture. Still, it is clear that the dominant force driving the rate of mobility between different occupational categories is their similarity with respect to socioeconomic status – the greater the similarity in status between any two occupational classes, the greater the rate of mobility – a point that Erikson and Goldthorpe somewhat underemphasize.

The major conclusion of *The Constant Flux* is that in industrial societies there is a core mobility pattern common to all countries and that the small observed differences between nations are due to idiosyncratic historical and political circumstances. Erikson and Goldthorpe also claim that there is little evidence that mobility has increased over time. Their first conclusion, that the *pattern* of mobility – that is, the relative likelihood of mobility between occupational classes (adjusting for variations in the size of occupational categories) – is largely invariant across industrial societies, ranks as a major discovery, although there is rather less certainty that the *amount* of mobility is as cross-nationally invariant. Other researchers have likewise demonstrated that the underlying pattern of mobility is relatively invariant over time once shifts in the distribution of the labor force over occupations are taken into account. Thus, there is strong evidence that the relative chance of ending up in specific occupational categories, given that one's father is in a particular category, was relatively invariant in industrial societies throughout the twentieth century. Erikson and Goldthorpe's second conclusion is suspect, since they have data for only one point in time and hence must rely on the dubious assumption that there are no age effects on mobility and hence that age differences may be interpreted as cohort effects. By contrast, Ganzeboom et al. (1989), in an analysis of 149 mobility tables from 35 countries, showed that the rate of intergenerational mobility has in general increased over time: in 16 of the 18 nations for which they had replicate data there was a significant increase in mobility chances, on the order of 1–2 percent per year over the second half of the twentieth century, which implies very substantial change in mobility regimes from one generation to the next. It is quite possible that the more-or-less universal trend toward greater societal openness is the consequence of processes posited by Treiman in a 1970 review that is still widely cited – industrialization, urbanization, and the increasing pervasiveness of mass communications – but these claims have yet to be put to an explicit test.

EDUCATIONAL ATTAINMENT

We have already noted that the highest level of education attained depends to some degree upon the socioeconomic status of parents. The obvious question to ask is, why is this so? Why should the children of men with high status occupations go further in school than men with low status occupations, and why should the children of well educated people attain high levels of education themselves? At least partial answers can be found in two theoretical developments, one an analysis of the way forms of capital affect education and other aspects of status attainment, and the other a conceptualization of final educational attainment as the culmination of a series of transitions between successive educational levels.

Forms of Capital

We can think of families as controlling three forms of "capital," all of which derive in part from the education and occupational status of parents:

- Cultural capital consists of information, knowledge, abilities, skills, and motivations. Cultural capital is thus similar to, but broader than, "human capital" as conceived by economists.
- Financial capital consists of permanent income, wealth, and property.
- Social capital consists of normative expectations and also of interpersonal relationships of obligation, influence, aid, and trust.

Here is how each form of capital affects educational attainment.

Cultural Capital

The main impact of cultural capital is in creating the skills, values, habits, and motivations that enhance the probability that children will do well at school. Since success at any level of schooling is the most important determinant of advancement to the next level, the consequence is that those who come from families with high cultural capital will tend to obtain more schooling than will others. Children from families with abundant cultural capital do better in school because in such families the attributes that facilitate school success – literacy and numeracy, abstract reasoning, and oral discussion and argumentation – are valued and practiced. Children in such families become proficient at these skills and are motivated to continue to improve them. Moreover, they usually begin their schooling with a head start over other children; in particular, often they have learned to read and count before beginning school. They are thus rewarded and encouraged by teachers, which reinforces their motivation to do well.

Financial Capital

The effect of financial capital (specifically, income and wealth) on educational attainment is quite straightforward. It operates in three ways: first, through the ability of parents to pay for schooling, where there are fees, or for high quality schooling, where schools vary in quality, or to afford housing in locales with superior schools; second, by enhancing access of children to facilities, products, and services that enhance learning, such as books, educational games, computers, and separate study rooms or desks; and, third, by enabling their children to forgo income – staying in school rather than dropping out to help support the family.

Social Capital

Parental expectations exert a powerful influence on the aspirations and expectations of their children, by conveying a sense of both what is possible and what is

appropriate. Thus, rates of substance abuse, delinquency, and teenage pregnancy, all of which promote early school leaving, are strongly related to the
nature of the family environment. Wider societal expectations may also affect
school performance and subsequent achievement. In particular, oppressed ethnic
or other social groups may on average do poorly in school simply because they
are expected to do so, by their teachers and other influential societal actors.
Arguing along similar lines, Steele (1997) has shown that the mean test performance of different categories of students can be experimentally manipulated by
evoking "stereotype anxiety"; that is, making salient stereotypes about group
differentials in ability. Finally, it has been widely observed, at least in the USA,
that educational attainment is negatively associated with the number of siblings,
net of other factors. In addition, children from non-intact families (that is, where
they do not grow up in households with both natural parents) tend get less
education than children from intact families. Both outcomes are the result of
reduced parental attention.

The evidence is by now fairly strong that cultural capital has by far the most
powerful effect on educational attainment of the three forms of capital. This is
hardly surprising, for two reasons. First, it is the most directly related to educational performance – intellectual skills acquired at home are readily transferred
to the classroom. Second, parental education, and the resulting cultural capital,
is permanent – once acquired it cannot be lost – whereas social capital is fairly
situationally specific and financial capital is subject to major variations over the
life course.

The odds of Continuing from One Educational Level to the Next

In a series of papers around 1980, Mare showed that the effect of parental status
on educational attainment depends on two factors: the effect of parental
status on the odds of moving from one educational level to the next (for
example, from middle school to upper secondary school) and the relative frequency of various transitions. Since the effect of parental status on the odds of
making a transition typically declines for successive transitions, it follows that
the higher the level of educational attainment in the population, the lower will be
the association between parental status and educational attainment. Thus, the
effect of parental status on educational attainment typically declined over the
course of the twentieth century even when the chances of making each transition
remained constant, simply because the average level of education increased in
most nations.

In sum, we now have a fairly clear idea both of the extent to which parental
socioeconomic status affects the level of education achieved by their offspring
(moderate) and of how this is accomplished (through family capital). But it is
important to recall that educational attainment is due largely to factors that
are uncorrelated with socioeconomic origins: individual differences in the intelligence, motivation, and tenacity of students; the influences of teachers
and peers; and simple luck, good or bad. Moreover, we also know that as
average educational levels have risen, the importance of socioeconomic origins

for the level of schooling people ultimate achieve has declined, even where the effect of origins in making any given transition have remained constant. Thus, systemic changes associated with societal development have had the unintended but salutary consequence of increasing equality of educational opportunity.

Methodological Developments

Interestingly, progress over the past 30 years, reflected in the findings reviewed above, has not been importantly influenced by theoretical innovations, with the partial exception of the theory of forms of capital discussed just above. Rather, the substantial increase in understanding of the structure and process of social stratification and social mobility in different societies has come about as a result of a series of related methodological advances: the introduction of new statistical techniques; improvements in measurement standardization (already discussed); organizational innovations that have resulted in the creation of a systematic body of comparative data; and design innovations, particularly multilevel designs, that facilitate comparative analysis.

Statistical Techniques

Structural equation modeling, introduced mainly by Otis Dudley Duncan in his monograph with Blau and in other work, and the introduction of log-linear modeling as a way of carrying out statistical inference for cross-tabulations of categorical variables, such as intergenerational occupational mobility tables, have already been mentioned. Another important innovation has been the adaptation of hazard rate models to the analysis of educational transitions. Such models are also increasingly being used to study both historical variations in mobility and status attainment processes and variations over the life course. These models have a clear advantage over the structural equation models estimated by Blau and Duncan in that they allow the representation of dynamic processes – that is, they permit researchers to adequately represent the way change occurs over the life course, as a series of sequential decisions. It is evident that when they first enter school, people do not know how much schooling they will ultimately attain. Rather, they face a series of decisions over the course of their educational careers: for example, in the USA, whether to drop out of high school or graduate; for graduates, whether to continue on to tertiary education; if so, what sort of tertiary institution to attend; and so on. Similarly, occupational mobility over the course of one's working life is the consequence of a set of decisions made one-by-one, either by the employee (whether to stay in a job or try to find something better or more suitable) or by the employer (whether to retain or lay off or fire a worker). Hazard rate (or "event history") models provide a statistically adequate way of modeling such sequences of events and, as such, are likely to be increasingly utilized in stratification research.

Standardized Data Sets for Cross-national Comparisons

Perhaps as a consequence of the increasing internationalization of quantitative competence, together with increases in computing power that have made feasible the analysis of large and complex data sets on desktop computers, there has been a shift in focus from the conduct of stand-alone cross-sectional surveys of specific populations to an interest in joining forces to produce comparable data over time or across nations. The initial model for this effort was the US General Social Survey (GSS), which began in 1972 and has been repeated thereafter every year or two with careful attention to comparability over time. As the series grew longer, sociologists began to exploit it to do various kinds of trend analysis, including stratification analysis (for example, DiPrete and Grusky, 1990). The success of the GSS inspired two highly salutary developments: (a) the launching of similar repeated cross-section surveys in other nations; and (b) the creation of the International Social Survey Program (ISSP), in which nations conducting annual social surveys on the GSS model collectively design a module of some 15 minutes worth of questions on a particular topic, which is then included in each national survey. From its inception in 1985 with five participating nations, the ISSP has grown to a 22–nation survey. Of particular interest to the stratification research community are the two social inequality modules designed by Jonathan Kelley and Mariah Evans, in 1987 (with nine nations participating) and 1992 (with 18 nations participating), which have generated invaluable information on subjective aspects of stratification; a third inequality module was carried out in 1999. In addition to the ISSP project, three other projects have provided highly comparable data of interest to stratification researchers: (a) the 12–nation International Social Justice Project conducted surveys in 1991 and 1996 that include many items concerned with subjective aspects of stratification (see Kluegal et al., 1995); (b) the International Survey of Economic Attitudes, recently launched by Jonathan Kelley and his colleagues, thus far includes data from six nations and plans tri-annual surveys on an expanding set of nations; (c) the six-nation survey of Social Stratification in Eastern Europe after 1989, headed by Szelenyi and Treiman (see Treiman and Szelenyi, 1993), includes extensive intergenerational and event history data for six formerly communist Eastern and Central European nations.

In addition to these new data collection efforts, Ganzeboom and Treiman have for some years been engaged in a project to collate and standardize unit-record data for all known national surveys conducted in the twentieth century that contain variables pertinent to the status attainment process, in order to develop a comprehensive account of to what extent and in what ways the processes of educational and occupational attainment vary over time and across societies and what macrosocial factors account for such variations – some of the results of which have been reported above. Thus far, they have obtained some 250 sample surveys from about 40 nations covering most of the twentieth century. Of these, 113 have been standardized and a common subset of variables has been made available for public use in the International Social Mobility and

Politics File (Nieuwbeerta and Ganzeboom, 1996). All of the internationally comparable data sets mentioned here are listed in the appendix to this chapter.

Multilevel Models

One of the most important recent developments in stratification research has been the ascendancy of multilevel analytic designs (for a review see DiPrete and Forristal, 1994). Generically, these are designs that include at least two levels of data: a micro-level – almost always individuals – and a macro-level, which specifies a social context. The basic idea is to study how the behavior of individuals varies according to the social context. There are several ways to analyze multilevel data. The most common approach is to carry out micro-level analysis for each context separately and then to compare the results, either formally or informally. This is the implicit design of any comparison of two or more contexts. Often such comparisons are limited to two points in time or to two or at most a handful of nations. Such comparisons suffer from what is known as the "degrees-of-freedom problem." Because any pair of nations or time points may differ in any number of ways, it is difficult to be certain that the particular macro-level differences one adduces to explain any particular differences in the micro-level outcomes arc, in fact, the causal agents. For this reason, comparisons of small numbers of contexts are more useful for establishing cross-context regularities than for explaining cross-context differences.

The obvious way around the degrees-of-freedom problem is to compare enough contexts to be able to treat contexts as observations. In this approach, a micro-level process is modeled separately for each context. Then, in a second step, the contexts are treated as observations and the coefficients from the micro-model are treated as dependent variables (by using multilevel modeling procedures, both levels can be estimated simultaneously, which is advantageous statistically). The variation in the micro-level coefficients is explained by variation in the contextual variables. Note that in this approach complete explanation of variation in the micro-level coefficients is not necessary; instead, the coefficients are treated as stochastic, i.e. themselves subject to error.

An interesting new development in stratification research, which exploits the multilevel approach, is the treatment of time as a variable, studying the impact of temporal change on various stratification outcomes. While many previous studies have compared outcomes at two points in time – which is logically equivalent to comparing two nations – until recently there have been few studies that have taken calendar time as a context, studying year-by-year variations in stratification outcomes, and linking variations in outcomes to macrosocial historical events, such as depressions, wars, revolutions, and social policy changes. This kind of research has burgeoned in recent years as comparable data have accumulated over time.

A limitation of both cross-national and cross-temporal multilevel designs is that it is difficult to generate enough cases to sustain anything other than the simplest analysis at the macro-level. We seldom have more than 30 or 40 nations or years, which is hardly enough cases from which to estimate a model with more than one or two contextual variables. An obvious solution is to cross years by nations. This is the approach Ganzeboom and Treiman are taking in the analysis of status attainment mentioned above: by crossing data from 40 nations by 15 five-year birth cohorts, it is possible to generate data for up to 600 ($= 15 \times 40$) contexts, although in practice there are fewer contexts since not all cohorts are available for every nation. With such data it is possible to systematically test hypotheses regarding the effect of contextual variables that vary both over time and across nations; for example, "parental occupational status has a smaller effect on educational attainment in welfare states than in *laissez-faire* systems," where the attributes of the welfare system are measured in each nation separately for each five-year period.

CONCLUSION

Great progress has been made in the study of social stratification and social mobility in the past half century, and particularly in the years since the publication of *The American Occupational Structure* by Blau and Duncan (1967). Advances in statistical methods, research designs, measurement standardization, and the availability of high quality cross-nationally comparable data have made it possible to show that modern societies have become increasingly open over the course of the twentieth century and as nations have industrialized, so that at the beginning of the twenty-first century inequality in occupational status and income arises more from differences in education than from direct occupational or income inheritance. Moreover, educational differences are mostly achieved rather than ascribed, depending more on personal attributes than on social status. This review has covered only a small fraction of these developments, but perhaps enough to give a sense both of the current accomplishments of this area of research and of the remaining challenges.

APPENDIX: CROSS-NATIONAL COMPARATIVE DATA SETS

International Social Survey Project (ISSP). Ann Arbor: Inter-university Consortium for Political and Social Research (distributor); consult http://www.icpsr.umich.edu/archive1.html

Kelley, J., Zagorski, K. and Evans, M. D. R. *International Survey of Economic Attitudes*. International Survey Centre, Institute for Advanced Study in the Behavioral Sciences, Australian National University, Canberra (distributor); consult http://www.international-survey.org/index.html

Nieuwbeerta, P. and Ganzeboom, H. G. B. (1996) *The International Social Mobility and Politics File* (a CD-ROM database) Amsterdam: Steinmetz Archive. This is a public use file of a selected set of internationally standardized variables from 113 surveys, a subset of the approximately 250 surveys collected by Harry B. G. Ganzeboom and Donald J. Treiman. The complete database is catalogued on the Internet: http://www.fss.uu.nl/soc/hg/ismf/index.htm. Access to the catalogued surveys must be arranged with Ganzeboom (ganzeboom@cc.ruu.nl) since use of some of the data sets requires the permission of the original investigators.

Szelenyi, I. and Treiman, D. J. (1993) *Social Stratification in Eastern Europe after 1989*. Los Angeles: Social Science Data Archive, Institute for Social Science Research, UCLA (distributor); download from http://www.sscnet.ucla.edu/issr/da/SSEE/SSEE. home.html

22

Social Networks

Bonnie Erickson

Network analysis is thriving in almost every corner of sociology, in every other social science, and in still further territories like mathematics and information science. Network analysis is so widely powerful because it is the serious study of social structure. Social structure is important everywhere, and in addition structural patterns can be abstracted from particular applications and freely applied to many other settings, so that theoretical and methodological approaches become very widely useful. Structure is as beautiful as it useful. It is lovely visually, since network structures have attractive patterns that are fun to look at and think about. It is lovely conceptually, since structural thinking produces both the sheer intellectual elegance and the paradoxical surprises that have made formal sociology a charmer since Simmel's day (and Simmel is every true net-worker's spiritual ancestor and continuing inspiration).

When I define network analysis as the serious study of social structure, some people are surprised: do not we all study social structure? Not really. Social structure means the pattern of social relationships linking social actors. The actors can be of many kinds: people, companies, families, nations, and so on. The social relationships can be of many kinds: love, hate, cooperation, competition, admiration, disdain, talking face-to-face, sending e-mail, and so on. But whatever the details, structure is the concrete network of some ties among some actors, and this is usually not what people study. Some describe overall features of a structure impressionistically, without actually recording and analyzing relationships. Many study individual attributes; for example, equating centrality in the world system with national wealth instead of powerful positions within networks of trade, diplomacy, war, and so forth. Some confuse social structure with the distribution of some variable, as in the "age structure" of a population, which provides important information about the relative size of age groups but gives us no information about anyone's social ties. Some study one relationship at a time, even though a single relationship is always subject to influence from surrounding relationships. For example, there are many studies of marriages that study each couple in isolation; yet the more wife and husband share their networks, the more they share domestic tasks.

To illustrate differences in approaches, consider elite Florentine families during Cosimo di Medici's rise to power. Why did some families support the Medici, while others supported the rival faction of oligarchs? Some have tried to explain this in terms of family attributes such as wealth, recency of elite status, or neighborhood. But Padgett and Ansell (1993) showed that supporters of the Medici and of the oligarchs were quite similar in such attributes. Padget and Ansell recorded marriage and business ties among the families and mapped their overall organization, grouping together families who had similar ties to other families. They found that families supported the faction they were most linked to, and also found good structural reasons for the Medici's eventual victory. Medici supporters had ties to the Medici and almost none to other elite families, including each other. This put the Medici in a powerful position, since their supporters depended on them for indirect ties to the rest of the elite, and their faction proved to be relatively centralized and cohesive. Meanwhile the oligarchs had many ties among themselves, with several well connected families whose competition for leadership weakened their party.

The power of the Medici's structural position was not just a fluke of Florentine society or politics, but is far more general. Burt (1992) finds much the same for very modern managers: the ones who get ahead faster are the ones who have more links to separate sets of people who are poorly (if at all) linked to each other, so that the fortunate manager who links them can control the flow of information to his or her advantage. The same kind of structural position pays off in laboratory studies of social exchange, in which the people who gain the most are the ones with exchange partners who have no one else to bargain with. Burt traces this analysis back to Simmel and his discussion of *tertius gaudens*, or the third party who profits from division between two others. The same structural pattern has the same outcome in classic theory and in modern experiments, in Florence centuries ago and in management hierarchies today.

Thus structural thinking can lead to generalizations that leap across time, place, and type of setting (as Simmel's examples do). There are many other examples. Consider the diffusion of innovations. If accepting some new thing depends on attributes such as how adventurous people are or how much attention they pay to the media, then an innovation moves steadily from the faster to the slower kinds of potential adopters. But if adoption is a social process, the pattern will be different. Adoption occurs when someone who has already taken up the innovation influences someone who has not, so the rate of adoption varies with the number who have adopted times the number who have not yet done so. Thus the rate of new adoption is slow at first (when there are few innovators to emulate) and at last (when almost everyone is on the bandwagon), while fastest in the middle of the process (when many innovators still have many holdouts to influence). Many examples of diffusion show the characteristic network profile, and many more refined details of adoption are rooted in network structure (Valente, 1995).

As still another example, consider social vacancies (Chase, 1991). White had the original theoretical insights while studying careers in a large church, for which he had records of people and positions over a long time. He realized that careers did not really consist of what people did, since a person could only move into a post after someone had moved out of it by promotion or retirement. What really drove the system was the empty spaces in it: a vacancy in one post attracted someone from another post, which then had a vacancy, and so forth, with vacancies flowing through the organizational structure. Looking at the flows of vacancies proved to be more informative than looking at the flows of people. The freshness of this idea, and the elegance of the models that White developed around it, have encouraged people to successfully apply them to quite different examples from empty apartments to empty hermit crab shells.

Again, consider what people think. Some people try to explain this through individual attributes, such as relating the politics of the wealthy to their desire to protect their interests. This approach constantly runs into trouble generalizing: the wealthy, women, white, or whatever keep having different views in different times and places. Structural analysis by-passes such difficulties by making an entirely different kind of generalization, not about what particular things people think but about how much people agree on whatever it is that they think (Erickson, 1988). The more that people are very strongly tied to each other in tight cliques with little outside influence, the more they agree. Their strong, frequent interaction, and their shared awareness of what everyone else is thinking, leads to strong conformity pressures. Note that this argument is indifferent to the content of people's beliefs, which can be anything their particular history, culture, and so on have generated, and equally indifferent to the contents of people's relationships, since social influence occurs in all kinds of networks. The argument is formal sociology in Simmel's sense: the abstracted form of ideas (amount of agreement) depends on the abstracted form of the structure (degree of density). This formal approach can be extended to other structural patterns; for example, if people are not in a clique but are exposed to the influence of the same third parties, they will also tend to agree, but not so much, because of the lack of direct mutual influence. Of course, ideas have effects on social structure too, since people are drawn to those they agree with or those they share knowledge with, and there are some interesting models of the dynamic duet between interpersonal similarity and interpersonal attraction over time (for example, Carley, 1991).

If social structure is so important, it is important to know how to identify it, and important to realize that special approaches are needed. Broadly there are two kinds of structural approaches: studying an entire network of all the ties of interest among the actors in some bounded setting (whole networks) or studying the ties among all the people tied in some way to particular actors (actor-centered approaches). For example, one might study ties of trade, diplomacy, war, and so on among all the countries of the world, or one might randomly survey people and ask them to report on their ties to their intimates. Whole network analysis is always best if feasible, because it gives the overall structure of the network as a whole as well as the limited network surrounding each individual actor.

Starting with whole networks, then, what has to be done to study one? First comes the sticky problem of boundaries. Networks naturally spread out, so no boundary is ever perfect. For example, Florentine elite families sometimes married and did business with families outside their group. Some boundaries are defined by populations of special interest, like the Florentine elite. Some are based on social definition of separate social entities, as in looking at all the ties of advice and friendship within a corporation. Some researchers start with one of these approaches, track ties to any social actor (whether in the initially selected group or not), and then add any actors with many ties to the initially selected group. Whatever the strategy, one hopes to find a set of actors with relatively good separateness from the rest of the world, separateness in the network sense: more ties within the set than between those in it and those outside it.

Second, what ties should one study? The best overall strategy is variety: friendship and enmity, business alliances and competition, trade, diplomacy, and war. Different kinds of ties have different causes and effects, and it is all of them together that makes up social structure. All too often we skip negative ties, in part because these can be a real challenge for research. People happily report whom they like, but when asked whom they dislike, insist that they dislike no one at all. When companies engage in illegal conspiracies, they do their best not to let researchers know.

Third, how can one make sense of all this information? People routinely store their relational data in matrices: rows for actors 1 through N, columns for actors 1 through N, and cell entries recording the tie from the row actor to the column actor. For example, a cell might record the number of times that the row actor sent the column actor e-mail last month, or whether the row nation sent an armed force to the column nation last year. Usually the order of the rows and columns is based on something meaningless like the order in which people were interviewed, so the information is unorganized and looks like visual static. Organization is imperative.

One popular, classic approach with a long history is to look for sets of actors who are relatively closely tied to each other, the small groups within the bigger networks. We recognize such groups in everyday life: cliques in a high school, business groups, political factions. And such groups can be important; for example, in encouraging similarity of thought among group members, as noted above. It would be easy to identify such groups if they were ideal-typical in some way – for example if all people had friendship ties only within their cliques and hostile ties only with outsiders – but social reality is just not that neat. Thus people have developed a number of ways to define groupings that are approximately cliques, in some modified sense of cliqueness. Different options have different theoretical rationales and suit different research issues. For example, conformity pressures are strongest when clique members have many ties to each other (hence are under each other's influence), so a student of attitudes might want to look for cliques in the sense of high density groups (density is the proportion of all possible linkages that actually exists). But information can flow among all members of a group as long as they are interconnected, directly or indirectly, even if many possible ties are missing; while at the same time the quality of the information tends to deteriorate if it is passed on many times. Thus students of information flow might want to look for groups such that everyone in the group can reach everyone else directly or through at most one intermediary. See Erickson (1988) for a more extended discussion of possible interpretations of group-finding strategies, and Wasserman and Faust (1994) for the procedures.

The search for groups has great intuitive appeal for most people, but it cannot handle some important features of social networks. First, some crucial parts of social structures are not groups in any sense, such as marginal actors whose defining (and crippling) characteristic is their *lack* of connections. Actors may have a common location in a structure without having ties to each other. Second, most structures include a variety of ties, each with a different pattern, yet the search for groups can handle only one tie at a time. For example, if we want groups in the sense of maximum density, we can maximize density on only one kind of tie; the maximum density groupings for other ties will normally be different. One may be involved in one cluster of co-workers while discussing work problems, and another while discussing sports. Problems like these fueled interest in a more general kind of search: the search for sets of actors who occupy the same kind of position in an overall social structure. Concern shifts from how well actors are connected to each other, to how similarly they are connected to everyone. The key idea is structural equivalence, or the extent to which actors have the same kinds of ties to the same third parties. Structurally equivalent actors share the same social location, the same position in all the relationships in a network. The Florentine elite provides examples of the important difference between the two ways to define groupings of actors. If we are looking for clique-like groupings, supporters of the oligarchs qualify because they were all interconnected by marriage and business ties, while supporters of the Medici do not because they had ties to the Medici but not each other. Yet both groupings were socially recognized and important. Structural equivalence includes both, since the Medici supporters were all in the same structural position of dependence on the Medici.

Structural equivalence includes more than one kind of relationship at a time. Consider a greatly simplified version of world systems theory. There are two structural locations: core and periphery. Core nations trade with each other at high rates, while periphery nations trade little with each other but a good deal with core nations. Core nations never send armed forces into each other's territory, but sometimes send them into peripheral nations, which never dare to return the favor but do occasionally invade each other. The same way of defining structural location organizes both trade relationships and attacks, even though each of these has a different pattern. (There are more detailed accounts of the world network, beginning with Snyder and Kick, 1979.) Once we identify structurally equivalent actors, and rearrange our data so that equivalent actors are together, it is easy to see the nature of the overall structure by direct visual inspection. Computers do the hard work (see Wasserman and Faust, 1994, for details). But people always have to make some tough judgment calls. How many structural locations should there be, and how alike do actors have to be to be in the same position? At present we have no convincing answers to such questions. Moreover, we have no joy for fans of statistical tests, since we build our models of structure from the same relational data that are all we have to test whether the model fits or not.

Analysis of whole network structure raises some intriguing questions that will take a long time to answer. What is the morphology of social structures: what kinds of structure are there? Some kinds of structure recur often in quite different settings; when and why? For example, a center–periphery structure has dense ties among central actors, few ties among peripheral ones, and a moderate number between more and less central actors. Trade among world nations is one example; so is recognition among members of a scientific specialty. Why does such a pattern occur sometimes but not at other times? Further, what difference does it make? The difference may be for actors; for example, peripheral actors may be too poorly connected to profit much from their trades or to be on top of current scientific trends. Or the difference may be for groups; for example, the social structure of a social movement helps to determine how effectively it can mobilize its membership for action.

Analysis of whole network structure also raises the problem of responsible portraiture. We always have a *choice* of ways to represent the overall structure of a network: in terms of cliques or in terms of structural locations; in terms either as determined by different methods, or as including more or fewer subdivisions; and so on. There is never a single, obviously right choice, but a series of judgments that call on the researcher's wider knowledge (does this version make sense in light of what the people in this structure think it is, or in light of what I have observed, or in terms of what structural location it is correlated with?), on the researcher's taste (does this version look better structured than that one?), on the ease of use of available computer packages, and so forth. The choice one makes is often the only one the rest of the world ever gets to see, so it is a weighty matter. It might seem that we could escape responsibility by sticking with the original data: use sociograms, in which all the actors are represented by symbols and all the relationships by various kinds of lines between them. This is getting to be a lot of fun, as people are developing nifty ways to show networks in three dimensions, from a mobile viewpoint, with gorgeous colors. (See Lin Freeman's delightful web page http://eclectic.ss.uci.edu/~lin/galery.html). Yet we still have to look at *an* arrangement at any one time, and the way the actors and lines are arranged affects how people interpret what they see; different arrangements of the same network lead people to different conclusions (for example, McGrath et al., 1997).

Centrality is another important structural topic that can be addressed only by studying whole networks. A more central actor is in some way better placed in the network as a whole: better able to get in touch with other actors, more visible to them, more able to control the flow of information among them, and so on.

This broad concept has alternative interpretations. One popular measure of centrality is *degree*, or the number of other actors to which an actor is linked. There is just one measure of degree if relationships are non-directional, or the same from actor A to actor B as from actor B to actor A, as in A and B are partners. But often ties are not the same both ways: A is B's superior, so A gives B orders but B cannot boss A around, or A loves B with unrequited passion. Then *indegree* is the number of ties an actor receives, and *outdegree* is the number the actor sends. Though these tend to be related, they can differ in interesting ways. Elite actors tend to attract more attention (indegree) than they return, like famous sociologists who are aware of only a fraction of the people who pay attention to them and their work. Sometimes one kind of degree is clearly the more theoretically appropriate. For example, in a network of competitive bridge players (Erickson and Nosanchuk, 1984), being known to a larger number of fellow players (having high indegree) means playing both one's good and bad performances before a larger audience. Thus more successful players get more esteem from fellow players, and get especially high esteem if they have high indegree. At the same time, more aggressive players receive more aversion, especially if they have high indegree.

Another popular version of centrality is *betweenness*, or the extent to which an actor is part of paths linking others and hence controls connections between them. The Medici had the highest betweenness in the elite of Florence, and it is this that Padgett and Ansell (1993) emphasize as the structural root of their power.

Studying whole networks gives us important information about the position of social actors within a social structure. Once we have this, we can easily combine it with attribute information to do more familiar kinds of work. For example, we can classify scientists into more or less central groups, and then consider how their later careers are affected by structural position, productivity, gender, and so forth.

Although whole network studies are wonderful they are not always feasible. A popular and powerful alternative is the study of actor-centered networks consisting of a focal actor and those tied to that actor. This approach combines neatly with sociology's most popular research tool, the survey: sample and interview people as usual, but include questions about each person's contacts. Not only is this strategy often the only practical one, but it is also one that lets us ask some profound questions. People's networks are their immediate social environment, the part of society they live in. What are such networks like, how do they get to be that way, and what difference do they make to people's lives?

Concerning what networks are like, we know a good deal about close ties and not nearly enough about weaker ones. It is much easier to ask people about those near or dear to them: there are not too many people to ask about, and people know the answers. Researchers have successfully asked people about the people they feel close to, the people they discuss important matters with, the people they can call on for help of various kinds, the closest people in particular role relationships like co-worker or friend, the people they talk to or e-mail most often, and so forth. We know that the close are few, ranging from a couple of people to a couple of dozen on average, depending on the kind of closeness. Close relationships call for a good deal of investment of time, emotion, commitment, risk, and so forth, so people cannot maintain a huge number of close ties – and the people who can maintain a larger number are, unfairly, the people with other useful resources such as better jobs and education (for example, Fischer, 1982). We know that, few though close ties are, they are specialized. For example, people get different types and amounts of help from ties of different degrees of closeness, from people in different role relationships, and from people with different attributes like gender (for example, Wellman, 1999). Specialization occurs partly because of convenience (it is neighbors who have lawnmowers next to your lawn), partly because of our cultural definitions of appropriateness (you would readily ask your neighbor to lend the mower, but ask your parents to lend the down payment on your house), and partly because of socialization (women learn to listen to people's troubles more patiently than men).

We know that the people we are close to tend to be very much like ourselves, and the closer they are the more alike they are. This similarity, which turns out to have far-reaching consequences (discussed below), arises from both choice and constraint. People feel more in common with, and more attracted to, other people who are like them in salient respects (*homophily*). In addition, people more often meet similar others because similar people spend time in the same places (Feld, 1982). Sometimes they obviously have no choice, like schoolchildren who spend most of their days with other pupils of the same age, but even apparently free choice of settings leads to constrained choice of friends because similar people make similar choices. People join voluntary associations that attract people like them in age, gender, occupation, and education, then, given a choice already narrowed to people rather like them, they make friends of people still more like them (McPherson and Smith-Lovin, 1987).

Close ties matter: people with better social support live longer, people with serious problems in their inner circles (like the death of a loved one) get depressed, people with strong ties to criminals go bad, while former criminals with good jobs and marriages go straight. Those near and dear are especially important for our access to the kind of support that depends primarily on another person's willingness and availability: getting companionship from friends, relying on long-term nursing care from a close relative. Just how this works varies from one context to another because cultures define appropriate help differently, people have different priorities of help to seek (with companionship high for some and survival necessities for others), the people they are close to have different resources to offer, and so on. There is a great deal of interesting work to be done on comparisons of different subgroups and countries. Wellman (1999) includes reports from some very different countries, while Degenne and Forse (1999) offer rich comparisons between France and other places. At the same time, some contextual differences widely thought to make a difference do not: people in the big, supposedly impersonal city have as many and as helpful supporters as do people living in the fabled coziness of small towns (Fischer,

1982). With all this rich brocade of detail, elegant universal generalizations are hard to come by, and much of the fun lies elsewhere: relishing and making sense of endless variations.

Meanwhile, weak ties matter too – more than people often realize. For example, people often get jobs through personal contacts, and often weaker ties produce more jobs or better jobs than do strong ties. Such surprising findings inspired one of the best known paradoxes of network analysis, "the strength of weak ties" (Granovetter, 1995). How can weak ties be strong? In part through sheer numbers. Though close to at most a few dozen people, the average North American knows about 1,400 (Killworth et al., 1990). Network size is important, as fundamentally important for as us as is the speed of light for others, yet our knowledge of it is quite crude. The fundamental problem is that we cannot ask people to report their network size: they do not know. Thanks to the remarkably ingenious and sustained research program of Bernard, Killworth, and collaborators, we have some still spotty and rough ideas. Notably, network size grows with social status, so the benefits of larger networks are unequally distributed and help to reproduce inequality. For example, the more people you know, the greater the chance that you will just happen to talk to one, who will just happen to learn you could be open to a job offer or who will just happen to mention an opening; many job changes occur in this apparently haphazard way that systematically favors the well connected (Granovetter, 1995).

Granovetter argues that weak ties are strong not because of their weakness as such, but because weak ties include structural bridges linking clusters of otherwise separated people who have different pools of resources. Not all weak ties are bridges (some weak ties link people in the same cluster) but almost all bridges are weak ties. Strong ties rarely bridge because the people close to us are too much like us: they know much the same things and much the same people as we do. Thus, despite their eagerness to help us, often they can do little to help us reach scarcely distributed resources like better jobs, while our mere acquaintances offer varied and wide-ranging contacts with many resources outside our and our intimates' reach. Granovetter's original research suggested that male managers, professionals, and technical workers got better jobs through weak ties, perhaps because weak ties combine the structural advantages of wide searches (by both the job seeker and potential employers) with the decision advantages of having a trusted contact vouch for some of the many assets that are vital to higher level work but very hard to measure. After 25 years of further research inspired by his, Granovetter (1995) thoughtfully assessed how and why the results of using weak or strong ties vary greatly, in a fascinating account too rich to review here.

Lin takes a somewhat different approach: weak ties matter because they connect us to a wider variety of people, including people varied in occupational prestige, and hence weak ties are more likely to include some people with higher occupational prestige than our own who can help us into better jobs than we already have. One interesting implication is that the game is different for elites: their strong ties to powerful people like themselves are worth more than their weaker ties to humbler folk. Lin has shown that people's acquaintances include more occupational diversity than their friends or kin, that people with more occupational diversity in their networks are better able to use a high prestige contact to get a job, and that the high prestige of the contact (not the weakness of the tie as such) predicts the higher prestige of the jobs obtained through weaker ties. See Lin (1999) for a useful review of his own and other work on networks and occupational status attainment.

Burt (1992) takes yet another view: what really matters is structural holes, or the gaps between groups of people to which a person is connected. It is these gaps which make the others dependent on that person (as discussed above) and hence help that person to profit. The ties the person has to these very separate groups are not likely to be strong ones, because people who have strong friends in common tend to know each other or soon come to do so. Again, like Granovetter and Lin, Burt carefully points out that weakness as such is not the strength of weak ties; instead the ties that give structural advantage are usually weak ones, for good network reasons. Burt goes on to argue that structural holes help people to use their resources to better advantage, getting higher rates of return from the same assets because of the bargaining power of brokerage positions; thus good networks are a multiplier for other forms of capital.

The value of diversity in weak ties is a common thread in these accounts, and also in some other intriguing work. Coser (1975) argues that people who interact with different kinds of people, in different role relationships, in different settings, develop a range of useful personal resources, including greater skill in the use of abstract language and a greater sense of personal autonomy. Other work suggests that these are considerable benefits, since (for example) more autonomous people get more autonomous jobs and maintain better health. Erickson (1996) shows that people who know others in a wider range of occupations also know more about each of a variety of cultural genres: artists, books, sports, business magazines, restaurants. On the one hand, diverse networks act as the continuing adult education school of culture: varied contacts have varied interests and talk to you about them. On the other, knowing at least about a lot of things helps you to find something in common with a wider range of the people you meet, and hence to add more variety to your network. The cultural diversity that varied networks help to teach is another valuable network benefit, since people in higher level work need to be able to deploy different kinds of culture for different purposes, such as discussing the latest *Harvard Business Review* with fellow managers to show command of business culture, but discussing sports with co-workers of all levels to smooth cross-class relationships through topics popular from high to low (Erickson, 1996).

We have done enough to know that network diversity is important; but given that, it is surprising how narrow is the research done so far. The study of diversity is largely limited to the variety of different occupations in which a person knows someone. For example, one may ask "Do you know anyone at all who is a lawyer? Anyone who is a plumber?" and so forth. Pioneered by Lin, this is a valuable approach because it allows us to by-pass the huge problems of studying people's weak ties. Instead, we ask about what matters in weak ties (at least in Lin's theoretical approach): to what kinds of resources do weak ties connect a person? Since occupation is a master role in modern society, it is an important indication of structural location, and of access to resources of many kinds. But since modern society is complex and includes multiple forms of important inequalities and differences, looking at occupation alone cannot suffice. What about ties to people in different ethnic groups, or ties to men and women? Almost everything we know about these is limited to close ties. Yet the gender and ethnicity of weak ties must matter too. For example, men and women tend to join voluntary associations of different kinds, and to work in gender segregated jobs, and hence to meet people of their own gender. Women tend to join smaller voluntary associations and to work in lower-level jobs, so their networks become smaller as well as female dominated. These networks then lead women into yet more jobs and other settings dominated by women. Such feedbacks between networks and locations lead to growing occupational, network, and other differences over the life course (Smith-Lovin and McPherson, 1993).

Analysis of this kind helps us to understand what it is about gender that makes it important (gender differences in work, network, culture, and so forth), which is a great improvement over the all too common practice of using gender as a variable in some statistical analysis and then speculating about why the observed effects occur. More generally, network analysis helps us to directly study the kinds of things that actually matter in social life, such as concrete social structures and the processes that go on within them, instead of relying on individual attributes that are often just crude proxies for the things we should be studying.

A review of the network benefits described above will help to illustrate another important benefit of network analysis: clarification of important but fuzzy structural concepts, which are endemic in sociological discussions. Social capital is one very trendy example. Broadly, social capital is the good things about social networks, the aspects of social networks that produce desirable results for people or for groups. But we have just seen that different aspects of networks are good for different outcomes: stronger ties for help that takes willingness but weaker ties for help that takes access to resources, kin for some kinds of help and neighbors for others, and so on. Moreover, every network feature produces *both* desirable and undesirable results: our intimates may help us or may grieve us by getting ill or betraying us; a diverse network may enrich our opportunities and our culture, but take time to maintain or create conflicting demands; density may help a politicized group to achieve unity of opinions, or may encourage a slew of equally well placed people to fight for leadership, as for the Florentine oligarchs. Thus there is not such a thing as social capital singular, and we need to carefully work out which aspects of networks have which outcomes (bad as well as good) under which conditions. Such conceptual refinement is bad for our ability to create catchy sound bites such as "social capital is declining," but good for getting us beyond a muddling of many different possible forms of social capital, as in Coleman's (1988) much cited but preliminary essay. More generally, network analysts have already developed a great many useful and precise structural concepts, while the network analysis orientation compels us to get specific and clear about any new structural thought we may be trying to have.

Returning yet again to rival accounts of the strength of weak ties brings us to the fascinating field of micro–macro integration in network terms. By any account, the structural point of weak ties is that they are the part of a personal network that connects someone to a wider social structure in the most advantageous ways. Accounts differ in the kind of wider social structure they assume, and hence in the ways that weak ties give advantage. Granovetter describes separated pockets of resources linked only by weak ties, while Lin describes a hierarchy of occupational prestige in which upward-leading ties are weak ties. But we actually know rather little about overall social structure in network terms, and about how personal networks plug into this wider picture.

Simmel (1955) provides the most ambitious and thought-provoking set of speculations about how personal networks and social structure have connected in changing ways in different societies and different times. The prime mover in his story is the complexity of the overall social structure. If people live in small repetitive units like villages, all the members of each village have much the same network with the available variety of people: everyone in town. But in a complex modern society, each person can seek out a special social circle for every taste or necessity: fellow mechanics, fellow birdwatchers, fellow conservatives, fellow neighbors, and so on and so on. Each social circle shares one limited thing in common, and everyone in the circle is in that sense alike, more alike than the village circle can be. Each person lives in the intersection of a unique combination of social circles, and thus in a unique social network of identities and influences, the opposite of the shared networks of villagers. The modern (or even postmodern) condition is thus one of individualism, but is not the individual's doing, being instead the result of massive elaborations of the division of labor and societal complexity. Simmel's work is unusual in its attention to history; too much of our work is very much limited to the present. Even our studies of the present are usually static snapshots of social structure with no attention to how networks change from year to year (though see Suitor et al., 1997).

Our incomplete knowledge of macro–micro network linkages is all the more important because we believe that networks are a major part of how overall social divisions and forms of inequality are reproduced over time. If the rich get richer and the poor get poorer (as has unfortunately been true in North America recently), and if in general those on top tend to stay on top, it is in part because advantaged social location provides every kind of network benefit needed to increase one's chances of staying happy, healthy, and wealthy. Those with better work and education have larger networks of close ties to higher status yet more varied people, *and* have larger overall networks with more variety of access to many kinds of resources. If people of a certain ascribed kind (men, women, members of ethnic groups, etc.) tend to keep getting into the same kinds of work, this is in part because a lot of hiring is done through networks and people know people like themselves. Tilly (1998) offers a fine analysis of such durable inequalities and the role of networks in them.

We have come full circle, from the study of whole networks to the study of actor-centered networks to the need to integrate both kinds of work. There has only been room, in this brief essay, to hint at the immense richness of network analysis. To learn more, one could read a good introductory book such as Scott (1991) or Degenne and Forse (1999). For network numbers, the definitive hand-book and text is Wasserman and Faust (1994). The journal *Social Networks* is a rich source of current work. But network analysis is not limited to such obviously network-centered publications. It is everywhere now, in journals and books of all substantive persuasions. Enjoy it as you find it, and consider adding it to your own repertoire.

23

Networks and Organizations

DAVID KNOKE

Organizational networks are increasingly pervasive social phenomena reaching into a variety of social contexts. They span the gamut from multinational corporate strategic alliances through community small enterprise systems to mentoring bonds between employees and their supervisors. Unraveling the complex economic, political, and interpersonal connections among organizations and their participants poses serious theoretical and methodological challenges. Over the past two decades, an explosive growth in scholarly research on organizational networks has moved the core concepts from suggestive metaphor to proto-theory, with powerful analytic tools at its disposal (for useful literature reviews see Alter and Hage, 1993; Knoke and Guilarte, 1994; Wasserman and Galaskiewicz, 1994; Grandori, 1998). Three main research themes emerge from this flourishing interdisciplinary field. First, many empirical researchers emphasize the development of rigorously defined concepts and precisely measured structural dimensions of organizational networks. Second, some analysts seek to specify the origins of network characteristics, in particular the formation and transformation of ties among actors. Third, other investigators examine the impacts of organizational networks on their members' attitudes and behaviors and try to explain the consequences for larger social systems within which multilevel organizational networks are embedded. This chapter offers an interpretive overview of these themes, emphasizing opportunities for deepening our already considerable knowledge about organizational networks.

The organizational network perspective is one manifestation of more general structural approaches to explaining social action. Structural action theorists explicate behavior in terms of patterned social relationships among actors rather than by analyzing actors' statuses or such internal psychological states as perceptions, attitudes, and beliefs. A key structural action assumption is that the totality of connections among multiple actors in a particular social system jointly affects the behaviors of both its individual members and the system as a whole. For example, small group theories of social action suggest that work team productivity primarily depends on neither employees' education levels nor their achievement drives, but on whether supportive or antagonistic interpersonal relations sustain or fragment group solidarity. Further, the actions of individual team members will also vary according to their structural locations within the network of interpersonal ties, with those employees who are more socially integrated into the team outperforming the more isolated workers. Similar emphases on patterned connections apply at more macrostructural levels; for example, to explain the investment and borrowing practices of banks and firms by analyzing their locations within networks of interlocking corporate directorates. The primacy of structural ties among social actors infuses the organizational network perspective with a vision distinct from other prominent organizational theories, such as transaction cost economics, organizational ecology, evolution, institutionalism, and resource dependence.

Both organization studies and network analysis are increasingly interdisciplinary enterprises. Investigating their central problems draws concepts, theories, data, and methods from the basic disciplines of sociology, economics, history, political science, anthropology, and such applied fields as law, management, and public administration. Although comprehensive detailed coverage of such a vast subject is impossible in this brief chapter, I sketch the broad contours of the organizational network perspective. Following a brief presentation of core network concepts and methods, I examine the application of network principles to three important topics: interorganizational economic behavior, interorganizational political action, and intraorganizational networks. I conclude with some speculations on future directions for organizational network analysis and possible policy implications.

CORE NETWORK CONCEPTS

Network theorists typically conceptualize social structures in terms of two fundamental components: actors and their relationships. For organizational networks, identifying which actors belong to a social system depends on the level of analysis at which researchers frame their theoretical expectations. At the most comprehensive level, the organizational society encompasses every for-profit, non-profit, and governmental organization operating within a geographically bounded community, region, nation, or even at the global economy level. An organizational population consists of all organizations exhibiting a specific form or type (usually defined as an industry providing an equivalent product or service), such as banks, churches, or semiconductor firms. The organizational field is a heterogeneous set of functionally interconnected organizations; for example, all firms, interest organizations, and government agencies that deal with agriculture, national defense, or health care. The population and field concepts cross-cut one another, since organizational fields typically draw their members from several diverse populations. At a meso-level of analysis, an organization is a goal-directed activity system whose boundary is legally defined by authority and property rights over its human and material resources. Organizational subsystems are various internal work units necessary for organizational survival, such as divisions, departments, and teams. At the lowest microanalytic level are persons – owners, directors, top executives, middle managers, and front-line employees – who perform both routine and exceptional activities. Network analysis can proceed within each organizational level, using different criteria to identify and observe the organizations, subunits, or persons belonging to an appropriately bounded system.

After identifying a bounded system and its members, an organizational analyst must decide which relation(s) among the actors can best characterize structures of interest. Rather than assuming that one type of tie completely captures "the" organizational network, analysts must acknowledge the simultaneous presence of multiple networks composed of several distinct relational contents. Each substantive type of tie may reveal a unique structural pattern among the system participants. For example, an advice-giving network among co-workers in the finance department of a large manufacturing corporation may bear little resemblance to their pattern of interpersonal trust, with contrasting implications for employee demoralization and subversion during periods of corporate downsizing or expansion. Despite the limitless substantive diversity of interorganizational and interpersonal ties, five general categories should suffice to classify most relational contents arising at every level of network analysis.

1   Resource exchanges involve transactions where one actor yields control over a physical good or service to another actor in return for some other kind of commodity (including money).
2   Information transmissions are inter-actor communications, including exhanges of strategic plans, scientific and technical data, work advice, political opinions, and even gossip.
3   Power relations consist of asymmetrical interactions in which one party exerts control over another's behaviors either by coercion or, more typically, by an authoritative superior exercising the taken-for-granted expectation that commands will be obeyed by subordinates (authority or "legitimate power" in Max Weber's meaning).
4   Boundary penetrations comprise coordinated actions to attain a common goal that could not be achieved individually. Familiar examples include interlocking boards of directors, industry committees to set technical standards, strategic alliances for innovation or production, and collective lobbying to obtain a public policy.
5   Sentimental attachments among individuals generate collective identities and liabilities for mutual assistance and emotional support. A trust relation is particularly important for sustaining many other kinds of interpersonal ties.

Researchers can choose to analyze the patterns connecting actors by their relationships from two complementary viewpoints. First, an egocentric perspective examines a focal organization or person ("ego") and its pattern of direct ties to others ("alters"). This procedure investigates such structural aspects as the number of ego's ties, their strengths and frequency, their multiplexity and reciprocity, the diversity of alters directly or indirectly reachable, and the density of ties among the alters in one's egocentric network. Second, a complete-network analysis examines total configurations of multiplex ties among all the actors in a social system; for example, all organizations in a field or all employees in a work team. Some macrostructural features parallel the egocentric approach: the density of existing to potential ties, the number of indirect links needed to connect every pair of actors, the extent to which multiplex ties directly connect the same pairs of actors. One crucial structural property for actors in complete networks is network centrality. This concept is intimately related to ideas about social power derived from an actor's ability to influence or control others' interactions; for example, by manipulating the flow of information, personnel, and resources, or by brokering political and economic deals between unconnected or hostile parties.

Researchers have developed and applied a large array of data collection and analysis methods for studying organizational networks (Wasserman and Faust, 1994). Primary methods include survey interviews and questionnaires, participant observations, and archival documents including news accounts and company reports. Complete-network studies impose particularly demanding response standards. Because the potential number of directed ties for a specific content among N actors is $N^2 - N$, missing data from even a small proportion of cases exponentially erodes the quality of research results. For example, if just 30 percent of respondents refuse to cooperate, confirming information would be unavailable for 53 percent of the possible connections.

INTERORGANIZATIONAL NETWORKS AND ECONOMIC BEHAVIOR

Vulnerable within an increasingly global economy, large corporations seek competitive advantages by slashing costs, improving quality, increasing productivity, and responding rapidly to technological innovations and fickle consumer tastes. A proliferation of several new interorganizational forms is one consequence of this churning environment. Pure market transactions require no recurring cooperation and collaboration among exchange parties. Hierarchical structures – multi-establishment firms, corporate acquisitions, and mergers – in which one firm absorbs another's assets and personnel into a unitary enterprise cannot be considered as true alliances because subunits preserve no ultimate independence of action. Strategic alliances, such as equity and non-equity partnerships, combine important aspects of both market and hierarchical arrangements between independent organizations. These hybrid structures, N-form or "networked" organizations, emphasize interorganizational exchange and collaborative relations. A strategic alliance is defined as at least two partner firms that: (a) remain independent after the alliance is formed; (b) share benefits and managerial control over the performance of assigned tasks; and (c) make continuing contributions in one or more strategic areas, such as technology or products (Yoshino and Rangan, 1995, p. 5).

The formation of a strategic alliance requires mutual trust among potential partners. Trust enables one firm to achieve some degree of social control over another's behavior under conditions of high uncertainty. From a transaction cost perspective, trust expectations mutually deter each partner's temptation to malfeasance or opportunism; that is, to dishonesty and dissembling about preferences and information (Williamson, 1981, p. 553). Writing explicit safeguards against every possible opportunistic outcome is unrealistic. To the extent that trust substitutes for more formal control mechanisms, such as written contracts, an alliance can reduce or avoid various transaction costs, including: searching for information about potential partners; writing formal agreements stipulating terms and conditions; monitoring partner performance; and enforcing the contract terms if a partner fails to honor the agreements. Far less costly protections can be built on a self-enforcing foundation of interfirm trust. Interorganizational alliances emerge over time, with trust occupying a pivotal role between antecedent conditions and consequent alliance formations. Interorganizational communication networks circumscribe an ego organization's capacity to screen and evaluate potential alliance partners. The more central a firm's position within an organizational field communication network, the greater its visibility and hence the larger the number of informants available to testify regarding its reliability and integrity. "The network structure that results from the accumulation of those ties increasingly becomes the repository of information on potential partners, helping organizations decide with whom to form new alliances" (Gulati and Gargiulo, 1999, p. 1475). Peripheral organizations positions enjoy fewer opportunities to become familiar with potential partners and for their own trustworthiness reputations to become vetted by the field. Unequal financial size or market share may hinder interorganizational trust formation because radically dissimilar partners often cannot fulfill their reciprocity obligations. Organizations sharing common characteristics are more likely to develop stronger bonds of trust. Many cross-border alliances, sought with foreign partners to gain access to local markets, founder on incompatible national and corporate cultures that prevent the development of mutual trust.

Because new partners generally have few grounds for trusting one another, equity-based contracts often initially protect both parties against the other's potential opportunism. After they gain confidence in one another through experience, "informal psychological contracts increasingly compensate or substitute for formal contractual safeguards as reliance on trust among parties increases over time" (Ring and Van de Ven, 1994, p. 105). This sequence is succinctly captured in the proverbial "familiarity breeds trust" (Gulati, 1995a). Reduced transaction and monitoring costs make informal social control the preferred cost-effective alternative to both market pricing and hierarchical authority. Consistent with these expectations, Gulati's (1995a) analysis of multisector alliances found strong evidence that formal equity-sharing agreements decreased with the existence and frequency of prior ties to a partner. Domestic alliances less often involved equity mechanisms than did international alliances, supporting claims that trust relations are more difficult to sustain cross-culturally.

Transaction cost economics and resource dependence theory offer alternative explanations for strategic alliance creation. Williamson (1981) asserted that asset specificity is a key factor propelling organizational efforts to economize. Interorganizational ties arise from specialized investments that would lose their value if transferred to another exchange partner. The more an investment is tailored specifically to recurrent transactions between a buyer–seller pair, the more likely these parties are to "make special efforts to design exchanges with good continuity properties" (Williamson, 1981, p. 555), thus effectively locking both partners both into prolonged bilateral transactions such as a strategic alliance. Resource dependence analyzes alliance ties as outcomes of innate power conflicts between organizational resource procurement needs and the desire to preserve freedom of corporate decision-making. Interorganizational relations emerge when one organization controls the critical resources – information, money, production and distribution skills, access to foreign markets – needed by another organization. Dependence theory argues that network ties arise from executives' attempts to control their firms' most problematic environmental contingencies through complete or partial absorption. Alliances tend to occur more often among interdependent than between autonomous firms. A company prefers partners best able to satisfy critical resource requirements while imposing minimal constraints on its own discretionary actions.

Resource dependence seems superior to transaction cost principles in explaining the cooperative research and development networks that emerged in the 1980s between new biotechnology firms and established agricultural, chemical, and pharmaceutical corporations (Smith-Doerr et al., 1999). Complementary resource needs drove these strategic alliances, primarily involving exchanges of financial support for technical expertise. The small, innovative research and development laboratories typically lacked funds, public legitimacy, and in-house capability to market their products and maneuver through the governmental regulatory labyrinth. They formed alliances with resource-rich diversified corporations that could provide badly needed financial infusions. In return, the large firms sought to acquire tacit knowledge and to learn new technological skills from their junior partners. In a study of equity joint ventures among US, Japanese, and European new materials, industrial automation, and automotive products firms, Gulati (1995b) found evidence consistent with both resource dependence and social structural explanations. Strategically interdependent companies (firms operating in complementary market niches) forged more alliances than did firms with comparable resources and capabilities. Previously allied partners had a higher probability of forming new alliances with one another, suggesting that "over time, each firm acquires more information and builds greater confidence in the partnering firm" (p. 644). But additional alliances eventually reduced the probability of forming further agreements because of fears of lost autonomy by becoming overly dependent on a single partner. Indirect connections through the prior alliance network also shaped succeeding alliances with new partners. That is, previously unconnected firms were more likely to collaborate if they both had ties to a common third party. Gulati concluded that "the social network of indirect ties is an effective referral mechanism for bringing firms together and that dense co-location in an alliance network enhances mutual confidence as firms become aware of the possible negative reputational consequences of their own or others' opportunistic behavior" (p. 644).

INTERORGANIZATIONAL NETWORKS AND POLITICAL ACTION

Political action by interorganizational networks is the primary theme of the organizational state theory, developed in Laumann and Knoke's (1987) research on US energy and health policy-making and elaborated in a comparative project on US, German and Japanese labor policy networks (Knoke et al., 1996). The core actors in the organizational state are formal organizations, both governmental and non-governmental, that attempt to realize their public policy interests through collective political action. Corporations pursue protected markets and greater profits, labor unions seek higher wages and better working conditions, professional associations try to protect their members' autonomy, political parties promote ideologies and solicit votes for re-election, and bureaucracies seek to enforce agency mandates and boost budgets. The main outcomes of organizational state processes are collectively binding decisions in specific policy events, such as legislative acts, regulatory decrees, court rulings, or strong bureaucratic leadership.

The policy domain is the largest unit of analysis in organizational state theory. It is defined as a social system within which collectively binding decisions are made, implemented, and evaluated with regard to a specific type of public policy. A domain is comprised of all the important actors holding common interests in those policies, regardless of whether they agree on preferred outcomes to policy events. Indeed, every policy domain is split among two or more opposing blocks of political organizations attempting to persuade policy-making authorities to approve different options. The alternative that eventually prevails results from more or less intense political struggles to assemble sufficient support to pass a bill or enact a regulation. Policy domains develop fairly stable power structures dominated by the most powerful peak interest groups and governmental actors. Gaining access to a domain's central positions requires an organization to acquire and deploy information (both technical expertise and political knowledge) and resources (both material and symbolic).

A central task for policy domain analysts is to uncover the key structural relations in the political networks among the core organizations. The two especially relevant networks are information exchange and resource networks. These relations most closely parallel Knoke's (1990, pp. 11–16) analytic distinction between two basic power dimensions: "influence," persuasive communications intended to change others' beliefs and perceptions regarding political actions, and "domination," resource transactions of physical benefits (or harms) in return for compliance with commands. Information is an intangible asset – such as scientific, legal, or political knowledge – whose transmission from one actor to another does not result in its loss to the first possessor. Resources are physical commodities – such as money, labor power, and facilities – whose control can be transmitted from one actor to another.

A fundamental organizational state proposition is that both information and resource networks shape organizational efforts to focus sufficient power on other policy domain organizations, most importantly on particular public authorities responsible for ultimately deciding a policy event, to sway the collective decision in their favor. Organizations on both sides of a policy conflict seek to increase the probability that these authorities will choose the outcome they prefer. To a great extent, actors use pre-existing information and resource exchange networks in their influence efforts on specific policy events. Hence, organizational positions in the already existing information and resource exchange networks are important factors both in stimulating participation and in determining the outcomes of policy events.

During the course of public policy struggles, opposing coalitions or alliances among organizations typically coalesce to undertake coordinated political actions aimed at furthering their members' common interests. A collective action involves three or more organizations working together in an effort to obtain their preferred policy event outcome. The necessary preconditions that lead to collective action involve mutual recognition by organizations that they share common goals, followed by formation of linkages that enable them to undertake cooperative activity. Some collective actions are aimed at supporters or potential supporters, while others are targeted toward neutral observers (e.g. the media and the general public) and against active opponents (more often to dissuade them from taking opposing action than to convert them). But the most important targets in any policy domain are the governmental officials who possess the legal or customary authority to make a decision about an event that is binding on the domain as a whole.

Network analysis reveals that global patterns of information exchange among political organizations in a policy domain are structured according to their common policy interests. Very dense communication networks typically connect a domain's core organizations. In each of the three US domains more than one hundred trade associations, labor unions, professional societies, public interest groups, federal executive agencies, and congressional committees were asked with which organizations they shared (i.e. both sent and received) important policy information (Laumann and Knoke, 1987; Knoke et al., 1996). The density of communication ties was 0.38 for the US labor domain and 0.30 in both the energy and health domains. Diagrams representing the communication network structures in the three domains showed that organizations expressing similar issue interests and policy preferences tended to occupy the same regions. In a two-dimensional plot of the labor policy organizations' path distances (i.e. the number of direct or indirect steps required to connect a pair of organizations), most unions, business associations, and federal agencies were located in three distinct sectors (Knoke et al., 1996, p. 112). Similarly, sharp cleavages occurred within the energy policy domain between consumers and several types of energy producers, and in the health policy domain between consumers, clients, medical researchers, and health care providers (Laumann and Knoke, 1987, pp. 242, 246). This partitioning into specialized policy segments reflects a tendency for political organizations to communicate primarily with their friends and potential allies, and to avoid giving information to organizations with which they share few common interests.

Every domain's communication structure also revealed that governmental actors and interest groups with broad policy agendas filled the central locations. Thus, the center of the energy domain was occupied by the White House, Department of Energy, and key House and Senate energy and resources committees. This core group was closely surrounded by such major labor unions and trade associations as the AFL-CIO, United Automobile Workers, American Petroleum Institute, Edison Electric Institute, American Gas Association, American Mining Congress, and National Automobile Dealers Association (Laumann and Knoke, 1987, pp. 243–5). Given the divergent and sometimes antagonistic policy interests of these organizations, their close proximity to the center of the domain's communication network indicates that these major political actors maintained high levels of information exchange with potential opponents. Open communication carries risks as well as benefits: "At a minimum, it can alert them that a policy change is afoot. It also conveys one's position, and it could convey extensive information about the political environment. As a strategic blunder, direct contact can provide the impetus for latent opposition to mobilize, expanding the scope of conflict. As a tactical matter, it is clearly in a group's interest to let its opponents address the information problems on their own" (Hula, 1999, p. 54). To lower the risks of aiding potential foes, political organizations confine their exchanges of sensitive tactical and strategic information only to other actors sharing their preferred policy outcomes. Communications with policy opponents are more likely to serve as warnings and deterrents, signaling the intensity of organizational interests and intentions to fight on particular policy events.

Exchanging policy-relevant information with other political organizations is an important prerequisite for engaging in political action, but is insufficient to explain organizational attempts to influence policy-makers' decisions. Engaging in policy discussions is a relatively low-cost activity, where participants can quickly move into or drop out of contact with one another. The complexity and density of interorganizational communication networks makes their boundaries amorphous and renders large, diffuse discussion groups unwieldy as effective policy influencing instruments. More promising insights accrue by examining the formation of advocacy coalitions whose member organizations cooperatively pursue collective policy goals. The expanding population of Washington political organizations and the complexities of gaining access to federal institutions noted above increasingly necessitate coalitional behavior. Organizations can leverage their political influence by pooling resources, especially their technical and political expertise, to create an effective division of labor for contacting governmental targets. Public officials may be more easily impressed, even convinced, by arguments advanced through a broadly united front than by clashing claims proffered by individual organizations. Hence, the main incentives for joining a collective action are reducing resource costs while increasing the chances of achieving a successful political outcome.

Organizations that form coalitions to pool their political resources are generally more successful in realizing their goals than are actors attempting by themselves to affect policies. Because considerable resource expenditures are involved, only organizations holding high interests in a particular policy event typically pursue their preferences collaboratively with others. The configurations of allied and opposing actors may be quite fluid and complex when examined over time. Further, because events reflect numerous decision points within a continuing policy stream, the interweaving of actors, relations, and actions is best considered across multiple, sequential policy events. A large sample of events can reveal both stability and change in policy network structures as well as the impact of event outcomes on subsequent policy struggles.

Comparative labor policy domains research found significant network effects on both organizational influence reputations and policy event activity (Knoke et al., 1996). The more central an organization in both the communication network (measured by policy information exchanges) and the support network (measured by resource exchanges), the higher its reputation as an especially influential player in labor policy. Similarly, greater centrality in both networks leads to more involvement across numerous legislative events in six types of political influence activities, including coalitions with other organizations. In the US and German cases, communication centrality exerted a much stronger effect than did political support centrality on both organizational reputations and political activities, while the Japanese pattern was just the reverse (Knoke et al., 1996, p. 120). Detailed analyses of specific legislative decisions showed that most national labor policy fights were conducted by relatively small "action sets," defined as coalitions of organizations that: hold the same preferred event outcome (passage or failure of a bill); communicate directly or indirectly with one another about policy affairs; and consciously coordinate their policy influence activities (pp. 21–2). Labor unions and business associations were the primary coalition leaders in all three nations, frequently taking opposing positions on legislative bills and almost never collaborating in the same action set even on those rare occasions when they preferred the same policy outcome. Only minorities of the 117 core US labor policy domain organizations expressed interest in the outcomes of each of the 25 congressional bills examined. On average fewer than 37 organizations advocated either the passage or failure of a bill (p. 140). Slightly more than half participated in action sets, which averaged fewer than ten members (however, two legislative events produced no action sets, and nine others just one action set favoring the bill's passage).

Most often, action sets are constructed as short-term coalitions to fight collectively over a specific policy event, then to disband after political authorities render a decision. Subsequently, new action sets coalesce, composed of different participants lured by the particular substantive interests at stake in a new policy proposal. These changing alliances are not random assemblages of political organizations. Policy domains are routinized political arenas comprising a limited range of potential participants, problems, and procedures for putting proposals onto the national agenda. Consequently, many coalitions are assembled and led by an enduring core group of organizations, primarily the peak or encompassing organizations possessing broad mandates to defend and advance the policy interests of sizable domain segments.

INTRAORGANIZATIONAL NETWORKS AND SOCIAL CAPITAL

The macro-level economic and political forces that reshaped interorganizational relations also produced a new employment contract between workers and their employers (Cappelli et al., 1997). The more daring or desperate corporations implemented flexible, high performance work practices. Rigid bureaucratic hierarchies yielded to experiments in cross-functional teams that devolved increasing volumes of information, technical skills, and managerial responsibility down to the front-line workers' level. Employees were prodded to contribute to restructured decision-making through quality circles, cross-training and job rotation, team work, and total quality management programs. Total quality management (TQM) principles emphasized the never-ending collaboration between management and workers for continuous learning and quality improvements, assessment of customer requirements, scientific monitoring of task performance, and process-management to enhance team effectiveness. New human resource management practices emphasized rewarding individual and group performances through incentive-based compensation schemes (profit- and gain-sharing, bonuses, and employee stock ownership plans). These diverse high performance innovations were all intended to lower supervisory costs and increase employees' work-life morale, thereby raising corporate productivity, quality, and profitability. By flattening managerial hierarchies and outsourcing formerly internalized staff functions, firms shortened or eliminated many traditional internal labor markets that had provided career ladders for regular promotions to ever-higher levels of responsibility, prestige, and pay. Instead, jobs evolved from fixed positions into flexible bundles of tasks that were subjected to periodic restructuring to grapple with organizational contingencies in turbulent world economic markets. Jobs mutated into project-based appointments through which multiply skilled employees passed in short-term assignments on their way to the next project inside the firm or with another employer.

From these gales of creative destruction a new corporate form emerged – the network organization, whose external alliances were discussed above. Its distinguishing internal features are multiplex exchange ties among the firm's loosely coupled divisions, departments, and work groups, and among managers and employees. It breaks down hierarchical and functional barriers, replacing them with task-specific units connected through communication, advice, and interpersonal trust networks. The networked organization "creates autonomous units, but it increases the volume, speed, and frequency of both vertical and horizontal communication within the organization to promote collaboration. . . .

Network management is, in the end, management by empowerment" (Limerick and Cunnington, 1993, p. 61).

N-form organizations provide structural opportunities to develop social capital relations for constructing employee careers under the new employment contract. Workers have always used networking activity as an important strategy for getting ahead in their companies. All organizations exhibit informal structures, at every level from the executive suite to the loading dock, which exist autonomously from formal structures stipulated by corporate policies, procedure manuals, and organization charts. Thus, any organization's actual internal structure combines formal authority and communication channels with informal networks for exchanging information, advice, and trust that simultaneously facilitate and constrain individual and group behavior. To succeed in obtaining power resources and better career opportunities, employees must learn to use informal network ties to extend beyond narrowly constrained formal role positions.

The new employment contract compels workers to survive and prosper by learning how to form and manipulate egocentric relations that yield competitive advantages in the contest for jobs, project assignments, promotions, recognition, and rewards. An employee's interpersonal ties comprise crucial social capital investments which may prove as beneficial for her career development as her human capital assets of knowledge, skills, and experience. A capacity "to network," in the everyday sense of contacting people who can help you, takes on great significance inside networked organizations, where formal positions are ill-defined and constantly changing. Social capital consists of manifest and latent social relationships that a person can mobilize, "making possible the achievement of certain ends that would not be attainable in its absence" (Coleman, 1990, p. 302). Embedded in pre-existing multiplex network ties, social capital is "created when the relations among persons change in ways that facilitate action" (p. 304). By proactively forging large volumes of contacts with numerous, diverse, and well endowed alters, an ego gains potential access to the assets controlled by others. "Social capital is at once the resources contacts hold and the structure of contacts in a network. The first term describes whom you reach. The second term describes how you reach" (Burt, 1992, p. 12).

Mixtures of competitive and cooperative modes characterize many multiplex intraorganizational networks. Sometimes actors activate their social capital connections to gain personal advantages over their adversaries, while under other circumstances they participate in collective actions for mutual benefit. For example, corporate employees engage in self-serving career moves, seeking out individual mentors or networking with superiors to get a leg up the promotion ladder. In contrast, high performance work practices, such as self-managed teams stressing group responsibility for production, encourage workers to pool their skills and social capital to increase group performance. Both networking styles also occur at a firm's strategy level, where top executives decide and implement plans to achieve global corporate objectives. Firms operating in the same industry generally form exclusive supplier relations and compete for customer loyalties, yet, as noted above, they also frequently collaborate in strategic alliances and joint ventures with expectations of mutual gains. An important challenge for network analysts is to explain which conditions encourage zero-sum or positive-sum behavior.

Ronald Burt's (1992) structural hole theory proposed a social capital explanation of competition at both inter-and intraorganizational levels of analysis. To succeed in a highly competitive arena, workers should invest in social contacts providing timely access to people controlling organizational resources vital for performing tasks and achieving objectives. An employee's "profit" is the rate of return on these social capital investments generated from using network alters, such as promotion recommendations and job referrals. Hence, a crucial networking skill is learning how to spot and develop ties to specific alters who can provide optimal information benefits, such as access, timing, and connections (Burt, 1992, pp. 13–15). A high-volume strategy, forming a large number of connections with many alters, is not sufficient. More crucially, a worker should enlarge her social capital by adding network alters who exhibit diverse qualities. That is, time and energy should be poured into cultivating relations with persons not otherwise connected to one another: "A structural hole is a relationship of nonredundancy between two contacts" (Burt, 1992, p. 18). Besides tapping into unique information sources, an employee who fills a structural hole thereby gains some control benefits through exploiting network gaps between non-redundant contacts. Ego becomes a valuable corporate player by occupying a unique informal position that connects vital constituencies, serving as a network broker or go-between who negotiates deals and extracts a commission. Structural holes thus provide employees with entrepreneurial opportunities for playing one party against another to reap a personal benefit.

Burt's (1992, pp. 115–80) analysis of 284 upper-level managers of a computer firm demonstrated that structural holes in egocentric networks contribute to early promotion and rapid rise to higher ranks. Different career paths ensued from two network forms: (a) an entrepreneurial form with network contacts outside a manager's immediate work group, which spanned corporate structural holes, led to early promotion and subsequent quick advancement to higher ranks; (b) a hierarchical or boss-centered form, centered on a manager's immediate work-group supervisor, also led to early promotion but subsequent prolonged stagnation in rank (p. 153). The gender gap in competitive networking was sharp: "The worst network for women and entry-rank men is the one best for high-ranking men. Women and entry-rank men with entrepreneurial, opportunity-oriented networks were promoted late to their current rank" (p. 159). Although women gained initially through using a boss-centered strategy, they faced subsequent barriers to career advancement. Lacking network contacts outside their immediate work group to vouch for a candidate's credentials, women mangers' mobility into top leadership positions was thwarted.

Herminia Ibarra's (1992, 1993a, b) research on ego-network dynamics revealed how men and women employees differentially converted their social capital into career advantages. She observed different homophily patterns (tendencies toward same-sex ties) among the 80 male and female employees in a New England advertising and public relations firm. Men formed multiplex network contacts mostly with other men (communication, advice-seeking, support, friendship, and influence relationships). Women employees differentiated their network contents, forming social support and friendship connections with female coworkers and instrumental ties with higher-status men. Hence, expressive and instrumental networks were reinforced for men, but were inversely correlated for women. Consequently, men seemed to receive higher career returns than women on their social capital investments, in the form of greater network centrality. Similar gender-differentiated network propensities occurred among 63 managers of four large corporations (Ibarra, 1993a). Men formed more weak-tie same-sex networks but women forged strong expressive bonds with other women. The impact of managers' ego-net strategies on potential for promotion also differed by gender. Both high-potential men and low-potential women concentrated on instrumental ties, while high-potential women and low-potential men emphasized expressive networks, such as trust and reciprocity. Ibarra concurred with Burt that women's preferred social capital strategies disadvantaged them getting ahead in the corporate game: "The 'entrepreneurial' network pattern characteristic of successful male managers is less effective for females who many require stronger network ties to achieve the same level of legitimacy and access to resources" (Ibarra, 1993a, p. 27).

A fundamental hypothesis of network analysis is that social actors that occupy more central network positions thereby control more resources and exercise greater political influence. Although intraorganizational centrality empowers employees, the reverse causal process may also operate: people seek connections to the most powerful players, in hopes of enhancing their own power through these connections. Occupants in central positions can derive several advantages over employees in peripheral locations: acquire more timely and useful information through their communication networks; mediate and broker deals between interested parties who lack direct ties to one another; better monitor and control resource exchanges and mobilize support for workplace initiatives; and, through ties to external organizations, participate in their organization's strategic activities. In sum, "network centrality increases an actor's knowledge of a system's power distribution, or the accuracy of his or her assessment of the political landscape.... Those who understand how a system really works can get things done or exercise power within that system" (Ibarra, 1993b, p. 494).

CONCLUSIONS

Theorizing and researching about organizational networks have largely proceeded at conceptually disjoint levels of analysis by investigators from differing disciplinary perspectives applying various methodologies and measurements to explain divergent substantive interests. A major challenge for the new millennium is to bring a closer integration among these disparate elements to achieve more comprehensive explanations of how network structures and processes form simultaneous constraints and opportunities for organizational populations, fields, firms, subunits, and employees. Examining the connections among cross-level network phenomena is crucial to unraveling their complex dynamics. The consequences of structural changes at one level ramify across other dimensions. Thus, the outcomes of strategic alliances, lobbying coalitions, and other interorganizational relations among firms transform the daily work routines and career opportunities available to top executives, middle managers, and production workers of the collaborating enterprises (Kanter and Myers, 1991). Similarly, aggregated webs of micro-level interactions among corporate departments and their employees change the configurations of larger organizational networks within which they are embedded. For example, an inability to develop trustful relations among a firm's managers and workers could obstruct successful implementation of interorganizational agreements. As employees occupying key boundary-spanning roles try to deal with uncertain company environments, they socially construct mutual trust relations with peers in other organizations, which tend to obscure the distinctions between persons and their roles as corporate agents. This confounding of interpersonal and interorganizational trust poses potential problems about social capital ownership and control. Tracking the co-evolution of network relations and their constituent actors across multiple organizational levels of analysis requires patient longitudinal data collection, analysis, and interpretation.

Network analysts have largely neglected to investigate how organizational networks affect employee political activities, such as their participation in work decisions, interpersonal disputes, conflicts with management, and social movements to change company policies. Most previous studies examined personal networks within only a single organization. We know relatively little about how alternative network structures empower entire workforces, in the sense of raising collective organizational capacities to get things done. How do different intra-organizational network structures affect corporate power to mobilize human and technical resources, perform productive tasks more efficiently, and achieve profitable outcomes? Answering these questions requires comparative research designs to measure multiple networks within many organizations.

On the applied side, an important implication of network analysis is that firms and employees must recognize the ubiquity of inter- and intraorganizational relations throughout corporate life. Identifying and building strong relationships can be beneficial strategies for both individual careers and the collective performances of work teams, departments, firms, and strategic alliances. As theoretical understanding and empirical findings about networking dynamics accumulate and diffuse, management schools and organizations should encourage explicit exposure to applied network management ideas as integral features of their formal curricula and training programs (Baker, 1994). At the same time, attention must be paid to the dark side of network practices – the potential for manipulation and abuse of power – that threaten to undermine the norms of reciprocity and trust crucial to sustaining fragile social ties in every organization.

Part VII
Individuals and Their Well-Being

24

Social Inequality, Stress, and Health

Joseph E. Schwartz

Research into the determinants of disease morbidity and mortality during most of the twentiethth century was dominated by a biological model of disease, as was the practice of medicine itself. Illnesses and other physical disorders were thought to be caused by harmful agents (bacteria or viruses causing infectious diseases, toxic chemicals, tobacco smoke, cholesterol, etc.) and/or a breakdown in one or more of the body's organ systems. Consistent with this biomedical model, primary prevention of disease has focused on reducing the population's exposure to toxic substances and procedures to control the spread of infections – for example, ensuring a clean water supply, quarantining infected individuals, and vaccinating individuals to make them immune to specific diseases.

It was not until 1977 that Engel published his seminal article setting forth the now widely accepted biopsychosocial model of disease. This article urged physicians and researchers to acknowledge and investigate the role of social, psychological, and behavioral factors in the prevention, etiology, and treatment of both physical and mental illnesses. Despite its wide acceptance, at least in principle, the vast majority of the medical literature ignores the role of psychological and sociological factors. A review of medical school curricula or the contents of leading journals (for example, *Journal of the American Medical Association* or *Lancet*) suggests that the medical establishment remains skeptical about the relevance of psychosocial factors in the etiology of disease.

The above not withstanding, the subfield of "psychosomatic medicine," historically dominated by psychiatrists, has a long tradition of emphasizing mind–body connections. Increasingly, a broader array of researchers have been investigating the impact of personality, behavior, and a variety of social factors on morbidity and mortality. While the majority are psychologists, there are also physicians, social epidemiologists, sociologists, anthropologists, and others. Many of these researchers identify themselves with one or more of the interdisciplinary fields of psychosomatic medicine, "behavioral medicine," and "health psychology."

In this chapter I review selected empirical findings and issues from behavioral medicine that are likely to interest sociologists. The first section is primarily descriptive, reviewing the fact that the risk of many diseases, and death itself, is socially patterned. Much of the emphasis is on mortality and cardiovascular disease, but the general point applies to other causes of death and many non-fatal diseases. Since, in my opinion, the subfield of social stratification lies at the core of sociology, this section emphasizes the link between stratification and health. While many mechanisms surely contribute to this relationship, I am particularly interested in the effect that *stress* may have on health and the possibility that differential exposure to stress in the social environment partially accounts for social class differences in health. The latter part of the chapter presents select findings from studies of animals and humans pertaining to the impact of social stress on health.

THE SOCIAL PATTERNING OF DISEASE AND MORTALITY

Demographic Factors

One of the goals of descriptive epidemiology is to document the extent to which mortality and disease prevalence varies by age, sex, and race/ethnicity. Many diseases are more frequent at older ages (heart disease, cancer, hip fracture), but others, such as AIDS and violence-related injuries, are more common in younger individuals. Similarly, some diseases are gender-specific for obvious biological reasons (uterine/cervical cancer, prostate cancer), others are more common in one gender (stroke, breast cancer, and fibromyalgia in women; AIDS and vio-lence-related injuries in men), and yet others are relatively gender-neutral (heart disease, diabetes, pneumonia, and flu). With respect to race/ethnicity, many genetic disorders are much more common in specific subgroups (for example, sickle cell anemia in blacks, Tay Sach's disease in Jews of East European descent). The same is true for several other disorders whose genetic basis is not clear: renal disease is much more prevalent in black Americans than in white Americans; stroke is more common in Asian Americans than white Americans; and several cancers are less common in Hispanic Americans than white Americans. Overall, mortality rates increase with age (after age five), are higher in men than women, and are higher in black Americans than in white or Asian Americans.

Of course it is one thing to document demographic differences in the rates of diseases and mortality, and quite another to explain their existence. Take hypertension as an example. In the United States, increased age and being black are two of the leading risk factors for hypertension. Prior to age 50, men are substantially more likely to have hypertension than women, but following menopause, the risk of hypertension increases substantially in women and probably surpasses that of men (Subcommittee on Definition and Prevalence of the 1984 Joint National Committee on Detection, Evaluation, and Treatment of High Blood Pressure, 1985). The causes of this social patterning are not well understood, though it is widely believed that genetics, behavior, and social/ cultural factors play a role.

We tend to consider the positive association between age and hypertension in the United States as reflecting the "natural aging process," but there are data suggesting that there is nothing innate about either the average level of blood pressure (BP) or its increase with age. Waldron et al. (1982) analyzed BP data for 84 different adult samples from throughout the world, nearly all available data sets satisfying a predefined set of criteria. Independent ratings of several cultural characteristics, based largely on anthropological data and reports, were also obtained for each sample. The authors found that the average age-matched BP of men and women were substantially lower in hunter-gatherer, herding, and traditional agricultural societies than in more "modern" agricultural and industrial societies in which most of the production was distributed through a market economy. These cross-cultural differences were greater in older adults (aged 50–60) than younger adults (aged 20–30), reflecting an age gradient of blood pressure that was flat or nearly flat in the more traditional societies but tended to increase by 0.5–1.0 mmHg with each year of age in market economies. The result in market economies was a difference of 15–30 mmHg between those who were 55 years old and those who were 25 years old.

In another intriguing study, Timio et al. (1988) followed 144 nuns from an order in Umbria, Italy, and 138 women from surrounding communities for 20 years. The nuns were completely secluded from urban life, prayed and worked in nearly absolute silence, and were not exposed to competition, insecurity about their future, or the economic, familial, and other stressors of modern Western society. The demographic and physiological characteristics, including BP, of the two groups were similar at recruitment into the study. While the nuns' BPs increased only about 1 mmHg over the entire 20 years, systolic BP in the control sample increased by an average of about 1 mmHg *per year* and diastolic BP increased about 1 mmHg every three years. The difference in age gradient between the two groups could not be explained by differences in alcohol, tobacco, coffee, or tea consumption, salt intake, cholesterol, or body weight change. It also could not be explained by differences in childbirth, since the age gradients were quite similar in the control women who had and had not had children. While unable to specify a mechanism, the authors suggested that the failure of nuns' BPs to increase with age must be due to the near absence of "conflict, aggression, and competition for power and money" in their social environment and their lifestyle of prayer, meditation, and silent work (p. 461).

Thus, it is a mistake to conclude from the observed age gradient of BP in Western societies that BP "naturally" increases with age. Similarly, it would be a mistake to conclude from the observed BP differences between Caucasian Americans and African Americans that racial differences are primarily genetic. While genes probably play a role, behavioral and other psychosocial factors also contribute.

Social Class

Unlike age, sex, and race, the constructs of social class and socioeconomic status (SES) are inherently socially defined. Whether the social stratification within a society is more accurately represented as a set of hierarchically ordered discrete classes or as relative positions along a more continuous gradient, those in higher status positions generally have a higher standard of living, greater access to scarce resources, and increased opportunities compared to those with lower status. While rarely conceptualized as a scarce resource, good health and a long life are two objectives to which almost everyone aspires. If those in the lower classes tend to have poorer health and a shorter life expectancy, this would augment the social and economic inequalities that are more traditionally the focus of social stratification research.

Governments and social reformers have gathered mortality data and analyzed them according to a variety of indicators of social class for more than a century (for example, Dublin, 1917; Britten, 1934; Guralnick, 1962). Antonovsky (1967) published one of the earliest systematic sociological reviews of the relationship of social class to longevity and mortality. He summarized data from more than 30 studies and concluded that the evidence was overwhelming that the lower class, often defined as unskilled manual laborers, had a substantially shorter life expectancy and a higher mortality rate than other social classes. What was less clear was whether longevity and mortality rates were similar across the remaining social classes, or whether those in intermediate classes (typically lower-level non-manual and skilled and semi-skilled manual workers) had mortality rates that were higher than those in the higher classes (for example, professionals, administrators, businessmen, upper and intermediate level managers and supervisors, and shopkeepers). Thus, an early question that emerged from this research was: is there a relatively continuous SES or social class gradient to mortality rates, or is there simply a marked difference between those at or near the bottom and everyone else?

Shortly after Antonovsky's review, Kitagawa and Hauser (1973) published an important monograph on the subject. The novel feature of their study was that they did not use the information on death certificates to assess people's social class or even their age. Instead, they matched the death certificates of individuals who died between May and August 1960 to US census data so that (a) information about the deceased and the full population would come from the same source (census) and (b) differential mortality with respect to education and income, in addition to occupation, could be examined. At the time of publication, their results were the most definitive available for the United States. In white and non-white males and females aged 25–64, there was a clear pattern of lower age-adjusted mortality rates with each increment in education. The same inverse relationship was observed between age-adjusted mortality rates and family income in white males and females aged 25–64. Even when adjusted for education, at least half of the income differential in mortality rates remained, and vice versa when the mortality rates were adjusted for income. This study also found a general, though not perfectly monotonic, inverse association in white males aged 25–64 between age-adjusted mortality and major occupational groups ranked roughly according to social status. Overall, this study supported the conclusion that there is an SES gradient in mortality across the entire SES distribution.

Some of the best evidence that mortality risk and the risk of cardiovascular disease increase steadily as one moves down the SES ladder comes from the Whitehall I Study of British civil servants (Marmot et al., 1984). This study followed 18,000 male civil servants, aged 40–64, all of whom had secure office-based jobs in and around London. Participants were classified into one of four categories, based on the civil service "grade" (ranking) of their position: (a) top administrative, (b) professional or executive, (c) clerical, and (d) other (for example, messengers, doormen). As shown in figure 24.1, a smooth gradient in mortality rates emerged within just a few years (Marmot et al., 1984) and the differences from one grade to the next have persisted as the cohort has continued to be followed (Marmot et al., 1995). Thus, even when looking at only a single industry (i.e. government), one in which employees are not exposed to absolute poverty, industrial accidents, or toxic substances in the workplace, there are clear differences in age-adjusted mortality risk among those in different non-manual occupational positions. We might expect the SES gradient to be even larger among private sector employees than among public sector employees. This study also shows that these differences are not due to differences in just one or two major causes of death, but exist for almost every major cause (Marmot et al., 1984). While smoking, obesity, and elevated blood pressure were all more common in the lower social grades, statistically controlling for these and other risk factors reduced the estimated differences in coronary heart disease mortality among the four grades by less than 25 percent (Marmot et al.,

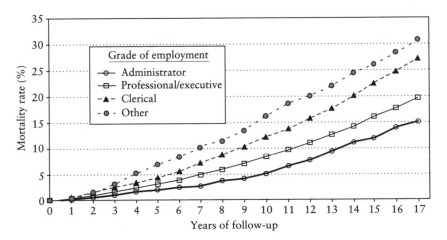

Figure 24.1 Mortality from all causes by year of follow-up and grade of employment, male civil servants, initially aged 40–64.

Source: M. G. Marmot and M. G. Shipley, Whitehall I Study, unpublished.

1984, 1995). Similar results have been reported in several other large epidemiological studies (see review by Kaplan and Keil, 1993).

In the United States, the National Longitudinal Mortality Study (NLMS; Sorlie et al., 1992) is a large ongoing study of mortality. A sample of nearly 1.3 million individuals of all ages was identified between 1978 and 1985 and basic physical and demographic data, including education, occupation, and income, were obtained. Using the National Death Index, the complete sample is being followed prospectively for deaths. The nine-year follow-up data became available in 1995 (Release 2, October 1, 1995) and can be used to examine the SES gradient and update the earlier analyses of Kitagawa and Hauser (1973) and others. Figures 24.2 and 24.3 show my estimates of the age-adjusted mortality ratios for different education and income groups, based on Cox proportional hazards regression analyses of all employed, 18–64 year old, men ($N = 162,216$) and women ($N = 128,865$) in the NLMS. The SES gradient is clear, and similar in magnitude to that reported by Kitagawa and Hauser (1973).

There are many potential explanations for why lower SES individuals, especially the poor, might be at increased risk for a variety of diseases and have a shorter life expectancy: more crowded living arrangements, poorer sanitary conditions, poorer diet, poorer access to medical care, access to poorer quality medical care, and differential rates of various health-related behaviors (for example, cigarette smoking, excessive alcohol consumption, and lack of regular physical exercise). It is less clear why those with average levels of education or income should be at higher risk than those with above average levels.

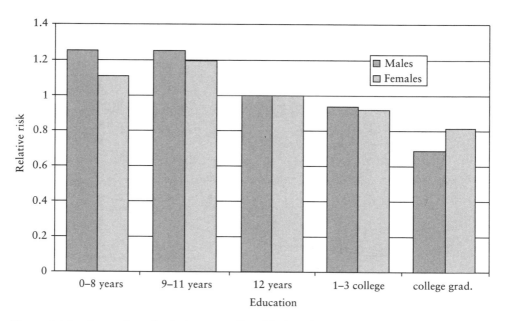

Figure 24.2 Age-adjusted relative mortality risk, by education category (reference is 12 years of education).

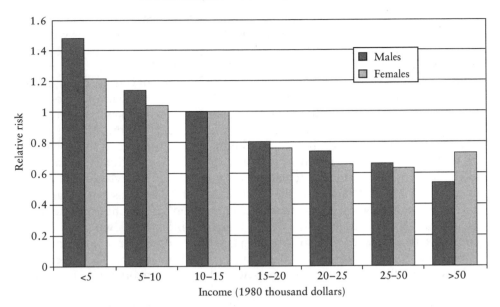

Figure 24.3   Age-adjusted relative mortality risk, by income category (reference is $10,000–15,000).

Areal Measures of Social Class

The preceding discussion has focused on individual level measures of SES: education, occupation, grade of employment, and income. However, there is a long tradition of treating geographic areas (nations, states, counties, neighborhoods, census tracts) as the unit of analysis and investigating whether SES differences – for example, in average education, average income, or average price of housing – predict differences in mortality rates. Historically, areal measures of SES were used as a proxy measure for the SES of individuals living in that area when individual level data on SES, mortality, and morbidity were unavailable. In most analyses, poorer SES areas have been found to have higher mortality rates. For example, Kitagawa and Hauser (1973) assigned each census tract in Chicago to one of five socioeconomic groups based on median family income in the US 1950 and 1960 censuses, and found that both infant mortality rates and age-adjusted all-cause mortality rates were highest in the lowest SES group of tracts, and next highest in the second lowest SES tracts. This pattern held for males and females, whites and non-whites, and, for all-cause mortality, in those under age 65 and those 65 and over. There were only slight differences among the three highest SES groupings of census tracts.

A small number of studies have simultaneously estimated the effects of individual-level and community-level measures of SES and found that the community-level measures have an independent effect over and above that of the individual-level measures. Using data from the Alameda County Study, Haan et al. (1987) found that after controlling for age, sex, race, baseline health in

1965, and any of four measures of individual's SES (education, income, employment status, or access to medical care), Oakland, California, residents who lived in federally designated "poverty areas" had an approximately 50 percent greater risk of dying during the subsequent nine years, 1965–74.

On a national scale, Anderson et al. (1997) merged census tract median income into the NLMS data set and found, for 25–64 year old black and white males and females, that while individuals' family incomes were more strongly related to mortality than median census tract income, the latter also had an independent and sizable effect. The increase in mortality risk associated with living in a low-income census tract was about twice as great for blacks (49 and 30 percent for male and female blacks) as it was for whites (26 and 16 percent for male and female whites). These results, like those of Haan et al. (1987), strongly suggest that there are contextual or neighborhood factors that increase the mortality risk of even high SES individuals who live in low-income areas. However, it also shows that, within any given area, those with higher income are at lower risk than those with low income. Together, these results suggest that both absolute income and relative income affect mortality risk.

There are several aspects of the physical and social environment that might contribute to an association between neighborhood SES and poor health. Air and water quality may be poorer in lower SES areas. Poor neighborhoods are often located in or near industrial areas, landfills, and toxic dumps for two reasons: (a) real estate in such areas is often less expensive, making it more affordable to lower SES families; and (b) poor neighborhoods usually have fewer political resources with which to resist the nearby location of polluting industries or dumping. The quantity and quality of available health care services also tend to be poorer in low SES areas.

Income Inequality and Mortality

At one level the question of whether there is too much or too little income inequality is largely a question of values and personal philosophy. Those who argue that there is an inherent conflict between those who have and those who do not have power, status, wealth, and control over the means of production usually view the existing income distribution as inequitable and unjust, imposed by the powerful on the powerless. In contrast, others view income inequality as reflecting differential rewards in a competition that is fundamentally fair – with better qualified or more productive individuals receiving higher incomes – and just. To my knowledge, no sociological or economic theory can adequately explain cross-national differences in income differentials. For example, why is it that salary differentials, and therefore income inequality, are substantially smaller in Scandinavian countries and Japan than in the United Kingdom and United States? These differences in inequality are even greater when one examines after-tax income. Even if there is a substantial consensus that some inequality is legitimate, there may be very little consensus on how much inequality is appropriate. The question of how much inequality is desirable and how much is too much is largely a matter of opinion, and individuals' opinions are likely to vary according to their relative position in the distribution.

But regardless of personal, or even collective, values, is there any evidence that the degree of income inequality matters? Using international data from a variety of sources, Wilkinson (1986, 1990, 1992) has pioneered the investigation of this question with respect to health, life expectancy, and mortality. First, it has been shown that while there is a very substantial association between per capita gross national product (GNP) and life expectancy in developing countries, this relationship is relatively modest for developed countries. Wilkinson (1992, p. 165) reported a correlation of 0.38 based on 1986–7 data for 23 Organization of Economic Cooperation and Development (OECD) countries and noted that changes in per capita GNP and changes in life expectancy during the preceding 16 years were uncorrelated ($r = 0.07$). In contrast, using various sources of data and various measures of inequality, he and others have found substantial correlations, in excess of 0.80, between inequality and both mortality (positive association) and life expectancy (negative correlation). Data from the Luxembourg Income Study for nine OECD countries exhibited correlations of 0.80 or higher between life expectancy and the percentage of income received by the bottom 60, 70, or 80 percent of the population (the higher the proportion, the less unequal the income distribution).

Within the Unites States, Kaplan et al. (1996) and Kennedy et al. (1996) have demonstrated that a variety of different measures of inequality (the Gini coefficient, the Robin Hood index, and the percentage of total income received by those at or below the median income) are all correlated 0.50 or greater with age-adjusted state mortality rates. The more unequal a state's distribution of income is, the higher that state's mortality rate tends to be. Kaplan et al. found that the correlation was highest ($r = 0.74$) when predicting mortality rates among those aged 25–64. Controlling for median state income (both articles) and proportion of the population having incomes below the federal poverty level (Kennedy et al., 1996) did not substantially alter the raw correlations. This is critical because if those states with greater income inequality were poorer or had higher poverty rates, their higher mortality rates might be attributable to the usual SES gradient.

These studies indicate that it is not simply poverty *per se* that increases mortality risk, at least in economically advanced societies. The authors, including Wilkinson, suggest that relative economic well being may be more important than absolute levels. However, it is possible that not only the relatively deprived but also those in the middle of the income distribution are at higher risk of death if they live in a less equal society. This possibility could be tested in a data set, such as the NLMS, that contains individual mortality data if appropriate aggregate measures of average income and income inequality were added.

Perhaps the most intriguing evidence supporting a causal relationship between economic inequality and mortality comes from longitudinal analyses examining *changes* in income distribution (Wilkinson, 1992). In an analysis of 12 European Community countries, increases between 1975 and 1985 in the proportion of the population living on less than half the national average disposable income, a cutpoint commonly used to define *relative* poverty, were strongly associated with smaller increases in life expectancy ($r = -0.73$). From a graph of the results (Wilkinson, 1992, p. 166, figure 3), it appears that over this ten-year period, a change of 4 percent in the proportion living in relative poverty is associated with about a one-year change in life expectancy for the entire population. In a second analysis of six OECD countries, increases in the percentage of total disposable income received by the bottom three quintiles (the bottom 60 percent of the population) were strongly associated with increases in life expectancy ($r = 0.80$). While the proportion of income received by the bottom 60 percent increased by more than 2 percnet during the 1970s in Japan, the life expectancy was increasing by almost 3.5 years. During the same period, the proportion of income received by the bottom 60 percent decreased by about 1 percent in Great Britain while the life expectancy increased by about two years. The notion that redistribution of as little as 3 percent of income might result in an increase of 1.5 to 2.0 years in life expectancy for the entire population is certainly provocative. Further research is necessary to ascertain which segments of the population – for example, which age groups and which SES groups – would see the greatest changes in life expectancy.

Kawachi et al. (1999) have integrated components of several sociological literatures to propose a model hypothesizing that the amount of absolute deprivation (poverty, unemployment), relative deprivation (inequality), and social disorganization (lack of social cohesion) in a community jointly influence the rates of violent and property crimes, poor health, and the age-adjusted mortality rate of the community. Using aggregate, state-level data from several sources, they had shown previously (Kawachi et al., 1997) that differences in income inequality among states are closely related to the percentage of residents who endorsed the following statements: "most people would try to take advantage of you if they got a chance," "you can't be too careful in dealing with people," and "people mostly look out for themselves" (all $r > 0.70$) in the 1986–90 General Social Survey. They interpret such statements of cynicism and mistrust as indicators of a relative lack of social cohesion, or social capital, and suggest that this may play a mediating role in the relationship between income inequality and mortality. Such analyses might help to explicate the social processes underlying previous macrosociological investigations of the consequences of social inequality (Blau and Blau, 1982; Blau and Schwartz, 1984).

I conclude this section with two comments. First, if the degree of economic inequality influences the social cohesion, crime rates, and even disease morbidity rates and life expectancy of a society, then significant social costs (what economists call "externalities") accompany the presumed economic benefits of a free market economy. In such a case, the issue of how much income inequality is appropriate should no longer be primarily a philosophical or economics question, but rather a political question that concerns the well-being and public health of the entire populace.

Second, much research remains to be done before we will understand how it is that income inequality can affect individuals' health, mortality risk, and life expectancy. If we consider the substantial increase in income inequality that occurred in the United States and several other West European nations during the last part of the twentieth century, it is clear that this was the conscious result of political decisions to reduce barriers to individuals and companies accumulating great wealth, while simultaneously increasing the risk of unemployment and a decline in income to the majority. In short, opportunities for greater success were accompanied by a net loss of economic security. As a result of becoming more competitive, there has been an increase in both the number of "winners" and the number of "losers," accompanied by an overall decrease in public concern for the well-being of the losers. I would suggest that collective economic security is an important determinant of social cohesion. Furthermore, an unintended consequence of increased competition is increased psychosocial stress, not only for the "losers," but for almost everyone who plays the game.

This brings us to the major transition point of the chapter. Thus far, I have presented some of the evidence showing that SES and income inequality are related to health and longevity. I have also indicated some of the macro- and micro-level factors that probably mediate this relationship. Interested readers should know that there are substantial literatures on the relationships of SES to diet and other known health-related behaviors, and a smaller literature examining the contribution of access to medical care to the SES gradient in mortality (for example, Kogevinas, 1991; Mackenbach et al., 1989). However, in the remainder of the chapter I review evidence that psychosocial stress plays a role in the etiology of several diseases. While I believe that a better understanding of the effects of stress on health will eventually help us to explain the SES gradient, I will not try to make this argument here.

STRESS AND ILLNESS

The belief that psychological or mental stress is a contributing factor to several diseases is widespread. Though all of us have experienced stress or felt stressed on multiple occasions, there is not a single, widely accepted definition of stress. Stress is often brought about by life events or situations, called stressors, but it can also result from contemplating past situations or anticipating future situations. Some of the more widely used questionnaires for assessing major and minor life events are the Schedule of Recent Experiences (Holmes and Rahe, 1967), the Life Experiences Survey (Sarason et al., 1978), and the Hassles and Uplifts Scale (Kanner et al., 1981). The Life Events and Difficulties Schedule (Brown and Harris, 1989) is an in-depth interview procedure for assessing the occurrence and significance of adverse events. Chronic situations pertaining to work (for example, heavy work demands, conflict with or lack of support from supervisor or co-workers, job insecurity, role conflict, lack of autonomy), family (marital conflict, financial strain, poor health of a family member), caregiver responsibilities, living in a high-crime neighborhood, and poverty are all associated with increased reports of stress/distress.

Stress is thought to affect health by altering both behavior and physiology. Stress is associated with increased alcohol consumption, increased nicotine consumption, risk of relapse among those who have quit smoking, reduced physical exercise, and adverse dietary changes, each of which increases the risk of multiple diseases and mortality. Nonetheless, most epidemiological studies indicate that changes in these and other health-related behaviors can only account for part of the observed relationship of stress with morbidity and mortality.

There is a great deal of research on the physiological effects of acute stress. While there is substantial variation across individuals and situations in the type and magnitude of response, it is well documented that acute stress is associated with: (a) activation of the sympathetic nervous system which triggers the release of catecholamines (adrenaline and noradrenaline) into the blood stream, which, in turn, increase heart rate and blood pressure (Cacioppo and Tassinary, 1990); (b) activation of the hypothalamic-pituitary-adrenal axis, which regulates the supply of corticosteroids (Kirschbaum and Helhammer, 1989); (c) changes in the number and functioning of various types of immune cells (Kiecolt-Glaser et al., 1992); and (d) gastric functioning (Wolf and Wolff, 1947). However, relatively shortly after exposure to an acute stressor has terminated, the sympathetic nervous system, neuroendocrine system, immune system, and cardiovascular system all return to pre-stress levels of activation. Thus, with one exception, it is not clear that physiological responses to acute stress are relevant to disease processes or mortality.

The exception is the possibility that acute stress may, on rare occasions, trigger a heart attack (myocardial infarction) or stroke. As might be imagined, it is very difficult to rigorously document this phenomenon. It would be nearly impossible to prospectively study enough individuals intensively enough to test whether such cardiovascular (CV) events are more likely to occur during or immediately following an acute stressor than at other times. Nonetheless, despite limitations pertaining to retrospective recall bias, there is evidence from case–control studies that CV morbid events can be triggered by episodes of anger and stress (Mittleman et al., 1995).

If stress plays a significant role in other disease processes, it is almost certainly through exposure to chronic stressors (or persistently repeated exposure to acute stressors). The physiological impact on humans of prolonged exposure to a stressor is less well known because such research cannot ethically be conducted under laboratory conditions. However, observational data indicate reduced immune system functioning following marital separation, divorce, or the death of a spouse, and during unemployment (see reviews by O'Leary, 1990; Herbert and Cohen, 1993). It still remains to be determined whether the observed changes in the immune system are sufficiently large to alter the risk of life-threatening infectious or autoimmune diseases.

Although the mechanisms are not well understood, some of the most convincing evidence of a relationship between stress and illness comes from epidemiological studies of work stress and cardiovascular disease. Excluding studies that have focused on specific occupations (for example, air traffic controllers, teachers, nurses), recent research has focused on two models of work stress, the "job strain" model and the "effort–reward imbalance" model.

According to the job strain (demand-control) model of Karasek et al. (1981), more demanding jobs are assumed to require more effort, but not necessarily to generate distress. Those with decision latitude in their job have greater flexibility to decide how best to meet the demands of their job and are therefore predicted to experience little or no distress. The jobs hypothesized to cause the most distress are those that combine high demands (workload) and low decision latitude, and this combination of job characteristics is labeled "high strain."

Two Swedish studies were the first to report an association in men between job strain and the risk of a heart attack (Karasek et al., 1981; Alfredsson et al., 1982). A US study reported evidence from two separate national health surveys that men in occupations that *other* incumbents rated as high in demands and low in decision latitude were more likely to have had a myocardial infarction (Karasek et al., 1988). There have now been more than twenty studies, with the vast majority showing that those in high strain jobs have a 20–300 percent greater risk of CV disease (reviewed in Belkic et al., 2000).

One plausible mechanism by which job strain may increase CV risk is by gradually increasing employees' resting blood pressures (BPs), eventually leading to the development of hypertension. Using 24–hour ambulatory blood pressure monitoring and controlling for age, body mass, and race/ethnicity, the Work Site Blood Pressure Study found that men in high strain jobs had systolic BPs that were 6–7 mmHg higher, both at work and at home, than those in jobs with high decision latitude or low demands (Schnall et al., 1992). This same pattern was observed when participants were re-evaluated three years later. Particularly interesting was the finding that those classified as having high strain jobs at both evaluations had systolic BPs that were 11 mmHg higher than those in non-high strain jobs on both occasions (Schnall et al., 1998).

Like the demand-control model, the effort–reward imbalance model of Siegrist (Matschinger et al., 1986; Siegrist et al., 1990; Siegrist, 1996) has two dimensions. It is hypothesized that the combination of high effort and low reward is pathogenic. Occupational rewards include aspects of control such as job stability and promotion prospects, as well as wages, fringe benefits, and status consistency. The combination of high effort and low reward has been found to predict heart attacks (Siegrist et al., 1990).

A common feature of these and several other models of stress is the importance of control. Whether a demanding situation is experienced as a challenge or a stressor may well depend on the degree of control and flexibility the individual has in determining how best to fulfill the demands. It is important to realize that control is both a personality characteristic (as in locus of control, sense of mastery) and a situational factor. Jobs vary enormously in the degree of control incumbents have over how to perform their tasks. In the Whitehall II Study, a second longitudinal study of a large cohort of British civil servants, low control at work was able to account for more of the SES gradient in new cases of coronary heart disease (over five years) than any other factor, including the traditional risk factors (Marmot et al., 1997). In this same data set, the effort–reward model predicted coronary heart disease better than the job strain model (Bosma et al., 1998).

Are the Effects of Stressors Psychologically Mediated?

Most models of stress and health tacitly assume that (a) stressors cause an emotional response (stress), (b) stress causes physiological changes in the body, and (c) these physiological changes contribute to morbidity and mortality (pathway ACD in figure 24.4). A major implication of this model is that if one can intervene at the second stage – for example, by teaching individuals stress management skills – one should be able to reduce the health consequences of a stressful environment. A less obvious implication is that if, for some reason, an individual does not become stressed by a situation that others find stressful, then he or she should not exhibit a physiological response. However, it is worth considering the possibility that environmental stressors can directly impact physiology (pathway BD in figure 24.4; see LeDoux, 1996), and that part of the association between emotions and physiology is spurious. This is consistent with the finding of Feldman et al. (2000) that emotional responses to acute stressors were not substantially correlated with cardiovascular (blood pressure and heart rate) responses. Perhaps job strain/stress is bad even for those who do not experience their jobs as stressful. If so, it would probably be more effective to alter work environments than to alter how individuals respond to these environments.

Animal Models of Stress

Sociologists interested in the role of stress on health should not ignore the findings from well controlled experimental studies of animals. Many animal researchers have used electric shock as a stressor. In one experiment, paired rats were exposed to shocks (Weiss, 1972). One member of each pair had no control over the situation, whereas the other could avoid the shock by pressing its nose to a panel. The rats with no control had higher levels of circulating cortisol and developed more gastric lesions than those rats who could avoid the shocks. Using this same stress paradigm, exposure to unavoidable shock

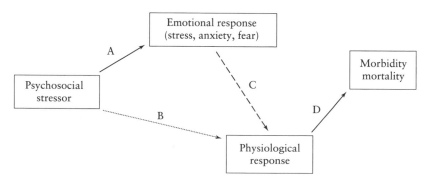

Figure 24.4   Two models of the linkage from psychosocial stressors to morbidity and mortality.

has been shown to suppress several parameters of the immune system and promote tumor growth, leading investigators to conclude that lack of control, or helplessness, alters the physiological response to a stressor (see review by Shavit, 1991).

In an extensive program of research on cynomolgus monkeys, Kaplan, Manuck, and collaborators have investigated the impact of social stability, experimentally manipulated, on dominant and non-dominant monkeys (Kaplan et al., 1982, 1991). In the socially stable condition, three sets of five male monkeys lived together for 22 months. In the unstable condition, 15 males were rotated among three cages 14 times during the 22 months. Much more overt conflict was observed among monkeys in the unstable condition, because the dominance hierarchy had to be re-established every 4–12 weeks. At the end of the 22 months, the coronary arteries of the dominant monkeys in the unstable condition were found to have substantially greater atherosclerosis than those of the dominant animals in the socially stable condition and the subordinate animals in either stability condition.

Animal research can also be used to identify factors that protect against the effects of stress. In a fascinating program of research at McGill University, Meaney and his colleagues have demonstrated that the amount of licking and grooming behavior of a mother mouse toward her newborn pups permanently alters brain physiology. Those pups who experience more licking and grooming (LG+) during the first three weeks of life develop a faster-acting negative feedback mechanism (relative to pups receiving less licking and grooming), causing plasma levels of the stress hormone cortisol to return to normal more quickly following the termination of a stressor. As adults, the LG+ mice are less fearful in new environments, are less reactive to a loud noise, and exhibit less hippocampal neuron loss and fewer spatial memory deficits at later ages (Meaney et al., 1991; Liu et al., 1997). Subsequent research has shown that this effect varies across genetic strains of mice, such that maternal licking and grooming (LG) matters more in genetically vulnerable strains, and matters very little in genetically hardy strains (Anisman et al., 1998).

Most recently, Meaney's group has conducted an elegant series of studies documenting a high degree of consistency in the LG behavior of mothers from one litter to the next and a high degree of intergenerational transmission of LG behavior (i.e. a high correlation between the LG behavior of mothers and that of their grown daughters). They then demonstrated that by having the daughter of a low-LG mother be raised by a high-LG mother, the daughter would grow up to become a high-LG mother herself *and* her daughters would also become high-LG mothers (Francis and Meaney, 1999). Similarly, through a manipulation involving handling of the pups, the researchers were able to make the naturally low-LG mothers engage in high levels of LG, which was also transmitted intergenerationally. These studies document that early social environment has profound and permanent effects on a mouse's stress physiology, that effects that might well be assumed to be genetically transmitted are in fact socially/behaviorally transmitted across generations, and that a psychosocial intervention can foster health-promoting behavior in mothers which is then transmitted to future generations. At this point, we can only speculate about possible parallels with parenting behavior towards newborn human infants.

Collectively, these and other studies have begun to document a variety of physiological pathways by which stress(ors) may promote the development of, or alter one's vulnerability to, disease. Current research is investigating the contribution of these pathways to observed associations between chronic stress exposure and illness in humans (for example, the association of work stress with blood pressure and cardiovascular disease). At a more general level, there is increased interest in trying to estimate the extent to which stress and other psychosocial factors can explain the association of socioeconomic status with morbidity and mortality.

25

Two Research Traditions in the Sociology of Education

Maureen T. Hallinan

The field of sociology of education is primarily a product of twentieth-century scholarship. The roots of the discipline may be traced to the late nineteenth- and early twentieth-century writings of Weber, Durkheim, Waller, and Parsons. Building on the theoretical foundation laid by these sociologists, a rich and comprehensive body of knowledge has accumulated over the past century about the institution of education and its role in society.

In this chapter, I illustrate research in the sociology of education by examining two research traditions in which systematic scholarship has accumulated over the past several decades. For each area I discuss theoretical and empirical studies, including both basic and applied work. I highlight these two traditions because they include conceptually rich and analytically rigorous research and because they encompass studies that are particularly relevant for contemporary American education. The areas are the organizational analysis of schools and the transition from school to work.

THE ORGANIZATIONAL ANALYSIS OF SCHOOLS

Conceptual Models of School Organization

Bidwell's (1965) seminal work on the school as a formal organization laid the foundation for a large body of research by sociologists of education on the organizational analysis of schools. Relying on Weber's (1946) description of a bureaucracy, Bidwell depicted the school as possessing characteristics of a bureaucracy, including a functional division of labor, staff roles defined as offices, a hierarchical arrangement of positions, and a set of rules of procedure. At the same time, Bidwell emphasized that schools, in contrast to other organizations, possessed a "structural looseness" in the relationships among their various components.

Early studies of school effects were based on an organizational perspective on schools. Coleman et al.'s (1966) landmark study on equality of educational opportunity estimated an input–output model of schools in which variation in school resources and student characteristics predicted student achievement. This input–output model failed to specify the mechanisms that linked organizational resources to student outputs and hence became known as the "black box" model. While research in this genre accomplished little in terms of explaining the processes that affect learning, it did contribute important insights into schooling. Not the least of these insights was demonstrated in the Coleman Report, namely that family background plays a predominant role in student achievement and must be considered along with the resources of schools when studying school effects.

In an effort to specify more precisely how schools affect student achievement, researchers in the late 1970s and 1980s focused on the processes that produce learning. A recognition of the importance of the context of learning led to the formulation of a "nested layers" model of school organization. From this perspective, the outputs at one level of the organization become the inputs to another level. For example, Gamoran and Dreeben (1986) discussed how resource allocation affected teaching. They described the way school officials disperse time to teachers who, in turn, make decisions about the use of time for pedagogical purposes. Teachers allocate time in various ways, such as distributing it across instructional groups, and ultimately dispense it to the individual student. Several empirical studies utilized the nested layers perspective as researchers focused on how resource allocation affected curriculum coverage and student learning (Bidwell and Kasarda, 1980; Alexander and Cook, 1982; Barr and Dreeben, 1983; Rowan and Miracle, 1983; Gamoran, 1987).

Once educational researchers conceptualized learning as a process that links student achievement to the allocation of resources within a school, they quickly expanded the nested layers model to include a number of other factors that channel learning opportunities to students. They focused on such factors as school climate, teacher characteristics, pedagogical practices, classroom interactions, and the content and organization of the curriculum. Many of these factors are interrelated; hence the model of schools as loosely structured organizations sheds light on these school processes.

Expanding Bidwell's notion of the "structural looseness" of school organization, Meyer and Rowan (1988) argued that schools are tightly coupled with respect to the assignment of teachers to students, but loosely coupled with respect to the content of instruction and pedagogical practices. Further, they characterized organizations not as open or closed systems that are internally independent of their social context, but as derived from and dependent upon their wider institutional environment.

Building on both the nested layers and the loosely coupled models of school organization, Gamoran et al. (2000) formulated a model of school organization that depicts organizational resources as the context for teaching and learning.

Assuming that teaching is the primary determinant of learning, they focus on the interactive relationship between the organizational context of the school and teaching. This conceptualization can encompass different views of teaching and various connections between the teacher and other members of the school organization. It informs the analysis of various aspects of instruction, including the professional role of teachers, curriculum standards, performance assessment, staff mobility, teacher morale, and student behavior.

Empirical Analyses of Organizational Effects of Schools

Using one or more of these models of school organization as a conceptual framework, researchers have conducted numerous empirical studies focusing on student outcomes. One organizational feature of schools that has attracted considerable attention over the past two decades is the organization of students for instruction. Aware that opportunities to learn are related to exposure to the curriculum and that the content of the curriculum can vary across groups of students, researchers have investigated how students are assigned to instructional groups and the consequences of these assignments. A large, systematic body of empirical research and literature has emerged on this topic.

Since most middle and secondary schools and a large number of elementary schools assign students to instructional groups on the basis of cognitive ability, much of the empirical research on the organization of students for instruction has focused on the determinants and consequences of ability grouping. Research has also focused on the process of assigning students to classes or groups on the basis of gender, age, and substantive interest.

In elementary schools, students typically are assigned to small, homogeneous ability groups for instruction in reading and often also in mathematics. In middle and high school, ability grouping may take the form of tracking in which students are assigned to an academic, general, or vocational curriculum. Recently, tracking has been replaced in most schools by course-based ability grouping, with students being assigned to advanced, honors, regular, or basic courses in English and mathematics, and often in other subjects as well. The courses differ somewhat in content and significantly in pace of instruction and depth of coverage.

Research on the determinants of ability group formation identify school and class size as factors largely determining the size and number of ability groups in a school. Examining within-class ability groups in elementary schools, researchers (Barr and Dreeban, 1983; Hallinan and Sorensen, 1983) found that regardless of the size or ability distribution of the class, teachers tended to form three ability groups of fairly equal size. Moreover, membership in these groups tended to remain stable over the school year. A reason for this identifiable pattern may be found in constraints on the availability of resources, including textbooks and other materials and space.

A number of studies identify factors that govern the assignment of students to ability groups at the elementary, middle, and secondary school levels. Some schools adhere to a policy of assignment based strictly on academic rank, as determined by grades or standardized test scores (Hallinan, 1994a). Other schools also rely on teacher evaluations of students' attitudes, motivation, aspirations, and behaviors (Cicourel and Kitsuse, 1963; Rosenbaum, 1976; Oakes, 1985). Rist's (1970) study of elementary students found that teachers placed students into ability groups based on their command of Standard American English, their appearance, and their ease of interaction with adults, in addition to their ability. Other studies have found that characteristics such as gender, socioeconomic status, age, and race play a role in determining a student's ability group level (Oakes, 1985; Hallinan, 1992, 1994a). Finally, some schools create more heterogeneous groups for various reasons, including efforts to insure demographic diversity in each group (Hallinan and Sorensen, 1983).

Many researchers have been concerned with possible discrimination in the assignment of students to ability groups. Most of the studies examining the effects of race, ethnicity, and gender, or ability group assignments, show a weak effect of ascribed characteristics on level of assignment (Patchen, 1982; Sorensen and Hallinan, 1984; Vanfossen et al., 1987; Oakes, 1990; Hoffer and Kamens, 1992; Kubitschek and Hallinan, 1996). For example, controlling for ability and performance (Kubitschek and Hallinan, 1996), non-whites are slightly more likely than whites to be assigned to lower level ability groups and females are more likely than males to be assigned to higher English groups.

Other studies have examined whether ability group assignments are fixed for a semester or year or whether students can change group level if desired (Rosenbaum, 1976; Eder, 1981; Hallinan and Sorensen, 1985; Oakes, 1985; Gamoran, 1989, 1992; Hallinan, 1990, 1996). These studies indicate that ability group mobility is a fairly frequent occurrence, at least at the secondary level. Moreover, change in ability group assignment varies by student background characteristics. Hallinan (1996) showed that males are more likely to be reassigned to a higher mathematics track than females, but less likely to be moved to a higher English track.

The main finding of this body of research is that ability grouping has significant effects on student achievement. Comparing the achievement of students in schools that group students homogeneously by ability to that of students in the few schools with heterogeneous grouping shows no direct effect of ability grouping on student achievement at the elementary (Slavin, 1987) or secondary (Slavin, 1990) levels. However, when student achievement is compared across ability groups, the results show that students assigned to higher ability groups have higher achievement than those assigned to lower groups, controlling for ability and past achievement (Rosenbaum, 1967; Alexander and McDill, 1976; Oakes, 1985; Kerckhoff, 1986; Gamoran, 1987; Vanfossen et al., 1987). Further, Hallinan (2000) found that assigning a student to a higher ability group than indicated by standardized test scores – that is, "mis-assigning" a student – results in greater growth in achievement than assignment to the "correct" group. The effects of ability group level on student achievement are robust across age, grade, school sector, subject area, and school characteristics.

These findings have led to considerable debate over the educational value of ability grouping. Proponents claim that ability grouping benefits higher achieving students. Moreover, while ability grouping may be detrimental to low ability students, improved instruction and a more interesting curriculum in low ability classes should rectify this inequity. Proponents also argue that the association of race, ethnicity, and gender with ability group placement can be eliminated by careful assignment practices (for a review of these arguments, see Hallinan, 1994b). Opponents of ability grouping claim that since ability grouping disadvantages the low achiever, it should be replaced by heterogeneous grouping to insure that all students have an equal opportunity to learn (Oakes, 1985, 1994). They argue that all students benefit from heterogeneous grouping because diversity stimulates learning (Good and Marshall, 1984; Mason and Good, 1993). Finally, critics of ability grouping state that the practice is embedded in a normative, cultural, and political context which makes eradicating the inequities of ability grouping impossible without eliminating the practice (Oakes, 1985, 1994). This debate continues to be played out in school districts across the country as educators evaluate the effects of ability grouping on student performance.

Organizational Characteristics of Schools and Student Cognitive and Social Outcomes

A second dimension of Bidwell's analysis of the school as a formal organization focused on the socialization function of schools. Bidwell argued that social psychological processes governing student interactions in school play a major role in socializing students to learning and to social behavior. In a recent analysis, Bidwell (2000) claimed that sociologists of education have not paid enough attention to the way school context affects student socialization. Researchers have focused primarily on how individual characteristics of students affect their academic achievement, educational aspirations, educational attainment, and occupational status. A primary example of this individualistic orientation is the psychological model of status attainment (Sewell and Hauser, 1980).

Some sociologists of education have examined contextual influences on students' educational and social outcomes. These studies have addressed three questions. First, how do peer groups influence student achievement and social behavior? Second, what is the effect of the formal organization of the school on student academic performance and social relations? Third, how does school or classroom climate affect student outcomes?

Peer Group Influences on Student Outcomes

Early writings of Waller (1932), Hollingshead (1949), Gordon (1957), Coleman (1961), Newcomb (1961), and Whyte (1967) focused primarily on peer influences in school. They described students' social interactions and the emergence of peer groups or cliques and student subcultures. They argue that peer groups develop a set of norms that govern the academic and social behavior of their members. These norms may support teachers' efforts to instruct students or may conflict with educational goals. Other early studies by Hollingshead (1949), Coleman (1961), and Newcomb (1961) identify the ascribed and achieved characteristics of students, including social class, athletic ability, and physical attractiveness, that qualify them for membership in a social clique.

More recent studies of student social groups, by Cusick (1973), Roistacher (1973), Cohen (1977), and Eder (1981), demonstrate that clique membership affects a student's attitudes, values, social status, and adherence to group norms. Moreover, cliques with different values, norms, and interests may coexist in the same school, and may have a differential impact on student academic and social behavior. In most of these studies, peer influences are explained by social psychological theories of normative and comparative reference groups, social exchange, role modeling, and labeling.

A number of survey analyses reveal the consequences of peer influences for student achievement (Spilerman, 1971; Felmlee et al., 1985; Schunk and Hanson, 1985; Mounts and Steinberg, 1995; Wentzel and Caldwell, 1997). These studies identify a number of these peer effects. Peers influence a student's choice of courses, time spent on homework, and engagement in classroom interaction. Students join with peers to exert pressure on teachers to negotiate grades, homework, and tests in exchange for class attendance and appropriate behavior. Peers have an impact on a student's motivation, effort, and attitudes toward school, which have immediate consequences for academic performance. Peers influence a student's educational aspirations, choice of college and educational attainment. Finally, peers affect a student's tendency to engage in deviant behavior, to be truant, and to drop out of school.

Effects of Organizational Context on School Outcomes

A few studies have examined the effects of the formal organization of the school or classroom on student cognitive and social outcomes. Bossert (1979) found that an elementary school classroom in which student competition was stressed had a wider achievement distribution than a classroom in which cooperative activities were encouraged. Schofield and Sagar (1977) showed that when middle-school classrooms were detracked, blacks and whites were more likely to mix socially. The organizational effects on student achievement observed in these studies are attributed to the influence of normative and comparative reference groups, though these mechanisms are not tested directly.

Studies also show the effects of the organization of a school or classroom on student peer relations and friendships. Students assigned to the same class or ability group are exposed to the same curriculum, share academic experiences, and usually work together on common projects. The propinquity and similarity imposed by membership in the same ability group encourages friendship. Moreover, student friendships that form within the boundaries of an instructional or social grouping in school are more likely to endure than those that form across organizational units.

Several empirical studies demonstrate how school and classroom context affect the likelihood that students become and remain friends. Hallinan and Sorensen (1985) found that assigning students to the same ability group increased the likelihood of their becoming friends and of forming cliques. In another study, Hallinan (1976) demonstrated that student-centered classrooms that encouraged student interaction had a less hierarchized distribution of friendship choices and fewer social isolates and sociometric leaders than teacher-centered classrooms with little student interaction. Similarly, Felmlee and Hallinan (1979) found that the greater the amount of peer interaction in a classroom, the more uniformly distributed are the students' friendship choices.

Organizational features of schools affect the likelihood of cross-race as well as same-race friendships (Hallinan and Teixeira, 1987; Hallinan and Williams, 1987, 1989). The interpersonal mechanisms that lead to same-race friendships, including propinquity, similarity, complementarity, and reciprocity, also govern cross-race friendships. Students of different races are more likely to become friends when they belong to the same group. In addition, when a school climate supports cross-race friendships and encourages cooperative behavior, and when school practices and policies reward students with various talents from all racial groups, cross-race friendships are likely to form. Hence, racially mixed academic or social groups are likely to promote cross-race friendships, while more segregated groups are likely to deter them.

Effects of School Climate on Student Outcomes

In one of the earliest studies of the effects of school climate on behavior, Coleman (1961) described a strong adolescent subculture in which boys esteem athletics, girls value beauty, and both respect academic achievement. Athletes, cheerleaders, and high academic achievers were more popular than their peers. The adolescent subculture affected pupils' self-image and achievement. Cusick (1973) portrayed a large public high school in which several cliques with different subcultures coexisted and exerted differential effects on student academic performance.

Following these studies, a number of survey analyses were conducted to examine the effects of school climate on student achievement. In the aftermath of mandatory school desegregation, researchers examined how the racial composition of a school (viewed as an indicator of academic climate or social class) affected student outcomes (for reviews of early empirical studies, see Spady, 1973; Crain and Mahard, 1978). The findings typically showed that black students attained higher achievement in majority white schools. Other studies show that the normative climate of a school, referred to as "environmental press" (Thistlewaite and Wheeler, 1966), influenced a student's aspirations, achievement, college plans, and career goals. In general, the research indicates that the stronger the academic climate of a school, the higher the academic outcomes.

While the interest of researchers in contextual effects on student outcomes declined in the 1980s and early 1990s, a study of public and private schools refocused attention on context as a socializing agent. In a comparison of public and private school achievement, Coleman et al. (1983) found that Catholic school students had higher academic achievement than public school students. Attempting to explain this Catholic school advantage, Bryk et al. (1993) analyzed both survey and observational data on Catholic schools. They concluded that the higher achievement of Catholic school students was due to a supportive communal school atmosphere, a common academic curriculum, and high educational expectations for all students.

Bryk et al. argue that Catholic school students participate in a voluntary community which provides personal support from peers who share a common commitment to the school's mission of working for social justice and the common good. This commitment leads students and teachers to attach greater value to education than they would if they were in a school without a communal environment and shared mission. Bryk et al. claim that any school that emphasizes community values and/or provides a moral or ethical context should improve student learning. Their study should motivate further research on how school context affects student behavior in order to identify ways public schools might create a community environment more supportive of students and of the school's educational goals.

In general, conceptualizing the school as a formal and informal organization has yielded a rich body of research that explains how schools operate in society. The theoretical ideas that motivated empirical research on organizational characteristics of schools and their effects on students' cognitive and social behavior provided an intellectual coherence to this research and allowed systematic progress to be made. This research tradition remains one of the most robust in the field of sociology of education.

TRANSITION FROM SCHOOL TO WORK

Since the main function of schooling is to prepare students to live effectively in adult society, the transition from school to work is of central interest to sociologists of education. The study of this transition has developed along two parallel lines. One body of research examines characteristics of US schools and the US labor market and how they facilitate or constrain the transition process. The other body of work compares the structural and organizational features of schools and the labor market in different countries and investigates how institutional differences across countries lead to variation in students' post-secondary opportunities.

Research on the transition from school to work may be located in a larger body of sociological research on social stratification and social mobility. Stratification research has described the hierarchical ordering of occupations and professions in society and how individuals are channeled into this stratified labor market. Sociologists of education have contributed to this research by studying the antecedents of educational achievement and attainment and the role these educational outcomes play in the process of social mobility.

Stratification and mobility research has concentrated primarily on individual-level determinants of occupational attainment. In contrast, research on the transition from school to work adopts an institutional perspective and focuses on the way characteristics of schools and of the labor market channel occupational opportunities to individuals leaving school and entering the labor force. The research concentrates on the transition from secondary school to work, but also examines the progression from higher education to an individual's occupational destination.

Transition from School to Work in the United States

High school graduates who do not attend college experience high unemployment, frequent job turnover, and low salaries (Rosenbaum and Kariya, 1989; Borman, 1991). Fewer than half of all high school students who choose not to attend college obtain jobs by the time they graduate, and more than half of these students continue to work the part-time jobs they held during high school (University Consultants, 1978). By the time they are 27 years old, high school graduates will have experienced approximately 4.5 spells of periods of unemployment (Veum and Weiss, 1993).

One reason for the difficult transition from school to work in the United States is the fact that the transition lacks structure. Students are not presented with a set of steps that would lead them to employment. In most comprehensive high schools in the United States, teenagers are offered a wide array of academic, general, and vocational courses. Schools allow students considerable leeway in constructing their high school programs. Graduation requirements include completion of a set of academic courses and a number of electives selected from across the curricular offerings.

The most definitive preparation for future employment is found in a high school's vocational program. Many students take one or more vocational courses out of interest in the area or to prepare for a particular career or occupation. Vocational programs may include various kinds of on-the-job training, such as internships, work-study programs, and summer employment. Some vocational programs lead to licensing in a craft or occupation or award a certificate of competence in a particular area.

Research shows that vocational training in high school increases the likelihood of a student's obtaining a job after graduation and has a positive impact on salary compared to similar students without vocational training (Campbell et al., 1986; Kang and Bishop, 1986). Nevertheless, only a minority of students with vocational training work in occupations that utilize their training (Bishop, 1988). Consequently, while vocational training may ease the transition from school to work for some students, the benefits of vocational education are lost for those students whose training is not utilized.

Other than vocational programs, schools provide little job preparation for students. Only 37 percent of American high schools offer job placement services (Arvey and Faley, 1988). These schools tend to focus on in-school training, such as how to fill out a job application and how to act during an interview, rather than formal outreach procedures to develop job openings.

Similarly, the search of employers for qualified workers is largely unstructured. Employers seldom seek contacts with high schools to identify qualified
candidates to fill their positions. While employers may require a high school
diploma as a job requisite, the diploma provides little information about a
student's job qualifications. Employers tend to ignore high school grades and
test scores in their recruitment efforts. Lacking critical information about students and their skills and preparation for a particular occupation, employers are
not in a position to make the most suitable hire, nor are employment agencies
able to direct students toward appropriate employment.

In the absence of a structured transition from school to work, informal
contacts play a critical role for some students. Granovetter's (1974) classic
research on getting a job has pointed to social contacts as a powerful tool to
expedite a job search. Granovetter showed that weak ties in the form of contacts
with acquaintances and casual friends can be more instrumental in a job search
than strong ties with close friends and relatives.

High school counselors and teachers are strategically located organizationally
to link students to future employers. Since US employers typically do not have
mechanisms to request information from high schools to help them identify
prospective employees, information provided informally by teachers and counselors is particularly useful.

Although not many employers utilize informal social contacts in their
search for new workers, those who do benefit from the help they receive. Bishop
(1993) reported that 5 percent of employers have contacts with schools
which, they claim, are a useful source of productive employees. Students
recruited from schools typically obtain higher status jobs (Holzer, 1995) than
those hired from other sources and earn higher salaries (Rosenbaum and Roy,
1996).

The difficulty that high school students have in obtaining their first job is also
experienced by students who have had some college education. Only half of the
population of students who begin college actually obtain a college degree
(Resnick and Wirt, 1996). Those who fail to graduate from college are often in
an even more difficult position than new high school graduates, with respect to
the job market. They typically receive no special assistance from their colleges in
looking for employment, and employers generally are unaware of students who
drop out of college to seek employment.

Moreover, many students fail to develop marketable skills through their
choice of college or of the courses they select in college. Recent research shows
that students receive little direct help in selecting a college that matches their
abilities and fits their ultimate career goals (Rosenbaum, 1996). As a result,
students often choose a college for which they are ill-prepared and that does not
serve their future needs well. Without proper guidance, college bound students,
especially those with weak academic records, often experience disappointment
and failure in college and drop out without furthering their career objectives
(Schneider and Stevenson, 1999). The negative consequences of poor college
choices are seen most readily in the difficulties these individuals have when they
enter the labor market.

Research in sociology of education has been an important source of information about the challenges and difficulties of entering the labor market directly from school. Studies have documented the weak links in the transition from school to work in the United States, and the consequences of an unstructured transition for students' job opportunities. Supplementing this body of research are a number of comparative studies that shed additional light on the way institutional and organizational characteristics of schools and the labor market affect the transition from school to work.

Cross-national Comparison of Transition from School to Work

Comparative research on stratification and mobility processes shows that while countries tend to be similar in the effects of social origin on occupational attainment, they differ markedly in the effects of educational attainment on job destination. Variation in the effect of educational qualifications on occupational attainment is usually attributed to the degree to which the transition between school and work is structured. In some countries, like Switzerland and Germany, students begin their preparation for the job market early in their school careers and follow clearly specified steps leading them to a specific occupation. In other countries, like the United States and Ireland, the path from school to work is ambiguous, and students follow quite different trajectories toward employment. The studies find that the more structured the transition, the greater the effect of educational attainment on occupational destination.

Several characteristics of industrialized countries affect the transition from school to work. The health of the economy determines the availability of work. The extent to which women participate in the labor market affects competition for jobs. Average level of educational attainment raises the level of skills required of new job holders. In addition to these general influences on the transition process, Kerckhoff (2000) identifies three other factors that directly relate to the structure of the transition from school to work: the degree of stratification of the educational system, the degree of standardization of educational programs, and the degree to which the educational credentials awarded are general academic ones or specialized vocationally relevant ones.

Comparing the structure of the transition to work in France, Germany, Great Britain, and the United States, Kerckhoff (2000) found that Germany is the most structured of the four countries, while the United States is the least structured. In Germany, students are divided as early as fifth grade into one of three curricula, which channel them to higher education, advanced vocational training, or early entrance into the labor market. This division marks students for particular kinds of employment and has a profound effect on their occupational attainment. The United States is characterized by a low degree of curriculum differentiation, despite the existence of tracks, and has virtually no points where educational decisions are irrevocable. As a result, the linkage between educational credentials and positions in the labor market is weak. Kerckhoff shows that countries with more standardized transitions have lower rates of return to full-time school, fewer increases in educational credentials, fewer job changes, and lower rates of early occupational mobility. In short, these countries exhibit a more orderly transition from school to work.

Making a similar comparison between the transition from school to work in the United States and Germany, Mortimer and Kruger (2000) found that the lack of structure in the US transition results in American youth's spending a longer period of time in trial and testing in the labor force than German youth. Americans new to the job market change jobs often in an effort to find a good fit between their skills and the requirements of a position. Similarly, employers view new graduates as an unstable workforce and tend to be unwilling to provide training for them unless or until they have spent a certain amount of time with the same employer. Often Americans react to the dissatisfactions they experience in their first jobs by returning to school to train for a specific occupation or career. Mortimer and Kruger claim that loosening the tight regulation of school-to-work pathways in Germany would make it easier for individuals to change careers or occupations in order to find greater job satisfaction and economic opportunity. Likewise, providing greater integration of school and work in the United States would make schooling more relevant to students, encourage them to attain further educational credentials, and create a better fit between educational training and job requirements.

One of the most ambitious cross-national studies of the transition from school to work was undertaken by Shavit and Muller (2000). Working with researchers from 13 industrialized nations, they investigated the association between educational qualifications and occupational attainment in Australia, Britain, France, Germany, Ireland, Israel, Italy, Japan, the Netherlands, Sweden, Switzerland, Taiwan and the United States. The researchers found marked differences in the degree to which the 13 countries exhibited four institutional features: educational stratification, educational standardization, occupationally specific vocational training, and a low percentage of students obtaining post-secondary education. These institutional characteristics were strong predictors of the strength of the association between educational and occupational attainment. For example, in countries exhibiting these characteristics, such as Germany, Switzerland, and the Netherlands, the effect of educational preparation on occupational destination was twice as large as in countries without these features, including Britain, Japan, and the United States.

The policy implications of these comparative studies for curricular reform are profound. The findings indicate that vocational education facilitates occupational attainment in those countries where training is directed toward a specific occupation but is of little value otherwise. Moreover, a more formalized transition process facilitates job acquisition, but decreases job mobility and a return to school.

Further research is needed, of course. Comparative analysis of survey data is limited by the few variables that are comparable across countries. The institutional data that are available need to be supplemented by contextual data describing the workplace, including characteristics of employers, employees, the structure of the workforce, and the involvement of other organizations that assist in job placement. Also needed is information about school context and the involvement of school personnel with students who are beginning a job search. In addition, an understanding of the transition from school to work would be informed by individual-level data, particularly students' ascribed and achieved characteristics. Finally, this body of research should be extended beyond new entrants to the labor market to further specify how schooling affects occupational attainment throughout the life cycle.

CONCLUSIONS

The two research traditions described in this chapter are similar in two ways. First, both the organizational analysis of schools and the study of the transition from school to work are grounded in theoretical perspectives that provide a solid foundation for empirical studies in these traditions. The study of school as an organization rests on general sociological theory about the structure, function, and processes of organizations, as well as their impact on their members and non-members. Research on the transition from school to work is located in broad sociological theories of stratification and social mobility, and its consequences for individuals' well-being and societal functioning.

Second, both research traditions have amassed a large body of empirical work that flows directly from and further expands the conceptual ideas that generated it. Informed by powerful sociological theories, the empirical studies in these areas tend to be systematic, integrated, and rigorous. Current empirical work can be related easily to previous studies, leading to the accumulation of a systematic body of research that broadens and deepens our understanding of the social processes that govern schooling.

In general, a strength of sociology of education is that it is grounded in comprehensive and powerful sociological theories of societal processes. These broad theories have had a major influence on the conceptual and empirical developments that characterize the sociological analysis of schools. At the same time, sociology of education has been slow to formulate its own more specific theories to explain schooling. While broad macro-level and micro-level sociological theories are valuable in providing ideas and direction to the study of schooling, a gap exists between these general formulations and the social processes that occur in the specific context of the school. Middle range theories and more contextualized conceptual frameworks that take into account the unique characteristics of schools and the populations they serve would lead to even greater progress in our understanding of the educational process. Moreover, conceptualizing the links between macro-and micro-level processes would increase our understanding of how school organization affects student learning and how youth culture influences student engagement.

Schools assume a major role in the transmission of knowledge and culture across generations and in the socialization of youth to their roles in adult life. The sociological analysis of schools reveals the various contributions schools make to society and how they shape and are shaped by societal institutions and events. The contributions of twentieth-century sociology of education are significant and of considerable consequence. The challenge for contemporary sociologists of education is to build and extend this body of work through theoretically rich and methodologically rigorous studies of schooling.

ACKNOWLEDGMENTS

The author is grateful to the National Science Foundation and the American Educational Research Association for Grant RED-9452861 for support of this research. The author thanks Amy Orr, Vladimir Khmelkov, and Warren Kubitschek for valuable research assistance. She is also grateful for support from the Institute for Educational Initiatives at the University of Notre Dame.

26

Aging and Aging Policy in the USA

MADONNA HARRINGTON MEYER AND PAMELA HERD

The study of aging and aging policy is always personal as well as social. How can we best prepare for our own old age? Or for that of our parents or grandparents? How can we as a society best prepare for a rapidly aging nation? Within the next 50 years, those over age 65 will comprise one-fifth of the population (US Bureau of the Census, 1993). Social gerontology includes the study of how our aging population will impact every facet of our lives, including health and health care, our family relationships, economics, and work.

Gerontology is a multidisciplinary approach, drawing on such fields as sociology, history, psychology, social work, medicine, public administration, political science, and biology. In recent decades, the discipline has changed – and in this chapter we highlight several emerging trends. First, gerontology has diversified from an initial tendency to focus primarily on white men to a more cross-cultural, racial, and gendered approach. Increasingly, scholars are paying careful attention to the ways that the processes and implications of aging vary for the poor, for women, and for persons of color. Second, gerontological research has moved away from a predominately individual or social-psychological approach to a more social structural approach that takes into account how political and economic structures impact the aging process. Third, social gerontologists have shifted from a focus on old age as an isolated point or stage in life, to a life course perspective that emphasizes links across life stages. Finally, the discipline has moved away somewhat from a problem-based to a solution-based approach by focusing on public policy and international comparisons that shed light on ways to effect change.

We begin this chapter with an overview of the development of gerontological theory. Next, we provide a primer on the demography of an aging population. We then turn to issues of health and health care in old age. Finally, we explore the factors that shape economic security for the aged and their families. Along the way we pay careful attention to inequalities linked to race, class, and gender and to the policy initiatives that do – and do not – mitigate these sources of inequality.

AGING THEORIES

Social theories provide a framework or context to examine an issue such as aging. The first aging theories found common ground in that they focused largely on the individual and what was normal aging. For example, *disengagement theory* stated that it was normal and natural for an older person to withdraw from society (Cumming and Henry, 1961). *Activity theory*, however, challenged this assertion by claiming the reverse, that aging well entailed remaining active (Havighurst et al., 1968). Both micro-level theories nonetheless emphasized how individuals age well rather than looking to external factors that impact the process of aging.

Gradually, however, aging scholars began to ask how the elderly fit into the larger social context (Quadagno, 1999). *Age stratification theory*, developed by Matilda White Riley (1971), suggested that like class, race, and gender, age is a key source of social inequality, bias, and discrimination. These contextual theories pointed out the importance of *age cohorts*. People born around the same time consequently experience similar events across their lives. For example, those who became adults during the Second World War, many of whom were able to rely on the GI Bill to obtain college degrees and buy their first homes, may have had more positive experiences than those who became adults during the Great Depression. Similarly, *life course theory*, championed by Glen Elder (1985), argued that to understand the diverse lifestyles of the aged, we must first understand the various paths and trajectories that people followed throughout their lives. For example, women who have moved in and out of the labor force because of child care and later parent care responsibilities tend to have very different social and economic conditions in old age than women who have prioritized their careers throughout their lives. Indeed, each cohort experiences the life course, and consequently old age, differently.

More recently, macro-level theories have employed *political economy* ideology by emphasizing how political and economic power differentially shapes the material conditions of various groups of the elderly. One such theory is *cumulative disadvantage theory*, which explains how one's place in the social structure throughout the life course, based upon gender, race, and class, defines experiences in old age. As you read this chapter, remember to think about the various advantages and disadvantages, related to your income, health, race, and gender, that are building across your life course. How will things look for you and for your cohort as you approach old age?

AGING POPULATIONS

The United States, like most industrialized countries, is in the midst of unprecedented demographic changes; these countries are increasingly comprised of growing numbers of older citizens. Even though they may not be warranted, the sharp increase in older people raises many social, economic, and political concerns.

A variety of indicators measure the changing age composition of a population. One way to tell whether a country is aging is to examine the median age of the population. In 1860, Americans' median age was under the age of 20, and by 1990, it was over 34 (Hobbs and Damon, 1996). A second way is to compute the proportion of those aged 65 and over. In 1900, only 4 percent of the population was aged 65 and over, by 1990, the proportion had reached 13 percent, and in 2030, the elderly may comprise 20 percent of the American population (US Bureau of the Census, 1993). A third method emphasizes the proportion of the oldest old, those aged 85 and over. In 1900, the oldest old comprised fewer than 0.1 percent of the population, but by 2030 this is estimated to increase to 8 percent (US Bureau of the Census, 1993). A final measure counts the number of centenarians. Between 1980 and 1990 alone, the number of those aged 100 and over grew from 14,000 to 28,000 (Hobbs and Damon, 1996).

The USA is not the only country experiencing an aging population. Currently, the elderly comprise 20 percent of Sweden's population, and by 2020 they will constitute between 20 and 25 percent of many European nations' populations. In Japan, those aged 65 and older will have grown from 14 percent of the total population in 1994 to over 25 percent in 2020. Less developed nations are also aging; between 1993 and 1994 the proportion of elderly grew by 2.3 percent in developed nations, compared to 3.2 percent in developing nations (Hobbs and Damon, 1996).

Why Populations Age

How do we explain this dramatic jump in the aged population? Social demographers emphasize three key factors: decreasing infant mortality rates, decreasing fertility rates, and longer, healthier lives. Generally, people are having fewer children, and those they do have are surviving and are increasingly likely to live longer. Thus, the old are making up a larger percentage of the population.

One of the easiest ways to show the process by which populations age is with a *population pyramid* that categorizes the population's distribution by age and sex. Figure 26.1a characterizes a country with a young population. Typically poor, agrarian, and lacking in public health care, less developed countries tend to have high fertility rates offset by high infant mortality and relatively low life expectancies (US Bureau of the Census, 1988). By contrast, figure 26.1b characterizes a country with a more middle-aged population. Societies that are developing, industrializing, and improving public health tend toward declining infant mortality rates, represented here through the squaring of the bottom part of the triangle. Finally, figure 26.1c characterizes a more developed nation with an older population. Like other developed nations, the USA is approaching this rectangular shaped population pyramid due to an overall declining mortality and a stabilized fertility rate.

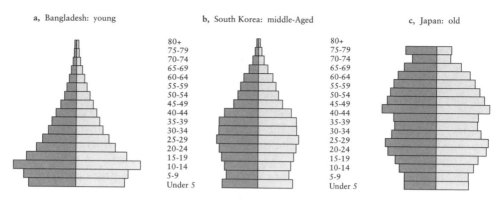

Figure 26.1   Illustrative population pyramids, 1998.

Source: US Bureau of the Census, International Database.

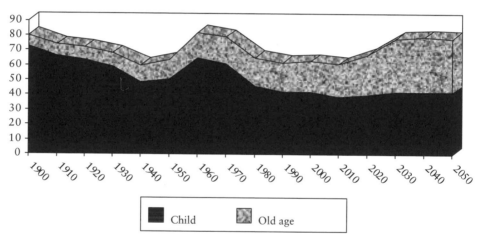

Figure 26.2   Dependency ratio changes in the USA, 1900–2050.

Source: US Bureau of the Census, *Historical Statistics of the United States.* Washington DC, US Government Printing Office, 1975, 1993.

The increasing proportion of the elderly in the US population, however, is also due to the post-Second World War babyboom (Levy and Michel, 1991). Between 1946 and 1958, fertility rates exploded to an average of 3.17 children per woman and then dropped dramatically to an all-time low of 1.7 (Quadagno, 1999). The great numbers of babyboomers, compared to the relatively small numbers in the generations immediately following them, have raised several concerns. Babyboomers have had enormous impacts on various institutions as they bulge through the population pyramid, overflowing schools in their child-hood and tightening the labor market in their middle years. In their latter years they will strain the economic stability of government social programs for the elderly. Figure 26.2 shows how these demographic shifts affect the *dependency ratio,* or the proportion of the population that is dependent on the working population. The *elderly dependency ratio* is a measure to compare the proportion of those over age 65, or retirees, to the working population. At the beginning of the twentieth century there were about 7 persons aged 65 and older for every 100 persons aged 18 to 65. But by 1990 there were 20 persons aged 65 and older for every 100 aged 18 to 65. The *child dependency ratio* compares the proportion of those under age 18 to those working age. At the beginning of the twentieth century the ratio was 73 children per 100 persons aged 18 to 65, but by 1990 the number of children dropped to 42 (United States Bureau of the Census, 1975; Hobbs and Damon, 1996). As figure 26.2 shows, the total dependency ratio for 2020 is quite similar to that of 1900, but the proportion made up by the elderly, rather than by children, has increased significantly.

Gender and Race Differences in Life Expectancy

While life expectancy rates from birth increased dramatically between 1900 and 1993, gender and racial differences in life expectancy remain significant (Treas, 1995). Figure 26.3 shows life expectancy at birth since 1900. In 1996, white men lived on average to age 74, white women lived to age 80, black men lived to age 66, and black women lived to age 74 (Hobbs and Damon, 1996). Generally, women live seven years longer than men. Researchers attribute much of the

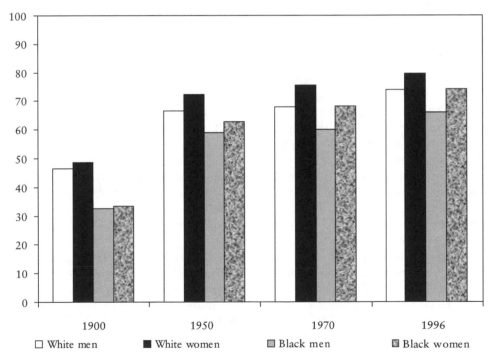

Figure 26.3 Life expectancy from birth by sex and race, 1900–1996.

Source: US Bureau of the Census, *65+ in the United States*, 1996, Current Population Report P23–190 and National Vital Statistic Report, volume 47, number 13, 1998.

ender difference in longevity to a combination of genetic differences and social and lifestyle differences. For example, women take better care of their health and are less likely to engage in high risk activities such as driving too fast or smoking. Similarly, whites live significantly longer than blacks; white men outlive black men by an average of eight years and white women outlive black women by an average of six years. Researchers link most of the racial gap in longevity to social, economic, and lifestyle factors, particularly racial differences in education, employment, poverty, infant mortality, exposure to violence, pollution, and other health hazards, and access to health care (Preston and Taubman, 1994; Treas, 1995; Ross and Wu, 1996).

Health

"At least I've got my health." No matter what hardships fall on older persons, you often hear them emphasize their gratitude that they have remained in good health – or carping loudly that they have not. No amount of savings and planning for a happy retirement will save the day if health fails dramatically. Most older people are in good health. Though the number of the oldest old has increased dramatically, the proportion of those who are chronically disabled has continued to drop throughout the past century (Manton et al., 1993). Generally, people are living longer and are in better health than ever before.

Most health problems in old age are the product of chronic conditions, namely illnesses that cannot be cured, though some might have been prevented. Heart disease is the leading cause of death among those aged 65 and over, followed by cancer and strokes. The leading health problems in old age are no doubt familiar; in 1991, 48 percent suffered from arthritis, 37 percent from hypertension, 32 percent from hearing impairments, and 30 percent from heart disease (National Center for Health Statistics, 1992).

People's health status often impacts their ability to function in everyday life, from taking out the trash to taking a bath. Those who study aging divide these functions of everyday living into two categories, Activities of Daily Living (ADLs) and Instrumental Activities of Daily Living (IADLs). ADLs are basic functional activities, such as eating, dressing, and bathing. IADLs include higher level activities like keeping track of money or going grocery shopping. Most older people, however, do not face significant limitations. In 1995, only about 5 percent of persons aged 65 to 79 needed help with one or more ADLs. The likelihood of needing assistance increases with age, however, and 15 percent of those 80 and over needed help with ADLs. The number of people who needed help with one or more IADLs was much higher, 11 percent among those aged 65 to 79 and 33 percent among those aged 80 and over (US Bureau of the Census, 1997).

Medicare

Most Americans obtain health insurance through their jobs, but because they are generally not employed, few older persons do. How do the elderly meet their health care needs? Nearly all rely on Medicare, which is a national health insurance benefit for the elderly and the permanently blind and disabled. Medicare is financed by the Health Care Financing Administration (HCFA) through the FICA tax. If you worked in 1999, 1.45 percent of your salary went to finance Medicare, and this amount was matched by your employer (Social Security Administration, 1998). Anyone aged 65 and over who receives Social Security is eligible. Medicare Part A, which is fully funded by the FICA tax, covers hospital stays and short-term nursing home stays for rehabilitation. Medicare Part B, which is financed by premiums and some general tax revenues, provides optional coverage of up to 80 percent of the cost of physicians' office visits (HCFA, 1998).

One of the largest drawbacks to Medicare is what it does not cover. Each year Medicare recipients pay a deductible, co-payments, and any costs above those Medicare allows. In addition, recipients cover those costs excluded under Medicare, notably prescriptions drugs, routine preventative care, and most dental, aural, and visual care. Moreover, Medicare excludes most chronic care for conditions, such as arthritis, Parkinson's, or Alzheimers's disease (HCFA, 1998). Because they are in worse health and have more chronic conditions, the poor, women, and African Americans are particularly likely to have to pay out of pocket for care excluded under Medicare. While Medicare provides health insurance for nearly all older people, its coverage is somewhat spotty (Verbrugge, 1990; Gibson, 1995). Indeed, in 1998 Medicare covered less than 50 percent of total health care costs for the elderly (HCFA, 1998). The economic consequences of this limited coverage are severe for many elderly people; each year one-third of the elderly with incomes between 100 and 150 percent of the poverty line are pushed into poverty by their health care costs (Commonwealth Fund, 1987).

To meet the costs of what Medicare does not cover, 66 percent of Medicare beneficiaries paid for Medigap policies to cover things like prescriptions, eye exams, or hearing aids (HCFA, 1998). Recent studies, however, show that access to Medigap coverage will become increasingly difficult for older people as prices are expected to rise (Alecxih et al., 1997). Additionally, a study cited by the Commonwealth Fund indicated race differences in Medigap coverage. While 48 percent of poor whites had coverage, only 17 percent of poor blacks and Hispanics had coverage (HCFA, 1998).

Despite its limitations, expansion of Medicare seems unlikely given that Medicare expenditures are expected to increase rapidly as the babyboomers get older. By 2040, when the average babyboomer will be aged 85, economists predict Medicare costs will have increased six times unless there are efforts toward cost containment (Schneider and Guralnik, 1990).

Medicaid

Medicaid and Medicare were both enacted in 1965, but the similarities in their names hide vast differences in their coverage. Medicaid provides health insurance for the poor elderly, and the permanently blind and disabled. For the poor elderly, Medicaid mainly covers things that Medicare does not: prescription drugs, co-payments, deductibles, and long-term nursing home care. Because eligibility for Medicaid requires that income be well below the poverty line, and assets be below $2000, fewer than one-third of the poor elderly receive it (US Bureau of the Census, 1990, table 148:98). In 1995, two-thirds of the Medicaid budget for the elderly went to institutional care, and only 8 percent was spent on long-term care in the community (Wiener and Stevenson, 1998). Greater resources devoted to home care would enable more elderly persons to live independently longer (Hooyman and Gonyea, 1995). Like Medicare, however, Medicaid is facing increasing costs. Medicaid long-term care expenditures are estimated to double between 1993 and 2018 (Wiener and Stevenson, 1998).

Cost Containment: Transferring the Costs of Long-term Care

The rising costs of Medicare and Medicaid have resulted in various cost containment policies. The Social Security Amendment of 1985 changed Medicare to a prospective payment system by creating Diagnostic Related Groupings (DRGs). The new structure of reimbursement provides a profit incentive for hospitals to release patients as soon as is possible. Although DRGs have reduced unnecessary medical treatments, and curbed rising medical costs, they have also lead to patients being released "quicker and sicker" (Estes, 1993). Medicaid cost containment strategies have included tightening eligibility rules (Harrington Meyer and Kesterke-Storbakken, 2000). Another strategy has been lowering reimbursement rates, setting them below private pay patient rates. Physicians, however, are not allowed to bill the patients the uncovered portion of the bill. The result has been many physicians, hospitals, and nursing homes refusing to provide services to Medicaid beneficiaries (Harrington Meyer and Kesterke-Storbakken, 2000). Consequently, families are providing services that hospitals, nursing homes, and even home health care agencies once provided (Glazer, 1990).

In fact, family or informal care constitutes 80 percent of long-term care provided in the United States. The term family care, however, as Hooyman and Gonyea (1995) argued, hides "the gendered nature of caring behind gender neutral terms such as family, caregiver, parent, spouse, or child" (p. 136). Overall, women provide 80 percent of informal long-term care (Stone et al., 1987). Among children who care for their elderly parents, 70–80 percent are daughters. In fact, studies have shown that daughter-in-laws are likely to provide more care than are sons; around 37 hours per week compared to 27 hours per week (Abel, 1986; Brody, 1990; Chang and White-Means, 1991).

Providing intense care for a frail older relative takes a toll on caregivers, economically, physically, and emotionally – though it may also be rewarding work. One study showed that 21 percent of caregivers compensated for their extra responsibilities by reducing work hours and 19 percent took time off without pay (Scharlach, 1994). Another study estimated that family members lose $8 billion dollars a year in lost wages (Ward, 1990). The resulting forgone wages, pensions, and Social Security places these women in a vulnerable economic situation (Smeeding et al., 1999). Physical repercussions of caregiving include sleeplessness and exhaustion, lack of exercise, increases in chronic conditions, and drug misuse (Brody 1990; Hoyert and Seltzer, 1992). Finally, the emotional consequences of caregiving include marital tension and depression (Gallagher et al., 1989; Stephens and Franks, 1995).

Medicare and Medicaid lessen the caregiving burden on young generations. Proposals to reduce Medicare or Medicaid expenditures typically overlook how beneficial these programs are for younger generations by enabling older people to provide for their own care. It is evident that cuts to Medicare and Medicaid may well reduce taxpayer burden, but they tend to increase caregiver burden. Are you willing and able to absorb these transferred costs? What types of policies would you like to see in place by the time your parents – or you – need long-term care?

ECONOMIC SECURITY

Economic security is tricky in old age because many older people no longer have jobs. As people age they tend to limit or terminate participation in the paid labor force. Their previous participation, however, which varies significantly by gender, race, and class, has a dramatic impact on whether or not they will be financially secure in retirement. Because of a lifetime of cumulative advantage or disadvantage, the elderly are the most economically diverse age group. While a significant proportion are well off and live a life of leisure and travel, a less visible group struggles to make ends meet. Poverty rates for the elderly are the lowest they have been in decades, and they are lower than poverty rates for other age groups. Still, about 12 percent of all older people are poor. Older women are twice as likely as older men to be poor, and older blacks and Hispanics are two to three times as likely as older whites to be poor (Hobbs and Damon, 1996). Those who live alone are particularly likely to be poor. Only one-fourth of older women, compared to three-fourths of older men, are married, and marriage rates are even lower for black than for white women. Thus, figure 26.4 reveals, 20 percent of white women, compared to 54 percent of Hispanic women and 40 percent of Black women, who lived alone in 1997, were at or below the poverty level (US Bureau of the Census, 1998a). Clearly, though the economic condition of the elderly has improved dramatically, pockets of poverty persist.

Retirement Income: Employer-based Pensions

Receipt of a private pension reduces the chances of being poor in old age substantially, but many older people are not fortunate enough to receive one. Indeed, among those aged 65 and over in 1992, pensions accounted for only 10 percent of total income (Grad, 1994). Pension eligibility, and pension size, vary markedly by gender and race. In 1994, while 48 percent of older men had a pension, only 30 percent of women did (National Economic Council, 1998). In 1992, 53 percent of white men and 30 percent of white women had a pension. Among Hispanics, 35 percent of men and 13 percent of women had a

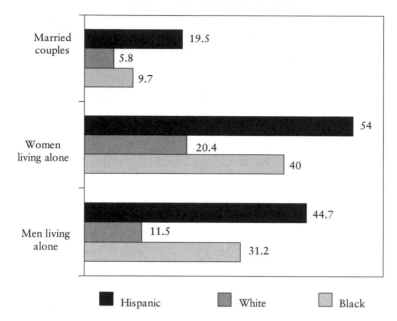

Figure 26.4   Percentage over age 65 living alone or married and in poverty, 1997.

Source: US Bureau of the Census, *Poverty in the United States, 1997.* Current Population Reports, Series P60–201. Washington DC, US Government Printing Office, 1998.

pension. And among African Americans, 32 percent of men and 19 percent of women had one (Grad, 1994). Among whites, the median pension varied from $8,045 for men to $4,725 for women. Black women actually had a median pension slightly higher than white women, $4,828, but black men's was only $5,428 (US House of Representatives, 1992).

Studies indicate that the main determinants of pension coverage include income, job tenure, full-time status, and union membership (Even and MacPherson, 1998). Despite women's increased labor force participation, many remain concentrated in low-wage, service, part-time, non-union, and small firm jobs that tend not to provide pensions (Hounsell, 1996). Even among professions that have high rates of pension coverage, women are less likely than men to be covered (DeViney, 1995). When women are covered by pensions, their pensions are smaller than men's because of both women's interrupted employment and their lower wages; women earn 70 percent of what men earn (Hooyman and Gonyea, 1995).

Racial differences in pension coverage are due to the same set of factors. In 1997, black men earned 69 percent of what white men did (US Bureau of the Census, 1998a), and they are two to three times more likely than whites to be unemployed (US Bureau of Labor Statistics, 1995). Additionally, African Americans suffer disproportionately from the plant closings that took place in the 1980s. During the 1990–1 recession, African Americans were the only racial group to experience a net job loss; that is, job loss associated with the recession was concentrated among African Americans relative to other racial groups, such as whites (Oliver and Shapiro, 1995). The combination of these factors makes pension coverage, and pension size, significantly less for black than for white Americans.

Pension coverage, already sporadic for today's elderly, is expected to be even less comprehensive for future generations. For example, pension coverage of men aged 21–36 declined from 62 percent in 1979 to only 49 percent in 1993; for women the comparable numbers increased slightly from 46 percent in 1979 to 48 percent in 1993 (Quadagno, 1999). Given a college degree, you may well be able to land jobs which include private pensions as fringe benefits, but how will the rest of your cohort fare?

Social Security

The most important source of income for the majority of Americans aged 65 and over is Social Security (Grad, 1994). The Social Security Act of 1935 created this old age income program as a means of helping to ensure economic security for older Americans who were particularly vulnerable to unemployment and poverty (Quadagno, 1999). Like private pensions, Social Security is based upon life course labor participation. Social Security is administered by the Social Security Administration (SSA) and is paid for by employees and employers through the FICA tax. If you worked in the USA in 1999, 6.2 percent of your gross income went toward Social Security, and your employer matched that with another 6.2 percent (SSA, 1998). Because Social Security has a maximum benefit, the tax is capped; thus in 1999, any earnings above $72,600 were not taxed (SSA, 1999).

Those who qualify for Social Security benefits include retired workers, their spouses, widows, and children, and disabled workers. Beginning in 2003, the eligibility age will gradually increase until 2027 when it will be 67. Those who take benefits at 62 face a 30 percent reduction in them (SSA, 1999). Those who qualify as spouses receive a benefit equal to 50 percent of the working spouse's benefit, even if they never contributed to the program themselves. Similarly, those who qualify as widows receive a benefit equal to 100 percent of their working spouse's benefit.

Although Social Security comprises close to 40 percent of the income of those aged 65 and older, one-fourth of the elderly rely on it for 90 percent or more of their income (SSA, 1995). Because of decreased access to private pensions and savings, in 1992, African Americans and Hispanics relied on Social Security for 48 and 44 percent of their annual incomes respectively (Grad, 1994). This is particularly troubling given the modest size of their benefits. While white women's average benefits in 1992 were $569, white men's were $748, black women's were only $490, and black men's were $569 (SSA, 1995). Women's benefits are less than men's because of a lifetime of lower earnings and frequent episodes out of the labor force to care for young children and frail older relatives, while black and Hispanic benefits are less than whites' because of a lifetime of lower earnings and a greater propensity to be unemployed or underemployed (Hooyman and Gonyea, 1998; Castro, 1995).

Social Security benefits are based upon years of work and income earned, yet they are calculated in a way that redistributes to low-income Americans. The replacement rate is the percentage of pre-retirement income that Social Security benefits replace. A high wage earner's replacement rate is 28 percent, whereas a low income earner's replacement rate is 78 percent (Koitz, 1996). Nonetheless, a worker who received a pre-retirement income of $3,877 a month in 1997 would have received $1,311 in Social Security benefits, whereas someone whose monthly income was $800 would have received $519 a month (Quadagno, 1999).

The future of Social Security has been at the forefront of policy debate in recent years. There are concerns that the fund will go bankrupt when babyboomers start collecting due to the small number of workers relative to recipients (Quadagno, 1996). A variety of proposals have been put forth to mitigate the effects of the babyboomers, which Quadagno (1999) summarizes. First, privatizing Social Security would allow workers to invest their own incomes in the stock market. However, while the stock market is presently strong, some argue that when the babyboomers retire they will sell their stocks and the market will crash or people simply risk making bad investments and losing their lifetime savings. Additionally, this would disadvantage women, mostly single mothers, who do not have strong rates of labor force participation due to their primary parenting responsibilities. It would also take a well educated (and lucky) person to know what are appropriate and strong investment strategies.

Making Social Security a means tested program is another option, whereby those who are wealthy will not receive benefits that they do not need. Many argue, however, that this move would threaten the program's present popularity and means testing would simply result in a scaled back and eventually ineffective Social Security program (Kingson, 1994). Australia tried this approach and each year the means test has tightened and fewer and fewer workers are eligible (Shaver, 1991).

Another option is raising the retirement age. This proposal would disproportionately affect women and minorities who tend to retire earlier due to their own or a family members' health problems or due to sex and race discrimination in the labor force (Burkhauser et al., 1996).

Despite the ongoing controversy, many scholars argue that there is no crisis with Social Security at all – and that minor changes such as raising the FICA payroll tax for employers and employees by just 1.1 percent – from 6.2 to 7.3 percent – would stabilize Social Security as we ride out the old age of the babyboomers (Quinn, 1997, p. 1c). Many fear that this 1.1 percent rise in taxes would be burdensome, but nearly 20 nations already have higher Social Security taxes than the USA (Quadagno, 1999).

Work and Retirement

Since the implementation of the Social Security Act in 1935, most workers have left the labor force by, or even before, age 65 (Haber and Gratton, 1994). Social gerontologists initially viewed retirement as the final major stage in the life course. But we now understand retirement as a process that may begin with being laid off or a voluntary reduction in hours, and may culminate a decade or two later with a shift to volunteering, golfing, or becoming homebound. Race differences in labor force participation are relatively smaller compared to gender differences. For example, in 1996, among those aged 35–39, the employment rate for white men was 91 percent and for white women it was 74 percent. The gap was smaller between black men and women with employment rates of 78 compared to 72 percent respectively. From age 30 to 65, employment rates for white men averaged 15–20 percent higher than those for white women. Between black men and black women the gap was between 5 and 10 percent (US Bureau of Labor Statistics, 1996). Among workers retiring in 1996, the median woman was employed for 27 years, compared to 39 years for the median man (National Economic Council, 1998). This has profound implications for financial security and retirement satisfaction for older women.

A great deal of research has focused on how we may plan for and enjoy a successful retirement period. Studies show that a pleasurable retirement is dependent upon economic security, physical health, and a strong social support network (Reitzes et al., 1991; Hayward et al., 1996). Many older people retire by choice when they think they are ready to, both socially and economically, and these retirees tend to be very satisfied with their retirements. But others leave the labor force due to job loss or their own – or a family member's – poor health and disability. Those who are pushed or pulled out, related to either job loss or health, tend to struggle more and are generally less satisfied with their retirement.

Early withdrawal from the labor force has been a dominant trend over the past two decades, but not all early withdrawal has been by choice. Middle-aged workers leave the labor force in their fifties due to "downsizing" layoffs and the difficulty of finding work, particularly well-paying work, above age 50. One study of those laid off from blue-collar manufacturing jobs revealed that only 40 percent of those 55 and over found new jobs, compared with 70 percent of individuals in their twenties (Barlett and Steele, 1992). By the 1990s, downsizing hit white-collar workers as well. Of the 4.5 million workers who lost jobs in the early 1990s recession, two-thirds were white-collar workers with college degrees (Gordon, 1996). White-collar downsizing has also proven to be problematic for older workers. While 80 percent of displaced younger workers found new jobs, only one-half of those aged 55–64 were as fortunate (Applebaum and Gregory, 1990). Many of these workers end up in "bridge" jobs, which span the time between one's original full-time career and retirement (Quinn and Kozy, 1996). Whether part-time or full-time, they tend to be low paid and a step down from previous employment (Couch, 1998).

Poor health often impinges on economic security by literally forcing some older people out of the labor force. African American men are significantly more likely than white men to leave the labor force early due to their chronic health, in part because they are two and a half times more likely to suffer from hypertension, circulatory problems, diabetes, and nervous disorders (Hayward et al., 1996). Additionally, they are more likely to work in blue-collar jobs, and these accompany more health problems than white-collar jobs (Daly and Bound, 1996). For women, health impacts labor force participation in two key ways. First, though women live longer than men, they have more chronic illnesses that interfere with their ability to work (George, 1996). Second, women are more likely to leave the labor force to care for a frail parent, spouse, or other family member (Stoller, 1994). Leaving the labor force by necessity, rather than by choice, causes women to be less satisfied with retirement (Mathews and Brown, 1987; Shaw, 1996). Sometimes these two factors intersect with unfortunate results: some older women with chronic conditions would like to retire but are unable to because previous caregiving responsibilities have left them financially insecure.

Clearly, concerns about financial security in old age revolve predominantly around women, particularly women of color. Most women who are old today worked sporadically throughout their life course. They generally have had extended periods of time out of the labor force raising children and caring for elderly parents (Hooyman and Gonyea, 1995). Lack of experience, training, and connections, combined with sexist, racist, and ageist hiring practices, means that women in the labor force in middle age face a difficult path. The "bridge jobs," which are perceived as a step down for men, may be the only career option available for many older women (Shaw, 1996). For women in younger generations, however, financial prospects in old age may be better. Overall labor force participation rates for women increased from 38 percent in 1960 to close to 60 percent in 1997, and their educational attainment since 1985 has been higher than men's (Castro, 1998). Our optimism is guarded, however, because recent projections for 2020 estimate that there will be no decline in poverty rates among women, largely due to increasing numbers of never married and divorced women and women's continued unpaid caregiving, both within and outside of marriage (Smeeding et al., 1999). The key issue is that families, particularly women, need to have more options in place to enable them to balance work and family responsibilities (Harrington Meyer, 2000).

CONCLUSIONS

The coming years are going to bring dramatic changes and challenges to the USA in terms of how we care for our aging population. From health care to economic policy, change will be an absolute necessity to accommodate the combination of increased longevity and the aging babyboomers. As Maggie Kuhn, founder of the Gray Panthers, remarked, "Instead of avoiding all the world's problems or becoming overwhelmed by them, I like to see them as an invitation" (Kuhn, 1991). The challenge, as we see it, is to ameliorate inequities in the present structure of government programs for the elderly and to mitigate the cumulative disadvantages produced by racism, sexism, and poverty throughout the life course. How do you think we should respond to the invitation?

27

Immigration and Ethnicity: the United States at the Dawn of the Twenty-first Century

Rubén G. Rumbaut

American ethnic groups have been forged, along with peculiarly American ideologies and classifications of "race," in the tumultuous course of the United States' national expansion. In myriad ways, their unequal modes of incorporation reflect fundamentally different starting points, contexts of reception, and attendant definitions of the situation. The development of social, political, and economic inequalities based on race and ethnicity has been not only a central theme but a central dilemma of the country's history, shaped over many generations by the European conquest of indigenous peoples and by massive waves of both voluntary and involuntary migration from all over the world. Indeed, immigration as well as enslavement, annexation, and conquest have been the originating processes by which American ethnicities have been formed and through which, over time, the United States has been transformed into what is arguably the world's most ethnically diverse society. The national self-image created by that history reflects the experience of a country that has time and again been revitalized and renewed by immigration. But chimerical conceptions of "race" also derive from those fateful encounters, those social relations formed between strangers: phenotypical and cultural differences came to be associated with steep gradients of privilege and power, and became hardened into invidious, indelible, outward markers of social status and identity in caste and class hierarchies. It took a bloody civil war in one century, and a civil rights revolution in the next, to end slavery and the legal underpinnings of racial exclusion, but not their bitter legacy.

Already in *The Souls of Black Folk*, written soon after Africa was partitioned by European colonial powers and Puerto Rico, the Philippines, Guam, and the Hawaiian islands were seized by the United States in the wake of the

Spanish-American-Cuban War, W. E. B. Du Bois had prophesied famously that "the problem of the twentieth century is the problem of the color line – the relation of the darker to the lighter races of men in Asia and Africa, in America and the islands of the sea" (Du Bois, 1903, p. 10). To be sure, much has changed since then in international and intergroup relations, mainly in the years after the Second World War, including the decolonization of Africa and Asia and the English-speaking Caribbean, and the dismantling of Jim Crow in the United States. But much has not, so that another pre-eminent African American scholar, John Hope Franklin, could "venture to state categorically that the problem of the twenty-first century will be the problem of the color line" (Franklin, 1993, p. 5).

That "color line" has historically defined the boundary between two broad modes of ethnic incorporation into American social life: one epitomized by "assimilation," the master process that purports to explain how it came to be that tens of millions of European immigrants from heterogeneous national and cultural origins and their descendants were absorbed into the mainstream of the society, their identities eventually becoming largely symbolic and fading into a "twilight of ethnicity" (Nahirny and Fishman, 1965; Gans, 1979; Alba 1985; Waters, 1990; but see also Glazer and Moynihan, 1963); and another largely resistant to such absorption into the majority regardless of level of acculturation or socioeconomic attainment, characterized instead by persistently high social distances in intergroup relations, discrimination, and segregation of racialized minorities (see Massey and Denton, 1993; Pedraza and Rumbaut, 1996). Thus, for example, in *The Social Systems of American Ethnic Groups* (1945), the most authoritative statement of the matter near mid-century, Warner and Srole described the straight-line "progressive advance" of eight immigrant groups in the major status hierarchies of Yankee City (Newburyport, Massachusetts), explicitly linking upward social mobility to assimilation, which they saw as determined largely by the degree of ethnocultural (religion and language) and above all racial difference from the dominant group. While "racial groups" were subordinated through caste restrictions on residential, occupational, associa-tional, and marital choice, the clash of "ethnic groups" with the dominant institutions of the "host society" was not much of a contest, particularly among the young. The polity, the industrial economy, the public school, popular culture, and the American family system all undercut and absorbed ethnicity in various ways, so that even when "the ethnic parent tries to orient the child to an ethnic past...the child often insists on being more American than Americans" (p. 284). And for the upwardly mobile, with socioeconomic success came inter-marriage and the further dilution of ethnicity.

Our conventional models of immigrant acculturation and ethnic self-identification processes largely derive from the historical experience of those (and earlier) European immigrants and their descendants. Indeed, only a few decades before, the large-scale "new" immigration of putatively "unassimilable" southern and eastern Europeans – Italians, Poles, Greeks, Russian Jews, and many others – had occasioned vitriolic public alarms and widespread fears about the "mongrelization of the race," culminating in forced Americanization cam-paigns and the passage of the restrictionist national-origins quota laws of the

1920s (see Higham 1955). But today a new era of mass immigration, now overwhelmingly non-European in composition, is again raising familiar doubts about the assimilability of the newcomers and the dark prospect that they might become consigned to a vast multiethnic underclass – and questions about the applicability of explanatory models developed in connection with the experience of European ethnics.

THE SIZE, COMPOSITION, AND CONCENTRATION OF CONTEMPORARY IMMIGRATION

At the dawn of the twenty-first century, new American ethnic groups are forming faster than ever before, an outcome now due entirely to international migration and once more accompanied by the official construction of ethnoracial categories into which to classify them. The emerging ethnic groups of the twenty-first century will be the children and grandchildren of today's immigrants. Their numbers and diversity will ensure that the process will have a profound societal impact, although it is too early to grasp except in opaque speculation their probable trajectories of incorporation. Four decades into a new era of mass immigration, it is now a commonplace to observe that the United States is in the midst of its most profound demographic transformation in a century. Whether in terms of its size, composition, or spatial concentration, the sheer magnitude of the phenomenon is impressive (see table 27.1). The "foreign [or immigrant] stock" population of the United States in 1997 numbered approximately 55 million people – that is, persons who are either foreign-born (27 million) or US-born children of immigrants (28 million). That figure is one-fifth (20.5 percent) of the total US population, and growing rapidly through ongoing immigration and natural increase (Rumbaut, 1998).

Still, as table 27.1 shows, the current *proportions* fall well short of those that obtained during the last era of mass immigration a century ago. During the period from 1880 to 1930, the foreign-stock population consistently comprised one-third of the national total (peaking at 35.3 percent in the 1910 census), with the foreign-born share reaching nearly 15 percent of the total in 1890 and again in 1910, compared to 8 percent in 1990 and 10 percent today. In that earlier period, it was not only the sheer size of the immigration flows but the sharp shift in national origins after 1890 from northwest to southern and eastern European countries that heightened nativist fears. Today's immigration is likewise large in volume and marked by an even sharper shift in its composition: while the proportion of immigrants arriving during 1880–1900 came overwhelmingly from Europe (97 percent), the proportion of European immigrants arriving during 1980–98 plummeted to just over 10 percent of the total number of legal admissions. Of today's 27 million foreign-born – already the largest immigrant population in world history – fully 60 percent had arrived after 1980, and 90 percent since 1960. Of those post-1960 immigrants, the latest Current Population Survey data available show that the majority (52 percent) had come from Latin America and the Caribbean; nearly a third (29 percent) had

Table 27.1   Decennial trends in the US foreign-born and foreign-stock population and in legal immigration by region of origin, 1890–1998

Census year	US Census Bureau data: foreign-born and foreign-stock population				Immigration and Naturalization Service (INS) data: legal immigration by decade and region of last residence				
	Foreign-born[a] no. (millions)	% of total US population	Foreign-stock[b] no. (millions)	% of total US population	Decade	Immigrants, no. thousands	Europe, Canada (%)	Latin America (%)	Asia (%)
1890	9.2	14.8	20.8	33.2	1881–90	5,247	97.8	0.6	1.3
1900	10.4	13.6	26.0	34.3	1891–00	3,688	96.5	1.0	2.0
1910	13.4	14.7	32.5	35.3	1901–10	8,795	93.9	2.1	3.7
1920	14.0	13.2	36.7	34.7	1911–20	5,736	88.3	7.0	4.3
1930	14.3	11.6	40.3	32.8	1921–30	4,107	82.5	14.4	2.7
1940	11.7	8.8	n.a.	n.a.	1931–40	528	86.3	9.7	3.1
1950	10.4	6.9	n.a.	n.a.	1941–50	1,035	76.6	14.9	3.6
1960	9.7	5.5	34.1	19.0	1951–60	2,515	67.8	22.2	6.1
1970	9.6	4.7	33.6	16.5	1961–70	3,322	46.3	38.6	12.9
1980	14.1	6.2	n.a.	n.a.	1971–80	4,493	21.6	40.3	35.3
1990	19.8	7.9	n.a.	n.a.	1981–90	7,338[c]	12.5	47.1	37.3
1997	25.8	9.7	54.7	20.5	1991–98	7,605[d]	14.8	50.4	30.1

[a]   Data on nativity from decennial censuses, 1890–1990, and from the Current Population Survey for 1997. Since the 1890 census, persons born in a foreign country but who had at least one parent who was a US citizen have been redefined as "native" rather than "foreign-born." In

1997, the estimate of 25.8 million "foreign-born" persons excludes more than one million persons born in a foreign country but counted as US "natives" under this definition, which privileges citizenship status over nativity. Persons residing in the USA who were born (or whose parents were born) in any "outlying areas" of the USA are also classified as "natives." These have included Puerto Rico since 1900, and others at different times, e.g. persons born in the Philippines were classified as native in 1900–40 and as foreign-born in 1950 (after independence in 1946) and since.

[b] The "foreign-stock" population is defined as the sum of the foreign-born population (the first generation) and the native population with at least one foreign-born parent (the second generation). The question on nativity or birthplace of parents was asked in censuses from 1870 to 1970, but dropped from the 1980 and 1990 (and 2000) censuses. The question has been asked in the (March) Current Population Surveys annually since 1994.

[c] Data include 1,359,186 formerly undocumented immigrants who had resided in the USA since 1982 and whose status was legalized in fiscal years 1989 and 1990 under the amnesty provisions of the Immigration Reform and Control Act (IRCA) of 1986.

[d] Data include another 1,329,209 formerly undocumented immigrants, mostly Special Agricultural Workers, whose status was adjusted to permanent resident under IRCA in fiscal years 1991 and since. Virtually all IRCA legalizations were completed by 1993.

Sources: US Census Bureau, *Statistical Abstracts of the United States* (112th edn), 1992, Tables 1, 5–6, 45; US Census Bureau, *Profile of the Foreign-born Population in the United States: 1997* (Current Population Reports, P23–195), 1999, Figure 8–1; US Immigration and Naturalization Service, *Statistical Yearbooks*, 1990–1998, Tables 1–2.

come from Asia and the Middle East. The Filipinos, Chinese, and Indochinese alone accounted for 15 percent of the total, or as much as all of those born in Europe and Canada combined. And African immigration, while smaller and less noticed, was also rapidly increasing, having grown to eight times its volume over the past three decades.

As in the past, today's newcomers are heavily concentrated in areas of settlement. Fully one-third of the immigrant-stock population of the country resides in California, and another third resides in Florida, Texas, and the New York–New Jersey region, with the ethnic concentrations being denser still within metropolitan areas in this handful of states. As of 1997 in Los Angeles County, for instance, a preponderant 62 percent of the area's 9.5 million people were of immigrant stock, as were 54 percent of New York City's and Orange County's, 43 percent of San Diego's, and 72 percent of Miami's (Rumbaut, 1998). In general, patterns of concentration or dispersal vary for different social classes of immigrants (professionals, entrepreneurs, manual laborers) with different types of legal status (regular immigrants, refugees, the undocumented). The likelihood of dispersal is greatest among immigrant professionals, who tend to rely more on their qualifications and job offers than on pre-existing ethnic communities; and, at least initially, among recent refugees who are sponsored and resettled through official government programs that have sought deliberately to minimize their numbers in particular localities (although refugee groups too have shown a tendency to gravitate as "secondary migrants" to areas where their compatriots have clustered, as have Cubans to South Florida, and Southeast Asians to California). The likelihood of concentration is greatest among the undocumented (for example, over 25 percent of the three million Immigration Reform and Control Act (IRCA) applicants who qualified for amnesty nationally were concentrated in the Los Angeles metropolitan area alone) and working-class immigrants, who tend to rely more on the assistance offered by pre-existing kinship networks; and among business-oriented groups, who tend to settle in large cities. Dense ethnic enclaves provide immigrant entrepreneurs with access to sources of cheap labor, working capital and credit, and dependable markets. Over time, as the immigrants become naturalized US citizens, local strength in numbers also provides opportunities for political advancement and representation of ethnic minority group interests at the ballot box. The research literature has shown that, among legal immigrants and refugees, the motivation and propensity to naturalize is higher among upwardly mobile younger persons with higher levels of education, occupational status, English proficiency, income, and property, and those whose spouses or children are US citizens. Undocumented immigrants by definition remain disenfranchised and politically powerless (Portes and Rumbaut, 1996).

But unlike the last great waves of European immigration, which were halted by the passage of restrictive legislation in the 1920s and especially by the back-to-back global cataclysms of the Great Depression and the Second World War, the current flows show no sign of abating. On the contrary, inasmuch as immigration is a network-driven phenomenon and the United States remains the premier destination for a world on the move, the likelihood is that it will continue indefinitely. To varying degrees of closeness, the tens of millions of immigrants and their children in the USA today are embedded in often intricate webs of family ties, both here and abroad. Such ties form extraordinary trans-national linkages and networks that can, by reducing the costs and risks of migration, expand and serve as a conduit to additional and thus potentially self-perpetuating migration. Remarkably, for example, a recent poll in the Dominican Republic found that *half* of the 7.5 million Dominicans have relat-ives in the USA and two-thirds would move to the USA if they could. Similarly, by the end of the 1980s, national surveys in Mexico (a country now of 100 million people) found that about half of adult Mexicans were related to someone living in the United States, and that one third of all Mexicans had been to the United States at some point in their lives; more recent surveys suggest still larger proportions (Massey and Espinoza, 1997). Immigrants in the USA in 1990 who hailed from the English-speaking Caribbean, notably from Jamaica, Barbados, Trinidad, Belize, and Guyana, already constituted between 10 and 20 percent of the 1990 populations of their respective countries – a growing double-digit group which now also includes El Salvador. By the same token, despite four decades of hostile relations, at least a third of Cuba's population of 11 million (and maybe half of Havana's) now have relatives in the USA and Puerto Rico, while over 75 percent of first-and second-generation Cubans in Miami have relatives in Cuba – ironically, a greater degree of structural linkage than ever before in the history of US-Cuban relations. Not surprisingly, when in July 1999 the US diplomatic mission in Havana held a lottery for 20,000 immigration visas to the USA, it received 541,000 applications in 30 days – meaning that about 10 percent of the total eligible population of Cuba applied to leave. Potentially vast social networks of family and friends are implied by these figures, microsocial structures that can shape both future migration and incorporation processes, as well as patterns of settlement in areas of destination, and may offer hints about the future of American pluralism (Rumbaut, 1997).

CAUSES AND CONTEXTS OF CONTEMPORARY IMMIGRATION

Changes in US immigration laws – in particular the amendments passed in 1965, which abolished the national-origins quota system and changed the preference system to give greater priority to family reunification over occupational skills – have often been singled out as the principal reason for the "new immigration" and the change in the national origins of its composition. But the ostensibly causal effects of the 1965 Act have been exaggerated, especially so with regard to Latin American immigration (legal or illegal) and the large-scale entry of Cold War refugees. It bears emphasizing that until this law was passed, Western Hemisphere immigration had been *unrestricted*, largely at the behest of Amer-ican agribusiness; and in fact, as Aristide Zolberg (1995, p. 155) has pointed out, the legislative history of the 1965 Act "indicates very clearly that the objective was to deter the growth of black and brown immigration" from Latin America and the Caribbean, while increasing that from Southern and Eastern Europe. For that matter, the 1965 law had nothing to do with determining, for instance, the huge Cuban exile flows of the early 1960s, or the even larger Indochinese refugee flows that would follow much later in the aftermath of the Vietnam War. What is more, the most important consequences of the 1965 Act, notably the rapid growth of previously barred immigration from Asian and African countries in the Eastern Hemisphere, were largely unintended.

The law does matter, of course: it influences migration decisions, regulates the migration process, and constitutes a key context of reception shaping the incorporation of newcomers, especially their right to full membership and future citizenship. Thus, the right of an immigrant to become a US citizen through naturalization was legally restricted on racial grounds until 1952. The first federal naturalization law of 1790 gave that right only to "free white persons," and a revised law in 1870 extended it to persons of African descent or nativity. Moreover, the original native inhabitants of the continent were presumed to be "loyal to their tribes" and not granted United States citizenship until 1924. Most Asian immigrants were excluded from access to American citizenship until the McCarran–Walter Act of 1952. Asian Indians had been able to naturalize on the grounds that they were Caucasians until the US Supreme Court, in a 1923 case, decided that they would no longer be considered white persons. The Chinese were removed from the classes of "aliens ineligible for citizenship" upon the repeal of the (1882) Chinese Exclusion Act in 1943, when China and the USA were Second World War allies. In all of these instances and many more, the law, backed up by the public force of the state, provides a source of *political capital* unavailable to residents without legal standing (see Aleinikoff and Rumbaut, 1998). But it cannot control historical forces or determine the size or source of migration flows.

International migrations are rooted in historical relationships established between the sending and receiving countries – rooted in colonialism, war and military occupation, labor recruitment, and economic interaction – through which migration footholds are formed, kinship networks expand, remittances (in the tens of billions of dollars annually) sent by immigrants to their families abroad link communities across national borders, and all of this turns migration into a social process of vast transformative significance, for both countries of origin and of destination, and one sustained by factors that extend beyond the realm of government action or the economic impulses that originally generated it. To be sure, migration pressures as a result of global inequality can only mount in a world that is more and more a place with a declining proportion of rich people and a growing proportion of poor people. Today, the biggest such development rift in the globe is located along the 2,000–mile USA–Mexico border, and indeed the longest, largest, and most continuous labor migration anywhere in the world is that from Mexico to the United States. The National Population Council predicted in 1999 that as many as eight million more Mexicans will migrate north of the border by 2020 unless Mexico manages to create one million jobs per year to meet population growth. But even in this paradigmatic instance the story is not reducible to a neoclassical economic function of wage differentials, employer demand, and labor supply.

While today's immigrants come from over 150 different countries, some regions and nations send many more than others, despite the equitable numerical quotas provided to each country by US law since 1965. Indeed, fewer than a dozen countries account for the majority of all immigration to the USA. One pattern, a continuation of trends already under way in the 1950s, is clear: immigration from the more developed countries has declined over time, while that from less developed countries has accelerated. However, among the less developed countries, the major sources of legal and illegal immigration are located in the Caribbean Basin – in the immediate periphery of the USA – or are a handful of Asian nations also characterized by significant historical ties to the USA. In fact, immigrants from Mexico and the Philippines alone account for a third of the total. These two countries share the deepest structural linkages with the USA, dating to the Mexican and Spanish-American Wars in the nineteenth century, and a long history of dependency relationships, external intervention, and (in the Philippines) direct colonization, as well as decades of active agricultural labor recruitment by the USA – of Mexicans to the Southwest, Filipinos to plantations in Hawaii and California – that preceded the establishment of family networks and chain migrations. The extensive US military presence in the Philippines has also fueled immigration through marriages with US citizens stationed there, through unique arrangements granting US citizenship to Filipinos who served in the armed forces during the Second World War, and through recruitment of Filipinos into the US Navy. Tellingly, in their analysis of spouse-immigrant flows, Jasso and Rosenzweig (1990) found that the most powerful determinant of the number of immigrants admitted as wives of US citizens was the presence of a US military base in the country of origin. Geopolitical factors thus shape the marriage market in immigrant visas, a vivid example of the connection between macro- and microsocial structures.

American foreign policy in the transformed post-Second World War world, notably the doctrine and practice of global communist containment, is itself a key factor in explaining several of the most sizable migrations from different world regions – indeed, in effectively helping to create the conditions that generated the flows in the first place (see Zolberg et al., 1989). During the Cold War this included direct US involvement in "hot" wars in Korea, Vietnam, Laos, Cambodia, and Central America, and interventions in Guatemala, Iran, Cuba, the Dominican Republic, and elsewhere – all of which, not coincidentally, are among the leading source countries of contemporary immigrants and refugees. Among the most numerous recent European arrivals have been (former) Soviet Jews and Poles, admitted mainly as political refugees, like other groups from communist countries. Emigration connections forged by US intervention and foreign policies were also a common denominator in the exodus of the Chinese after the 1949 revolution (and more recently in the issuance of immigrant visas to tens of thousands of Chinese students in the USA after the events of Tienanmen Square in 1989), and Iranians after the 1978 revolution. Indeed, immigrants from the four communist countries figuring most prominently in American foreign policy – Cuba, Vietnam, China, and the (former) Soviet Union

– accounted in 1997 for nearly one-sixth of the total US foreign-born population (exceeded only by Mexico and the Philippines). In short, contemporary immigration to the USA and the creation and consolidation of social networks that serve as bridges of passage have taken place within this larger historical context and cannot be adequately understood outside of it, or reduced to a cost–benefit economic calculus of individual migrants or to the immigration laws of particular states.

The size and source of new immigrant communities in the USA today are thus directly if variously related to the history of American military, political, economic, and – pervasively – cultural involvement in the major sending countries, and to the linkages that are formed in the process which (often unintentionally) open a surprising variety of legal and illegal migration pathways. Ironically, immigration to the United States – and the pluralization of American ethnicity – may be understood as a dialectical consequence of the expansion of the nation to its post-Second World War position of global hegemony. As the United States has become more deeply involved in the world, the world has become more deeply involved in America – indeed, in diverse ways, it has come to America (Rumbaut, 1994). As such, American pluralism today is not and cannot be construed as solely an internal matter of intergroup relations, of purely domestic concern; it is also fundamentally international and transnational in its nature and scope, and reflects the US role in the world.

Contemporary Immigration and Ethnic Stratification

A widespread point of view in the contentious debate about the new immigration is that it constitutes, relative to those who came in earlier decades, a "declining stock" of less educated and more welfare dependent populations, partly because of its national origins, and partly because of putatively nepotistic family reunification preferences in US law (Borjas, 1990). This latter contention has been rebutted by recent research that shows that immigrants who are admitted through family ties are as successful in their economic contributions as those who come under employment preferences (see Rumbaut, 1997). Furthermore, the fact that most immigrants to the USA since the 1960s have come from comparatively poorer nations does not mean that the immigrants themselves are drawn from the uneducated, unskilled, or unemployed sectors of their countries of origin. In fact, a substantial proportion of contemporary immigrants *exceed* the human capital of native workers by a wide margin, especially in education (Portes and Rumbaut, 1996). These highly educated, professional or managerial immigrants are more likely to speak English, to live in the suburbs, and to accommodate to "American ways" – and "invisibly" at that, meaning that they are not publicly perceived as a "problem." Available occupational data from the Immigration and Naturalization Service (INS) – indicating the number employed as professionals, executives, and managers at the time of immigrant admission – show that over the past three decades, well over two million immigrant engineers, scientists, university professors, physicians, nurses, and other professionals and executives and their immediate families have been admitted into the USA. From the late 1960s to the late 1990s, one-third of all legal immigrants worldwide to the USA (excluding dependents) were high-status professionals, executives, or managers in their countries of origin – a higher percentage than that of the native-born American population – despite the fact that the overwhelming majority of immigrants were admitted under family preferences over this period (Rumbaut, 1997).

Still, there are very sharp differences in the class, and "ethclass" (Gordon, 1964), character of contemporary immigration to the USA. In fact, the diversity of contemporary immigration is such that, among all ethnic groups in America today, native and foreign-born, different immigrant nationalities account at once for the *highest* and the *lowest* rates of education, self-employment, home ownership, poverty, welfare dependency, and fertility – as well as the lowest rates of divorce and of female-headed single-parent families, and the highest proportions of children under 18 residing with both natural parents. These differential starting points, especially the internal socioeconomic diversification of particular waves and "vintages" within the same nationalities over time, augur differential modes of incorporation and assimilation outcomes that cannot be extrapolated simply from the experience of earlier immigrant groups of the same nationality, let alone from immigrants as an undifferentiated whole.

Table 27.2 ranks the principal US immigrant groups by their proportion of college graduates among adults aged 25 and older, and compares them to native racial-ethnic groups on various indicators of socioeconomic status (as of the last census). The foreign-born as a whole had the same proportion of college graduates (20 percent) as the native-born population, as well as an equivalent rate of labor force participation and self-employment. They were, however, more likely than natives to be poor and to work in low status jobs. But decontextualized data at this level of analysis conceal far more than they reveal, although that is often the level at which arguments about the supposedly "declining stock" of new immigrants are made. It is worth repeating that, by far, the most educated *and* the least educated ethnic groups in the USA today are immigrants, a reflection of polar-opposite types of migrations embedded in very different historical contexts. Disaggregated by region and country of birth, the huge differences among them are made clear, underscoring the fact that these groups cannot sensibly be subsumed under pan-national, one-size-fits-all, made-in-the-USA racialized categories like "Asians" or "Latinos" – or "blacks" or "whites." Not, that is, without obliterating the entire histories, cultures, and identities of distinct peoples in the process – an unintended consequence of official ethno-racial classifications. (Since 1977, those categories have been set by Statistical Directive 15 of the US Office of Management and Budget, the agency responsible for determining standard classifications of racial and ethnic data on all federal forms and statistics, including the census. OMB Directive 15 fixed the identities of Americans in five broad categories for statistical and administrative purposes, but through widespread public use the categories soon began to shape those identities and have evolved into political entities, with their own constituencies, lobbies and vested interests.)

Table 27.2 Social and economic characteristics of principal immigrant groups in the USA in 1990, in rank order of college graduates, by region and country of birth, compared to native US racial–ethnic groups

Region/country of birth	Persons (no.)	Median age	Education[a] college graduates (%)	Labor force and occupation[b] In labor force (%)	Self-employed (%)	Upper white-collar (%)	Lower blue-collar (%)	Poverty rate (%)	Income[c] Public assistance (%)	Own home (%)
Africa	363,819	34	47.1	75.1	7.1	37	12	15.7	4.7	34
Asia	4,979,037	35	38.4	66.4	7.8	32	13	16.2	10.7	50
Europe and Canada	5,095,233	53	18.6	52.2	9.5	32	12	9.3	5.7	68
Latin America/Caribbean	8,416,924	33	9.1	70.7	5.0	12	26	24.3	11.3	37
Above US average										
India	450,406	36	64.9	74.6	6.3	48	8	8.1	3.4	54
Taiwan	244,102	33	62.2	64.9	7.5	47	4	16.7	3.7	66
Iran	210,941	35	50.6	67.9	12.0	42	6	15.7	7.7	55
Hong Kong	147,131	30	46.8	75.1	5.5	41	7	12.7	3.5	62
Philippines	912,674	39	43.0	76.3	3.3	28	11	5.9	10.4	61
Japan	290,128	38	35.0	54.2	7.9	39	7	12.8	2.2	46
Korea	568,397	35	34.4	63.9	18.0	25	13	15.6	7.9	48
China	529,837	45	30.9	62.3	7.8	29	16	15.7	10.6	56
Near US average										
Soviet Union*	333,725	55	27.1	39.7	10.1	31	11	25.0	16.7	47
United Kingdom	640,145	50	23.1	57.3	8.3	40	6	6.6	3.7	69
Canada	744,830	53	22.1	52.1	9.5	38	8	7.8	4.8	71
Germany	711,929	53	19.1	54.7	9.1	33	9	7.7	4.3	73
Poland*	388,328	57	16.3	50.4	7.9	21	20	9.7	5.4	64
Vietnam*	543,262	30	15.9	64.4	5.8	17	21	25.5	26.2	47
Cuba*	736,971	49	15.6	64.1	7.3	23	18	14.7	16.2	56
Colombia	286,124	35	15.5	73.7	6.6	17	22	15.3	7.5	38
Jamaica	334,140	36	14.9	77.4	4.0	22	11	12.1	7.8	44
Greece	177,398	49	14.8	60.9	14.7	29	12	9.1	5.3	67

Nicaragua	168,659	30	14.6	73.1	4.7	11	24	24.4	8.4	26
Ireland	169,827	56	14.6	51.5	7.3	29	9	8.4	4.1	60

Below US average

Haiti	225,393	35	11.8	77.7	3.5	14	21	21.7	9.3	37
Italy	580,592	59	8.6	46.4	10.1	20	18	8.0	5.5	81
Dominican Republic	347,858	34	7.5	63.8	5.1	11	31	30.0	27.8	16
Guatemala	225,739	30	5.8	75.7	5.2	7	28	25.8	8.3	20
Cambodia*	118,833	29	5.5	48.4	5.2	9	23	38.4	49.5	23
Laos*	171,577	27	5.1	49.7	2.2	7	41	40.3	45.5	26
Portugal	210,122	40	4.6	71.6	5.1	9	36	7.0	8.4	62
El Salvador	485,433	29	4.6	76.3	4.7	6	27	24.9	7.1	19
Mexico	4,298,014	30	3.5	69.7	4.5	6	32	29.7	11.3	36
Total foreign-born	19,767,316	37	20.4	64.3	6.9	22	19	18.2	9.1	49
Total native-born	228,942,557	33	20.3	65.4	7.0	27	14	12.7	7.4	65

Native racial–ethnic groups

Asian (native-born)	2,363,047	15	35.9	68.8	5.5	34	8	9.8	4.5	63
White (non-Hispanic)	188,128,296	35	22.0	65.3	7.7	29	13	9.2	5.3	68
Black (non-Hispanic)	29,216,293	28	11.4	62.7	2.8	18	21	29.5	19.7	43
Pacific Islanders	365,024	25	10.8	70.1	4.1	18	16	17.1	11.8	44
Puerto Rican	2,727,754	26	9.5	60.4	2.8	17	21	31.7	26.9	26
American Indian/ Alaskan	1,959,234	27	9.3	62.1	5.8	18	19	30.9	18.6	54
Mexican (native-born)	8,933,371	18	8.6	67.2	4.4	16	19	24.5	13.5	54

a Educational attainment for persons aged 25 years or older.

b Labor force participation and occupation for employed persons 16 years or older; Upper white-collar, professionals, executives, and managers; Lower blue-collar, operators, fabricators, and laborers.

c Percentage of persons below the federal poverty line; and of households receiving public assistance income.

* Denotes country from which most recent migrants to the USA have been officially admitted as refugees.

Sources: US Bureau of the Census, *The Foreign Born Population in the United States*, CP-3–1, July 1993, Tables 1–5; *Persons of Hispanic Origin in the United States*, CP-3-3, August 1993, Tables 1–5; *Asian and Pacific Islanders in the United States*, CP-3-5, August 1993, Tables 1–5; and data drawn from a 5 percent Public Use Microdata Sample (PUMS) of the 1990 US Census, subject to sample variability.

One point that stands out in table 27.2 is the extremely high degree of educational attainment among immigrants from the developing countries of Africa and Asia – 47 and 38 percent were college graduates, respectively. An upper stratum is composed of the most sizable foreign-born groups whose educational and occupational attainments significantly exceeded the average for the native-born American population. Note that all of them are of Asian origin – from India, Taiwan, Iran, Hong Kong, the Philippines, Japan, Korea, and China – with recently immigrated groups reflecting the highest levels of attainment. Also in this upper stratum (although not shown in table 27.2) were smaller immigrant groups, notably those from Nigeria, Egypt, South Africa, Kenya, Israel, Lebanon, Ghana, and Argentina. In fact, by the mid-1970s, one-fifth of all US physicians were immigrants, and there were already more foreign medical graduates from India and the Philippines in the USA than native African American physicians. By the mid-1980s, over half of all doctoral degrees in engineering awarded by US universities were earned by foreign-born students, with one-fifth of all engineering doctorates going to students from Taiwan, India, and South Korea alone; and one-third of all engineers with a doctorate working in US industry were immigrants. These "brain drain" immigrants are perhaps the most skilled ever to come to the United States. Their class origins help to explain the popularization of Asians as a "model minority" and to debunk nativist calls for restricting immigrants to those perceived to be more "assimilable" on the basis of color, language, and culture.

By contrast, as table 27.2 shows, the lower socioeconomic stratum includes recent immigrants from Mexico, El Salvador, Guatemala, the Dominican Republic, and to a lesser extent Haiti – many of whom were undocumented. They had higher rates of labor force participation but much lower levels of educational attainment, were concentrated in low-wage unskilled jobs, and had poverty rates as high as those of native minority groups, though much lower proportions of households on welfare. Here also were less educated but less visible and older European immigrants from Italy and Portugal (34 percent of Portuguese adult immigrants had less than a fifth grade education, compared to less than 2 percent of the total US-born population). And two Asian-origin nationalities, Laotian and Cambodian refugees, exhibited by far the highest rates of poverty and welfare dependency in the USA. Southeast Asians and to a lesser extent Chinese and Korean workers are much in evidence, along with undocumented Mexican and Central American immigrants, in a vast underground sweatshop economy that expanded during the 1980s and 1990s in Southern California. These data too debunk stereotypes that have been propounded in the mass media as explanations of "Asian" success, and point instead to the contextual diversity of recent immigration and to the class advantages and disadvantages of particular groups.

A middle stratum, composed of groups whose educational and occupational characteristics are close to the US average, is even more heterogeneous in terms of national origin, as seen in table 27.2. It includes older immigrants from the Soviet Union, Britain, Canada, and Germany, and more recent immigrants from Vietnam, Cuba, Colombia, and Jamaica. However, not at all evident in table 27.2 is the fact that *within* particular nationalities there are often also many class differences which reflect different "waves" and immigration histories. For example, while 31 percent of adult immigrants from China have college degrees, 16 percent have less than a fifth grade education. Desperate Haitian boat people arriving by the thousands in the 1980s and 1990s mask an upper middle-class flow of escapees from the Duvalier regime in the early 1960s; by 1972 the number of Haitian physicians in the USA represented an incredible 95 percent of Haiti's stock. Similarly, the post-1980 waves of Cuban Mariel refugees and Vietnamese "boat people" from modest social class back-grounds differed sharply from the elite "first waves" of the 1959–62 Cubans and the 1975 Vietnamese, underscoring the internal diversification of particular national flows over time – and the complexities of contemporary "ethclass" formations.

Among the employed, the percentage of older, longer-established Canadian and certain European immigrants in professional specialties exceeds the respect-ive proportion of their groups who are college graduates; but the percentage of recently arrived Asian immigrants who are employed in the professions is gen-erally far below their respective proportions of college graduates. These discre-pancies between educational and occupational attainment point to barriers such as English proficiency and strict licensing requirements that regulate entry into the professions and that recent immigrants – most of them non-white, non-European, and non-English speakers – must confront as they seek to make their way in America. In response, some immigrants shift instead to entrepre-neurship as an avenue of economic advancement and as an alternative to employment in segmented labor markets. As table 27.2 shows, Korean immi-grants are the leading example of this entrepreneurial mode of incorporation, with self-employment rates that are higher by far than any other native-born or foreign-born groups.

SOME QUESTIONS AND REFLECTIONS ON AMERICAN PLURALISM

The rapid growth of this emerging population – unprecedented in its diversity of color, class, and cultural origin – is changing fundamentally the ethnic and racial composition and stratification of the American population, and perhaps also the social meanings of race and ethnicity, and of American identity. All of this has led to a burgeoning research literature (see Smith and Edmonston, 1997; Hirschman et al., 1999), and an intensified, at times xenophobic, public debate about the new immigration and its manifold impacts on American society. Less noticed has been the fact that a new second generation of Americans raised in immigrant families has been coming of age – transforming their adoptive society even as they themselves are becoming transformed into the newest Americans. Over time, its members will decisively shape the character of their ethnic com-munities and their success or failure (Gans, 1992; Portes, 1996; Portes and Rumbaut, 1996, 2000; Zhou, 1997; Rumbaut, 1998). Hence, the long-term effects of contemporary immigration will hinge more on the trajectories of these youths than on the fate of their parents. These children of today's immigrants – a post-immigrant generation oriented not to their parents' immigrant pasts but to their own American futures – are here to stay, and they represent the most consequential and lasting legacy of the new mass immigration to the United States.

What will the long-term national consequences will be? Will the new ethnic mosaic reinvigorate the nation or spell a quantum leap in its social problems? Will the newcomers move into the mainstream of American life or will they be marginalized into an expanded multiethnic underclass? Will their social mobility be enabled by the structure of opportunities or blocked by racial discrimination and a changed economy? Will their offspring's search for identity fade with time, acceptance, and intermarriage into the "twilight of ethnicity" or will a hostile reception and a color line lead instead with heightened salience into the "high noon" of ethnicity? Different groups' frames of remembrance and retellings of their past – their definitions of the situation – tell much about who has been included and excluded in the national narrative, and hence about the society's contexts of reception and terms of belonging (Aleinikoff and Rumbaut, 1998). As these newest members "become American," in their own plural ways, what kinds of narratives will they tell, and on what terms of belonging? Will their children and grandchildren "repeat" the history and experience of previous waves of European immigrants? If we can learn something from that checkered past, it may be to harbor few illusions about the value of gazing into crystal balls. When those now-legendary millions of young European strangers were disembarking at Ellis Island early in the twentieth century, who could have imagined what the world would be like for their children in the 1930s, or their grandchildren in the 1960s? And today, who can foresee what world will await the children of millions of Latin American and Caribbean and Asian and African strangers in the 2020s, or their grandchildren in the 2050s? In a world changing faster than we seem to learn about it, it may be a fool's errand to extrapolate naively and myopically from the present in order to divine the distant future.

Still, in the context of today's debates about the one and the many, about multiculturalism and the "disuniting of America," about the contested meaning of race, the rise of ethnic consciousness, and the politics of identity, it might help to gain some distance from the objects of contention and listen for a moment to a different voice, less ethnocentric, more cosmopolitan. In *The Buried Mirror* (1992), his quincentennial reflections on Spain and the New World, the Mexican writer Carlos Fuentes, himself a progeny of that original encounter between the Old World and the New, put the matter this way:

> History begs the question, How to live with the Other? How to understand that I am what I am only because another person sees me and completes me? This question, which arises every time that white and black, East and West, predecessor and immigrant, meet in our times...became the central question of conquest and colonization in the Americas. (Fuentes, 1992, p. 89)

Writing before the passage of Propositions 187, 209, and 227, Fuentes sees "the universal question of the coming century" posed most forcefully in California, especially in Los Angeles, the world's premier immigrant metropolis and a gateway to both Asia and Latin America. "How do we deal with the Other?" He seeks his answer in his hybrid origins: "We [Hispanics] are Indian, Black, European, but above all mixed, *mestizo*. We are Iberian and Greek, Roman and Jewish, Arab, Gothic and Gypsy." Indeed, after nearly 800 years of Arab rule in Spain, lasting until the triumph of the *reconquista* with the fall of the last Moorish kingdom in 1492, the Arab cultural influence was pervasive, so that today fully a quarter of all Spanish words are of Arab origin. For Fuentes the answer lies in forging

> centers of incorporation, not of exclusion. When we exclude, we betray ourselves. When we include, we find ourselves.... People and their cultures perish in isolation, but they are born or reborn in contact with other men and women, with men and women of another culture, another creed, another race. If we do not recognize our humanity in others, we shall not recognize it in ourselves. Often we have failed to meet this challenge. But we have finally seen ourselves whole in the unburied mirror of identity, only when accompanied – ourselves with others. (Fuentes, 1992, pp. 348, 353)

As long as ethnoracial and economic inequalities remain deeply entrenched in American institutions, such a "post-ethnic" cosmopolitan vision will fail to be fulfilled. But the United States today is in the midst of a profound transformation, and inexorable processes of globalization, especially international migrations from Asia, Africa, and the Americas, will diversify further still the polyethnic composition of its constituent populations – and make more exigent the challenge of their incorporation. At such times, and in a field as dynamic and controversial as this one, when issues of immigration, race, and ethnicity command national policy attention and have become the stuff of acrimonious public debates – from assimilation to affirmative action to bilingual education to multiculturalism to border control to citizenship – there is an urgent need for an inclusive sociological vision with wide-angle lenses that can grasp the complexity of the ever-changing present within its larger historical context.

American pluralism is Janus-faced – looking behind to vastly different and even antithetical pasts, looking ahead to scarcely predictable if polyethnic futures – mixing a plurality of interests, origins, and outlooks capable of interpreting the nation's "foundational fictions" and the ethno-national experience from very different vantage points. It is bound to remain thus unless and until this "permanently unfinished" country manages to reconcile the erstwhile irreconcilable dualities of its history: a country stamped at once with all of its alluring, perennial promise as a land of opportunity and fresh starts for the ambitious stranger and the tempest-tost, and with all of its enduring, bitter legacy of racial exclusion and color lines, of blocked opportunities and deferred dreams. Still, the challenge of (and to) American pluralism is not a peremptory challenge, imperious and impervious to debate; rather, it is played out in the context of a civic culture that offers room for open discussion and question. What is past is prologue, yes; but it need not be the epilogue too. An inclusive, not intolerant, American pluralism need not produce bitter legacies, but better ones, while teaching us at once some poignant lessons of empirical sociology and universal history.

28

Social Psychology

LYNN SMITH-LOVIN

Social psychology in sociology has three distinct intellectual faces: the study of group processes, the study of symbolic interaction, and the study of social structure and personality. These intellectual traditions have different questions and methods, but share a strong focus on the relational character of human activity. The group processes tradition uses experimental methods to look at how patterns of relationships determine individual outcomes. It also looks at how relational structures evolve, through coalition formation, the dissolution of ties, or the creation of hierarchy. The symbolic interactionists often use qualitative data to study how meanings are developed through social interaction, and how interpretation of situations using those meanings generates lines of action. They focus on how the social relationships in which we are embedded become incorporated into an organized sense of self, which then serves to motivate future actions. The social structure and personality tradition often uses symbolic interactionist logic to study the impact of institutional positions on individual outcomes like well-being, attitudes, values, or behavior patterns. These researchers typically use survey methods, since people can reliably report their location in institutional structures (for example, martial status, employment status, education) and the outcomes of interest are measured at the individual level.

A comprehensive book-length summary of the findings in the three faces of sociological social psychology is offered in a volume sponsored by the American Sociological Association Section on Social Psychology (Cook et al., 1995). Rather than duplicating that encyclopedic review, this chapter concentrates on developments in two areas where major advances have come in the past decade, and where current controversies still brew. The two areas are the analysis of instrumental action in social structures and the analysis of affective, emotional processes that interaction in these structures evokes. The first is centered in the group process tradition; the second encompasses work in both the symbolic interactionist and the social structure and personality areas. In recent years, several scholars have begun to look at how the instrumental and affective processes are interrelated. The chapter ends by reviewing this convergence, as well as highlighting some new areas for development.

RATIONAL ACTION WITHIN SOCIAL STRUCTURES

The intuitive idea that actors attempt to maximize outcomes that they value led to the development of several closely related theories of social exchange in the late 1950s and early 1960s (Thibaut and Kelley, 1959; Homans, 1961; Blau, 1964). While these early theories sparked considerable controversy (some scholars charged they were tautological or reductionist), the early exchange perspectives led directly to some of the most productive theoretical research programs in sociological social psychology. The most direct descendants are the modern theories of social exchange (see review in chapter 8 of Cook et al., 1995).

Social Exchange Theory

Most modern social exchange theories draw heavily on the work of Emerson (1972), who answered many of the controversies surrounding the original exchange theories by focusing on (a) the power–dependence relationship and (b) the exchange network. Emerson defined the power of an actor A over actor B as equal to the dependence of actor B on actor A for valued resources. Thus, power was a property of a relationship, not a characteristic of an individual. Focusing on the relationship allowed sociologists to predict how power would vary in enduring, stable configurations of relationships. Indeed, a great deal of work in the past two decades has focused on how the structure of a network affects the relative dependence of actors, and thus their relative power.

Researchers usually study social exchange in laboratory settings using money as the valued good that is exchanged. Money is convenient because it is widely valued, satiation occurs relatively slowly, and it is easily quantified. The theory, however, applies to all types of valued things that people can want from other people: positive evaluation, desirable behaviors, goods, or services. In the lab, people (often strangers who are isolated from one another) have the opportunity to exchange with one or more potential partners. The most common type of network studied is a negatively connected network – one in which exchange with one partner makes exchange with another less likely (often impossible) during a given time period. For example, both car sales and marriage occur in negatively connected networks. Buying a car from one person decreases to almost zero the chance that you will buy a car from another in a short time frame. Marrying one person eliminates the possibility of marrying another (until a divorce has occurred).

Two major types of exchange dominate the literature: negotiated and reciprocal. In negotiated networks, people make offers to one another until a deal is struck or until the round ends without an agreement. The important feature here is that each actor knows what he or she will receive for the value he or she offers. Actors receive rewards for the joint behavior of reaching an agreement, and that agreement is strictly binding. In reciprocal exchange, on the other hand, the terms of exchange are not negotiated. Actors individually choose behaviors that have consequences for their interaction partners, without knowing what those people will choose to do to them. This situation more closely represents many interpersonal interactions: the exchange of smiles, favors, etc. When I do something helpful for you, I often do not obtain explicit agreement that you will return the kindness at a later time (that would be negotiated exchange). Any benefit that I receive results from the individual action of the other person, and the extent of that benefit (if any) is unknown at the time that I make my decision about whether to act to help the other. This doesn't mean, of course, that reciprocal exchange is not contingent. Obviously, if no behavior resulting in value to me occurs, I am unlikely to continue sending rewarding behaviors indefinitely. For the first 15 or 20 years, the research on negotiated and reciprocal exchange proceeded in parallel. Molm (2000a) has recently reported experiments in which negotiated and reciprocal exchange are compared directly. She found that power use was lower in reciprocal exchange than in negotiated exchange. She also found that powerful actors in reciprocal exchanges were more likely to opt for patterns of exchange that produced predictable, steady exchange with their disadvantaged partners, rather than adopting a strategy of intermittent rewarding that would have maximized their outcomes in the long run. In other words, reciprocal exchange tends to produce satisficing rather than maximizing patterns of interaction that produce more equality than does negotiated exchange.

Position in both negotiated and reciprocal exchange networks determines how often an actor exchanges with various partners, how many valued goods an actor accumulates, etc. Actors are more dependent when they are connected to fewer potential exchange partners, especially if those partners have many other good options for exchange. Dependent actors are excluded from exchange more often, get smaller quantities of valued goods in negotiated exchanges, and receive fewer benefits from their relationships. The important feature here is that this result requires no particular conscious or strategic action on the part of actors in less dependent positions. To have power is to use it. Less dependent (more powerful) actors will receive better offers (in negotiated exchange) or receive more frequent rewards from others (in reciprocal exchange) simply by virtue of their position.

Much controversy in social network research has centered on formal measures of structural power – the advantage that a position derives from the availability of alternative exchange relations, the limits on the availability of their relations' alternatives, and so on throughout a network. (See the June 1992 issue of the journal *Social Networks* for a set of papers highlighting this topic.) Some approaches have used network concepts like centrality or reachability, while others use more formal graph analytic approaches. Other scholars have challenged the usefulness of these purely structural descriptions of power by combining the influence of the network's structure and the actor's behavior pattern on exchange outcomes (Molm, 1990; Freidkin, 1992). Actors who create strong, contingent reinforcement patterns for their interaction partners achieve better outcomes than those who use inconsistent patterns. The effects of these patterns are especially important for those who occupy relatively disadvantaged network positions.

Because of Emerson's influence, much exchange research in the past 20 years has focused on the voluntary exchange of positively valued things. The more traditional (and colloquial) sense of power as coercive, negative control of another's behavior has received much less attention. Most theorists who did treat both reward-based power dependence and coercive, punitive power explicitly dealt with the two types of power as entailing different processes. Molm (1997), however, incorporated both rewards and punishments within the power dependence framework. She argued that you can be dependent on someone else both as a source of valued things and to avoid things that you don't want to happen. In experiments, this punishment power often is operationalized as the ability to take points (worth money) away from another actor. This format allowed Molm to investigate how reward power and punishment power worked together to create outcomes in an exchange network.

Molm showed that people don't use punishment power very often, because it is risky and people are generally risk-averse. They experience losses more sharply than gains. If you punish someone who has something that you want, that person will often retaliate by withholding rewards or punishing you back, rather than doing what you want him or her to. So the only actors who use punishment strategies very often are the people who don't have much to lose: coercion is the tool of people who are disadvantaged on reward power and who are imbedded in highly imbalanced relationships (Molm, 1997, pp. 270–1). They have less to lose and more to gain by using punishment. Punishment can be very effective, however, if used with an effective behavioral strategy. As Molm (1997, p. 268) puts it, "successful coercion requires diligence in monitoring another's behavior, skill in applying punishment contingently, and the willingness to accept short-term losses (including normative censure) in return for uncertain long-term gains."

In addition to the new work by Molm comparing negotiated and reciprocal exchange, new threads in the exchange literature highlight the structure itself as a dependent variable. More studies on coalition formation, network expansion, and other forms of network transformation are making the relationship even more central to this area. Some of this research explores how affective response as a social exchange outcome can promote cohesion and commitment in exchange relationships; this work is reviewed below in an examination of the convergence of instrumental and affective research interests. Other new research questions shift the focus from negatively connected, competitive exchanges to positively connected networks in which resources gained through exchange with one actor actually make exchange with another partner *more* likely. Since most production systems have this character – supplies need to be obtained from multiple sources before a good can be produced – these positively connected networks are very important for our understanding of social systems. There is also a lively literature on how rational, goal-oriented actors can solve social dilemmas – situations where cooperation is mutually advantageous, but the highest-payoff individual strategy is not to cooperate (see review in chapter 12 of Cook et al., 1995).

Expectation States Theory

The other major research tradition spawned by the early exchange theorists has ventured much farther from its roots. Influenced by Homans's early exchange theory and by Bales's (1950) observations of behavior in small task groups, Joseph Berger and his colleagues (Berger et al., 1974) tried to explain why a large number of group behaviors, like talking, being spoken to, evaluating the ideas of others, receiving positive evaluations from others, tended to occur together in what they called a *power and prestige order*. They proposed an expectation states theory of how these observable status hierarchies developed. They argued that under certain conditions – a collective task orientation where all group members stand to gain from better performance on a group enterprise – inequalities in task-related behaviors develop out of group members' expectations about the value of their own and others' contributions to the group task. Effectively, deference is granted to group members in exchange for the recipient engaging in behaviors that produce rewards for the other group members.

Performance expectations are the central concept in the theory. Group members form performance expectations, then give or take action opportunities to produce the best group outcome, given their beliefs about group members' relative abilities to contribute. Despite the fact that expectations are formed by individuals, however, the interactional encounter is the unit of analysis in the theory. In expectation states theory, it is the comparison of expectations for two group members that allows the prediction of the behavior that they will engage in *vis-à-vis* one another. Like power, status is a relational concept rather than an individual characteristic.

Performance expectations can form from several sources. In a group of highly similar people, behavioral cues early in the interaction can be crucial. People who engage in positive task behaviors, seizing early action opportunities, generate high performance expectations. But much of the expectation states research focused on how status characteristics that were valued in outside society were used to differentiate group members. When group members differed on some evaluated characteristic, Berger argued that this characteristic became salient in forming performance expectations. Unless there was evidence to the contrary, the group member with the more valued state of the status characteristic would be presumed by group members to have higher competence at the group task than someone with the less valued status.

Berger and his colleagues adopted the strategy of isolating status processes from other things that could go on in small groups (like emotional dynamics or identity processes). They used a standardized experimental setting in which a subject interacted with a simulated actor. Both the subject and the simulated actor made judgments about an ambiguous stimulus, under conditions where they were motivated to make accurate judgments. After the individual judgments were reported back to the subject, he or she was given a chance to change his or her individual decision if the two disagreed. The proportion of "stay" responses – sticking with one's own opinion in the face of disagreement from the simulated other – was the key dependent variable. Independent variables typically were characteristics like gender, race, ethnicity, personal attractiveness, or education, that are evaluated in our society and that were assigned to the simulated actor in order to produce status advantage or disadvantage for the subject. The important thing about this research tradition is that these status characteristics (for example, being male as opposed to female) are *not* seen as directly determining task behavior. Instead, the theory predicts that gender will determine the power and prestige order only when it is salient (because it differentiates group members) and when it is linked to expectations about the task in particular ways. For example, men are generally presumed in our society to be more competent than women, but this is an indirect link to a non-gendered task. If the task is male-stereotypic, the link could be stronger; if it is female-stereotypic, the link could be reversed in direction (with women receiving higher performance expectations).

Later work explored how demeanor, rewards from other tasks, and formal positions could influence expectations (and therefore group behavior). After the basic structure of the theory was well supported, researchers devoted many studies to exploring how different types of information combined to form performance expectations (see review in chapter 11 of Cook et al., 1995). A related thread of research investigated how status structures became legitimated, and how this legitimacy helped to stabilize the inequalities that result.

Expectation states theory has been very successful in applied research as well. A number of experiments demonstrate how initial status differences, imported from the external societal structure, can be reduced or eliminated by employing interventions that shape group members' expectations. Elizabeth Cohen (1982), for example, showed how group tasks and strategic interventions could help racial minorities to become more active in school settings. Others have demonstrated how gender inequalities can be reduced or reversed (see Wagner et al., 1986, for an example and summary of this work).

Recent research has moved back from the rigorously controlled standardized experiment to the analysis of small group interaction. For example, Cathy Johnson (1993) has explored how being assigned to a managerial or worker role in a simulated work environment influenced conversational behaviors like interruption or suggesting ideas. As a consequence of this move to the study of open interaction, researchers are beginning to investigate how status-organizing processes interact with other dynamics in groups (see discussion below of status and emotion). Another major focus of recent research is a new attention to the dynamics of group interaction. Skvoretz and Fararo (1986), for example, attempted to specify how information imported from outside status structures combined with information that unfolds as the group interacts to form a cumulating status structure. New event history methods that allow the analysis of behavior as it unfolds over time have allowed researchers to examine these dynamics empirically.

Another important development in this tradition, also based partially on exchange principles, is Cecilia Ridgeway's theory of status value (Ridgeway, 1991). Ridgeway asked the question: how do nominal characteristics (categories like male/female, young/old, black/white) acquire consensual status value in society? Using expectation states logic, she argued that if the nominal characteristic is correlated initially with some material resource, interactions between people who differ on both resource levels and the nominal characteristic will lead to inferences about performance expectation that will eventually diffuse through the society, creating status value for the nominal categories. New simulation work by Mark et al. (1999) indicates that in small societies, a correlation between resources and the nominal characteristic is not needed; uncorrelated differentiation on both resources and the nominal characteristic is enough to create status value in some instances.

The research traditions above – social exchange and expectation states – both look at how people attempt to gain valued rewards, the first through exchange with others and the second in the context of a group performing a collective task. We now turn to research traditions that are based on a different conception of the actor.

MEANING AND EMOTION IN SOCIAL INTERACTION

The symbolic interactionist tradition in sociology has at its root three central principles: (a) people act toward things, including each other, on the basis of the meanings that those things hold for them; (b) the primary source of these meanings is social interaction; and (c) meanings are managed and transformed through an interpretative process (Snow, 2000). The fundamental conception of the actor is that of a meaning-creator, who actively works to interpret what is happening around him or her in terms of meanings accrued from past interactions and who actively generates new lines of action to maintain a coherent, meaningful view of self and others. Historically a heavily cognitive perspective, symbolic interaction has turned its eye toward affective meaning and emotion in the past 20 years (MacKinnon, 1994). There are two dominant perspectives in this new work. The first views emotion as a signal about how well events are maintaining identities. The second takes a more cultural approach, concentrating on the norms associated with emotion.

Control Theories of Identity

Sociologists use the term "identity" to refer to the many meanings attached to a person, both by the self and by others. The concept embraces both (a) structural features like group affiliations, role occupancy, and category memberships, and (b) the character traits that the individual displays or that others attribute to him or her. There has historically been some tension between symbolic interactionists who focus on the creative, actively negotiated process through which people make their identities within social interaction and the symbolic interactionists who emphasize the extent to which our identities are shaped by the social structures in which we live. (See Stryker (1980) for a nice overview of the history of interactionist thought and Snow (2000) for a short summary of differences and communalities between the two schools.) In recent years, theoretical thinking in the latter camp (often called structural symbolic interactionism) has been dominated by a control system model that makes it much more dynamic, creative and processual.

David Heise (1979) initially developed the control system view, borrowing control models from engineering and measurement technology from psychology. He argued that people acquire general meanings for role-identities (like mother and daughter) and social actions (like compliment or criticize) through interaction. The meanings are affective in character and universal in their form. People respond to all concepts in terms of three basic dimensions: goodness, powerfulness, and liveliness. After people acquire these meanings, they are quite stable. Therefore, when people recognize an interaction as an instance of a certain type of situation (a mother and a daughter), they perceive events and engage in actions that maintain the meanings that those role-identities evoke. So a woman who sees herself as a mother interacting with a daughter will do things that maintain the good, powerful, and lively meanings associated with that identity, and will expect her daughter to do things to maintain that somewhat less potent but more lively identity. Thus the role-identity meanings and action meanings act as reference signals that are maintained by social interaction. When events do not maintain identity meanings, emotions signal the extent and direction of the deflection away from the reference value (Smith-Lovin and Heise, 1989; Smith-Lovin, 1990).

There are several important ways in which this affect control theory represented a major advance over earlier formulations. The control model focuses explicitly on the relational context of interaction. The unit of analysis here is the event (an actor–behavior–object combination), not the individual. The use of universal dimensions of meaning (goodness, powerfulness, and liveliness) allows all types of social entities (actors, behaviors, emotions, traits, settings) to be characterized in the same system. Using an impression formation paradigm from psychology, the theory specifies exactly how the many elements of a situation combine to form a situation-specific meaning that is then compared to the reference value to ascertain how well events are maintaining meanings. Most importantly, the control view of the relationship between role-identity and social action accurately represented the extraordinary flexibility of actors' application of cultural information as they moved through varying situations. Role occupants (for example, mothers) did not follow a simple, static script of role expectations *vis-à-vis* a particular alter (a daughter). What they did was powerfully shaped by events that occurred and their interpretation of them. A mother who has just been appreciated by her daughter is expected to behave very differently than a mother who has been ignored. A final insight from affect control theory is the sense in which cognition and affect are intertwined inexorably. One cannot process a cognitive understanding of an interpersonal situation without responding to it emotionally. Nor is emotion likely to occur (in any but the simplest stimulus–response modes) without the active work of defining the situation.

Burke (1991) later developed an alternative identity control model. He used a more intricate, role-specific method for measuring meaning (so that meanings cannot be compared across role domains). Burke's model focused only on the maintenance of the focal actor's identity meanings; he assumed that people tried to maintain their own identities, but are concerned with the identities of others only insofar as they impact self-meanings. In contrast, affect control theory attempts to maintain meanings associated with all elements of a situation.

The most marked difference between the two control models is in their view of emotion, however. In Heise's theory, people may feel exceptionally good, potent or lively if their immediate experiences deflect them upward on one or more of the affective dimensions. An employee who receives an unexpectedly good performance evaluation might feel "high as a kite." While people are predicted to act in ways that bring situated meanings back into line with reference signals, emotions can signal deflections above *or* below the reference standard. In Burke's identity control formulation, failure to confirm meanings is always assumed to produce a negative emotion, stress (Burke, 1991).

Researchers have tested the control theories successfully using a wide array of experimental, survey and qualitative methods (see reviews in chapters 2 and 5 of Cook et al., 1995). Experiments showed that affect control theory does a good job of predicting the emotions of both actors and the recipients of actions. Experiments also have confirmed the counterintuitive prediction that people will choose to interact with others who confirm a negative self-identity (as a poor public speaker) *even when the other option is someone who evaluates them more positively than they evaluate themselves.* Qualitative data from two church congregations showed how gay Christians created new identities and rituals to generate positive emotions in a religious context (while more traditional identity meanings for homosexual and religious identities generated negative emotion). Burke and his colleagues have tested their control theory extensively in a data set of newly married couples in Washington state who were followed for three years. Gender identities, personal identities about control, and parental/spousal identities all appear to be maintained by the respondents in that survey.

New research focuses on three areas. First, both control theories have developed such substantial research traditions at this point that scholars are beginning to consider how to judge their relative strengths. The key points of disagreement – the measurement of meaning, the location of the reference standard, and the valence of emotion – will focus research in the future. Second, both research traditions have begun to explore how the multiple identities that constitute the self are processed during interaction. These studies deal with the salience of identities within a relatively stable self-structure (Stryker, 1980) and the parallel processing of multiple identities that may be evoked within a single situation (Smith-Lovin, 2001). Third, researchers are applying the control theories in the context of instrumental interaction to view the interaction of affective and instrumental processes. This work is discussed more extensively in the final section of the chapter.

Feeling Rules, Emotion Work, and Emotional Labor

While the control models use identity dynamics to generate emotions, most work in the sociology of emotion emphasizes cultural norms. Arlie Hochschild (1979) drew upon Erving Goffman's insights about the management of self-presentation to discuss how people manage their emotions to make them appropriate to a situation. Hochschild developed the concept of emotion work to describe the act of trying to change the type or intensity of emotion that one was experiencing. People use cognitive thoughts, physical manipulation, or expressive display to try to change how they feel. Often people manage emotions in order to conform to feeling rules – norms about what type or intensity of emotion we *should* feel. Peggy Thoits (1985) has linked emotion work to mental health. She argued that when emotions routinely fail to match our cultural expectations and management efforts fail, the emotional deviance could be labeled as mental illness. Such deviance could be created by inadequate socialization or by structurally induced stress.

When emotion work is done for pay, and feeling rules are job requirements that represent a "commoditization of feeling," Hochschild argued that workers could lose touch with their real, unmanaged emotional responses. She speculated that the consequences would be a disturbing sense of inauthenticity and burnout on the job. Her study of the emotional labor that flight attendants were required to perform to put up a pleasant, friendly face in interaction with sometimes annoying, abusive passengers (Hochschild, 1983) illustrates the process. Emotional labor in many other occupations – bill collectors, supermarket checkers, medical students, nurses, and library workers – has been observed using similar ethnographic methods. Researchers have also studied emotion norms in non-work contexts using undergraduate students, advice books, women's magazine columns, and ethnographic work in other cultures. This work convincingly demonstrates that norms for both feelings and emotion display are an important component of many roles. These norms can change over time and vary from culture to culture. Research on the psychological effects of managing one's emotions for pay is less convincing; this is a promising area for future work.

Social Structural Positions and Emotional Experience

Survey researchers often study mental well-being while drawing on both the symbolic interactionist and cultural perspectives on emotion. This research tradition looked at how social structural positions (and the role-identities that they imply) affect emotional experience. In general, this research showed that those who are disadvantaged or lower status report more emotional distress than those who have greater control and more resources to cope with trouble (see review in Mirowsky and Ross, 1989). Women report more emotional distress than men. The uneducated poor report more than the educated rich. Poor racial minorities experienced more distress than poor whites (although the effect is non-existent or occasionally reversed among the middle class). People who experience undesirable life events (for example, loss of a job, death of a spouse, accidents) report more distress than those who do not. The young and the very old are more unhappy than the middle-aged. Those who have few network ties and few social roles have less happiness than those with more resources. The basic argument in this work is that positive emotional experience is more likely when people occupy positive, high status identities, when they have control over interactions in which they are embedded, and when they have coping mechanisms available to them to handle any misfortunes that do occur. As the sturctural symbolic interactionists would predict, those who occupy high status, high power positions are more likely to experience pleasant, efficacious emotions as they maintain those identitites.

The Interplay of Affect and Instrumental Action

While the research on instrumental action and on emotional processes proceeded without much cross-fertilization for a long time, several recent research projects look at how the two interact. The convergence of interests began with a theory of emotions based on social exchange principles. Kemper (1978) proposed a theory based on two dimensions of relationships that he argued were universal: status and power. Relative positions on these two dimensions defined the key aspects of a relationship and determined its emotional character (what Kemper called structural emotions). Changes in status or power and attributions about who was responsible for causing those changes led to specific emotions. For example, status loss led to anger if the other person was responsible. The anger then motivated action to regain status. Status loss by another, if caused by oneself, led to guilt.

Since Kemper's theory, several research streams have developed to examine how instrumental exchanges affect emotional outcomes. The oldest and most developed stream focuses on how perceptions of justice, equity, or fairness develop from exchange interactions (see review in chapter 10 of Cook et al., 1995). Indeed, this was a central concern of the original exchange theorists, Homans, Blau, and Emerson. Not surprisingly, people feel they have been unjustly treated and express anger when their rewards are lower than their investments. Past reward experiences, status structures, power structures, and reference groups all serve to complicate the process, however. People quickly acclimate to any given levels of rewards (or a stable trajectory, like steadily rising rewards) and experience outcomes that fall below that expected level with a sense of distressing loss (Molm, 1997). Closely related to expectation states theory, status value theory argues that people generally expect congruence between status value within a group and the level of rewards that one receives. Therefore, people perceive fairness and are satisfied with their outcomes when they receive what people like them generally get.

Power is related to perceptions of fairness in a somewhat more complicated way. Power use (and its lack of reciprocity) lead to perceptions of unfairness, but coercive power use causes much more negative emotion than reward withholding (Molm, 1997, pp. 190–218). Even when the two types of power use result in equivalent departures from reciprocity, coercive power is seen as more nasty and intentional. These negative feelings by the low power person lead to behavioral resistance – reward withholding and even retaliation. This reaction, in turn, makes the high power user lose part of the ability to reward; since loss is experienced very sharply, the retaliation generally helps to mute coercive power use below what would be expected in the absence of the emotional response.

A more recent research thread in social exchange deals with the related question of how trust and affective commitment (positive feeling) build up in exchange relationships. Edward Lawler and his colleagues have posited a model through which repeated exchanges each create small amounts of positive emotion, cumulating over time to create a positive attitude toward the exchange partner and behavioral commitment (high levels of exchange) to the exchange relationship (Lawler and Yoon, 1998). One of the most interesting elements of this work is its analysis of how networks evolve over time in response to emotional outcomes. In systems with some equal and some unequal relations, pockets of positive, cohesive, committed relations tend to form among the power-equals, cutting them off from the more powerful actors within the system. Since the more powerful actors generally have more potential exchange partners, they spread their interactions among a large number of alters and develop committed relationships with very few. On the other hand, when somewhat lower power, but power-equal, actors can exchange more frequently with each other, they form highly cohesive subgroups.

Other network theorists have concentrated on the link between uncertainty, behavioral commitment and trust. Basically, these researchers show that trust can only develop when an exchange is risky (i.e. the situation allows for untrustworthy behavior) *and* the trading partner acts in a reliable, trustworthy manner. Kollock (1994), for example, showed that trust and behavior commitment develops more quickly when the quality of the traded good is difficult to determine (and therefore the opportunity to deceive is present). Molm (2000b) showed that trust and affective commitment developed to highest levels in reciprocal exchange (where partners did not negotiate to binding agreements), especially when the power structure made behavioral commitment advantageous for both.

Just as exchange researchers have shown how emotions are embedded in exchange structures, expectation states researchers have begun looking at how identity meanings and emotions can shape status processes. When status hierarchies form in small, task-oriented groups, the high status people often experience more positive emotions, since they are encouraged to make contributions and their contributions are more often marked by positive evaluation. Conversely, the lower status people often feel negative emotions about being ignored or having their contributions commented on negatively. Lovaglia and Houser (1999) demonstrated that these emotions tend to mute the status structure.

The lower status group members are resistant to influence because of their negative emotion, while the higher status members may be unusually accepting because of their good feelings. Exchange researchers have noted the same thing in the interaction of power, influence, and emotion: the negative emotion felt by low power people makes them much less likely to accept influence from high power people for whom they would normally hold high expectations (Willer et al., 1997).

The group processes researchers are also beginning to explore how identity interacts with status and power processes. Identity that links low and high power positions seems to mute power use in exchange networks (Lawler and Yoon, 1998). If the subject in an expectation states experiment shares an identity with a simulated actor, that piece of positive identity information seems to combine just like other status information to form performance expectations (Kalkhoff and Barnum, 2000).

CONCLUSIONS ABOUT THE STATE OF SOCIOLOGICAL SOCIAL PSYCHOLOGY

The research strategy chosen by the major theoretical programs in sociological social psychology has paid off handsomely. Isolating power, status, and identity processes so that they could be studied in pure form has led to a dramatic growth of theoretical knowledge in the past 25 years. Indeed, we have progressed so far that researchers are starting to put the picture back together again. In just the past five years, several studies have appeared that examine how status, power, identity, and emotion interact in more complex situations. Our increasing understanding of these interactions has also increased the interplay between experimental, survey, and ethnographic researchers. As the experimentalists, who primarily test theories, develop more complex views of how basic processes interact, their theories become more useful to survey and ethnographic researchers, who necessarily deal with a more complex social situation.

It is, of course, more difficult to say where we are going than to say where we have been. One expects the current trend toward studying the interactions between status, power, identity, and emotion to continue. But advances will certainly come *within* the faces of social psychology as well.

In social exchange, people are beginning to think about how exchange networks change. Studies of network dynamics – how networks evolve through different power structures – will constitute much future work. Since the research has focused so heavily on networks where exchange in one relation is negatively correlated with exchange in another, the future might lie in the study of positively connected networks – those where different resources are obtained from alters or where resources must be passed through an intermediary to obtain rewards. And ultimately, of course, we will have to study how complex exchange networks that mix the different types of connections operate.

In the study of status processes, theorists are beginning to consider what happens when you relax the basic scope conditions under which the theory should operate: the collectively oriented, goal seeking group. The exchange-based logic of the theory depends on these scope conditions (they are the only reason why we would expect an actor to defer to a higher expectation alter in order to obtain the collective reward). So the puzzle is why so many of the expectation states processes seem to operate *outside* the range of these situations. Researchers will explore a variety of avenues before understanding the phenomenon, but one suspects that issues of identity will play a major role in the answer.

The study of identity and emotion must focus to some degree on exploring the differences between the Heise and Burke models that now dominant the field. There also may be a return to the more network-ecological view of the self that characterized the structural symbolic interactionists' early efforts (Stryker, 1980). Once we understand how the social actor attempts to maintain identity meanings through social interaction and emotion display, we can return to the central question of how those identities and their meanings are obtained, and what evokes them in one situation as opposed to another.

The research on emotion management and emotion norms has been largely descriptive until now. Now that the existence of such norms (and their variation across historical time and across societies) is well established, we need additional work to establish the sources of the norms. What explains cultural variations in normative structure? How do emotion norms and other aspects of the social fabric co-evolve over history? In addition, Hochschild's (1983) original work suggested a number of hypotheses that we need to explore. She suggested that the class structure influences emotional socialization, so that middle-class children learn skills that better suit them for emotional labor. She also argued that participation in emotional labor over a long period tends to alienate workers from their authentic feelings, creating mental health problems. Data about emotional experience over many occupations and class backgrounds will be necessary to test such hypotheses.

Part VIII
Social Action

29

Immigrant Women and Paid Domestic Work: Research, Theory, and Activism

Pierrette Hondagneu-Sotelo

Many commentators refer to paid domestic work as the "invisible occupation."
The work occurs in private households; it is generally performed in isolation,
without the company of co-workers or managers; and in the United States it has
historically been the province of marginalized women, of women of color and of
immigrant women. The occupation did achieve national visibility for a moment
in 1993 with the revelation that two female nominees for attorney general had
hired undocumented immigrant workers to care for their children in their
homes. Yet even as national attention focused on nannies as domestic workers,
the objections raised by the Senate inquisitors, the media, and the constituents
centered on the "illegality" of hiring unauthorized immigrant workers and in
particular on Zoe Baird's failure to pay the requisite taxes and make social
security payments. This focus obscured issues that have to do with basic work
rights of domestic workers. In fact, the media attention ignored the voices and
concerns of the domestic workers themselves.

Who performs paid domestic work in the United States today? While domestic
employees are a diverse group that include European au pairs, college students,
and laid-off aerospace workers, the principal entrants into the occupation are
Latina and Caribbean immigrant women. They represent a group of workers
who, due to their class, race, gender, and legal status, are among the most
disenfranchised and vulnerable in our society. Little wonder, then, that their

needs and concerns remained largely "invisible," even when highlighted in a national controversy labeled by some pundits as "nannie-gate."

Paid domestic work encompasses multiple tasks – cleaning, serving, child care, gardening, and so forth – and is currently organized in various ways. In this chapter, I discuss only the employment of immigrant women who do house-cleaning according to job work arrangements, where they maintain a weekly or bi-weekly route of employers. Under job work, domestic workers are able to position themselves as experts to sell their labor services in much the same way a vendor sells a product to various customers, and since they work for different employers on different days, they are less likely to become involved in deeply personal employer–employee relations than are live-in domestics or those who work for the same employer on a daily basis (Romero, 1988).

While job work holds the potential to provide better working conditions and pay than those encountered by live-in domestic workers, it is still problematic. Job terms and pay are generally negotiated without the benefit of guidelines established by government, unions, employment agencies, or private firms, and domestic workers must locate and secure multiple sources of employment to survive. My research in a San Francisco Bay area community examined how immigrant women domestic workers devised ways to improve their employment in job work, and some of these findings were utilized in an innovative informa-tion and outreach project in Los Angeles that seeks to upgrade the occupation for Latina immigrant women. In both the research process and the dissemination of the research findings, I attempted to incorporate cultural models resonant with Latino communities. As I gathered research materials, I often acted as a *servidora*, an informal social worker, and later in the outreach project, some of the research findings were disseminated through *novelas*, a popular form of Latin American print media.

This chapter addresses research, theory, and activism in the context of immi-grant women who do paid domestic work. I argue that interaction between sociological research and activism informed by feminism can yield new theor-etical insights and understandings. First, I discuss and reflect on how a research process informed by feminism shaped a particular set of findings. Feminist principles shaped the research process by first encouraging me to see immigrant women as experts in defining their most urgent concerns, thus restraining me from imposing my own preconceived research agenda, and second inspiring me to rely on reciprocity. In particular, feminist concerns with reciprocity in field-work relationships inspired me to act as a *servidora*, and this revealed aspects of the occupation that may have otherwise remained concealed. Next, I discuss how I utilized these research findings in an information and outreach project aimed at Mexican and Central American immigrant women who do paid domestic work in Los Angeles. Finally, I reflect on how this process stimulated further theoretical insights for me. When I returned to ask women in the original community of study for suggestions on some of the materials I had prepared for use in the Los Angeles outreach project, the comments revealed new insights.

Discussions of theory and praxis often privilege the manner in which research and theory inform or direct political practices and activities. In this chapter, I suggest a less unilinear relationship between research and theory on the one hand and political activism on the other. In the instance discussed here, the dissemination of the research findings in an advocacy project led to a new understanding and theoretical interpretations of the research. Research, theory, and activism run on a feedback loop.

RESEARCH AND RECIPROCITY

My research on domestic employment comprises part of a larger study on migration patterns and changing gender relations among Mexican undocumented immigrant women and men that I conducted in a Mexican immigrant community located in the San Francisco Bay area. I chose qualitative methods – in-depth interviews and participant observation – in order to develop an explanation of processes as they unfold at the microstructural level. The materials discussed in this chapter draw mainly from observation and informal conversations that occurred in various public and private locales, supplemented by interviews with 17 women who were working as non-live-in domestic housecleaners or had done so in the recent past. All interactions and interviews were conducted in Spanish and research began in November 1986, just as the Immigration Reform and Control ACt was passed, and continued for 18 months.

I had not initially entered the field with the intention of examining how women organize paid domestic work. As I became immersed in many activities and groups in this community, I learned that the undocumented immigrant women there were concentrated in jobs as paid domestic workers in private households, usually working for different employers on different days. In many settings, everywhere, it seemed, I saw women talking about how they managed paid domestic work; I began to focus part of my research on these issues, and as I did, I read books such as Judith Rollins's *Between Women: Domestics and Their Employers* (1985) and Evelyn Nakano Glenn's *Issei, Nisei, Warbride: Three Generations of Japanese Women in Domestic Service* (1986). The ideas and approaches used in these studies prompted new questions for me, and so my ethnographic and interview research emerged in dialogue with some of this literature.

To date, most studies of domestics are largely based on information gathered from interviews and historical materials (Katzman, 1981; Dudden, 1983; Glenn, 1986; Romero, 1988, 1992). An exception is Rollins's study (1985), which is based on interviews with domestic employers and employees and on participant-observation material gathered by Rollins when she went "undercover" as a domestic worker, a method that provided a wealth of insights. The novelty and strength of participant-observation in this study is that it occurred in multiple settings. I did not seek employment as a paid domestic worker, but I interacted on a regular basis with the women who do the work and I gathered information at parties, church and community events, and in their homes. Observing paid domestic workers in their daily social life reveals that many social connections and exchanges undergird what appears to be a privatized economic relationship.

Ethnographic research involves constant face-to-face interaction over a prolonged period of time, and playing different roles offers the researcher different perspectives on social reality. The vantage point from which the researcher interacts and observes constitutes an important part of the research strategy; it structures the investigation's findings and shapes the parameters of the investigator's research roles and findings (Hondagneu-Sotelo, 1988). My different roles, besides student/researcher, included activist and community organizer, friend, nosy person, and *servidora*. Reciprocity was a central component to all these roles, but here I wish to focus on how this played out as I assumed elements of what appears to be an autochthonous woman's role in Latino immigrant communities.

Servidoras are Latina women who act as informal purveyors of information and who provide referrals and personal services to immigrant families. Two Chicana women and two immigrant women, one Mexican and the other Guatemalan, served a large number of families as community brokers, and I used them both as role models and sources of information. Although I worked in legal services and in a bilingual education program in this particular community seven years prior, it was not my old contacts so much as my English language and literacy skills, and my concurrent involvement in community organizations, that were valuable. I regularly accompanied individuals and families to collection agencies and doctor's and lawyer's offices, translated bank statements and insurance policies, provided updated information on amnesty-legalization provisions, and so forth. My activities as a *servidora* opened windows to immigrant lives that would have otherwise remained closed to me. These activities also opened the windows to a series of ethical issues.

The Ethics of Reciprocity

Ethics in field research generally refers either to covert research, where the true identity and purpose of the investigator remains unknown to those who are studied, or to the protection of human subjects (Bulmer, 1982). The practice of reciprocity, a practice consonant with feminist principles, also raises several ethical issues.

Why use reciprocity in the first place? Reciprocity offers a way to lessen the asymmetry of doing research among people lacking basic resources, rights, and power in society. For me, reciprocity was a way to avoid a more colonialist way of doing research or just entering the field to pillage "raw data" for export. It allowed me to engage in more of a mutual exchange, whereby people's time, efforts, and energy in helping me with my research project were compensated by some of the resources to which I had access.

But was it less exploitative? In some cases, reciprocity served as an informal quid pro quo, as an IOU for participation in research. In several instances, people – most often men – offered to pay me cash for my assistance with filling out forms, translations, or transportation and instead I negotiated their participation in a formal interview (to which they had already agreed, but were procrastinating). Some of the women with whom I spent a good deal of time often thanked me for being such a good friend, such a ready and patient listener. One older woman compared me to a public health nurse she had known, and another referred to me as a "saint" for helping poor people in the community. Although initially flattered, I grew uncomfortable with these rituals of deference. The results of my assistance were minimal, and, more importantly, these same people helped me too. Often when I was praised I would interject something to the effect of, "Well I'm a student and I appreciate the help you give me with my project too." Although it seemed cold and calculated, I tried to remind them of my research interest, as it more adequately reflected the exchange.

Some of the most revealing information I collected did not come from the in-depth interviews but was disclosed to me in the context of being a friend. People enmeshed in explosive family conflicts or problematic decisions often produced unedited, but reflective, outpourings of emotions, motives, and private incidents. Like the best letters and the best diary entries, these outpourings resulted from personal crises. People offer some of the most revealing details of their lives when they are not relating to one as a researcher. This is double-edged, for although all the respondents consented to serve as "human subjects" in the research project, it was when I served in capacities other than "questioning researcher" that I obtained some of the most telling information. Acting as a *servidora*, I gained detailed knowledge of personal finances, marital intimacies, and conflicts. With regard to paid domestic work, I sometimes wrote letters or made phone calls on the women's behalf when they asked for pay raises, I observed the women complain about particular employers or other domestic workers, and I listened very carefully when they discussed their strategies for dealing with these problems.

Although all the women knew I was conducting research, my reciprocity obscured my research intent and availed more information to me. Yet rather than seeing reciprocity as constituting unbridled coercion or deceit, I believe it made the research process more egalitarian. Although my primary goals were clearly different than the respondents' interests, our interests did not necessarily conflict. Reciprocity allowed me to exchange a service for what the subjects were giving to me.

Judith Stacey (1988) has argued that researchers acting as friends or advocates leave subjects open to betrayal, exploitation, and abandonment. While research relationships are problematic, I maintain that reciprocity in field research can represent an instance where the means justify the means. The traditional appeal to non-exploitative research generally argues that the ends, or the finished research product, justifies the means. In this scheme, the dangers and risks assumed by research participants are outweighed by the potential benefits, such as a cure for a disease. This justification for the effects of research on people's lives derives from the physical sciences, and human subjects protocol in the social sciences generally mimics this approach, despite how poorly the protective clauses translate from the physical to the social sciences (Duster et al., 1979).

The standard human subjects protocol informs respondents that the end product might shape policies that may ultimately benefit people like themselves. As I read a formatted statement to research participants, I placed little conviction in those words, and I believe that the study participants interpreted those words as empty promises as well. People engaged in the research less in expectation that by doing so they would help to formulate more just immigration policies but more, I believe, in the expectation that their research relationship with me could be a non-threatening and even a personally beneficial, advantageous one. Rarely did subjects or others in the community inquire about the potential benefits that they might derive from the finished research product.

RESEARCH FINDINGS

In various social settings – at picnics, at baby showers, at parish legalization clinic, and in people's homes – I observed immigrant women engaged in lively conversation about paid domestic work. Women traded cleaning tips; tactics about how best to negotiate pay, how to geographically arrange jobs so as to minimize daily travel, how to interact (or more often avoid interaction) with clients, and how to leave undesirable jobs; remedies for physical ailments caused by the work; and cleaning strategies to lessen these ailments. The women were quick to voice disapproval of one another's strategies and to eagerly recommend alternatives.

The ongoing activities and interactions among the undocumented Mexican immigrant women led me to develop the organizing concept of "domestics' networks," immigrant women's social ties among family, friends, and acquaintances that intersect with housecleaning employment. These social networks are based on kinship, friendship, ethnicity, place of origin, and current residential locale, and they function on the basis of reciprocity, as there is an implicit obligation to repay favors of advice, information, and job contacts. In some cases these exchanges are monetized, as when women sell "jobs" (i.e. leads for customers or clients) for a fee. Information shared and transmitted through the informal social networks was critical to domestic workers' abilities to improve their jobs. These informational resources transformed the occupation from one single employee dealing with a single employer to one in which employees were informed by the collective experience of other domestic workers.

The Job Search and Contracting

Although the domestics' networks played an important role in informally regulating the occupation, jobs were most often located through employers' informal networks. Employers typically recommended a particular housecleaner among friends, neighbors, and co-workers. Although immigrant women helped one another to sustain domestic employment, they were not always forthcoming with job referrals precisely because of the scarcity of well paid domestic jobs.

Competition for a scarce number of jobs prevented the women from sharing job leads among themselves, but often male kin who worked as gardeners or as horse stable hands provided initial connections. Many undocumented immigrant women were constantly searching for more housecleaning jobs and for jobs with better working conditions and pay.

Since securing that first job is difficult, many newly arrived immigrant women first find themselves subcontracting their services to other more experienced and well established immigrant women who have steady customers. This provides an important apprenticeship and a potential springboard to independent contracting (Romero, 1987). Subcontracting arrangements can be beneficial to both parties, but the relationship is not characterized by altruism or harmony of interests. In this study, immigrant women domestics who took on a helper did so in order to lighten their own workload and sometimes to accommodate newly arrived kin.

For the new apprentice, the arrangement minimizes the difficulty of finding employment and securing transportation, facilitates learning expected tasks and cleansers, and serves as an important training ground for interaction with employers. Employee strategies were learned in the new social context. Women sometimes offered protective advice, such as not to work too fast or be overly concerned with all crevices and hidden corners when first taking on a new job.

A subcontracted arrangement is informative and convenient for an immigrant woman who lacks her own transportation or possesses minimal English-language skills, but it also has the potential to be a very oppressive labor relationship. The pay is much lower than what a woman might earn on her own. In some instances, the subcontracted domestics may not be paid at all. These asymmetrical partnerships between domestic workers continue for relatively long periods of time. Although subcontracting arrangements may help domestics to secure employment with multiple employers, the relationship established between the experienced, senior domestic and the newcomer apprentice is often a very exploitable one for the apprentice.

The Pay

Undocumented immigrant women in this study averaged $35–50 for a full day of domestic work performed on a job basis, although some earned less and others double that amount. What determines the pay scale for housecleaning work? There are no government regulations, corporate guidelines, management policy, or union to set wages. Instead, the pay for housecleaning work is generally informally negotiated between two women, the domestic and the employer. The pay scale that domestics attempt to negotiate for is influenced by the information that they share among one another and by their ability to sustain a sufficient number of jobs, which is in turn also shaped by their English-language skills, legal status, and access to private transportation. Although the pay scale remains unregulated by state mechanisms, social interactions among the domestics themselves serve to informally regulate pay standards.

Unlike employees in middle-class professions, most of the domestic workers that I observed talked quite openly with one another about their level of pay. At informal gatherings, such as a child's birthday party or community event, the women revealed what they earned with particular employers and how they had achieved or been relegated to that particular level of pay. Working for low-level pay was typically met with murmurs of disapproval or pity, but no stronger sanctions were applied. Conversely, those women who earned at the high end were admired.

As live-out, day workers, these immigrant women were paid on either an hourly or a "job work" basis, and most women preferred the latter. Being paid *por trabajo*, or by the job, allowed the women greater flexibility in caring for their own families' needs. And with regard to income, being paid by the job instead of an hourly rate increased the potential for higher earnings. Women who were able to work relatively fast could substantially increase their average earnings by receiving a set fee for cleaning a particular house. If they could schedule two houses a day in the same neighborhood, or if they had their own car, they could clean two and sometimes even three houses in one day.

Using Ethnographic Findings for Advocacy

In every major US city with a large immigrant population, large umbrella coalitions that include community, church, legal, and labor groups are now working to establish and defend civil rights and workplace rights for immigrants and refugees. Two key features distinguish these efforts. First, the claims are typically made outside the traditional and exclusive category of US citizenship. Second, until recently many of these efforts were aimed only at male immigrants. For various reasons, among them the "invisibility" of immigrant women's employment, immigrant rights advocates have been slower to defend immigrant women's labor rights. But this is changing.

A year and a half after completing the research, I began meeting with a group of lawyers and community activists associated with the Coalition for Humane Immigrant Rights in Los Angeles to plan an information and outreach program for paid domestic workers, the majority of whom in Los Angeles are Latina immigrant women. It was in this context that I utilized some of the research findings on immigrant women and domestic employment.

The newly formed committee met for one year before launching an innovative informational outreach program. The planning stage was long because of the obstacles that this occupation poses for organizing strategies and because the group was not working from an existing blueprint. How to organize paid domestic workers who work in isolated, private households is neither easy nor obvious. There are no factory gates through which all employees pass, and instead of confronting only one employer, one finds that the employers are nearly as numerous as the employees. Traditional organizing strategies with paid domestic workers encompass both trade unions and job cooperatives (see Chaney and Castro, 1989; Salzinger, 1991), but both models necessarily build in

TRABAJADORA DOMESTICA:
Si Ud. es recien llegada, cuidado con desconocidos que prometan presentarte supuestos empleadores

Figure 29.1 Domestic workers: if you have just arrived be careful with strangers who promise to introduce you to supposed employers.

Mantenga en mente estos tres consejos

1 Si Ud. puede
Trabajar
rapidamente
le conviene
cobrar por casa
en vez
de cobrar
por hora.

2 mantengase bién
informada con
amigas, comadres
y vecinas que
también hacen
trabajo doméstico,
sobre problemas
y soluciones.

3 Siempre
comunique
al patrón o
la patrona, los
productos que
se necesitan
para hacer
la limpieza.

Recuerde: Ud. tiene derecho a recibir el sueldo
mínimo de $4.25 por hora, aunque
esté entrenando.
Comparta sus problemas de trabajo con
sus amistades, para aprender más.

Figure 29.2   Keep these three things in mind.

numerical limitations. Our group decided that reaching workers isolated within multiple residential workplaces could best be accomplished through mass media and distribution of materials at places where paid domestic workers are likely to congregate, such as on city buses and in public parks. The key materials in our program were *novelas*.

Novelas are booklets with captioned photographs that tell a story, and they are typically aimed at working-class men and women. In recent years immigration rights advocates in California have successfully disseminated information regarding legalization application procedures, legal services, and basic civil rights to Latino immigrants using this method, and in southern California, even the Red Cross has developed a *novela* on AIDS awareness. Our group developed the text for several *didactic novelas*, and in lieu of photographs, we hired an artist to draw the corresponding caricatures. One *novela* centers on hour and wage claims, and another was designed as an emergency measure to alert domestic workers that a rapist was getting women into his car by offering domestic work jobs to women waiting at bus stops. Based on the research with paid domestic workers, I prepared a two-sided *novela* sheet that cautions women about the abuses in informal subcontracting relations, underlines that payment by the "job" or house yields higher earnings than hourly arrangements, and recommends that domestic workers share cleaning strategies and employment negotiation strategies with their friends. The text also reminds women of their entitlement to receive minimum wage ($4.25).

With a small grant, the advocacy group hired four Latina immigrant outreach workers, two Salvadoran women and two Mexican women, to distribute these materials to Latina immigrant domestic workers. Posters were printed up and placed on over 400 municipal buses that run along east–west routes. In large black print written across a red background the text reads (in Spanish): "Domestic Worker: Do You Have a Problem at Work? For Help or Free Information, Call the Labor Defense Network"; an accompanying illustration shows a domestic worker with octopus-like arms, with one hand balancing a crying baby while the other hands hold a feather duster, an iron, a baby bottle, a stirring spoon, and a soapy sponge. The posters also included tear-off sheets with information on where to solicit legal counsel for domestic work issues, such as salary disputes or sexual harassment. As they distributed the materials, the outreach workers advised domestic workers on their employment rights and provided resource information on where to obtain legal assistance for job-related problems. The outreach workers also distributed small notebooks and encouraged domestic workers to record daily all work hours, tasks performed, and pay received, so that if a labor dispute should arise, they would have documentation to present in court.

RESEARCH, ACTIVISM, THEORY

After I had prepared the text for the *novela*, I sent the Spanish-language text to several of the immigrant women respondents in my study so that I might elicit their feedback. Most of them had little to say, and when I spoke with them, they agreed that the project and the materials were useful, but they did not offer recommendations or suggestions. There was, however, one exception. The woman who had been most active in using the domestics' network resources and successful in accumulating an enviable list of jobs, Maria Alicia N., did voice strong views on the *novela* text. She expressed these views in the form of a lengthy tape-recorded "letter." Verbal letters recorded on cassettes are sometimes used by some Mexican immigrants to communicate with their family back home, and Maria Alicia favored this form of communication as she was trying to control her already steep phone bills. In the cassette she sent me, she spoke of the recent challenges she had faced as a single working mother, her worries about her 12 year old son's affinity with a local gang, and her disappointment in discovering that her boyfriend of seven years was still married to another woman in Mexico. But on the upside, her work was going well, as she still maintained a steady route of employers and was earning more than ever before. On the subject of the text, she offered many insightful remarks on the subcontracting relationship that are worth quoting:

> You asked for my opinion on these *novelas* that you're making. Look, with my sister it took me a lot of work to make her independent, and little by little she got out on her own with her own houses [to clean], right. Now she works for herself, but it took me a lot of work because at the beginning she didn't like to be left alone. She didn't want to drive, she didn't want to do this or that, but now she realized that she is independent and it would be terrible if she was working for me. Perhaps something would have happened, we probably would have broken off our association.
>
> There have been other occasions. Once I tried to help a woman, and I told her I would leave her a house. I showed her the house, I took her there, and I told the señora that she was my sister. I wanted to give her that house [to clean] and do you believe it? She didn't go the day that she was supposed to do so! So then I looked bad with the señora. So I say how is it possible that one can have such great need and not have the desire to work? They are asking god for work, but they don't want to work. I mean, they are looking for work and praying to god that they don't find it!
>
> So then a cousin, no a sister, of Amador also came here. I told her it was a good business with houses, "Little by little I'll leave you a few, little by little because now it's really slow." I told her, "You'll make a lot of money very fast, because this is a good job, you earn well." So we went to do some houses, and in one of them it seemed to her that I charged too little, and in another, it seemed to her that I did too much work, that I should only do this and do that. What happens is that people are not conscious that they must make merits. . . . And people just don't want to make that kind of sacrifice.

Maria Alicia responded defensively to the materials I had sent for her commentary. Rather than recalling her experiences as a "helper" hired to assist another paid domestic worker, she cited three more recent examples in which her own hired "helpers" had not performed up to the standard she set. In the above quote she blames her sister for being too dependent, her friend for being irresponsible and lazy, and her boyfriend's sister for being unwilling to work hard and accept a low level of pay initially.

The subcontracting relationship embodies and reproduces inequality among paid domestic workers. Maria Alicia responded defensively to the text warning women of the abuses that occur among Latina domestics themselves because the position that Maria Alicia identified with was as a moderately successful paid domestic worker who occasionally took on her own helpers. But in fact she herself had entered the occupation by working as a subcontracted helper for virtually nothing and living rent free with another Mexican immigrant woman domestic worker. That relationship seemed too distant for her to even recall, but when I had interviewed her several years earlier, she had complained about it. At that time, she related disappointment and anger with her experiences as a "helper" subcontracted by another domestic worker who exploited her labor and her situation: "I helped her to work a lot, and she did not pay me. Nothing, nothing. I would help her to do three or four houses a day. No, no, no, no, they were giving me nothing! It would have been better if I had never accepted such an arrangement."

Maria Alicia's divergent responses in the interview, and then in reaction to the research findings in the form of the *novela* text, prompted me to see the dual nature of the domestic workers' networks. Although the subcontracting relationship is just one facet of the network relations, it provides an important means of entry into the occupation for women who lack sufficient contacts with employers. For domestic workers who hire their own helpers, the subcontracting relationship is a way to yield enough labor to cover an increasing number of lucrative jobs. I began to see Maria Alicia's comments as reflections of different positions in the network, and I began to conceptualize paid domestic work as a career where movement is governed in part by the domestic worker's networks (Hondagneu-Sotelo, 1994).

This revelation allowed me to see that there is mobility within an occupation that is generally held to be either static or the route to upward mobility by changing occupation. Paid domestic work has typically been seen either as a "bridging occupation" that facilitates acculturation and mobility into industrial employment for rural–urban migrant or immigrant women (Broom and Smith, 1963; McBride, 1976) or as an "occupational ghetto" for women of color (Glenn, 1986; Romero, 1987, 1988). For women such as Maria Alicia, paid domestic work is neither a static position nor the route to jobs in the formal sector of the economy. Even in paid domestic work conducted outside the purview of formal regulations, some immigrant women can move up the ranks and obtain better employers who offer higher pay and better working conditions, more houses to clean, and, eventually, their own "hired help."

ARE FEMINIST SOCIOLOGY AND ACTIVISM COMPATIBLE?

Francesca M. Cancian (1996) discusses some of the ways in which mainstream academic power structures and careerism dissuade sociologists from incorporating social change into their research agendas, and she correctly, I think, emphasizes that vast structural changes in universities and academic publishing are necessary to change traditional approaches to scholarship. These broad, structural changes are necessary and will require a concerted, organized effort on the part of feminist sociologists, especially those in relatively senior, decision-making positions. But in the interim, or simultaneously perhaps, more limited, circumscribed innovations might be pursued by individuals.

The interactions between research, activism, and theory related in this chapter suggest that feminists with academic careers can combine traditional academic scholarship with social change activism. In fact, feminists working within academic careers may find a double pay-off, as I did, to integrating social research and activism. On the one hand, there is the satisfaction of having an impact, however modest, on enhancing the social conditions of the people one has studied. This advances the notion of reciprocity to another level, and, if one is predisposed to asking existential "so what?" questions about the social significance of one's research, it may provide some answers. On the other hand, the experience of seeking outlets in which to implement research findings may also advance previous interpretations and theoretical implications drawn from the original research. The prospects for sociologists who wish to apply their findings toward women's equality would seem to have increased with the proliferation of new feminist research. In the instance I have discussed here, research and theory informed activism, but it was the dissemination and advocacy work that in turn allowed me to gain new insights from my findings and interpretations.

30

The Subject and Societal Movements

ALAIN TOURAINE

It is initially essential to distinguish three types of collective action. The first type of collective action involves social demands, and occurs at the level of organizations; and the second involves political crisis and occurs at the level of institutions and decision-making centers. The third, which is increasingly important and with which I am concerned, is one that responds to conditions in a deinstitutionalized society in which common beliefs no longer unify and where the Self is fractured. These conditions give rise to societal movements that involve the personal and collective struggle for the unification of the Subject. In contrast with collective action involving social demands, which are based on economic calculation, or those involving political crisis, which lead to political demands, a societal movement relies on a collective determination to acquire a fundamental cultural resource, such as knowledge, recognition, a model of morality, and, most especially, the will to become a Subject.

To make this more concrete, in collective actions involving social demands or under a political crisis, the language is political, even though the collective action may occur in an industry, firm, hospital, university or neighborhood. For example, whenever a recession throws people out of work and lowers wages, a population may rise up with strong demands, but they have few chances of raising consciousness by fostering an understanding of the situation or even an ideology. The actors' consciousness focuses on their own situation, on calculations for proving the validity of their claims, justifying demands about living standards or the strain of their work, or making comparisons with people in other socioeconomic categories. There is no reference to power relationships, or to the society's basic cultural orientations. Nor is there a reference to a social Subject, or to conflictive relations about the social uses of a cultural model, or to shared cultural orientations.

THE DISTINCTIVENESS OF SOCIETAL MOVEMENTS

Just as the sociology of rational choice and interests has diligently studied social demands, and functionalist sociology has dwelled on institutions in crises, the third type of collective action requires analyses that center attention on how actors aim to change a society's key cultural models and how they are managed. Such a movement is recognizable because it brings together three characteristics: a conflict between social actors contending over the social relations whereby a society reproduces itself; a positive reference to the cultural values at stake in the conflict; and an idea as to how the Subject is joined to the societal movement.

It is never easy to detect whether a collective action contains a societal movement, with long-lasting consequences. The long, massive strike of May 1968 (with its demonstration on May 13, for which a million persons turned out) appeared at the time to have been a political crisis with only short-term effects. Yet a quarter of a century afterwards, there is no denying that it changed society and introduced cultural themes into politics. Therefore, we must consider it to have been a major societal movement with continuing consequences.

A societal movement is based on neither an economic calculation nor political pressure. It relies on the will to acquire a fundamental cultural resource (knowledge, a model of morality such as socialism or equality) and on the will to become a Subject. This will is not expressed in a vacuum – not in the solitude of a personal experience but in social relations and in a way that respects and advances personal and collective freedoms. Societal movements criticize social relations involving inequality, domination, and power, but they go beyond that in appealing to an ethics of collective responsibility.

Many sociologists have concentrated on how societal movements mobilize resources. This approach is useful insofar as a movement's orientations can be reduced to the collective pursuit of individual interests. But why does the pursuit of individual interests spawn collective action? This question is especially pertinent given the strong temptation to be a free-rider, as Olson (1965) pointed out in his now classical analysis. This we might consider to be a sociology of resource mobilization, and involves actors and their objectives. Also, by focusing on societal movements, I am also not considering rebellions, namely actions taken against suffering, poverty, or slavery. Rebellions are defined by what they reject – by what they designate as unbearable – whereas societal movements have a positive orientation and accompany political, cultural, or social objectives. A rebellion is centered on its own suffering, whereas, in a societal movement, we find both conflict and hope.

In considering the role of hope, idealism, and an altered conscience, which are the seeds of societal movements, I can refer to some concrete examples. These would include: the popular movements that put an end to apartheid in South Africa; the Polish and Czech solidarity movements that prepared the fall of the Soviet system; the Tiananmen uprising; ongoing student actions in Korea, Taiwan, and Iran; and, also, as I indicated, the French student movement of May 1968. Societal movements are the real place where liberation and liberty join together. Although the public (sometimes with the help of the media) have recognized the importance of these movements, sociology has usually resisted interpreting them, except in the most reductionist of ways. A main emphasis in sociology since Olson's (1965) earlier work has been to state that such movements involve the rational pursuit of ends. This implies that many or most stay out of the conflict so they can benefit from those who take risks without taking risks themselves. But how can we explain that so many men and women have taken risks – have fought and made sacrifices in the hope of achieving goals, a hope in which they themselves could not believe?

As I have defined societal movements as those that are transformative, and infused by shared energy, they involve subjective elements. Although it must be recognized that societal movements, such as the ones I have mentioned, accompany anti-social and sometimes destructive behaviors, it is important not to attach too much importance to such behaviors. The active Subject that lies within the societal movement and its concrete expressions has helped to erode the state's logic of power and the reproduction of inequality within the state, and, thereby, societal movements have further global consequences.

Two ways of thinking have obscured the very idea of a social movement. The first, which has always prevailed in France, only considers anything having to do with the state's power as important. Accordingly, only political actions have a broad scope, whereas social actions are always confined in narrow bounds. This, I believe, stems from historical features in France, and the fact that the French demanded, early on, a political democracy but have lagged behind in building a social democracy. The preference of the people in France, and in other Latin countries, for revolutionary radicalism stems from the strong bonds that, in these lands, united the state with the traditional oligarchy and, even more, with the Catholic Church. This has set the revolutionary tone of politics, a tone that has often had (and can still have) ringing effects. As a consequence, so many observers enthusiastically saluted the long workers' strike in May 1968 but scorned the students' cultural movement, which they qualified *as petit bourgeois*.

The second way of thinking that has obscured the nature of social movements seems the opposite of the foregoing. It is based on completely splitting the social apart from the political system. It is then easy to show how, in order to attain its objectives or grow, a political action must mobilize social resources but without a connection with the objectives or conceptions of social actors. This way of thinking is just as political as the first, but it endows politics with a different meaning. From this vantage point, social action is subordinate to political action, which aims specifically at acquiring or maintaining power. Such thinkers see social movements nearly everywhere, since, constantly (especially in democracies), politicians strengthen their hand by presenting themselves as the only actors capable of responding to social pressure. The extreme form of this is Leninism, which, by assigning the political vanguard the central role, places directly under its control movements or organizations, which are soon reduced to being relay mechanisms for the party.

The idea of a societal movement is different from these two conceptions. Above all else, it asserts that, under certain circumstances at least, social actors can define a central social cause and oppose opponents in the name of dominant cultural values, while also defending their particular interests. To talk about a societal movement is to affirm that social actors have pre-eminence over political authorities. This entails the idea of representative democracy and, in particular, of social democracy, wherein the party is the union's political muscle. To detect societal movements means inquiring into the conditions under which, at the level of conflicting social relations, actions emerge that have a general scope and are capable of commanding political actors and resources instead of being used by them.

In contrast with political conceptions of a revolutionary or a strategic sort, for which only political action can broaden the scope of demands that are always particularistic, the idea of a societal movement is based on the idea that there exists a central conflict. This is particularly the case in the contemporary world, which we could describe as postindustrial, computerized, and information-based. As I analyze the current situation, social conflicts in our society pit the Subject against the triumph of the marketplace and technology and also against authoritarian communitarian (exclusive) powers. For me, this cultural conflict seems as central as the economic conflict was in industrial society or the political conflict was during the first centuries of the modern era. If we reject the idea of a social movement from the start or use this phrase to refer only to demands or to reactions in a political crisis, we keep ourselves from corroborating, or even understanding, it.

SOCIETAL MOVEMENTS AND THE SUBJECT

A societal movement exists only if it combines a social conflict with a cultural cause defined with reference to a Subject. The Subject has assumed religious and political forms, and even taken on the form of a class or nation. I would like to argue that the Subject can emerge "finally as it is in itself' – as the personal Subject – only in our type of society. In all societies, however, the Subject reveals itself through moral values that oppose the social order. A societal movement defends a way of putting moral values to use that is different from the one its social opponent defends and tries to impose. Moral references and the consciousness of direct conflict with a social opponent who is defined by its way of appropriating common values and cultural resources are two inseparable aspects of a societal movement. This reference to morals should not be confused with claims based on needs or working conditions. Such claims back up demands for modifying the ratio of costs to benefits, whereas the moral discourse of a societal movement refers to freedom, a cause, fairness, justice, and the respect for fundamental rights.

Specifically, as we pass from the depiction of the working-class movement as a reaction to capitalism's contradictions to the image of a working-class movement with a cause that is both defensive and offensive, we see the growing importance of freedom, justice, and social rights. But we must go much further to detect and then understand contemporary societal movements during this transition period involving the postindustrial society. We must give up defining the social actor objectively as a socioeconomic category, because a societal movement does not aim at changing the relative positions of individuals on a scale of revenue or power. It seeks, instead, to rally a dominated, alienated, "fragmented" Subject. In this sense, the word "consciousness" must be used not to refer to the consciousness that a class or nation develops of its own situation but to emphasize the emergence of the actor.

But how does the actor constitute its own self? This question lies at the heart of a sociology that has stopped analyzing systems in order to understand the Subject. For some sociologists, reflection of the Subject upon itself leads it to seek a principle of order and control over the prevailing disorder and arbitrariness. For others, the Subject can assert itself only by referring to common values, a general interest. Sociologists of the first sort are often called "liberals"; those of the second, "communitarians." The first try to discover rules, procedures, and laws; the second, the contents, or substantial definition, of the Good. But the two are not so clearly or fully opposed as it seems, since laws transcribe a conception of the Good, and procedures never stay neutral whenever social interests come into play. The opposition between liberals and communitarians is played out within an objectivist conception of society, even though this conception is more traditional among communitarians (who may be traditionalists or even Tocquevillians). Quite different are those sociologists, such as Habermas (1989) or Taylor (1989), who, in contrast with both liberals and communitarians, assign a central place to the construction of the Subject. What must be added to their different approaches is the idea that the Subject constitutes itself only through social conflict.

Every societal movement has two sides: the one, utopian; the other, ideological. As utopian, the actor identifies the self in terms of the Subject's rights. As ideological, the actor concentrates on the struggle with a social opponent. Without a doubt, the class struggle is ideological. It emphasizes social conflict more than shared issues. On the other hand, the student movements of 1964 and 1968 in France were so utopian that they defined their opponent in excessively vague terms. Even though every societal movement is lopsided, stressing utopian or ideological aspects at the expense of the other, a societal movement requires both.

In contemporary social thought, we see two conceptions of individualism opposing each other. The one defends the multiplicity of choices offered to the large majority of individuals by our society of consumption and mass communications. For it, the market is the place of freedom, since it takes the place of the power of faith, doctrine, or established hierarchies. Opposite this conception, the second argues for the idea of a personal and collective Subject capable of endowing its situations and experiences with a general meaning. The first conception refers to freedom of choice; the second to autonomy and meaningful life experiences. These two conceptions form the grounds for social movements that, though opposite, both defend the individual.

Nothing sheds a brighter light on the Subject than the analysis of societal movements, because both the Subject and movements involve a moral principle about social relations. A societal movement cannot be reduced to moral protest; nor can the Subject be reduced to the pursuit of individual interests or pleasure. The Subject cannot be separated from a societal movement. They form two sides of a single reality. We thus see how much the idea of the Subject differs from that of conscience, especially when the latter, as classically formulated, means self-control or skeptical self-detachment (as in the case of Montaigne). The Subject is neither a being, nor a place, nor an autonomous space and time. It is a call to protest and to self-assertion.

A societal movement only exists if it succeeds in defining a conflictual social relation and the broad, societal issues underlying this conflict. It thus links together the assertion of an identity, a definition of the opponent, and an understanding of the issues that underlie contention. Can we draw the conclusion that a societal movement is more thoughtful, better controlled, and more responsible than protest or crisis behavior? Not at all. The degree of violence of a collective action has nothing to do with its nature. The violence depends on whether or not there is room for negotiations. A societal movement may assume a revolutionary form; but it stops being a movement only if it loses its autonomy and becomes a social resource in the hands of political leaders whose objectives are quite different from those of the original movement.

At this point, a historical question crops up: can societal movements still exist in societies under the sway of the market economy? Or does the marketplace tend to eliminate what I have called the system of historical action and, consequently, replace societal movements with simple demands or occasional political crises? Many postmodernists, reflecting on the contemporary global economy, contend that hyper-industrialized societies that have moved beyond historicity can only experience chaos or make adjustments to limited, controlled change. Clearly, this pessimistic view is shortsighted and ignores the human capacity for reflection and for possessing an historical awareness. I take the view that societal movements emerge in all types of societies, and, in particular, they emerge in those endowed with historicity – capable of cognitively, economically, and morally investing in themselves. For that reason, contemporary neoliberalism, even on a near global scale, does not preclude societal movements.

SOCIETAL MOVEMENTS AND DEMOCRACY

One of the reasons why I have analyzed societal movements for such a long time is that I felt it necessary to radically and intellectually criticize revolutionary actions and ideologies, which, from the Reign of Terror to Leninism, have always resulted in essentially totalitarian governments or even in fascism. My central thesis is that we cannot separate the forming of social actors and, therefore, of societal movements from the autonomy of the issues underlying their actions – hence from the political mediation that constitute democracy's central, indispensable element. The Subject, societal movements, and democracy are as inseparable as historical necessity, revolutionary action, and totalitarianism, which represent their darker side. Societal movements, of whatever sort, bear them within democratic aspirations. They seek to give a voice to those who have no voice and bring them into political and economic decision-making. In contrast, revolutionary actors dream of cultural, ethnic, political, or social purification, of a unified and transparent society, of creating a new mankind, and of eradicating whatever counters a unanimity that soon has no other reason for being than to organize political support for a totalitarian power.

This general conception leads us, as sociologists, to maintain that the presence of a societal movement is linked neither to a revolutionary situation nor to the force of an ideological discourse or line of politics. Rather, it is linked to the actor's capacity for working out a praxis – to a commitment to societal conflict and the defense of societal values, i.e. values that cannot be reduced to interests and, consequently, that cannot lead to the annihilation of one's opponent. A movement's meaning lies neither in the situation where the movement forms nor in the consciousness that ideologists ascribe to it or impose on it. The meaning is in its ability to undertake a certain type of action and place social conflict and issues on a certain level. In opposition to an "economicist" tradition often linked to Marxism, I have constantly defended the idea of a societal movement and a historical actor. In my first study of the working-class movement (Touraine, 1965), I stated that this movement was defending workers' autonomy. We would be caricaturing the study of the consciousness of social movements were we to reduce it to its most ideological forms. In effect, the latter often lie the furthest from praxis; and when they do not, the movement has, in fact, turned into an authoritarian or totalitarian anti-movement. All forms of absolute ideological mobilization – the identification of a social actor with God, Reason, History or the Nation – entail the destruction of societal movements. The latter are open to conflict, debate, and democracy, whereas ideological movements risk replacing plurality with unanimity, conflict with homogeneity, and participation with manipulation. Revolutionary intellectuals and leaders, demagogues and fundamentalists, are the active agents in the destruction of social movements. How can this escape our notice at the end of a century teeming with neo-communitarian movements, the most powerful of which call for a theocratic society?

Nowadays, given the globalization of the economy, we see arising, on the one hand, societal movements for minority rights, immigrant rights, and, more generally, human rights, but we are also witnessing anti-movements, which are giving birth to sects and cults in democratic lands and to new totalitarian movements on a national, ethnic, or religious basis. Here I am using a notion that many commentators – without giving it much thought – have avoided because they wish to ignore the difficulties of comparing the Nazi and communist systems with contemporary nationalist and religious fundamentalist movements. Is it so hard to admit that each totalitarian system, despite its specific aspects, belongs to a general type? Recourse to a "faith," whether Islam, Christianity, or Hinduism, leads to religious warfare, which communism and the revolutionary Mexican system, despite their violently anti-religious campaigns, avoided. Beyond the specific aspects of each totalitarian system, all of them share one characteristic, namely an absolute political power that speaks in the name of a people (a particular historical, national, or cultural group) and an assertion of absolute superiority (as being representative of a reality above politics and the economy). A totalitarian system is always popular, national, and doctrinaire. It subordinates social practices to a power that claims to incarnate the idea that a people represent and defends a faith, race, class, history, or territory.

Obviously, totalitarianism destroys democracy, but it also annihilates social, cultural, and historical movements and actors. It reduces historicity by using economic or cultural resources for constructing a closed mythical identity, itself reduced in practice to the justification of an absolute power. The idea of a people has always been a disguise for an absolutist state. It is no accident that the totalitarian, then authoritarian, governments in the communist countries dependent on the Soviet Union chose to call themselves "people's republics." Totalitarianism is the central problem of the twentieth century. In like manner, when political activists reject elections or bring excessive moral or material pressure to bear on those who do not share their point of view, they destroy the social movement for which they claim to be speaking. They act like dema- gogues (or Red Guards) rather than like the vanguard leading a class, nation or socioeconomic category. In short, a societal movement is praxis and not just a consciousness, and is fully linked to the affirmation that there is no societal movement without democracy, and vice versa.

Social Movements in a Non-democratic Situation

An objection immediately comes to mind. Does this vision not focus solely on developed lands, where modernization is self-sustaining? Does it not overlook situations where democracy does not exist, because of the arbitrary power imposed by a national or foreign state or an oligarchy interested in speculation and social power more than in economic rationality? This is such an important objection that the answers to it serve to guide the analysis of social movements. It calls for two complementary answers.

The first answer is that there can be no development without popular societal movements and democracy. Development results from combining three major factors: the abundance and quality of investment; the distribution of the fruits of growth; and public consciousness of the political unit. In effect, nation and modernization cannot be separated, since a developed economy is a dense, coherent, convergent network of exchanges, transactions, and interactions among all societal sectors. More simply, development supposes a ruling elite accumulating resources and making long-term decisions; but it also requires redistributive and leveling forces, universal participation in the process of mod- ernization, and the reduction of social and cultural privileges. These forces, born out of popular mobilization, have recourse to political institutions. Instead of saying, as many do, that development is a condition for democracy, I contend that democracy is a condition for development. The inability of the Soviet Union to really develop and its increasing paralysis provided evidence in support of this. But is the fast growth of China and of other lands in Asia, or elsewhere, not counter-evidence? We must answer no. In China, we observe the breakup of a totalitarian system and, in the coastal provinces, the rapid growth of a market economy under the leadership of decision-making centers located abroad. This breakup has positive effects, especially coming as it does after the Cultural Revolution's destructive violence. But if social movements do not form, if democracy is not born, the historical process under way in China will disintegrate into a new authoritarianism or else into chaos. The Soviet Union's former satellites and former Yugoslavia, too, are looking for a way between democratic development and regression into authoritarianism. Such regression has had tragic consequences in Serbia and has negatively affected Romania and several other ex-Soviet countries. Meanwhile, the communists' comeback in Poland, Hungary, Bulgaria, and Lithuania, and their success in elections in Russia and elsewhere, cannot – at present – be interpreted as a defeat for democracy and modernization.

Self-sustaining growth is a worthy objective, but this conception must be broadened to take into account other factors. When the dominant mode of development is of a domestic sort, there is a risk that authoritarian agencies will attempt to control the people or reduce them to mere resources. And when the dominant mode of development is of a market sort, social movements inevitably disintegrate into a multitude of pressure groups whose demands make social inequality worse. Can social movements exist in non-democratic situations? Let us push these questions even further. Are there democratic elements, hence movements, whose actions tend toward a despotic or market model instead of a democratic one?

This second answer takes us back to the analysis of the Subject, which can assert itself only through struggling against both the marketplace and commodified community. This means that the Subject arises as a form of opposition and liberation within the world of the marketplace and within the universe of the community. Indeed, societal movements, like the Subject itself, arise within a mode of development or even in forms of social power.

The major historical case is that of collective movements in authoritarian societies ruled by a despotic power, a national oligarchy, or a foreign colonial power. In this case, movements are forced to combine the defense of the oppressed and the demands for democracy with a revolutionary action for destroying the powers that be. Even in democratic lands, the working-class movement has always borne its share of violence in reaction to the violence of employers or governments. The strategy of a collective movement and of its leaders consists in combining actions for breaking with the existing order with democratic actions – the "logic" of the struggle against the powers that be with actions for defending freedom and, thus, political consciousness. This combination often fails. For instance, the labor movement has sometimes been an instrument, lacking autonomy, in the service of a new political power; and, sometimes, it has only defended relatively privileged socioeconomic categories. But these failures, however many times they have happened, must not keep us from realizing that a cultural, historical, or societal movement was present, despite the non-democratic outcome. True, the Algerian national movement has led to a military dictatorship that quells popular opposition. Nonetheless, it was an anti-colonial movement for national liberation. Nor does the horror of the Reign of Terror detract from the events of June 1789 that introduced democracy in France. A movement is never purely democratic, nor does a revolution ever entirely lack democratic contents.

DESPAIR OR HOPE?

We would weaken the idea of a societal movement were we to reduce it to naming a particular – more ideal than real – type of collective action. It is a concept or theoretical formulation. The idea of a societal movement (and, more broadly, of a social movement) forces us to give up the too easy quests of conservative thought, which looks for factors of integration, and of revolutionary thought, which denounces a system of domination as incapable of being either restrained or reformed.

This idea also protects us against the fragmentation that menaces collective action and, indeed, all aspects of social life. On the one hand, social movements seem to be less focused on being interest groups currently than on efforts for defending social integration from "social fractures" and ruptures of social bonds. The theme of exclusion, which has replaced exploitation, contains this idea. On the other hand, "identity movements" are abounding, in the United States where women, homosexuals, African Americans, and ethnic or national communities are asserting cultural autonomy while also fighting against discrimination, but also in countries obsessed with ideas of purity and homogeneity. The increasing separation between these two types of collective action, which are foreign to each other, is not just a given fact. It is a reality as pathological as the wider separation between the world of instrumentality and the world of identity, a separation that entails the collapse of social and especially political mediation between the economy and cultures.

There is a risk of too easily defining the idea of a societal movement only in terms of its twofold refusal of communitarianism and of economic globalization, and also some risk of considering any pressure group or identity movement as a significant societal movement. It is also important for sociologists to look for such movements underneath extreme ideologies where they are often hidden. Let us take two opposite examples. In Algeria (and other Islamic countries, Egypt in particular), there are political groups that use Islam to attain power and construct a fundamentally anti-modern, Iranian type of society. To survive, they use the techniques of modernity. However, we should not forget that this also gives expression to an uprooted population, to young people without jobs who use the *trabendo* (black market), or sports, as a means of forcing open the doors of the society of consumption. Those who oppose lay reactions to the dangerous politics of religious mobilization are right up to a point, but they are wrong in that they fail to see that many movements draw their force from the culture and society they defend because they feel threatened. The second example is the 1995 strike in the French public services. The events that took place then cannot be reduced to a defense of vested interests or privileges. They manifested a popular rejection of an economic policy that subordinated all of social life to deficit reduction, considered to be the key for developing a single European currency (which, in and of itself, is supposed to bring prosperity and jobs for all).

Let us try to clear up, at least a little, our confusion by recalling the "natural history" of any movement. It starts when the denunciation of misery goes along with a moral appeal to the dignity of everyone and the solidarity of all. Only thereafter is the opponent identified; and the conflict becomes central, before being institutionalized – as the organized social movement turns into a political force or party, which intervenes in economic and social policy-making. This ultimate phase usually accompanies a return to ideological discourses that, cut off from strategic actions, call for a return either to open conflict or to the denunciation of misery. In each phase, this history may be interrupted. This natural history teaches us useful lessons, even if these are too general to account for the wide diversity of historical situations. But these lessons are of less use for understanding the present than is a historical reflection that pays more attention to the effects of demodernization.

How could the split between the economic and cultural worlds not affect societal movements? The "civil/civic" movements of the seventeenth and eighteenth centuries worked for the creation of a national, republican political order. The working-class movement has drawn its strength from its consciousness that it was a means of progress, that it was pulling society "history-wise" through its struggle against the irrationality of capitalistic profit-seeking. These movements were borne by collective actors, which we label as social classes because they were defined by their political, economic, or social situations. This linkage between an objective meaning and a consciousness necessarily tears apart in the current situation of demodernization. Such movements are becoming increasingly moral, while fighting an opponent that is defined less as a power or class than as an agent of "dehumanization" and of domination through globalized networks of production, consumption, and communication. In this very concrete sense, the identity between the Subject and social movements compels recognition. In industrialized nations particularly, movements are less and less instrumental but more and more expressive.

The awareness of exclusion has spread with poverty, segregation, and joblessness. The societal movement against exclusion is arising out of the efforts of persons who, working in humanitarian organizations, increasingly think and act in terms not of the crisis of capitalism but of the conditions for the destruction or creation of the individual as Subject. There is no evidence that, in France, the leaders of the 1995 protests will be the forerunners of a movement that will organize, undertake a strategic action, and change into a party (as environmentalists have done in Germany). These groups, associations, and movements seem to be constituting themselves as historical, independent actors who mobilize volunteers, who actively use and criticize the media, but who critically stand aloof from a political system that, in their eyes, is subject to the constraints of the international economy. Meanwhile, the weak and threatened sectors of the vast middle class are organizing political actions for defending their vested interests. More diffuse, "everyday" movements – which are also more enthusiastic and more generous – are undertaking exemplary actions, decrying the denial of truth and justice, and combining the personal with collective solidarity. How can we not see in them the already constituted force of a new societal movement? To do so fits into a broader reflection on the conditions for political action and, therefore, for social control over both globalization and technological revolutions, in particular over the effects directly bearing on personality and culture.

Neither liberals nor revolutionaries believe in the capacity of social actions for producing their history through their cultural orientations and social conflicts. In contrast, I maintain that we should recognize the importance of demands for a sense of identity or of strategies for pressing demands. But only the idea of a societal movement enables us to recognize the existence of actions combining a fundamental social conflict with the pursuit of societal objectives (such as modernization, social integration or the respect for human rights) defined in concrete situations and social relations. The idea of a societal movement is not satisfied with completing a sociology that is mainly oriented toward the quest for social integration. It associates integration with conflict and, as a consequence, takes the central place in analyzing the social organization and social change. It is indispensable for any political sociology.

I am not insisting on placing the idea of the Subject at the center of analysis in order to "desocialize" societal movements, i.e. to separate them from the conflictual social relations where they have their origins. On the contrary, this insistence is intended to distinguish a societal movement from the political instruments and ideological apparatuses that keep us from seeing that a societal movement always appeals to the Subject's liberty. These appeals are not situated in the social vacuum of natural law, but in the social relations of domination, property, and power. A societal movement is thus both a struggle for and a struggle against.

Societal movements are important not just because they reveal the contradictions within modem societies, which is defined by their historicity, by the concentration of the means for changing society, and by the distance between the rulers and ruled. What best defines a societal movement is the linkage it establishes between cultural orientations and a social conflict bearing demands that are political and societal. If a societal movement does not form, all these elements separate from each other and, doing so, degrade. On the one hand, cultural orientations, when they are split off from social and political conflicts, turn into moral principles of belonging or of exclusion, mechanisms of cultural control, and norms of social conformity. On the other hand, political conflicts, when they are split off from societal movements, are reduced to struggles for power. Finally, demands, left to themselves, tend to reinforce established inequalities, since the most powerful and influential have the most vested interests to defend and are best equipped to press demands. We thus see a juxtaposition of pressure groups; movements of rejection that comprise categories defined as minorities, deviants or foreigners; and a communitarian populism that appeals to an indeterminate people against leaders and intellectuals. Each of these aspects of social or political life could, it initially seems, be studied by itself, but that is impossible. All collective actions bear evidence of an absent or disintegrated societal movement.

Societal movements do not always exist; but they do represent a hypothesis that must be worked out in order to understand contemporary collective life. Sociological positivism that takes as starting point not social relations and historicity but principles of order (whether based on personal interests or communitarian values) provides poor explanations that are insufficient because positivists place nothing between the individual and society. In actual fact, however, neither the individual nor society exists as principles that can be isolated from social relations and processes that constantly join order with change, and integration with conflict.

Our need for these concepts and principles of analysis is all the greater now, in that we are living in a "fragmented" society that has been deprived of a consciousness of itself. Under these conditions, issues and actors of historical change are obscure, and discourses and ideologies lag behind practices or become artificially radicalized practices. Our societies are not just hypermodern; they lack meaning, since they suffer from the dissociation of practices from consciousness, and of acts from discourses. Nowadays, the center of society is an empty field where are scattered the remains of past combats and old discourses, which have become second-hand merchandise acquired by the merchants of power and ideologies. For this reason, the idea of a societal movement must be defended because it interprets this emptiness and gives a coherent meaning to all the behaviors, contradictory with each other, that originate in the disappearance and breakup or breakdown of the former social movements.

Translated from the French by Noal Mellott, CNRS, Paris.

31

The Myth of the Labor Movement

Rick Fantasia

There is a current of change flowing through the US labor movement that is really quite remarkable. After a half century of bureaucratic complacency and organizational torpor, and a quarter century of employer aggression and unfavorable economic shifts that have caused a steady decline in union membership and significantly diminished political influence, labor is suddenly experiencing all of the pains and the possibilities of a rebirth. The new reform leadership of the AFL-CIO, headed by the triumvirate of John Sweeney, Richard Trumka, and Linda Chavez-Thompson, came to power in 1995 as the "New Voice" slate in the first contested presidential election in the history of the union federation. Instead of simply anointing the designated successor to Lane Kirkland (the consummate bureaucrat, who had himself been plucked from the dim corridors of the trade union bureaucracy as designated heir to former President George Meany), a slim majority of an Executive Council made up of the Presidents of the member unions broke with tradition by encouraging and supporting the opposition "New Voice" ticket.

Its ascent representing more of a "palace coup" than a revolution, the new leadership nevertheless immediately set out to clean out all the closets, to overhaul the bureaucracy and the budget in an effort to redirect substantial resources toward organizing new members, while simultaneously stirring the long-dormant arsenal of union militancy by encouraging tactical creativity among the new heads of the various departments within the federation (Brecher and Costello, 1998; Lerner, 1998; Mort, 1998). While the results may not be evident for several years, the initiatives undertaken have been impressive. For example, a newly formed Department of Field Mobilization has taken on the ambitious task of resuscitating the system of over five hundred regionally organized and city-wide Central Labor Councils that currently exist nationwide (Dean, 1998; Gapasin and Wial, 1998). Central Labor Councils are institutionalized networks of local unions that once served as powerful sources of inter-union solidarity and mobilization, but that were allowed to atrophy and grow moribund under decades of a bureaucratic leadership that eschewed most forms of collective mobilization (Fantasia, 1988, p. 244).

To underscore organizing as the central focus of union activity, the leadership has established a new Organizing Department to provide strategic assistance to member unions as well as to facilitate inter-union cooperation in organizing campaigns by coordinating large-scale, multi-union organizing projects in various parts of the country, several of which have emerged as experimental models for both cross-union and union–community organization and solidarity (Bensinger, 1998; Fine, 1998; Waldinger et al., 1998). In order to meet the supply demanded by such efforts, a new generation of labor organizers, drawn from both worker and student ranks, are being systematically trained and placed by the AFL-CIO funded Organizing Institute. Such efforts as these require the establishment of ongoing links to university campuses, ethnic communities, and religious organizations, and in contrast to the insularity and mistrust that too often characterized its predecessors, the current AFL-CIO leadership has actively facilitated such ties (Fraser and Freeman, 1997).

The reason for such an intensive focus on organizing is that for several decades it was largely overlooked in favor of servicing the needs of the existing membership, who, after all, were the constituencies that union leaders depended upon for reelection. According to Richard Bensinger, the Director of Organizing in the first four years of the reforms, "When John Sweeney was elected the new president of the AFL-CIO, 97 percent of locals had no existing organizing programs and no membership involvement in organizing. At best, less than 5 percent of our total resources went to new-member organizing, and unions operated in almost complete isolation of the community" (Bensinger, 1998, p. 28). With union density currently under 10 percent in the private sector, down from a high of 39 percent in 1954, according to Clawson and Clawson (1999, p. 97), a heavy stress on organizing is now viewed as a matter of basic institutional survival, and union locals are being urged to devote as much as one-third of their total resources to organizing activities. It is estimated that at a national level, unions must be able to organize a minimum of 350,000 new workers per year *just to stay even with current membership levels*, and must organize 1.2 million new workers annually to grow by a modest rate of 1 percent (Bensinger, 1998, p. 30).

THE MYTHIC IS REAL

These numbers help to explain the centrality of organizing in the work of the new leadership of the federation, and also perhaps the emphasis in much of the recent sociological and labor relations literature as well. Generally speaking, analytical attention to the labor movement by social scientists and others has largely focused on various dimensions of the movement's corporeal forms, probing its proportions, organizational structure, institutional leverage, political efficacy, membership characteristics, etc., while disregarding or minimizing its evocative dimensions, its place in the symbolic vocabulary of societies. However, I would suggest that it might be reasonably argued that the very strength and efficacy of the labor movement's embodied forms depends, to a considerable degree, on its capacity to evoke something larger than itself; that is, to spawn and to be able to sustain a sacred narrative, a transcendent myth. One might, in fact, nudge this point even further by suggesting that the most fundamental reality of the labor movement is its mythic quality.

I do not mean myth that sustains the social order, as Roland Barthes has demonstrated they may surely do (1972), nor do I mean myth as a "fabulous narration," an untrustworthy or deliberately false construction that obscures the field of vision (Williams, 1977, pp. 176–8). Instead, I mean myth as an enabling and mobilizing force, "a means of acting on the present" as Georges Sorel put it a century ago in his classic essay on the General Strike:

> The General Strike groups all of the noblest, deepest, and most moving sentiments that the proletariat possess in a coordinated picture, and by bringing them together, gives to each one of them its maximum of intensity; appealing to their memories of particular conflicts, it colors with an intense life all the details of the composition presented to consciousness.... [We] thus obtain that intuition of socialism which language cannot give us with perfect clearness – and we obtain it as a whole, perceived instantaneously. (Sorel, 1906, pp. 112, 128)

In Sorel's "myth of the general strike," the truly potent social force was the myth itself, always appearing larger in the social imagination than any concrete historical action, its symbolic presence looming large over every actual strike, every skirmish in the class war.

Mythical compositions or themes are generally created in the pursuit of some certitude in an insecure world, and in his analysis of the symbolic life of the Italian Communist Party, David Kertzer draws from the anthropologist Girardet to identify the three central thematic elements of political mythology: (a) the presence of an evil conspiracy; (b) the presence of a Savior; (c) the coming of a Golden Age (Kertzer 1996, p. 17). Of course, such mythic forms may be effectively mobilized and invoked by social forces across political fields, by the right as well as the left (as Sorel's own flirtations with Fascism partly demonstrate), by capital or labor, by the socially powerful as well as the socially stigmatized. However, in a period like our own when the market, the individual, and the entrepreneur have taken on mythical proportions in the social imagination, through acts of construction that have rendered alternative ways of being essentially unimaginable, the recitation of mythic solidarity can serve a crucial mobilizing function as counter-mythology.

For any myth to attain a social life it must be expressed in a practical, embodied form. Antonio Gramsci's view of myth was as a "concrete phantasy" embodied in The Prince (his jailhouse euphemism for the Italian Communist Party), whose essential quality was as a "'live' work, in which political ideology and political science are fused in the dramatic form of a 'myth'" (quoted in Kertzer, 1996, p. 17). Similarly, in their analysis of the mythic status of the law in everyday life, Ewick and Silbey (1998) argue that for legality to be enacted, it must be believed to be, simultaneously, *of* this world and *not of* this world, both a temporal and practical product of human activity and a timeless product of otherworldly forces. As they point out, the Church represents an institutional reality that not only hosts the transcendent, but authorizes "the sacred to break through to the profane" (p. 232).

An important element of the foundational myth of labor movements every-where has been solidarity, a potent sacred narrative with remarkably transcen-dent qualities. Under certain conditions and at certain moments, demonstrations of solidarity are capable of summoning powerful spiritual forces in the social world (in groups, collective activities, organizational forms), forces that can produce extraordinary degrees of selflessness and collective identification. This is not a tautology, for the dramatic display of solidarity can demonstrate that the impossible is possible, and thus beget a broader and bolder expression of solidar-ity. This may even be all the stronger in a society rife with social division and group mistrust, where there is a constant scramble to get ahead and to stay afloat, and where, amidst the inevitable disappointments and the relentless atomization, solidarity can represent an unusually potent mythic theme. Within the regime of industrial relations, a system established to channel and domesticate social con-flict, worker solidarity is capable of "charming" the social world by levitating that which was a mundane event in one moment (a meeting, a grievance, a contract negotiation) and raising it to a "higher," "sacred" level the next (an individual voice becomes the collective chant, "her" grievance is transformed into "our" protest, the picket line becomes the site of a powerful moral crusade.) It is unfortunate that the term "labor metaphysic" has been employed so derisively, for it expresses quite reasonably an important dimension of collective action.

I would agree that such terms can seem almost quaint in the American context, where for the past half-century the leadership of the AFL-CIO actively discouraged any collective recitation of mythic solidarity that might be con-strued as a threat to the existing order. Emblematic of the impulse to inhibit the ritualization of its own history is the irony that labor's May Day is commemo-rated almost everywhere except in its birthplace, the United States (Foner, 1986). But though institutionally quite peripheral through much of labor's history, the solidarity myth has, at certain times and in certain sectors, been symbolically central in the United States. One example is the legend of the "Wobblies," the Industrial Workers of the World (IWW), active from 1905 to 1917. As Rothen-buhler (1988) has argued, the Wobblies crossed the threshold of meaningful social categories, residing in a "liminal zone" in which their actions had no meaningful place within the terms of the governing myths of an industrial society. Whereas labor organizations bargain and negotiate with employers, file formal grievances, strike over wages, and otherwise operate within a struc-ture designed to channel and accommodate "labor relations," the Wobblies refused to be a "labor organization" at all. Celebrating their marginal status in their theme song, "Halleluja, I'm a Bum," their members rode the rail lines from conflict to conflict, organizing the most marginal segments of the labor force (immigrants, the unskilled, migratory laborers), while "filling the jails" in their battles over free speech. As Rothenbuhler notes, their membership dues were too low to have maintained a budget (with no system for collecting them), they had no strike fund, they refused to sign labor–management contracts (the very basis of the collective bargaining system), and they rotated their officials in order to prevent the hardening of loyalties and the creation of organizational hierarchy (behind the slogan "we are all leaders").

Because the Wobblies refused to be a responsible "labor organization," their actions and their demands were not resolvable by the mythic structure of industrial society, Rothenbuhler argues, but because he views myth solely as a symbolic expression of incorporation that "preserves rather than changes structure" (p. 73), he tends to see the Wobblies only as a force disrupting the governing myths of the time (which they surely did), rather than as the myth-making, legendary social embodiment of labor solidarity in its own right, one that lives on symbolically, over eighty years after the Wobblies were destroyed as an organization. Clearly, their potential as a mythic force was strongly impeded by the dominance of bureaucratic forms of business unionism that prevailed for most of the twentieth century, but it should also be recognized that the very character of the Wobblies was, to a significant degree, a relational product of this, its obverse, the "pure and simple trade unionism" of Samuel Gompers and the American Federation of Labor. As Buhle has noted in his study of business unionism, "In its vision and practice, the IWW was everything that the AFL refused to be and did not wish to be" (Buhle, 1999, p. 66).

The post-Second World War versions of business unionism have not only upheld the myths of capitalism (though some more firmly than others) but also sought to erase the myth of the labor movement; not only in an ideological sense, but in a practical, organizational sense as well, where the relentless pragmatism of business unionism has been a powerful counterweight to the invocation of mythic solidarity. Business unions are characterized by a highly centralized and unabashedly top-down hierarchical structure, with a heavy reliance on *both* the formal procedural requirements of the labor relations system and closed channels of communication networks at the top that tend to facilitate secretive, "backroom" deal-making (thus requiring and encouraging an ill-informed and passive membership). Business unionism is socially exclusive, rather than inclusive, more undemocratic than democratic. Business unionism reacts to employer initiatives, rather than taking a proactive stance, it engages in aggressive anti-radicalism (often the source of internal political opposition), and it eschews union militancy except on rare occasions when it can be tightly controlled by the union staff (Banks and Russo, 1996). It is because these organizational forms and practices are inimical to the "sacred narrative" of solidarity that they have been dominant within the American context.

A Social Drama in Two Acts

What I am underlining is the necessity of the labor movement to recover or create a mythic status and the requirement for that recovery or creative process to embody solidarism in actions, in organizational forms, and in the relation of the movement to social groups and institutions beyond it. Group formation and collective action are social representations, which means that while they may represent a certain social "reality" (like worker solidarity, or a labor movement), it is a reality that is uneven, never fully formed, in flux, a point of contention, and thus always partly allegorical. Where social groups are contenders for power and influence in a hostile social universe, like unions in American society, they must constantly "demonstrate" their efficacy and potential, not only to those with no experience with unionism, but also to unionized workers whose experience of solidarity must be constantly reinforced.

"Demonstrations" are, after all, just that. They demonstrate to participants and potential participants, friend and foe alike, not what a group "is" at any given time, but what it is potentially, with respect to mobilization, commitment, or social disruption. This is often what is at stake in the inescapable disparities and disagreements between activists and authorities over the "actual numbers" of participants in demonstrations (see Bourdieu, 1984b, p. 175). Not only are the numbers objects of contention, but so is the collective bodily pose of the demonstrators (militant or peaceful, disruptive or orderly, use of symbols and slogans that are reassuring or provocative), which are partly a product of the representational struggle itself (the goals, organizing styles, and circumstances of an action) and partly a product of the social backgrounds and positions of the participants (what and how much they have to gain or lose by the form of their participation, their relative security and position within a labor market, etc.).

In other words, the symbolic character of a labor movement is reflected (and formed) in the nature of the vehicles that are advancing it at any given time and place, and so a key part of the work of mythical construction involves the social act of assembly. But there is a second kind of social act at work in the process of mythical construction, a process of invocation by which leaders and spokespersons perform the act of symbolic construction of the group, a process which has received close attention in the writings of Pierre Bourdieu (1991). It is work that involves petitions, pronouncements, slogans, reports, and press releases, and that involves the leaders, activists, spokespersons, and journalists for the putative group or collectivity, as well as the institutions (the think tanks, periodicals and journals, academic centers, foundations, both established institutions and institutions seeking an established place) that may lend the spokespersons the necessary legitimacy, in symbolic weight, to be widely heard; as well as the relationship between leaders and the group-in-formation that they seek to lead by speaking in their name. In other words, it is a process requiring attention to the social production of the leader or spokesperson, who, once granted the authority of invocation, is able to invoke and therefore to establish the identity of the collectivity, thus participating in an important part of the process whereby a group is brought into being as an identifiable group. As Bourdieu (1991, pp. 248–9) has written:

> The spokesperson . . . as the personification of a fictitious person, of a social fiction, he raises those whom he represents out of their existence as separate individuals,

enabling them to act and speak through him as a single person. In return he receives the right to take himself for the group, to speak and act as if he were the group incarnate in a single person . . . the group is created by the person who speaks in its name, thus appearing as the source of the power that he exerts over those who are its real source. This circular relation is at the root of the charismatic illusion which means that, ultimately, the spokesperson may appear, to others as well as to himself, as *causa sui*.

The construction of the solidarity myth is not just a matter of "public relations," for public relations would simply require that the designation be adjusted to the widest possible market, disconnected from the process of group formation (mobilization, collective action), which cannot be just summoned in any case since it is a relational and interactive phenomenon, and that requires a long and arduous task of mobilizing and organizing. The process of naming a group and getting that name to stick takes place within a conflictual context, so that who and what gets named as a legitimate collectivity – the labor movement, the working class – is the result of a social struggle. It also has important consequences, not only for what a society thinks it is, but for how its citizens act and for what social and political actions appear reasonable or unreasonable within it. Consider the longstanding academic disagreement (it cannot even be considered a "debate" at this point) within the social sciences about the legitimacy of the concept of a "working class" (and therefore its very existence), with each side marshalling its methodological strategies and its data to advance a case that has enormous political consequences, but that is not even recognized as a debate in public political discourse. The result is that neither the term nor the social group can exist there, while a variety of euphemisms are employed ("the middle class," "the working poor," "hard working families") when some designation is necessary.

In some respects, the process I am describing approximates the practice of "framing", a concept adapted by students of social movements to designate the "interpretive schemata that simplifies and condenses the 'world out there' by selectively punctuating and encoding objects, situations, events, experiences, and sequences of actions within one's present or past environment" (Snow and Benford, 1992, pp. 136–7; see also Gamson, 1992a). The myth of solidarity, enacted and demonstrated in the actions of a labor movement, could be viewed as the "master frame" of a labor movement, and in an illustration of the framing perspective one analyst has drawn attention to the fact that the Polish labor movement, *Solidarnosc*, was named for the solidarity that it expressed in action (Tarrow, 1994, p. 133).

Both in contrast to Bourdieu's framework of the social construction of collectivities and despite some very fruitful applications of the framing perspective, it is an approach that seems to put both too little and too much emphasis on the purposive role of leaders in attributing, articulating, and punctuating meaning frames. Too little, to the extent that it tends to take the framers (the leaders, activists, and spokespersons who articulate the frame) at face value, without the necessary systematic attention to the processes and struggles through which leaders are socially produced, selected, and designated as leaders; while simultaneously, putting too much emphasis on leaders to the extent that it takes the social groups or social movements at face value, without the necessary systematic attention to their relational positions, the processes of institutional consecration (the state and the university being two such institutions), and the various symbolic and material processes and struggles (and the stakes involved) that lead to the formation of a social movement or collectivity (which usually entails the denial of group or movement status to others). Whereas frame analysis takes the existence of groups as a given, showing the ways in which symbolic meaning is constructed therein, Bourdieu's perspective views group formation itself as a crucial symbolic process (and sociological problem), and therefore seems to offer a deeper and more comprehensive analytical strategy.

While it is not possible to pursue such a comprehensive analysis in the context of this short chapter, it might be useful to consider a recent example of another labor movement's rebirth, one that has occurred contemporaneously with the attempt to rejuvenate American labor movement. In France, where union membership comprises an even smaller percentage of the labor force than in the USA (although these are not really comparable, since the strength of French unions is institutionalized at the national level and thus individual union membership is less important than in the USA), events over the past several years illustrate some of the points that I have been making about the myth of the labor movement. Drawn from press accounts, informants, and various secondary sources, what follows is a selective outline of the events in France, with a focus on their mythic qualities.

ALL THE MAKINGS OF A MYTH

In the midst of the largest of the demonstrations in mid-December of 1995, *Le Monde* announced "The first great strike against globalization," and although there were some Indonesians and South Koreans who might have wanted to argue the accuracy of that headline, from most vantage points within the French hexagon the "new world order" seemed to have been suddenly turned upside down. In the months and years that have followed, a remarkably broad and cohesive "social movement" has mushroomed that was germinated in the strikes and that has been cultivated by a labor movement that was emboldened by them. The result has been the creation of Europe's (and perhaps the world's) strongest bulwark against the harsh terms of global capitalism.

While to much of the world the French strikes of November and December 1995 seemed to explode out of nowhere, there were definite signs in the months leading up to them. Indeed, within only 24 hours after the results of the second and final round of the presidential elections had been announced in June, that Jacques Chirac had been elected President, union leaders assembled a press conference to warn of a "third, social round" that could be expected were the right to attempt to cut social benefits as the solution to high unemployment. Skirmishes followed in October and November, with a successful 24-hour national strike by public employees here, a student demonstration there, while the Minister of Industry warned a group of assembled bankers that if unemployment not soon reduced there existed the possibility of a social explosion on the scale of May 1968 (an event whose practical mythical status has now been both extended and revivified).

Then, in November 1995, Prime Minister Juppé announced the government's "employment plan," which was immediately recognized for what it was: an effort in the drive toward deficit reduction dictated by the European Union's development of a common currency. The plan would have reduced the deficit by cutting state-run health insurance and pension systems, raising health premiums on retirees, taxing the monthly child allowance payment, and assuring that more reductions would surely follow, by transferring control over most social spending from committees jointly controlled by employers and employees to the Parliament, where further cutting would be made easier. The group most directly hit by the plan would have been public employees (a group constituting a full 40 percent of the French labor force of 22.5 million), whose retirement benefits would be cut and delayed, and whose workplaces would be trimmed (schools and post offices to be cut, some 3,750 miles of rail lines to be closed).

It was from such "mundane details" that a movement with mythic proportions was created. It began with a series of marches and demonstrations, by students on November 21, by civil servants on November 24, then a women's march the next day, another march by civil servants on November 28, and students again on November 30. This was prior to the largest of the strikes, which began when railway workers, the "shock troops" of the strikes, shut down the nation's transport system, and were then followed by other public sector workers (teachers, postal workers, health care workers), as well as students and retirees. Workers in the private sector did not join the strikes (the possibility of which was a valuable card held by the movement throughout), although many private businesses were forced to close due to the transportation stoppage.

According to press accounts, a remarkable "democracy of distress" prevailed. With massive traffic jams clogging the arteries around major cities, hundreds of thousands of commuters were forced to walk, bicycle, rollerblade, and hitchhike to work. Instead of this generating widespread resentment against the strikers, the press reported an extraordinary carnival-like atmosphere of public spiritedness and mutual assistance, with surprisingly strong support for the strikes throughout (polls showed 55–65 percent support for the strikes). The *sense* of public support at the street level was further enhanced when a rare Parisian snowfall brought large numbers of children – out of school because of the strike – into the streets.

The strikes lasted for a month, and a series of demonstrations brought record numbers of supporters into the streets. "Official" (Interior Ministry) sources reported the following figures on the number of demonstrators:

- 490,000 on November 24;
- 160,000 on November 30;
- 520,000 on December 5;

- 700,000 on December 7;
- 985,000 on December 12;
- 600,000 on December 16.

It must be noted, in light of my earlier remarks, that strike leaders argued vigorously that the Interior Ministry figures should be doubled for a fully accurate count, particularly on December 12 and 16, they asserted, when scores of cities reported having the largest demonstrations in their history (the unions and some of the press reported 1.7 million marchers on December 12). Even according to the Interior Ministry figures, on certain days the number of marchers in provincial cities was said to have been unprecedented (100,000 in Marseille; over 75,000 in Bordeaux, Clermont-Ferrand, Dijon, Grenoble, Limoges, Lyon, Rouen, and Toulouse; and 28 cities altogether had demonstrations of over 20,000 on December 16).

The scope and depth of the events presented the press with the difficult problem of reconciling what was under way with over a decade of "conventional wisdom" – itself a mythic construction – of a depoliticized, privatized, French working-class consumer, a sort of French version of the "embourgoisement" thesis that had been advanced earlier and elsewhere, and expressed in popularized social statistics emphasizing the consumerism, the rates of private home ownership, the variety of lifestyles, as well as the increasing distance from traditional left parties of French working-class people (see, for example, Mendras, 1991; Forse et al., 1993; Mermet, 1995). In effect, the events of 1995 "colored with an intense life all the details of the composition," to repeat Sorel's terminology, of an alternative myth that was embodied, enacted, and therefore illustrative of that *other* working-class reality, the one that is certainly much more ephemeral socially, but which can have enormous symbolic and material effects. Writing in the December 19 issue of the newspaper *Liberation*, the sociologist Edgar Morin wrote of the upheaval:

> This general awakening and multiplication of solidarity between workers at their work stations, and between these workers and their families, their friends, and neighbors, and the birth of communication and mutual aid between neighbors at home and at work showed that the paralysis of the strike served as a spontaneous regeneration of the social tissue and helped us to rediscover a basic psychic health that brings openness toward the other.... We can see that the strikes have generated a great source of good will that underscores just how much it is trapped and locked up by our everyday existence in contemporary society. (p. 10)

The judgments and public observations of intellectuals had an important place in the process of constructing the strikes and their effects in mythic terms. Perhaps not coincidentally, Pierre Bourdieu has played a central role during and since the strikes by putting the considerable symbolic capital that he has accumulated (as holder of the prestigious Chair in Sociology at the Collège de France) at the service of the developing movement. His speech, in "solidarity with those who are now fighting to change society," which was made to railway workers at the Gare de Lyon, and reprinted in at least four national newspapers, immediately placed the strike in mythic terms: "I have come here to express our support to those who have been fighting for the last three weeks against the destruction of a *civilization*, associated with the existence of public service, the civilization of republican equality of rights, rights to education, to health, culture, research, art, and, above all, work" (Bourdieu, 1998, p. 24).

Such pronouncements (by various intellectuals, as well as Bourdieu, who has sought to organize them in various collective bodies) not only *placed* the strike in an epic context, but served to *raise* the strike by separating it from the mundane ("just another strike by self-interested civil servants"). That is, they used the powers granted by their symbolic capital (accumulated in other domains) to perform acts of "symbolic levitation," simultaneously raising the stakes and lifting events into the realm of the sacred. Of course, such symbolic gesturing might appear groundless were the other social act, that of assembly and collective action, not demonstrating in vivid fashion the existence (and therefore the plausibility) of a movement. As I suggested above, a fuller analysis would require a social inquiry of the strike supporters (and opponents) themselves, including their social and institutional backgrounds and trajectories, and the stakes involved in taking this or that stance, an analysis that has been attempted elsewhere (Duval et al., 1998).

As might be expected, the opponents of the strikes sought to "frame" the events differently, by attempting to keep them within the realm of the mundane, expressing the inevitability of the Juppé plan, or some similar version, emphasizing utopianism of the strikers, their divorce from "reality," etc. This symbolic conflict between the two sides was illustrated in the "battle of the lists," two competing petitions on the strikes that were circulated among intellectuals, and then placed prominently in the press. The one petition, viewed as being "headed" by the sociologist Bourdieu (by virtue of the prominence of his name), expressed unambiguous support of the strikers, while the other, "headed" by Touraine and Wieviorka (authors of a well known book on the worker's movement) as well as others, took a view which, while not explicitly supporting the program of the right (a politically untenable position for an intellectual in France), but recognizing the inevitability of reform, offered unambiguous support for the only trade union leader *not* supporting the strikes (lauding Nicole Notat for the "courage" of her pragmatism).

The reverberations from the strikes have been enormous on several levels. The immediate issues were mostly settled favorably for the workers, for while the government did retain the ability to control social service spending in the future, it was forced to retreat on every other issue, including job cuts, reform of the pension systems, and the raising of health premiums (in fact, the movement that emerged agreed that reforms might be needed, but that they should be preconditioned on the right to a decent existence, in employment, housing, health, and education, which would retain a priority over the rights of property and finance (Bensaid, 1996). In the political realm, the left was returned to power in the next set of parliamentary elections, though the presence of an ongoing extra-parliamentary social movement opposition has served as strict discipline for the Jospin government, just as it did the previous one.

The strikes generated potentially important shifts within the French labor movement, as two old political and institutional antagonists, the communist-dominated CGT trade union federation and the anti-communist FO (a product of the Cold War), reached a historic rapprochement after the strikes, when their leaders (the communist Louis Viannet and the anti-communist Marc Blondel) shook hands and embraced on national television. They are now both a part of a "common front" that has animated the broader social movement that has developed since the strikes. The other significant result of the strikes has been the emergence and growth of two new militant trade union groupings, SUD ("Solidarity, Unity, Democracy"), an autonomous movement of postal and tele-communications workers, and FSU ("Unitary Union Federation"), a radical faction of the Teacher's Union that has emerged as a significant force within the labor movement and that has helped to animate and coordinate an important movement of high school students.

The student movement, which has mobilized several nationwide strikes of high school students demanding improvements in the educational system and the labor market, is but one of a number of mobilizations among "excluded" social groups that has swept France in the past several years, and which has been bound together with – both in the "public imagination" and organizationally – the labor movement and groups of intellectuals. For example, within two years following the strikes there was formed a movement of the homeless, centered on the occupation of an unoccupied building for several months in an affluent Left Bank neighborhood, which became a sort of mecca for thousands seeking social absolution, and which was widely linked to the social impulses unleashed by the strikes.

Later, a movement of the unemployed was forged out of the occupation of government social service offices nationwide, and forced the immediate social needs of the unemployed onto the national table. Supported by the labor move-ment (a particularly meaningful institutional link), the level of organization was remarkable for those normally considered demoralized, and for those with such few resources. Still later "illegal aliens" were added to the growing "Mouvement Sociale," as scores of African immigrants barricaded themselves in a cathedral, on hunger strike, ringed by hundreds of supporters, and forced the government to reduce deportations and provide for further immigration appeals. The recent "sacking" of McDonald's outlets in southwest France, in protest over trade requirements that allow for hormone-fed beef, has been the latest in a series of what are no longer separate initiatives, but are capable of being drawn into the vortex of a wider social movement umbrella.

Together, these movements have joined with the labor movement in ongoing dialogue in an "Etats Generaux du Mouvement Sociale," a sort of popular congress to chart future developments, share resources, and coordinate actions. While there have been extraordinary displays of mutual aid across these move-ments, the linkages between them in the public imagination and within the movements themselves have been equally the result of the coordinated activities of intellectuals to counter the media tendency to emphasize the sectional and parochial interests of each. Indeed, an important outcome of the uprising has been the remobilization of the intellectuals, who had been increasingly considered depoliticized and politically indifferent.

This process has been expressed in various ways since the strikes. The group "Raisons d'Agir" ("reasons to act") was formed by several senior editors, journalists, and professors (*Le Monde Diplomatique, Le Canard Enchaine, Liber,* etc.) to coordinate publishing schedules and to work together to increase the critical impact of their work, with a strong emphasis on the social movements themselves and critiques of the neoliberal orthodoxy (the best-selling "Raisons d'Agir" book series, under the direction of Bourdieu, has produced a number of short, inexpensive, and politically charged books, geared to challenging the neoliberal consensus, several of which have sold upwards of 200,000 copies). In addition, within just the first three years, the number of publications devoted to the strikes has been quite remarkable. There have been no fewer than 13 books, 41 journal articles, 14 special issues of journals or magazines, four conferences (with published transcripts), six student theses ("memoires universitaires") and 12 union or employer publications.

The French strikes and the solidarity that they demonstrated, combined with the intellectuals' symbolic power to invoke, authorize, and "name" the events, have spawned a broad "social movement" that is, by all accounts, a significant social force in France and in Europe. In the strikes and their aftermath, a "working class" was essentially remade, becoming not a "universal class" so much as a more cohesive social group whose demands and concerns have become increasingly syncretized with the needs and demands of other social groups. Further, what has developed in relation to this is a more coordinated and elaborated myth-making apparatus that is able to begin to offer an alternative to the myths of neoliberal "globalization" (and, above all, the myth of its inevitability and invincibility). For although opposed in content and much grander in scale, the myths of global capitalism have a status comparable to the myth of the labor movement, to the extent that the myths of capitalism are also enacted (through the seriality and enforced atomization of everyday life) and are denominated by an extraordinarily powerful set of myth-making machines (including the forces of mass media, the political process, academia, and the economic realm to which everything else has become subordinate). Indeed, societies everywhere are radically reconstructed to make the neoliberal mythology seem completely self-evident, so that, for example, the privatization of public goods has become the practical context in which the market is posed as the supreme arbiter of all human affairs, thus producing a reciprocally confirming "reality" that seems to foreclose any other. What the French strikes have accomplished, therefore, is a breach in a socially constructed hermetic seal in which the agents and institutions of global capitalism have sought to actively institute – symbolically and materially – their own inevitability.

For both historical and cultural reasons, the specific lessons the French case can offer for the American labor movement are few. In the USA, labor relations are much more decentralized (unionism based in individual workplaces and individual companies, with a relatively weak national presence), there has been a very different political legacy, and employers enjoy an unusually large degree of freedom to mobilize economic and political resources to counter unions (Freeman, 1994). At the same time, the movement to reform the US labor movement, if successful, will have a substantial impact on social relations in American society. Unions will be larger and more socially representative of the labor force as a whole, they will be more aggressive and will have more political influence, and they will be linked to a broader set of social institutions (academic, religious, ethnic) that will, in turn, root unionism in the society more deeply than it has been for many decades. However, to the extent that the reforms under way are being animated at the top, the lack of a strong national structure means that there may be only minimal influence that the top leadership can exert in constructing a genuine "social movement," if indeed that is what it would be willing to unleash.

While the institutional elements necessary for reforming the labor movement are being put into place, the one lesson that American labor can surely learn from the French example is that the revival of the labor movement hinges on the revival of the myth of the labor movement. This requires both the visual and tangible expressions of militant solidarity in collective action (as a counterweight to existing society) and an autonomous and committed myth-making apparatus that can "name" that which has been virtually unmentionable for the past half century. Ultimately, it is on these two acts that everything else will depend.

Appendix: Data Resources on the World Wide Web

Kathryn Harker

High quality social science data and resources are increasingly available on the Internet. The purposes of this appendix are to aid sociologists and other social scientists in their search for data and resources, and to promote international, comparative, and interdisciplinary research.

Most web sites listed have been developed and are maintained by major research centers and government agencies. They were selected for inclusion because of the quality of their data, clear documentation, usefulness to researchers, and the likelihood of their long-term stability. However, as the Internet is constantly changing, the permanence of these web sites and their addresses, as well as the comprehensiveness of this listing, cannot be guaranteed.

This appendix is divided into three sections: (a) resources and locators that provide general information and links to web sites; (b) specific databases, archives, and data sets listed alphabetically by country (or Europe and international); and (c) an alphabetical listing of web sites by topic.

Helpful Resource Lists and Locators

American Sociological Association (ASA), Data Resources for Sociologists
   http://www.asanet.org/data.htm
American Sociological Association (ASA), Sections
   http://www.asanet.org/Sections/general.htm
DATA and Program Library Service, Internet Crossroads in the Social Sciences
   http://dpls.dacc.wisc.edu/internet.html
Family Sociology Resources
   http://osiris.colorado.edu/SOC/RES/family.html
ICPSR, Other Social Science Data Sites
   http://www.icpsr.umich.edu/websites.html
Internet Data Archives for Social Scientists
   http://www.irss.unc.edu/cassell/courses/IDATARC2.htm

Internet Resources for Sociology Students
  http://www.xu.edu/depts/socdept/resources.html
Law Enforcement Agencies on the Web
  http://www.fsu.edu/~crimdo/police.html
Research Resources for the Social Sciences
  http://www.socsciresearch.com/
Scholars' Guide to WWW
  http://home.nycap.rr.com/history/
Sites Related to Demography and Population
  http://www.prc.utexas.edu/e-resources/other_sites.htm
Sociosite, Social Science Data Archives (SSDA)
  http://www.pscw.uva.nl/sociosite/DataBases.html
Statistical Data Locators
  http://www.ntu.edu.sg/library/statdata.htm
Statistics Sweden (SCB), Other Statistical Sources
  http://www.scb.se/scbeng/statbuen.htm
UCSD, Social Science Data on the Internet
  http://odwin.ucsd.edu/idata/
United Nations WWW and Gopher Servers
http://www.undcp.org/unlinks.html
Voice of the Shuttle: Gender Studies Page
  http://vos.ucsb.edu/shuttle/gender.html
WWW Virtual Library, Demography and Population Studies
  http://demography.anu.au/VirtualLibrary/

Alphabetical by Country

Algeria

Statistics Algeria

The National Office of Statistics is a public establishment in charge of collecting, processing and diffusing socio-economic statistical information. From this webpage, users can download statistical information and offical publications.
  http://www.ons.dz/

Australia

Australian Consortium for Social and Political Research, Inc. (ACSPRI)

ACSPRI is an organization of 35 universities and nine research organizations whose objectives are to collect and facilitate access to Australian and overseas machine-readable data. ACSPRI is administratively fused with the SSDA, which handles the Australian national membership in the ICPSR Archives.
  http://ssda.anu.edu.au/ACSPRI/index.html

Social Science Data Archives (SSDA)

The SSDA, financed by the Australian National University, has collected and preserved data relating to social, political, and economic affairs in Australia and New Zealand since 1981.

The Archives include over 500 academic and government studies and 480 polls and censuses. The SSDA is a member of IFDO (International Federation of Data Organizations) and the ICPSR Archives. Any researcher in an Australian academic institution has access to data through SSDA. Fees are minimal, with charges of approximately US$60 per data set request.

http://ssda.anu.edu.au/

Austria

WISDOM (Wiener Institut für Sozialwissenschaftliche Dokumentation und Methodik)

WISDOM, established in 1984, collects and disseminates Austrian and German social science data. The data archive is a member of CESSDA (Council of European Social Science Data Archive) and the IFDO (International Federation of Data Organizations). Data are available through WISDOM on a cost-recovery basis. Discounts are available to students.

http://www.ifdo.org/org_archives/at_wisdom.htm

Belgium

Belgian Archive for the Social Sciences (BASS)

Affiliated with the Université Catholique de Louvain, BASS collects and disseminates Belgian and European social science survey data and statistical files. The Archive contains over 400 data sets in the fields of political science, sociology, social medicine and mental health, history, demography, and economics. A catalogue of the Archive is available; US$28 paperback, $10 floppy disk.

http://www.ssd.gu.se:80/ifdo/BASS.html

Brazil

Centro de Estudos de Opinião Publica (CESOP)

CESOP is an interdisciplinary initiative located at the University of Campinas-UNI-CAMP Brazil. Its objective is to gather and organize survey data, provide consulting services to researchers, and develop research projects and training programs in public opinion methodology and quantitative analysis. CESOP organizes the National Survey Data Bank on Public Opinion, which includes Brazilian surveys on behavior, attitudes, and opinions. This data bank has raw data, questionnaires and research reports and is accessible to the public. CESOP serves as the Brazilian link to the Roper Center (University of Connecticut) and the ICPSR Archive.

http://www.unicamp.br/cesop/

Pesquisa Nacional de Amostra de Domicilios [Brazilian Household Surveys] (PNAD)

PNAD provides statistical data regarding Brazilian households. It is located in the ISSR Data Archives at the University of California at Los Angeles. However, use of the data may be restricted to individuals associated with the university. Contact information is made available in the description of each individual data set.

http://www.sscnet.ucla.edu/issr/da/index/framet.htm

Bulgaria

National Statistical Institute of Bulgaria (NSI)

The NSI collects and disseminates statistical data, for which it develops, maintains, and applies unified national nomenclatures and classifications based upon international standards. Surveys include economic, demographic, and social information and indicators. The NSI also provides analyses and forecasts for social, economic, and demographic processes and trends in Bulgaria. The annual Catalogue of Statistical Publications is provided free of charge in both Bulgarian and English versions.

http://www.acad.bg/BulRTD/nsi/index.htm

Canada

Canadian Centre on Substance Abuse (CCSA)

The CCSA is a non-profit organization that provides information about the nature, extent, and consequences of the use of alcohol, tobacco, and other drugs and assists organizations dedicated to dealing with these issues. This website provides statistical information, as well as links to discussion papers, the 1997 National Household Survey on Drug Abuse (SAMHSA), and summaries and highlights of many Canadian studies covering alcohol, drugs, gambling, and AIDS.

http://www.ccsa.ca/

Canadian Election Study (CES), 1997

The CES, a nationally representative election study, is conducted by the Institute for Social Research at York University. This site provides access to the 1997 election data frequencies and allows researchers to download questionnaires, documentation, and survey data, in either French or English, in SPSS format.

http://www.isr.yorku.ca/projects/ces/index.html

The Canadian Legislator Study

In June 1997, the Canadian Legislator Study surveyed over 550 legislators about the role of government in health promotion, specifically with regard to smoking and tobacco control. The study's web site provides highlights of the national findings and brief summaries of survey results for each territory of Canada.

http://www.isr.yorku.ca/projects/csl/index.html

Central East Health Information Partnership (CEHIP)

CEHIP collects and disseminates data sets related to health planning, research, and education to the partners. These data sets include information regarding both Ontario and the nation as a whole. CEHIP also provides community health status indicators for all public health units and district health councils in the Central East Region of Canada. These indicators are freely available via this web site.

http://www.cehip.org/

Centre for Research on Work and Society

The Centre, located at York University, Toronto, promotes research on work and labor, provides resources to researchers, and organizes working groups. The Centre's web site provides access to working papers, and comprehensive lists of links to other work-related research centers and government departments (federal and regional).
http://www.yorku.ca/research/crws/centres.htm

Centre for the Study of Democracy, Queens University

The Centre's objective is to promote and conduct research on democratic development and stability. The Centre's web site provides a link to the Canadian Public Opinion Data Archive and to the Archive of Ukranian Public Opinion Data. Data from these archives are available via the Internet.
http://csd.queensu.ca/

"Challenge" Canadian Research Information Database

The "Challenge," established by the Humanities and Social Sciences Federation of Canada, is an information resource for researchers, policy-makers, journalists, and students. Challenge provides short descriptions of current Canadian research in the humanities and social sciences. This site, available in both English and French, contains a listing of current research projects and information regarding how to post descriptions.
http://www.hssfc.ca/introEng.html

Data Liberation Initiative (DLI)

The DLI provides Canadian academic institutions with affordable access to Statistics Canada data files and databases. Under the DLI, universities acquire data that are available at the institutional level for a set annual fee. Public use microdata files (from surveys such as the General Social Survey, the Census, and the Survey of Labour and Income Dynamics), Census profiles, CANSIM time-series data, and trade statistics are all available from the DLI via FTP.
http://www.statcan.ca/english/Dli/dli.htm

Data Resource Center (DRC)

Based at the University of Guelph, the DRC acts as a central repository for statistical and social science data and provides user support to researchers. It includes a web-based retrieval system that allows access to Canadian census files, statistics, historical information, climate data, World Bank files, and the ICPSR data archive. Additional data are under restricted access, and available by CD-ROM. The DRC also provides links to other external data sources and resource centers.
http://drc.uoguelph.ca/

Institute for Social Research (ISR)

The ISR at York University, Toronto houses the largest university-based survey research unit in Canada. Survey data collected by the ISR and other major Canadian surveys (e.g. The Canadian Election Study, The Canadian Legislator Study) are kept in the data archive. These studies include major national election, quality of life, and attitudinal surveys, and are available in SPSS, SAS, Excel, Access, and dBase formats. Those not affiliated with York University are charged a fee for each data set. This web site is available in both English and French.

http://www.isr.yorku.ca/

National Archives of Canada

The National Archives preserve, store, and provide access to Canada's archival heritage through publications, exhibitions, special events, and reference and researcher services. The archives include millions of records, texts, photos, films, maps, videos, books, paintings, prints, and government files. These resources are available to the general public, and access to them can be arranged for non-local researchers.

http://www.archives.ca/www/com/english/memories.html

Ontario Ministry of Health

The Ontario Ministry of Health web site contains information regarding health programs, research developments, and community contacts. The site also provides links to Ministry of Health publications and a useful set of links to other health-related Canadian web sites.

http://www.gov.on.ca/health/

QualPage

The QualPage website provides resources to qualitative researchers. Included in this site is information regarding conferences and workshops, qualitative approaches, disciplines and foundations, discussion forums, grant information, and methodology. Additionally, the site provides links to electronic journals, organizations and interest groups, papers, and software resources.

http://www.ualberta.ca/~jrnorris/qual.html

Social Science Computing Library (SSCL)

The SSCL is a computing facility operated by the Faculty of Social Science. Its objective is to provide software and services to researchers. Researchers can access Statistics Canada's computerized data bank, which includes the time-series database CANSIM through the SSCL. CANSIM includes 55,000 time series on retail trade, national accounts, energy, labor force earnings, etc.

http://www.sscl.uwo.ca/explore/datainfolib.html

Statistics Canada

The Statistics Canada website, available in both English and French, provides researchers with free tabular data on aspects of Canada's economy, land, people, and government. Further, it provides free census data, education resources, daily news updates, and access to the CANSIM time series and trade statistics databases, research papers, and publications. Researchers can also order CD-ROM copies of the *Labour Force Historical Review* (US$195) and the *Inter-Corporate Ownership 1998* guide.

http://www.statcan.ca/start.html

China

China Health and Nutrition Survey (CHNS)

Conducted by an international team of researchers, the CHNS examines the effects of health, nutrition, and family planning policies and programs implemented by national and local governments, and explores the impact of social and economic transformation upon the health and nutritional status of the Chinese population. The CHNS used a multistage, random cluster design to draw a sample of about 3,800 households in eight provinces of China. Detailed community data were collected in surveys of food markets, health facilities, family planning officials, and other social services and community leaders. The 1989, 1991, and 1993 CHNS data are available via anonymous FTP. Copies of the 1989, 1991, and 1993 CHNS questionnaires are available in Adobe Acrobat format.
http://www.cpc.unc.edu/projects/china/china_home.html

China in Time and Space (CITAS)

CITAS aims to collect and disseminate contemporary and historical data on China to scholars and other non-commercial users. The project utilizes geographic information system technology (GIS) to integrate map data, and allows for longitudinal and historical comparative research. CITAS data include vectorized base maps of China, geo-referenced socioeconomic data, bibliographic references, and utilities for coding data. Data are provided at minimal cost and are available in SPSS, ASCII, or ARC/INFO interchange formats.
http://citas.csde.washington.edu/org/org_guide.html

Databank for China Studies (DCS)

The DCS has collected social science data for the People's Republic of China since 1995. The archive includes over 20 large and medium-sized data sets, covering topics such as household surveys, economics, women, fertility, and the elderly. Access to data is restricted to academic researchers, who must apply to the center. Usage fees are determined on a case by case basis.
http://www.usc.cuhk.edu.hk/databank.asp

Croatia

Croatian Bureau of Statistics (CBS)

The CBS collects, processes, analyzes, and publishes Croatian statistical data and provides aid to researchers. Most of its publications are published in portable document format (PDF), which is readable in Adobe Acrobat.
http://www.dzs.hr/Eng/Default.htm

Czech Republic

Czech Statistical Office (CzSo)

The CzSo provides statistical publications to the Czech government, experts, and the public. Most publications are in Czech, unless otherwise stated, and can be ordered online. The CzSo charges US$1 for every five pages of text, excluding postal charges.
http://infox.eunet.cz/csu/csu_e.html

Denmark

Danish Data Archives (DDA)

Part of the Danish State Archive, the DDA serves as the national data bank for researchers and students in Denmark. The archive holds over 1,800 survey data and statistical files in the fields of political science, sociology, social medicine, history, demography, economics, and regional studies. Documents are available in machine-readable form and in book form. The DDA also includes the Danish Demographic Database, which contains census and emigration data from the eighteenth and nineteenth centuries. A catalogue of holdings and newsletter are available from the archives.

http://www.dda.dk/

Estonia

The Estonian Social Science Data Archives (ESSDA)

The ESSDA, located in the University of Tartu, is an interdisciplinary center that acts as the national data bank of Estonia. Its objective is to contribute to the maintenance and use of Estonian social science information. Coordinating its efforts with the Academic Union of Estonian Sociologists (AUES), it has collected 214 data sets between 1975 and 1994.

http://sys130.psych.ut.ee/esta/essda.html

France

Banque de Données Socio-politique (BDSP)

The BDSP collects, archives, and distributes machine-readable data related to political science, sociology, and history. These data include spatial data and time series of French electoral results, survey data, and public opinion polls. It is a member of CESSDA, IFDO, and the ICPSR Archive.

http://solcidsp.upmf-grenoble.fr

Institut de l'Information Scientifique et Technique (INIST)

INIST, associated with the National Center of Scientific Research (CNRS), is one of the premier centers of scientific and technical information in Europe. The mission of INIST is to collect and disseminate the results of scientific and technical research.

http://www.inist.fr/

Germany

Central Archive (Zentralarchiv – ZA)

An institute of the Cologne Association for Social Research, the ZA archives data from all fields of empirical research, with an emphasis upon survey data. The data collections include national election studies, consumer studies, leisure and tourism studies, communication and mass media research, the German General Social Surveys, and Eurobarometer research.

http://www.za.uni-koeln.de/index-e.htm

Center for Survey Research and Methodology (ZUMA)

ZUMA aims to assist and advise researchers on the design and execution of social science research, especially surveys. It also prepares census data and provides access to income and consumer research, microdata, and social indicators.

http://www.zuma-mannheim.de/index-e.htm

German Socio-economic Panel (GSOEP)

The GSOEP, begun in 1984, is an ongoing representative longitudinal study of private households in Germany. The GSOEP originally included only individuals living in West Germany, but was expanded in 1990 to include East Germans as well. The study explores living conditions and changes over time. This web site also provides links to working papers.

http://www.diw-berlin.de/soep/soepe.htm

Guatemala

1995 Guatemalan Survey of Family Health (EGSF)

The Guatemalan Family Life Survey is a non-representative set of detailed household and community surveys conducted by RAND. The EGSF examines rural Guatemalan families, the ways in which they cope with childhood illnesses and pregnancy, and the roles of ethnicity, poverty, social support, and health beliefs in these processes. In all, 4,792 households and 2,872 women aged 18–35 have been interviewed for this survey.

http://www.rand.org/FLS/

Hong Kong

Social Sciences Research Center (SSRC)

Established by the Faculty of Social Science at the University of Hong Kong, the SSRC promotes interdisciplinary research, fosters ties with other research institutions, and offers consulting services. The SSRC is currently developing a Social Science Data Archive containing data sets relevant to Hong Kong and China, and includes an index of outside data sets.

http://www.ssrc.hku.hk/

Hungary

Social Research Informatics Centre (TARKI)

TARKI was founded in 1985 by ten major social science research institutions in Hungary. The purpose of TARKI is to collect, process, archive, and publish relevant social science data. The data archive includes over 300 sociological and socio-statistical surveys from the past 15 years. TARKI also conducts several policy-oriented research projects that study the size and development of the private sector, the public perception of privatization, and the effectiveness of welfare programs within Hungary. Data are available online in SPSS format or through the mail.

http://www.tarki.hu/

Indonesia

Indonesian Family Life Survey, 1993 (IFLS)

The IFLS was conducted by RAND as a set of household and community surveys. In 1993, individuals from 13 provinces in 7,224 households (83 percent of the population) were surveyed regarding issues such as fertility, family planning, infant and child health, migration, employment, the elderly, and children.

http://www.rand.org/organization/drd/labor/FLS/ or ICPSR

Israel

Central Bureau of Statistics (CBS)

The CBS provides researchers with updated statistical information, including the previous month's price indices, the Census of Population and Housing, and monthly bulletins of prices. Statistical publications are also available online.

http://www.cbs.gov.il/engindex.htm

Geobase, Israel Regional Database

Developed and run by the SSDA, Geobase is a geographic data warehouse which stores statistical information on topics such as economics, labor, population, transportation, tourism, housing, and education. This information is collected from statistical publications, local authorities, public service records, and the Central Bureau of Statistics.

http://geobase.huji.ac.il/docs/overview.htm

Social Sciences Data Archive (SSDA)

Established by the Faculty of Social Sciences at Hebrew University of Jerusalem, the SSDA collects, preserves, and distributes social science data. It includes more than 800 data sets, covering subjects such as survey data, census micro-data, government records, immigration, and macroeconomic series. Its user community includes all Israeli universities, professionals, and policy-makers. Others may request access to data but are charged for the cost of the data set. Data are supplied through FTP, floppy disks, CD-ROM, and/or computer cassettes.

http://ssda.huji.ac.il/intmenu.htm

Italy

Archivio Dati e Programmi per le Scienze (ADPSS)

Part of the Istituto Superiore di Sociologia, the ADPSS specializes in the collection of ecological and survey data files in Italian urban and political studies.

http://www.nsd.uib.no/cessda/adpss.html

Jamaica

Derek Gordon Data Bank

The Derek Gordon Data Bank, located at the University of the West Indies at Mona, collects and provides access to social and economic data and promotes comparative data analysis on a regional level. Access to data is free for Caribbean social science researchers and policy-makers and is provided on a user-charge basis to researchers elsewhere. The Data Bank's holdings include the Survey of Living Conditions (Jamaica) 1989–1993 and the Labour Force Survey 1990, 1992–1993.

http://www.chass.utoronto.ca:8080/datalib/other/dgdb.htm

Japan

Information Center for Social Science Research on Japan (SSJ Data Archive)

Established by the Institute of Social Science at the University of Tokyo, the SSJ Data Archive provides a collection of data from social and statistical surveys. Data from the archive are available only to academic researchers in Japan.

http://www.iss.u-tokyo.ac.jp/pages/ssjda-re/

National Survey of Japanese Elderly 1987

This study, a national probability sample of non-institutionalized persons aged 60 or older, was designed for use in cross-cultural analyses of aging in the United States and Japan. Data collected by the study include information on demographics, social integration, health status, subjective well-being and mental health, psychological indicators, financial situation, memory, and interviewer observations. Data can be obtained in SAS or SPSS formats, and the codebook is available via a PDF file.

http://www.icpsr.umich.edu/NACDA/archive.html

Korea

Korean Social Science Data Center (KSDC)

The KSDC, established in 1997, collects and manages domestic and international social science data. The Center is a contributing member of the ICPSR, and translates Korean data into English for foreign researchers. The Korean data are composed primarily of election surveys. Both institutions and individuals may obtain KSDC membership for a specified fee.

http://www.ksdc.re.kr/m1/me1.html

Latvia

Central Statistical Bureau (CSB)

The CSB collects and disseminates important Latvian socioeconomic indicators via the Internet.

http://www.csb.lv/

Lithuania

Lithuanian Department of Statistics (StD)

The StD collects and disseminates important Lithuanian statistical information via the Internet.

http://www.std.lt/

Luxembourg

Luxembourg Employment Study (LES Project)

The LES, a project associated with LIS (see below), was begun in 1994. The purpose of the project has been to construct a databank of labor force surveys, beginning in the early 1990s, for 13 countries of varying labor market structures. The data from these surveys have been standardized to allow for comparative research.

http://www.lis.ceps.lu/index.htm

Luxembourg Income Study (LIS)

The LIS is an interdisciplinary cooperative research project including micro-data from more than 25 countries. The LIS allows analysis of labor market behavior on both individual and household levels, industrial and educational patterns, and retirement decisions. It includes the Comparative Welfare States Data Set, which can be downloaded in zip-file format online.

http://www.lis.ceps.lu/index.htm

Malaysia

Malaysian Family Life Surveys, 1976–1977 and 1988–1989 (MFLS)

The MFLS was conducted by RAND as a set of representative household and community surveys. These surveys collected detailed information on such issues as family structure, fertility, economic status, education, and migration. Some of the 1988–9 survey was collected as panel data.

http://www.rand.org/organization/drd/labor/FLS/ or ICPSR

Mexico

Encuesta Nacional de la Dinamica Demografica 1992 [National Survey of Population Dynamics] (ENADID)

ENADID provides comprehensive national data on the Mexican population. It is located in the Data Archive in the Population Research Center at the University of Texas at Austin and the Universidad Autonoma Metropolitana Data Base, but may be available only to account holders at those universities. Contact information is provided.

http://www.prc.utexas.edu/

Encuesta Nacional De Empleo Urban (ENEU)

ENEU provides national employment data for the country of Mexico. It is located in the Data Archive in the Population Research Center at the University of Texas at Austin and

the Universidad Autonoma Metropolitana Data Base, but may be available only to account holders at those universities. Contact information is provided.
http://www.prc.utexas.edu/

Instituto Nacional de Estadistica, Geografia, e Informatica (INEGI)

INEGI provides geographic, economic, and demographic information about Mexico, and coordinates the Informatic Development Programme. The site provides access to a catalogue of products. This catalogue, however, is available only in Spanish.
http://www.inegi.gob.mx/

Netherlands

CentER Savings Survey (formerly known as the VSB Panel [Dutch Socio-Economic Panel Study]), Netherlands

The VSB Project conducts research on household decision-making and savings patterns. VSB includes panel data on Dutch households (DSEP), which are similar to PSID data and include around 5,000 households in every wave. Starting in 1993, the VSB also includes the VSB Savings Panel of 3,000 households, 2,000 of which form a representative sample of the Dutch population and 1,000 of which are from the top 10 percent income bracket. Research is conducted by economists and psychologists.
http://center-ar.kub.nl/css/

Central Bureau of Statistics (CBS)

The CBS collects, processes, and analyzes statistical data pertaining to the Netherlands. Statistical results are available in published form.
http://www.cbs.nl/

Economy Data Archives (Econdata)

Econdata is a database of national and regional economic studies, both those which are a part of the main Steinmetz Archive (Dutch Social Science Data Archive) and those registered with the Steinmetz Archive.
http://www.niwi.knaw.nl/nl/projects/proecon.htm

Longitudinal Aging Study Amsterdam (LASA)

LASA, begun in 1992 by the Netherlands Institute of Gerontology, is an interdisciplinary, longitudinal study used to develop and evaluate policy in the field of aging. The main topics addressed in this study include autonomy and quality of life (functioning) of older persons. The sample, obtained from the cross-sectional NESTOR study, is constructed to reflect the national distribution of urbanization and population density in the Netherlands.
http://www.nig.nl/onderzoek/index_en.html

Netherlands Institute for Scientific Information Services (NIWI)

NIWI collects and registers social science data, and mediates the acquisition of that data by researchers. NIWI provides access to the Econdata and Steinmetz Archives and the History Data Archives (NHDA).
http://www.niwi.knaw.nl/welcome.htm

Steinmetz Archive

The Dutch Social Science Data Archive collects, documents, processes, and distributes Dutch and international social science data to interested researchers. The archive holds 2,000 data sets, including collections of public opinion polls, election studies, and the Continuous Social Survey.

http://www.niwi.knaw.nl/us/dd_star/starinfo.htm

SocioSite

SocioSite, established at the University of Amsterdam, is a comprehensive resource to hundreds of web sites that are sociological in nature. Web site links are categorized according to subject matter, and are often accompanied by a short description. SocioSite also provides links to course syllabi, online journals, libraries, data archives, sociology departments, research centers and associations, publishers, newsgroups, and mailing lists.

http://www.pscw.uva.nl/sociosite/

New Zealand

New Zealand Social Research Data Archives (NZSRDA)

Located in Massey University, the NZSRDA collects, cleans, documents, and preserves social, political, and economic data. It includes over 33 New Zealand data sets, as well as international data sets. Data access is limited to academic researchers.

http://www.massey.ac.nz/~NZSRDA/nzsrda/archive.htm

New Zealand Election Study

The New Zealand Election Study provides an analysis of political behavior over five successive New Zealand elections. It focuses on democratic processes during a period of social and economic change and a transition between electoral systems. The web site includes a list of publications and working papers.

http://www.nzes.org

Norway

Norwegian Social Science Data Services (NSD)

The NSD, directed under the Research Council of Norway, is a national research center that maintains access for researchers to social science data and services. Data available through the NSD include: the Commune Database, census tract information, the Criminal Justice Archive, the Nordic Database on Regional Time Series (1950–90), a Polling Archive, the Norwegian Survey Archive, the Census Databank, the KIRUT Database, and data on the political system. This site also has a clickable map with links to other data archives around the world.

http://www.nsd.uib.no/english/

Norwegian Historical Data Centre (NHDC)

Located at the University of Tromsø, the NHDC strives to provide a national Norwegian population register for the eighteenth and nineteenth centuries. The NHDC has computerized census data from 1865 to the present linked with eighteenth- and nineteenth-century parish registers. Data are available as hard copy and on floppy disk, and statistics are available on the Internet.

http://www.isv.uit.no/seksjon/rhd/indexeng.htm

Statistics Norway

Statistics Norway collects, analyzes, and disseminates Norwegian statistical information. The web site includes selected statistics by subject, weekly bulletin updates, and information about publications utilizing these statistical data.

http://www.ssb.no/www-open/english/

Philippines

The Cebu Longitudinal Health and Nutritional Survey (CLHNS)

Conducted as a joint effort between researchers in the United States and the Philippines, the CLHNS is an ongoing study of a cohort of Filipino women who gave birth to a child between May 1, 1983 and April 30, 1984. The first follow-up, in 1991–2, included information on a total of 2,260 children. The study addresses issues of infant feeding patterns, as well as other health, demographic, and nutritional outcomes. The 1983–4 data are available on CD-ROM free of charge, and the 1991–2 follow-up data are available via FTP on the Internet. Copies of questionnaires and codebooks are also available via the Internet.

http://www.cpc.unc.edu/projects/cebu/cebu_home.html

Russia

Euro-Asian Bank of Social Data (DB)

Formerly the All-Union Data Bank, the Euro-Asian Bank of Social Data archives and disseminates machine-readable data on sociological research projects conducted in the USSR/Russia. The DB now stores a comprehensive collection of 25 years of empirical social research, covering a wide range of topics.

http://www.berlin.iz-soz.de/extern/isras/eurodb.htm

Russia Longitudinal Monitoring Survey (RLMS)

This web site seeks to provide easy access to public use data on Russia. The RLMS, which began in 1992, is an interdisciplinary series of nationally representative surveys studying the impact of economic reforms on the health and economic welfare of the Russian Federation. Researchers on the project include economists, statisticians, sociologists, nutritionists, and public health scholars from the USA and Russia. Data are currently available for four series (1992–4), and can be obtained in SAS format through anonymous FTP or on diskette. Documentation is available over the Internet in Adobe Acrobat format.

http://www.cpc.unc.edu/projects/rlms/rlms_home.html

Slovenia

Statistical Office of the Republic of Slovenia

The Statistical Office collects, analyzes, and provides statistical data to researchers interested in the Republic of Slovenia. Data are available on tape or diskette.
http://www.sigov.si/zrs/

South Africa

Statistics South Africa (Stats SA)

Stats SA collects, analyzes and provides statistical data to researchers interested in South Africa. Statistical releases and reports, as well as economic indicators and time-series data, are available from the site.
http://www.statssa.gov.za/

South African Data Archive (SADA)

SADA was established in 1993 to provide and promote the use of domestic and international social science data and documentation. It is a member of IASSIST, IFDO, and the ICPSR. The Archive includes political science, election, criminology, demography, sociology, economic, business, education, history, health, psychology, and census data. A listing of data holdings is available online, as is a listing of other relevant archives. Archive data can be obtained through FTP, on diskette, or in some cases on CD-ROM, and are available in ASCII or SPSS format. Researchers are charged for the direct costs of the data delivery.
http://www.nrf.ac.za/sada/

Spain

Análisis Sociológicos Económicos y Políticos, SA (ASEP)

One of Spain's leading public opinion institutes, ASEP provides researchers with data and documentation from their public opinion surveys. The data bank at ASEP includes more than 120 national studies conducted since 1986. ASEP is also participating in numerous international projects, such as the World Values Survey, the International Social Survey Program (ISSP), and the Comparative Study of Electoral Systems. Data on CD-ROM can be ordered online. Prices vary. This website is only available in Spanish. However, many of the CD-ROMs include both Spanish and English translations.
http://www.asep-sa.com/

Centro de Investigaciones Sociologicas (CIS)

The CIS, a state agency attached to the Office of the Presidency, was established to conduct surveys in an attempt to study Spanish society. Over 1,200 social and political public opinion surveys are available in the CIS data bank. Surveys include monthly barometer polls, monographic surveys, regional and municipal surveys, electoral surveys, and international surveys. Data can be purchased in tabular form or in raw form and are available to all Spanish citizens. Other interested researchers can contact the CIS.
http://www.cis.es/

Sweden

Karolinska Institutet

Sweden's only medical university, the Karolinska Institutet strongly emphasizes medical research and maintains the Karolinska Institutet Library (KIB), the country's largest medical library and national resource library for medicine, ontology, and care sciences. This site contains a research database, which provides researchers with descriptions of ongoing projects, and links to project leaders and published results.

http://www.ki.se/ki/

National Archives of Sweden

The National Archives of Sweden, located in Stockholm, have established the National Archival Database (NAD), which provides individuals with information regarding the state. NAD includes the National Registry of Private Archives, which is available on CD-ROM and will soon be available via the Internet. This web site also includes links to regional and military archives. Access to archival information is public, unless otherwise stated in the Act of Secrecy.

http://www.ra.se/index.htm

Social Citizenship Indicator Program (SCIP)

Located at the Swedish Institute for Social Research at Stockholm University, SCIP provides data for comparative research in the areas of social policy, standard of living, and labor market research. The web site also provides free access to working papers and publications.

http://www.sofi.su.se/

Statistics Sweden (SCB)

The Statistics Sweden web site provides a wonderful, comprehensive listing of links to the public authorities responsible for disseminating official Swedish statistics. Additionally, this site provides useful links for statistical information pertaining to Africa, Asia, Europe, the Middle East, North America, Oceania, and South America, and information collected by international organizations.

http://www.scb.se/scbeng/statbuen.htm

Swedish Social Sciences Data Service (SSD)

An independent service at the University of Goteborg, the SSD collects, processes, and archives Swedish and international data from over 130 countries. The Archive includes social science survey and statistical data, and provides thorough documentation. However, all documentation is in Swedish. Data can be requested by e-mail. Non-Swedish researchers should contact the Data Archive representative in their home country (IFDO Archives, ICPSR, IRSS, ISSR-UCLA). Each data set costs US$25.

http://www.ssd.gu.se:80/enginfo.html

Switzerland

SIDOS

SIDOS acts as the Swiss information and data archival service for the social sciences. This site, offered in English, French, and German, provides information regarding data access, links to other resources, and SIDOS news updates.

http://www-sidos.unine.ch/Commun/DE/toc00D.html

Taiwan

Office of Survey Research, Academia Sinica

The Office of Survey Research maintains the Survey Research Data Archive (SRDA) for the purpose of promoting and supporting Taiwanese research. The archive is for academic use only, and includes social, political, educational, and economic data. Major data sets include the Social Image Survey in Taiwan, the Taiwan Social Change Survey, the Public Opinion Polls, and the Influence of Air Pollution on the Health of Human Beings study. Data and documentation are available at the cost of US$1 per floppy disk, US$0.10 per page of documentation, plus shipping and handling. Data are available in raw, SAS, or SPSS format.

http://www.sinica.edu.tw/as/survey/index_e.html

Turkey

State Institute of Statistics (SIS)

The SIS provides access to data on Turkish economic and social indicators. The web site includes a financial statistics page, the 1997 Population Register results, and information on IMF economic and financial data for Turkey.

http://www.die.gov.tr/

United Kingdom

British General Household Study (GHS)

The General Household Survey is a national survey conducted quarterly by the Social Survey Division of the Office for National Statistics. Begun in 1971, the GHS provides information on housing, employment, education, health and social services, transport, population, and social security. The survey is based on a sample of approximately 9,000 households. SPSS files were created for all years from 1973 to 1982. Data for 1971 and 1972, however, are only available as ASCII files. Since 1983, the data have been supplied in SIR format and can be distributed to researchers in a variety of formats. There was no data collection for 1997–8. Data are currently available through the Data Archive at Essex.

http://biron.essex.ac.uk/cgi-bin/biron/

The British Household Panel Study

The BHPS is a household-based multipurpose panel study of adults. The survey includes large numbers of elderly individuals and single parents, and can be linked with data from other surveys. The first wave included 5,500 households and 10,300 individuals from

250 areas of Great Britain. Waves 1 through 6 are currently available through the Data Archive at Essex and are disseminated in SPSS, SAS, STATA, and SIR formats.
http://www.irc.essex.ac.uk/bhps/

Centre for Applied Social Surveys (CASS) Question Bank

The CASS Question Bank was established to help researchers to devise their own survey questionnaires by providing examples of how other surveys have operationalized and measured specific concepts. The questionnaires of many of the major British surveys are stored in the Question Bank, and can be searched by survey, year, topic area, and keywords. Questionnaire information is transferred through PDF and can be read using Adobe Acrobat. CASS also provides aid to analysts trying to identify appropriate secondary data to use in their research.
http://www.scpr.ac.uk/cass

Centre for Longitudinal Studies, University of London

The Centre focuses upon the use of longitudinal methods to study the citizens of Britain. Three major multidisciplinary longitudinal studies located here include: The 1970 British Cohort Study, a continuing study of all people born April 5–11, 1970; The National Child Development Study, a continuing study of all people born March 3–9, 1958; The National Survey of Health and Development, a continuing study of those born in March of 1946. Data for the cohort studies are available through the ESRC Data Archive.
http://www.cls.ioe.ac.uk

Edinburgh Data and Information Access (EDINA)

EDINA provides free access to a national data library for students and researchers in the United Kingdom. EDINA houses agricultural, environmental and life science, art, humanities, social science, census, geographic, and Scottish regional data. The data library (EUDL) heads several major projects, including: the British Survey of Fertilizer Practice, the Scottish Data Initiative, the Scottish Migration and Housing Choice Survey, and Digimap (digital map data via the web). Data can be converted to SPSS, SIR, Excel, Arc/Info, MapInfo, and ASCII formats.
http://edina.ed.ac.uk/

ESRC Data Archive, University of Essex

The ESRC Data Archive contains the largest collection of social science and humanities data in the United Kingdom. Initiated in 1967, it now contains 7,000 data sets, including cross-sectional academic, government, and commercial studies, as well as time series, longitudinal, panel, and cross-national studies. Areas studied include agriculture, crime, social and political attitudes, family expenditures, health, and the labor force. Data are available to domestic and foreign researchers.
http://dawww.essex.ac.uk

Manchester Information and Associated Services (MIMAS)

MIMAS provides national research support services, free to researchers in the UK, at the University of Manchester. MIMAS allows easy access to a limited number of data sets. These include census and census-related data sets, government and continuous studies, macroeconomic time-series data sets, spatial data sets, and scientific data sets. Documentation is available in hardcopy.

http://mimas.ac.uk/

Qualitative Data Archival Resource Centre (Qualidata)

Qualidata was established in 1967 at the University of Essex in response to the lack of archived qualitative data. Qualidata salvaged past research and continued to locate, assess, and document current data, arranging for it to be deposited in public archives. It maintains an information database about the extent and availability of qualitative research dating back to 1970. The Qualidata catalog (Qualicat) is available via the Internet. Some of the archives referenced by Qualidata are: the National Social Policy and Social Change Archive; the National Sound Archive, the British Library; the Modern Records Centre, University of Warwick; the Institute of Criminology, University of Cambridge; Archives and Business Records Centre, University of Glasgow; and the School of Scottish Studies, University of Edinburgh.

http://www.essex.ac.uk/qualidata/current/backg.htm

Social Science Information Gateway (SOSIG)

SOSIG provides an excellent online catalogue of Internet resources. SOSIG screens sources for high quality standards and the ability to support serious educational and research aims. Researchers can search SOSIG by keyword, or can browse SOSIG's "virtual shelves" by subject area or geographical region.

http://sosig.esrc.bris.ac.uk/

United States of America

The Administration for Children and Families (ACF), US Department of Health and Human Services

The ACF homepage provides updates on recent research and political developments relevant to ACF, a news archive, access to an HHS listserv, a variety of fact sheets, and fiscal and statistical information. The information provided deals with child care, child support, child welfare, Head Start programs, refugees, and welfare.

http://www.acf.dhhs.gov/

Aggression Research Program, University of Michigan

The Aggression Research Program studies the etiology and prevention of aggressive and anti-social behavior through laboratory experiments, longitudinal surveys, and clinical field trials. The Program also addresses issues such as peer relations, social judgment, and mass media. Links are provided to major studies, such as the Children's TV and Aggression Study, the Evaluating the Metropolitan Area Child Study, and the C-2 Believe Prevention Study.

http://www.isr.umich.edu/rcgd/aggr/index.html

American Religion Data Archive (ARDA)

Sponsored by the Lilly Endowment, the ARDA collects, preserves, and provides access to quantitative data sets for the study of American religion. Archived data include

surveys of the general population, of selected religious groups, of religious professionals, and of religious aggregations. Documentation can be viewed and data downloaded from this web site. This site also has an excellent list of links to related web
sites.

http://www.arda.tm

Americans Changing Lives

This study constitutes both the 1986 and 1989 waves of a national longitudinal panel
survey covering a wide range of sociological, psychological, mental, and physical health
items. It was designed to investigate the differences between black and white Americans
in middle and late life. Among the topics covered are interpersonal relationships, satisfaction, social interactions and leisure activities, traumatic life events, retirement, health
behaviors, and utilization of health care. Also included are measures of physical health,
psychological well-being, and cognitive functioning. Data are available in SPSS and SAS
formats.

http://www.icpsr.umich.edu/cgi/ab.prl?file=6438

American Society of Criminology – Divisions and Other Sources

This site provides information on the four divisions of the American Society of Criminology (Critical Criminology, International Criminology, People of Color and Crime, and
Women and Crime) and a helpful list of links to other criminal justice sites. Included in
this list are sites dealing with general criminal justice, international criminal justice, the
courts, juvenile justice, corrections, police, white collar crime, drugs, government sites,
criminal justice newsletters, and available listservs.

http://www.asc41.com/four.html

ASA Section on International Migration

The purpose of this ASA Section is to encourage and promote the development of theory
and research in the field of international migration. This site provides links to the
Section's newsletter, World on the Move, and includes updates on conferences, awards
and calls for papers. It also has an excellent listing of links to web sites containing
information and data dealing with immigration, race, and ethnicity.

http://www.ssc.msu.edu/~intermig/

Assessing the New Federalism

A multiyear project of the Urban Institute, ANF is designed to analyze changes in government funding of income support programs, social services, health programs, and programs
aimed at children and families. This site offers access to 872 variables for all 50 US states
and the District of Columbia. These data allow researchers to explore changes over time
and conduct comparative analyses. Data can be viewed online or downloaded to a PC.
Look for a button on the Urban Institute's homepage that is labeled with the project name.

http://www.urban.org

Behavioral Risk Factor Surveillance System (BRFSS)

The BRFSS, administered and supported by the Division of Adult and Community
Health at the National Center for Chronic Disease Prevention and Health Promotion

of the CDC, is an ongoing data collection program. Its main objective is to collect and analyze data regarding the state-level prevalence of the major behavioral risks among adults that are associated with premature morbidity and mortality. Since 1994, all states, the District of Columbia, and three territories were participating in the BRFSS. Prevalence data and questionnaires are available online.

http://www.cdc.gov/nccdphp/brfss/

Bureau of Justice Statistics (BJS)

The BJS collects, analyzes, and distributes information on crime, criminal offenders, victims, and the justice system. This site provides access to key facts at a glance, publications, and press releases. It also provides links to other sites that provide criminological and justice data. Selected public-use data can also be downloaded here via the Internet.

http://www.ojp.usdoj.gov/bjs/

Bureau of Labor Statistics (BLS)

The BLS is the principal fact-finding agency for the federal government in the field of labor economics and statistics. It collects, processes, analyzes, and disseminates data to the public, Congress, state and local governments, and labor organizations. The BLS data include time-series data, as well as surveys dealing with the labor force, unemployment, prices and living conditions, compensation and working conditions, and productivity and technology. The BLS also maintains the National Longitudinal Surveys (NLS) homepage. Data provided by the BLS are relevant to current issues and of high accuracy and statistical quality.

http://www.bls.gov/

Center for Disease Control (CDC) Web Search

The CDC Web Search web page allows researchers to directly search the CDC database for health-related statistics and studies using keywords or phrases.

http://www.cdc.gov/search.htm

Country Studies, Library of Congress

A continuing series of books is prepared by the Federal Research Division of the Library of Congress to provide detailed information on foreign countries. These books, compiled by interdisciplinary authors, describe and analyze the politics, economy, social system, and national security systems of 85 countries. They also provide photos, tables, maps, glossaries, and bibliographies. Maps and charts are in PDF format and require Adobe Acrobat Reader 3.0 or higher.

http://lcweb2.loc.gov/frd/cs/cshome.html

County and City Data Books

This web site allows access to electronic version of the 1988 and 1994 County and City Data Books. These data books provide information regarding such areas as population, race, households, health, crime, education, and income for both the state/county and city levels. Researchers are able to obtain information on CD-ROM, or can receive customized printouts or data subsets. Data can be converted into SPSS files.

http://fisher.lib.Virginia.EDU/ccdb/

Current Population Surveys (CPS)

Conducted by the Bureau of the Census for the Bureau of Labor Statistics for over 50 years, the CPS is a monthly survey of approximately 50,000 households. The primary purpose of the CPS is to provide nationally representative information on the labor force characteristics of the US population. To access data, researchers must register at this web site.
http://www.bls.census.gov/cps/

Data and Program Library Service (DPLS)

Founded at the University of Wisconsin-Madison in 1966, the DPLS is a member of the ICPSR and provides free data access to over 5,000 data sets to students, staff, and faculty of the university. Outsiders may obtain access to non-ICPSR archival data (locally produced data) by purchasing data files or arranging access via anonymous FTP on a cost-recovery basis. Data holdings include: census data; IMF data; World Bank data; longitudinal surveys; macroeconomic indicators; election studies; population studies; data pertaining to aging, urban studies, conflict, socialization, poverty, and labor force participation; public opinion polls; educational and health data; and government statistics. Data can be obtained in either SPSS or SAS files.
http://dpls.dacc.wisc.edu/

Demographic and Health Surveys Data Archive (DHS)

The Demographic and Health Program is a 14–year project to help developing countries to conduct and analyze population and health surveys. The Data Archive holds data from 47 countries in Africa, Asia, Latin America, and the Near East. These data include surveys of women, men, households, and data regarding the availability of services. Data are available in raw and recoded forms, which allow cross-national comparisons. Data can be accessed through direct FTP or the mail. Mailed data cost US$200 per data set ($50 for those in developing countries).
http://www.measuredhs.com/

The Dialog Corporation

The Dialog Corporation is the world's largest online information company, which maintains a database 50 times as large as the World Wide Web. The database includes a collection of data from the social sciences. Data may be purchased by researchers.
http://www.dialog.com/

Disability and Managed Care Data Archive

This data archive includes national survey databases that may be useful for research on managed care and the disabled. The archive includes the National Health Inventory Survey-Disability Supplement (NHIS), the Medicare Current Beneficiary Survey, the National Long-Term Care Surveys 1982–1994 (NLTCS), the Survey of Income and Program Participation (SIPP), the Medical Expenditure Panel Survey (MEPS), the Research Archive on Disability in the United States, and Americans with Disabilities. The site also provides links to other web sites of interest and a summary table of the variables in each data set that might interest managed care researchers.
http://managedcare.hhs.gov/research/data/index.html

Economic Research Service (ERS), US Department of Agriculture

The ERS serves as the primary source of federal economic information on agriculture, food, natural resources, and rural America. This site provides researchers with recent agricultural reports, links to publications, and access to state fact sheets and maps. Also available are ERS data products, which address topics ranging from farm sector economics and banking and farm credit to international agriculture and land, water and conservation. Data products can be downloaded off the web free of charge or can be purchased in CD-ROM form.

http://www.ers.usda.gov/

Fedstats (Federal Statistics)

Maintained by the Federal Interagency Council on Statistical Policy, Fedstats provides easy access to US government statistics free of charge. Statistics provided online are supplied by more than 70 agencies affiliated with the US government.

http://www.fedstats.gov/

The Feminist Majority Foundation (FMF), Feminist Gateway

The Feminist Gateway provides access to information regarding issues of women's health, history and education, involvement in sports, politics, science, and work, women's organizations, violence against women, reproductive rights, lesbian issues, feminist arts, literature, and entertainment, and global feminism. Further, this site contains links to other more general women's Internet sites.

http://www.feminist.org/gateway/1_gatway.html

The Gallup Organization

The Gallup Organization has been a leading source of public opinion data since 1935. The Gallup Poll covers new social and business-related issues each week. Up-to-date press releases on opinion data can be obtained via the Internet at this web page, but data files cannot be accessed.

http://www.gallup.com/

General Social Survey (GSS)

Conducted by NORC since 1972, the GSS is an ongoing nationally representative personal interview survey of US households (includes black oversamples). The GSS measures trends in American attitudes, experiences, practices, and concerns. It is also a good source for data on religiosity. The GSS study takes part in the International Social Survey Program (ISSP), which administers identical questionnaires in 25 countries. This site also provides access to the General Social Survey Data and Information Retrieval System (GSSDIRS), which allows for easier analysis of GSS data.

http://www.icpsr.umich.edu/gss

General Social Survey Resources, Queens College

This site allows researchers to download the General Social Survey free of charge and provides access to extraction software. Online versions of the GSS bibliography, index to questions, and codebooks are also available.

http://www.soc.qc.edu/QC_Software/GSS.html

GeoLytics, Demographics

GeoLytics provides CD-ROM products that integrate US Census, other government, and private data with sophisticated statistical and mapping tools. Four CDs are currently available: CensusCD Blocks, CensusCD 1980, StreetCD, and CensusCD+Maps. These products are expensive, ranging from US$200 to 1,000. However, GeoLytics provides 50 percent discounts for academic, government, and non-profit organizations.

http://www.geolytics.com/

Government Information Sharing Project

This web site, maintained at Oregon State University, allows easy access to statistical data and information provided by the Bureau of the Census, the Bureau of Economic Analysis, the National Center for Education Statistics, and the MESA Group. The data include USA Counties, 1996; the 1990 Census of Population and Housing; Population Estimates by Age, Sex and Race, 1990–97; the Equal Employment Opportunity File, 1990; School District Data Book Profiles, 1989–90; the Regional Economic Information System, 1969–96; the 1992 Economic Census; the Census of Agriculture, 1982, 1987, and 1992; US Imports/Exports History 1993–97; Consolidated Federal Funds Report, 1987–96; and the Earnings by Occupation and Education, 1990. The site also provides links to other government web sites, the Oregon Population Survey, and Oregon Statistics.

http://govinfo.kerr.orst.edu/

Health and Retirement Study (HRS)

The HRS is a national panel study intended to provide data for those having to make policy decisions affecting retirement, health insurance, savings, and economic well-being. The study, including data from 7,600 households, has had three waves of data collection. Data from Waves I and II are available on the web site.

http://www.umich.edu/~hrswww/

High School and Beyond (HS&B)

The HS&B study, which was conducted between 1980 and 1992, explored the activities of seniors and sophomores as they progressed through high school, post-secondary education, and into the workplace. A total of 58,270 high school students (28,240 seniors and 30,030 sophomores) and 1,015 secondary schools participated. Many items overlap with the NCES 1972 high school senior cohort study. Data are available from the ICPSR in both SPSS and SAS formats, and can also be obtained through the National Center for Education Statistics (see below).

http://www.icpsr.umich.edu/IAED/hsb.html

Hispanic Health and Nutrition Examination Survey (HHANES)

The HHANES, conducted from July 1982 to December 1984, is a nationwide probability sample of approximately 16,000 persons of Hispanic heritage who were between the ages of 6 months and 74 years. This study provides information on the health history, status, and behaviors of Hispanic Americans. Data from this study are only available on tape, and can be ordered online, through the mail, by telephone or by fax for US$265 per tape.

http://www.cdc.gov/nchswww/products/catalogs/sitemap.htm

Institute for Research in Social Science (IRSS) Data Archive, UNC-CH

One of the oldest and largest archives of machine-readable data in the USA, the IRSS holds more than 2,800 studies and surveys. The IRSS is the exclusive national repository of the Louis Harris Public Opinion Polls, a local repository for World Fertility Surveys and Demographic and Health Surveys (DHS), and the repository for North Carolina state surveys. The archive acquires data from the Roper Center, the ICPSR, and the North Carolina State Data Center, and holds public opinion data from the Louis Harris Poll, the National Network of State Polls, the Carolina Poll, the Southern Focus Poll, and a small collection of polls from Latin America and Spain. The archive also contains census, economic, political, and educational datasets. Data can be accessed via FTP over the Internet, and are available in ASCII, SAS, and SPSS formats.

http://www.irss.unc.edu/data_archive/

Institute for Social Research (ISR), University of Michigan

The ISR is the longest-standing laboratory for interdisciplinary research in the social sciences. It comprises four centers: the Survey Research Center, the Research Center for Group Dynamics, the Center for Political Studies, and the Population Studies Center. Some of the ISR's major studies include the PSID, AHEAD/HRS, and the National Election Studies. The data from many of the larger studies conducted by the centers within the ISR are available to researchers through the ICPSR.

http://www.isr.umich.edu/isrsites.html

Inter-University Consortium for Political and Social Research (ICPSR)

Located within the Institute for Social Research at the University of Michigan, the ICPSR is a membership-based organization serving colleges and universities in the United States and many foreign countries. For those not at a member institution, direct purchase of data can be arranged. The ICPSR provides access to the world's largest archive of social science data, training facilities for the study of quantitative technology, and resources for researchers. The archive includes data in the following areas: census data, community and urban studies, conflict and aggression studies, economic behavior, attitudes, education, elites and leadership, geography and environment, government, health care facilities, international systems, legal systems, legislative bodies, mass political behavior, organizational behavior, social indicators, and social institutions. Further, the ICPSR maintains the National Archive of Criminal Justice Data (NACJD), the National Archive of Computerized Data on Aging (NACDA), and the Substance Abuse and Mental Health Data Archive (SAMHDA).

http://www.icpsr.umich.edu/index.html

Integrated Public Use Microdata Series (IPUMS)

The IPUMS is possibly the richest source of information regarding long-term social and economic change in America. It includes 25 high precision samples of the American population drawn from 13 federal censuses (1850–1990). Data for these samples include information on fertility, nuptiality, immigration, labor force participation, education, household composition, etc. Researchers can access the data online in SAS, SPSS, STATA, or BMDP formats.

http://www.ipums.umn.edu/

Longitudinal Retirement History Study, 1969–1979 (LRHS)

The LRHS, conducted by the US Department of Health and Human Services, is a nationally representative survey of individuals who were between the ages of 58 and 63 years in 1969. The initial sample of 11,162 people was followed up in five additional waves taking place in 1971, 1973, 1975, 1977, and 1979. Data are available in raw form, in SPSS format, or in SAS format.

http://www.socio.com/srch/summary/dasra/age03–14.htm

Longitudinal Study of Aging 1984–1990 (LSOA) and 1994–1996 (LSOA-II)

Part of the National Health Interview Survey Series, the LSOA studies explore the causes and correlates of changes in health and functioning among older adults. The LSOA studies are based upon a large nationally representative sample of the US non-institutionalized population that were 70 years and older in 1984. These data can be purchased on CD-ROM from either the Government Printing Office (GPO) or the National Technical Information Service (NTIS) for US$16–30. The LSOA-II is also stored at the National Opinion Research Center (NORC) archives.

http://www.norc.uchicago.edu/studies/homepage.htm

Mexican Migration Project

Collected between 1982 and 1996, the Mexican Migration Project is a comprehensive data set on Mexican migration to the United States. This study, a joint project of the University of Guadalajara and the University of Pennsylvania, employs the ethno-survey approach, combining the techniques of ethnographic fieldwork and representative survey sampling methods in order to gather both qualitative and quantitative data regarding migration patterns. Researchers can download the data in SPSS format from this site through FTP. Codebooks are available online as well.

http://lexis.pop.upenn.edu/mexmig

Michigan Prevention Research Center (MPRC)

The MPRC focuses upon prevention research dealing with problems of employment, economic stress, and well-being throughout the lifecourse. Center projects and studies which can be accessed via the Internet include JOBS, the Welfare to Work Program, and the Monitoring the Future Study.

http://www.isr.umich.edu/src/seh/mprc/index.html

The Monitoring the Future Study (MTF)

Conducted by the University of Michigan's Survey Research Center since 1975, the MTF study has surveyed a nationally representative sample of high school seniors, who receive identical follow-up surveys by mail for several years following their initial participation. Since 1991, nationally representative samples of eighth and tenth graders have been surveyed as well. The purpose of the MTF is to study changes in young Americans' beliefs, attitudes, and behaviors. Of particular interest, this study is used to document trends in substance use among youth. Statistics, data tables and figures, and publications are available via the Internet. This site also includes links to related sites.

http://www.isr.umich.edu/src/mtf/index.html

Murray Research Center

The Murray Research Center of Radcliffe College focuses its research upon the changing lives of American women. The Center, which maintains a national archive of over 200 studies, promotes the use of existing social science data. The studies cover topics including work, education, mental health, political participation, family, widowhood, and aging. Included in the archive are studies such as Lives in Progress, the Baltimore Longitudinal Study of Attachment, and the Life Cycle Study of Children with High Ability, the Harlem Longitudinal Study and the Colorado Adoption Project. Data are available free of charge to all researchers. This site also offers information regarding conferences, workshops, and publications.

http://www.radcliffe.edu/murray/

National Aging Information Center (NAIC)

The NAIC is a national resource center providing researchers and the public with information and data on issues related to aging. This web site provides a searchable bibliographic database, links to publications, statistical resources, and links to other relevant Internet sites.

http://www.aoa.dhhs.gov/naic/

National Archive of Computerized Data on Aging (NACDA)

Located within the ICPSR and funded by the National Institute on Aging, the purpose of the NACDA is to collect, preserve, disseminate, and facilitate the use of data relevant to gerontological research. Abstracts and data sets are available online through this web site. ICPSR rules regarding data access apply.

http://www.icpsr.umich.edu/NACDA/index.html

National Archives and Records Administrations Center for Electronic Records (NARA)

NARA acquires, preserves and disseminates US Federal Government electronic records. Data holdings include over 30,000 files created by Congress, the Courts, the Executive Office, and Presidential Commissions. These files include genealogical, agricultural, attitudinal, demographic, medical, economic, educational, environmental, military, scientific, and international data, as well as interesting collections such as the JFK Assassination Records Collection. The NARA Archival Information Locator (NAIL) is available to assist in record searches. Records are available for purchase on magnetic tape, cartridges, CD-ROM, or floppy disk on a cost-recovery basis (usually US$80–90). Hard-copy documentation is also available on a cost-recovery basis.

http://www.nara.gov/nara/electronic/

National Center for Charitable Statistics (NCCS)

Established in 1982, NCCS has been a program of the Center on Nonprofits and Philanthropy (CNP) at the Urban Institute since July 1996. NCCS serves as the national repository of information on non-profit institutions. It builds compatible national, state, and regional databases and develops uniform standards for reporting on the activities of charitable organizations. This site provides access to IRS information, fact sheets, state profiles, and links to other relevant sites.

http://nccs.urban.org

National Center for Education Statistics (NCES)

The NCES is the primary federal organization responsible for collecting, analyzing, and disseminating data related to education in the USA and other nations. NCES puts out approximately 100 publications per year and conducts surveys regarding elementary/ secondary and post-secondary education. Some of the major studies that this web site provides links to are the National Household Education Survey (NHES), High School and Beyond (HS&B), and NELS 1988.

http://nces.ed.gov/

National Center for Health Statistics (NCHS)

The NCHS is the primary federal organization responsible for collecting, analyzing, and disseminating health statistics. This web site allows researchers to view publications and statistical tables, and to download selected public-use data files. It provides links to ChildStats, a federal interagency forum on child and family statistics, and to health studies concerning aging, natality, mortality, health care and health services utilization, health care expenditures, nutrition, health promotion, health status, marriage and divorce, maternal and child health, reproductive health and behavior, and health risk factors. Some of NCHS's major studies include: the Hispanic Health and Nutrition Examination Survey (HHANES), the National Health Interview Survey (NHIS), the National Health Interview Survey on Disability (NHIS-D,) the National Health and Nutrition Examination Surveys (NHANES I, II, and III), the National Survey of Family Growth (NSFG), the National Immunization Survey, and the National Vital Statistics System.

http://www.cdc.gov/nchswww/default.htm

National Clearinghouse for Alcohol and Drug Information (NCADI)

The NCADI is a major resource center providing current information and statistics regarding alcohol and drug use. It provides reports of research findings and publications, and links to 12 databases of alcohol and drug information, to alcohol and drug resources/ referrals and to related Internet sites.

http://www.health.org/

National Clearinghouse on Child Abuse and Neglect Information

The National Clearinghouse is a major resource center providing current information and statistics regarding child abuse to professionals and researchers concerned with issues of child maltreatment. It provides reports of research findings, a database of documents and audiovisuals, and information regarding state child abuse statutes and laws.

http://www.calib.com/nccanch

National Data Archive on Child Abuse and Neglect (NDACAN)

The NDACAN, maintained at Cornell University, acquires, processes, stores, and facilitates the analysis of high quality data sets relevant to the study of child abuse and neglect. The Current Holdings List provides abstracts of the archive's data. Data and documentation can be obtained on a choice of media, and are available in SAS and SPSS format. For selected studies, a user's guide and frequency tables of the most commonly requested data are available online. Data sets and their documentation cost US$75, or US$25 for students. This web site also provides links to NDACAN's mailing list and publications.

http://www.ndacan.cornell.edu/

National Education Longitudinal Study of 1988 (NELS:88)

Beginning with an eighth grade cohort in 1988, and followed up in 1990, 1992, and 1994, NELS:88 provides longitudinal data about the transitions adolescents experience as they develop, attend school, and embark on their careers. This nationally representative sample resulted in the participation of 24,599 eighth grade students. Data are available through the ICPSR in SAS or SPSS, and can also be obtained through the National Center for Education Statistics (NCES).

http://www.icpsr.umich.edu/IAED/nels.html

National Election Studies (NES)

The National Election Studies include national surveys of the American electorate in presidential and midterm election years, time-series data for biennial elections over the past five decades, and pilot studies conducted in odd-numbered years. As well as providing election data, the NES provide excellent information on American religious beliefs and involvement. The web site allows access to data and to the NES Guide to Public Opinion and Electoral Behavior. This site also provides a link to the Comparative Study of Electoral Systems (CSES).

http://www.umich.edu:80/~nes/overview/overview.htm

National Health Interview Survey (NHIS)

The NHIS is a continuing nationwide survey of the US household population. In 1992 over 125,000 people were involved in the survey, which questions them regarding their health, disability, and hospitalization history. Data are available on magnetic tape and CD-ROM. This web site also provides a link to the 1994 National Health Interview Survey on Disability, Phase 1, and the 1984 and 1994 Supplements on Aging (SOA). The

NHIS-D includes disability statistics and studies the social, administrative, and mobility patterns of the disabled.

http://www.cdc.gov/nchswww/products/catalogs/subject/nhis/nhis.htm

National Health and Nutrition Examination Surveys (NHANES I, II, and III)

The NHANE surveys, conducted in 1971–5, 1976–80, and 1988–94, are nationwide probability samples of individuals between the ages of 6 months and 74 years. The purpose of these surveys was to obtain information regarding nutrition, health status, and health behaviors of Americans. Data can be ordered via the Internet, and are available on tape and CD-ROM (CD-ROM only for NHANES III). Prices vary.

http://www.cdc.gov/nchswww/products/catalogs/sitemap.htm

1995 National Household Survey on Drug Abuse (NHSDA)

Conducted since 1971, the NHSDA collects statistical information on the use of illegal drugs, alcohol, and tobacco products by the US population. The study uses a nationally representative sample of the civilian non-institutionalized population of the United States, 12 years and older. The 1995 NHSDA included a sample of 17,747 persons, with an oversample of blacks, Hispanics and young people. Reports and tables of information obtained from this study are available at this web site.

http://www.health.org/pubs/95hhs/ar18txt.htm

National Criminal Justice Reference Service (NCJRS), Juvenile Justice

The NCJRS refers researchers to Internet resources dealing with the criminal justice system. The Juvenile Justice page contains fact sheets, information regarding juvenile justice issues, links to general resources, and links to other relevant Internet sites and listservs.

http://www.ncjrs.org/jjhome.htm

The National Longitudinal Study of Adolescent Health, the Add Health Project

Add Health is a nationally representative school-based study of the health and health-related behaviors of adolescents in grades 7–12. The study has been designed to explore the causes of adolescent health and behaviors, with an emphasis on the influence of social context. Due to issues of confidentiality, the distribution of data requires great security. Thus, public-use data include only a subset of respondents, which can be ordered on CD-ROM. Restricted-use data will be distributed only to certified researchers who commit themselves to maintaining limited access. Contact information concerning access to data is provided at this web site. Codebooks can also be downloaded here.

http://www.cpc.unc.edu/addhealth/

National Longitudinal Surveys (NLS)

The National Longitudinal Surveys (NLS), begun in 1966 with the sponsorship of the Bureau of Labor Statistics, US Department of Labor, are a set of cohort surveys which have gathered information on the labor market experiences of five groups of American men and women. Sample selection procedures insured that the labor market experiences of minorities, youth, women, and the economically disadvantaged would be represented.

The NLS include the National Longitudinal Survey of Youth (NLSY79), surveys of youth between 14 and 22 years of age in 1979, and the Children of the National Longitudinal Survey of Youth, surveys of a group of children born to women of one of the national survey groups. NLS data are available for US$20 per cohort-specific compact disc.

http://stats.bls.gov/nlshome.htm

National Long Term Care Survey (NLTCS)

The NLTCS, conducted in 1982, 1984, 1989, and 1994, is a nationally representative sample of the US elderly population. This survey places a particular emphasis upon the aged who are functionally impaired, and links interview data with Medicare Part A and B service record information. This site provides online access to free public use files and documentation.

http://cds.duke.edu/

National Opinion Research Center (NORC)

NORC, a non-profit survey research center located at the University of Chicago, focuses upon important issues facing government organizations and the public. NORC studies cover topics including economics, education, epidemiology and public health, health services, statistics and methodology, substance abuse, mental health, and disability. Some of the larger datasets available through NORC are the NLSY, LSOA II, the National Household Survey on Drug Abuse, the National Health and Social Life Survey, the Occupational Prestige Study, and NELS.

http://www.norc.uchicago.edu/about/homepage.htm

National Survey of America's Families (NSAF)

Part of the Assessing the New Federalism Project at the Urban Institute, the NSAF focuses on the economic, health, and social characteristics of children, adults under 65, and their families. Conducted in 1997, the NSAF is nationally representative and contains data for over 100,000 people. This site allows researchers to register for and access public-use data free of charge. A second wave, conducted in 1999, will be also be available as soon as possible.

http://newfederalism.urban.org/nsaf/

National Survey of Black Americans Waves I–IV

The four waves of this national multistage probability sample survey were conducted in 1979–80, 1987–8, 1988–9, and 1992. This survey focused upon neighborhood–community integration, services, crime and community contact, the role of religion and the church, physical and mental health, self-esteem, life satisfaction, employment, the effects of chronic unemployment, the effects of race on the job, interaction with family and friends, racial attitudes, race identity, group stereotypes, and race ideology. Data and documentation can be acquired from the ICPSR. ICPSR rules regarding acquisition of data apply.

http://www.icpsr.umich.edu/cgi/search.prl

National Survey of Families and Households (NSFH)

The NSFH is a comprehensive survey of American family life. The survey interviewed a national probability sample of over 13,000 respondents in 1987–8. The sample was followed up in 1992–4, with interviews of the original respondent, the original spouse or cohabiting partner of the respondent, and the current spouse or partner of the respondent. In addition, interviews were conducted with a randomly selected child age 10–23 and with a parent of the respondent. This site provides online access to preliminary data from the second wave of the NSFH. Data is only available in FTP format at this time.

http://www.ssc.wisc.edu/nsfh/

National Survey of Family Growth (NSFG)

The NSFG survey is based on interviews with a national sample of non-institutionalized American women aged 15–44 years. The purpose of the survey, conducted in 1973, 1976, 1982, 1988, 1990, and 1995, is to collect data on factors affecting pregnancy and women's health. Public-use data files can be purchased on CD-ROM (US$15–22) or tape (US$265–395). Documentation can be downloaded via FTP from this site.

http://www.cdc.gov/nchs/default.htm

Panel Study of Income Dynamics (PSID), ISR at University of Michigan

The PSID is a longitudinal survey of a representative sample of US indviduals and families that has been conducted annually since 1968. The survey emphasizes the dynamic aspects of economic and demographic behavior. Data and comprehensive documentation are available to the public, distributed through the ICPSR on magnetic tape or via FTP online. Since 1987, data have also been available by CD-ROM. Researchers are charged US$30 for CD-ROMs if they are affiliated with ICPSR member institutions, US$55 if they are associated with a non-ICPSR academic institution, and US$105 if they are non-academic. A PSID bibliography, newsletter, and SAS and SPSS examples are also available online.

http://www.isr.umich.edu/src/psid/

Population Index 1986–1998 (Volumes 52–64)

The Population Index serves as a primary reference tool for population literature searches. The index provides an annotated bibliography of recent books, journal articles, working papers, and other materials. The entire published database (1986–98) is available to perform online searches by author, subject, geographical region, or year of publication. This web site also provides helpful links to other population research sites.

http://popindex.princeton.edu/index.html

Population Studies Center (PSC), University of Michigan

The PSC is an interdisciplinary center conducting both domestic and international research in the areas of fertility, family planning, marriage, inequality, migration, aging, and education. Studies can be located at this web page through a subject search. Some of the major studies archived here are the Cebu Longitudinal Health and Nutrition Survey, the World Fertility Surveys, and the China Health and Nutrition Survey.

http://www.psc.lsa.umich.edu/intro.html

Princeton University Office of Population Research Data Archive

This site contains descriptions of fertility data sets maintained by the OPR. Included are several studies on American fertility, European fertility decline, the World Fertility Survey (WHS), the Demographic and Health Surveys (DHS), and Chinese fertility surveys. This site also contains links to the Latin American Development Archive at Johns Hopkins University and the Central American Population Program in San José, Costa Rica.

http://www.opr.princeton.edu/archive/

Roper Center for Public Opinion Research

The Roper Center is the largest archive of public opinion data in the world, containing more than 12,500 studies conducted in over 75 countries. The Center provides machine-readable datasets, data analysis, customized searches, and access to POLL, an online database of data holdings and documentation. Academic and non-academic subscriptions to the Center's services are available, as is the purchase of *ad hoc* access to specific data sets or questions. This web site also provides links to other survey research organizations.

http://www.ropercenter.uconn.edu/

Sites Related to Demography and Population

This webpage, located at the Population Research Center at the University of Texas at Austin, contains links to demography and population-related sites. Included are links to population websites located outside of the United States and within Texas. Further, this page includes links to US government and international, intergovernmental and non-governmental organizations.

http://www.prc.utexas.edu/e-resources/other_sites.htm

Social Gerontology and the Aging Revolution

This web site provides links to helpful resources, references, academic programs, and research pertaining to aging and the elderly.

http://www.trinity.edu/~mkearl/geron.html

Social Security Online

The Social Security Administration's (SSA) homepage provides access to information regarding the SSA, electronic publications, and online direct services. Additionally, the site provides links to policy and research information and statistical publications and tables.

http://www.ssa.gov/SSA_Home.html

Sociometrics Data Archives

Sociometrics is a research and development firm specializing in social science research applications and the provision of public access to social science data. The Social Science Data Library includes nearly 350 data sets in several separate data archives: the Data Archive on Adolescent Pregnancy and Pregnancy Prevention (DAAPPP), the American

Family Data Archive (AFDA), the Data Archive of Social Research on Aging (DASRA), the Maternal Drug Abuse Data Archive (MDA), the AIDS/STD Data Archive (AIDS), and the Research Archive on Disability in the US (RADIUS). A Contextual Data Archive is also under construction. All studies have been selected by national panels of researchers for their technical quality and their utility. This web site also provides links to program archives for the public dissemination and replication of prevention programs in key health areas. Orders are placed online for a fee.

http://www.socio.com/s_sall.htm

The State of the Nation's Cities: a Comprehensive Database on American Cities and Suburbs

In 1996 the US Department of Housing and Urban Development (HUD) contracted with the Center for Urban Policy Research to assemble a database of 77 American cities and suburbs. In 1998, the database included information on over 3,000 variables, allowing easy comparability of indicators on employment, economic development, demographics, housing and land use, income and poverty, fiscal conditions, health, social and environmental indicators. Database and documentation are available in paper copy, as an ASCII file, a SPSS portable file, an Excel file, or a SAS file.

http://www.policy.rutgers.edu/cupr/cuprlite/sonc.htm

Survey of Asset and Health Dynamics Among the Oldest-Old (AHEAD)

A Health and Retirement Study auxiliary study, AHEAD is a national panel study that focuses on the interplay of resources and late life health transitions. The sample includes individuals born in or before 1923 and any younger spouses, and includes oversamples of blacks, Hispanics, and Florida residents. Three waves of data collection have been conducted (1994, 1996, 1998). Public-release Wave I data are available on the web site to those who register for an account.

http://www.umich.edu/~hrswww/overview/ahdover.html

Survey of Income and Program Participation (SIPP)

SIPP is a continuous series of nationally representative surveys begun in 1984. The purpose of these surveys is to collect information regarding income, labor force participation, government program participation and eligibility, and general demographic characteristics. It is used to measure the effectiveness of existing federal, state, and local programs, such as food stamps, to estimate future costs, and to provide information on American income distribution. Researchers can access the public-use data and documentation from the Census homepage.

http://www.bls.census.gov/sipp/sipphome.htm

UC Data, Data Archive and Technical Assistance

UC Data maintains an archive of over 2,000 computerized social science and health statistical data sets. The data sets cover topics such as public opinion, voting patterns, ethnic populations, income distribution, health and aging, and international relations. The archive obtains data from the ICPSR, the National Center for Health Statistics, the US Bureau of Economic Analysis, and the Census. It is also the exclusive repository of the Mervin Fields' California Polls, a time-series social and political attitude data set. Data are available to University of California at Berkeley faculty, staff, and students on

CD-ROM or tape cartridges. Outsiders may obtain access to data not offered elsewhere, such as the Mervin Fields' California Polls, for a fee.

http://ucdata.berkeley.edu/new_web/welcome.html

The Urban Information Center (UIC)

The UIC is a special data center housed within the Campus Computing center at the University of Missouri's St Louis campus (UMSL). The UIC provides data processing expertise and promotes the application of demographic data to a wide variety of marketing and planning problems. This web site provides free access to a variety of census and demographic data, some of which pertain to the entire USA and some of which pertain only to St Louis, Missouri, or Illinois.

http://www.oseda.missouri.edu/uic/intro.html

The Urban Institute

The Urban Institute is a non-partisan policy research organization that investigates social and economic problems in the United States. The Institute's web site offers access to the latest research reports and publications, and information regarding upcoming events. It also provides links to the Institute's current research projects (in the areas of federalism, economics, social welfare, community building, and policy briefs) and related institutions/networks.

http://urban.org/

US Census Bureau

The Census Bureau's web page offers official census statistics. Researchers are able to extract data from the 1990 Census and from surveys like the Current Population Survey and the Survey of Income and Program Participation and obtain summary tables from the County and City Data Books and the Statistical Abstracts of the United States. Further, the site provides a link to the International Database (IDB), a computerized data bank containing statistical tables of demographic and socioeconomic data for all countries in the world.

http://www.census.gov

Voice of the Shuttle: Gender Studies Page

This Gender Studies page provides links to general resources, women's studies and feminist theory, studies on homosexuality, information on men's movements, and cyber/tech-gender.

http://vos.ucsb.edu/shuttle/gender.html

Wisconsin Longitudinal Studies (WLS)

The WLS is a long-term study of a men and women who graduated from Wisconsin high schools in 1957. Data were collected from a random sample of 10,317 respondents or their parents in 1957, 1964, 1975, and 1992 and a randomly selected sibling in 1977 and 1993. The data provide information on social background, aspirations, schooling, military service, family, labor market experiences, mental ability tests, etc. The study is representative of white, non-Hispanic Americans who have completed at least high school. Data are available via the Internet.

http://dpls.dacc.wisc.edu/WLS/wlsarch.htm

1997 World Factbook, Central Intelligence Agency

The World Factbook is prepared by the CIA for the use of government officials. It includes information regarding the flags, maps, and descriptions of foreign countries.
http://www.odci.gov/cia/publications/factbook/index.html

Uruguay

Economic Information Unit and Social Science Faculty's Data Archive (UISDP)

Maintained by the Social Science Faculty Council at the Universidad de la República since 1992, UISDP has collected and archived data and provided support for social researchers. The UISDP provides access to 72 data sets, and imposes no special limitations on foreign researchers.
http://www.rau.edu.uy/fcs/banco/banco.htm

Europe

Council of European Social Science Data Archives (CESSDA)

CESSDA promotes the acquisition, storage, and dissemination of social science machine-readable data throughout Europe. Its web page provides very easy access to over 30 major high quality social science data archives located throughout the world. CESSDA's web page also offers links to catalogues of member organizations and provides a central news forum about CESSDA activities.
http://www.nsd.uib.no/Cessda/

Economic Commission for Europe (UN/ECE) Population Activities Unit, Population Aging

The Population Activities Unit is the only United Nations office specializing in European and North American population issues. The Unit promotes dialogue between policy-makers, government officials, and population experts on various facets of demographic change, coordinates region-wide activities to collect and share data, and disseminates findings to experts and policy-makers. The Unit is also involved in a project to collect cross-national comparative data to study the social and economic conditions of the elderly.
http://www.unece.org/ead/age/

Eurodata Research Archive

A structure within the Mannheim Centre for European Social Research (MZES), Eurodata supports comparative European research. The data archive focuses on socioeconomic and political data collected at the national and regional levels. This web site, available in both English and German, includes links to Eurodata publications, the Luxembourg Income Study (LIS), the Luxembourg Employment Study (LES), the Panel Comparability Project (PACO), and other major European social science organizations, data archives, and studies.
http://www.mzes.uni-mannheim.de/eurodata/eurodata.html

European Documentation Centre (EDC)

The EDC at the University of Mannheim is part of a large information network created by the European Communities in the 1960s. The Centre provides information on the European Union, EU institutions, and EU programs. This site, available in both English and German, provides access to a large number of EU databases, some of which are available for free over the Internet.

http://www.uni-mannheim.de/users/ddz/edz/eedz.html

Europinion

Europinion provides access to data from European public opinion polls and surveys. This web site includes links to the Standard Eurobarometer (EB), the European Continuous Tracking Survey (CTS), Flash Eurobarometers, Top-Decision Makers EBs, Central and Eastern Eurobarometers, and Qualitative Studies requested by the European Commission Services. Data can be downloaded in PDF format, and read using Adobe Acrobat Reader 3.0 or higher (which can be downloaded at this site).

http://europa.eu.int/en/comm/dg10/infcom/epo/eo.html

Eurostat (Statistical Office of the European Communities)

Eurostat provides the European Union with high quality statistical information. The use of uniform rules to collect statistical data from the National Statistical Institutes of each of the 15 member states allows global and comparative data analysis. The collected data include information regarding economy and finance, population and social conditions, energy and industry, agriculture, external trade, environment, research, and development. The web site provides graphs, tables, and maps of the data.

http://europa.eu.int/en/comm/eurostat/serven/home.htm

International

Aboriginal Resources

This web page provides links to a variety of resources concerned with aboriginal culture, arts, law, legislation, environmental concerns, newsgroups, and publications.

http://www.bloorstreet.com/300block/aborl.htm

Archivos de Fecundidad y Salud, Programa Centroamericano de Poblacion, Universidad de Costa Rica

This archive contains a collection of fertility and health surveys conducted in Belize, Guatemala, El Salvador, Honduras, Nicaragua, Costa Rica, and Panama between the years of 1976 and 1995. These surveys contain information on pregnancies, contraceptive use and knowledge, marriage, maternal-infantile health, immunization, oral rehydration use and knowledge, health service use, AIDS knowledge, child mortality, and other related topics. Data files are available to researchers in ASCII format.

http://www.opr.princeton.edu/populi/archiv/index.html

Center for International Earth Science Information Network (CIESIN)

Established in 1989, CIESIN provides information to help scientists, policy-makers, and the general public to understand our changing world and promotes global and regional network development. CIESIN houses the World Data Center A (WDC-A) for human interactions in the environment. The Data Archive provides access to demographic and socioeconomic data, metadata resources, and interactive applications. Holdings include US Decennial Census products, some Chinese data, Mexican data, a global population database, and the World Bank's Social Indicators of Development.
http://www.ciesin.org/

Center for International Health Information (CIHI)

CIHI, a USAID information management activity, works to provide reliable information on the population, health and nutrition of developing countries aided by USAID. This web site allows access to country health profiles and health statistics, and USAID program information. It also provides a link to the Health Statistics Database (HSD).
http://www.cihi.com

Centro Latinamericano de Demografia [Latin American Demographic Center] (CELADE)

CELADE provides researchers with technical assistance and population information and statistics about Latin American and Caribbean countries, carries out applied research in related subjects, and works on the development of related computer systems and programs. CELADE also offers population workshops, courses, and seminars, and publishes three periodical publications (in Spanish).
http://www.eclac.org/Celade-Eng/

The Global Observatory

Developed in 1996, the Global Observatory serves as a specialist trans-state data archive. The active development of the Observatory is currently located at the Globalization and World Cities (GAWC) Research Group and Network. The archive, organized on a topic basis, maintains information concerning world cities, environmental regions, social movements (environmental, indigenous peoples, local, feminist, labor, religious, terrorism, peace, etc.), global corporations, cultural areas, core–periphery structures, migration (refugees, tourism, etc.), energy flows, information and control, media communications, financial transactions, and commodity flows. Topics are linked to other resources, additional related information, and helpful bibliographies.
http://www.stile.lut.ac.uk/global.html

Hunger Web

The Hunger Web provides links to high quality Internet data regarding international hunger, food, poverty, and population issues. Further, this site contains links to informative publications, important hunger-related research institutions, international financial institutions dealing with hunger-related issues, relevant US government sites, and other helpful resources.
http://www.brown.edu/Departments/World_Hunger_Program/hungerweb/researchers.html

IASSIST

IASSIST is an international membership organization that promotes the development of social science data information centers, technology for secondary research, archiving standards, and information center staff development. Members are affiliated with academic, government, non-profit, and commercial institutions worldwide. IASSIST offers workshops and conferences, and publishes IASSIST Quarterly.

http://datalib.library.ualberta.ca/iassist/

Infonation, United Nations

Infonation provides free access to an easy-to-use database that allows researchers to view and compare up-to-date statistical data for the member states of the United Nations. Data include information regarding geography, economy, population, and social indicators.

http://www.un.org/Pubs/CyberSchoolBus/infonation/e_i_map.htm

Institute for Global Communications (IGC)

The IGC is a non-profit organization that promotes the use of computer technology to advance movements for international peace, economic and social justice, human rights, and environmental sustainability. This site provides mailing lists and discussion forums, consulting services, and news regarding non-profit activist organizations. Further, it provides links to Peacenet, Econet, Labornet, Womensnet, and Conflictnet, online networks of organizations dedicated to disseminating information and promoting activism.

http://www.igc.org/igc/gateway/index.html

International Archive of Education Data

This archive acquires, processes, and disseminates data collected by national, state or provincial, local, and private organizations, concerning all levels of education in countries for which data is available. The Archive allows for comparative and longitudinal research in the field of education. Data include information on such topics as funding, personnel, teaching resources, facilities, teacher and student preparation, graduation and matriculation rates, drop-out rates, test scores, job placements, life histories, and life assessments. Data files, documentation, and reports are downloadable through the ICPSR web site in public-use format. The web site features an online data analysis system (DAS) that allows users to conduct analyses on selected data sets within the Archive.

http://www.icpsr.umich.edu/IAED/

International Monetary Fund (IMF)

Established in 1945, the IMF currently has 128 country members. The IMF aims to promote international monetary cooperation, facilitate international trade, and assist members with temporary difficulties. This web site offers information about the IMF and its member countries.

http://www.imf.org/external/np/exr/facts/glance.htm

International Network for Social Network Analysis (INSNA)

INSNA, established in 1978, is a professional association of researchers interested in social network analysis. The INSNA web site contains general information, news, and updates about the association, lists of journals and textbooks dealing with social network analysis, and links to people and institutions conducting social network analysis. Online resources also include links to software packages for social networks, links to sources of social network data, and links to other social network related web sites.

http://www.heinz.cmu.edu/project/INSNA

International Social Survey Programme (ISSP)

The ISSP is a continuing, annual program of cross-national collaboration. The program serves to link data from the General Social Survey (GSS) in the United States to that of its counterparts in Germany, Britain, Australia, and 27 other countries. Cross-national study modules on 11 different topics, ranging from the environment, government, and religion, to social inequality and the role of the government, have been utilized. Data and documentation are maintained and distributed by the Zentralarchiv at the University of Cologne, Germany. A link to the Zentralarchiv is included on the ISSP web site. The ISSP is a valuable resource for researchers undertaking comparative analysis or studying attitudes, behaviors, and attributes of adult populations in other countries.

http://www.issp.org/homepage.htm or
http://www.norc.uchicago.edu/

International Stratification and Mobility File (ISMF)

The ISMF is a collection of standardized sample survey data dealing with issues of social stratification and social mobility. This site allows access to a catalogue of social mobility data and codebooks, provides tools for standardizing occupation codes, occupational mobility tables, and more. Access to data can be obtained only by request. However, there is information regarding access and links to other data archives that maintain ISMF data sets.

http://www.fss.uu.nl/soc/HG/ismf/

International Survey Center

The ISC conducts cross-national research on social, economic, and political issues. This web site provides access to the ISSP, publications, reports, and several ready-to-use ISSP data sets. The background variables in these public-use data sets have been recoded into common categories to allow for easy international comparative research. Data are available in SPSS format and can be downloaded from the Internet for free. Great for classroom exercises or student research.

http://www.international-survey.org

Lijphart Election Archive

The Lijphart Election Archive is a collection of district level election results for approximately 350 national legislative elections in democratic nations. The Archive data represent 43 countries in Africa, Central America and the Caribbean, North America, South America, Asia, Eastern Europe, Western Europe, the Middle East, and

Oceania. As well as providing access to data, this site also provides links to other online election information and data.

http://dodgson.ucsd.edu/lij/

Living Standards Measurement Study, World Bank (LSMS)

The LSMS is a multitopic survey designed to study household welfare and behavior in developing countries. This survey is used to evaluate the effectiveness of government policies on living conditions and poverty. The household questionnaires include questions regarding consumption, expenditures, income, employment, health, education, fertility, and migration. Questionnaires are also conducted to determine community conditions and resources, regional prices of common goods, and information on schools and clinics. This site provides access to data, questionnaires, documentation, reports, and newsletters. Some data can be obtained free of charge via the Internet. Minimal handling charges are applied to data that must be shipped to interested researchers.

http://www.worldbank.org/html/prdph/lsms/lsmshome.html

Most Research Themes

Most Research Themes, under the direction of UNESCO, supplies social science information to policy-makers worldwide through workshops and seminars, publications, conferences, and computer networks. Most's research areas of focus include: multicultural and multiethnic societies; cities as arenas of accelerated social transformation; and coping locally and regionally with economic technological and environmental transformation.

http://www.unesco.org/most/restheme.htm

North American Jewish Data Bank

Established in 1986, the North American Jewish Data Bank acts as a repository for computer-based population and survey data on Jewish communities in the United States and Canada. Along with the 1981 Canadian Census data and the 1970 and 1990 National Jewish Population Survey, the Data Bank has in its holding 46 local studies from 41 Jewish communities. Raw data are available for analysis on request and can be supplied in a variety of formats. This site also provides links to publications and results from the 1990 NJPS.

http://web.gc.cuny.edu/dept/cjstu/na.htm

Organization for Economic Co-operation and Development (OECD)

Founded following the Second World War to rebuild war-ravaged economies, OECD brings together countries sharing the principals of a market economy, pluralist democracy, and human rights in an attempt to encourage economic development and cooperation. The OECD collects statistical data, which can be used for cross-national comparisons, conducts macro- and microeconomic research, and provides policy advice. OECD archives are deposited at the Historical Archives of the European Communities in Italy. Historical monographs are sold by OECD, and free documents of statistical and policy-related information are available online.

http://www.oecd.org

The Panel Comparability Project (PACO)

The PACO project's goal is to create an international comparative database that integrates longitudinal micro-data from national household panel studies. The PACO Database contains harmonized variables and data structures for seven countries, allowing for cross-national comparisons. The complete database (250MB) is available to researchers on CD-ROM. The PACO Panel Archive includes the original panel data sets from ten countries (in Europe and the USA) in SPSS format, but is restricted to CEPS/INSTEAD affiliates. Documentation for these studies has also been collected and is available in paper form or online.

http://www.ceps.lu/paco/pacopres.htm

Rapid Demographic Change and the Welfare of the Elderly

This is a multi-year study conducted in the Philippines, Taiwan, Thailand, and Singapore. The study focuses upon issues of kin, exchange, living arrangements, income, labor force participation, health, etc. The data were obtained through censuses, official statistics, national surveys, focus groups, and case and village studies. This site also provides links to other aging surveys conducted in East and Southeast Asia.

http://www.psc.lsa.umich.edu/asia/index.shtml

r•cade®

r•cade® is a resource center providing public access to key statistical information about Europe. The center's statistics are drawn from Eurostat, UNESCO, and the International Labour Organisation (ILO). The center holds thousands of data sets on economics, labor, agriculture, demographics, environment, research and development, and education. Data are available to all for a charge. This web site allows online access to an integrated database, on which data orders can be placed. Data can also be ordered through the mail.

http://www-rcade.dur.ac.uk/

Research@WorldBank.org

Maintained by the World Bank's Development Research Group, this web site provides access to research and analysis of data regarding key economic issues relevant to development. Various research findings, data, and publications are available via this site, including the Policy Research Reports and Working Papers, Global Economic Prospects, World Development Indicators, links to economic journals, and the Living Standards Measurement Study (LSMS) Working Papers. This site also provides free e-mail newsletters on development research.

http://www.worldbank.org/research/index.htm

REVES International Database on Healthy Life Expectancy

Presented in both English and French, the REVES homepage provides access to the REVES yearbook, a statistical world yearbook on health expectancy. Bibliographical references are also provided, along with links to other relevant sites and conference information.

http://sauvy.ined.fr/reves/

Scholar's Guide to WWW

This guide provides access to a large number of internet links to population and demography websites, and to more general sociology websites as well. The guide is easy to navigate, and provides a good starting point when searching for population-related information.

http://home.nycap.rr.com/history/

SocioSite, Social Science Data Archives (SSDA)

SocioSite, established at the University of Amsterdam, is an extremely comprehensive resource to hundreds of web sites that are sociological and demographic in nature. Easy to use web site links are categorized according to region of the world and country.

Third International Mathematics and Science Study (TIMSS)

Conducted by the United States' National Center for Education Statistics (NCES), the TIMSS is an international study of schools and over half a million students in 41 countries. TIMSS is the largest, most comprehensive comparative educational study ever conducted. Findings regarding the educational performance and knowledge of fourth, eighth, and twelfth graders are summarized according to country, and are available online.

http://nces.ed.gov/timss/

United Nations Children's Fund (UNICEF)

The UNICEF homepage provides information regarding social issues, world events, programs, and political movements that impact children. The site also allows access to UNICEF publications, such as *The State of the World's Children 1999* and *The Progress of Nations 1998*, and statistical data regarding women, infants, and children.

http://www.unicef.org/fhpright.htm

United Nations Development Programme (UNDP)

The UNDP aspires to help countries to achieve sustainable human development by assisting in the development of programs to eradicate poverty, create employment, empower women, and protect the environment. This web site provides information regarding UNDP programs and the UN system, and links to publications and documents, such as *Human Development Reports* and *Office of Development Studies Publications*. The site also provides useful links to other web sites pertaining to poverty, gender, the environment, and governance.

http://www.undp.org/

United Nations Educational, Scientific, and Cultural Organization (UNESCO)

UNESCO aims to contribute to world peace and security by promoting collaboration among nations in an attempt to advance universal respect for justice, law, human rights, and freedom. UNESCO's web page allows access to 87 bibliographic, referral, factual, and statistical databases, covering such topics as education, natural sciences, communication, culture, social and human sciences, and world heritage. These databases can be searched by keyword, geographical region, and information type. Data (most) can be obtained in CD-ROM format in either English or French, and printed copies of documentation are free.

http://www.unesco.org/general/eng/index.html

War-torn Societies Projects (WSP), Documents Database

The WSP Database is an annotated bibliographic database of texts ranging from policy documents and evaluation reports to research and academic articles on the subject of war-torn societies. The WSP aims to encourage main actors in war-torn countries to analyze their activities and situations and to use research as a tool to develop and define political, social, and economic policy.

http://www.unrisd.org/wsp/

The World Bank

The World Bank provides loans, advice, and resources to more than 100 developing countries and countries in transition. The World Bank's homepage contains information regarding development topics (agriculture, education, health, poverty, etc.) and its projects. The site also provides free access to data pertaining to the World Bank countries, including statistics, indicator tables and sectoral data, and data that can be viewed by topic. Additionally, this site has links to working papers, online publications, and a publications catalogue, through which publications such as *The World Bank Atlas 1999* and *World Development Indicators 1999* can be purchased.

http://www.worldbank.org/

World Database of Happiness

This database acts as a register of scientific research on the subjective appreciation of life. The web site offers access to: a Bibliography of Happiness, which focuses on contemporary publications; a Catalogue of Happiness in Nations, which provides comparable cross-national observations; a Catalogue of Happiness Correlates; and a Directory of Happiness Investigators, which provides a listing of researchers in this area of study. Both published and unpublished data are referenced.

http://www.eur.nl/fsw/research/happiness/

World Health Organization (WHO)

WHO acts as the authority on international health work and promotes the attainment of the highest level of health among all people. WHO works interactively with researchers, medical care providers, governmental organizations, non-governmental organizations, and educators in an attempt to reach this goal. This web site provides a wonderful source of health information and statistics and includes links to World Health Reports and other WHO publications. The site also contains a large number of links to other related sites.

http://www.who.int/

Alphabetical by Topic

Aggression and War

Aggression Research Program, University of Michigan, USA
  See description in the USA section.
  http://www.isr.umich.edu/rcgd/aggr/index.html
The Global Observatory
  See description in the International section.
  http://www.stile.lut.ac.uk/global.html
Peacenet
  Found under the Institute for Global Communications in the International section.
  http://www.igc.org/igc/gateway/index.html
War-torn Societies Projects (WSP), Documents Database
  See description in the International section.
  http://www.unrisd.org/wsp/

Aging

Centre for Longitudinal Studies, University of London, UK
  See description in the United Kingdom section.
  http://www.cls.ioe.ac.uk
Disability and Managed Care Data Archive, USA
  See description in the USA section.
  http://managedcare.hhs.gov/research/data/index.html
Health and Retirement Study (HRS), USA
  See description in the USA section.
  http://www.umich.edu/~hrswww/overview/hrsover.html
Longitudinal Aging Study Amsterdam (LASA), Netherlands
  See description in the Netherlands section.
  http://www.nig.nl/onderzoek/index_en.html
Longitudinal Retirement History Study, 1969–1979 (LRHS), USA
  See description in the USA section.
  http://www.socio.com/srch/summary/dasra/age03–14.htm
Longitudinal Study of Aging 1984–1990 (LSOA) & 1994–1996 (LSOA-II),USA
  See description in the USA section.
  http://www.norc.uchicago.edu/studies/homepage.htm
Murray Research Center, USA
  See description in the USA section.
  http://www.radcliffe.edu/murray/
National Aging Information Center (NAIC), USA
  See description in the USA section.
  http://www.aoa.dhhs.gov/naic/
National Archive of Computerized Data on Aging (NACDA), USA
  See description in the USA section.
  http://www.icpsr.umich.edu/NACDA/index.html
National Center for Health Statistics (NCHS), USA
  See description in the USA section.
  http://www.cdc.gov/nchswww/default.htm

National Long Term Care Survey (NLTCS), USA
  See description in the USA section.
  http://cds.duke.edu/
National Survey of Japanese Elderly 1987, Japan
  See description in the Japan section.
  http://www.icpsr.umich.edu/NACDA/archive.html
Rapid Demographic Change and the Welfare of the Elderly, USA
  See description in the International section.
  http://www.psc.lsa.umich.edu/asia/index.shtml
Social Gerontology and the Aging Revolution, USA
  See description in the USA section.
  http://www.trinity.edu/~mkearl/geron.html
Social Security Online, USA
  See description in the USA section.
  http://www.ssa.gov/SSA_Home.html
Sociometrics Data Archives, USA
  See description in the USA section.
  http://www.socio.com/s_sall.htm
Survey of Asset and Health Dynamics Among the Oldest-Old (AHEAD), USA
  See description in the USA section.
  http://www.umich.edu/~hrswww/overview/ahdover.html

Agriculture and Environmental Conservation

Economic Research Service (ERS), US Department of Agriculture, USA
  See description in the USA section.
  http://www.ers.usda.gov/
The Global Observatory
  See description in the International section.
  http://www.stile.lut.ac.uk/global.html
Government Information Sharing Project, USA
  See description in the USA section.
  http://govinfo.kerr.orst.edu/
United Nations Development Programme (UNDP)
  See description in the International section.
  http://www.undp.org/
The World Bank
  See description in the International section.
  http://www.worldbank.org/

Children and Adolescents

The Administration for Children and Families (ACF), US Department of Health and Human Services, USA
  See description in the USA section.
  http://www.acf.dhhs.gov/
The Cebu Longitudinal Health and Nutrition Survey (CLHNS), Philippines
  See description in the Philippines section.
  http://www.cpc.unc.edu/projects/cebu/cebu_home.html

High School and Beyond (HS&B), USA
   See description in the USA section.
   http://www.icpsr.umich.edu/IAED/hsb.html
The Monitoring the Future Study (MTF), USA
   See description in the USA section.
   http://www.isr.umich.edu/src/mtf/index.html
Murray Research Center, USA
   See description in the USA section.
   http://www.radcliffe.edu/murray/
National Center for Education Statistics (NCES), USA
   See description in the USA section.
   http://nces.ed.gov/
National Center for Health Statistics (NCHS), USA
   See description in the USA section.
   http://www.cdc.gov/nchs/default.htm
National Clearinghouse on Child Abuse and Neglect Information, USA
   See description in the USA section.
   http://www.calib.com/nccanch
National Criminal Justice Reference Service (NCJRS), Juvenile Justice, USA
   See description in the USA section.
   http://www.ncjrs.org/jjhome.htm
National Data Archive on Child Abuse and Neglect (NDACAN), USA
   See description in the USA section.
   http://www.ndacan.cornell.edu/
National Education Longitudinal Study of 1988 (NELS:88), USA
   See description in the USA section.
   http://www.icpsr.umich.edu/IAED/nels.html
The National Longitudinal Study of Adolescent Health, The Add Health Project, USA
   See description in the USA section.
   http://www.cpc.unc.edu/
National Longitudinal Surveys (NLS), USA
   See description in the USA section.
   http://stats.bls.gov/nlshome.htm
Sociometrics Data Archives, USA
   See description in the USA section.
   http://www.socio.com/s_sall.htm
Third International Mathematics and Science Study (TIMSS)
   See description in the International section.
   http://nces.ed.gov/timss/
United Nations Children's Fund (UNICEF)
   See description in the International section.
   http://www.unicef.org/fhpright.htm

Economy and Income

Assessing the New Federalism, USA
   See description in the USA section.
   http://www.urban.org

CentER Savings Survey (formerly known as the VSB Panel [Dutch Socio-Economic Panel Study]), Netherlands
　　See description in the Netherlands section.
　　http://center-ar.kub.nl/css/
Country Studies, Library of Congress, USA
　　See description in the USA section.
　　http://lcweb2.loc.gov/frd/cs/cshome.html
County and City Data Books, USA
　　See description in the USA section.
　　http://fisher.lib.Virginia.EDU/ccdb/
Econet
　　Found under the Institute for Global Communications in the International section.
　　http://www.igc.org/igc/gateway/index.html
Economic Information Unit and Social Science Faculty's Data Archive (UISDP), Uruguay
　　See description in the Uruguay section.
　　http://www.rau.edu.uy/fcs/banco/banco.htm
Economic Research Service (ERS), US Department of Agriculture, USA
　　See description in the USA section.
　　http://www.ers.usda.gov/
Economy Data Archives (Econdata), Netherlands
　　See description in the Netherlands section.
　　http://www.niwi.knaw.nl/nl/projects/proecon.htm
Eurodata Research Archive
　　See description in the Europe section.
　　http://www.mzes.uni-mannheim.de/eurodata/eurodata.html
Government Information Sharing Project, USA
　　See description in the USA section.
　　http://govinfo.kerr.orst.edu/
Luxembourg Employment Study (LES Project), Luxembourg
　　See description in the Luxembourg section.
　　http://www.lis.ceps.lu/index.htm
Luxembourg Income Study (LIS), Luxembourg
　　See description in the Luxembourg section.
　　http://www.lisceps.lu/index.htm
The Panel Comparability Project (PACO)
　　See description in the International section.
　　http://www.ceps.lu/paco/pacopres.htm
Panel Study of Income Dynamics (PSID), USA
　　See description in the USA section.
　　http://www.isr.umich.edu/src/psid/
Russia Longitudinal Monitoring Survey (RLMS), Russia
　　See description in the Russia section.
　　http://www.cpc.unc.edu/projects/rlms/rlms_home.html
Social Security Online, USA
　　See description in the USA section.
　　http://www.ssa.gov/SSA_Home.html
The State of the Nation's Cities: a Comprehensive Database on American Cities and Suburbs, USA
　　See description in the USA section.
　　http://www.policy.rutgers.edu./cupr/cuprlite/sonc.htm

Survey of Income and Program Participation (SIPP), USA
  See description in the USA section.
  http://www.bls.census.gov/sipp/sipphome.htm
US Census Bureau, Income, USA
  See US Census Bureau in the USA section.
  http://www.census.gov/ftp/pub/hhes/www/income.html
The World Bank
  See description in the International section.
  http://www.worldbank.org/

Education

Government Information Sharing Project, USA
  See description in the USA section.
  http://govinfo.kerr.orst.edu/
High School and Beyond, USA
  See description in the USA section.
  http://www.icpsr.umich.edu/IAED/hsb.html
International Archive of Education Data
  See description in the International section.
  http://www.icpsr.umich.edu/IAED/
Murray Research Center, USA
  See description in the USA section.
  http://www.radcliffe.edu/murray/
National Center for Education Statistics (NCES), USA
  See description in the USA section.
  http://nces.ed.gov/
National Education Longitudinal Study of 1988 (NELS), USA
  See description in the USA section.
  http://www.icpsr.umich.edu/IAED/nels.html
The Panel Comparability Project (PACO)
  See description in the International section.
  http://www.ceps.lu/paco/pacopres.htm
Third International Mathematics and Science Study (TIMSS)
  See description in the International section.
  http://nces.ed.gov/timss/
The World Bank
  See description in the International section.
  http://www.worldbank.org/

Elections, Government, Political Systems

Assessing the New Federalism, USA
  See description in the USA section.
  http://www.urban.org
Canadian Election Study (CES), 1997, Canada
  See description in the Canada section.
  http://www.isr.yorku.ca/projects/ces/index.html

The Canadian Legislator Study (CLS), Canada
   See description in the Canada section.
   http://www.isr.yorku.ca/projects/cls/index.html
Centre for the Study of Democracy, Canada
   See description in the Canada section.
   http://csd.queensu.ca/
Centro de Investigaciones Sociologicas (CIS), Spain
   See description in the Spain section.
   http://www.cis.es
Country Studies, Library of Congress, USA
   See description in the USA section.
   http://lcweb2.loc.gov/frd/cs/cshome.html
Eurodata Research Archive
   See description in the Europe section.
   http://www.mzes.uni-mannheim.de/eurodata/eurodata.html
Korean Social Science Data Center (KSDC), Korea
   See description in the Korea section.
   http://www.ksdc.re.kr/m1/me1.html
Lijphart Election Archive
   See description in the International section.
   http://dodgson.ucsd.edu/lij/
Murray Research Center, USA
   See description in the USA section.
   http://www.radcliffe.edu/murray/
National Archives and Records Administrations Center for Electronic Records (NARA), USA
   See description in the USA section.
   http://www.nara.gov/nara/electronic/
National Election Studies (NES), USA
   See description in the USA section.
   http://www.umich.edu:80/~nes/overview/overview.htm
New Zealand Election Study, New Zealand
   See description in the New Zealand section.
   http://www.nzes.org
Social Citizenship Indicator Program (SCIP), Sweden
   See description in the Sweden section.
   http://www.sofi.su.se/
1997 World Factbook, Central Intelligence Agency, USA
   See description in the USA section.
   http://www.odci.gov/cia/publications/factbook/index.html

Health and Nutrition

Archivos de Fecundidad y Salud, Programa Centroamericano de Poblacion, Universidad de Costa Rica
   See description in the International section.
   http://www.opr.princeton.edu/populi/archiv/index.html
Behavioral Risk Factor Surveillance System, USA
   See description in the USA section.
   http://www.cdc.gov/nccdphp/nccdhome.htm

The Cebu Longitudinal Health and Nutrition Survey (CLHNS), Philippines
See description in the Philippines section.
http://www.cpc.unc.edu/projects/cebu/cebu_home.html

Center for Disease Control (CDC) Web Search, USA
See description in the USA section.
http://www.cdc.gov/search.htm

Center for International Health Information (CIHI)
See description in the International section.
http://www.cihi.com

Central East Health Information Partnership (CEHIP), Canada
See description in the Canada section.
http://www.cehip.org/

China Health and Nutrition Survey (CHNS), China
See description in the China section.
http://www.cpc.unc.edu/projects/china/china_home.html

Demographic and Health Surveys Data Archive (DHS), USA
See description in the USA section.
http://www.measuredhs.com/

Disability and Managed Care Data Archive, USA
See description in the USA section.
http://managedcare.hhs.gov/research/data/index.html

1995 Guatemalan Survey of Family Health (EGSF), Guatemala
See description in the Guatemala section.
http://www.rand.org/organization/drd/labor/FLS/

Health and Retirement Study (HRS), USA
See description in the USA section.
http://www.umich.edu/~hrswww/

Hispanic Health and Nutrition Examination Survey (HHANES), USA
See description in the USA section.
http://www.cdc.gov/nchswww/products/catalogs/sitemap.htm

Karolinska Institutet, Sweden
See description in the Sweden section.
http://www.info.ki.se/ki/

Murray Research Center, USA
See description in the USA section.
http://www.radcliffe.edu/murray/

National Center for Health Statistics (NCHS), USA
See description in the USA section.
http://www.cdc.gov/nchswww/default.htm

National Clearinghouse for Alcohol and Drug Information (NCADI), USA
See description in the USA section.
http://www.health.org/

National Health Interview Survey (NHIS), USA
See description in the USA section.
http://www.cdc.gov/nchswww/products/catalogs/subject/nhis/nhis.htm

National Health and Nutrition Examination Surveys (NHANES I, II, and III), USA
See description in the USA section.
http://www.cdc.gov/nchswww/products/catalogs/sitemap.htm

1995 National Household Survey on Drug Abuse (NHSDA), USA
　　See description in the USA section.
　　http://www.health.org/pubs/95hhs/ar18txt.htm
The National Longitudinal Study of Adolescent Health, The Add Health Project, USA
　　See description in the USA section.
　　http://www.cpc.unc.edu/
National Long Term Care Survey (NLTCS), USA
　　See description in the USA section.
　　http://cds.duke.edu/
Ontario Ministry of Health, Canada
　　See description in the Canada section.
　　http://www.gov.on.ca/health/
REVES International Database on Healthy Life Expectancy
　　See description in the International section.
　　http://sauvy.ined.fr/reves/
Russia Longitudinal Monitoring Survey (RLMS), Russia
　　See description in the Russia section.
　　http://www.cpc.unc.edu/projects/rlms/rlms_home.html
Sociometrics Data Archives, USA
　　See description in the USA section.
　　http://www.socio.com/s_sall.htm
Substance Abuse and Mental Health Data Archive (SAMHDA), USA
　　Found under ICPSR in the USA section.
　　http://www.icpsr.umich.edu/index.html
Survey of Asset and Health Dynamics Among the Oldest-Old (AHEAD), USA
　　See description in the USA section.
　　http://www.umich.edu/~hrswww/overview/ahdover.html
United Nations Children's Fund (UNICEF)
　　See description in the International section.
　　http://www.unicef.org/fhpright.htm
The World Bank
　　See description in the International section.
　　http://www.worldbank.org/
World Health Organization (WHO)
　　See description in the International section.
　　http://www.who.int/

Justice, Criminology, Delinquency

American Society of Criminology – Divisions and other Sources, USA
　　See description in the USA section.
　　http://www.asc41.com/four.html
Bureau of Justice Statistics (BJS), USA
　　See description in the USA section.
　　http://www.ojp.usdoj.gov/bjs/
Canadian Centre on Substance Abuse (CCSA), Canada
　　See description in the Canada section.
　　http://www.ccsa.ca/

Law Enforcement Agencies on the Web, USA
   http://www.fsu.edu/~crimdo/police.html
The Monitoring the Future Study (MTF), USA
   See description in the USA section.
   http://www.isr.umich.edu/src/mtf/index.html
National Archive of Criminal Justice Data (NACJD), USA
   Found under ICPSR in the USA section.
   http://www.icpsr.umich.edu/NACJD/home.html
National Clearinghouse for Alcohol and Drug Information (NCADI), USA
   See description in the USA section.
   http://www.health.org/
National Clearinghouse on Child Abuse and Neglect Information, USA
   See description in the USA section.
   http://www.calib.com/nccanch
National Criminal Justice Reference Service (NCJRS), Juvenile Justice, USA
   See description in the USA section.
   http://www.ncjrs.org/jjhome.htm
1995 National Household Survey on Drug Abuse (NHSDA), USA
   See description in the USA section.
   http://www.health.org/pubs/95hhs/ar18txt.htm
*The National Longitudinal Study of Adolescent Health, The Add Health
Project, USA*
   see description in the USA section.
   http://www.cpc.unc.edu/
Substance Abuse and Mental Health Data Archive (SAMHDA), USA
   Found under ICPSR in the USA section.
   http://www.icpsr.umich.edu/index.html

Labor, Work, Organizations

Bureau of Labor Statistics (BLS), USA
   See description in the USA section.
   http://www.bls.gov/
Centre for Research on Work and Society, Canada
   See description in the Canada section.
   http://www.yorku.ca/research/crws/centres.htm
Current Population Survey (CPS), USA
   See description in the USA section.
   http://www.bls.census.gov/cps/
Derek Gordon Data Bank, Jamaica
   See description in the Jamaica section.
   http://www.chass.utoronto.ca:8080/datalib/other/dgdb.htm
Encuesta Nacional De Empleo Urban (ENEU), Mexico
   See description in the Mexico section.
   http://www.prc.utexas.edu/
The Global Observatory
   See description in the International section.
   http://www.stile.lut.ac.uk/global.html

Labornet
   Found under the Institute for Global Communications in the International section.
   http://www.igc.org/igc/gateway/index.html
Luxembourg Employment Study (LES Project), Luxembourg
   See description in the Luxembourg section.
   http://www.lis.ceps.lu/index.htm
Murray Research Center, USA
   See description in the USA section.
   http://www.radcliffe.edu/murray/
National Longitudinal Surveys (NLS), USA
   See description in the USA section.
   http://stats.bls.gov/nlshome.htm
The Panel Comparability Project (PACO)
   See description in the International section.
   http://www.ceps.lu/paco/pacopres.htm
The State of the Nation's Cities: A Comprehensive Database on American Cities and Suburbs, USA
   See description in the USA section.
   http://www.policy.rutgers.edu./cupr/cuprlite/sonc.htm

Living Conditions

Derek Gordon Data Bank, Jamaica
   See description in the Jamaica section.
   http://www.chass.utoronto.ca:8080/datalib/other/dgdb.htm
Hunger Web
   See description in the International section.
   http://www.brown.edu/Departments/World_Hunger_Program/hungerweb/research-ers.html
Living Standards Measurement Study (LSMS)
   See description in the International section.
   http://www.worldbank.org/html/prdph/lsms/lsmshome.html
REVES International Database on Healthy Life Expectancy
   See description in the International section.
   http://sauvy.ined.fr/reves/
The State of the Nation's Cities: A Comprehensive Database on American Cities and Suburbs, USA
   See description in the USA section.
   http://www.policy.rutgers.edu./cupr/cuprlite/sonc.htm
United Nations Development Programme (UNDP)
   See description in the International section.
   http://www.undp.org/
The Urban Information Center (UIC), USA
   See description in the USA section.
   http://www.oseda.missouri.edu/uic/intro.html
The Urban Institute, USA
   See description in the USA section.
   http://urban.org/

The World Bank
See description in the International section.
http://www.worldbank.org/

Methodology

Center for Survey Research and Methodology (ZUMA), Germany
See description in the Germany section.
http://www.zuma-mannheim.de/index-e.htm
Centre for Applied Social Surveys (CASS) Question Bank, UK
See description in the United Kingdom section.
http://www.scpr.ac.uk/cass
International Network for Social Network Analysis (INSNA)
See description under the International section.
http://www.heinz.cmu.edu/project/INSNA
QualPage, Canada
See description in the Canada section.
http://www.ualberta.ca/~jrnorris/qual.html

Non-profit Organizations

Institute for Global Communications (IGC)
See description in the International section.
http://www.igc.org/igc/gateway/index.html
National Center for Charitable Statistics (NCCS), USA
See description in the USA section.
http://nccs.urban.org
The Urban Institute, USA
See description in the USA section.
http://urban.org/

Peace and Happiness

The Global Observatory
See description in the International section.
http://www.stile.lut.ac.uk/global.html
World Database of Happiness
See description in the International section.
http://www.eur.nl/fsw/research/happiness/
Peacenet
Found under the Institute for Global Communications in the International section.
http://www.igc.org/igc/gateway/index.html

Population and Demography

Archivos de Fecundidad y Salud, Programa Centroamericano de Poblacion, Universidad de Costa Rica
See description in the International section.
http://www.opr.princeton.edu/populi/archiv/index.html
ASA Section on International Migration, USA
See description in the USA section.
http://www.ssc.msu.edu/~intermig/

Centro Latinamericano de Demografia [Latin American Demographic Center] (CELADE)
    See description in the International section.
    http://www.eclac.org/Celade-Eng/
Demographic and Health Surveys Data Archive (DHS), USA
    See description in the USA section.
    http://www.measuredhs.com/
Economic Commission for Europe (UN/ECE) Population Activities Unit, Population Aging
    See description in the Europe section.
    http://www.unece.org/ead/age/
Encuesta Nacional de la Dinamica Demografica 1992 [National Survey of Population Dynamics] (ENADID), Mexico
    See description in the Mexico section.
    http://www.prc.utexas.edu/
GeoLytics, Demographics, USA
    See description in the USA section.
    http://www.geolytics.com/
The Global Observatory
    See description in the International section.
    http://www.stile.lut.ac.uk/global.html
Government Information Sharing Project, USA
    See description in the USA section.
    http://govinfo.kerr.orst.edu/
Hunger Web
    See description in the International section.
    http://www.brown.edu/Departments/World_Hunger_Program/hungerweb/research-ers.html
Institute for Research in Social Science (IRSS) Data Archive, USA
    See description in the USA section.
    http://www.irss.unc.edu/data_archive/
Integrated Public Use Microdata Series (IPUMS), USA
    See description in the USA section.
    http://www.ipums.umn.edu/
Mexican Migration Project, USA
    See description in the USA section.
    http://lexis.pop.upenn.edu/mexmig
Murray Research Center, USA
    See description in the USA section.
    http://www.radcliffe.edu/murray/
National Center for Health Statistics (NCHS), USA
    See description in the USA section.
    http://www.cdc.gov/nchswww/default.htm
Norwegian Historical Data Centre (NHDC), Norway
    See description in the Norway section.
    http://www.isv.uit.no/seksjon/rhd/indexeng.htm
The Panel Comparability Project (PACO)
    See description in the International section.
    http://www.ceps.lu/paco/pacopres.htm

Population Index, USA
  See description in the USA section.
  http://popindex.princeton.edu/index.html
Population Studies Center (PSC), University of Michigan, USA
  See description in the USA section.
  http://www.psc.lsa.umich.edu/intro.html
Princeton University Office of Population Research Data Archive, USA
  See description in the USA section.
  http://www.opr.princeton.edu/archive/
Scholars' Guide To WWW
  See description in the International section.
  http://home.nycap.rr.com/history/
Sites Related to Demography and Population
  This web page, located at the Population Research Center at the University of Texas at
  Austin, contains links to demography and population-related sites. Included are links
  to population websites located outside the United States and within Texas. Further, this
  page includes links to US government and international, intergovernmental and non-
  governmental organizations.
  http://www.prc.utexas.edu/e-resources/other_sites.htm
The Urban Information Center (UIC), USA
  See description in the USA section.
  http://www.oseda.missouri.edu/uic/intro.html
US Census Bureau, USA
  See description in the USA section.
  http://www.census.gov
The World Bank
  See description in the International section.
  http://www.worldbank.org/
World Health Organization (WHO)
  See description in the International section.
  http://www.who.int/

Poverty

Hunger Web
  See description in the International section.
  http://www.brown.edu/Departments/World_Hunger_Program/hungerweb/research-
  ers.html
Living Standards Measurement Study, World Bank (LSMS)
  See description in the International section.
  http://www.worldbank.org/html/prdph/lsms/lsmshome.html
*The State of the Nation's Cities: A Comprehensive Database on American Cities and
Suburbs, USA*
  See description in the USA section.
  http://www.policy.rutgers.edu./cupr/cuprlite/sonc.htm
United Nations Children's Fund (UNICEF)
  See description in the International section.
  http://www.unicef.org/fhpright.htm

United Nations Development Programme (UNDP)
  See description in the International section.
  http://www.undp.org/
US Census Bureau, Poverty, USA
  Found under US Census Bureau in the USA section.
  http://www.census.gov/ftp/pub/hhes/www/poverty.html
The World Bank
  See description in the International section.
  http://www.worldbank.org/

Public Opinion

Análisis Sociológicos Económicos y Políticos, SA (ASEP), Spain
  See description in the Spain section.
  http://www.asep-sa.com/
Centro de Estudos de Opinião Publica (CESOP), Brazil
  See description in the Brazil section.
  http://www.unicamp.br/cesop/
Centro de Investigaciones Sociológicas (CIS), Spain
  See description in the Spain section.
  http://www.cis.es/
Europinion
  See description in the Europe section.
  http://europa.eu.int/en/comm/dg10/infcom/epo/eo.html
The Gallup Organization, USA
  See description in the USA section.
  http://www.gallup.com/
Institute for Research in Social Science (IRSS) Data Archive, USA
  See description in the USA section.
  http://www.irss.unc.edu/data_archive/
National Opinion Research Center (NORC), USA
  See description in the USA section.
  http://www.norc.uchicago.edu/about/homepage.htm
Office of Survey Research, Academia Sinica, Taiwan
  See description in the Taiwan section.
  http://www.sinica.edu.tw/as/survey/index_e.html
Roper Center For Public Opinion Research, USA
  See description in the USA section.
  http://www.ropercenter.uconn.edu/
UC Data, Data Archive and Technical Assistance, USA
  See description in the USA section.
  http://ucdata.berkeley.edu/new_web/welcome.html

Religion and Culture

American Religion Data Archive, USA
  See description in the USA section.
  http://www.arda.tm
General Social Survey (GSS), USA
  See description in the USA section.
  http://www.icpsr.umich.edu/gss

General Social Survey Resources, USA
  See description in the International section.
  http://www.soc.qc.edu/QC_Software/GSS.html
International Social Survey Programme (ISSP)
  See description in the International section.
  http://www.issp.org/homepage.htm
National Election Surveys (NES), USA
  See description in the USA section.
  http://www.umich.edu:80/~nes/overview/overview.htm
North American Jewish Data Bank, USA
  See description in the International section.
  http://web.gc.cuny.edu/dept/cjstu/na.htm

Social, Family, Household Surveys

British General Household Study (GHS), UK
  See description in the United Kingdom section.
  http://biron.essex.ac.uk/cgi-bin/biron
The British Household Panel Study, UK
  See description in the United Kingdom section.
  http://www.irc.essex.ac.uk/bhps/
General Social Survey, USA
  See description in the USA section.
  http://www.icpsr.umich.edu/gss
General Social Survey Resources, USA
  See description in the USA section.
  http://www.soc.qc.edu/QC_Software/GSS.html
German Socio-economic Panel (GSOEP), Germany
  See description in the Germany section.
  http://www.diw-berlin.de/soep/soepe.htm
Guatemalan Family Life Survey (GFLS), Guatemala
  See description in the Guatemala section.
  http://www.rand.org/organization/drd/labor/FLS/
Indonesian Family Life Survey (IFLS), Indonesia
  See description in the Indonesia section.
  http://www.rand.org/organization/drd/labor/FLS/
International Social Survey Program (ISSP)
  See description in the International section.
  http://www.issp.org/homepage.htm
Malaysian Family Life Survey (MFLS), Malaysia
  See description in the Malaysia section.
  http://www.rand.org/FLS/
Murray Research Center, USA
  See description in the USA section.
  http://www.radcliffe.edu/murray/
1995 National Household Survey on Drug Abuse (NHSDA), USA
  See description in the USA section.
  http://www.health.org/pubs/95hhs/ar18txt.htm

The National Longitudinal Study of Adolescent Health, The Add Health Project, USA
    See description in the USA section.
    http://www.cpc.unc.edu/
National Longitudinal Surveys (NLS), USA
    See description in the USA section.
    http://stats.bls.gov/nlshome.htm
National Survey of America's Families (NSAF), USA
    See description in the USA section.
    http://newfederalism.urban.org/nsaf/
National Survey of Black Americans Wave I–IV, USA
    See description in the USA section.
    http://www.icpsr.umich.edu/cgi/search.prl
The National Survey of Families and Households (NSFH), USA
    See description in the USA section.
    http://www.ssc.wisc.edu/nsfh/
National Survey of Family Growth (NSFG), USA
    See description in the USA section.
    http://www.cdc.gov/nchs/default.htm
The Panel Comparability Project (PACO)
    See description in the International section.
    http://www.ceps.lu/paco/pacopres.htm
Panel Study of Income Dynamics (PSID), ISR at University of Michigan, USA
    See description in the USA section.
    http://www.isr.umich.edu/src/psid/
Pesquisa Nacional de Amostra de Domicilios [Brazilian Household Surveys] (PNAD), Brazil
    See description in the Brazil section.
    http://www.sscnet.ucla.edu/issr/da/index/framet.htm
Wisconsin Longitudinal Study, USA
    See description in the USA section.
    http://dpls.dacc.wisc.edu/WLS/wlsarch.htm

Stratification

Hunger Web
    See description in the International section.
    http://www.brown.edu/Departments/World_Hunger_Program/hungerweb/researchers.html
International Stratification and Mobility File (ISMF)
    See description in the International section.
    http://www.fss.uu.nl/soc/HG/ismf/

Women and Feminism

The Administration for Children and Families (ACF), US Department of Health and Human Services, USA
    See description in the USA section.
    http://www.acf.dhhs.gov/

The Feminist Majority Foundation (FMF), Feminist Gateway, USA
See description in the USA section.
http://www.feminist.org/gateway/1_gatway.html
Murray Research Center, USA
See description in the USA section.
http://www.radcliffe.edu/murray/
National Survey of Family Growth (NSFG), USA
See description in the USA section.
http://www.cdc.gov/nchs/default.htm
Sociometrics Data Archives, USA
See description in the USA section.
http://www.socio.com/s_sall.htm
United Nations Development Programme (UNDP)
See description in the International section.
http://www.undp.org/
Voice of the Shuttle: Gender Studies Page, USA
See description in the USA section.
http://vos.ucsb.edu/shuttle/gender.html
Womensnet
Found under the Institute for Global Communications in the International section.
http://www.igc.org/igc/gateway/index.html

Bibliography

Abbott, A. (1999) *Discipline and Department: Chicago Sociology at One Hundred.* Chicago: University of Chicago Press.

Abel, E. K. (1986) Adult daughters and care for the elderly. *Feminist Studies*, 12, 479–97.

Abers, R. (1998) From clientalism to cooperation. *Politics and Society*, 26, 511–38.

Abolafia, M. Y. (1996) *Making Markets: Opportunism and Restraint on Wall Street.* Cambridge, MA: Harvard University Press.

Abramovitz, M. (1993) The search for the sources of growth: Areas of ignorance, old and new. *Journal of Economic History*, 53, 217–43.

Abramovitz, M. (1996) *Regulating the Lives of Women: Social Welfare Policy from Colonial Times to the Present.* Boston: South End Press.

Adam, B. (1998) *Timescapes of Modernity.* London: Routledge.

Adams, P. L. (1990) Prejudice and exclusion as social traumata. In J. D. Noshpitz and R. D. Coddington (eds), *Stressors and the Adjustment Disorders.* New York: Wiley.

Adams, T. K. and Duncan, G. J. (1992) Long-term poverty in rural areas. In C. M. Duncan (ed.), *Rural Poverty in America.* New York: Auburn House.

Aglietta, M. (1979) *A Theory of Capitalist Regulation: the US Experience.* London: NLB.

Ainslie, R. C. (1998) Cultural mourning, immigration, and engagement: vignettes from the Mexican experience. In M. Suárez-Orozco (ed.), *Crossings: Mexican Immigration in Interdisciplinary Perspectives.* Cambridge, MA: Harvard University Press.

Ake, C. (1994) *Democratization of Disempowerment in Africa.* Lagos: Malthouse Press Limited.

Alba, R. D. (1985) *Italian Americans: Into the Twilight of Ethnicity.* Englewood Cliffs, NJ: Prentice Hall.

Albelda, R. and Tilly, C. (1997) *Glass Ceiling and Bottomless Pits: Women's Work, Women's Poverty.* Boston: South End Press.

Albrow, M. (1997) *The Global Age: State and Society beyond Modernity.* Stanford, CA: Stanford University Press.

Alecxih, L. et al. (1997) *Key Issues Affecting Access to Medigap Insurance.* Washington, DC: The Commonwealth Fund.

Aleinikoff, T. A. and Rumbaut, R. G. (1998) Terms of belonging: are models of membership self-fulfilling prophecies? *Georgetown Immigration Law Journal*, 13, 1–24.

Alesina, A. and Perotti, R. (1994) The political economy of growth: a critical survey of the recent literature. *World Bank Economic Review*, 8, 351–71.

Alexander, J. (1998a) *Neofunctionalism and After*. Malden, MA: Blackwell.

Alexander, J. C. (1978) Formal and substantive voluntarism in the work of Talcott Parsons: a theoretical and ideological reinterpretation. *American Sociological Review*, 43, 177–98.

Alexander, J. C. (1995) *Fin de Siècle Social Theory*. London: Verso.

Alexander, J. C. (1998b) Citizens and enemy as symbolic classification. In J. C. Alexander (ed.), *Real Civil Societies. Dilemmas of Institutionalization*. London: Sage.

Alexander, K. A. and Cook, M. A. (1982) Curricula and coursework: a surprise ending to a familiar story. *American Sociological Review*, 47, 26–64.

Alexander, K. A. and McDill, E. L. (1976) Selection and allocation within schools: some causes and consequences of curriculum placement. *American Sociological Review*, 41, 963–80.

Alford, R. and Friedland, R. (1985) *Powers of Theory: Capitalism, the State, and Democracy*. New York: Cambridge University Press.

Alford-Cooper, F. (1998) *For Keeps: Marriages that Last a Lifetime*. Armonk, NY: Sharpe.

Alfredsson, L., Karasek, R., and Theorell, T. (1982) Myocardial infarction risk and psychosocial work environment: an analysis of the male Swedish working force. *Social Science and Medicine*, 16, 463–7.

Allan, K. (1998) *The Meaning of Culture: Moving the Postmodern Critique Forward*. New York: Praeger.

Allen-Smith, J. E. (1995) Blacks in rural America: socioeconomic status and policies to enhance economic well-being. In J. B. Stewart and J. E. Allen-Smith (eds), *Blacks in Rural America*. New Brunswick, NJ: Transaction Publishers.

Allensworth, E. M. and Rochin, R. I. (1996) White exodus, Latino repopulation and community well-being: trends in California's rural communities, Research Report No. 13 (June), Julian Samora Research Institute, Michigan State University, East Lansing.

Alter, C. and Hage, J. (1993) *Organizations Working Together*. Newbury Park, CA: Sage.

Amato, J. A. (1996) *To Call It Home: the New Immigrants of Southwestern Minnesota*. Marshall, MN: Crossings Press.

Amato, P. R. and Booth, A. (1997) *A Generation at Risk: Growing up in an Era of Family Upheaval*. Cambridge, MA: Harvard University Press.

Amenta, E. (1998) *Bold Relief: Institutional Politics and the Origins of Modern American Social Policy*. Princeton, NJ: Princeton University Press.

American Anthropological Association (1998) Executive Board statement (May 17) [http://www/ameranthassn.org/racepp.htm].

Ammerman, N. (ed.) (1997) *Congregation and Community*. New Brunswick, NJ: Rutgers University Press.

Amnesty International (1998) From San Diego to Brownsville: human rights violation on the USA–Mexico border. New Release, May 20, 1998. [http://www.amnesty.org].

Anderson, B. (1991) *Imagined Communities: Reflections on the Origins and Spread of Nationalism*, 2nd edn. London: Verso.

Anderson, R. T., Sorlie, P., Backlund, E., Johnson, N. and Kaplan, G. A. (1997) Mortality effects of community socioeconomic status. *Epidemiology*, 8, 42–7.

Anderson, W. F. (1999) A new front in the battle against disease. In G. Stock and J. Campbell (eds), *Engineering of the Human Germline*. Oxford: Oxford University Press.

Andreas, P. (1998) The US immigration control offensive: constructing an image of order on the southern border. In M. Suárez-Orozco (ed.), *Crossings: Mexican Immigration in Interdisciplinary Perspectives*. Cambridge, MA: Harvard University Press.

Angel, R. J. and Angel, J. L. (1997) *Who Will Care for Us? Aging and Long Term Care in Multicultural America*. New York: New York University Press.

Anheier, H. and Salamon, L. (eds) (1998) *The Nonprofit Sector in the Developing World: a Comparative Analysis*. Manchester: Manchester University Press.

Anisman, H., Zaharia, M. D., Meaney, M. J. and Merali, Z. (1998) Do early-life events permanently alter behavioral and hormonal responses to stressors? *International Journal of Developmental Neuroscience*, 16, 149–64.

An-Na'im, A. A. (ed.) (1992) *Human Rights in Cross-cultural Perspectives: Quest for Consensus*. Philadelphia: University of Pennsylvania Press.

An-Na'im, A. A. and Deng, F. M. (eds) (1990) *Human Rights in Africa: Cross-cultural Perspectives*. Washington, DC: Brookings Institution.

Annie E. Casey Foundation (1996) *Kids Count Data Book*. Washington, DC: Center for the Study of Social Policy.

Antonovsky, A. (1967) Social class, life expectancy and overall mortality. *Millbank Quarterly*, 45, 31–73.

Appadurai, A. (1996) *Modernity at Large: Cultural Dimensions of Globalization*. Minneapolis: University of Minnesota.

Applebaum, E. and Gregory, J. (1990) Flexible employment: union perspectives, bridges to retirement. In P. Doeringer (ed.), *Older Workers in a Changing Labor Market*. Ithaca, NY: ILR Press.

Arato, A. (1981) Civil society against the state: Poland 1980–81. *Telos*, 47, 23–47.

Archibugi, D., Held, D. and Köhler, M. (1998) *Re-imagining Political Community*. Stanford, CA: Stanford University Press.

Ardener, S. (ed.) (1993) *Women and Space*. Oxford: Berg.

Arendt, H. (1969) *The Human Condition*. Chicago: University of Chicago Press.

Arendt, H. (1973) *The Origins of Totalitarianism*. San Diego: Harcourt, Brace and Company.

Ariarajah, S. W. (1991) *Hindus and Christians*. Grand Rapids, MI: Eerdmans.

Arnason, J. P. (1989) The imaginary constitution of modernity. In *Autonomie et autotransformation de la société. La philosophie militante de Cornelius Castoriadis, Giovanni Busino et al.* Geneva: Droz.

Arnason, J. P. (1998) Multiple modernities and civilizational contexts: reflections on the Japanese experience. Unpublished paper.

Aron, R. (1955) L'Opium des intellectuels (trans. T. Kilmartin as *The Opium of the Intellectuals*. Garden City: Doubleday, 1957).

Aronowitz, M. (1984) The social and emotional adjustment of immigrant children: a review of the literature. *International Review of Migration*, 18, 237–57.

Arrendondo-Dowd, P. (1981) Personal loss and grief as a result of immigration. *Personnel and Guidance Journal*, 59, 376–8.

Arvey, R. D. and Faley, R. H. (1988) *Fairness in Selecting Employees*. Reading, MA: Addison-Wesley.

Athey, J. L. and Ahearn, F. L. (1991) *Refugee Children: Theory, Research, and Services*. Baltimore, MD: Johns Hopkins University Press.

Augé, M. (1994) *An Anthropology for Contemporaneous Worlds*. Stanford, CA: Stanford University Press.

Axtmann, R. (1997) Collective identity and the democratic nation-state in the age of globalization. In A. Cvetkovich and D. Kellner (eds), *Articulating the Global and the Local: Globalization and Culture Studies*. Boulder, CO: Westview Press.

Babbie, E. (1982) *Understanding Sociology: a Context for Action*. Belmont, CA: Wadsworth Publishing Company.

Babbie, E. (1988) *The Sociological Spirit*. Belmont, CA: Wadsworth Publishing Company.

Bachelard, G. (1969) *The Poetics of Space*. Boston: Beacon Press.

Bagguley, P. (1995) Protest, poverty and power – a case-study of the anti-poll tax movement. *American Sociological Review*, 43, 693–719.

Bagguley, P., Mark-Lawson, J., Shapiro, D., Urry, J., Walby, S. and Warde, A. (1990) *Restructuring. Place, Class and Gender*. London: Sage.

Baker, W. E. (1994) *Networking Smart: How to Build Relationships for Personal and Organizational Success*. New York: McGraw-Hill.

Bales, R. F. (1950) *Interaction Process Analysis: a Method for the Study of Small Groups*. Cambridge, MA: Addison-Wesley.

Bane, M. J. and Ellwood, D. T. (1994) *Welfare Realities: from Rhetoric to Reform*. Cambridge, MA: Harvard University Press.

Banks, A. and Russo, J. (1996): Teaching the organizing model of unionism and campaign-based education: national and international trends. Unpublished manuscript, presented to AFL-CIO/Cornell University Research Conference on Union Organizing, Washington, DC.

Barber, B. (1998) *Intellectual Pursuits: Toward an Understanding of Culture*. Lanham, MD: Rowman and Littlefield.

Barkan, S. E. (n.d.) What is to be done? Strategy, organization, and the study of social movements. Unpublished manuscript.

Barlett, D. and Steele, J. (1992) *America: What Went Wrong?* Kansas City, MO: Andrews and Meel.

Barnes, B. (1977) *Interests and the Growth of Knowledge*. London: Routledge and Kegan Paul.

Barnes, B. (1995) *The Elements of Social Theory*. Princeton, NJ: Princeton University Press.

Barnet, R. and Cavanagh, J. (1996) Homogenization of global culture. In J. Mander and E. Goldsmith (eds), *The Case against the Global Economy and for a Turn toward the Local*. San Francisco: Sierra Club Books.

Barr, R. and Dreeben, R. (1983) *How Schools Work*. Chicago: University of Chicago Press.

Barthes, R. (1972) *Mythologies*. New York: Hill and Wang.

Bartle, X. (1998) Left–right position does matter but does social class? Causal models of the 1992 British general election. *British Journal of Political Science*, 28, 501–28.

Bates, T. (1991) Discrimination and the capacity of New Jersey area minority and women-owned businesses. Working paper, Graduate School of Management and Urban Policy, New School for Social Research.

Bates, T. (1997) *Race, Self-employment and Upward Mobility: an Illusive American Dream*. Baltimore: Johns Hopkins University Press.

Bauman, Z. (1990) *Thinking Sociologically*. Oxford: Blackwell.

Bauman, Z. (1992) *Intimations of Postmodernity*. London: Routledge.

Bauman, Z. (1998) *Globalization: the Human Consequences*. Cambridge: Polity Press.

Bayat, A. (1997) *Street Politics: Poor People's Movements in Iran*. New York: Columbia University Press.

Bean, F. D., de la Garza, R. O., Roberts, B. and Weintraub, S. (1997) *At the Crossroads: Mexican Migragion and US Policy*. Lanham, MD: Rowman and Littlefield.

Beaulieu, L. J. and Mulkey, D. (eds) (1995) *Investing in People: the Human Capital Needs of Rural America*. Boulder, CO: Westview Press.

Bebbington, A. (1999) *Capitals and Capabilities: a Framework for Analyzing Peasant Viability, Rural Livelihoods and Poverty in the Andes*. London: International Institute for Environment and Development.

Beck, U. (1992) *Risk Society*. Beverly Hills, CA: Sage.

Beck, U. (1997) *The Reinvention of Politics: Rethinking Modernity in the Global Social Order*. Cambridge: Polity Press.

Beck, U., Giddens, A. and Lash, S. (eds) (1994) *Reflexive Modernization*. Cambridge: Polity Press.

Becker, G. (1981) *A Treatise on the Family*. Cambridge, MA: Harvard University Press.

Becker, H. P. and Boskoff, A. (eds) (1957) *Modern Sociological Theory in Continuity and Change*. New York: Dryden Press.

Beckett, K. (1997) *Making Crime Pay: Law and Order in Contemporary American Politics*. New York: Oxford University Press.

Belkic, K., Schnall, P., Landsbergis, P. and Baker, D. (2000) The workplace and CV health: conclusions and thoughts for a future agenda. *Occupational Medicine*, 15, 307–22.

Bell, C. and Newby, H. (1976) Communion, communalism, class and community action: the sources of new urban politics. In D. Herbert and R. Johnston (eds), *Social Areas in Cities*. Chichester: Wiley.

Bell, D. (1980) *The Winding Passage*. Cambridge, MA: Abt Books.

Bell, D. and Valentine, G. (1997) *Consuming Geographies. We Are Where We Eat*. London: Routledge.

Bell, D. A. (1998) Civil society versus civic virtue. In A. Gutmann (ed.), *Freedom of Association*. Princeton, NJ: Princeton University Press.

Bellah, R., Madsen, R., Sullivan, W., Swidler, A. and Tipton, S. (1985) *Habits of the Heart: Individualism and Commitment in American Life*. Berkeley: University of California Press.

Benabou, R. (1997) Inequality and growth. In B. Bernanke and J. Rotemberg (eds), *NBER Macreconomics Annual*. Cambridge, MA: MIT Press.

Ben-David, J. (1971) *The Scientist's Role in Society: a Comparative Study*. Englewood Cliffs, NJ: Prentice Hall.

Bendix, R. (1967) Tradition and modernity reconsidered. *Comparative Studies in Society and History*, 9, 292–346.

Bendix, R. (1970) *Embattled Reason: Essays on Social Knowledge*. New York: Oxford University Press.

Benhabib, S. (1992) Models of public space: Hannah Arendt, the liberal tradition, and Jürgen Habermas. In C. Calhoun (ed.), *Habermas and the Public Sphere*. Cambridge: MIT Press.

Benjamin, W. (1979) *One-way Street and Other Writings*. London: Verso.

Bensaid, D. (1996) Neo-liberal reform and popular rebellion. *New Left Review*, 215, 109–16.

Bensinger, R. (1998) When we try more, we win more: organizing the new workforce. In J.-A. Mort (ed.), *Not Your Father's Union Movement*. New York: Verso.

Benton, T. (1989) Marxism and natural limits. *New Left Review*, 178, 51–86.

Benton, T. (1997) Reflexive modernization or green socialism? Paper presented at the RC 24 Conference on Sociological Theory and the Environment, Woudschoten Conference Center, Zeist, the Netherlands.

Benton, T. and Redclift, M. (1994) *Social Theory and the Global Environment*. London: Routledge.

Berger, A. (1999) Private company wins rights to Icelandic gene database. *British Medical Journal*, 318, 11.

Berger, J., Conner, T. L. and Fisek, M. H. (1974) *Expectation States Theory: a Theoretical Research Program*. Cambridge, MA: Winthrop.

Berger, P. (1983) From the crisis of religion to the crisis of secularity. In M. Douglas and S. Tipton (eds), *Religion and America*. Boston: Beacon Press.

Berger, P. (1996) Secularism in retreat. *The National Interest*, 46, 3–12.

Berger, P. L. (1998) Conclusion: general observations on normative conflicts and mediation. In P. L. Berger (ed.), *The Limits of Social Cohesion*. Boulder, CO: Westview Press, pp. 352–72.

Berlin, I. (1969) The two concepts of liberty. In *Four Essays on Liberty*. Oxford: Clarendon Press.

Berman, M. (1983) *All That Is Solid Melts into Air. The Experience of Modernity*. London: Verso.

Berman, S. (1997) Civil society and the collapse of the Weimar Republic. *World Politics*, 49, 401–29.

Bernstein, M. A. and Adler, D. E. (eds) (1994) *Understanding American Economic Decline*. New York: Cambridge University Press.

Berry, J. (1998) Acculturative stress. In P. Organista, K. Chun, and G. Marín (eds) *Readings in Ethnic Psychology*. New York: Routledge.

Bertram, E., Blachman, M., Sharpe, K. and Andreas, P. (1996) *Drug War Politics: the Price of Denial*. Berkeley: University of California Press.

Bertraux, D. and Thompson, P. (1997) *Pathways to Social Class: a Qualitative Approach to Social Mobility*. Oxford: Clarendon Press.

Besser, T. L. (1996) *Team Toyota: Transplanting the Toyota Culture to the Camry Plant in Kentucky*. Albany, NY: SUNY Press.

Best, J. (1999) *Random Violence: How We Talk about Crimes and New Victims*. Berkeley: University of California Press.

Bethel, E. R. (1997) *The Roots of African-American Identity: Memory and History in Free Antebellum Communities*. New York: St Martin's Press.

Bhabha, H. (ed.) (1990) *Nation and Narration*. London: Routledge.

Bidwell, C. E. (1965) The school as a formal organization. In J. B. March (ed.), *Handbook of Organizations*. Chicago: Rand McNally.

Bidwell, C. E. (2000) A social psychological approach to the study of schooling. In M. T. Hallinan (ed.), *Handbook of Sociology of Education*. New York: Plenum Publishing Corp.

Bidwell, C. E. and Kasarda, J. D. (1980) Conceptualizing and measuring the effects of school and schooling. *American Journal of Education*, 88, 401–30.

Birdsall, N. and Londono, J. L. (1997) Asset inequality matters: an assessment of the World Bank's approach to poverty reduction. *American Economic Review*, 87, 31–7.

Birdsall, N. and Sabot, R. (1995) Inequality and growth reconsidered: lessons from East Asia. *World Bank Economic Review*, 9.

Bishop, J. (1988) Vocational education for at-risk youth: how can it be made more effective? Working paper no. 88–11, New York State School of Industrial and Labor Relations, Cornell University.

Bishop, J. (1993) Improving job matches in the US labor market. *Brookings Papers on Economic Activity: Microeconomics*, 335–400.

Bittles, A. H. and Roberts, D. F. (eds) (1992) *Minority Populations: Genetics, Demography and Health*. London: Macmillan.

Blau, F. D. and Beller, A. (1992) Black–white earnings over the 1970s and 1980s: gender differences in trends. *Review of Economics and Statistics*, 74, 276–86.

Blau, F. D. and Graham, J. W. (1990) Black–white differences in wealth and asset composition. *Quarterly Journal of Economics*, 105, 321–39.

Blau, J. R. (1993) *Social Contracts and Economic Markets*. New York: Plenum.

Blau, J. R. and Blau, P. M. (1982) The cost of inequality: metropolitan structure and violent crime. *American Sociological Review*, 47, 114–29.

Blau, J. R., Redding, K. and Land, K. (1993) Ethnocultural cleavages and the growth of church membership in the United States, 1860–1930. *Sociological Forum*, 8, 609–37.

Blau, P. M. (1964) *Exchange and Power in Social Life*. New York: Wiley.

Blau, P. M. and Duncan, O. D. (1967) *The American Occupational Structure*. New York: Wiley.

Blau, P. M. and Schwartz, J. E. (1984) *Crosscutting Social Circles*. New York: Academic Press.

Blomstrom, M., Lipsey, R. E. and Zeijan, M. (1993) Is fixed investment the key to economic growth? NBER working paper no. 4436.

Bloor, D. (1976) *Knowledge and Social Imagery*. Chicago: University of Chicago Press (1991).

Blossfeld, H. and Hakim, C. (1997) *Between Equalization and Marginalization: Women Working Part-time in Europe and the United States of America*. New York: Oxford University Press.

Bluestone, B., Stevenson, M. H. and Tilly, C. (1991) The deterioration of labor market prospects for young men with limited schooling: assessing the impact of "demand side" factors. Paper presented at the Eastern Economic Association Meeting, Pittsburgh, PA.

Blumberg, R. L. (1978) *Stratification: Socioeconomic and Sexual Inequality*. Dubuque, IA: Wm C. Brown.

Blumstein, P. and Schwartz, P. (1983) *American Couples*. New York: William Morrow.

Boas, F. (1909) Race problems in America. In G. W. Stocking, Jr (ed.), *The Shaping of American Anthropology: 1883– 1911. A Frank Boas Reader*. Chicago: University of Chicago Press (1974), pp. 318–26.

Bobbio, N. (1988) Gramsci and the concept of civil society. In J. Keane (ed.), *Civil Society and the State*. London: Verso.

Bok, D. (1996) *The State of the Nation: Government and the Quest for a Better Society*. Cambridge, MA: Harvard University Press.

Bokemeier, J. L. (1997) Rediscovering families and households: Restructuring rural society and rural sociology. *Rural Sociology*, 62, 1–20.

Boli, J. and Thomas, G. M. (1997) World culture in the world polity: a century of international non-governmental organizations. *American Sociological Review*, 62, 171– 90.

Boli, J. and Thomas, G. M. (eds) (1999) *Constructing World Culture: International Nongovernmental Organization Since 1875*. Stanford, CA: Stanford University Press.

Booth, A. and Crouter, A. C. (eds) (1998) *Men in Families: When Do They Get Involved? What Difference Does It Make?* Mahwah, NJ: Lawrence Erlbaum Associates.

Borjas, G. J. (1990) *Friends or Strangers: the Impact of Immigration on the US Economy*. New York: Basic Books.

Borman, K. M. (1991) *The First "Real" Job: a Study of Young Workers*. Albany: State University of New York Press.

Bosma, H., Peter, R., Siegrist, J. and Marmot, M. (1998) Two alternative job stress models and the risk of coronary heart disease. *American Journal of Public Health*, 88, 68–74.

Bossert, S. (1979) *Tasks and Social Relationships in Classrooms*. Cambridge: Cambridge University Press.

Boudon, R. (1973) *Education, Opportunity, and Social Inequality*. New York: Wiley.

Boudon (1981) *The Logic of Social Action*. London: Routledge and Kegan Paul.

Bound, J. and Freeman, R. B. (1992) What went wrong? The erosion of relative earnings and employment among young black men in the 1980s. *Quarterly Journal of Economics*, 107, 201– 32.

Bourdieu, P. (1966) Intellectual field and creative project. In M. F. Young (ed.), *Knowledge and Control: New Directions for the Sociology of Education*. London: Collier Macmillan (1971).

Bourdieu, P. (1975) The specificity of the scientific field and the social conditions of the progress of reason. *Social Science Information*, 14, 19–47.

Bourdieu, P. (1979) *La distinction: critique sociale du judgment* (trans. R. Nice as *Distinction: a Social Critique of the Judgment of Taste*. Cambridge, MA: Harvard University Press, 1984).

Bourdieu, P. (1980) *Le sens pratique* (trans. R. Nice as *The Logic of Practice*. Stanford, CA: Stanford University Press, 1990).

Bourdieu, P. (1984a) Homo Academicus (trans. P. Collier as *Homo Academicus*. Stanford, CA: Stanford University Press, 1988).

Bourdieu, P. (1984b) *Questions de Sociologie. Sociology in Question*. Thousand Oaks, CA: Sage Publications (1993).

Bourdieu, P. (1991) *Language and Symbolic Power* (ed. J. B. Thompson). Cambridge, MA: Harvard University Press.

Bourdieu, P. (1998) *Contre-feux. Acts of Resistance: Against the Tyranny of the Market*. New York: The New Press.

Bourdieu, P. and Wacquant, L. (1992) *An Invitation to Reflexive Sociology*. Chicago: Chicago University Press.

Bourdieu, P. and Wacquant, L. (1999) On the cunning of imperialist reason. *Theory, Culture and Society*, 16, 41–58.

Bowles, S. and Gintis, H. (1976) *Schooling in Capitalist Society*. New York: Basic.

Boyer, R. (1990) *The Regulation School: a Critical Introduction*. New York: Columbia University Press.

Bradshaw, T. K. (1993) In the shadow of urban growth: bifurcation in rural california communities. In T. A. Lyson and W. W. Falk (eds), *Forgotten Places: Uneven Development in Rural America*. Lawrence: University Press of Kansas.

Brandon, N. (1994) *The Six Pillars of Self-esteem*. New York: Bantam.

Braun, B. and Castree, N. (eds) (1998) *Remaking Reality*. London: Routledge.

Breault, K. (1989) New evidence on religious pluralism, urbanism, and religious participation. *American Sociological Review*, 54, 1048–53.

Brecher, J. and Costello, T. (1998) A "New labor movement" in the shell of the old? In G. Mantsios (ed.), *A New Labor Movement for the New Century*. New York: Monthly Review Press.

Brechin, S. and Kempton, W. (1994) Global environmentalism: a challenge to the post-materialism thesis? *Social Science Quarterly*, 75, 245–69.

Breyman, S. (1998) *Movement Genesis: Social Movement Theory and the West German Peace Movement*. Boulder, CO: Westview Press.

Brines, J. (1994) Economic dependency, gender, and the division of labor at home. *American Journal of Sociology*, 100, 652–88.

Brines, J. and Joyner, K. (1999) Principles of cohesion in cohabitation and marriage. *American Sociological Review*, 64, 333–55.

Brinton, M. C. and Nee, V. (eds) (1998) *The New Institutionalism in Sociology*. New York: The Russell Sage Foundation.

Britten, R. H. (1934) Mortality rates by occupational class in the US. *Public Health Reports*, 49, 1102.

Brody, E. (1990) *Women in the Middle: Their Parents Care Years*. New York: Springer.

Brooks, C. and Manza, J. (1997a) Class politics and political change in the United States, 1952–1992. *Social Forces*, 76, 379–408.

Brooks, C. and Manza, J. (1997b) Social cleavages and political alignments: US presidential elections, 1960 to 1992. *American Sociological Review*, 62, 937–46.

Broom, L. and Smith, J. H. (1963) Bridging occupations. *British Journal of Sociology*, 14, 321–34.

Brown, C. (1984) Black–white earnings ratios since the Civil Rights Act of 1964: The importance of labor market dropouts. *Quarterly Journal of Economics*, 99, 31–44.

Brown, D. L. and Hirschl, T. A. (1995) Household poverty in rural and metropolitan-core areas of the United States. *Rural Sociology*, 60, 44–66.

Brown, E. R., Wyn, R., Yu, H., Valenzuela, A. and Dong, L. (1998) Access to health insurance and health care for Mexican American children in immigrant families. In M. Suárez-Orozco (ed.), *Crossings: Mexican Immigration in Interdisciplinary Perspectives*. Cambridge, MA: Harvard University Press.

Brown, G. W. and Harris, T. O. (1989) *Life Events and Illness*. New York: Guilford Press.

Browne-Miller, A. (1995) *Intelligence Policy*. New York: Plenum.

Brubaker, R. (1996) *Nationalism Reframed: Nationhood and the National Question in the New Europe*. Cambridge: Cambridge University Press.

Brustein, W. (1996) *The Logic of Evil: the Social Origins of the Nazi Party, 1925–1933*. New Haven, CT: Yale University Press.

Bryant, C. G. A. (1992) Civil society and pluralism: a conceptual analysis. *Sisyphus*, 1(8), 103–16.

Bryant, J. M. (1996) *Moral Codes and Social Structure in Ancient Greece:a Sociology of Greek Ethics from Homer to the Epicureans and Stoics*. Albany: State University of New York Press.

Bryk, A. S., Lee, V. E. and Holland, P. B. (1993) *Catholic Schools and the Common Good*. Cambridge, MA: Harvard University Press.

Buchmann, M. (1989) *The Script of Life in Modern Society: Entry into Adulthood in a Changing World*. Chicago: University of Chicago Press.

Buck-Morss, S. (1989) *The Dialectics of Seeing: Walter Benjamin and the Arcades Project*. Cambridge, MA: MIT Press.

Buhle, P. (1999) *Taking Care of Business*. New York: Monthly Review Press.

Bulmer, M. (ed.) (1982) *Social Research Ethics*. New York: Holmes and Meier.

Bumpass, L. L., Sweet, J. A. and Cherlin, A. (1991) The role of cohabitation in declining rates of marriage. *Journal of Marriage and the Family*, 53, 913–27.

Burdick, J. (1993) *Looking for God in Brazil*. Berkeley: University of California.

Burke, P. (1991a) Overture: the new history, its past and its future. In P. Burke (ed.), *New Perspectives in Historical Writing*. University Park: The Pennsylvania University Press.

Burke, P. J. (1991b) Identity processes and social stress. *American Sociological Review*, 56, 836–49.

Burkhauser, R., Couch, K. and Phillips, H. (1996) Who takes early Social Security benefits? The economic and health characteristics of elderly beneficiaries. *The Gerontologist*, 36, 789– 99.

Burstein, P. (1998) Interest organizations, political parties, and the study of democratic politics. In A. N. Costain and A. S. McFarland (eds), *Social Movements and American Political Institutions*. Lantham, MD: Rowman and Littlefield.

Burt, R. S. (1992) *Structural Holes: The Social Structure of Competition*. Cambridge, MA: Harvard University Press.

Busch, B. G. (1998) Faith, truth, and tolerance: religion and political tolerance in the United States. PhD thesis, University of Nebraska, Lincoln.

Butler, D. and Stokes, D. (1969) *Political Change in Britain; Forces Shaping Electoral Choice*. New York: St Martin's Press.

Butler, R. and Heckman, J. (1977) The Government's impact on the labor market status of Black Americans: a critical review. In L. J. Hansman (ed.), *Equal Rights and Industrial Relations*. Madison, WI: Industrial Relations Research Association.

Buttel, F. H. (2000a) Classical sociological theory and contemporary environmental sociology: some reflections on the antecedents and prospects for reflexive modernization theories in the study of environment and society. In G. Spaargaren, A. Mol, and F. H. Buttel (eds), *Environmental Sociology and Global Modernity*. London: Sage.

Buttel, F. H. (2000b) Ecological modernization as social theory. *GeoForum*, 31.

Butterfield, F. (1996) US has plan to broaden availability of DNA testing. *New York Times*, July 14.

Buvinic, M. (1997) Women in poverty: a new global underclass. *Foreign Policy*, 108, 38–53.

Byrne, D. (1998) *Complexity Theory and the Social Sciences*. London: Routledge.

Cacioppo, J. T. and Tassinary, L. G. (1990) *Principles of Psychophysiology: Physical, Social, and Inferential Elements*. New York: Cambridge University Press.

Calhoun, C. (1996) Social theory and the public sphere. In B. S. Turner (eds), *The Blackwell Companion to Social Theory*. Oxford: Blackwell.

Calhoun, C. (1997) Nationalism and the public sphere. In J. Weintraub and K. Kumar (eds), *Public and Private in Thought and Practice*. Chicago: University of Chicago Press.

Camic, C. (1991) Introduction: Talcott Parsons before the structure of social action. In C. Camic (ed.), *Talcott Parsons: the Early Essays*. Chicago: University of Chicago Press.

Camic, C. (1992) Reputation and predecessor selection: Parsons and the institutionalists. *American Sociological Review*, 57, 421–45.

Camic, C. (1995) Three departments in search of a discipline: localism and interdisciplinary interaction in American sociology, 1890–1940. *Social Research*, 62, 1003–13.

Campbell, A. (1960) *The American Voter*. New York: Wiley.

Campbell, D. (1999) The deterritorialization of responsibility. In D. Campbell and M. J. Shapiro (eds), *Rethinking Ethics and World Politics*. Minneapolis: University of Minnesota Press.

Campbell, P. B., Basinger, K. S., Dauner, M. B. and Parks, M. A. (1986) *Outcomes of Vocational Education*. Columbus, OH: Ohio State University, National Center for Research in Vocational Education.

Cancian, F. (1996) Participatory research and alternative strategies for activist sociology. In H. Gottfried (eds), *Feminism and Social Change*. Urbana: University of Illinois Press.

Cantril, H. and Allport, G. W. (1935) *The Psychology of Radio*. New York: Harpers.

Capek, S. (1993) The "environmental justice" frame: a conceptual discussion and an application. *Social Problems*, 40, 5–24.

Cappelli, P., Bassi, L., Katz, H., Knoke, D., Osterman, P. and Useem, M. (1997) *Change at Work*. New York: Oxford University Press.

Card, D. and Lemieux, T. (1996) Wage dispersion, returns to skill and the black–white wage differential. *Journal of Econometrics*, 74(2), 319–61.

Carey, J. W. (1989) *Communication as Culture: Essays on Media and Society*. Boston: Unwin Hyman.

Carley, K. (1991) A theory of group stability. *American Sociological Review*, 6, 331–54.

Carpenter, J. A. (1997) *Revive Us Again: the Reawakening of American Fundamentalism*. New York: Oxford University Press.

Carrere, S. and Gottman, J. M. (1999) Predicting the future of marriages. In E. M. Hetherington (eds), *Coping with Divorce, Single Parenting, and Remarriage: a Risk and Resiliency Perspective*. Mahwah, NJ: Lawrence Erlbaum Associates, Publishers.

Carrol, C. D. and Weil, D. N. (1994) Saving and growth: a reinterpretation. *Carnegie-Rochester Conference Series on Public Policy*, 40, 133–92.

Carruthers, B. G. (1996) *City of Capital: Politics and Markets in the English Financial Revolution*. Princeton, NJ: Princeton University Press.

Carruthers, B. G. and Halliday, T. (1998) *Rescuing Business: the Making of Corporate Bankruptcy Law in England and the United States*. New York: Oxford University Press.

Castells, M. (1977) *The Urban Question*. London: Edward Arnold.

Castells, M. (1978) *City and Power*. London: Macmillan.

Castoriadis, C. (1990) *Le monde morcelé. Les carrefours du labyrinthe III*. Paris: Seuil.

Castro, I. (1998) *Equal Pay: a Thirty-five Year Perspective*. Washington, DC: US Department of Labor.

Catton, W. R., Jr (1976) Why the future isn't what it used to be (and how it could be made worse than it has to be). *Social Science Quarterly*, 57, 276–91.

Catton, W. R., Jr (1980) *Overshoot: the Ecological Basis of Revolutionary Change*. Urbana: University of Illinois Press.

Catton, W. R., Jr (1994) Foundations of human ecology. *Sociological Perspectives*, 37, 74–95.

Catton, W. R., Jr and Dunlap, R. E. (1978) Environmental sociology: a new paradigm. *The American Sociologist*, 13, 41–9.

Chaney, E. M. and Castro, M. G. (eds) (1989) *Muchachas No More: Household Workers in Latin America and the Caribbean*. Philadelphia: Temple University Press.

Chang, C. and White-Means, S. (1991) The men who care: an analysis of primary caregivers who care for the frail elderly at home. *Journal of Applied Gerontology*, 10, 343–58.

Chapman, M. (ed.) (1993) *Social and Biological Aspects of Ethnicity*. New York: Oxford University Press.

Chartier, R. (1982) Intellectual history or sociocultural history? The French trajectories. In D. LaCapra and S. L. Kaplan (eds), *Modern European Intellectual History: Reappraisals and New Perspectives*. Ithaca, NY: Cornell University Press.

Chase, I. D. (1991) Vacancy chains. *Annual Review of Sociology*, 17, 133–54.

Chase-Dunn, C. and Hall, T. D. (1997) *Rise and Demise, Comparing World Systems*. Boulder, CO: Westview Press.

Chaves, M., Konieczny, M. E., Beyerlein, K. and Barman, E. (1999) The national congregations study: background, methods, and selected results. *Journal for the Scientific Study of Religion*, 38, 458–76.

Chavez, L. (1992) *Shadowed Lives: Undocumented Immigrants in American Society*. Fort Worth, TX: Hartcourt Brace College Publishers.

Chavez, L. (1998) *The Color Bind: California's Battle to End Affirmative Action*. Berkeley: University of California Press.

Cheah, P. (1997) Posit(ion)ing human rights in the current global conjuncture. *Public Culture*, 9, 233–66.

Chiteji, N. and Stafford, F. S. (1999) Portfolio choices of parents and their children as young adults: asset accumulation of African American Families. Paper presented at the American Economic Association meeting, New York.

Cicourel, A. and Kitsuse, J. (1963) *The Educational Decision Makers*. Indianapolis: Bobbs-Merrill.

Cilliers, P. (1998) *Complexity and Postmodernism*. London: Routledge.

Clawson, D. and Clawson, M. A. (1999) What has happened to the US labor movement? *Annual Review of Sociology*, 25, 95–119.

Clayton, O., Jr (1996) *An American Dilemma Revisited: Race Relations in a Changing World*. New York: Russell Sage.

Clemens, E. (1997) *The People's Lobby*. Chicago: University of Chicago Press.

Clifford, J. (1997) *Routes*. Cambridge, MA: Harvard University Press.

Clydesdale, T. (1999) Toward understanding the role of Bible beliefs and higher education in American attitudes toward eradicating poverty, 1964–1996. *Journal for the Scientific Study of Religion*, 38, 103–18.

Coase, R. H. (1988) *The Firm, the Market and the Law*. Chicago: University of Chicago Press.

Cobb, S. (1988) Social support as a moderator of life stress. *Psychosomatic Medicine*, 3(5), 300–14.

Cohen, E. G. (1982) Expectation states and interracial intervention in the classroom. *Annual Review of Sociology*, 8, 209–35.

Cohen, J. L. and Arato, A. (1992) *Civil Society and Political Theory*. Cambridge, MA: MIT Press.

Cohen, J. M. (1977) Sources of peer group homogeneity. *Sociology of Education*, 50, 227–41.

Cohen, R. (1997) *Global Diasporas*. London: UCL Press.

Cohen, S. and Syme, S. L. (1985) Issues in the study and application of social support. In S. Cohen and S. L. Syme (eds), *Social Support and Health*. Orlando, FL: Academic Press.

Cole, S. (1992) *Making Science: Between Nature and Society*. Cambridge, MA: Harvard University Press.

Coleman, E. (1997) Banking on the poor. *Report*, 19–23.

Coleman, J. S. (1961) *The Adolescent Society: the Social Life of the Teenager and Its Impact on Education*. Glencoe, IL: The Free Press.

Coleman, J. S. (1988) Social capital in the creation of human capital. *American Journal of Sociology*, 94, S95–S120.

Coleman, J. S. (1990) *Foundations of Social Theory*. Cambridge, MA: Harvard University Press.

Coleman, J. S., Campbell, E. Q., Hobson, C. J., McPartland, J., Mood, A. M., Weinfeld, F. D. and York, R. L. (1966) *Equality of Educational Opportunity*. Washington, DC: US Government Printing Office.

Coleman, J. S., Hoffer, T. and Kilgore, S. (1983) *High School Achievement: Public, Catholic, and Private Schools Compared.* New York: Basic.

Coleman, J. S., Mosteller, F. and Moynihan, D. P. (eds) (1972) *On Equality of Educational Opportunity.* New York: Random House.

Colignon, R. A. (1997) *Power Plays: Critical Events in the Institutionalization of the Tennessee Valley Authority.* Albany: State University of New York Press.

Collins, H. and Pinch, T. (1993) *The Golem: What Everyone Should Know about Science.* Cambridge: Cambridge University Press.

Collins, P. H. (1998a) *Fighting Words: Black Women and the Search for Justice.* Minneapolis: University of Minnesota Press.

Collins, R. (1975) *Conflict Sociology: toward an Explanatory Science.* New York: Academic Press.

Collins, R. (1994) *Four Sociological Traditions: Selected Readings.* Oxford: Oxford University Press.

Collins, R. (1998b) *The Sociology of Philosophies: a Global Theory of Intellectual Change.* Cambridge, MA: Harvard University Press.

Commission on Behavioral and Social Sciences Education and Policy Division (CBSSEPD) (1999) *Human Dimensions of Global Environmental Change.* Washington, DC: National Academy Press.

Committee on Human Genetic Diversity (1997) *Scientific and Medical Value of Research on Human Genetic Variation.* Washington, DC: National Academy Press.

Commonwealth Fund (1987) *Medicare's Poor.* Washington, DC: Commission on Elderly People Living Alone.

Conley, D. (1999) *Being Black, Living in the Red: Race, Wealth, and Social Policy in America.* Berkeley: University of California Press.

Conroy, M. (1999) Social and environmental certification. Paper presented at the University of North Carolina, Chapel Hill, November 9.

Cook, K. S., Fine, G. A. and House, J. S. (eds) (1995) *Sociological Perspectives on Social Psychology.* Boston: Allyn and Bacon.

Cooley, C. H. (1909) *Social Organization: a Study of the Larger Mind.* New Brunswick, NJ: Transaction (1993).

Cornelius, W. A. (1982) Interviewing undocumented immigrants: methodological reflections based on fieldwork in Mexico and the US. *International Migration Review,* 16, 378–411.

Cornelius, W. (1998) The structural embeddedness of demand for Mexican immigrant labor. In M. Suárez-Orozco (ed.), *Crossings: Mexican Immigration in Interdisciplinary Perspectives.* Cambridge, MA: David Rockefeller Center for Latin American Studies, Harvard University Press.

Cornia, G. and Danziger, S. (1997) *Child Poverty and Deprivation in the Industrialized Countries, 1945–1995.* New York: Oxford University Press.

Coser, L. (1965) *Men of Ideas: a Sociologist's View.* New York: Simon & Schuster (1997).

Coser, L. (1968) Sociology of knowledge. In D. L. Sills (ed.), *International Encyclopedia of the Social Sciences.* New York: Macmillan.

Coser, R. L. (1975) The complexity of roles as a seedbed of individual autonomy. In L. A. Coser (ed.), *The Idea of Social Structure: Papers in Honor of Robert K. Merton.* New York: Harcourt Brace Jovanovich.

Coser, R. L. (1991) *In Defense of Modernity.* Stanford, CA: Stanford University Press.

Cotton, J. (1988) On the decomposition of wage differentials. *Review of Economics and Statistics,* 70(2), 236–43.

Couch, K. (1998) Later life job displacement. *The Gerontologist*, 38, 7–17.

Cousineau, M. (ed.) (1998) *Religion in the Age of Transformation*. New York: Praeger.

Coveney, P. and Highfield, R. (1990) *The Arrow of Time*. London: Flamingo.

Crain, R. L. and Mahard, R. E. (1978) School racial composition and black college attendance and achievement test performance. *Sociology of Education*, 51, 81–101.

Crane, D. (1972) *Invisible Colleges: Diffusion of Knowledge in Scientific Communities*. Chicago: University of Chicago Press.

Cresswell, T. (1997) Imagining the nomad: mobility and the postmodern primitive. In G. Benko and U. Strohmayer (ed.), *Space and Social Theory*. Oxford: Blackwell.

Crewe, I., Day, N. and Fox, A. (1991) *The British Electorate 1963–1987: a Compendium of Data from the British Election Studies*. New York: Cambridge University Press.

Crewe, I. and Sarlvik, B. (1983) *Decade of Dealignment: the Conservative Victory of 1979 and Electoral Trends in the 1970s*. Cambridge, MA: Cambridge University Press.

Crewe, I. and Thompson, K. (1999) Party loyalties: dealignment or realignment? In G. Evans and P. Norris (eds), *Critical Elections: British Parties and Voters in Long Term Perspective*. Newbury Park, CA: Sage.

Crouter, A. C. and Manke, B. (1997) Development of a typology of dual-earner families: a window into differences between and within families in relationships, roles, and activities. *Journal of Family Psychology*, 11, 62–75.

Cullen, L. M., Gao, X., Easteal, S. and Jazwinska, E. C. (1998) The hemochromatosis 845 G→A and 187 C→G mutations: prevalence in non-Caucasian populations. *American Journal of Human Genetics*, 62,1403–7.

Cumming, E. and Henry, W. (1961) *Growing Old: the Process of Disengagement*. New York: Basic Books.

Curran, J. (1998) Crisis of public communication: a reappraisal. In T. Liebes and J. Curran (eds), *Media, Ritual and Identity*. London: Routledge.

Cusick, P. A. (1973) *Inside High School*. New York: Holt, Rinehart, and Winston.

Cvetkovich, A. and Kellner, D. (1997) Introduction: thinking global and local. In A. Cvetkovich and D. Kellner (eds), *Articulating the Global and the Local: Globalization and Cultural Studies*. Boulder, CO: Westview Press.

Dahl, R. (1971) *Polyarchy*. New Haven, CT: Yale University Press.

Dahl, R. (1989) *Democracy and Its Critics*. New Haven, CT: Yale University Press.

Dahl, R. (1998) *On Democracy*. New Haven, CT: Yale University Press.

Dahrendorf, R. (1968) *Essays in the Theory of Society*. Stanford, CA: Stanford University Press.

Dahrendorf, R. (1979) *Life Chances: Approaches to Social and Political Theory*. Chicago: University of Chicago Press.

Dalaker, J. (1999) Poverty in the United States: 1998. *Current Population Reports, Series 60–207*. Washington, DC: US Government Printing Office.

Dalton, R. (1996) *Citizen Politics: Public Opinion and Political Parties in Advanced Industrial Democracies*, 2nd edn. Chatham, NJ: Chatham House.

Daly, M. and Bound, J. (1996) Worker adaptation and employer accommodation following the onset of a health impairment. *Journal of Gerontology*, 51B, 7–17.

Dandaneau, S. P. (1996) *A Town Abandoned: Flint, Michigan Confronts Deindustrialization*. Albany: State University of New York Press.

D'Anjou, L. (1996) *Social Movements and Cultural Change: the First Abolition Campaign Revisited*. New York: Aldine de Gruyter.

Darity, W., Jr (1980) Illusions of Black economic progress. *Review of Black Political Economy*, 10, 154–68.

Darity, W., Jr (1998) Intergroup disparity: economic theory and social science evidence. *Southern Economic Journal*, 64, 805–26.

Darity, W., Jr, Dietrich, J., Guilkey, D. and Hamilton, D. (1999) Passing on Blackness: Latinos, race, and economic outcomes. Unpublished manuscript, University of North Carolina at Chapel Hill.

Darity, W., Jr, Guilkey, D. and Winfrey, W. (1996) Explaining differences in economic performance among racial and ethnic groups in the US: the data examined. *American Journal of Economics and Sociology*, 55, 411–25.

Darity, W., Jr and Myers, S., Jr (1980) Changes in Black–White income inequality, 1968–1978: a decade of progress? *Review of Black Political Economy*, 10, 355–79.

Darity, W., Jr and Myers, S., Jr (1998) *Persistent Disparity: Race and Economic Inequality in the United States since 1945*. London: Edward Elgar.

Darity, W., Jr, Myers, S., Jr, Carson, E. and Sabol, W. (1994) *The Black Underclass: Critical Essays on Race and Unwantedness*. New York: Garland Publishers.

Davidman, L. (1991) *Tradition in a Rootless World*. Berkeley: University of California.

Davis, M. (1990) *City of Quartz*. London: Verso.

Davis, N. and Robinson, R. (1999) Their brothers' keepers? Orthodox religionists, modernists, and economic justice in Europe. *American Journal of Sociology*, 104, 1631–65.

Dean, A. (1998) The road to union city: building the American labor movement city by city. In J.-A. Mort (ed.), *Not Your Father's Union Movement*. New York: Verso.

Deavers, K. L. and Hoppe, R. A. (1992) Overview of the rural poor in the 1980s. In C. M. Duncan (eds), *Rural Poverty in America*. New York: Auburn House.

Deegan, M. J. (1998) *The American Ritual Tapestry: Social Rules and Cutlural Meanings*. New York: Greenwood Press.

Degenne, A. and Forse, M. (1999) *Introducing Social Networks*. London: Sage.

DeGré, G. (1939) *The Social Compulsions of Ideas: toward a Sociologial Analysis of Knowledge*. New Brunswick, NJ: Transaction.

Della Porta, D. and Reiter, H. (eds) (1997) *Policing Protests: The Control of Mass Demonstrations in Contemporary Democracies*. Minneapolis: University of Minnesota Press.

Delors, J. (1996) Education: the necessary utopia. In *Learning: the Treasure Within*. Report to UNESCO of the International Commission on Education for the Twenty-first Century. Paris: UNESCO.

DeMaris, A. and Rao, K. V. (1992) Premarital cohabitation and subsequent marital stability in the United States: a reassessment. *Journal of Marriage and the Family*, 54, 178–90.

Demerath, N. J. III, Hall, P. D., Schmitt, T. and Williams, R. H. (eds) (1998) *Sacred Companies: Organizational Aspects of Religion and Religious Aspects of Organizations*. New York: Oxford University Press.

D'Emilio, J. and Freedman, E. B. (1988) *Intimate Matters*. New York: Harper and Row.

DeParle, J. (1999) Project to rescue needy stumbles against the persistence of poverty. *New York Times*, May 15, A1, 15.

Devlin, B. and Risch, N. (1992a) Ethnic differentiation at VNTR loci, with specific reference to forensic applications. *American Journal of Human Genetics*, 51, 534–48.

Devlin, B. and Risch, N. (1992b) A note on the Hardy–Weinberg equilibrium of VNTR data by using the Federal Bureau of Investigation's fixed-bin method. *American Journal of Human Genetics*, 51, 549–53.

DeViney, S. (1995) Life course, private pension, and financial well-being. *American Behavioral Scientist*, 39, 172–85.

De Vos, G. (1973) *Socialization for Achievement: Essays on the Cultural Psychology of the Japanese*. Berkeley: University of California Press.

De Vos, G. and Suárez-Orozco, M. (1990) *Status Inequality: the Self in Culture*. Newbury Park, CA: Sage.

Dhesi, A. and Singh, H. (1989) Education labour market distortions and relative earnings of different religion–caste categories in India (a case study of Delhi). *Canadian Journal of Development Studies*.

Dickens, P. (1992): *Society and Nature*. Philadelphia: Temple University Press.

Dietz, T. and Rosa, E. A. (1997) Effects of population and affluence on CO_2 emissions. *Proceedings of the National Academy of Sciences*, 94, 175–9.

Diken, B. (1998) *Strangers, Ambivalence and Social Theory*. Aldershot: Ashgate.

Dill, B. T. (1998) A better life for me and my children: low income single mothers' struggle for self-sufficiency in the rural south. *Journal of Comparative Family Studies*, 29, 419–28.

Dill, B. T. and Williams, B. B. (1992) Race, gender and poverty in the rural south: African American single mothers. In C. M. Duncan (eds), *Rural Poverty in America*. New York: Auburn House.

Dilthey, W. (1883) *Introduction to the Human Sciences: an Attempt to Lay a Foundation for the Study of Society and History* (trans. and intro. R. J. Betanzos). Detroit: Wayne State University Press (1998).

DiMaggio, P., Evans, J. and Bryson, B. (1996) Have Americans' social attitudes become more polarized? *American Journal of Sociology*, 102, 690–755.

DiPrete, T. A. and Forristal, J. D. (1994) Multilevel models: methods and substance. *Annual Review of Sociology*, 20, 331–57.

DiPrete, T. A. and Grusky, D. B. (1990) Structure and trend in the process of stratification for American men and women. *American Journal of Sociology*, 96, 107–43.

Dohrenwend, B. P. (1986) Theoretical formulation of life stress variables. In A. Eichler, M. M. Silverman and D. M. Pratt (eds), *How to Define and Research Stress*. Washington, DC: American Psychiatric Press.

Dougherty, K. J. (1994) *The Contradictory College*. Albany: State University of New York.

Dowd, N. E. (1997) *In Defense of Single-parent Families*. New York: New York University Press.

Dreze, J. and Sen, A. (1989) *Hunger and Public Action*. Oxford: Clarendon Press.

Dublin, L. I. (1917) *Causes of Death by Occupation* (Bureau of Labor Statistics Bulletin No. 207). Washington, DC: US Government Printing Office.

Du Bois, W. E. B. (1903) The souls of black folk. In J. H. Franklin (ed.), *Three Negro Classics*. New York: Bantam (1965).

Dudden, F. (1983) *Serving Women: Household Service in Nineteenth-century America*. Middletown, CT: Wesleyan University Press.

Dugger, C. (1996) Queens old timers uneasy as Asian influence grows. *The New York Times*, March 31.

Duncan, C. M. (1992) *Rural Poverty in America*. New York: Auburn House.

Duncan, C. M. (1999a) *Worlds Apart: Why Poverty Persists in Rural America*. New Haven, CT: Yale University Press.

Duncan, C. M. (1999b) Equality of social capital in poor rural communities. Unpublished paper.

Duncan, O. D. (1961) A socioeconomic index for all occupations. In Albert J. Reiss, Jr (ed.), *Occupations and Social Status*. New York: Free Press.

Dunlap, R. E. (1991) Trends in public opinion on environmental issues: 1965 to 1990. *Society and Natural Resources*, 4, 285–312.

Dunlap, R. E. (1993) From environmental to ecological problems. In C. Calhoun and G. Ritzer (eds), *Social Problems*. New York: McGraw-Hill.

Dunlap, R. E. (1997) Global environmental concern: an anomaly for postmaterialism. *Social Science Quarterly*, 78, 24–9.

Dunlap, R. E. and Catton, W. R., Jr (1994) Struggling with human exemptionalism: the rise, decline, and revitalization of environmental sociology. *The American Sociologist*, 25, 5–30.

Dunlap, R. E. and Mertig, A. G. (1996) Weltweites Umweltbewusstsein: eine Herausforderung für die sozialwissenschaftliche Theorie. *Kölner Zeitschrift für Soziologie und Sozialpsychologie*, 36, 193–218.

Dunlap, R. E. and Van Liere, K. D. (1984) Commitment to the dominant social paradigm and concern for environmental quality. *Social Science Quarterly*, 65, 1013–28.

Dunleavy, P. and Husbands, C. (1985) *British Democracy at the Crossroads: Voting and Party Competition in the 1980s*. Boston: Allen and Unwin.

Durkheim, E. (1893) *The Division of Labour in Society*. London: Macmillan (1984).

Durkheim, E. (1903) *Moral Education*. New York: Free Press (1973).

Durkheim, E. (1912) *The Elementary Forms of the Religious Life*. London: George Allen and Unwin (1968).

Duster, T., Matza, D. and Wellman, D. (1979) Fieldwork and the protection of human subjects. *American Sociologist*, 14, 136–42.

Duval, J., Gaubert, C., Lebaron, F., Marchetti, D. and Pavis, F. (1998) *Le "decembre" des intellectuels français*. Paris: Editions LIBER.

Eagleton, T. (1991) *Ideology: an Introduction*. London: Verso.

Ebaugh, H. R. and Chafetz, J. (2000) *Religion and the New Immigrants: Continuities and Adaptations in Immigrant Congregations*. Walnut Creek, CA: AltaMira Press.

Eckersley, R. (1989) Green politics and the new class. *Political Studies*, 37, 205–33.

Eder, D. (1981) Ability grouping as a self-fulfilling prophecy: a micro-analysis of teacher–student interaction. *Sociology of Education*, 54, 151–62.

Edwards, B. and Foley, M. (1998) Civil society and social capital: beyond Putnam. *American Behavioral Scientist*, 42, 124–40.

Eide, A., Grause, C. and Rosas, A. (eds) (1994) *Economic, Social and Cultural Rights: a Textbook*. Dordrecht, the Netherlands: Martinus Nijhoff.

Eisenstadt, S. N. (1996) *Japanese Civilization: a Comparative View*. Chicago: University of Chicago Press.

Eisenstadt, S. N. (1998) *Antinomien der Moderne*. Frankfurt am Main: Suhrkamp.

Elder, G. (1985) *Life Course Dynamics: Trajectories and Transitions, 1968–1980*. Ithaca, NY: Cornell University Press.

Elder, K. (1996) *The Social Construction of Nature: a Sociology of Ecological Enlightenment*. Thousand Oaks, CA: Sage.

Ellis, A. (1992) *Reason and Emotion in Psychotherapy*. Secaucus, NJ: Lyle Stuart.

Ellison, C. and Levin, J. S. (1998) The religion–health connection: evidence, theory, and future directions. *Health Education and Behavior*, 25, 700–20.

Ellwood, D. (1986) The spatial mismatch hypothesis: are there jobs missing from the ghetto? In R. Freeman and H. Holzer (eds), *The Black Youth Employment Crisis*. Chicago: University of Chicago Press.

Emerson, R. M. (1972) Exchange theory, parts I and II. In J. Berger, M. Zelditch Jr and B. Anderson (eds), *Sociological Theories in Progress*. Boston: Houghton-Mifflin.

Engel, G. L. (1977) The need for a new medical model: a challenge for biomedicine. *Science*, 196, 129–36.

Enserink, M. (1998) Physicians wary of scheme to pool Icelanders' genetic data. *Science*, 281, 890–1.

Epstein, W. M. (1997) *Welfare in America: How Social Science Fails the Poor*. Madison, WI: University of Wisconsin Press.

Erickson, B. H. (1988) The relational basis of attitudes. In B. Wellman and S. D. Berkowitz (eds), *Social Structures: a Network Approach*. Cambridge: Cambridge University Press.

Erickson, B. H. (1996) Culture, class, and connections. *American Journal of Sociology*, 102, 217–51.

Erickson, B. H. and Nosanchuk, T. A. (1984) The allocation of esteem and disesteem. *American Sociological Review*, 49, 648–58.

Erickson, E. (1964) *Identity, Youth, Crisis*. New York: W. W. Norton.

Erikson, K. (1976) *Everything in Its Path*. New York: Simon and Schuster.

Erikson, R. and Goldthorpe, J. H. (1992) *The Constant Flux: a Study of Class Mobility in Industrial Societies*. Oxford: Clarendon Press.

Eschbach, K., Hagan, J., Rodriguez, N., Bailey, S. and Hernandez-Leon, R. (1997) Death at the border – June 1997 [http://www.nnirr.org].

Espanshade, T. and Balinger, M. (1998) Immigration and public opinion. In M. Suárez-Orozco (ed.), *Crossings: Mexican Immigration in Interdisciplinary Perspectives*. Cambridge, MA: Harvard University Press.

Espeland, W. N. (1998) *The Struggle for Water: Politics, Rationality, and Identity in the American Southwest*. Chicago: University of Chicago Press.

Espin, O. M. (1987) Psychological impact of migration on Latinas. *Psychology of Women Quarterly*, 11, 489–503.

Estes, C. (1993) *The Long Term Care Crisis*. Newbury Park, CA: Sage.

Evans, G. (1992) Testing the validity of the Goldthorpe class schema. *European Sociological Review*, 8, 211–32.

Evans, G., Heath, A. F. and Payne, C. (1999) Class: Labour as a catch-all party. In G. Evans and P. Norris (eds), *Critical Elections: British Parties and Voters in Long Term Perspective*. Newbury Park, CA: Sage.

Evans, P. (1995) *Embedded Autonomy*. Princeton, NJ: Princeton University Press.

Even, W. and MacPherson, D. (1998) Racial and ethnic differences in pension coverage and benefit levels. Tallahassee, FL: Working Paper Series, Pepper Institute on Aging and Public Policy.

Evett, I. W. (1993) Criminalistics: the future of expertise. *Journal of the Forensic Science Society*, 33, 173–8.

Evett, I. W., Buckleton, I. S., Raymond, A. and Roberts, H. (1993) The evidential value of DNA profiles. *Journal of the Forensic Science Society*, 33, 243–4.

Evett, I. W., Gill, P. D., Scranage, J. K. and Wier, B. S. (1996) Establishing the robustness of short-tandem-repeat statistics for forensic application. *American Journal of Human Genetics*, 58, 398–407.

Ewick, P. and Silbey, S. (1998) *The Common Place of Law*. Chicago: University of Chicago Press.

Eyerman, R. and Jamison, A. (1998) *Music and Social Movements: Mobilizing Traditions in the Twentieth Century*. New York: Cambridge University Press.

Fainstein, N. (1987) The underclass/mismatch hypothesis as an explanation for Black economic deprivation. *Politics and Society*, 15, 403–51.

Falcón, A. (1995) Puerto Ricans and the politics of racial identity. In H. Harris et al. (eds), *Racial and Ethnic Identity: Psychological Development and Creative Expression*. New York: Routledge.

Fantasia, R. (1988) *Cultures of Solidarity*. Berkeley: University of California Press.

Fararo, T. J. and Skvoretz, J. (1986) E-state structuralism: a theoretical method. *American Sociological Review*, 51, 591–602.

Farley, R. (1996) *The New American Reality: Who We Are, How We Got Here, Where We Are Going*. New York: Russel Sage Foundation.

Featherman, D. L., Jones, F. L. and Hauser, R. M. (1975) Assumptions of social mobility research in the US: the case of occupational status. *Social ScienceResearch*, 4, 329–60.

Feld, S. (1982) Social structural determinants of similarity among associates. *American Sociological Review*, 47, 797–801.

Feldman, P., Cohen, S., Lepore, S., Matthews, K. A., Kamarck, T. W. and Marsland, A. L. (2000) Negative emotions and acute physiological responses to stress. *Annals of Behavioral Medicine*.

Felmlee, D., Eder, D. and Tsui, W. Y. (1985) Peer influence on classroom attention. *Social Psychological Quarterly*, 48, 215–26.

Felmlee, D. and Hallinan, M. T. (1979) The effect of classroom interaction on children's friendships. *Journal of Classroom Interaction*, 14, 1–8.

Ferber, A. L. (1998) *White Man Falling: Race, Gender, and White Supremacy*. Lanham, MD: Rowman and Littlefield.

Ferguson, R. (1995) Shifting challenges: fifty years of economic change toward Black–White earnings equality. *Daedalus: Proceedings of the American Academy of Arts and Sciences*, 124(1), 37–77.

Fields, G. S. (1989) Changes in poverty and inequality in developing countries. *World Bank Research Observer*, 4, 167–86.

Figart, D. M. and Kahn, P. (1997) *Contesting the Market: Pay Equity and the Politics of Economic Restructuring*. Detroit: Wayne State University Press.

Fillieule, O. (1998) Plus ça change, moins ça change. Demonstrations in France during the nineteen-eighties. In D. Rucht, R. Koopmans and F. Neidhardt (eds), *Act of Dissent: New Developments in the Study of Protest*. Berlin: Wissenschaftszentrum Berlin für Sozialforschung.

Fine, J. (1998) Moving innovation from the margins to the center. In G. Mantsios (eds), *A New Labor Movement for a New Century*. New York: Monthly Review Press.

Finke, R. and Stark, E. (1992) *The Churching of America*. New Brunswick, NJ: Rutgers University Press.

Fischer, C. (1982) *To Dwell among Friends*. Berkeley: University of California Press.

Fischer, C. S., Hout, M., Janowski, M. S., Lucas, S. R., Swidler, A. and Voss, K. (1996) *Inequality by Design: Cracking the Bell Curve Myth*. Princeton, NJ: Princeton University Press.

Fishbein, M. and Ajzen, I. (1975) *Belief, Attitude, Intention, and Behavior*. Reading, MA: Addison-Wesley.

Fitchen, J. M. (1992) *Poverty in Rural America*. Boulder, CO: Westview Press.

Fitchen, J. M. (1995) Spatial redistribution of poverty through migration of poor people to depressed rural communities. *Rural Sociology* 60, 181–201.

Fitzpatrick, M. A. and Mulac, A. (1995) Relating to spouse and stranger: gender preferential language use. In P. J. Kalbfleisch and M. J. Cody (eds) *Gender, Power, and Communication in Human Relationships*. Hillsdale, NJ: Lawrence Erlbaum.

Flanagan, K. (1996) *The Enchantment of Sociology: a Study of Theology and Culture*. New York: St Martin's Press.

Flaskerud, J. H. and Uman, R. (1996) Acculturation and its effects on self-esteem among immigrant Latina women. *Behavioral Medicine*, 22, 123–33.

Fleischacker, S. (1998) Insignificant communities. In A. Gutmann (ed.), *Freedom of Association*. Princeton, NJ: Princeton University Press.

Flora, C. B. (1989) Domestic service in the Latin American *Fotonovela*. In E. M. Chaney and M. G. Castro (eds), *Muchachas No More: Household Workers in Latin America and the Caribbean*. Philadelphia: Temple University Press.

Flyvberg, B. (1998) *Rationality and Power: Democracy in Practice*. Chicago: University of Chicago Press.

Foley, M. W. and Edwards, B. (1996) The paradox of civil society. *Journal of Democracy*, 7, 38–52.

Foner, P. S. (1986) *May Day: a Short History of the International Workers' Holiday, 1886–1986*. New York: International Publishers.

Ford Foundation, New Dehli Office (1994) Saving the village tank. *Bulletin*, Summer, 3–5.

Forse, M., Jalin J.-P., Lemel, Y., Mendras, H., Stoclet, D. and Dechaux, J.-H. (1993) *Recent Social Trends in France 1960– 1990*. Montreal and Kingston, Ont.: McGill-Queen's University Press.

Foster, J. B. (1999a) Marx's theory of metabolic rift: classical foundations for environmental sociology. *American Journal of Sociology*, 105, 366–405.

Foster, J. B. (1999b) *Marx's Ecology: Materialism and Nature*. New York: Monthly Review Press.

Foucault, M. (1969) *L'Archéologie du savoir* (trans. A. M. Sheridan Smith as *The Archaeology of Knowledge*. New York: Pantheon, 1972).

Foucault, M. (1979) *Discipline and Punish*. New York: Vintage.

Fowler, B. (1997) *Pierre Bourdieu and Cultural Theory: Critical Investigations*. Newbury Park, CA: Sage.

Francis, D. and Meaney, M. J. (1999) Variations in maternal care form the basis for a non-genomic mechanism of inter-generational transmission of individual differences in behavioral and endocrine response to stress. Abstract for poster presentation at New York Academy of Sciences Conference on Socioeconomic Status and Health in Industrial Nations: Social, Psychological and Biological Pathways, Washington, DC.

Frankenberg, R. (1966) *Communities in Britain: Social Life in Town and Country*. Harmondsworth, Penguin.

Franklin, J. H. (1993) *The Color Line: Legacy for the Twenty-first Century*. Columbia: University of Missouri Press.

Franklin, M. (1985): *The Decline of Class Voting in Britain: Changes in the Basis of Electoral Choice, 1964–1983*. Oxford: Clarendon Press.

Franklin, M. (1992) *Electoral Change: Responses to Evolving Social and Attitudinal Structures in Western Countries*. Cambridge: Cambridge University Press.

Fraser, N. (1992) Rethinking the public sphere. In C. Calhoun (ed.), *Habermas and the Public Sphere*. Cambridge, MA: MIT Press.

Fraser, S. and Freeman, J. B. (ed.) (1997) *Audacious Democracy: Labor, Intellectuals, and the Social Reconstruction of America*. New York: Houghton Mifflin Company.

Freeman, R. (1981) Black economic progress after 1964: who has gained and why? In S. Rosen (ed.), *Studies in Labor Markets of Chicago*. Chicago: University of Chicago Press.

Freeman, R. B. (ed.) (1994) *Working under Different Rules*. New York: Russell Sage Foundation.

Freeman, R. B. and Rodgers, W. M. III (1999): Area economic conditions and the labor market outcomes of young men in the 1990s expansion. National Bureau of Economic Research working paper no. W7073, April [http://papers.nber.org/papers/W7073].

Freud, S. (1919) The uncanny. In J. Strachey (ed.), *The Standard Edition of the Complete Psychological Works of Sigmund Freud*. London: The Hogarth Press (1968).

Freud, S. (1927) *The Future of an Illusion*. New York: Norton (1961).

Friedkin, N. E. (1992) An expected value model of social power: predictions for selected exchange models. *Social Networks*, 14, 213–29.

Friese, H. and Wagner, P. (1999) Modernity and contingency. Not all that is solid melts into air. But what does and what does not? In M. Featherstone and S. Lash (eds), *Spaces of Identity. City – Nation – World*. London: Sage.

Frisby, D. (1983) *The Alienated Mind: the Sociology of Knowledge in Germany, 1918–33*. London: Routledge.

Frisby, D. (1992a) *Simmel and Since*. London: Routledge.

Frisby, D. (1992b) *Sociological Impressionism*. London: Routledge.

Frisby, D. and Featherstone, M. (eds) (1997) *Simmel on Culture*. London: Sage.

Fröbel, F., Heinrichs, J. and Kreye, K. (1977) *The New International Division of Labour*. Cambridge: Cambridge University Press.

Fuentes, C. (1992) *The Buried Mirror: Reflections on Spain and the New World*. New York: Houghton Mifflin.

Fujimura, J. H. (1998) Authorizing knowledge in science and anthropology. *American Anthropologist*, 10, 347–60.

Furnham, A. and Bochner, S. (1986) *Culture Shock*. London: Methuen.

Fürster, M. F. (1994) Measurement of low incomes and poverty in a perspective of international comparisons. *Labour Market and Social Policy Occasional Papers*, no. 14. Paris: Organisation for Economic Co-Operation and Development.

Gager, C. T. (1998) The role of valued outcomes, justifications, and comparison referents in perceptions of fairness among dual-earner couples. *Journal of Family Issues*, 19, 622–48.

Galbraith, J. K. (1999) Globalization and pay. *Proceedings of the American Philosophical Society*, 143, 178–86.

Gallagher, D., Rose, J., Rivera, P., Lovett, S. and Thompson, L. (1989) Prevalence of depression in family caregivers. *The Gerontologist*, 26, 449–56.

Gallagher, S. and Smith, C. (1999) Symbolic traditionalism and pragmatic egalitarianism: contemporary evangelicals, families, and gender. *Gender and Society*, 13, 211–33.

Gallie, D., Penn, R. and Rose, M. (eds) (1996) *Trade Unionism in Recession*. New York: Oxford University Press.

Gallup, J. L. (1997) Ethnicity and earnings in Malaysia. Development Discussion Paper No. 593. Harvard Institute of International Development.

Game, A. (1995) Time, space, memory, with reference to Bachelard. In M. Featherstone, S. Lash and R. Robertson (eds), *Global Modernities*. London: Sage.

Gamoran, A. (1987) The stratification of high school learning opportunities. *Sociology of Education*, 60, 135–55.

Gamoran, A. (1989) Rank, performance, and mobility in elementary school grouping. *Sociological Quarterly*, 30, 109–23.

Gamoran, A. (1992) Access to excellence: assignment to honors English classes on the transition from middle to high school. *Educational Evaluation and Policy Analysis*, 14, 185– 204.

Gamoran, A. and Dreeben, R. (1986) Coupling and control in educational organizations. *Administrative Science Quarterly*, 31, 612–32.

Gamoran, A., Secada, W. G. and Marrett, C. B. (2000) The organizational context of teaching and learning: changing theoretical perspectives. In M. T. Hallinan (ed.), *Handbook of Sociology of Education*. New York: Plenum/Kluwer.

Gamson, J. (1996) The organizational shaping of collective identity: the case of lesbian and gay film festivals in New York. *Sociological Forum*, 11, 231–61.

Gamson, W. A. (1992a) The social psychology of collective action. In A. D. Morris and C. M. Mueller (ed.), *Frontiers in Social Movement Theory*. New Haven, CT: Yale University Press.

Gamson, W. A. (1992b) *Talking Politics*. Cambridge, UK: University of Cambridge Press.

Gans, H. J. (1967) *The Levittowners: Ways of Live and Politics in a New Suburban Community*. New York: Pantheon Books.

Gans, H. J. (1979) Symbolic ethnicity: the future of ethnic groups and cultures in America. *Ethnic and Racial Studies*, 2, 1–20.

Gans, H. J. (1986) Urbanism and suburbanism as ways of life. In R. Pahl (ed.), *Readings in Urban Sociology*. Oxford: Pergamon.

Gans, H. J. (1992) Second generation decline: scenarios for the economic and ethnic futures of the post-1965 American immigrants. *Ethnic and Racial Studies*, 15, 173–92.

Gans, H. J. (1995) *The War Against the Poor*. New York: Basic Books.

Ganzeboom, H. B. G. and Treiman, D. J. (1996) Internationally comparable measures of occupational status for the 1988 international standard classification of occupations. *Social Science Research*, 25, 201–39.

Ganzeboom, H. B. G., de Graaf, P. and Treiman, D. J. (1992) An international scale of occupational status. *Social Science Research*, 21, 1–56.

Ganzeboom, H. B. G., Luijkx, R. and Treiman, D. J. (1989) Intergenerational class mobility in comparative perspective. *Research in Social Stratification and Mobility*, 8, 3– 84.

Ganzeboom, H. B. G., Treiman, D. J. and Ultee, W. (1991) Comparative intergenerational stratification research: three generations and beyond. *Annual Review of Sociology*, 17, 277–302.

Gapasin F. and Wial, H. (1998) The role of central labor councils in union organizing in the 1990s. In K. Bronfenbrenner et al. (eds), *Organizing to Win*. Ithaca, NY: Cornell University Press.

Garcia-Coll, C. and Magnuson, K. (1997) The psychological experience of immigration: a developmental perspective. In A. Booth, A. Crouter and N. Landale (eds), *Immigration and the Family: Research and Policy on US Immigrants*. Malwah, NJ: Lawrence Erlbaum Associates.

Garrett, P. and Lennox, N., with Fitchen, J., Hardesty, C., Johnson, C. and Thompson, M. (1993) Rural families and children in poverty. In Rural Sociological Society Task Force on Persistent Rural Poverty, *Persistent Poverty in Rural America*. Boulder, CO: Westview Press.

Gautier, A. H. (1996) *State and the Family: a Comparative Analysis of Family Policies in Industrialized Countries*. Oxford: Clarendon Press.

Gay, D. A., Ellison, C. and Powers, D. A. (1996) In search of denominational subcultures: religious affiliation and "pro-family" issues revisited. *Review of Religious Research*, 38, 3–17.

Geertz, C. (1983) *Local Knowledge: Further Essays in Interpretive Anthropology*. New York: Basic Books.

Gellner, E. (1994) *Conditions of Liberty*. London: Hamish Hamilton.

George, L. (1996) Social factors in illness. In R. Binstock and L. George (eds), *Handbook of Aging and the Social Sciences*. San Diego, CA: Academic Press.

George, L. (1999) Religion and physical health. Paper presented at the American Sociological Association annual meeting, Chicago.

Gibson, R. (1995) The black American retirement experience. In J. Quadagno and D. Street (eds), *Aging for the Twenty-first Century*. New York: St Martin's Press.

Giddens, A. (1977) *Studies in Social and Political Theory*. New York: Basic Books.

Giddens, A. (1979) *Central Problems in Social Theory*. London: Macmillan.

Giddens, A. (1981) *A Contemporary Critique of Historical Materialism*. London: Macmillan.

Giddens, A. (1984) *The Constitution of Society*. Cambridge: Polity Press.

Giddens, A. (1991) *Modernity and Self-identity*. Cambridge: Polity Press.

Giddens, A. (1994) *Beyond Left and Right*. Stanford, CA: Stanford University Press.

Giddens, A. (1998) *The Third Way*. Cambridge: Polity.

Giddens, A. and Turner, J. H. (eds) (1987) *Social Theory Today*. Stanford, CA: Stanford University Press.

Gieryn, T. F. (1999) *Cultural Boundaries of Science: Credibility on the Line*. Chicago: University of Chicago Press.

Gill, A. (1998) *Rendering unto Caesar: the Catholic Church and the State in Latin America*. Chicago: University of Chicago Press.

Gilroy, P. (1993) *The Black Atlantic. Modernity and Double Consciousness*. London: Verso.

Glasberg, D. S. and Skidmore, D. (1997) *Corporate Welfare Policy and the Welfare State: Bank Deregulation and the Savings and Loan Bailout*. New York: Aldine de Gruyter.

Glassner, B. (1999) *The Culture of Fear: Why Americans Are Afraid of the Wrong Things*. New York: Basic Books.

Glazer, N. (1990) The home as workshop: women as amateur nurses and medical care providers. *Gender and Society*, 4, 479– 99.

Glazer, N. (1997) *We Are All Multiculturalists Now*. Cambridge, MA: Harvard University Press.

Glazer, N. and Moynihan, D. P. (1963) *Beyond the Melting Pot: the Negroes, Puerto Ricans, Jews, Italians, and Irish of New York City*. Cambridge, MA: MIT Press.

Glenn, E. N. (1986) *Issei, Nisei, Warbride: Three Generations of Japanese American Women in Domestic Service*. Philadelphia: Temple University Press.

Goffman, E. (1959) *The Presentation of Self in Everyday Life*. New York: Anchor Books.

Goffman, E. (1963) *Stigma: Notes on the Management of Spoiled Identity*. New York: Simon and Schuster.

Goldblatt, D. (1996) *Social Theory and the Environment*. Boulder, CO: Westview Press.

Goldfarb, J. C. (1998) *Civility and Subversion: the Intellectual in Democratic Society*. New York: Cambridge University Press.

Goldsmith, A., Veum, J. and Darity, W. Jr (1997) The impact of psychological and human capital on wages. *Economic Inquiry*, 35, 815–29.

Goldstein, S. and Goldstein, A. (1996) *Jews on the Move: Implications for Jewish Identity*. Albany: State University of New York.

Good, T. L. and Marshall, S. (1984) Do students learn more in heterogeneous or homogeneous groups? In P. L. Peterson, L. C. Wilkinson and M. T. Hallinan (eds), *The Social Context of Instruction: Group Organization and Group Process*. Los Angeles: Academic Press.

Goodwin, J. and Jasper, J. M. (1999) Caught in a winding, snarling vine: The structural bias of political process theory. *Sociological Forum*, 14, 27–54.

Goodwin, J. L. (1997) *Gender and the Politics of Welfare Reform: Mothers' Pensions in Chicago, 1911–1929*. Chicago: University of Chicago Press.

Gordon, C. W. (1957) *Social System of the High School*. Glencoe, IL: The Free Press.

Gordon, D. (1996) *Fat and Mean*. New York: Free Press.

Gordon, M. (1964) *Assimilation in American Life*. New York: Oxford University Press.

Gorham, L. (1992) The growing problem of low earnings in rural areas. In C. M. Duncan (eds), *Rural Poverty in America*. New York: Auburn House.

Gornick, J. C. and Jacobs, J. A. (1998) Gender, the welfare state and public employment: a comparative study of 7 industrialized countries. *American Sociological Review*, 63, 688–710.

Gorsuch, R. L. (1988) Psychology of religion. *Annual Review of Psychology*, 39, 201–21.

Gottlieb, R. (1994) *Forcing the Spring*. Washington, DC: Island Press.

Gould, K. A., Schnaiberg, A. and Weinberg, A. S. (1996) *Local Environmental Struggles*. Cambridge: Cambridge University Press.

Gouldner, A. W. (1965) *Enter Plato: Classical Greece and the Origins of Social Theory*. New York: Basic Books.

Gouldner, A. W. (1970) *The Coming Crisis of Western Sociology*. New York: Basic Books.

Gouldner, A. W. (1979) *The Future of Intellectuals and the Rise of the New Class*. New York: The Seabury Press.

Gouldner, A. W. (1980) *The Two Marxisms*. New York: The Seabury Press.

Gouveia, L. and Stull, D. D. (1995) Dances with cows: beefpacking's impact on Garden City, Kansas, and Lexington, Nebraska. In D. D. Stull et al. (eds), *Anyway You Cut It: Meatpacking and Small-town America*. Lawrence: University Press of Kansas.

Grabher, G. and Stark, D. (1997) *Restructuring Networks in Post-Socialism: Legacies, Linkages, and Localities*. New York: Oxford University Press.

Grad, S. (1994) Income of the population 55 or older, 1992, Publication No. 13–11871. Washington DC: Social Security Administration, Office of Research and Statistics.

Gramling, R. (1996) *Oil on the Edge: Offshore Development, Conflict, Gridlock*. Albany: State University of New York Press.

Grandori, A. (ed.) (1998) The organizational texture of inter-firm relations. Special issue of *Organization Studies*, 19, 549–741.

Granovetter, M. (1995) *Getting a Job: a Study of Contacts and Careers*, 2nd edn. Chicago and London: University of Chicago Press.

Grant, J. (1998) *Raising Baby by the Book*. New Haven, CT: Yale University Press.

Green, J., Guth, J., Smidt, C. and Kellstedt, L. (1996) *Religion and the Culture Wars: Dispatches from the Front*. Lanham, MD: Rowman and Littlefield.

Green, S. (1994) Del Valle a Willmar: settling out of the migrant stream in a rural Minnesota community. Working paper no. 19, Julian Samora Research Institute, Michigan State University.

Greer, S. (1969) Sociology and Political Science. In S. M. Lipset (ed.), *Politics and the Social Sciences*. New York: Oxford University Press.

Greider, W. (1997) *One World, Ready or Not: the Manic Logic of Global Capitalism*. New York: Simon and Schuster.

Grinberg, L. and Grinberg, R. (1989) *Psychoanalytic Perspectives on Migration and Exile*. New Haven, CT: Yale University Press.

Groves, J. M. (1997) *Hearts and Minds: the Controversy over Laboratory Animals*. Philadelphia: Temple University Press.

Grusky, D. B. (1994) *Social Stratification: Class, Race, and Gender in Sociological Perspective*. Boulder, CO: Westview Press.

Gundel, M. (1926) Einige Beobachtungen bei der rassenbiologischen Durchforschung Schleswig-Holsteins. *Klinische Wochenschrift*, 5, 1186.

Gulati, R. (1995a) Does familiarity breed trust? The implications of repeated ties for contractual choices in alliances. *Academy of Management Journal*, 38, 85–112.

Gulati, R. (1995b) Social structure and alliance formation patterns: a longitudinal analysis. *Administrative Science Quarterly*, 40, 619–52.

Gulati, R. and Gargiulo, M. (1999) Where do networks come from? *American Journal of Sociology*, 104, 1439–93.

Gulbenkian Commission on the Restructuring of the Social Sciences (1996) *Open the Social Sciences: Report of the Gulbenkian Commission on the Restructuring of the Social Sciences*. Stanford, CA: Stanford University Press.

Guralnick, L. (1962) Mortality by occupation and industry among men 20 to 64 years of age, US, 1950. *Vital Statistics*, Special Reports, 53, 56.

Gurr, T. R. (1970) *Why Men Rebel*. Princeton, NJ: Princeton University Press.

Gustafsson, B. and Johansson, M. (1999) In search of smoking guns: what makes income inequality vary over time in different countries? *American Sociological Review*, 64, 585–605.

Gutmann, A. (1999) *Democratic Education*. Princeton, NJ: Princeton University Press.

Haan, M., Kaplan, G. A. and Camacho, T. (1987) Poverty and health: Prospective evidence from the Alameda County Study. *American Journal of Epidemiology*, 125, 989–98.

Haber, C. and Gratton, B. (1994) *Old Age and the Search for Security*. Bloomington: Indiana University Press.

Habermas, J. (1973) *Theory and Practice* (trans. J. Viertel). Boston: Beacon Press.

Habermas, J. (1989) *The Structural Transformation of the Public Sphere*. Cambridge, MA: MIT Press.

Habermas, J. (1996) *Between Facts and Norms: Contributions to a Discourse Theory of Law and Democracy*. Cambridge, MA: MIT Press.

Haddad, Y. Y. and Esposito, J. L. (1998) *Islam, Gender, and Social Change*. New York: Oxford University Press.

Hagan, J. and McCarthy, B. (1997) *Mean Streets: Youth Crime and Homelessness*. Cambridge: Cambridge University Press.

Hagstrom, W. O. (1965) *The Scientific Community*. New York: Basic Books.

Haines, H. H. (1996) *Against Capital Punishment: the Anti-death Penalty Movement in America, 1972–1994*. New York: Oxford University Press.

Hall, J. A. (1998) The nature of civil society. *Society*, 34, 32–41.

Hallinan, M. T. (1976) Friendship patterns in open and traditional classrooms. *Sociology of Education*, 49, 254–65.

Hallinan, M. T. (1990) The effects of ability grouping in secondary schools: a response to Slavin's best-evidence synthesis. *Review of Educational Research*, 60, 501–4.

Hallinan, M. T. (1992) The organization of students for instruction in the middle school. *Sociology of Education*, 65, 114–27.

Hallinan, M. T. (1994a) School differences in tracking effects on achievement. *Social Forces*, 72, 799–820.

Hallinan, M. T. (1994b) Tracking: From theory to practice. *Sociology of Education*, 67, 79–91.

Hallinan, M. T. (1996) Track mobility in secondary school. *Social Forces*, 74, 983–1002.

Hallinan, M. T. (2000) Linkages between sociology of race and sociology of education. In M. T. Hallinan (ed.), *Handbook of Sociology of Education*. New York: Plenum Publishing.

Hallinan, M. T. and Sorensen, A. B. (1983) The formation and stability of instructional groups. *American Sociological Review*, 48, 838–51.

Hallinan, M. T. and Sorensen, A. B. (1985) Ability grouping and student friendships. *American Educational Research Journal*, 22, 485–99.

Hallinan, M. T. and Teixeria, R. A. (1987) Opportunities and constraints: black–white differences in the formation of interracial friendships. *Child Development*, 58, 1358–71.

Hallinan, M. T. and Williams, R. A. (1987) The stability of students' interracial friendships. *American Sociological Review*, 52, 653–64.

Hallinan, M. T. and Williams, R. A. (1989) Interracial friendship choices in secondary schools. *American Sociological review*, 54, 67–78.

Hajer, M. (1995) *The Politics of Environmental Discourse*. New York: Oxford University Press.

Hall, J. R. (1997) *Reworking Class*. Ithaca, NY: Cornell University Press.

Hamilton, M. (1998) *Sociology and the World's Religions*. New York: St Martin's Press.

Hammond, J. L. (1998) *Fighting to Learn: Popular Education and Guerrilla War in El Salvador*. New Brunswick. NJ: Rutgers University Press.

Hann, C. 1996: Introduction: civil society. In C. Hann and E. Dunn (eds), *Challenging Western Models*. London: Routledge.

Hannerz, U. (1991) Scenarios for peripheral cultures. In A. D. King (ed.), *Culture, Globalization and the World-System*. London: Macmillan.

Hannerz, U. (1996) *Transnational Connections*. London: Routledge.

Hannigan, J. A. (1995) *Environmental Sociology: a Social Constructionist Perspective*. London: Routledge.

Hansen, K. V. (1997) Rediscovering the social. In J. Weintraub and K. Kumar (cds), *Public and Private in Thought and Practice*. Chicago: University of Chicago Press.

Haraway, D. (1991) *Simians, Cyborgs, and Women: the Reinvention of Nature*. London: Routledge.

Harding, R. J., Fullerton, S. M., Griffiths, R. C., Bond, J. B., Cox, M. J., Schneider, J. A., Moulin, D. S. and Clegg, J. B. (1997) Archaic African and Asian lineages in the genetic ancestry of modern humans. *American Journal of Human Genetics*, 60, 772–89.

Harding, S. (1998) *Is Science Multi-cultural? Postcolonialisms, Feminisms, and Epistemologies*. Bloomington: Indiana University Press.

Hare, R. M. (1976) Ethical theory and utilitarianism. In H. D. Lewis (ed.), *Contemporary British Philosophy*. London: Allen and Unwin.

Harrington Meyer, M. (ed.) (2000) *Care Work: Gender, Labor, and the State*. New York: Routledge.

Harrington Meyer, M. and Kesterke-Storbakken, M. (2000) How the states shape access to long term care: does payment source affect admission to nursing homes. In M. Harrington Meyer (ed.), *Care Work: Gender, Labor, and the State*. New York: Routledge.

Harris, K. M. (1997) *Teen Mothers and the Revolving Welfare Door*. Philadelphia: Temple University Press.

Harrison, B. (1972) The intra metropolitan distribution of minority economic welfare. *Journal of Regional Science*, 12(1), 23–43.

Harrison, B. (1974) *Urban Economic Development: Suburbanization, Minority Opportunity, and the Condition of the Central City*. Washington, DC: Urban Institute

Harrison, B. (1994) *Lean and Mean*. New York: Basic Books.

Harsanyi, J. (1975) Can the maximin principle serve as a basis for morality? A critique of John Rawls's theory. *American Political Science Review*, 64, 594–606.

Hastings, A. (ed.) (1999) *A World History of Christianity*. Grand Rapids, MI: Eerdmans.

Harvey, D. (1989) *The Condition of Postmodernity*. Oxford: Blackwell.

Harvey, D. (1996) *Justice, Nature and the Geography of Difference*. Oxford: Blackwell.

Hauser, R. M. and Warren, J. R. (1997) Socioeconomic indexes for occupations: a review, update, and critique. In A. E. Raftery (ed.), *Sociological Methodology*. Oxford: Blackwell.

Havighurst, R., Neugarten, B. and Tobin, S. (1968) Disengagement and patterns of aging. In B. Neugarten (ed.), *Middle Age and Aging: a Reader in Social Psychology*. Chicago: University of Chicago Press.

Hay, C. (1996) *Re-stating Social and Political Change*. Philadelphia: Open University Press.

Hayles, N. K. (ed.) (1991) *Chaos and Order*. Chicago: University of Chicago Press.

Hays, S. (1996) *The Cultural Contradictions of Motherhood*. New Haven, CT: Yale University Press.

Hayward, M. D., Friedman, S. and Chen, H. (1996) Race inequities in men's retirement. *Journal of Gerontology*, 51B, S1– 10.

Health Care Financing Administration (1998) *A Profile of Medicare: Chart Book, 1998*. Washington, DC: US Government Printing Office.

Heath, A. F., Curtice, J., Jowell, R., Evans, G., Field, J. and Witherspoon, S. (1991) *Understanding Political Change: the British Voter 1964–1987*. New York: Pergamon Press.

Heath, A. F., Jowell, R. and Curtice, J. (1985) *How Britain Votes*. New York: Pergamon Press.

Heath, A. F., Jowell, R. and Curtice, J. (1994) *Labour's Last Chance? The 1992 Election and Beyond*. Brookfield, VT: Dartmouth.

Heath, A. and Savage, M. (1995) Political alignments within the middle classes, 1972– 1989. In D. Butler and M. Savage (eds), *Political Change in Britain: Forces Shaping Electoral Choice*. New York: St Martin's Press.

Hedstrom, P. and Swedberg, R. (eds) (1998) *Social Mechanisms: an Analytical Approach to Social Theory*. Cambridge: Cambridge University Press.

Hefner, R. W. (1998a) Civil society: cultural possibility of a modern ideal. *Society*, 35, 16– 27.

Hefner, R. W. (ed.) (1998b) *Democratic Civility: the History and Cross-cultural Possibility of a Modern Political Ideal*. New Brunswick, NJ: Transaction Publishers.

Heise, D. R. (1979) *Understanding Events*. New York: Cambridge University Press.

Heller, K. and Swindle, R. W. (1983) Social networks, perceived social support, and coping with stress. In R. D. Felner (ed.), *Preventative Psychology: Theory, Research, and Practice in Community Intervention*. New York: Penguin Press.

Henslin, J. M. (ed.) (1995) *Down to Earth Sociology*. New York: Free Press.

Henson, K. D. (1996) *Just a Temp*. Philadelphia: Temple University Press.

Herbert, M. (1998) *Camouflage Isn't Only for Combat: Gender, Sexuality, and Women in the Military*. New York: New York University Press.

Herbert, T. B. and Cohen, S. (1993) Stress and immunity in humans: a meta-analytic review. *Psychosomatic Medicine*, 55, 364–79.

Hernandez, D. J. (1995) *America's Children*. New York: Russell Sage Foundation.

Hernandez, D. and Charney, E. (eds) (1998) *From Generation to Generation: the Health and Well-being of Children in Immigrant Families*. Washington, DC: National Academy Press.

Herrnstein, R. J. and Murray, C. (1994) *The Bell Curve: Intelligence and Class Structure in American Life*. New York: The Free Press.

Hersch, C. (1998) *Democratic Artworks: Politics and the Arts from Trilling to Dylan*. Albany: State University of New York Press.

Hertz, R. (1986) *More Equal than Others: Women and Men in Dual Career Marriages*. Berkeley, Los Angeles: University of California Press.

Hess, D. J. (1997) *Science Studies: an Advanced Introduction*. New York: New York University Press.

Hetherington, K. (1994) The contemporary significance of Schmalenbach's concept of the bund. *Sociological Review*, 42, 1–25.

Hetherington, K. (1998) *Expressions of Identity: Space, Performance, Politics*. Thousand Oaks, CA: Sage.

Higham, J. (1955) *Strangers in the Land: Patterns of American Nativism, 1860–1925*. New York: Atheneum.

Higham, J. (1997) *Civil Rights and Social Wrongs: Black–White Relations since World War II*. University Park: Pennsylvania State University Press.

Himmelfarb, G. (1999): *The Two Cultures: a Moral Divide*. New York: A. A. Knopf.

Himmelstein, J. L. (1997) *Looking Good and Doing Good: Corporate Philanthropy and Corporate Power*. Bloomington: Indiana University Press.

Hirschfeld, L. and Hirschfeld, H. (1919) Serological difference between the blood of different races. *Lancet*, October 18, 675–9.

Hirschman, C., Kasinitz, P. and DeWind, J. (eds) (1999) *The Handbook of International Migration: the American Experience*. New York: Russell Sage Foundation.

Hobbs, F. and Damon, B. (1996) *65+ in the United States*. Washington, DC: US Bureau of the Census.

Hobsbawm, E. (1994) *Age of Extremes: the Short Twentieth Century 1914–1991*. London: Michael Joseph.

Hochschild, A. R. (1979) Emotion work, feeling rules and social structure. *American Journal of Sociology*, 85, 551–75.

Hochschild, A. R. (1983) *The Managed Heart: Commercialization of Human Feeling*. Berkeley: University of California Press.

Hochschild, A. R. (1989) *The Second Shift: Working Parents and the Revolution at Home*. New York: Viking.

Hochschild, A. R. (1997) *The Time Bind: When Work Becomes Home and Home Becomes Work*. New York: Metropolitan Books.

Hoffer, T. and Kamens, D. (1992) Tracking and inequality revisited: secondary school course sequences and the effects of social class on educational opportunities. Paper presented at the Annual Meeting of the American Sociological Association, Pittsburg.

Hoffman, E. (1989) *Lost in Translation: a Life in a New Language*. New York: Penguin Books.

Hollingshead, A. B. (1949) *Elmtown's Youth*. New York: Wiley.

Holmes, T. H. and Rahe, R. H. (1967) The social readjustment rating scale. *Journal of Psychosomatic Research*, 11, 213–18.

Holzer, H. J. (1994) Black employment problems: new evidence, old questions. *Journal of Policy Analysis and Management*, 13(4), 699–722.

Holzer, H. (1995) *What Employers Want: Job Prospects for Less-educated Workers*. New York: Russell Sage.

Homans, G. C. (1961) *Social Behavior: Its Elementary Forms*. New York: Harcourt, Brace & World.

Hondagneu-Sotelo, P. (1988) Gender and fieldwork. *Women's Studies International Forum*, 11, 611–18.

Hondagneu-Sotelo, P. (1994) Regulating the unregulated: domestic workers' social networks. *Social Problems*, 41, 201–15.

Hoogvelt, A. 1997: *Globalization and the Postcolonial World: the New Political Economy of Development*. Baltimore: Johns Hopkins University Press.

Hooks, B. (1991) *Yearning: Race, Gender and Cultural Politics*. London: Turnaround.

Hooyman, N. R. and Gonyea, J. (1995) *Feminist Perspectives on Family Care: Politics for Gender Justice. Volume 6, Family Caregivers Application Series.* Thousand Oaks, CA: Sage.

Hopkins, T. K. and Wallerstein, I. (coord.) (1996) *The Age of Transition: Trajectory of the World-system, 1945–2025.* London: Zed Press.

Horkheimer, M. and Adorno, T. (1944) *Dialectic of Enlightenment.* New York: Herder and Herder.

Hounsell, C. (1996) *Women and Pensions: a Policy Agenda.* New York: Norton.

Howard, J. and Hollander, J. (1997) *Gendered Situations, Gendered Selves: a Gender Lens on Social Psychology.* Thousand Oaks, CA: Sage.

Howard, R. E. (1995) *Human Rights and the Search for Community.* Boulder, CO: Westview Press.

Howell, D. R. (1994) The collapse of low-skill male earnings in the 1980s: skill mismatch or shifing wage norms? Working paper, New York School for Social Research.

Howes, D. (1996) Commodities and cultural borders. In D. Howes (ed.), *Cross-cultural Consumption.* London: Routledge.

Hoyert, D. and Seltzer, M. (1992) Factors relating to well being and life activities of family caregivers. *Family Relations*, 41, 74–81.

Hula, K. W. (1999) *Lobbying Together: Interest Group Coalitions in Legislative Politics.* Washington, DC: Georgetown University Press.

Hunter, J. D. (1991) *Culture Wars.* New York: Basic Books.

Huntington, S. (1968) *Political Order in Changing Societies.* New Haven, CT: Yale University Press.

Huntington, S. (1991) *The Third Wave.* Norman: Oklahoma University Press.

Huntington, S. (1996) *The Clash of Civilizations and the Remaking of World Order.* New York: Simon and Schuster.

Hutchison, W. (1987) *Errand to the World: American Protestant Thought and Foreign Missions.* Chicago: University of Chicago Press.

Huxley, T. H. (1881) Science and Culture. In *Science and Education*, volume 3 of *Collected Essays.* New York: Greenwood Press (1968), pp. 134–59.

Hyland, S. and Timberlake, M. (1993) The Mississippi Delta: changes or continued trouble? In T. A. Lyson and W. W. Falk (eds), *Forgotten Places: Uneven Development in Rural America.* Lawrence: University Press of Kansas.

Iannaconne, L. (1993) Heirs to the Protestant ethic? The economics of American fundamentalism. In M. Marty and S. Appleby (eds), *Fundamentalism and the State.* Chicago: University of Chicago Press.

Iannaconne, L. (1994) Why strict churches are strong. *American Journal of Sociology*, 99, 1180–212.

Ibarra, H. (1992) Homophily and differential returns: sex differences in network structure and access in an advertising firm. *Administrative Science Quarterly*, 37, 422–47.

Ibarra, H. (1993a) Personal networks of women and minorities in management: a conceptual framework. *Academy of Management Review*, 18, 56–87.

Ibarra, H. (1993b) Network centrality, power and innovation involvement: determinants of technical and administrative roles. *Academy of Management Journal*, 36, 471–501.

Idler, E., Ellison, C., George, L., Krause, N., Levin, J., Ory, M., Pargament, K., Powell, L., Williams, D. and Underwood-Gordon, L. (1977) National Institute on Aging/ Fetzer Institute Working Group Brief Measure of Religiousness and Spirituality: Conceptual Development. Unpublished manuscript.

Ihlanfeldt, K. and Sjoquist, D. (1990) Job accessibility and racial differences in youth employment rates. *American Economic Review* (March).

Inglehart, R. (1977) *The Silent Revolution*. Princeton, NJ: Princeton University Press.

Inglehart, R. (1995) Public support for environmental protection: objective problems and subjective values in 43 societies. *Political Science and Politics*, 28, 57–72.

Inkeles, A. (1964) *What Is Sociology? An Introduction to the Discipline and Profession*. Englewood Cliffs, NJ: Prentice Hall.

International Labour Office (1969) *International Standard Classification of Occupations*, rev. edn. Geneva: International Labour Office.

International Labour Office (1990) *International Standard Classification of Occupations: ISCO-88*. Geneva: International Labour Office.

Jackson, R. M. (1998) *Destined for Equality: the Inevitable Rise of Women's Status*. Cambrige, MA: Harvard University Press.

Jacobson, C. K. (ed.) (1995) *American Families: Issues in Race and Ethnicity*. New York: Garland Press.

James, E. (1987) The nonprofit sector in comparative perspective. In W. Powell (ed.), *The Nonprofit Sector: a Research Handbook*. New Haven, CT: Yale University Press.

Jänicke, M. (1986) *State Failure. The Impotence of Politics in Industrial Society*. Cambridge: Polity Press.

Jasper, J. M. (1997) *The Art of Moral Protest: Culture, Biography, and Creativity in Social Movements*. Chicago: University of Chicago Press.

Jasso, G. and Rosenzweig, M. R. (1990) *The New Chosen People: Immigrants in the United States*. New York: Russell Sage Foundation.

Jaynes, G. (1990) The labor market status of black Americans: 1939–1985. *Journal of Economic Perspectives*, 4, 24.

Jencks, C. and Riesman, D. (1969) *The Academic Revolution*. Garden City, NY: Anchor.

Jenkins, J. C. (1999) Grassrooting the system? The development and impact of social movement philanthropy, 1953–1990. Paper presented at the annual meeting of the American Sociological Association, Chicago.

Jenkins, J. C. and Eckert, C. M. (1986) Channeling black insurgency. *American Sociological Review*, 51, 812–30.

Jenkins, J. C. and Klandermans, B. (1995) *The Politics of Social Protest: Comparative Perspectives on States and Social Movements*. Minneapolis/London: University of Minnesota Press/UCL Press.

Jenness, V. and Broad, K. (1997) *Hate Crimes: New Social Movements and the Politics of Violence*. New York: Aldine de Gruyter.

Jensen, L. and Eggebeen, D. J. (1994) Nonmetropolitan poor children and reliance on public assistance. *Rural Sociology*, 59, 45–65.

Jensen, L. and Tienda, M. 1989: Nonmetropolitan minority families in the United States: trends in racial and ethnic stratification, 1959–1986. *Rural Sociology*, 54, 509–32.

Jessop, B. (1983) *Nikos Poulantzas*. Basingstoke: Macmillan.

Jessop, B. (1991) *The Politics Of Flexibility: Restructuring State and Industry in Britain, Germany, and Scandinavia*. Brookfield, VT: E. Elgar.

Jessop, B. (1995) The regulation approach, governance and post-Fordism – alternative perspectives on economic and political change. *Economy and Society*, 24, 307–33.

Jessop, B., Bonnett, K., Bromley, S. and Ling, T. (1988) *Thatcherism: a Tale of Two Nations*. New York: Polity Press.

Johnson, C. (1993) Gender and formal authority. *Social Psychology Quarterly*, 56, 193–210.

Jones, B. (1997) *Forcing the Factory of the Future: Cybernation and Societal Institutions*. Cambridge: Cambridge University Press.

Jones, G. S. (1983) *Languages of Class: Studies in English Working Class History, 1832–1982*. Cambridge: Cambridge University Press.

Jones, J. H. (1981) *Bad Blood. The Tuskegee Syphilis Experiment: a Tragedy of Race and Medicine*. New York: Free Press.

Jones, J. (1998) *American Work: Four Centuries of Black and White Labor*. New York: W. W. Norton.

Jones, R. A. (1986) Durkheim, Frazer, and Smith: the role of analogies and exemplars in the development of Durkheim's sociology of religion. *American Journal of Sociology*, 92, 596–627.

Jones-Correa, M. (1998) Commentary: immigration and public opinion. In M. Suárez-Orozco (ed.), *Crossings: Mexican Immigration in Interdisciplinary Perspectives*. Cambridge, MA: Harvard University Press.

Joyce, P. (1990) *Visions of the People*. Cambridge: Cambridge University Press.

Joyce, P. (1993) The imaginary discontents of social history: a note of response to Mayfield and Thorne, and Lawrence and Taylor. *Social History*, 18, 1.

Joyce, P. (1994) *Democratic Subjects: the Self and the Social in Nineteenth-century England*. Cambridge, MA: Cambridge University Press.

Kain, J. F. (1968) Housing segregation, Negro employment and metropolitan decentralization. *Quarterly Journal of Economics*, 82(2), 175–97.

Kalleberg, A. L., Knocke, D., Marsden, P. V. and Spaeth, J. L. (1996) *Organizations in America: Analyzing Their Structures and Human Resource Practices*. Thousand Oaks, CA: Sage Publications.

Kalkoff, W. and Barnum, C. (2000) The effects of status-organizing and social identity processes on patterns of social influence: Experimental data and conclusions, *Social Psychology Quarterly*, 63.

Kang, S. and Bishop, J. (1986) The effect of curriculum on labor market success. *Journal of Industrial Teacher Education*, 133–48.

Kanner, A. D., Coyne, J. C., Schaefer, C. and Lazarus, R. S. (1981) Comparison of two methods of stress measurement: daily hassles and uplifts versus major life events. *Journal of Behavioral Medicine*, 4, 1–39.

Kanter, R. M. and Myers, P. S. (1991) Interorganizational bonds and intraorganizational behavior: how alliances and partnerships change the organizations forming them. In A. E. Lawrence and P. R. Lawrence (eds), *Socioeconomics: toward a New Synthesis*. Armonk, NY: M. E. Sharpe.

Kao, G. and Tienda, M. (1995) Optimism and achievement: the educational performance of immigrant youth. *Social Science Quarterly*, 76, 1–19.

Kaplan, C. (1996) *Questions of Travel*. Durham, NC: Duke University Press.

Kaplan, G. A. and Keil, J. E. (1993) Socioeconomic factors and cardiovascular disease: a review of the literature. *Circulation*, 88, 1973–98.

Kaplan, G. A., Pamuk, E. R., Lynch, J. W., Cohen, R. D. and Balfour, J. L. (1996) Inequality in income and mortality in the United States: analysis of mortality and potential pathways. *British Medical Journal*, 312, 999–1003.

Kaplan, J. R., Manuck, S. B., Adams, M. R., Williams, J. K., Selwyn, A. P. and Clarkson, T. B. (1991) Nonhuman primates as a model for evaluating behavioral influences on atherosclerosis, and cardiac structure and function. In A. P. Shapiro and A. Baum (eds), *Behavioral Aspects of Cardiovascular Disease*. Hillsdale, NJ: Lawrence Erlbaum.

Kaplan, J. R., Manuck, S. B., Clarkson, T. B., Lusso, F. M. and Taub, D. M. (1982) Social status, environment, and atherosclerosis in cynomolgus monkeys. *Arteriosclerosis*, 2, 359–68.

Karasek, R. A., Baker, D., Marxer, F., Ahlbohm, A. and Theorell, T. (1981) Job decision latitude, job demands, and cardiovascular disease: a prospective study of Swedish men. *American Journal of Public Health*, 75, 694–705.

Karasek, R. A., Theorell, T., Schwartz, J. E., Schnall, P. L., Pieper, C. F. and Michela, J. L. (1988) Job characteristics in relation to the prevalence of myocardial infarction in the US Health Examination Survey (HES) and the Health and Nutrition Examination Survey (HAINES). *American Journal of Public Health*, 78, 910–18.

Kasarda, J. D. (1985) Urban change and minority opportunities. In P. E. Paterson (ed.), *The New Urban Reality*. Washington, DC: Brookings Institution, pp. 33–67.

Katz, E. (1998) And deliver us from segmentation. In R. G. Noll and M. E. Price (eds), *A Communications Cornucopia*. Washington, DC: Brookings Institution.

Katz, M. B. (1986) *In the Shadow of the Poorhouse: a Social History of Welfare in America*. New York: Basic Books.

Katz, M. B. (1989) *The Undeserving Poor: from the War on Poverty to the War on Welfare*. New York: Pantheon Books.

Katz, S. H. (1995) Is race a legitimate concept for science? *The AAPA Revised Statement on Race: a Brief Analysis and Commentary*. Universtiy Park: University of Pennsylvania.

Katz Rothman, B. (1998) *Genetic Maps and Human Imaginations: the Limits of Science in Understanding Who We Are*. New York: W. W. Norton.

Katzman, D. M. (1981) *Seven Days a Week: Women and Domestic Service in Industrializing America*. Urbana: University of Illinois Press.

Kavanagh, D. (1990a) *British Politics: Continuities and Change*. New York: Oxford University Press.

Kavanagh, D. (1990b) Ideology, sociology, and the strategy of the British Labour Movement. In J. Clark and J. H. Goldthorpe (eds), *Consensus and Controversy*. London: Falmer.

Kawachi, I., Kennedy, B. P., Lochner, K. and Prothrow-Stith, D. (1997) Social capital, income inequality, and mortality. *American Journal of Public Health*, 87, 1491–8.

Kawachi, I., Kennedy, B. P. and Wilkinson, R. G. (1999) Crime: social disorganization and relative deprivation. *Social Science and Medicine*, 48, 719–31.

Keane, J. (1988) Introduction. In J. Keane (ed.), *Civil Society and the State*. London: Verso.

Keane, J. (1998) *Civil Society. Old Images, New Visions*. Cambridge: Polity Press.

Keith, M. and Pile, S. (eds) (1993) *Place and the Politics of Identity*. London: Routledge.

Kellough, G. (1996) *Aborting Law: an Exploration of the Politics of Motherhood and Medicine*. Toronto: University of Toronto Press.

Kemper, T. D. (1978) *A Social Interactional Theory of Emotion*. New York: Wiley.

Kennedy, B. P., Kawachi, I. and Prothrow-Stith, D. (1996) Income distribution and mortality: cross sectional study of the Robin Hood index in the United States. *British Medical Journal*, 312, 1004–7. (See important correction. *BMJ*, 312, 1194.)

Kennedy, M. D. (ed.) (1995) *Envisioning Eastern Europe: Postcommunist Cultural Studies*. Minneapolis: Univeristy of Michigan Press.

Kerckhoff, A. C. (1986) Effects of ability grouping in British secondary schools. *American Sociological Review*, 51, 842–58.

Kerckhoff, A. C. (2000) Transition from school to work in comparative perspective. In M. T. Hallinan (ed.), *Handbook of Sociology of Education*. New York: Plenum/Kluwer.

Kerckhoff, A. C. and Bell, L. (1998) Early adult outcomes of students at risk. *Social Psychology of Education*, 2, 81–102.

Kern, S. (1983) *The Culture of Time and Space, 1880–1918*. London: Weidenfeld and Nicolson.

Kertzer, D. I. (1996) *Politics and Symbols: the Italian Communist Party and the Fall of Communism*. New Haven, CT: Yale University Press.

Kidd, Q. and Lee, A.-R. (1997) Postmaterialist values and the environment: a critique and reappraisal. *Social Science Quarterly*, 78, 1–15.

Kiecolt-Glaser, J. K., Cacioppo, J. T., Malarkey, W. B. and Glaser, R. (1992) Acute psychological stressors and short-term immune changes: what, why, for whom, and what extent? *Psychosomatic Medicine*, 54, 680–5.

Killworth, P. D., Johnson, E. C., Bernard, H. R., Shelley, G. A. and McCarty, C. (1990) Estimating the size of personal networks. *Social Networks*, 12, 289–312.

Kim, E. H. and Yu, E. (1996) *East to America: Korean American Life Stories*. New York: New Press.

Kingson, E. (1994) Testing the boundaries of universality. What's mean? What's not? *The Gerontologist*, 34, 733–40.

Kirschbaum, C. and Helhammer, D. (1989) Salivary cortisol in psychobiological research: an overview. *Neuropsychobiology*, 22, 150–69.

Kitagawa, E. M. and Hauser, P. M. (1973) *Differential Mortality in the United States: a Study in Socioeconomic Epidemiology*. Cambridge, MA: Harvard University Press.

Kitschelt, H. (1986) Political opportunity structures and political protest: anti-nuclear movements in four democracies. *British Journal of Political Science*, 16, 57–85.

Klandermans, B. (1984) Mobilization and participation: social psychological expansions of resource mobilization theory. *American Sociological Review*, 49, 583–600.

Klandermans, B. (1992) The social construction of protest and multi-organizational fields. In A. Morris and C. Mueller (eds), *Frontiers in Social Movement Theory*. New Haven, CT: Yale University Press.

Klandermans, B. (1997) *The Social Psychology of Protest*. Oxford: Blackwell.

Klein, A. M. (1997) *Baseball on the Border: a Tale of Two Laredos*. Princeton, NJ: Princeton University Press.

Kleinman, S. (1996) *Opposing Ambitions*. Chicago: Univeristy of Chicago Press.

Kluegal, J. R., Mason, D. S. and Wegener, B. (eds) (1995) *Social Justice and Political Change: Public Opinion in Capitalist and Post-communist States*. New York: Aldine de Gruyter.

Knapp, P., Kronick, J. C., Marks, R. W. and Vosburgh, M. G. (1996) *The Assault on Equality*. New York: Praeger.

Knoke, D. (1990) *Political Networks: the Structural Perspective*. Cambridge: Cambridge University Press.

Knoke, D. and Guilarte, M. (1994) Networks in organizational structures and strategies. *Current Perspectives in Social Theory, Supplement*, 1, 77–115.

Knoke, D., Pappi, F. U., Broadbent, J. and Tsujinaka, Y. (1996) *Comparing Policy Networks: Labour Politics in the US, Germany, and Japan*. Cambridge: Cambridge University Press.

Knorr-Cetina, K. D. (1981) *The Manufacture of Knowledge: an Essay on the Constructivist and Contextual Nature of Science*. Oxford: Pergamon Press.

Kogevinas, M., Marmot, M. G., Fox, A. J. and Goldblatt, P. O. (1991) Socioeconomic differences in cancer survival. *Journal of Epidemiology and Community Health*, 45, 216–19.

Kohut, H. (1971) *The Analysis of Self: a Systematic Approach to the Psychoanalytic treatment of Personality Disorders*. New York: International Universities Press.

Koitz, D. (1996) *The Entitlement Debate*. Washington, DC: Congressional Research Service.

Kollock, P. (1994) The emergence of exchange structures: an experimental study of uncertainty, commitment and trust. *American Journal of Sociology*, 100, 313–45.

Kollock, P., Blumstein, P., and Schwartz, P. (1994) The judgment of equity in intimate relationships. *Social Psychology Quarterly*, 57, 340–51.

Korgen, K. O. (1998) *From Black to Biracial: Transforming Racial Identity among Americans*. New York: Praeger.

Korpi, W. and Palme, J. (1998) The paradox of redistribution and strategies of equality: welfare state institutions and inequality and poverty in the western countries. *American Sociological Review*, 63, 661–87.

Kosmin, B. and Lachman, S. (1993) *One Nation under God*. New York: Harmony Books.

Kraus, V., Schild, E. O. and Hodge, R. W. (1978) Occupational prestige in the collective conscience. *Social Forces*, 56, 900–18.

Kriesi, H. (1995) The political opportunity structure of new social movements: its impact on their mobilization. In J. C. Jenkins and B. Klandermans (eds), *The Politics of Social Protest: Comparative Perspectives on States and Social Movements*. Minneapolis/London: University of Minnesota Press/UCL Press.

Kriesi, H., Koopmans, R., Duyvendak, J.-W. and Giugni, M. G. (1995) *The Politics of New Social Movements in Western Europe. A Comparative Analysis*. Minnesota: University of Minnesota Press.

Kroll-Smith, S. and Floyd, H. H. (1997) *Bodies in Protest: Environmental Illness and the Struggle over Medical Knowledge*. New York: New York University Press.

Kubitschek, W. N. and Hallinan, M. T. (1996) Race, gender, and inequity in track assignments. *Research in Sociology of Education and Socialization*, 11, 121–46.

Kuhn, M., Long, C. and Quinn, L. (1991) *No Stone Unturned: the Life and Times of Maggie Kuhn*. New York: Ballantine Books.

Kuhn, T. S. (1962) *The Structure of Scientific Revolutions*. Chicago: University of Chicago Press.

Kumar, K. (1993) Civil society: an Inquiry into the usefulness of an historical term. *British Journal of Sociology*, 44, 375–96.

Kumar, K. (1994) Civil society again. *British Journal of Sociology*, 45, 127–31.

Kurthen, H., Bergmann, W. and Erb, R. (eds) (1997) *Anti-Semitism and Xenophobia in Germany after Unification*. New York: Oxford University Press.

Kusch, M. (1995) *Psychologism: a Case Study in the Sociology of Philosophical Knowledge*. London: Routledge.

Kuznets, S. (1955) Economic growth and income equality. *American Economic Review*, 45, 1–28.

Kymlicka, W. (1995) *Multicultural Citizenship*. New York: Oxford University Press.

Land, K., Deane, G. and Blau, J. (1991) Religious pluralism and church membership. *American Sociological Review*, 56, 237–49.

Laosa, L. (1989) *Psychological Stress, Coping, and the Development of the Hispanic Immigrant Child*. Princeton, NJ: Educational Testing Service.

LaRossa, R. (1997) *The Modernization of Fatherhood: A Social and Political History*. Chicago: University of Chicago Press.

Laumann, E. O. and Knoke, D. (1987) *The Organizational State: a Perspective on the Social Organization of National Energy and Health Policy Domains*. Madison, WI: University of Wisconsin Press.

Lavin, D. E. and Hyllegard, D. (1996) *Changing the Odds: Open Admissions and the Life Chances of the Disadvantaged*. New Haven, CT: Yale University Press.

Lawler, E. J. and Yoon, J. (1998) Network structure and emotion in exchange relations. *American Sociological Review*, 63, 871–94.

Lawlor, J. and Potts, J. (1991) Job hunt: blacks face more bias. *USA Today*, May 15, p. A1.

Lawrence, J. (1998) *Speaking for the People: Party, State and Popular Politics in England 1867–1914*. Cambridge: Cambridge University Press.

Lazarsfeld, P. F. and Katz, E. (1955) *Personal Influence: the Part Played by People in the Flow of Mass Communications*. New York: Free Press.

Lazarsfeld, P. F. and Merton, R. K. (1948) Mass communication, popular taste, and organized social action. In L. Bryson (ed.), *The Communication of Ideas*. New York: Harper.

Lazarus, R. S. and Folkman, S. (1984) *Stress, Appraisal and Coping*. New York: Springer Publishing Company.

Lazear, E. (1979) The narrowing of black–white differentials is illusory. *American Economic Review*, 69(4), 553–64.

Lazerwitz, B., Winter, A. J., Dashefsky, A. and Tabory, E. (1998) *Jewish Choices: American Jewish Denominationalism*. Albany: State University of New York Press.

Lecaillon, J., Paukert, F., Morrisson, C. and Germidis, D. (1984) *Income Distribution and Economic Development: An Analytical Survey*. Geneva: International Labour Office.

LeDoux, J. (1996) *The Emotional Brain: the Mysterious Underpinnings of Emotional Life*. New York: Simon and Schuster.

Lee, C. K. (1998) *Gender and the South China Miracle: Two Worlds of Factory Women*. Berkeley: University of California Press.

Lee, J. Z. and Campbell, C. (1997) *Fate and Fortune in Rural China: Social Organization and Popular Behavior in Liaoning, 1774–1873*. Cambridge: Cambridge University Press.

Lee, R. E. (1996) Structures of knowledge. In T. K. Hopkins and I. Wallerstein (coord.), *The Age of Transition: Trajectory of the World-system, 1945–2025*. London: Zed Press.

Lee, R. E. (1999) After history? The last frontier of historical capitalism. *Protosoziologie*, 13, 48–65.

Leege, D. and Kellstedt, L. A. (1993) *Rediscovering the Religious Factor in American Politics*. Armonk, NY: M. E. Sharpe.

Leege, D. and Welch, M. (1988) Religious predictors of Catholic parishioners' socio-political attitudes. *Journal for the Scientific Study of Religion*, 27, 536–52.

Leege, D. and Welch, M. (1991) Dual reference groups and political orientation. *American Journal of Political Science*, 35, 28–56.

Lefebvre, H. (1991) *The Production of Space*. Oxford: Blackwell.

Lehman, E. C. Jr (1993) *Gender and Work: the Case of the Clergy*. Albany: State University of New York Press.

Lembecke, J. (1998) *The Spitting Image: Myth, Memory, and the Legacy of Vietnam*. New York: New York University Press.

Lemert, C. C. (1997) *Social Things : an Introduction to the Sociological Life*. Lanham, MD: Rowman & Littlefield.

Lemert, C. C. (ed.) (1999) *Social Theory: the Multicultural and Classic Readings*. Boulder, CO: Westview Press.

Lenski, G. (1966) *Power and Privilege*. Chapel Hill: University of North Carolina.

Lenski, G. and Lenski, J. (1982) *Human Societies: an Introduction to Macrosociology*. New York: McGraw-Hill.

Lerner, S. (1998) Taking the offensive, turning the tide. In G. Mantsios (ed.), *A New Labor Movement for the New Century*. New York: Monthly Review Press.

Levinas, E. (1982) Ideology and idealism. In S. Hand (ed.), *The Levinas Reader*. Oxford: Basil Blackwell.

Levinas, E. (1998) *On Thinking of the Other: Entre Nous*. New York: Columbia University Press.

Levine, M. P. (1998) *Gay Macho: the Life and Death of the Homosexual Clone*. New York: New York University Press.

Levinger, G. (1966) Sources of marital dissatisfaction among applicants for divorce. *American Journal of Orthopsychiatry*, 36, 803–7.

Levy, F. (1987) *Dollars and Dreams: the Changing American Income Distribution*. New York: Russell Sage.

Levy, F. and Michel, R. (1991) *The Economic Future of American Families: Income and Wealth Trends*.Washington, DC: The Urban Institute Press.

Lewis, O. (1959) *Five Families: Mexican Case Studies in the Culture of Poverty*. New York: Basic Books.

Lichter, D. T. (1997) Poverty and inequality among children. *Annual Review of Sociology*, 23, 121–45.

Lichter, D. T. and Constanzo, J. A. (1987) Nonmetropolitan underemployment and labor-force composition. *Rural Sociology*, 52, 329–44.

Lichter, D. T., Cornwell, G. and Eggebeen, D. (1993) Harvesting human capital: family structure and education among rural youth. *Rural Sociology*, 58, 53–75.

Lichter, D. T. and Eggebeen, D. (1992) Child poverty and the changing rural family. *Rural Sociology*, 57, 151–72.

Lichter, D. T. and McLaughlin, D. K. (1995) Changing economic opportunities, family structure, and poverty in rural areas. *Rural Sociology*, 60, 688–706.

Lichter, D. T., McLaughlin, D. K. and Cornwell, G. T. (1995) Migration and the loss of human resources in rural America. In L. Beaulieu, and D. Mulkey (eds), *Investing in People: the Human Capital Needs of Rural America*. Boulder, CO: Westview Press.

Lie, J. (1998) *Han Unbound: the Political Economy of South Korea*. Stanford, CA: Stanford University Press.

Lieberman, R. C. (1998) *Shifting the Color Line: Race and the American Welfare State*. Cambridge, MA: Harvard University Press.

Lieberson, S. (1933) *A Piece of the Pie*. Berkeley: University of California Press.

Liebes, T. and Katz, E. (1990) *The Export of Meaning: Cross-cultural Readings of Dallas*. New York: Oxford University Press.

Limerick, D. and Cunnington, B. (1993) *Managing the New Organization: a Blueprint for Networks and Strategic Alliances*. San Francisco: Jossey-Bass.

Lin, N. (1999) Social networks and status attainment. *Annual Review of Sociology*, 25, 467–87.

Lindert, P. H. and Williamson, J. G. (1985) Growth, equality and history. *Explorations in Economic History*, 22, 341–77.

Linz, J. L. and Stepan, A. (eds) (1978) *The Breakdown of Democratic Regimes*. Baltimore: Johns Hopkins University Press.

Linz, J. L. and Stepan, A. (1996) *Problems of Democratic Transition and Consolidation*. Baltimore: Johns Hopkins University Press.

Linz, J. L. and Valenzuela, A. (1994) *The Failure of Presidential Democracy*. Baltimore: Johns Hopkins University Press.

Lipset, S. M. (1959) *Social Mobility in Industrial Society*. Berkeley, University of California Press.

Lipset, S. M. (1960) *Political Man: the Social Bases of Politics*. Garden City, NY: Doubleday.

Lipset, S. M. (ed.) (1969) *Politics and the Social Sciences*. New York: Oxford University Press.

Lipset, S. M. and Rokkan, S. (1967a) Cleavage structures, party systems, and voter alignments: an introduction. In S. M. Lipset and S. Rokkan (eds), *Party Systems and Voter Alignments: Cross-national Perspectives*. New York: The Free Press.

Lipset, S. M. and Rokkan, S. (eds) (1967b) *Party Systems and Voter Alignments: Cross-national Perspectives*. New York: Free Press.

Liu D., Diorio, J., Tannenbaum, B., Caldji, C., Francis, D., Freedman, A., Sharma, S., Pearson, D., Plotsky, P. M. and Meaney, M. J. (1997) Maternal care, hippocampal glucocorticoid receptors, and hypothalamic-pituitary-adrenal responses to stress. *Science*, 277, 1659–62.

Lockwood, D. (1995) Marking out the middle class(es). In T. Butler and M. Savage (eds), *Social Change and the Middle Classes*. London: UCL Press.

Lofland, L. (1998) *The Public Realm: Exploring the City's Quintessential Social Territory*. New York: Aldine de Gruyter.

Lovaglia, M. and Houser, J. (1996) Emotional reactions, status characteristics and social interaction. *American Sociological Review*, 61, 867–83.

Lowenhardt, J. (1995) *The Reincarnation of Russia*. Durham, NC: Duke University Press.

Lowenthal, D. (1985) *The Past Is a Foreign Country*. Cambridge: Cambridge University Press.

Lukes, S. (1977) *Essays in Social Theory*. New York: Columbia University Press.

Lutz, M. A. (1999) *Economics for the Common Good*. London: Routledge.

Lyotard, J. F. (1979) *La condition postmoderne* (trans. G. Bennington and B. Massumi as *The Postmodern Condition: a Report on Knowledge*. Manchester: Manchester University Press, 1994).

Lyotard, J. F. (1989) Universal history and cultural differences. In A. Benjamin (ed.), *The Lyotard Reader*. Oxford: Blackwell.

McAdam, D. (1982) *Political Process and the Development of Black Insurgency*. Chicago: Chicago University Press.

McAdam, D., McCarthy, J. D. and Zald, M. N. (eds) (1996a) *Comparative Perspectives on Social Movements*. Cambridge: Cambridge University Press.

McAdam, D., Tarrow, S. and Tilly, C. (1996b) To map contentious politics. *Mobilization*, 1, 17–34.

McBride, T. (1976) *The Domestic Revolution*. New York: Holmes.

McCarthy, E. D. (1966) *Knowledge as Culture: the New Sociology of Knowledge*. London: Routledge.

McCarthy, J. (1998) Environmentalism, wise use, and the nature of accumulation in the rural West. In B. Braun and N. Castree (eds), *Remaking Reality*. London: Routledge.

McCarthy, J. D., Britt, D. W. and Wolfson, M. (1991) The institutional channelling of social movements by the state in the United States. *Research in Social Movements, Conflict, and Change*, 13, 45–76.

McCarthy, J. D. and Zald, M. (1976) Resource mobilization and social movements: a partial theory. *American Journal of Sociology*, 82, 1212–41.

McGrath, C., Blythe, J. and Krackhardt, D. (1997) The effect of spatial arrangement on judgments and errors in interpreting graphs. *Social Networks*, 19, 223–42.

Machonin, P. (1997) *Social Transformation and Modernization: on Building Theory of Societal Changes in the Post-European Countries*. Prague: Sociologicke Nakladetelstvi.

MacIntyre, A. (1984) *After Virtue*. Notre Dame: University of Notre Dame Press.

Mckay, G. (1996) *Senseless Acts of Beauty*. London: Verso.

Mackenbach, J. P., Stronks, K. and Kunst, A. E. (1989) The contribution of medical care to inequalities in health: differences between socio-economic groups in decline of mortality from conditions amenable to medical intervention. *Social Science and Medicine*, 29, 369–76.

MacKinnon, N. J. (1994) *Symbolic Interactionism as Affect Control*. Albany: State University of New York Press.

McLaughlin, N. (1998) Why do schools of thought fail? Neo-Freudianism as a case study in the sociology of knowledge. *Journal of the History of the Behavioral Sciences*, 34, 113–34.

Macnaghten, P. and Urry, J. (1998) *Contested Natures*. London: Sage.

McPherson, J. M. and Smith-Lovin, L. (1987) Homophily in voluntary associations. *American Sociological Review*, 52, 370–9.

Madriz, E. (1997) *Nothing Happens to Good Girls: Fear of Crime in Women's Lives*. Berkeley: University of California Press.

Mair, P. (1997) *Party System Change: Approaches and Interpretations*. London: Sage.

Mannheim, K. (1925) The problem of a sociology of knowledge. In *Essays on the Sociology of Knowledge* (ed. and trans. P. Kecskemeti). New York: Oxford University Press (1952).

Mannheim, K. (1929) *Ideology and Utopia: an Introduction to the Sociology of Knowledge* (trans. L. Wirth and E. A. Shils). New York: Harcout, Brace, and Company (1936).

Mannheim, K. (1962) *Essays on the Sociology of Culture*. London: Routledge.

Mannheim, K. (1997) *Collected Works of Karl Mannheim*. London: Routledge.

Manski, C. (1989) Anatomy of the selection process. *Journal of Human Resources*, 24, 343–60.

Manton, K., Corder, L. and Stallard, E. (1993) Estimates of change in chronic disability and institutional evidence and prevalence rates in the US elderly population from the 1982, 1984, and 1989 Long Term Care Survey. *Journal of Gerontology* 48, S153–66.

Marcuse, H. (1964) *One-dimensional Man: Studies in the Ideology of Advanced Industrial Society*. Boston: Beacon Press.

Mare, R. D. (1980) Social background and school continuation decisions. *Journal of the American Statistical Association*, 75, 295–305.

Mark, N., Smith-Lovin, L. and Ridgeway, C. L. (1999) The emergence of status value. Paper presented at the American Sociological Association meetings.

Markoff, J. (1996a) *Waves of Democracy: Social Movements and Political Change*. Thousand Oaks, CA: Pine Forge Press.

Markoff, J. (1996b) *The Abolition of Feudalism: Peasants, Lords, and Legislators in the French Revolution*. University Park: Pennsylvania State University Press.

Marks, J. (1995) *Human Biodiversity: Genes, Race, and History*. New York: Aldine de Gruyter.

Marmot, M. G., Bobak, M. and Smith, G. D. (1995) Explanations for social inequalities in health. In B. C. Amick, S. Lovine, A. R. Tarlov, and D. C. Walsh (eds), *Society and Health*. New York: Oxford University Press.

Marmot, M. G., Bosma, H., Hemingway, H., Brunner, E. and Stansfeld, S. (1997) Contribution of job control and other risk factors to social variations in coronary heart disease incidence. *Lancet*, 350, 235–9.

Marmot, M. G., Shipley, M. G. and Rose, G. (1984) Inequalities in death – specific explanations of a general pattern? *Lancet*, i, 1003–6.

Marshall, G. (ed.) (1998) *A Dictionary of Sociology*. New York: Oxford University Press.

Marshall, G., Newby, H., Rose, D. and Vogler, C. (1988) *Social Class in Modern Britain.* London: Hutchinson.

Marshall, T. H. (1950) *Citizenship and Social Class, and Other Essays.* Cambridge: Cambridge University Press.

Marshall, T. H. (1964) *Class, Citizenship, and Social Development: essays.* Garden City, NY: Doubleday.

Martell, L. (1994) *Ecology and Society.* Amherst: University of Massachusetts Press.

Martin, G. D. (1996) *Promoting Participation in Development – a Case Study of PRADAN.* Madurai, Tamil Nadu, India: Research and Documentation Resource Centre; and Professional Assistance for Development Action (PRADAN).

Martinez-Alier, J. (1995) Commentary: the environment as a luxury good or "too poor to be green." *Ecological Economics*, 13, 1–10.

Marwell, G. and Oliver, P. (1993) *The Critical Mass in Collective Action: A Micro-Social Theory.* Cambridge: Cambridge University Press.

Marx, A. (1998) *Making Race and Nation: a Comparison of South Africa, The United States, and Brazil.* Cambridge: Cambridge University Press.

Marx, K. (1956) *Selected Writings in Sociology and Social Philosophy.* London: Watts.

Marx, K. and Engels, F. (1848) *Manifesto of the Communist Party.* Moscow: Foreign Languages.

Mason, D. A. and Good, T. L. (1993) Effects of two-group and whole-class teaching on regrouped elementary students' mathematics achievement. *American Educational Research Journal*, 30, 328–60.

Mason, P. (1994) Decomposing the unobservable: educational attainment and wage discrimination among African-Americans, Latinos and Whites. Working paper, Wayne State University.

Massey, D. (1984) *Spatial Divisions of Labour.* London: Macmillan.

Massey, D. (1990) American apartheid: Segregation and the making of the underclass. *American Journal of Sociology*, 96, 329–57.

Massey, D. (1994) *Space, Class and Gender.* Cambridge: Polity.

Massey, D. and Denton, N. A. (1993) *American Apartheid: Segregation and the Making of the Underclass.* Cambridge, MA: Harvard University Press.

Massey, D. and Espinosa, K. E. (1997) What's driving Mexico–US migration? A theoretical, empirical, and policy analysis. *American Journal of Sociology*, 102, 939–99.

Mathews, A. M. and Brown, K. (1987) Retirement as a critical life event. *Research on Aging*, 9, 548–71.

Matschinger, H., Siegrist, J., Siegrist, K. and Dittmann, K. H. (1986) Type A as a coping career: towards a conceptual and methodological redefinition. In T. Schmidt, M. Dembroski and G. Blumchen (eds), *Biological and Psychological Factors in Cardiovascular Disease.* Berlin: Springer Verlag.

Maume, D. J. Jr, Cancio, A. S. and Evans, T. D. (1996) Cognitive skills and racial inequality: reply to Farkas and Vicknair. *American Sociological Review*, 61, 561–4.

Maxson, C. and Klein, M. (1997) *Responding to Troubled Youth.* New York: Oxford University Press.

Maxwell, N. (1994) The effect on black–white wage differences of differences in the quantity and quality of education. *Industrial and Labor Relations Review*, 47, 249–64.

May, H. (1976) *The Enlightenment in America.* New York: Oxford University Press.

Mayer, S. E. (1997) *What Money Can't Buy: Family Income and Children's Life Chances.* Cambridge, MA: Harvard University Press.

Mead, L. (1992) *The New Politics of Poverty.* New York: Basic Books.

Meadwell, H. (1995) Post-Marxism, no friend of civil society. In J. A. Hall (ed.), *Civil Society*. Cambridge: Polity Press.

Meaney, M. J., Mitchell, J. B., Aitken, D. H., Bhatnagar, S., Bodnoff, S. R., Iny, L. J. and Sarrieau, A. (1991) The effects of neonatal handling on the development of the adrenocortical response to stress: implications for neuropathology and cognitive deficits in later life. *Psychoneuroendocrinology*, 16, 85–103.

Mellor, E. (1987) Workers at the minimum wage or less: who they are and the jobs they hold. *Monthly Labor Review*, 110, 34–8.

Menchik, P. L. and Jianakoplos, N. A. (1997) Black–white wealth inequality: is inheritance the reason? *Economic Inquiry*, 35(2), 428–42.

Mendras, M., with Cole, A. (1991) *Social Change in Modern France*. Cambridge: Cambridge University Press.

Mermet, G. (1995) *Francoscopie 1995*. Paris: Larousse.

Merrill, D. M. (1997) *Caring for Elderly Parents: Juggling Work, Family, and Caregiving in Middle and Working Class Families*. New York: Greenwood Press.

Merry, S. E. (1997) Global human rights and local social movements in legally plural world. *Canadian Journal of Law and Society*, 12, 247–71.

Merton, R. K. (1949) *Social Theory and Social Structure*. New York: The Free Press.

Meyer, D. S. and Tarrow, S. (1998) A movement society: contentious politics for a new century. In D. S. Meyer and S. Tarrow (eds), *The Social Movement Society: Contentious Politics for a New Century*. Lanham, MD: Rowman and Littlefield.

Meyer, J. W. and Rowan, B. (1988) The structure of educational organizations. In M. Meyer (ed.), *Environments and Organizations*. San Francisco: Jossey-Bass.

Michaels, J. and Wiggins, J. A. (1976) Effects of mutual dependency and dependency asymmetry on social exchange. *Sociometry*, 39, 368–76.

Michels, R. (1949) *First Lectures in Political Sociology*. Minneapolis: University of Minnesota Press.

Miles, S. (1998) *Consumerism as a Way of Life*. Newbury Park, CA: Sage.

Milkman, R. (1997) *Farewell to the Factory: Auto Workers in the Late Twentieth Century*. Chicago: University of Chicago Press.

Miller, E. (1997) Intellectual history after the earthquakes: a study in discourse. *The History Teacher*, 30, 357–71.

Miller, L. S. (1995) *An American Imperative: Accelerating Minority Educational Advancement*. New Haven, CT: Yale University Press.

Mills, C. W. (1942) *Sociology and Pragmatism: the Higher Learning in America*. New York: Oxford University Press.

Mills, C. W. (1959) *The Sociological Imagination*. London: Oxford University Press.

Minkoff, D. C. (1994) From service provision to institutional advocacy: the shifting legitimacy of organizational forms. *Social Forces*, 72, 943–69.

Minkoff, D. C. (1997a) The sequencing of social movements. *American Sociological Review*, 62, 779–99.

Minkoff, D. C. (1997b) Producing social capital: national social movements and civil society. *American Behavioral Scientist*, 40, 606–19.

Mirowsky, J, and Ross, C. (1989) *Social Causes of Psychological Distress*. New York: Aldine de Gruyter.

Misztal, B. A. (1996) *Trust in Modern Society*. Cambridge: Polity Press.

Mittleman, M. A., Maclure, M., Sherwood, J. B., Mulry, R. P., Tofler, G. H., Jacobs, S. C., Friedman, R., Benson, H. and Muller, J. E. (1995) Triggering of acute myocardial infarction onset by episodes of anger. *Circulation*, 92, 1720–5.

Moffett, S. H. (1992) *A History of Christianity in Asia, Volume 1: Beginnings to 1500.* San Francisco: Harper San Francisco.

Mol, A. P. J. (1995) *The Refinement of Production: Ecological Modernization Theory and the Chemical Industry.* Utrecht: Van Arkel.

Mol, A. P. J. (1997) Ecological modernization: industrial transformation and environmental reform. In M. Redclift and G. Woodgate (eds), *The International Handbook of Environmental Sociology.* London: Edward Elgar.

Mol, A. P. J. and Spaargaren, G. (2000) Ecological modernization theory in debate: a review. *Environmental Politics.*

Molm, L. D. (1989) The structure and use of power: a comparison of reward and punishment power. *Social Psychology Quarterly,* 51, 108–22.

Molm, L. D. (1990) Structure, action and outcomes: the dynamics of power in exchange relations. *American Social Review,* 55, 427–47.

Molm, L. D. (1997) *Coercive Power in Social Exchange.* New York: Cambridge.

Molm, L. D. (2000a) Power in negotiated and reciprocal exchange. *American Sociological Review,* 65.

Molm, L. D. (2000b) Risk and trust in social exchange: an experimental test of a classical proposition. *American Journal of Sociology,* 105.

Molm, L. D. and Cook, K. S. (1995) Social exchange and exchange networks. In K. S. Cook, G. A. Fine and J. S. House (eds), *Sociological Perspectives on Social Psychology.* Boston: Allyn and Bacon.

Moore, B. (1966) *The Social Origins of Dictatorship and Democracy.* Boston: Beacon Press.

Moore, B. L. (1996a) *To Serve My Country, to Serve My Race: the Story of the Only African American Wacs Stationed Overseas during World War II.* New York: New York University Press.

Moore, T. S. (1996b) *The Disposable Work Force: Worker Displacement and Employment Instability in America.* New York: Aldine de Gruyter.

Morris, A. (1984) *The Origins of the Civil Rights Movement: Black Communities Organizing for Change.* New York: Free Press.

Morris, M. and Western, B. (1999) Inequality in earnings at the close of the twentieth century. *Annual Review of Sociology,* 25, 623–57.

Mort, J.-A. (ed.) (1998) *Not Your Father's Union Movement: Inside the AFL-CIO.* New York: Verso.

Mortimer, J. T. and Kruger, H. (2000) Transition from school to work in the United States and Germany: formal pathways matter. In M. T. Hallinan (ed.), *Handbook of Sociology of Education.* New York: Plenum/Kluwer.

Moss, P. and Tilly, C. (1991) *Why Black Men Are Doing Worse in the Labor Market: a Review of Supply-side and Demand-side Explanations.* New York: Social Science Research Council.

Mounts, N. S. and Steinberg, L. (1995) An ecological analysis of peer influence on adolescent grade point average and drug use. *Developmental Psychology,* 31, 915–22.

Mueller, M. (1999) Digital convergence and its consequences. *Javnost: The Public,* 6, 11–27.

Mullins, N. C. (1973) *Theories and Theory Groups in Contemporary American Sociology.* New York: Harper and Row.

Murphy, R. (1994) *Rationality and Nature.* Boulder, CO: Westview Press.

Murphy, R. (1997) *Sociology and Nature.* Boulder, CO: Westview Press.

Murray, C. (1984) *Losing Ground: American Social Policy, 1950–1980.* New York: Basic Books.

Myers, D. (1998a) Dimensions of economic adaptation by Mexican-origin men. In M. Suárez-Orozco (ed.), *Crossings: Mexican Immigration in Interdisciplinary Perspectives*. Cambridge, MA: Harvard University Press.

Myers, M. A. (1998b) *Race, Labor, and Punishment in the New South*. Columbus: Ohio State University Press.

Myers, S. Jr (1989) How voluntary is black unemployment and black labor forse withdrawal? In S. Shulman and W. Darity Jr (eds), *The Question of Discrimination: Racial Inequality in the US Labor Market*. Middletown, CT: Wesleyan University Press.

Nahirny, V. C. and Fishman, J. A. (1965) American immigrant groups: ethnic identification and the problem of generations. In W. Sollors (ed.), *Theories of Ethnicity: a Classical Reader*. New York: New York University Press (1996).

Nairn, T. (1997) *Faces of Nationalism: Janus Revisted*. London: Verso.

Nakao, K. and Treas, J. (1994) Updating occupational prestige and socioeconomic scores: how the new measures measure up. In P. V. Marsden (ed.), *Sociological Methodology*. Oxford: Blackwell.

National Center for Health Statistics (1992) *Monthly Vital Statistics, Report 41*. Washington, DC: US Government Printing Office.

National Economic Council (1998) *Women and Retirement Security: Executive Summary*. Washington, DC: NEC.

National Research Council (1998) *Children of Immigrants: Health Adjustment, and Public Assistance*. Washington, DC: National Research Council.

Neal, D. and Johnson, W. (1995) The role of premarket factors in black–white wage differenccs. Working paper no. 5124, NBER.

Negengast, C. and Turner, T. (1997) Universal human rights versus cultural relativity. *Journal of Anthropological Research*, 53, 269–72.

Neidhardt, F. and Rucht, D. (1993) Auf dem Weg in die Bewegungsgesellschaft? Uber die stabilisierbarkeit sozialer Bewegungen. [On the way to a movement society? The stabilization of social movements.] *Sozialer Welt*, 44, 305–26.

Neill, S. (1986) *A History of Christian Missions*. New York: Penguin.

Nelkin, D. and Andrews, L. (1999) DNA identification and surveillance creep. *Sociology of Health and Illness*, 21, 689–706.

Nesbitt, P. D. (1997) *Feminization of the Clergy in America: Occupational and Organizational Perspectives*. New York: Oxford University Press.

Neuman, W. R. (1991) *The Future of the Mass Audience*. Cambridge: Cambridge University Press.

Newby, H. (1979) *Green and Pleasant Land?* London: Hutchinson.

Newcomb, T. M. (1961) *The Acquaintance Process*. New York: Holt, Rinehart, and Winston.

New Scientist (1995) Genes in black and white, *New Scientist*, July 8, 34–7 (no by-line).

Nisbet, R. A. (1966) *The Sociological Tradition*. New York: Basic Books.

Nock, S. L. (1998) *Marriage in Men's Lives*. New York: Oxford University Press.

Nollert, M. (1995) Neocorporatism and political protest in the western democracies: a cross-national analysis. In J. C. Jenkins and B. Klandermans (eds), *The Politics of Social Protest: Comparative Perspectives on States and Social Movements*. Minneapolis/London: University of Minnesota Press/UCL Press.

Nord, M. (1994) Keeping the poor in their place: the proximate processes that maintain spatial concentration of poverty in the United States. PhD dissertation, Pennsylvania State University, University Park.

Nord, M. and Luloff, A. E. (1995) Homeless children and their families in New Hampshire: a rural perspective. *Social Science Review*, 69, 461–78.

Nord, M., Jemison, K. and Bickel, G. (1999) Measuring food security in the United States: prevalence of food insecurity and hunger, by state, 1996–1998. *Food Assistance and Nutrition Research Report Number 2.* Washington, DC: United States Department of Agriculture.

Noshpitz, J. D. and Coddington, R. D. (1990) *Stressors and the Adjustment Disorders.* New York: John Wiley and Sons.

Nozick, R. (1973) Distributive justice. *Philosophy and Public Affairs*, 3.

Nozick, R. (1974) *Anarchy, State and Utopia.* Oxford: Blackwell.

Oakes, J. (1985) *Keeping Track: How Schools Structure Inequality.* New Haven, CT: Yale University Press.

Oakes, J. (1990) *Multiplying Inequalities: the Effects of Race, Social Class, and Tracking on Opportunities to Learn Mathematics and Science.* Santa Monica, CA: RAND.

Oakes, J. (1994) More the misapplied technology: a normative and political response to Hallinan on tracking. *Sociology of Education*, 67, 84–9, 91.

O'Brien, M. and Penna, S. (1998) *Theorizing Welfare: Enlightenment and Modern Society.* Newbury Park, CA: Sage.

O'Connor, J. (1994) Is sustainable capitalism possible? In M. O'Connor (ed.), *Is Capitalism Sustainable?.* New York: Guilford.

O'Donnell, G. (1973) *Modernization and Bureaucratic-Authoritarianism.* Berkeley: University of California, Institute of International Studies.

O'Donnell, G. and Schmitter, P. (1986) *Transition from Authoritarian Rule: Tentative Conclusions about Uncertain Democracies.* Baltimore: Johns Hopkins University Press.

O'Donnell, G., Schmitter, P. and Whitehead, L. (eds) (1986) *Transitions from Authoritarian Rule: Latin America.* Baltimore: Johns Hopkins University Press.

Offe, C. and Wisenthal, H. (1980) Two logics of collective action: Theoretical notes on social class and organizational form. In M. Zeitlin (ed.), *Political Power and Social Theory.* Greenwich: Connecticut University Press.

Ogbu, J. and Simons, H. D. (1998) Voluntary and involuntary minorities: a cultural-ecological theory of school performance with some implications for education. *Anthropology and Education Quarterly*, 29, 1155–88.

Oldenburg, R. (1989) *The Great Good Places.* New York: Marlowe and Company.

O'Leary, A. (1990) Stress, emotion and human immune function. *Psychological Bulletin*, 108, 363–82.

Oliver, M. and Shapiro, T. (1995) *Black Wealth/White Wealth: a New Perspective on Racial Inequality.* New York: Routledge.

Oliver, P. E. (1984) If you don't do it, nobody else will: active and token contributors to local collective action. *American Sociological Review*, 49, 601–10.

Olsen, L. (1998) *Made in America: Immigrant Students in Our Public Schools.* New York: The New Press.

Olson, D. (1998) Religious pluralism in contemporary US counties. *American Sociological Review*, 63, 759–61.

Olson, M. (1965) *The Logic of Collective Action.* Cambridge, MA: Harvard University Press.

Omni, M. and Winant, H. (1986) *Racial Formation in the United States.* New York: Routledge.

O'Neill, J. (1990) The role of human capital in earnings differences between black and white men. *Journal of Economic Perspectives*, 4, 25–46.

O'Neill, J. (1994) *The Missing Child in Liberal Theory.* Toronto: University of Toronto Press.

Oommen, T. K. (1997) *Citizenship, Nationality, and Ethnicity: Reconciling Competing Identities*. Cambridge: Polity Press.

Ophuls, W. (1977) *Ecology and the Politics of Scarcity*. San Francisco: W. H. Freeman.

Orfield, G. (1998) Commentary on the education of Mexican immigrant children. In M. Suárez-Orozco (ed.), *Crossings: Mexican Immigration in Interdisciplinary Perspectives*. Cambridge, MA: Harvard University Press.

Owen, D. (ed.) (1997) *Sociology after Postmodernism*. Thousand Oaks, CA: Sage Publications.

Padgett, J. F. and Ansell, C. K. (1993) Robust action and the rise of the Medici, 1400–1434. *American Journal of Sociology*, 98, 1259–319.

Padilla, A., Cervantes, R., Maldonado, M. and Garcia, R. (1988) Coping responses to psychosocial stressors among Mexican and Central American immigrants. *Journal of Community Psychology*, 16, 418–27.

Pareto, V. (1935) *The Mind and Society*. New York: Harcourt, Brace and Company.

Park, R. E. and Burgess, E. W. (1921) *Introduction to the Science of Sociology*. Chicago: University of Chicago Press.

Parkin, F. (1968) *Middle Class Radicalism*. Manchester: Manchester University Press.

Parry, G., Moyser, G. and Day, N. (1992) *Political Participation and Democracy in Britain*. Cambridge: Cambridge University Press.

Parsons, T. (1959) An approach to the sociology of knowledge. In J. E. Curtis and J. W. Petras (eds), *The Sociology of Knowledge: a Reader*. London: Duckworth (1970).

Passas, N. and Agnew, R. (1997) *The Future of Anomie Theory*. Boston: Northeastern University Press.

Patchen, M. (1982) *Black–White Contact in Schools: Its Social and Academic Effects*. West Lafayette, IN: Purdue University Press.

Patterson, O. (1998) *Rituals of Blood: Consequences of Slavery in Two American Centuries*. Washington, DC: Civitas Counterpoint.

Payne, C. M. (1995) *I've Got the Light of Freedom*. Berkeley: University of California Press.

Pearlin, L. I. and Schooler (1978) The structure of coping. *Journal of Health and Social Behavior*, 19, 2–21.

Pedraza, S. and Rumbaut, R. G. (eds) (1996) *Origins and Destinies: Immigration, Race, and Ethnicity in America*. Belmont, CA: Wadsworth.

Perlo, V. (1996) *Economics of Racism II: the Roots of Inequality, USA*. New York: International Publishers.

Perotti, R. (1996) Growth, income distribution and democracy: what the data say. *Journal of Economic Growth*, 1, 149–87.

Peters, J. D. (1999) *Speaking into the Air: a History of the Idea of Communication*. Chicago: University of Chicago Press.

Petersen, A. (1998) *Unmasking the Masculine: Men and Identity in a Sceptical Age*. Newbury Park, CA: Sage.

Petersen, W. (1997) *Ethnicity Counts*. New Brunswick, NJ: Transaction.

Phinney, J. (1998) Ethnic identity in adolescents and adults. In P. Organista, K. Chun and G. Marín (eds), *Readings in Ethnic Psychology*. New York: Routledge.

Pierce, J. L. (1995) *Gender Trials: Emotional Lives in Contemporary Law Firms*. Berkeley: University of California Press.

Pinkney, T. (1991) *Raymond Williams*. Bridgend: Seren Books.

Piven, F. F. and Cloward, R. (1992) Normalizing collective protest. In A. D. Morris and C. M. Mueller (eds), *Frontiers in Social Movement Theory*. New Haven, CT: Yale University Press.

Plotnick, R. D., Smollensky, E., Evenhouse, E. and Reilly, S. (1998) *The Twentieth Century Record of Inequality and Poverty in the United States*. Discussion paper no. 1166–98. Madison, WI: Institute for Research on Poverty.

Polednak, A. P. (1989) *Racial and Ethnic Differences in Disease*. New York: Oxford University Press.

Pollard, K. M. and O'Hare, W. (1990) Selective migration of rural high school seniors in the 1980s. Paper delivered at the Rural Sociological Society Meetings.

Polletta, F. (1997) Culture and its discontents: recent theorizing on the cultural dimensions of protest. *Sociological Inquiry*, 67, 431–50.

Popkin, S. (1979) *The Rational Peasant*. Berkeley: University of California Press.

Portes, A. (ed.) (1996) *The New Second Generation*. New York: Russell Sage Foundation.

Portes, A. (1998) Social capital: its origins and applications in modern sociology. *American Review of Sociology*, 24, 1– 24.

Portes, A., Dore-Cabral, C. and Landolt, P. (1997) *The Urban Caribbean: Transitions in the New Gobal Economy*. Baltimore: Johns Hopkins University Press.

Portes, A. and Rumbaut, R. G. (1990) *Immigrant America: a Portrait*. Berkeley: University of California Press (2nd edn, 1996).

Portes, A. and Rumbaut, R. G. (2000) *Legacies: the Story of the New Second Generation*. Berkeley and New York: University of California Press and Russell Sage Foundation.

Portes, A. and Zhou, M. (1993) The new second generation: segmented assimilation and its variants. *Annals of the American Academy*, 530, 74.

Potuchek, J. L. (1997) *Who Supports the Family: Gender and Breadwinning in Dual Earner Marriages*. Stanford, CA: Stanford University Press.

Powell, W. W. (1990) Neither market nor hierarchy: network forms of organization. In B. M. Staw and L. L. Cummings (eds), *Research in Organizational Behavior*. Greenwich, CT: JAI Press.

Powell, W. W. and Clemens, E. S. (eds) (1998) *Private Action and the Public Good*. New Haven, CT: Yale University Press.

Prades, J. A. (1999) Global environmental change and contemporary society: classical sociological analysis revisited. *International Sociology*, 14, 7–32.

Preston, S. and Taubman, P. (1994) Socioeconomic differences in adult mortality and health status. In L. Martin and S. Preston (eds), *Demography of Aging*. Washington, DC: National Academy Press.

Prigogine, I. and Stengers, I. (1984) *Order out of Chaos: Man's New Dialogue with Nature*. New York: Bantam Books.

Przeworski, A. (1977) Proletariat into class: the process of class formation from Karl Kautsky's "the class struggle" to recent controversies. *Politics and Society*, 7, 343–401.

Pulver, G. C. (1995) Economic forces shaping the future of rural America. In by L. J. Beaulieu and D. Mulkey (eds), *Investing in People: the Human Capital Needs of Rural America*. Boulder, CO: Westview Press.

Pulzer, P. G. J. (1967) *Political Representation and Elections: Parties and Voting in Great Britain*. New York: Praeger.

Punch, M. (1996) *Dirty Business: Exploring Corporate Misconduct, Analysis, and Cases*. Thousand Oaks, CA: Sage.

Putnam, R. (1993) *Making Democracy Work: Civic Tradition in Modern Italy*. Princeton, NJ: Princeton University Press.

Pyle, R. E. (1996) *Persistence and Change in the Protestant Establishment*. Westport, CT: Praeger Publishers.

Quadagno, J. (1996) Social Security and the myth of the entitlement crisis. *The Gerontologist*, 36, 391–9.

Quadagno, J. (1999) *Aging and the Life Course*. New York: McGraw-Hill College.

Quinn, J. and Kozy, M. (1996) The role of bridge jobs in the retirement transition: gender, race, and ethnicity. *The Gerontologist*, 36, 363–72.

Quinn, J. B. (1997) Social Security in better shape than many say. *Washington Post*, May 3, 1C.

Ramirez, F. O., Soysal, Y. and Shanahan, S. (1997) The changing logic of political citizenship: cross national acquisition of women's suffrage rights, 1890–1990. *American Sociological Review*, 62, 735–43.

Rapaport, L. (1997) *Jews in Germany after the Holocaust: Memory, Identity, and Jewish–German Relations*. Cambridge: Cambridge University Press.

Rawls, J. (1971) *A Theory of Justice*. Cambridge, MA: Harvard University Press.

Redclift, M. and Woodgate, G. (1997) Sustainability and social construction. In M. Redclift and G. Woodgate (eds), *The International Handbook of Environmental Sociology*. London: Edward Elgar.

Reddy, W. (1987) *Money and Liberty in Modern Europe: a Critique of Historical Understanding*. Cambridge: Cambridge University Press.

Redfield, R. (1947) The folk society. *American Journal of Sociology*, 52, 293–308.

Reich, R. B. (1991) *The Work of Nations*. New York: Vantage.

Reinarman, C. and Levine, H. G. (1997) *Crack in America: Demon Drugs and Social Justice*. Berkeley: University of California Press.

Reis, E. R. (1998) Banfield's amoral familism revisited: implication of high inequality structures for civil society. In J. C. Alexander (ed.), *Real Civil Societies. Dilemmas of Institutionalization*. London: Sage.

Reitz, J. G. (1998) *Warmth of the Welcome: the Social Causes of Economic Success for Immigrants in Different Nations and Cities*. Boulder, CO: Westview.

Reitzes, D. C., Mutran, E. and Pope, H. (1991) Location and well-being among retired men. *Journal of Gerontology*, 46, 195–203.

Resnick, L. B. and Wirt, J. G. (1996) The changing workplace. In L. B. Resnick and J. G. Wirt (eds), *Linking School and Work*. San Francisco, CA: Jossey Bass.

Reynolds, L.T. (1998) Two deadly diseases and one nearly fatal cure: the sorry state of American sociology. *American Sociologist*, 29, 20–37.

Ridgeway, C. L. (1991) The social construction of status value: gender and other nominal characteristics. *Social Forces*, 70, 367–86.

Riley, M. W. (1971) Social gerontology and the age stratification of society. *American Sociological Review*, 52, 1–14.

Rindfuss, R. R. and Vandenheuvel, A. (1990) Cohabitation: a precursor to marriage or an alternative to being single. *Population and Development Review*, 16, 703–26.

Rinehart, J., Huxley, C. and Robertson, D. (1997) *Just Another Car Factory? Lean Production and Its Discontents*. Ithaca, NY: Cornell University Press.

Ring, P. S. and Van de Ven, A. H. (1994) Developmental processes of cooperative interorganizational relationships. *Academy of Management Journal*, 19, 90–118.

Ringer, F. (1990) The intellectual field, intellectual history, and the sociology of knowledge. *Theory and Society*, 19, 269–94.

Risman, B. J. (1998) *Gender Vertigo: American Families in Transition*. New Haven, CT: Yale University Press.

Rist, R. (1970) Student social class and teacher expectations: the self-fulfilling prophecy in ghetto education. *Harvard Educational Review*, 40, 411–51.

Roberts, J. T. and Grimes, P. (1997) Carbon intensity and economic development, 1962–1971: a brief exploration of the environmental Kuznets curve. *World Development*, 25, 191–8.

Roberts, R., Roberts, C. and Chen, Y. R. (1998) Ethnocultural differences in prevalence of adolescent depression. In P. Organista, K. Chun and G. Marín (ed.), *Readings in Ethnic Psychology*. New York: Routledge.

Robinson, R. and Johnson, W. (1997) *The Buddhist Religion*. Belmont, CA: Wadsworth.

Rodgers, W. III (1994) The relationship between macroeconomic conditions and male black–white earnings ratios: the 1980s in an historical context. Working paper, College of William and Mary.

Rodgers, W. III and Spriggs, W. E. (1996) What does the AFQT really measure? Race, wages, and schooling and the AFQT score. *Review of Black Political Economy*, 24, 13–46.

Rodriguez, L. (1993) *Always Running*. New York: Touchstone Books.

Rogler, L. (1998) Research on mental health services for Hispanics: targets of convergence. In P. Organista, K. Chun and G. Marín (eds), *Readings in Ethnic Psychology*. New York: Routledge.

Roistacher, R. C. (1973) Peer nominations, clique structures and exploratory behavior in boys at four junior high schools. *Dissertation Abstracts International*, 33B, no. 9.

Rollins, J. (1985) *Between Women: Domestics and Their Employers*. Philadelphia: Temple University Press.

Romero, M. (1987) Domestic service in the transition from rural to urban life: the case of La Chicana. *Women's Studies*, 13, 199–222.

Romero, M. (1988) Chicanas modernize domestic service. *Qualitative Sociology*, 11, 319–34.

Romero, M. (1992) *Maid in the USA*. New York: Routledge.

Rosa, E. A. and Dietz, T. (1998) Climate change and society: speculation, construction, and scientific investigation. *International Sociology*, 13, 421–55.

Rosenbaum, J. E. (1976) *Making Inequalities: the Hidden Curriculum of High School Tracking*. New York: Wiley.

Rosenbaum, J. E. (1996) Policy issues of research on the high school-to-work transition. *Sociology of Education*, 69, 102–22.

Rosenbaum, J. E. and Jones, S. A. (2000) Interactions between high schools and labor markets. In M. T. Hallinan (ed.), *Handbook of Sociology of Education*. New York: Plenum/Kluwer.

Rosenbaum, J. E. and Kariya, T. (1989) From high school to work: Market and institutional mechanisms in Japan. *American Journal of Sociology*, 94, 1334–65.

Rosenbaum, J. E. and Roy, K. (1996) Trajectories for success in the transition from school to work. Paper presented at the annual meetings of the American Educational Research Association, New York.

Ross, C. and Wu, C. (1996) Education, age, and the cumulative advantage in health. *Journal of Health and Social Behavior*, 37, 104–20.

Rothenbuhler, E. W. (1988) The liminal fight: mass strikes as ritual and interpretation. In J. C. Alexander (ed.), *Durkheimian Sociology*. Cambridge: Cambridge University Press.

Rothenbuhler, E. W. and Streck, J. M. (1998) The economics of the music industry. In A. Alexander, J. Owers and R. Carveth (eds), *Media Economics: Theory and Practice*. Mahwah, NJ: LEA.

Rowan, B. and Miracle, A. W. Jr (1983) Systems of ability grouping and the stratification of achievement in elementary schools. *Sociology of Education*, 56, 133–44.

Roy, W. G. (1997) *Socializing Capital: the Rise of the Large Industrial Corporation in America*. Princeton, NJ: Princeton University Press.

Rubin, L. B. (1976) *Worlds of Pain*. New York: Basic Books.

Rubin, L. B. (1994) *Families on the Fault Line*. New York: HarperCollins.

Rucht, D. (1998) The structure and culture of collective protest in Germany since 1950. In D. S. Meyer and S. Tarrow (eds), *The Social Movement Society*. Lanham, MD: Rowman and Littlefield.

Ruggles, P. (1990) *Drawing the Line: Alternative Poverty Measures and Their Implications for Public Policy*. Washington, DC: The Urban Institute Press.

Rumbaut, R. G. (1994) Origins and destinies: immigration to the United States since World War II. *Sociological Forum*, 9, 583–621.

Rumbaut, R. G. (1995) The new Californians: comparative research findings on the educational progress of immigrant children. In R. Rumbaut and W. Cornelius (eds), *California's Immigrant Children*. La Jolla, CA: Center for US–Mexican Studies.

Rumbaut, R. G. (1996) Becoming American: acculturation, achievement, and aspirations among children of immigrants. Paper presented at the Annual Meeting of the American Association for the Advancement of Science, Baltimore, Maryland.

Rumbaut, R. G. (1997a) Ties that bind: immigration and immigrant families in the United States. In A. Booth, A. C. Crouter and N. S. Landale (eds), *Immigration and the Family: Research and Policy on US Immigrants*. Mahwah, NJ: Lawrence Erlbaum.

Rumbaut, R. G. (1997b) Achievement and ambition among children of immigrants in Southern California. Paper presented to the Jerome Levy Economics Institute of Bard College, Annandale-on-the-Hudson, NY.

Rumbaut, R. G. (1998) Coming of age in immigrant America. *Research Perspectives on Migration*, 1, 1–14.

Runciman, D. (1997) *Pluralism and the Personality of the State*. Cambridge: Cambridge University Press.

Rural Sociological Society Task Force on Persistent Rural Poverty (1993) *Persistent Poverty in Rural America*. Boulder, CO: Westview Press.

Rutter, V. and Schwartz, P. (1996) Same-sex couples: courtship, commitment, context. In A. E. Auhagen and M. von Salisch (eds), *The Diversity of Human Relationships*. Cambridge: Cambridge University Press.

Said, E. (1979) *Orientalism*. New York: Random House.

Salzinger, L. (1991) A maid by any other name: the transformation of "dirty work" by Central American immigrants. In M. Burawoy, A. Burton, A. A. Ferguson, K. J. Fox, J. Gamson, N. Gartrell, L. Hurst, C. Kurzman, L. Salzinger, J. Schiffman and S. Ui (eds), *Ethnography Unbound: Power and Resistance in the Modern Metropolis*. Berkeley: University of California Press.

Sanderson, S. K. (1995) *Civilizations and World Systems: Studying World Historical Change*. Walnut Creek, CA: Altamira.

Sanneh, L. (1989) *Translating the Message: the Missionary Impact on Culture*. Maryknoll, NY: Orbis.

Sarason, I., Jonson, J. H. and Siegel, J. M. (1978) Assessing the impact of life changes: Development of the Life Experiences Survey. *Journal of Consulting and Clinical Psychology*, 46, 932–46.

Sartori, G. (1969) From the sociology of politics to political sociology. In S. M. Lipset (ed.), *Politics and the Social Sciences*. New York: Oxford University Press.

Sassen, S. (1998) *Globalization and Its Discontents: Essays on the New Mobility of People and Money*. New York: New Press.

Savage, M. (1987) *The Dynamics of Working-class Politics: the Labour Movement in Preston, 1880–1940*. New York: Cambridge University Press.

Savage, M. (2000) *Class Analysis and Social Transformation*. Buckingham: Open University Press.

Savage, M., Barlow, J., Dickens, P. and Fielding, A. J. (1992) *Property, Bureaucracy, and Culture: Middle Class Formation in Contemporary Britain*. New York: Routledge.

Sayer, A. (1992) *Method in Social Science*. London: Routledge.

Sayer, L., Kahn, J. and Falk, W. W. (1998) Considering the country cousin determinants of poverty for rural and urban blacks and whites. Unpublished paper, Center for Population, Gender and Social Inequality, University of Maryland, College Park.

Scanlon, T. (1975) Preference and urgency. *Journal of Philosophy*, 72.

Scannell, P. (1991) *Broadcast Talk*. London: Sage.

Scharlach, A. (1994) Caregiving and employment: competing or complementary roles. *The Gerontologist*, 34, 378–85.

Schlossberg, N. (1984) *Counseling Adults in Transition: Linking Practice to Theory*. New York: Springer.

Schmalenbach, H. (1977) *Herman Schmalenbach: On Society and Experience*. Chicago: University of Chicago Press.

Schmaus, W., Segerstrale, U. and Jesseph D. (1992) A manifesto. *Social Epistemology*, 6, 243–65.

Schnaiberg, A. (1975) Social syntheses of the societal– environmental dialectic: the role of distributional impacts. *Social Science Quarterly*, 56, 5–20.

Schnaiberg, A. (1980) *The Environment*. New York: Oxford University Press.

Schnaiberg, A. and Gould, K. A. (1994) *Environment and Society*. New York: St Martin's Press.

Schnaiberg, A., Weinberg, A. and Pellow, D. (1999) The treadmill of production and the environmental state. Paper presented at the conference on The Environmental State, Northwestern University, Chicago, August.

Schnall, P. L., Schwartz, J. E., Landsbergis, P. A., Warren, K. and Pickering, T. G. (1992) Relation between job strain, alcohol, and ambulatory blood pressure. *Hypertension*, 19, 488– 94.

Schnall, P. L., Schwartz, J. E., Landsbergis, P. A., Warren, K. and Pickering, T. G. (1998) A longitudinal study of job strain and ambulatory blood pressure: results from a 3–year follow-up. *Psychosomatic Medicine*, 60, 697–706.

Schneider, B. and Stevenson, D. (1999) *America's Teenagers: Motivated but Directionless*. New Haven, CT: Yale University Press.

Schneider, B., Swanson, C. B. and Riegle-Crumb, C. (1998) Opportunities for learning: Course sequences and positional advantages. *Social Psychology of Education*, 2, 25–53.

Schneider, G. L. and Guralnik, J. M. (1990) The aging of America. Impact on health care costs. *Journal of the American Medical Association*, 263, 2335–40.

Schneider, W. H. (1996) The history of research on blood group genetics: initial discovery and diffusion. *History and Philosophy of the Life Sciences*, 18(3), 277–303.

Schofield, J. W. and Sager, H. A. (1977) Peer interaction patterns in an integrated middle school. *Sociometry*, 40, 130–8.

Schunk, D. H. and Hanson, A. R. (1985) Peer models: influence on children's self-efficacy and achievement. *Journal of Educational Psychology*, 77, 313–22.

Schusterov, G. A. (1927) Isohaemagglutinierenden Eigenschaften des menschlichen Blutes nach den Ergebnissen einer Untersuchung an Straflingen des Reformatoriums (Arbeithauses) zu Omsk. *Moskovskii Meditsinksii Jurnal*, 1, 1–16.

Schutz, A. (1967) *The Phenomenology of the Social World*. Evanston, IL: Northwestern University Press.

Schwalbe, M. (1998) *The Sociologically Examined Life*. Mountain View, CA: Mayfield.

Schwartz, P. (1994) *Peer Marriage: How Love between Equals Really Works*. New York: The Free Press.

Schweizer, T. and White, D. R. (eds) (1998) *Kinship, Networks, and Exchange*. New York: Cambridge University Press.

Scott, A. (1990) *Ideology and the New Social Movements*. London: Unwin Hyman.

Scott, J. (1991) *Social Network Analysis: a Handbook*. London: Sage.

Seligman, A. B. (1992) *The Idea of Civil Society*. New York: Free Press.

Seligman, A. B. (1997) *The Problem of Trust*. Princeton, NJ: Princeton University Press.

Seligman, A. B. (1998) Between public and private. *Society*, 35, 30–6.

Sen, A. (1973) *On Economic Inequality*. Clarendon Press: Oxford.

Sen, A. (1979) Utilitarianism and welfarism. *Journal of Philosophy*, 76.

Sen, A. (1980) Equality of what? In S. McMurrin (ed.), *The Tanner Lectures in Human Values, volume 1*. Cambridge: Cambridge University Press.

Sen, A. (1981) *Poverty and Famines: an Essay on Entitlement and Deprivation*. Oxford: Clarendon Press.

Sen, A. (1987) *On Ethics and Economics*. Oxford: Blackwell.

Sen, A. (1992) *Inequality Reexamined*. Oxford: Clarendon Press.

Sennett, R. (1991) *The Conscience of the Eye*. London: Faber and Faber.

Serafini, M. W. (1996) Dream machine. *National Journal*, 4, 932–5.

Sewell, W. and Hauser, R. M. (1980): The Wisconsin longitudinal study of social and psychological factors in aspirations and achievements. In *Research in Sociology of Education and Socialization, volume 1*. Greenwich, CT: JAI Press.

Shapin, S. (1992) Discipline and bounding: the history and sociology of science as seen through the externalism–internalism debate. *History of Science*, 30, 333–69.

Shapin, S. (1994) *A Social History of Truth: Civility and Science in Seventeenth-Century England*. Chicago: University of Chicago Press.

Shapiro, I. (1989) *Laboring for Less: Working but Poor in Rural America*. Washington, DC: Center on Budget and Policy Priorities.

Shapiro, T. and Wolff, E. (2000) *Assets and the Disadvantaged: the Benefits of Spreading Asset Ownership*. New York: The Russell Sage Foundation.

Shaver, S. (1991) Considerations of mere logic: the Australian age pension and the politics of means-testing. In J. Myles and J. Quadagno (eds), *States, Labor, and Markets: the Future of Old Age Policy*. Philadelphia: Temple University Press.

Shavit, Y. (1991) Stress-induced immune modulation in animals: Opiates and endogenous opioid peptides. In R. Ader, D. L. Felten and N. Cohen (eds), *Psychoneuroimmunology*. San Diego: Academic Press.

Shavit, Y. and Muller, W. (eds) (1998) *From School to Work: a Comparative Study of Educational Qualifications and Occupational Destinations*. Oxford: Clarendon.

Shavit, Y. and Muller, W. (2000) Vocational secondary education, tracking, and social stratification. In M. T. Hallinan (ed.), *Handbook of Sociology of Education*. New York: Plenum/Kluwer.

Shaw, L. (1996) Special problems of older women workers. In J. Quadagno and D. Street (eds), *Aging for the Twenty-first Century*. New York: St Martin's Press.

Sheley, J. F. and Wright, J. D. (1995) *In the Line of Fire: Youth, Guns, and Violence in Urban America*. New York: Aldine de Gruyter.

Sheller, M. and Urry, J. (2000) The city and the car. *International Journal of Urban and Regional Research*, 24 (in the press).

Sherkat, D. E. and Ellison, C. G. (1999) Recent developments and current controversies in the sociology of religion. *Annual Review of Sociology*, 25, 363–94.

Sherman, A. (1992) *Falling by the Wayside: Children in Rural America*. Washington, DC: Children's Defense Fund.

Sherraden, M. (1991) *Assets and the Poor: a New American Welfare Policy*. New York: M. E. Sharpe.

Sherraden, M. (1997) Building assets among African-American males. Unpublished manuscript. Washington University, St Louis.

Shields, R. (1991) *Places on the Margin*. London: Routledge.

Shils, E. (1958) *The Intellectuals and the Powers and Other Essays*. Chicago: University of Chicago Press.

Shils, E. (1991) The virtue of civil society. *Government and Opposition*, 26, 3–20.

Shipman, P. (1994) *The Evolution of Racism: Human Differences and the Use and Abuse of Science*. New York: Simon and Schuster.

Short, J. F. Jr (1997) *Poverty, Ethnicity, and Violent Crime*. Boulder, CO: Westview Press.

Shuval, J. (1980) Migration and stress. In I. L. Kutasshm et al. (eds) *Handbook on Stress and Anxiety: Contemporary Knowledge, Theory, and Treatment*. San Francisco: Jossey-Bass.

Siegrist, J. (1996) Adverse health effects of high-effort/low-reward conditions. *Journal of Occupational Health Psychology*, 1, 27–41.

Siegrist, J., Peter, R., Junge, A., Cremer, P. and Seidel, D. (1990) Low status control, high effort at work and ischemic heart disease: prospective evidence from blue collar men. *Social Science and Medicine*, 331, 1127–34.

Sills, D. L. (ed.) (1968) *International Encyclopedia of the Social Sciences*. New York: Macmillan.

Simmel, G. (1950) *The Sociology of Georg Simmel* (trans., ed. and intro K. H. Wolff). Glencoe, IL: Free Press.

Simmel, G. (1955) *Conflict and the Web of Group Affiliations*. Glencoe, IL: Free Press.

Sisk, D. T. (1995) *Democratization in South Africa: the Elusive Contract*. Princeton, NJ: Princeton University Press.

Skeggs, B. (1997) *Formations of Class and Gender: Becoming Respectable*. Thousand Oaks, CA: Sage.

Skilton, A. (1997) *A Concise History of Buddhism*. Birmingham: Windhouse.

Skinner, Q. (1969) Meaning and understanding in the history of ideas. *History and Theory*, 8, 3–53.

Skinner, Q. (1996) *Reason and Rhetoric in the Philosophy of Hobbes*. Cambridge: Cambridge University Press.

Skirbekk, G. (1993) Modernization of the lifeworld. Universality and plurality in the process of modernization. In *Rationality and Modernity. Essays in Philosophical Pragmatics*. Oslo: Skandinavian University Press.

Skocpol, T. (1979) *States and Social Revolutions: a Comparative Analysis of France, Russia, and China*. Cambridge: Cambridge University Press.

Skocpol, T. (1992) *Protecting Soldiers and Mothers: the Political Origins of Social Policy in the United States*. Cambridge, MA: Belknap Press.

Skocpol, T. (1996) Unravelling from above. *The American Prospect*, 25, 20–5.

Skocpol, T., Evans, P. and Rueschemeyer, D. (eds) (1985) *Bringing the State Back*. Cambridge: Cambridge University Press.

Skolnick, J. and Currie, E. (1998) *Crisis in American Institutions*. Glenview, IL: Scott, Foresman/Little, Brown College Division.

Skrentny, J. D. (1996) *The Ironies of Affirmative Action: Politics, Culture, and Justice in America*. Chicago: University of Chicago Press.

Skvoretz, J. and Fararo, T. J. (1996) Status and participation on task groups: a dynamic network model. *American Journal of Sociology*, 101, 1366–49.

Slavin, R. E. (1987) Ability grouping and student achievement in elementary schools: a best-evidence synthesis. *Review of Educational Research*, 57, 293–336.

Slavin, R. E. (1990) Ability grouping in secondary schools: a best-evidence synthesis. *Review of Educational Research*, 60, 471–99.

Slevin, K. F. and Wingrove, C. R. (1998) *From Stumbling Blocks to Stepping Stones: the Life Experiences of Fifty Professional African American Women*. New York: New York University Press.

Sluzki, C. (1979) Migration and family conflict. *Family Process*, 18(40), 379–90.

Smajkic, A. and Weane, S. (1995) Special issues of newly arrived refugee groups. In S. Somach (eds), *Issues of War Trauma and Working with Refugees: a Compilation of Resources*. Washington DC: Center for Applied Linguistics Refugee Service Center.

Smart, J. F. and Smart, D. W. (1995) Acculturation stress of Hispanics: loss and challenge. *Journal of Counseling and Development* 75, 390–6.

Smeeding, T., Estes, C. and Glasse, L. (1999) Social Security reform and older women: Improving the system. *Income Security Policy Series, Paper No. 22*. Syracuse, NY: Center for Policy Research.

Smelser, N. (1959) *Social Change in the Industrial Revolution: an Application of Theory to the British Cotton Industry*. Chicago: University of Chicago Press.

Smelser, N. (1963) *The Sociology of Economic Life*. Englewood Cliffs, NJ: Prentice Hall.

Smelser, N. (1994) *Sociology*. Cambridge, MA: Blackwell.

Smith, C. (1996a) *Disruptive Religion: the Force of Faith in Social Movement Activism*. New York: Routledge.

Smith, C. (1996b) *Resisting Reagan: the US Central American Peace Movement*. Chicago: University of Chicago Press.

Smith, C. (1998) *American Evangelicalism: Embattled and Thriving*. Chicago: University of Chicago Press.

Smith, C. (2000) *Christian America? What Evangelicals Really Want*. Berkeley: University of California Press.

Smith, C., Emerson, M., Gallagher, S., Kennedy, P. and Sikkink, D. (1998) *American Evangelicalism: Embattled and Thriving*. Chicago: University of Chicago Press.

Smith, E. and Sapp, W. (eds) (1997) *Plain Talk about the Human Genome Project*. Tuskegee, AL: Tuskegee University.

Smith, J. P. (1978) The convergence to racial equality in women's wages. RAND Paper Series P-6026.

Smith, J. P. (1986) *Closing the Gap, Forty Years of Economic Progress for Blacks*. Santa Monica, CA: The Rand Corporation.

Smith, J. P. (1989) Black economic progress after Myrdal. *Journal of Economic Literature*, 27, 519–64.

Smith, J. P. and Edmonston, B. (eds) (1997) *The New Americans: Economic, Demographic, and Fiscal Effects of Immigration*. Washington, DC: National Academy Press.

Smith, J. P. and Welch, F. R. (1977) Black–white male wage ratios: 1960–1970. *American Economic Review*, 67(3), 323–38.

Smith, J. P. and Welch, F. R. (1978) *Race Differences in Earnings: a Survey and New Evidence*. Santa Monica, CA: The Rand Corporation.

Smith, P. B. and Bond, M. H. (1998) *Social Psychology across Cultures*. New York: Prentice Hall.

Smith-Doerr, L., Owen-Smith, J., Koput, K. W. and Powell, W. W. (1999) Networks and knowledge production: collaboration and patenting in biotechnology. In R. T. A. J. Leenders and S. Gabbay (eds), *Corporate Social Capital*. Reading, MA: Addison Wesley.

Smith-Lovin, L. (1990) Emotion as confirmation and disconfirmation of identity: an affect control model. T. D. Kemper (ed,), *Research Agendas in the Sociology of Emotion*. Albany: State University of New York Press.

Smith-Lovin, L. (2001) Role-identities, action and emotion: parallel processing and the production of mixed emotions. In Y. Kashima, M. Foddy and M. Platow (eds), *Self and Identity: Personal, Social, and Symbolic*. New York: Erlbaum.

Smith-Lovin, L. and Heise, D. R. (1989) *Affect Control Theory: Research Advances*. London: Gordon and Breach Scientific Publishers.

Smith-Lovin, L. and McPherson, J. M. (1993) You are who you know: a network approach to gender. In P. England (ed.), *Theory on Gender/ Feminism on Theory*. New York: Aldine De Gruter.

Snipp, M., Horton, H. D., Jensen, L., Nagel, J. and Rochin, R. (1993) Persistent rural poverty and racial and ethnic minorities. In Rural Sociological Society Task Force on Persistent Rural Poverty, *Persistent Poverty in Rural America*. Boulder, CO: Westview Press.

Snow, D. A. (2000) Symbolic interactionism. In N. J. Smelser and P. B. Baltes (eds), *International Encyclopedia of the Social and Behavioral Sciences*. London: Elsevier Science.

Snow, D. A. and Benford, R. D. (1992) Master frames and cycles of protest. In A. D. Morris and C. M. Mueller (eds), *Frontiers in Social Movement Theory*. New Haven, CT: Yale University Press.

Snow, D. A., Rochford, E. B. Jr, Worden, S. K. and Benford, R. D. (1986) Frame alignment processes, micro-mobilization and movement participation. *American Sociological Review*, 51, 464– 81.

Snyder, D. and Kick, E. L. (1979) Structural position in the world system and economic growth, 1955–1970: a multiple-network analysis of transnational interactions. *American Journal of Sociology*, 84, 1096–126.

Social Security Administration (1995) *Research and Statistics: Fast Facts and Figures about Social Security*. Washington, DC: US Government Printing Office.

Social Security Administration (1998) *Facts and Figures*, Publication No. 05–10011. Washington, DC: US Government Printing Office.

Social Security Administration (1999) *Social Security Update*, Publication no. 05–10003. Washington, DC: US Government Printing Office.

Soeffner, H. (1997) *The Order of Rituals: the Interpretation of Everyday Life*. New Brunswick, NJ: Transaction.

Soja, E. (1989) *Postmodern Geographies*. London: Verso.

Somach, S. (ed.) (1995) *Issues of War Trauma and Working with Refugees: Compilation of Resources*. Washington, DC: Center for Applied Linguistics Refugee Service Center.

Sorel, G. (1906) *Reflections sur la violence* (trans. T. E. Hulme and J. Roth as *Reflections on Violence*. New York: Free Press, 1950).

Sorensen, A. B. and Hallinan, M. T. (1984) Race effects on the assignment to ability groups. In P. L. Peterson, L. C. Wilkinson and M. T. Hallinan (eds), *The Social Context of Instruction: Group Organization and Group Process*. Los Angeles: Academic Press.

Sorlie, P., Rogot, E., Anderson, R., Johnson, N. J. and Backland, E. (1992) Black–white mortality differences in family income. *Lancet*, 340, 346–50.

Sorokin, P. A. (1927) *Social and Cultural Mobility*. New York: Free Press.

Spaargaren, G. (1996) The ecological modernization of production and consumption. PhD thesis, Wageningen University.

Spady, W. G. (1973) The impact of school resources on students. In F. N. Kerlinger (ed.), *Review of Research in Education*. Itasca, IL: Peacock Publishers.

Spilerman, S. (1971) Raising academic motivation in lower class adolescents: a convergence of two research traditions. *Sociology of Education*, 44, 103–18.

Spillman, L. (1997) *Nation and Commemoration: Creating National Identities in the United States and Australia*. Cambridge: Cambridge University Press.

Sreberny-Mohammadi, A. and Mohammadi, A. (1994) *Small Media, Big Revolution: Communication, Culture, and the Iranian Revolution*. Minneapolis: University of Minnesota.

Stacey, J. (1988) Can there be a feminist ethnography? *Women's Studies International Forum*, 1, 21–7.

Stack, C. (1996) *Call to Home: African Americans Reclaim the Rural South*. New York: Basic Books.

Staggenborg, S. (1988) The consequences of professionalization and formalization in the pro-choice movement. *American Sociological Review*, 53, 585–605.

Stallings, B. (ed.) (1995) *Global Change, Regional Response*. Cambridge: University of Cambridge Press.

Staples, W. G. (1997) *The Culture of Surveillance: Discipline and Social Control in the United States*. New York: St Martin's Press.

Stark, R. and Finke, R. (2000) *The Human Side of Religion*. Berkeley: University of California Press.

Stark, W. (1958) *The Sociology of Knowledge: an Essay in Aid of a Deeper Understanding of the History of Ideas*. Glencoe, IL: The Free Press.

Steele, C. (1997) A threat in the air: how stereotypes shape intellectual identity and performance. *American Psychologist*, 52, 613–29.

Steensland, B. S., Park, J., Regnerus, M. D., Robinson, L. D., Wilcox, W. B. and Woodberry, R. D. (2000) The measure of American religion: toward improving the state of the art. *Social Forces* (in the press).

Stein, A. (1997) *Sex and Sensibility: Stories of a Lesbian Generation*. Berkeley: University of California Press.

Steinberg, S. (1996) *Beyond the Classroom: Why School Reform Has Failed and What Parents Need to Do*. New York: Simon and Schuster.

Steiner, H. J. and Alston, P. (1996) *International Human Rights in Context, Law, Politics, Morals*. Oxford: Clarendon Press.

Stepan-Norris, J. and Zeitlin, M. (1996) *Talking Union*. Urbana: University of Illinois Press.

Stephens, L. (1998) *Anti-disciplinary Protest: Sixties Radicalism and Postmodernism*. Cambridge: Cambridge University Press.

Stephens, M. A. P. and Franks, M. (1995) Spillover between daughter's roles as caregiver and wife: Interference or enhancement? *Journal of Gerontology*, 50, B9–17.

Stevens-Arroyo, A. and Cadena, G. (1995) *Old Masks, New Faces: Religion and Latino Identities*. New York: Bildner Center Books.

Stewart, J. B. and Allen-Smith, J. E. (eds) (1995) *Blacks in Rural America*. New Brunswick, NJ: Transaction Publishers.

Stillman, P. G. (1980) Hegel's civil society. *Polity*, 12(4), 622–46.

Stinchcombe, A. L. (1968) *Constructing Social Theories*. New York: Harcourt, Brace & World.

Stinchcombe, A. L. (1983) *Economic Sociology*. New York: Academic Press.

Stoller, E. P. (1994) Why women care: gender and the organization of lay care. In E. Stoller and R. Gibson (eds), *Worlds of Difference: Inequality in the Aging Experience*. Thousand Oaks, CA: Pine Forge Press.

Stone, R., Cafferata, G. L. and Sangl, J. (1987) Caregivers of the frail elderly: A national profile. *The Gerontologist*, 27, 616–26.

Stonequist, E. V. (1937) *The Marginal Man: a Study in Personality and Cultural Conflict*. New York: Scribners.

Strenski, I. (1997) *Durkheim and the Jews of France*. Chicago: University of Chicago Press.

Stryker, S. (1980) *Symbolic Interactionism*. Menlo Park, CA: Benjamin/Cummings.

Stull, D. D., Broadway, M. J. and Griffith, D. (1995) *Anyway You Cut It: Meatpacking and Small-Town America*. Lawrence: University Press of Kansas.

Suárez-Orozco, C. (1998) The transitions of immigration: how do men and women differ? *DRCLAS News*, 6–7.

Suárez-Orozco, C. (2000) Identities under seige: immigration stress and social mirroring among the children of immigrants. In A. Robben and M. Suárez-Orozco (eds), *Cultures under Seige: Violence and Trauma in Interdisciplinary Perspective*. Cambridge: Cambridge University Press.

Suárez-Orozco, C. and Suárez-Orozco, M. (1995) *Transformations: Migration, Family Life, and Achievement Motivation Among Latino Adolescents*. Palo Alto, CA: Stanford University Press.

Suárez-Orozco, C. and Suárez-Orozco, M. (2000) *Children of Immigration*. Cambridge, MA: Harvard University Press.

Suárez-Orozco, M. (1998) *Crossings: Mexican Immigration in Interdisciplinary Perspectives*. Cambridge, MA: Harvard University Press.

Suárez-Orozco, M. (1996) California dreaming: Proposition 187 and the cultural psychology of ethnic and racial exclusion. *Anthropology and Education Quarterly*, 27, 151–67.

Subcommittee on Definition and Prevalence of the 1984 Joint National Committee on Detection, Evaluation, and Treatment of High Blood Pressure (1985) Hypertension prevalence and the status of awareness, treatment, and control in the United States. Final report of the Subcommittee on Definition and Prevalence of the 1984 Joint National Committee. *Hypertension*, 7, 457–68.

Suitor, J. J., Wellman, B. and Morgan, D. L. (eds) (1997) Change in networks. Special issue of *Social Networks*, 19(1).

Summers, G. F. (1995) Persistent rural poverty. In E. N. Castle (eds), *The Changing American Countryside: Rural People and Places*. Lawrence: University Press of Kansas.

Summers, G. F., Bloomquist, L., Buttel, F., Garrett, P., Glasgow, N., Humphrey, C., Lichter, D. T., Lyson, T., Snipp, M. and Tickamyer, A. (1993) Introduction. In Rural Sociological Society Task Force on Persistent Rural Poverty, *Persistent Poverty in Rural America*. Boulder, CO: Westview Press.

Suro, R. (1998) *Strangers among Us: How Latino Immigration Is Transforming America*. New York: Alfred Knopf.

Swanson, L. E., Harris, R. P., Skees, J. R. and Williamson, L. (1995) African Americans in southern rural regions: the importance of legacy. In J. B. Stewart and J. E. Allen-Smith (eds), *Blacks in Rural America*. New Brunswick, NJ: Transaction Publishers.

Swartz, D. (1997) *Culture and Power: the Sociology of Pierre Bourdieu*. Chicago: University of Chicago Press.

Swidler, A. and Arditi, J. (1994) The new sociology of knowledge. *Annual Review of Sociology*, 20, 305–29.

Szmatka, J., Skvoretz, J. and Berger, J. (1997) *Status, Network, and Structure: Theory Development in Group Processes*. Stanford, CA: Stanford University Press.

Sztompka, P. (ed.) (1994) *Agency and Structure: Reorienting Social Theory*. Yverdon, Switzerland: Gordon and Breach.

Tajfel, H. (1978) *The Social Psychology of Minorities*. New York: Minority Rights Group.

Tamir, Y. (1998) Revisiting the civic sphere. In A. Gutmann (ed.), *Freedom of Association*. Princeton, NJ: Princeton University Press.

Tarrow, S. (1994) *Power in Movement*. New York: Cambridge University Press.

Taylor, C. (1989) *Sources of the Self: the Making of Modern Identity*. Cambridge: Cambridge University Press.

Taylor, C. (1996) *Philosophical Arguments*. Cambridge: Cambridge University Press.

Taylor, L. C. (1999) Work attitudes, employment barriers, and mental health symptoms. Unpublished manuscript.

Taylor, P. J. and Buttel, F. H. (1992) How do we know we have global environmental problems? *GeoForum*, 23, 405–16.

Taylor, V. (1989) Social movement continuity: the women's movement in abeyance. *American Sociological Review*, 54, 761–75.

Telles, S. M. (1996) *Whose Welfare? AFDC and Elite Politics*. Lawrence: University Press of Kansas.

Tellegen, E. and Wolsink, M. (1998) *Society and Its Environment: an Introduction*. Yverdon, Switzerland: Gordon and Breach.

Tester, K. (1992) *Civil Society*. Routledge: London.

Therborn, G. (1976) *Science, Class and Society: On the Formation of Sociology and Historical Materialism*. London: Verso.

Therborn, G. (1980) *The Ideology of Power and the Power of Ideology*. London: NLB.

Thibaut, J. W. and Kelley, H. H. (1959) *The Social Psychology of Groups*. New York: Wiley.

Thistlewaite, D. L. and Wheeler, N. (1966) Effects of teacher and peer subcultures upon student aspirations. *Journal of Educational Psychology*, 57, 35–47.

Thoites, P. (1985) Self-labeling processes in mental illness: the role of emotional deviance. *American Journal of Sociology*, 92, 221–49.

Thompson, E. A. and Neal, J. V. (1997) Allelic disequilibrium and allele frequency distribution as a function of social and demographic history. *American Journal of Human Genetics*, 60, 197–204.

Thompson, E. P. (1963) *Making of the English Working Class*. New York: Pantheon Books.

Thompson, J. B. (1990) *Ideology and Modern Culture: Critical Social Theory in the Era of Mass Communication*. Cambridge: Polity Press.

Thornton, A. (1985) Changing attitudes toward separation and divorce: Causes and consequences. *American Journal of Sociology*, 90, 856–72.

Thurow, L. (1999) *Building Wealth*. New York: HarperCollins.

Tickamyer, A., Bokemeier, J., Feldman, S., Harris, R., Jones, J. P. and Wenk, D. (1993) Women and persistent rural poverty. In Rural Sociological Society Task Force on Persistent Rural Poverty, *Persistent Poverty in Rural America*. Boulder, CO: Westview Press.

Tickamyer, A. R. (1992) The working poor in rural labor markets: the example of the southeastern United States. In C. M. Duncan (ed.), *Rural Poverty in America*. New York: Auburn House.

Tilly, C. (1978) *From Mobilization to Revolution*. Reading, MA: Addison-Wesley.

Tilly, C. (1984) Social movements and national politics. In C. Bright and S. Harding (eds), *Statemaking and Social Movements*. Ann Arbor, MI: University of Michigan Press.

Tilly, C. (1994) *Popular Contention in Great Britain, 1758–1834*. Cambridge, MA: Harvard University Press.

Tilly, C. (1998) *Durable Inequality*. Berkeley, CA: University of California Press.

Timio, M., Verdecchia, P., Venanzi, S., Gentili, S., Ronconi, M., Francucci, B., Montanari, M. and Bichisao, E. (1988) Age and blood pressure changes. A 20–year follow-up study in nuns in a secluded order. *Hypertension*, 12, 457–61.

Tittle, C. R. (1995) *Control Balance: toward a General Theory of Deviance*. Boulder, CO: Westview Press.

Tocquvelle, A. de (1835) *Democracy in America, volume 1* (ed. J. P. Mayer). Garden City, NY: Doubleday (1969).

Tocquvelle, A. de (1856) *The Old Regime and the French Revolution*. New York: Anchor (1955).

Tong, R. (1998) *Feminist Theory*, 2nd edn. Boulder, CO: Westview.

Tönnies, F. (1957) *Community and Society (Gemeinschaft und Gesellschaft)* (trans. and ed. C. P. Loomis. East Lansing: Michigan State University Press.

Torfing, J. (1998) *Politics, Regulation and the Modern Welfare State*. New York: St Martin's Press.

Torres, C. A. (1998) *Democracy, Education and Multiculturalism*. Lanham, MD: Rowman and Littlefield.

Touraine, A. (1965) *Sociologie de l'action*. Paris: Seuil.

Touraine, A. (1969) *La société post-industrielle*. Paris: Denoël (*The Post-industrial Society*, trans. L. F. X. Mayhew. London: Wildwood House, 1974).

Touraine, A. (1997) *What Is Democracy?* Boulder, CO: Westview.

Tracy, P. E. and Kempf-Leonard, K. (1996) *Continuity and Discontinuity in Criminal Careers*. New York: Plenum Press.

Treas, J. (1995) Older Americans in the 1990s and beyond. *Population Bulletin*, 50, 1–47.

Treas, J. and Torrecilha, R. (1995) The older population. In R. Farley (ed.), *State of the Union: America in the 1990s. Volume 2: Social Trends*. New York: The Russell Sage Foundation.

Treiman, D. J. (1970) Industrialization and social stratification. In E. O. Laumann (ed.), *Social Stratification: Research and Theory for the 1970s*. Indianapolis: Bobbs-Merrill.

Treiman, D. J. (1977) *Occupational Prestige in Comparative Perspective*. New York: Academic Press.

Treiman, D. J., McKeever, M. and Fodor, E. (1996) Racial differences in occupational states and income in South Africa, 1980 and 1991. *Demography*, 33(1), 111–32.

Treiman, D. J. and Szelényi, I. (1993) Social stratification in eastern Europe after 1989. In *Transformation Processes in Eastern Europe* (Proceedings of a Workshop held at the Dutch National Science Foundation, December 3–4, 1992). The Hague: NOW.

Tuan, M. (1998) *Forever Foreigners or Honorary Whites? The Asian Ethnic Experience Today*. New Brusnwick, NJ: Rutgers University Press.

Tuck, R. (1991) History of political thought. In P. Burke (ed.), *New Perspectives in Historical Writing*. University Park: Pennsylvania University Press.

Tucker, K. H. Jr (1996) *French Revolutionary Syndicalism and the Public Sphere*. Cambridge: Cambridge University Press.

Tuch, S. A. and Martin, J. K. (1997) *Racial Attitudes in the 1990s: Continuity and Change*. New York: Praeger.

Turner, B. (ed.) (1993a) *Citizenship and Social Theory*. Newbury Park, CA: Sage.

Turner, B. S. (1993b) Outline of a theory of human rights. *Sociology*, 27, 489–512.

Turner, B. S. (1997) Citizen studies: a general theory. *Citizenship Studies*, 1, 5–18.

Turner, J. H. (1986) *The Structure of Sociological Theory*. Chicago: Dorsey Press.

Turow, J. (1997) *Breaking up America: Advertisers and the New Media World*. Chicago: University of Chicago Press.

Tyler, T. R. and Smith, H. (1998) Social justice and social movements. In D. Gilbert, S. T. Fiske and G. Lindzey (eds), *Handbook of Social Psychology*, 4th edn. New York: McGraw-Hill.

UNAIDS (1998) *Aids Epidemic Update: December 1998*. New York: UNAIDS Joint United Nations Programme on HIV/AIDS.

UNESCO (1998) Statistics (age-specific enrollment rates and illiteracy rates) [http://unescostat.unescoorg/Indframe.htm].

United Nations Development Programme (1999) *Human Development Report 1999*. New York: Oxford University Press.

University Consultants (1978) *Experiences of Recent High School Graduates: the Transition to Work or Postsecondary Education*. Lexington, MA: Lexington.

Urban, M., Igrunov, V. and Mitrokhin, S. (1997) *The Rebirth of Politics in Russia*. Cambridge: Cambridge University Press.

Urry, J. (1995) *Consuming Places*. London: Routledge.

Urry, J. (2000) *Sociology Beyond Societies*. London: Routledge.

US Bureau of the Census (1975) *Historical Statistics of the United States*. Washington, DC: US Government Printing Office.

US Bureau of the Census (1988) *Aging in the Third World*. Washington, DC: US Government Printing Office.

US Bureau of the Census (1990) *Statistical Abstract of the United States*. Washington, DC: US Government Printing Office.

US Bureau of the Census (1991) *Money Income of Households, Families and Persons in the United States: 1990*. Current Population Reports, P60–74. Washington, DC: US Government Printing Office.

US Bureau of the Census (1992) *The Black Population in the United States: March 1991*. Current Population Reports, P20–464. Washington, DC: US Government Printing Office.

US Bureau of the Census (1993) *We the American Elderly*. Washington, DC: US Government Printing Office.

US Bureau of the Census (1997) *Americans with Disabilities, 1994–95*. Current Population Reports, Series P70–61. Washington, DC: US Government Printing Office.

US Bureau of the Census (1998a) *Poverty in the United States, 1997*. Current Population Reports, Series P60–201. Washington, DC: US Government Printing Office.

US Bureau of the Census (1998b) *Statistical Abstract of the United States: 1998*. Washington, DC.

US Bureau of the Census (1999) *Marital Status and Living Arrangements: March 1998* (update). Current Population Reports, Series P20–514. Internet release, January 7.

US Bureau of Labor Statistics (1995) *Employment, Hours, and Earnings*. Washington, DC: US Government Printing Office.

US Bureau of Labor Statistics (1996) *Current Population Survey* [http://ferret.bls.census.gov/macro/171996/empearn/3_000.htm].

US Department of Agriculture (1997) *Rural Conditions and Trends* 8. Washington, DC: US Department of Agriculture.

US Department of Education (1997) *Digest of Education Statistics*. Washington, DC: National Center for Education Statistics.

US House of Representatives (1992) *How Well Do Women Fare under the Nation's Retirement Policies?* Subcommittee on Retirement Income. Washington, DC: US Government Printing Office.

Useem, B., Camp, C. G. and Camp, G. M. (1996) *Resolution of Prison Riots: Strategies and Policies*. New York: Oxford University Press.

Valente, T. (1995) *Network Models of the Diffusion of Innovations*. New Jersey: Hampton Press.

Valenzuela, A. (1999) Gender roles and settlement activities among children and their immigrant families. *American Behavioral Scientist*, 42, 720–42.

van den Berghe, P. L. (1975) *Man in Society: a Biosocial View*. New York: Elsevier.

Vanfossen, B., Jones, J. and Spade, J. (1987) Curriculum tracking and status maintenance. *Sociology of Education*, 60, 104–22.

Vedder, R., Gallaway, L. and Klingaman, D. C. (1990) Black exploitation and white benefits: the Civil War income revolution. In R. F. America (ed.), *The Wealth of Races: the Present Value of Benefits from Past Injustices*. Westport, CT: Greenwood Press.

Verbugge, L. M. (1990) Pathways of health and death. In R. D. Apple (ed.), *Women, Health and Medicine in America*. New York: Garland.

Vernez, G., Abrahamse, A. and Quigley, D. (1996) *How Immigrants Fare in US Education*. Santa Monica, CA: Rand.

Vernon, J. (1993) *Politics and the People: a Study in English Political Culture, c.1815–1867*. New York: Cambridge University Press.

Vernon, J. (1994) Who's afraid of the "linguistic turn"? The politics of social history and its discontents. *Social History*, 19, 81–98.

Veum, J. R. and Weiss, A. B. (1993) Education and the work histories of young adults. *Monthly Labor Review*, 116, 11–20.

Vichinsky, E. P., Earles, A., Johnson, R. A., Hoag, M. S., Williams, A. and Lubin, B. (1990) Alloimmunization in sickle cell anemia and transfusion of racially unmatched blood. *New England Journal of Medicine*, 322, 1617–21.

Vigil, D. (1988) *Barrio Gangs: Street Life and Identity in Southern California*. Austin: University of Texas Press.

Vinitzky-Seroussi, V. (1998) *After Pomp and Circumstance: High School Reunion as an Autobiographical Occasion*. Chicago: University of Chicago Press.

Volkan, V. D. (1993) Immigrants and refugees: a psychodynamic perspective. *Mind and Human Interaction*, 4, 63–9.

Vroman, W. (1986) Transfer payments, sample selection, and male black–white earnings differences. *American Economic Review*, 76, 351–4.

Wacquant, L. (1989) The ghetto, the state and the new capitalist economy. *Dissent*, 508–20.

Wagner, D. G., Ford, R. S. and Ford, T. W. (1986) Can gender inequalities be reduced? *American Sociological Review*, 51, 47–61.

Wagner, P. (1994) *A Sociology of Modernity: Liberty and Discipline*. London: Routledge.

Wagner, P. (1999) The resistance that modernity constantly provokes. Europe, America and social theory, *Thesis Eleven*, 58, 39–63.

Wagner, P. (2000) *Vanishing Points of Modernity: Inescapability and Attainability in Social Theory*. London: Sage.

Waldinger, R. (1996) *Still the Promised City? African-Americans and New Immigrants in Postindustrial New York*. Cambridge, MA: Harvard University Press.

Waldinger, R. (1997) *Social Capital or Social Closure? Immigrant Networks in the Labor Market*. Los Angeles: Lewis Center for Regional Policy Studies, UCLA.

Waldinger, R. and Bozorgmehr, M. (1996) *Ethnic Los Angeles*. New York: Russell Sage Foundation.

Waldinger, R., Erickson, C., Milkman, R., Mitchell, D. J. B., Valnzuela, A., Wong, K. and Zeitlin, M. (1998) Helots no more: a case study of the justice for janitors campaign in Los Angeles. In K. Bronfenbrenner et al. (eds), *Organizing to Win*. Ithaca, NY: Cornell University Press.

Waldron, I., Nowotarski, M., Freimer, M., Henry, J. P., Post, N. and Witten, C. (1982) Cross-cultural variation in blood pressure: a quantitative analysis of the relationship of blood pressure to cultural characteristics, salt consumption, and body weight. *Social Science and Medicine*, 16, 419–30.

Wallace, A. (1966) *Religion: an Anthropological View*. New York: Random House.

Wallace, W. L. (1997) *The Future of Ethnicity, Race, and Nationality*. New York: Praeger.

Waller, W. (1932) *Sociology of Teaching*. New York: Wiley.

Wallerstein, I. (1979) *The Capitalist World-economy*. Cambridge: Cambridge University Press.

Wallerstein, I. (1991) *Unthinking Social Science: the Limits of Nineteenth-century Paradigms*. Cambridge: Polity Press.

Wallerstein, I. (1995) *Historical Capitalism*. London: Verso.

Walzer, M. (1992) The civil society argument. In C. Mouffe (ed.), *Dimensions of Radical Democracy: Pluralism, Citizenship, Community*. New York: Verso.

Walzer, M. (1997) *On Toleration*. New Haven, CT: Yale University Press.

Ward, D. (1990) Gender, time, and money in caregiving. *Scholarly Inquiry for Nursing Practice*, 4, 223–39.

Warner, R. S. (1993) Work in progress toward a new paradigm for the sociological study of religion in the United States. *American Journal of Sociology*, 98, 1044–93.

Warner, R. S. and Wittner, J. G. (eds) (1998) *Gatherings in Diaspora: Religious Communities and the New Immigration*. Philadelphia: Temple University Press.

Warner, W. L. and Srole, L. (1945) *The Social Systems of American Ethnic Groups*. New Haven, CT: Yale University Press.

Warren, J. and Twine, F. (1997) White Americans, the new minority? Non-blacks and the ever-expanding boundaries of whiteness. *Journal of Black Studies*, 28, 200–18.

Wasserman, S. and Faust, K. (1994) *Social Network Analysis: Methods and Applications*. Cambridge: Cambridge University Press.

Wasserman, S. and Galaskiewicz, J. (eds) (1994) *Advances in Social Network Analysis*. Thousand Oaks, CA: Sage.

Waters, M. (1990) *Ethnic Options: Choosing Identities in America*. Berkeley: University of California Press.

Waters, M. (1996a) West Indian family resources and adolescent outcomes: trajectories of the second generation. Paper presented at the Annual Meeting of the American Association for the Advancement of Science, Baltimore, Maryland, February 10.

Waters, M. (1996b) Human rights and the universality of interests: toward a social constructionist approach. *Sociology*, 30, 593–600.

Weakliem, D. L. (1995) Two models of class voting. *British Journal of Political Science*, 25, 254–70.

Weber, M. (1921) *The City*. New York: Free Press (1958).

Weber, M. (1946) *From Max Weber: Essays in Sociology* (trans. and ed. H. H. Gerth and C. W. Mills). New York: Oxford University Press.

Weber, M. (1957) *The Theory of Social and Economic Organization*. Glencoe, IL: Free Press.

Weintraub, J. and Kumar, K. (eds) (1997) *Public and Private in Thought and Practice: Perspectives on a Grand Dichotomy*. Chicago: University of Chicago Press.

Weiss, J. M. (1972) Influence of psychological variables on stress-induced pathology. *Physiology, Emotion and Psychosomatic Illness, Ciba Foundation Symposium*, 8, 253– 65.

Weissbourd, R. (1996) *The Vulnerable Child*. Reading, MA: Perseus Books.

Welch, F. (1990) The employment of black men. *Journal of Labor Economics*, 8, 226–74.

Wellman, B. (ed.) (1999) *Networks in the Global Village*. Boulder, CO: Westview.

Wellman, D. T. (1993) *Portraits of White Racism*. Cambridge: Cambridge University Press.

Wentzel, K. R. and Caldwell, K. (1997) Friendships, peer acceptance, and group membership: relations to academic achievement in middle school. *Child Development*, 68, 1198–209.

Weston, K. (1991) *Families We Choose: Lesbians, Gays, Kinship*. New York: Columbia University Press.

Wheaton, B. (1983) Stress, personal coping resources, and psychiatric symptoms: an investigation of interactive models. *Journal of Health and Social Behavior*, 24, 208–29.

White, H. (1973) *Metahistory: the Historical Imagination in Nineteenth-century Europe*. Baltimore: Johns Hopkins University Press.

White, H. C. (1993) *Careers and Creativity: Social Forces in the Arts*. Boulder, CO: Westview Press.

Whitley, R. (1984) *The Intellectual and Social Organization of the Sciences*. Oxford: Oxford University Press.

Whittier, N. (1995) *Feminist Generations: the Persistence of the Radical Women's Movement*. Philadelphia: Temple University Press.

Whyte, W. (1967) *Street Corner Society*. Chicago: University of Chicago Press.

Wiener, J. M. and Stevenson, D. G. (1998) *Long-term Care for the Elderly: Profiles of Thirteen States*. Washington, DC: Urban Institute Press.

Wilcox, B. (1998) Conservative Protestant childrearing. *American Sociological Review*, 63, 796–809.

Wilkinson, R. G. (ed.) (1986) *Class and Health: Research and Longitudinal Data*. London: Tavistock Publications.

Wilkinson, R. G. (1990) Income distribution and mortality: a "natural" experiment. *Sociology of Health and Illness*, 12, 391–412.

Wilkinson, R. G. (1992) Income distribution and life expectancy. *British Medical Journal*, 304, 165–8.

Willer, D., Lovaglia, M. and Markovsky, B. (1997) Power and infleunce: A theoretical bridge. *Social Forces*, 76, 571–603.

Willey, M. M. and Rice, S. A. (1933) *Communication Agencies and Social Life*. New York: McGraw-Hill.

Williams, R. (1973) *The Country and the City*. London: Chatto and Windus.

Williams, R. (1974) *Television: Technology and Cultural Form*. New York: Schocken.

Williams, R. (1977) *Keywords*. New York: Oxford University Press.

Williams, R. (1988) *Border Country*. London: Hogarth Press.

Williams, R. H. (1997) *Cultural Wars in American Politics: Critical Reviews of a Popular Myth*. New York: Aldine de Gruyter.

Williamson, O. E. (1975) *Markets and Hierarchies*. New York: Free Press.

Williamson, O. E. (1981) The economics of organization: The transaction cost approach. *American Journal of Sociology*, 87, 548–77.

Wills, T. A. (1985) Supportive functions of interpersonal relationships. In S. Cohen and S. L. Symee (eds), *Social Support and Health*. Orlando, FL: Academic Press.

Wilson, E. (1991) *The Sphinx in the City*. London: Virago.

Wilson, W. J. (1980) *The Declining Significance of Race*. Chicago: University of Chicago Press.

Wilson, W. J. (1987) *The Truly Disadvantaged: the Inner City, the Underclass, and Public Policy*. Chicago: University of Chicago Press.

Wilson, W. J. (1993) *The Ghetto Underclass: Social Science Perspectives*. Newbury Park, CA: Sage.

Wilson, W. J. (1996) *When Work Disappears: the World of the New Urban Poor*. New York: Alfred A. Knopf.

Wilson, W. J. and Neckerman, K. (1986) Poverty and family structure: The widening gap between evidence and public policy issues. In S. Danziger and D. Weinberg (eds), *Fighting Poverty: What Works, What Doesn't*. Cambridge, MA: Harvard University Press.

Winnicott, D. W. (1971) *Playing and Reality*. Harmondsworth: Penguin.

Wirt, J. G., Muraskin, L. D., Goodwin, D. A. and Meyer, R. H. (1989) *National Assessment of Vocational Education*. Washington, DC: US Department of Education.

Wirth, L. (1938) Urbanism as a way of life. *American Journal of Sociology*, 44, 1–24.

Wolf, S. and Wolff, H. G. (1947) *Human Gastric Function: an Experimental Study of a Man and His Stomach*. New York: Oxford University Press.

Wolfe, A. (1989) Whose keepers? In *Social Science and Moral Obligation*, Berkeley: University of California Press.

Wolfe, A. (1992) Democracy versus sociology: boundaries and their sociological consequences. In M. Lamont and M. Fournier (eds), *Cultivating Differences. Symbolic Boundaries and the Making of Inequality*. Chicago: University of Chicago Press.

Wolfe, A. (1997) Public and private in theory and practice. In J. Weintraub and K. Kumar (eds), *Public and Private in Thought and Practice*. Chicago: University of Chicago Press.

Wolff, J. (1995) *Resident Aliens*. Cambridge: Polity Press.

Wong-Fillmore, L. (1991) When learning a second language means losing the first. *Early Childhood Research*.

Wood, J. T. (1996) She says/he says: communication, caring, and conflict in heterosexual relationships. In J. T. Wood (ed.), *Gendered Relationships*. Mountain View, CA: Mayfield Publishing Company.

Woodberry, R. D. (1997) The place of religion in American sociology. Presented at the national meeting of the Association for the Sociology of Religion, Toronto, Canada.

Woodberry, R. D. (1998) Religiosity: does one "size" fit all? Unpublished paper.

Woodberry, R. D. and Smith, C. S. (1998): Fundamentalism et al.: conservative Protestants in America. *Annual Review of Sociology*, 24, 25–56.

Woodiwiss, A. (1996) Review essay. Searching for signs of globalization. *Sociology*, 30, 799–810.

Woolcock, M. (1998) Social capital and economic development: toward a theoretical synthesis and policy framework. *Theory and Society*, 27, 151–208.

World Bank (1999a) *World Development Indicators*. Washington, DC: World Bank.

World Bank (1999b) *Knowledge for Development: World Development Report*. Washington, DC: World Bank.

World Bank Group (1999) *Poverty Trends and Voice of the Poor*. Poverty Reduction and Economic Management, Human Development, Development Economics, September 29.

World Health Organization (1999) *The World Health Report 1999: Making a Difference*. Geneva: World Health Organization.

Wright, J. D., Rubin, B. A. and Devine, J. A. (1998) *Beside the Golden Door: Policy, Politics, and the Homeless*. New York: Aldine de Gruyter.

Wright, P. (1992) *A Journey through Ruins*. London: Paladin.

Wrong, D. H. (1998) *The Modern Condition: Essays at Century's End*. Stanford, CA: Stanford University Press.

Wuthnow, R. (1987) *Meaning and Moral Order: Explorations in Cultural Analysis*. Berkeley: University of California Press.

Wuthnow, R. (1989) *Communities of Discourse: Ideology and Social Structure in the Reformation, the Enlightenment, and European Socialism*. Cambridge, MA: Harvard University Press.

Wuthnow, R. (1998) *After Heaven*. Berkeley: University of California Press.

Wynne, B. (1992) Uncertainty and environmental learning: reconciling science and policy in the preventive paradigm. *Global Environmental Change*, 2, 111–27.

Wynne, B. (1994): Scientific knowledge and the global environment. In M. Redclift and T. Benton (eds), *Social Theory and the Global Environment*. London: Routledge.

Yearley, S. (1991) *The Green Case*. London: HarperCollins.

Yearley, S. (1996): *Sociology, Environmentalism, Globalization*. London: Sage.

Yoon, I. (1997) *On My Own: Korean Businesses and Race Relations in America*. Chicago: University of Chicago Press.

Yoshino, M. Y. and Rangan, U. S. (1995) *Strategic Alliances: an Entrepreneurial Approach to Globalization*. Cambridge, MA: Harvard University Press.

Young, L. (1997) *Rational Choice Theory and Religion: Summary and Assessment*. New York: Routledge.

Yunus, M. (1998) *Banker to the Poor*. Dhaka, Bangladesh: The University Press Limited.

Zald, M. N. (1992) Looking backward to look forward: Reflections on the past and future of the resource mobilization research program. In A. D. Morris and C. M. Mueller (eds), *Frontiers in Social Movement Theory*. New Haven, CT: Yale University Press.

Zelizer, V. A. (1985) *Pricing the Priceless Child: the Changing Social Value of Children*. New York: Basic Books.

Zerjal, T., Dashnyam, B., Pandya, A., Kayser, M., Roewer, L., Santos, F. R., Schiefenhovel, W., Fretwell, N., Jobling, M. A., Harihara, S., Shimizu, K., Semjidmaa, D., Sajantila, A., Salo, P., Crawford, M. H., Ginter, E. K., Evgrafov, O. V. and Tyler-Smith, C. (1997) Genetic relationships of Asians and Northern Europeans revealed by Y-Chromosomal DNA analysis. *American Journal of Human Genetics*, 60, 1174–83.

Zhou, M. (1997) Growing up American: the challenge confronting immigrant children and children of immigrants. *Annual Review of Sociology*, 23, 63–95.

Zhou, M. and Bankston, C. L. III (1998) *Growing up American: How Vietnamese Children Adapt to Life in the United States*. New York: Russell Sage Foundation.

Zimmerer, K. (1994) Human geography and the new ecology. *Annals of the Association of American Geographers*, 84, 108–25.

Zohar, D. and Marshall, I. (1994) *The Quantum Society*. New York: William Morrow.

Zimmermann, B., Didry, C. and Wagner, P. (eds) (1999) *Le travail et la nation. Histoire croisée de la France et de l'Allemagne*. Paris: Editions de la Maison des Sciences de l'Homme.

Zimmerman, M. (1990) *Heidegger's Confrontation with Modernity*. Bloomington: Indiana University Press.

Znaniecki, F. (1940) *The Social Role of the Man of Knowledge*. New York: Columbia University Press.

Zolberg, A. R. (1995) From invitation to interdiction: US foreign policy and immigration since 1945. In M. S. Teitelbaum and M. Weiner (eds), *Threatened Peoples, Threatened Borders: World Migration and US Policy*. New York: W. W. Norton.

Zolberg, A. R., Shurke, A. and Aguayo, S. (1989) *Escape from Violence: Conflict and the Refugee Crisis in the Developing World*. New York: Oxford University Press.

Zukin, S. (1992) *Landscapes of Power*. Berkeley: University of California Press.

Index